MEDIEVAL
COSTUME AND FASHION

HERBERT NORRIS

DOVER PUBLICATIONS, INC.
Mineola, New York

Copyright

Publisher's Note copyright © 1999 by Dover Publications, Inc.
All rights reserved under Pan American and International Copyright
Conventions.

Published in Canada by General Publishing Company, Ltd., 30 Lesmill
Road, Don Mills, Toronto, Ontario.

Bibliographical Note

This Dover edition, first published in 1999, is an unabridged republi-
cation of the work originally published in 1927 by J. M. Dent and Sons
Ltd., London, under the title *Costume & Fashion, Volume Two: Senlac to
Bosworth, 1066–1485.*

Library of Congress Cataloging-in-Publication Data

Medieval costume and fashion / Herbert Norris.
     p.   cm.
  ISBN 0-486-40486-2 (pbk.)
   1. Costume—History—Medieval, 500–1500. 2. Costume—
Europe—History.
GT575.M43   1999
391'.0094'0902—dc21
                                             98-49856
                                               CIP

Manufactured in the United States of America
Dover Publications, Inc., 31 East 2nd Street, Mineola, N.Y. 11501

I DEDICATE THIS VOLUME

TO

ALL LOVERS OF

ARCHÆOLOGY AND RESEARCH

PUBLISHER'S NOTE

Herbert Norris was renowned in his time as a costume architect and archaeologist. He designed historical and theatrical costume and stage sets for one hundred plays in England and America, as well as for a number of British films and pageants. Nevertheless, his series of books, *Costume and Fashion,* is considered his finest achievement.

Originally intended to be a six-volume series that would tell the story of costume and fashion from the time of ancient Greece until the end of the nineteenth century, only four volumes were completed and published before his death in 1950. They include *Volume 1: The Evolution of European Dress through the Earlier Ages* (1924); *Volume 2: Senlac to Bosworth, 1066-1485* (1927); *Volume 3: The Tudors, 1485-1603,* 2 vols. (1938); and *Volume 6: The Nineteenth Century* (1933). The fourth and fifth volumes, if completed, would have covered the Stuart and Hanoverian periods of fashion history, respectively. This book is the unabridged reprint of Volume 2 of the series: *Senlac to Bosworth, 1066–1485*, originally published in 1927. The reader may notice a few references to the other volumes in the text of this work.

Volume 1 of the series is currently out of print. Volume 3 is available in a one-volume (unabridged) Dover edition published in 1997. It combines Books I and II, and is entitled *Tudor Costume and Fashion* (ISBN 0-486-29845-0). Volume 6 of the series (*The Nineteenth Century*) is also available in a Dover reprint published in 1998. It is entitled *Nineteenth Century Costume and Fashion* (ISBN 0-486-40292-4).

FOREWORD

THE gratifying reception accorded to Volume I. of this History, particularly in America, has encouraged the publishers and others to suggest its continuation, here presented. Volume II. follows the same general plan as that used in the first volume, with certain modifications and considerable additions.

In order to identify the period discussed with events and personalities familiar to the reader, the practice employed in Volume I., of prefacing each chapter with a list of contemporary historical events, is continued in this book.

The accuracy of information given in the chapter on Heraldry, and the sections dealing with Chivalry, the Order of the Garter, the Order of the Bath, and Peers' Parliamentary Robes, is guaranteed by the fact that I am indebted for supervision of their details to Mr. G. Ambrose Lee, C.B., C.V.O., Clarenceux King-of-Arms, whose expert knowledge and kind assistance have been of the utmost value.

Again, my most grateful thanks are due to my wife and daughter, whose help with French and German translations has been most useful; to Major D. S. Paterson for his most able work in editing the MS., and to Mrs. Paterson for her talented aid in preparing drawings. To Messrs. J. M. Dent and Sons Ltd. I am more than indebted for the courtesy they have shown to a harassed author and the care they have devoted to the publication of his work.

HERBERT NORRIS.

LONDON, 1927.

INTRODUCTION

CHANGES in fashion arise from strange and diverse causes: sometimes a vanquished foe revenges himself by revolutionising the dress of his conquerors, or of their wives—sometimes a whim or deformity of empress or courtesan imprints its seal on the mode of the century—again, the arrival of some new royal consort or great notability from afar brings its train of consequences, either to enrich or simplify the nation's dress—some "precious" cult revives an art or manner of yesteryear, and behold, its votaries array themselves in the garments of its earlier vogue, although with a temerity usually tempered by the addition of comfort-giving modern accessories.

In studying the costume of the periods comprised in this volume, it is not sufficient to know the cut, shape and decoration of each garment; one must also know the manner of wearing, and the general effect aimed at by the wearer. Complaint is often heard that a given period is not suited to the player cast for a certain part. This may be occasionally true, but much can be done by a judicious combination of art, knowledge and consistency. Not every figure is well adapted to carry off with ease and dignity a prevailing fashion, but almost all will endeavour to approximate shape and carriage to the mode of the moment. This can be done as effectively in wearing historical costume as in conformity to the ever-changing fashions of to-day. It requires the same devotion to detail, courageously adopted and consistently followed, with rigid avoidance of the temptation to incorporate "becoming" features or accessories from another age. For example, results fatal to an artistic triumph would follow the wearing of the fifteenth-century "butterfly" headdress, which should project almost horizontally from the back of the head, tilted over the eyes in the manner of the latest hat of 1927. Nor is artifice necessarily confined to costume.

It is a curious fact that a certain type of face seems to be associated with each definitely marked period of history. True, the far-reaching effects of contemporary fashions cannot alter the shape of the bony structure of the face; but, nevertheless, it is certain that clearly differentiated types, considered beautiful at a given time, influenced the physiognomy and the apparent shape of the features, so that the heads of a given period acquired a general character to which individuals succeeded in adapting their own appearance.

It may be well to record here certain items of general interest which it has been found difficult to weave into the later structure of the book.

In selecting costumes for a given set of characters, their social position is not the only consideration to be borne in mind. Another factor bearing on the appropriate attire is the part of the country in which they lived. For example, a noble lady living on the borders of Scotland or Wales would be considerably behind the metropolitan mode of the day; and of course the same thing applies to men.

Dress of children. Babies of all classes were swathed in swaddling bands, and, for the christening and baptismal ceremony, the chrysom cloth was used—a piece of linen put upon the head, the ends being bound round the body. On these and other special occasions, "The child (of royal and noble parents) must be wrapped in a velvet cloak of any desired colour, which must be at least three ells long . . . and must be furred with miniver; and when the child is wrapped in the velvet, then must be put over the child (when the person carrying it has it on her arm) a long couvrechef or kerchief of violet silk, extending from the child's head down to the ground, and at the feet end as long as the cloak or longer " (La Viscomtesse de Furnes, fifteenth century).

The dress of boys throughout the period treated in this volume may be taken as exactly similar to that of their elders.

Girls wore a simplified version of their mothers' dress, but invariably had their hair flowing, often confined by a fillet or snod, or perhaps a wreath of flowers.

Women's arms and legs. An important fact to remember is that during the Middle Ages women's arms were never bare. In the four-teenth and fifteenth centuries, when low necks and extremely bare shoulders were the vogue, it was a rigid rule with Dame Fashion that the arms were entirely covered. It is curious that in the fifteenth century the cuffs of sleeves concealed even the hands to the second knuckle, and that at the same time the décolletage hardly rose above the waistbelt.

It would be interesting to know what the ladies of mediæval times had on their legs, but unfortunately scarcely any representations of leg-coverings are shown in illuminated MSS. The little that is seen indicates that their legs were clothed in the same manner as those of the men—

in braies, hosen, garters, crossgartering and footgear, the shoes being
of the same type as those worn by the men.

Women's riding-dress. Up to the beginning of the thirteenth
century there was no special dress prescribed for women to wear when
mounted on horseback. Before this time they simply wore the most
ample gown they possessed, with perhaps the paenula added. It was
not until the thirteenth century that they adopted, as a riding-habit,
the most useful of men's garments, the gardcorp, which they wore
over the ordinary gown, as seen in Fig. 215.

Night attire. The question of night attire in the Middle Ages is
a delicate one.

During the eleventh and twelfth centuries the sherte and camise
fulfilled the dual purpose of day and night intimacies among the best
people. "Even with the publicity inseparable from the absence of
special bedrooms, mediæval modesty did not provide a nightgown"
(*Social England*). Documents of the thirteenth and fourteenth centuries
indicate that, with exceptions, both men and women went to bed as
nature made them. Frequent mention is made of great personages
being roused suddenly in the night and forced to rise. To hide their
nakedness they anxiously seized whatever happened to be the nearest
possible vesture—a peliçon, houpeland—but often only the bed-clothes.
A "robe de chambre" or dressing-gown was used only in exceptional cases.

In illuminated MSS. of the fourteenth century one finds representations of kings and queens in bed, with no visible garment, but wearing
their crowns,[1] and in one instance a queen wears only a crown and
crespinette. In another MS. the Three Magi are shown together in
bed, their three crowned heads resting on three pillows, but apparently
naked; and in yet another the coif is the only covering worn by a man
in bed with a woman.

A picture of Charles V. of France in bed shows him wearing a low-
necked white nightgown, tied in front and having long close sleeves.
He wears his crown, and his head rests upon a cloth-of-gold pillow partly
covered with a white head-sheet. Mention of nightgowns and nightcaps
—coifs—is found in writings of the fifteenth century; and a picture of
this time shows a man wearing a nightgown with long close sleeves of
cloth of gold! Sir Richard Whittington, however, is represented on his
deathbed, naked, with his head swathed in a turban. In pictures of this
century and earlier, the inmates of mediæval hospitals are shown in

---

[1] Probably the fancy of an inventive artist, for purposes of identification.

bed quite naked; and it appears to have been a habit, reprobated by careful housewives, for servants and others to flick out the candle with the tail of their shertes or camises after getting into bed.

Meals. In Anglo-Saxon times and until the middle of the twelfth century it was usual for kings and nobles to have their tables laid four times a day, with "royal sumptuousness," for the whole court or household. After this date we find it recorded that "it is the custom, whether from parsimony, or as they themselves say, from fastidiousness, for princes to provide only one meal a day for their court."

About this time an improvement occurred in the standard of behaviour, at table, and as regards ordinary social intercourse. William of Malmesbury, writing about David of Scotland (1123–1153), tells us that he "rubbed off all the rust of barbarism. He released from the payment of taxes for three years all such of his countrymen as would pay more attention to their dwellings, dress more elegantly and feed more nicely." Another historian of the time writes that "all men, clerics and laymen alike, shall be content with two courses."

In the thirteenth century the fashionable hour for dinner was 11 a.m. and for supper 6 o'clock. Before retiring to bed, cakes and comfits (creations of the confectioner's art: round, square, or oblong sweetmeats made of sugar and what not) were handed round in gold or silver dishes, covered with a cloth. These were usually kept upon the "dressoir," at hand in case a visitor should call. Spiced wines, especially concoctions called "hippocras"[1] and "clarry"[2] were the chief beverages drunk by the upper classes "in company."

From early times, and during the whole of the Middle Ages, and indeed onwards into Tudor days, it was customary in the great houses for minstrels and gleomen to precede the entry of important dishes at any great feast.

The middle classes took their chief meal about eight in the evening. One kind of potage and two varieties of meat only at one meal were allowed. Each diner had his own knife and spoon, which were placed beside him in a case made to contain them.

The lower classes carried their knife and spoon in the wallet which served for many purposes; and among the peasantry the spoon, often of wood or horn, was tucked into the hood or cap.

---

[1] *Hippocras :* a white or red wine in which different aromatic ingredients were infused. It took its name from the particular kind of bag, termed "Hippocrates sleeve," through which it was strained.

[2] *Clarry :* a mixed wine, two-thirds white and one-third red, mingled with honey.

More details of the table are to be found in records of the fourteenth century. Among fashionable people the usual hours for dinner and supper remained the same as in the previous century, and continued so during the following.

For a great feast or banquet given by a prince or great noble the arrangement of the tables was as follows: The " chairs of estate " for the prince's family and his guests were set at the end of the great hall upon the dais under the canopy and " cloth of estate "; the tables for the nobility were lower and arranged on either side. The lesser nobility occupied seats and tables along the two sides of the hall, the buffets and dressoirs being placed at the farther end opposite the chairs of estate.

The *tables* used for important people on these occasions were long and narrow, about two feet in width, having ornamental supports at the ends, and strengthened by a tie-rod which also served as a foot-rest (*see* Fig. 677). Other kinds of tables in use at earlier periods and during the fourteenth and fifteenth centuries were formed of boards laid on two trestles connected by a tie-rod. The end of a trestle is shown in Fig. 421.

The *table-cloths* were of fine white linen or double damask, with borders of velvet, gold, and silk fringes. Two cloths were used; the under one fell to the ground at either end, and to a depth of about ten to twelve inches at the sides. Over this a cloth the same size as the top of the table was laid. The dressoirs and buffets were also covered with rich cloths.

In *setting the table* the elaborate salt-cellar, Fig. 679, was placed on the host's right hand, and rolls of bread arranged in groups, platters, trenchers, forks (*see* p. 141), spoons and cups were set by the pages and servitors for each guest. Each guest supplied his own knife, but large carving-knives were placed in certain positions upon the tables.

The "cornet l'eau" was sounded to announce the time of the repast, and all guests were served with water for the *washing of hands*. In the case of princes the ceremony was performed in a special way with the "double basin." The major-domo proceeded to the buffet and fetched two basins placed one on top of the other, the under one, with spout, containing aromatic water. These were presented to the cupbearer, who, kneeling on one knee at the side of the honoured guest, took the under basin of water in the right hand and poured the water over the hands of the guest, the water falling into the empty basin held in the cupbearer's left hand. A towel or napkin was presented by an esquire.

The hands of less important personages were washed by an esquire who poured water over them from the ewer (*see* Fig. 680) carried in the right hand, the water falling into a basin held in the left hand.

The *service* was performed by esquires, pages and servitors. All the viands and wines were kept on the buffets, and the esquires brought each dish and presented it across the table to the diner for his or her inspection, and when selected the esquire carved—"an art which every gentleman should not neglect"—the platters being placed before the guests by pages.

It was considered the height of good form for a gentleman to feed off the same platter or trencher as the lady whom he escorted into dinner.

Wines, having been tasted, were handed by kneeling cupbearers, who held the cup (Figs. 182, 184, 423, and 438, No. 9) in the left hand and removed its cover with the right.

For each course five or six dishes were served, often more, accompanied by many rich sauces. Between each course and the next, at an important banquet, a "sotelte"[1] was brought in—a confection of jelly, pasties, pies and sugar made in all kinds of fantastic devices, ships, castles, etc., some bearing mottoes. A contemporary description of one such sotelte runs as follows: "The Holy Virgyne and Gabrielle gretynge hur with an Ave." A "comedy" was another name for a quaint dish. The chef d'œuvre of the banquet would be a roast peacock, brought to table on the best dish, with head and fully displayed tail.[2] Frequently at an important banquet musicians, actors and acrobats gave performances during or between the courses; these took place in the centre of the hall.

After the repast the ceremony of washing hands was repeated, and the table-cloths were removed. Spices, comfits, wines, especially hippocras, were handed round, and the signal for the games, etc. to begin was given by the host.

At the end of the fourteenth century it became usual for the lord and his family to dine in "an upper chamber," and the old custom of the whole household partaking of supper together in the great hall began to die out, except on any auspicious occasion.

Breakfast made its first appearance in the fifteenth century. It consisted of bread, beef, brawn and herrings, with wine or ale as the accompanying beverage.

The usual titivating took place among ladies and gentlemen about

---

[1] *Sotelte* = a subtlety.   [2] For a fourteenth-century menu, *see* p. 285.

PLATE II. SCULPTURE IN FRANCE. TWELFTH CENTURY

A. Le Roi Clovis } From Notre Dame Corbeil
B. La Reine Clotilde }

C. La Reine de Saba } In Saint Louis de Naud
D. Le Roi Salomon }

E. A Saint }
F. Do. } In Cathedrale de Chartres
G. Do. }

to enter the hall for either dinner or supper, but the only mention of "dinner dress" to be met with in mediæval writings is a garment called a "seurcot à mangier." Ladies of fashion retired after a strenuous day and discarded their daytime gowns, robing themselves in the surcote à manger before sitting down to dine. The particular shape of this garment is not described; but as the sideless gown came into fashion during the second half of the fourteenth century, and some illuminations show it worn at dinner, it is safe to surmise that this was the same garment.

Table manners in mediæval times are usually thought of as having been anything but nice. Most of the common decencies of to-day, however, were practised in the fifteenth century, and probably much earlier. Regulations for good behaviour, to be found in contemporary writings, present a fresh aspect for our contemplation, as evidenced by the undernoted extracts:

Byt not thy brede, but breke as myche as thou wyll ete.

Do not cram thy cheeks out wyth food like an ape.

Drye thy mouthe when thou schall drynke.

Yf thou spitt over the borde or elles upon it thou schalle be holden an uncurtayse mon.

Clense not thy tethe at mete with knyfe, styk or wande, or drynke with food in thy mouthe.

Nor blow not on thy drynke nor mete or put thy knyfe in the mouthe nor with the borde-clothe thi tethe thou wype.

After mete when thou shal wasshe spitt not in the basyn.

Whenne that so ys that ende shalle kome of mete your knyffes clene (and put them where they ouhte to be (in the case), and foule tales noone to other telle.

Withe fulle mouthe drynke in no wyse.

Whenne ye shalle drynke, your mouthe clence withe a clothe.

Thy mouthe not to full when thou dost eate.

> Not smackynge thy lyppes as comonly do hogges,
> Nor gnawynge the bones as it were dogges.
> Such rudenes abhorre, suche beastlynes flie.
> At the table behave thy selfe manerly.
>
> Pyke not thy teethe at the table syttynge
> Nor use at thy meate over muche spytynge.
> Ley not thyne elbowe nor thy fyst
> Upon the tabylle whylis that thou etist.
> Bulk (belch or hiccup) not as a beene were yn thy throte.
>
> Thy spone with pottage to full do not fyll
> For fylynge the cloth, if thou fortune to spyll.
> For rudnes it is thy pottage to sup
> Or speak to any, his head in the cup.
>
> Nor suppe not with grete sowndynge
> Nother potage nor other thynge.

Cleanliness and the bath. In justice to our ancestors of the Middle Ages it should be made clear that the opinion of their uncleanliness entertained in these later times is without foundation. Advice as to thorough washing is frequently given in mediæval writings.

"And loue (love) you to be cleane and wel apparelled, for from our cradles let us abhor uncleannes, which neither nature or reason can endure."

With the coming of the Romans the bath was introduced into Roman Britain. Romans of all classes paid great attention to cleanliness and the performance of the toilet. These customs were adopted by the Roman Briton, and in Roman settlements of any importance buildings were erected in which hot and cold baths were the principal attraction; and here the people spent the leisure which we pass to-day in cafés and clubs.

During the Anglo-Saxon period there is meagre evidence of the continuance of this wholesome practice in England, but by the eleventh and twelfth centuries plenty of references to the use of the bath in France are to be found. These suggest that if the English were not too clean, such was not the case with the Normans and French. It may be safely surmised that the bath was an important detail in the toilet of the luxurious Eleanor of Aquitaine, even during her "Grand Tour" of Europe to the Holy Land.

In troubadour songs and stories mention is frequently made of the bath, taken at home or in an establishment erected for the purpose. By this time, the thirteenth century, public baths had lost their importance as a facility for reunion, and had an exclusively hygienic use. It may be surprising to some that in the unsophisticated (!) days of the thirteenth century "bath salts" were used — aromatic baths were a favourite indulgence with the upper and middle classes.

General abhorrence of "the unwashed" and of dirty clothes is proved by many references, most emphatic in their disapproval, to be found in romances of the time. It is true, however, that we have some evidence to the contrary: a certain washing bill from December to May only amounts to fifteen pence, and, even taking into consideration the value of money at that time, this does not speak highly for the fastidiousness of a royal lady of the early thirteenth century.

During the periods when it was the fashion to wear many garments, with numerous etceteras and an elaborate coiffure, it must have taken hours to dress; when garments were difficult to change it followed that this happened infrequently. Simplicity of dress promotes cleanliness of body. A fact which indicates that at least the upper classes were accustomed to the luxury of conveniences for ablutions is that nearly all monastic establishments had bathrooms or baths installed for the use of the inmates, and special ones were reserved for visitors. The clergy did *not* condemn cleanliness of person, but they were very much opposed to meticulous care of the body and hair, and the long ceremony of the toilet which took up so much time among fashionable society. Incessant complaints by the clergy on this point are met with in the writings of various periods.

The baths. The baths of Roman times were sunk in the floor, but this was not always the case in the Middle Ages. There are some representations of baths in illuminated MSS. of various dates. One twelfth-century drawing shows the use of a large metal bowl or basin set upon a wooden stand, very highly ornamented and therefore clearly regarded as an important item of domestic equipment. Another drawing (*see* Fig. 597) illustrates an ordinary wooden wash-tub such as had been in use for some centuries.

In the thirteenth century and onwards, it was customary to have the bath enclosed in a tent-like arrangement of linen, hung from a hoop fixed to the ceiling, and in this the bather could perform ablutions without fear of spectators, or of splashing the contents of the apartment. It is probable that a shower-bath or douche was arranged in this tent. In a wardrobe account of Queen Isabella of Valois, 419 yards of linen to hang round the bath is mentioned.

It is evident that baths were considered a great comfort, and an illuminated MS. dating about 1475 illustrates the various luxuries indulged in at that time. In one miniature, circular wooden tubs are shown, hung by chains from the ceiling, with two or three persons bathing in each.

In the fifteenth century three beautiful bathrooms were fitted up at Windsor and Westminster for the use of the royal family.

Fifteenth-century directions for giving a bath or "stewe" to a gentleman run as follows:

> If your lord will to the bath his body to wasche clene
> Hang sheets round about the roof; do thus as I mean.
> Every sheet full of flowers and herbs sweet and green,
> And look ye have sponges five or six thereon to sit or lean.
> Look there be a great sponge thereon your lord to sit
> Thereon a sheet as so he may bathe him there afit.
> Under his feet also a sponge if there be any to put,
> And always be sure of the door and see that he be shut.
> A bason full in your hand of herbs hot and fresh
> And with a soft sponge in hand his body that ye wasche,
> Rince him with rose water warm and fair upon him sprinkle

Wardrobe accounts give many details not only as regards clothes but other items of interest; and one dating 1349 proves the existence of a certain toilet utensil which is in common use to-day.

Portable tripod washstands with urn and tap, basin and waste-pipe, and slop-pail complete, were in use during the fifteenth century; one is shown in Fig. 597.

With regard to sanitation, one has only to visit a Norman castle—Newcastle, Orford, Castle Hedingham, etc.—and examine for oneself the excellent domestic and sanitary arrangements.

———

A word of warning may be apposite. The conclusions of any one authority should be carefully checked against the observations of others, for interpretation of these ancient records is full of traps for the unwary.

Study of illuminated MSS. or sculpture of early times requires care and knowledge if the information they contain is to be absorbed without error. For example, it is difficult to distinguish between the ordinary fashionable dress of his time which an artist may portray, and the occasional differences which he may introduce when depicting some Biblical characters, or a "fancy" costume of his own invention. Again, it has to be remembered that the practice of clothing in "modern" dress any representation of people of ancient times was almost universal among illuminators and sculptors during the Early Ages and Mediæval days.

Archæologists should be thanked for these anachronisms: they give valuable information about the costume of the period *in which the artist lived*. The explanation is that fashion changed so seldom and so slowly, that for long periods the younger generation wore very much the same style of dress as the older (this was the *rule*, not the exception); therefore, an artist whose father or even grandfather dressed as he did himself, imagined that the same style had been handed down for centuries. He believed that men and women living two or six centuries earlier must have dressed in the same way. There were no costume books in those days.

One shudders to think how the archæologist of future centuries may be handicapped in his researches by discovery of records of such stage presentations as the Georgian productions of Shakespeare in powdered wigs and "square cuts," and the present Neo-Georgian versions of the same dramatist's works in plus-fours and bowlers.

CONTENTS

LIST OF ILLUSTRATIONS

IN COLOUR AND HALF-TONE

*NOTE: For this edition, the color plates, each marked by an asterisk, appear between pages 188 and 189.

LIST OF ILLUSTRATIONS

BLACK AND WHITE

LIST OF AUTHORITIES QUOTED

Hugh Arnold (Stained Glass)
G. H. Birch
Beriah Botfield
Charles Boutell (Heraldry)
Rev. Dr. Cobham Brewer
Sir Edmund Burke
Albert F. Calvert
Geoffrey Chaucer
Rev. H. J. Chaytor (Troubadours)
Dictionary of National Biography
Herbert Druitt (Brasses)
Thomas Elmham
Camille Enlart
F. W. Fairholt
Rohault de Fleury
Frank Rede Fowke
Edward A. Freeman
Sir John Froissart
Viscomtesse de Furnes
Samuel Rawson Gardiner
H. de B. Gibbins
J. R. Green
Carl Gross (Guilds)
Guy of Amiens
Rev. James Hastings
J. A. Herbert (Illuminated MSS.)
John Hoveden
George Leland Hunter (Tapestry)
Sir Thomas Graham Jackson
Sire de Joinville
Jules J. Jusserand
A. F. Kendrick
Patrick Kirwan
Henry Knighton
Paul Lacroix
William Langland

G. Ambrose Lee (Heraldry, etc.)
W. R. Lethaby
Walter Lowrie
John Lydgate
Herbert W. Macklin (Brasses)
William Maitland
Arazio Marucchi
Michaud. Biographie Universelle
Eric G. Millar (Illuminated MSS.)
Enguerrand de Monstrelet
Poul Nörlund
Matthew Paris
Paston Letters
Piers of Langtoft
Sir James Henry Ramsay, Bart.
Robert of Gloucester
James Harvey Robinson
Roger de Hoveden
Roger of Wendover
G. McN. Rushforth (Brasses)
Justin H. Smith (Troubadours)
Toulmin Smith (Guilds)
Alexander Speltz
C. A. Stothard
John Stow
Agnes Strickland
Father Herbert Thurston
H. D. Traill
George Unwin (Guilds)
E. Viollet-le-Duc
Ordericus Vitalis
Thomas Walsingham
J. S. M. Ward
William of Malmesbury
William of Newburgh

CHAPTER I
1066–1154

CONTENTS

XIcent

Fig. 1. Border

COSTUME AND FASHION

CHAPTER I

1066–1154

CONTEMPORARY EMPERORS AND KINGS

	ENGLAND	FRANCE	GERMANY
1066	William I. Matilda of Flanders	Philippe I., 1060–1108 1. Bertha of Holland 2. Bertrade de Montford	Henry IV., 1056–1099 Bertha of Susa
1087	William II.		
1099			Henry V., 1099–1125 Matilda of England
1100	Henry I. 1. Matilda of Scotland 2. Adelicia of Louvaine		
1108		Louis VI. le Gros, 1081–1137 1. de Crécy 2. Adelaide of Savoy	
1125			Lothaire II., 1125–1138 Richèze, daughter and heiress of Henri le Gros END OF FRANCONIAN DYNASTY
1135	Stephen Matilda of Boulogne		
1137		Louis VII., 1137–1180 1. Eleanor of Aquitaine 2. Constance of Castile 3. Alice of Champagne	
1138			Conrad III. of Franconia 1138–1152 Bertha of Salzbach END OF HOHENSTAUFEN DYNASTY
1152			Frederick I. Barbarossa (Redbeard), 1152–1190 1. Adela von Vohbourg 2. Béatrix de Bourgoyne

HISTORICAL DATA

1066-1154

1066. The Battle of Senlac, or Hastings, was fought on 14 October, 1066. The subsequent conquest of England by William, Duke of Normandy, occupied a very short time; in marked contrast to the protracted course of Saxon subjugation of Britain five centuries earlier.

The English nobles and gentry who supported William continued to hold their estates under him. The lands of those who had fallen in fight against him, or fled the country, were confiscated and given to the Norman nobles and military attendants who had helped William to conquer the country, and the names of these are set out in the Battle Abbey Roll. Among them were many who married English heiresses and widows—the Norman ancestors of noble families who hold estates in England to-day, or did so at any rate yesterday.[1]

But many, the flower of English youth, made their way to distant lands, and some served valiantly in the armies and the Varangian Guard (see Vol. I., p. 187) of Alexius, Emperor of Byzantium.

No formal change was made in the constitution of the country, but the English were brought into closer contact with the Continent, thereby gaining a new culture and wider political relations. The everyday life of the people continued much the same as before the Conquest.

"In the course of three months, by God's providence, tranquillity was restored throughout England, and the bishops and barons of the realm, having made their peace with William, entreated him to be crowned, according to the custom of the English kings."—ORDERICUS VITALUS.

The coronation took place at Westminster on Midwinter Day (Christmas Day) 1066.

"Stigand, Archbishop of Canterbury, refused to 'lay hands' on one who, as he alleged, was a bloody man, and the invader of another's rights. However, Ealdred, Archbishop of York, a good and wise man, discharged this function, realising, more astutely, that one should yield to the times, and not resist the dispensation of Providence."—WILLIAM OF NEWBURGH.

1067. The tranquillity of the country was so reassuring, that within three months of his coronation King William was able to leave England and return to Normandy (1067), with a splendid company of nobles, both Norman and English.

1068. The city of Exeter had been held by the late King Harold's mother, Gytha, and her two sons, but it was stormed by William's faithful friend William Fitz-Osbern, and its fall in 1068 completely overthrew the power of Wessex.

William returned from Normandy shortly after this event. Having been in England a few months he sent persons of high rank to Normandy to fetch his wife Matilda, who crossed the Channel attended by many knights and noble ladies, and by her chaplain, Guy, Bishop of Amiens. She was crowned at Winchester, at Whitsuntide of the same year, by Ealdred, Archbishop of York. William was re-crowned with her, the ceremony being more splendid than his first coronation, by reason of the charm and majestic personality of the new queen, and the number of her ladies.

At this coronation the office of King's Champion, unknown among Anglo-Saxon monarchs, was introduced into England. It was discharged by William's "dispenser" or steward, a Norman knight named Robert, Lord of Fontenaye-le-Marmion, in whose family this privilege was hereditary. William bestowed upon him the castle and lands of Tamworth. He also granted to Marmion the Manor of Scrivelsbye in Lincolnshire, and at a later date the office of King's Champion descended, through a co-heiress of Philip Marmion, to the Dymocks of Scrivelsbye.

1070. The last struggle of the English for freedom from William's domination was made by the Earls Eadwine and Morkere, together with the famous Hereward the Wake, "the Last of the English," at their camp of refuge at Ely in the midst of the Fens. Vanquished by the king, Hereward fled, but in 1070 became reconciled to William, to whom he paid homage. At last William was in deed, as well as in name, king over England. Soon afterwards the

[1] Lloyd George's Budget, 1911.

Norman barons gave cause for anxiety by faithlessness to their sovereign, and this, together with trouble arising through the turbulence of his sons, overshadowed the remainder of William's reign.

Lanfranc, Archbishop of Canterbury.

Successful invasion of Scotland against Malcolm Canmor.

William, a monk of Jumiéges and chronicler, flourished 1070; died 1090.

1071. William, ninth Duke of Aquitaine and Count of Poitiers. The earliest troubadour known. Born 1071; died 1127.

1073. Henry IV. of Germany wages war against the Saxons, whom he conquers in 1075.

1075. Ordericus Vitalis, the historian, born at Atcham, near Shrewsbury. Died 1143.

The first of many risings took place in 1075. The occasion, curiously enough, was the first of many society weddings which influenced fashions. Unfortunately, no description of the bride's trousseau, or the gowns of the guests, remains for our edification. Ralph of Wader, Earl of Norfolk, without permission from the king, wedded Emma, the daughter of William Fitz-Osbern and sister of Roger, Earl of Hereford. The "bride-ale" was celebrated at Exning,[1] probably in the old royal residence, and to it were bidden many great men, including Earl Waltheof. Here a plot to dethrone William was hatched. Waltheof refused participation, but promised secrecy. The two earls (Norfolk and Hereford) raised an army of mercenaries, but were defeated by the English and Norman forces. The bridegroom fled overseas, leaving his bride to defend Norwich, which charge she most bravely fulfilled. Roger of Hereford was taken and Waltheof surrendered.

1076. Ingulf (born 1030), Abbot of Crowland 1076, and secretary to William I. Died 1109.

1082. Sugar, Abbat of S. Denis. One of the most illustrious ministers of France, author of Life of Louis VII., and founder of the great Chronicles of S. Denys. Died 1152.

1083. Florence of Worcester, chronicler, born some years previously. In 1083 he continued the Chronicles of Marianus Scotus. Died 1118.

Henry of Huntingdon, English chronicler, born this year; died 1155.

1086. Domesday Book, or Liber Wintoniæ, begun in 1080, completed this year, and kept in the Treasury at Winchester.

1087. Death of William the Conqueror.

Accession of William II. (Rufus).

Robert Curthose succeeds William I. as Duke of Normandy.

1093. Anselm, Archbishop of Canterbury.

War with Scotland, and death of Malcolm Canmor.

1095. Second revolt of the barons.

Foulcher de Chartres, historian, chaplain to Baldwin I., King of Jerusalem.

William of Malmesbury, historian, born this year; died 1143.

1096–7. First Crusade.

1099. Jerusalem captured, and Latin kingdom founded.

1100. Death of William II.

Accession of Henry I.

"Maistre" Wace born in Jersey; historian and author of Roman de Rou. Died 1175.

1101. Third revolt of the barons.

Geoffrey of Monmouth, chronicler, born about this time; died 1154.

1104. Guibert, born 1055, Abbé de S. Marie de Nogent-sous-Coucy, 1104. Died 1124.

1106. Battle of Tenchebrai. Robert of Normandy defeated and the dukedom ceded to the English crown.

Simeon, monk of Durham, born 1061. Historian and mathematician. Died 1131.

1109. War between England and France.

1110. Henry V. of Germany goes to Rome, and forces Pope Paschal II. to crown him emperor (1111). He is excommunicated.

1114. Matilda, daughter of Henry I., marries the Emperor Henry V.

Otto of Freising, German historian, born this year.

1118. John of Salisbury, scholar and writer, "for thirty years the central figure of English learning." Bishop of Chartres 1176. Died 1180.

[1] Anna, King of the East Angles, established his royal residence at Exning, whence he could command the surrounding dykes which had been an important defence since the days of the Iceni. His daughter, Etheldreda, queen, saint and foundress of Ely (673), was born here (630), and baptised at the Seven Springs in the vicinity. The site of this residence to-day is but a mound covered with trees, surrounded by a moat, and set in the midst of fields, wherein graze worn-out racers, less than one mile from Newmarket.

From ancient times Exning was the centre of the horse trade. The old mart in this amphitheatre was deserted in 1227 on account of an outbreak of plague, and on the Icknield Way, between Cambridgeshire and Suffolk, was established another—New Market.

1120. After the festivities which marked the close of the French wars, Henry I. and his retinue returned to England, followed shortly afterwards by his only son, William the Ætheling. Embarking at Barfleur, the prince and all on board save one were lost in the tragic wreck of the *White Ship*. Through this catastrophe, Henry's daughter, Matilda, widow of the Emperor Henry V. of Germany, became heiress to the throne of England—by right of her birth, and of her acknowledgment by the English people, who called her "The Lady of the English."

1122. Christiens de Troyes, poet and romancer. Author of *Lancelot du Lac*. Died 1195.

1124. Renewal of hostilities between England and France.

1127. Geoffrey Plantagenet (later Duke of Normandy, 1144), Count of Anjou, Maine and Touraine, marries Matilda, daughter and heiress of Henry I., and widow of the Emperor Henry V.

1129. Peace.

1135. Death of Henry I.
Accession of Stephen.
Piers or Peter of Blois born. Chancellor to Archbishop of Canterbury. Author, and secretary to Eleanor of Aquitaine. One of the most distinguished men of the twelfth century. Died before 1203.

1136. William of Newburgh, historian, born; died 1208.

1137. Nicholas Brakespeare born near St. Albans. Elected Abbot of S. Rufus, Avignon, 1137; Cardinal-Bishop of Albano, 1146; and Pope, 1154. The only Englishman who sat upon the papal throne. He took the name of Adrian IV. Died 1159.

1138. David of Scotland invades England in support of Matilda's claim to the throne, but is defeated at the Battle of the Standard.

1139. Beginning of Civil War in England.

1143. Walter Mapes, romance writer, born; died 1196.

1147. The Second Crusade preached by S. Bernard and undertaken by the Emperor Conrad and Louis VII. of France.

1150. Rigord, a monk of S. Denis, historiographer of Philippe Augustus. Died 1207.
Roger Hoveden, chronicler, continued Bede's *History*; died 1202.
Gervase of Tilbury born. English chronicler, and Marshal of the Kingdom of Arles; died 1235.

1152. Giraldus Cambrensis, or Gerald de Barri, historian, born; died 1223.
Henry, Duke of Normandy (Matilda's son), invaded England in support of his mother's claims and his own. After the death of Stephen's elder son Eustace, the king was induced to make peace, and by the Treaty of Wallingford (1153) the long-fought dispute was settled. Stephen was to retain the crown for life, and at his death, to the exclusion of his other children, Matilda's son was to succeed to his mother's inheritance.

1154. Death of Stephen.
Accession of Henry II.

Fig. 2. Border

THE ARTS

ARCHITECTURE

THE work of the Western artists who followed Classic traditions, combined with that of the Byzantine artists (both employed by Charlemagne), developed into what is known as Romanesque Art, a general term for all the debased styles which sprang from attempts to imitate Roman work. This style—the Romanesque—made very little progress in Germany until the beginning of the eleventh century, when its influence spread westward into France.

In England the style in vogue was termed Norman, and was simply an imitation of the Romanesque of the Norman-French. It gradually developed into a definite national style, its period dating approximately from 1050 to 1150. Norman architecture is characterised chiefly by the round arch, supported on short massive columns, with plain capitals and bases. The narrow round-headed windows were seldom filled with glass, wooden shutters being used instead to keep out the wind and rain. Decoration was exceptional, although zig-zag and billet mouldings, and dog's-tooth ornament, came into use later. The interior stone walls were invariably plastered over to give an even surface.

After William I. had established himself as King of England he sent for the most competent architects and artists from Normandy, France and Italy—in all cases, priests—who commenced building operations on a large scale, and the superior quality of Norman work, indicative of their national thoroughness, stands as a landmark in the history of English art and architecture. Much credit is due to William, for, having a passion for building, he was indefatigable in his supervision of all details.

The Normans can scarcely be said to have introduced a new style of art into England, for already the English were accomplished in a somewhat similar type of architecture, although definitely inferior to theirs. In the chief towns and cities, existing stone buildings erected by the English were demolished, and in their places arose new buildings of a much more solid nature. It is interesting to note that Lanfranc, the Norman, began to rebuild Canterbury Cathedral in 1070, the earlier buildings having been entirely destroyed by the Danes (1011) and by fire (1067). Lanfranc's work was completed in 1077.

Churches built at this period are numerous, as are also castles. The latter were constructed solely as fortresses, and as such the White Tower is of first importance. It was begun about the year 1077 by Gundulf, a monk of the Abbey of Bec in Normandy, who was a celebrated architect. He was Bishop of Rochester from 1076 to 1108, and rebuilt the cathedral there; the beautiful west door is one of the few survivals of his work. He was also the architect for the keep at Dover Castle. The building of Durham Castle is due to Earl Waltheof, and must have been completed by the year 1075. Domesday Book names forty-nine Norman castles.

In the twelfth century, a large number of castles were erected by the great nobles. They were built with two objects in view—to provide a military station and a fortified dwelling. These castellated residences became the strongholds of lawless barons, who frequently held them against the king, instead of for him. In the reign of Stephen, as many as one thousand one hundred and fifteen were in existence. Many of the Norman castles of which portions still remain are interesting examples of the domiciles of the upper classes, and show the great hall, kitchens, bedrooms, passages, stairs and domestic offices. A castle of the reign of Henry I. is well typified by the existing pile known as Castle Hedingham, Essex. The architect was Archbishop William de Curbellio (1128–1136), who built it for Aubrey de Vere about 1130.

In 1099, "William (II.) King of England, returning to England out of Normandy, held his Court for the first time in the New Hall at Westminster. When he first entered with a large retinue of soldiers to inspect it, some said that it was much larger than was necessary, but the King replied that it was not half so grand as it ought to be, and would be only a bedroom in proportion to the palace which he intended to build."

Besides this noble hall, Rufus erected a curtain wall to the inner ward around the Tower, and also repaired London Bridge. All these buildings cost an enormous sum, which he wrung from Norman and English alike, and from the Church.

"A rare piece of work," Bow Bridge, was built in stone over the Old Forde, Stratford, by Matilda, wife of King Stephen; "before that time the like had never been seen in England."

ARCHITECTURE IN FRANCE

The Abbey of S. Denis,[1] dedicated to the patron saint of France, was refounded by Dagobert the Great. After five hundred years of vicissitudes by fire and strife, this stately mausoleum of the French monarchs, from Clovis to Louis XVI., was rebuilt in 1140 in the new Gothic style.[2]

[1] S. Denis came from Rome as a Christian missionary in 251. He was founder of the Gallic Church, and first Bishop of Paris. In 272, he suffered martyrdom at the hands of the Roman governor, and his body was thrown into the Seine, but it was recovered by a Gaulish lady, who later became a Christian, and buried in her garden. A church dedicated to this saint was afterwards built upon the site of his grave.

[2] See also p. 77 (Chap. II.).

Chartres was a centre of Druidical worship in pre-Christian times, and, from the fourth century A.D., a Christian church existed there which lasted for over seven hundred years. Various successive buildings were destroyed by fire, until, in the year 1110, it was entirely rebuilt, including the existing western front. In 1194 fire again destroyed the whole church with the exception of the western front and the statues thereon, which may be studied to-day.

SCULPTURE

In the eleventh century Western Europe saw a noteworthy revival in the sculptor's art. It began in Italy, influenced directly by the Romanesque style of earlier generations; and that country remained pre-eminent throughout the movement until the end of the sixteenth century. What has been called the "Artistic Crusade" extended from Italy through Southern France, where interesting links between the ancient Classic and Mediæval styles are to be found at Arles (Provence), Metz (Austrasia), and in Burgundy. Thence it spread onwards to Normandy, Germany, Flanders. Early sculpture in all these countries is very closely connected with the revival of art in Italy, but, as progress was made, national characteristics of a distinct kind developed in each. In Normandy masons and sculptors formed a large and powerful corporation, a fact which had its bearing, later, on the development of guilds in this country.

After the Norman Conquest many French and Norman artists were employed to undertake the renovation of various English churches and abbeys. Some of these buildings contained already sculpture of French and Byzantine origin, for from the seventh century onwards French "masters in stone" had been called to the aid of the English authorities for the building and ornamentation of their finest ecclesiastical edifices.

Prior to the renewal of Norman influence on art in England, sculpture in the late Anglo-Saxon period had been applied mainly to the decoration of incised memorial slabs, and to simple architectural details; in character it consisted of carved scroll-work and conventional foliage. During the second part of the eleventh century, sculpture was used considerably for the ornamentation of fonts, and for reliefs over church doors, the tympanum, and the earlier subject-matter was sometimes enlivened by the introduction of figures. As yet, however, sculpture in this country was a somewhat crude copy of Byzantine and Romanesque styles, and these themselves were but a feeble imitation of Classic work.

In addition to some interesting statues referred to below, the early part of the twelfth century saw the beginning (in France) of another important branch of sculpture of the time, which took the form of sepulchral effigies. Early examples in England were about fifty years later than those in France, and were executed in Purbeck marble. The hardness of this material explains why many details are somewhat indefinite, but later on a softer stone was employed, which permitted a greater freedom of treatment and resulted in a much improved technique; indeed, sculpture appears to have been peculiarly the form of artistic expression which best suited the English faculty—early examples show a pronounced "feeling" for its decorative possibilities—and this was pursued and elaborated by Gothic artists.

SCULPTURE IN FRANCE

The most beautiful examples of early figure sculpture are not in England. They are to be found in the statues ornamenting the Abbey of S. Denis, which was reconstructed under Abbat Sugar between the years 1137–1180. This collection, including several early twelfth-century examples removed from Notre Dame de Corbeil, on the destruction of that church, is noted for its wonderful statues of kings and queens of France, represented in costumes of the twelfth and thirteenth centuries (Plate II., A and B). Other fine examples are to be seen at Chartres, Etampes, Bourges, and Saint Louis de Naud. All represent historical personages of various periods, but each is shown in the style of costume fashionable at the middle of the twelfth century (Plate II., C and D).

The western front (1130–1150) or Porte Royale at Chartres Cathedral comprises three arches, and every available space is occupied by sculptured figures of various sizes, ranging from over life-size to miniature figures of a few inches (Plate II., E, F, G). The figures are somewhat elongated, but are excellent authorities for costume of this period, and the less exposed statues still retain traces of decoration in gold and colour. At Bourges there are many statues of the early twelfth century, some still showing the original colouring. The central porch of Notre Dame at Châlons-sur-Marne contains many interesting statues dating about 1140.

SCULPTURE IN ENGLAND

To some extent copied from these French examples, the statues of Henry I. and Matilda, on either side of the west door of Rochester Cathedral, are the oldest known sculptured effigies of an English king and queen. These statues must have been erected after the queen's death in 1118, as details in the costumes of both show the fashions of 1130. During the Civil War of Charles I.'s time they were much mutilated, and scarcely any trace of the faces or crowns is left.

The portraits sculptured on either side of the chancel window in Furness Abbey, and formerly thought to portray King Stephen and his wife Matilda, are now proved to represent Henry IV. and his queen. Discoveries of this kind with regard to historical subjects in all branches of art have been made frequently of late years. In some instances this may be disappointing, but the gain in historical accuracy more than compensates for the loss of some cherished misconception.

(*Continued on p.* 78.)

STAINED GLASS

The earliest example in Western Europe of stained glass used for windows is to be found in the cathedral at Augsburg, and dates about 1065. One of the figures, that of King David, shows the costume of a king or noble of this period.

The stained glass in Le Mans Cathedral dates between 1081–1097, and shows a series of figures in white and coloured draperies, against backgrounds of alternate blue and red glass. The delineation of the figures displays the same treatment as the figures in contemporary illuminated MSS.

Stained glass of the twelfth century is to be seen in the west window at Chartres Cathedral, 1142–1150. At S. Denis a window consisting of ten pictures illustrating the First Crusade is intensely valuable as an authority for Western armour, and for the costumes of the Saracens. It was erected about 1140 by Abbat Sugar, but destroyed in the Revolution of 1789. Fortunately, copies are extant.

Some windows in Canterbury Cathedral were the first in England to be filled with stained glass, about 1130. Several panels of twelfth-century stained glass were removed in the nineteenth century from their original positions in the choir clerestory to the window in the south transept, and to the west window. They represent various saints, dressed in costumes very similar to that shown in Fig. 10. These, together with the stained glass at Chartres and S. Denis, represent the first examples of a new school—a change from Byzantine characteristics to Gothic. The Crucifixion window at Poitiers is of the older school, although it dates from the second half of the twelfth century.

XII th.

Fig. 3. Border

ILLUMINATED MANUSCRIPTS

The art of illustrating MSS. by drawings in outline appeared in Western Europe early in the ninth century. A century later, Anglo-Saxon artists adopted this style, and figure-drawing in outline is the characteristic feature of illuminated MSS. of the tenth as well as of the eleventh century. For the whole of this period the art of the illuminator in England was practised chiefly at Winchester and Canterbury. The work of this southern Anglo-Saxon school attained perfection during the second half of the eleventh century, and maintained its standard during the twelfth and first part of the thirteenth centuries.

Human figures, in brown or black ink, are elongated, and the drawing shows an indifferent sense of proportion. The lines are slightly thickened at various points to suggest shadows, and the draperies have a wrinkled appearance, and float around and away from the body and limbs, as if wafted in a breeze. The zig-zag or ragged effect seen at the edges of the garments shows the influence of early Classic models. To this outline of brown or black ink, artists of this time added a tinted line, often in a brilliant hue, apparently intended to hint at the use of different colours in the robes.

A very favourite subject with these artists was to picture the lower orders engaged in such work as was consistent with the seasons of the year, and illustrations of this type are generally found in calendars prefixed to psalters or other religious MSS.

Anglo-Saxon and other early illuminators adopted the Roman custom of painting the first words or initial letter of an important sentence in vermilion, or *red lead* (Latin, *minium*). As early as the eighth century these first letters were elaborated with decorative designs in colours, and eventually developed into delightful little pictures, usually painted on a groundwork of red lead. The name "miniature," [1] derived from *minium*, was given to these small pictures even when they were not enclosed in an initial letter.

After the Norman Conquest many branches of art, including that of the illuminator, were affected by a new influence which greatly improved and changed their character. In illuminated MSS. this is not noticeable until the beginning of the twelfth century, when the Anglo-Saxon style began to die out.

As regards illuminated MSS., the first part of the twelfth century is a period of transition. The drawing of the human figure improved but slightly, and its treatment was still somewhat archaic: the body was emaciated, the arms and legs long and thin. This type of figure-drawing is distinctive of English draftsmanship of the time.

---

[1] In the sixteenth century the term "miniature" was slightly strained to signify any picture on a small scale, particularly portraits, and the word gradually acquired its modern function of denoting a small version of something usually presented on a larger scale.

In addition to the coloured pigments used during the eleventh century gold was now employed, but sparingly, and it was not burnished. Decorated initial letters began to make their appearance in this century, and were filled with curious animal subjects in conjunction with floral motifs.

(Continued on p. 79.)

Fig. 4. Border, twelfth century

TAPESTRY

References to tapestry at various periods are apt to mislead the student unless care be taken to ascertain the sort of tapestry in use at a given time. Brief references are made, therefore, to the development of the material itself, and to the changing purposes for which it was used. The following note is continued in later chapters.

The Latin "aulaeum," plural "aelaea," signified a curtain, carpet or hanging. "Circundo cubiculum aelaeis"="to hang the chamber." "Tapete" in Latin meant the same, and was applied to a material of brilliant colour displaying human and animal figures, hunting scenes, etc., *embroidered* or *woven* upon it. Originally Oriental in character, it was introduced into archaic Greece and Rome, and there used for draping over furniture, or hung upon the wall.

Embroidered material was used for wall hangings and door curtains during the Byzantine epoch. In Western Europe this method of covering the walls came into use, to a moderate degree, among those nations influenced by Roman taste and culture, and later by that of Byzantium. Any rich fabric imported from the East, either figured or plain, might be used in this way. Hangings of precious stuffs (palls) were used principally for the decoration of churches.

Probably the first mention of hangings used in England dates from the eighth century, when Bishop Eagberht of York adorned several churches with silken material covered with strange figures. France led the way, however, in the decoration of churches in this manner, and frequent mention is found in records from this time onwards.

In the eleventh century, tapestries were *woven* at Poitiers, and as early as 1025 they had become so famous that foreign clerics acquired pieces to garnish their churches.

An important point arises at this date as regards the name "tapestry" and its variations. Hitherto it was applied to plain material or hangings embroidered or woven with figures, but henceforth the name "tapestry" was properly applied exclusively to *woven picture wall hangings*. These woven hangings of French make—tapestries —of the eleventh and twelfth centuries have been described [1] as having plain-coloured or decorative backgrounds whereon were represented figures of emperors, kings, biblical personages, heroes, animals and flowers. These subjects were delineated in a strange conventional manner and the draftsmanship was considerably cruder and more primitive than any drawings to be found in contemporary illustrated MSS.

A description of an apartment in a palace in Normandy occupied by Adela (died 1137), Countess of Blois, a daughter of William I., is given in a poem dated 1107.[2] The walls of the long hall were covered with tapestries woven in wool, silk, gold and silver. On one of the long walls was a hanging representing Chaos, the Creation, the Fall and Death of Abel, and the Deluge. On the other were scenes from Grecian mythology [3] and Roman history. At one end were displayed subjects from biblical history, and at the other, around the alcove which contained the bed, were hangings depicting the Conquest of England. The ceiling counterfeited the firmament and its constellations, and the floor was set with a mosaic showing a map of the then known world. The head of the bed was carved with figures representing Philosophy, Music, Arithmetic, Astronomy and Geometry; at the foot, Rhetoric, Logic and Grammar, and Medicine, Galen and Hippocrates.

On the occasion of public festivities, a royal wedding or the state entry of a king or queen, tapestry was hung in the streets before the houses. This custom dates from this time and it continued for many centuries. The tapestries used for this purpose generally represented moral stories, caricatures, satires, etc.

The nature of the design of these tapestries just described is exemplified in the so-called Bayeux "Tapestry" now in the Hôtel de Ville, Bayeux. This shows a very crude treatment of human figures, animals, architecture, etc., and is said to have been executed by Matilda of Flanders and her ladies.[4] It consists of a piece of linen 220 feet long

---

[1] In his *Spanish Royal Tapestries*, Mr. Albert F. Calvert makes the following interesting remarks:

"The term tapestry is often applied to any hangings of mediæval workmanship whether woven in a frame or not. This use of the word is incorrect.

"Tapestry is a fabric woven with coloured wools on to warp threads in a loom or frame in which the weft completely conceals the warp. It is woven all in one piece. This distinguishes it from embroidery or other needlework to which stitches are added after the groundwork of the fabric has been detached from the frame. The worker weaves directly from a design or cartoon which is supplied to him."

[2] Written by Baudri, Abbat of Bourgueil, afterwards Bishop of Dol.

[3] The Siege of Troy was a very favourite subject from these early times and continued to be popular until the seventeenth century.

[4] In the Introduction to his book on the Bayeux Tapestry, Mr. Frank Rede Fowke says:

"I conclude the tapestry to be a contemporary work in which Queen Matilda had no part, and that it was probably ordered for his cathedral by Bishop Odo, and made by Norman workpeople at Bayeux."

by 20 inches high and *worked with the needle*—embroidered—in eight different-coloured woollen threads. It was made to hang upon the wall of the nave of the cathedral at Bayeux, and in consequence has been erroneously called a tapestry.

Tapestry was not only ornamental but a very useful adjunct to a castle where walls were cold and gloomy in appearance and the rooms large and draughty. Tapestries were often used to divide a large chamber into smaller chambers, and frequently hung between arches from rods fixed at the top of the capitals of the columns or piers. Few windows were set with glass, in fact it was exceptional during the Norman period, the apertures being closed with wooden shutters. When light and air were not required, or draughts unwelcome, tapestry was drawn over the windows. As entrances to rooms were frequently only bays, three feet at the widest and six feet high, often without doors, tapestry was used to conceal them. Entrance or exit was made through vertical divisions in the centre of the fabric. Often one side would be draped back for constant passage through the doorway.

The Saracens of Spain were expert in weaving tapestry, but in the twelfth century the Flemings appropriated the craft and became their successful competitors.

(*Continued on p. 139.*)

Early 12th Cent

Fig. 5. Border

COSTUME IN GENERAL
1066–1154

DRESS OF THE SECOND HALF OF THE ELEVENTH CENTURY

Men. During the Anglo-Saxon period and up to the end of the eleventh century, costume was well adapted to freedom of action. The short, close-fitting garments of the men facilitated natural movement. The arms were carried away from the body, and gesture was animated; in walking, the gait was lively. It was a period of energy.

The portion of Norman costume introduced into England which differed materially from the dress in use here was essentially that of the Court and aristocracy. Figs. 7 and 9 are very different in character from the Anglo-Saxon styles, although the former was known in England prior to the Conquest (*see* Vol. I., pp. 252 and 262). At the same time, the everyday dress worn by the Norman nobility and upper classes, exemplified by Fig. 10, was in a measure similar to the Anglo-Saxon style. This "simple habit" was extolled by Ordericus Vitalis in the following lines:

"They used a modest dress, well fitted to the proportions of their bodies, which was convenient for riding and walking, and for all active employments as common sense dictated."

William of Malmesbury also says: "The Normans were . . . exceedingly particular in their dress and delicate in their food, but not so to excess."

Women. From the earliest times the women of the upper classes were accustomed to wearing long garments. They wore them from infancy, and, for countless generations, their ancestresses had worn them. They had become second nature. The various methods of arranging draperies in use during the Anglo-Saxon period have been dealt with already. Norman ladies of the second half of the eleventh century adopted similar modes.

The shoulders and bust were unrestricted by the easy-fitting upper part of the gown, which fell in ample trailing folds around the legs. The arms were not hampered by the wide sleeves, since constant use had made the manipulation of full garments an easy matter.

DRESS OF THE FIRST HALF OF THE TWELFTH CENTURY

Men. At the end of the eleventh century long robes came into fashion, and remained, with slight variations, until the accession of the Plantagenets. These robes necessitated slow and dignified movements; short steps were essential if the wearer wished to avoid catching the legs and feet in the drapery. Long sleeves likewise obliged the wearer desirous of grace to hold the elbows close to the side.

In Anglo-Saxon times costume in both England and France had been influenced strongly by the prevailing modes of Byzantium, which swayed the fashions of Western Europe.

By the eleventh century these influences had become merged in the characteristic dress of the Anglo-Saxons and Normans, but towards the middle of the twelfth century another Byzantine impulse, due to the First Crusade, transformed the fashions of the nobility.

Having mastered the inconvenience of the earlier modes, it was not difficult for the men to adapt themselves to the shorter draped tunics, or bliauts, which sometimes had moderately wide sleeves and often close-fitting ones.

It was a convenient custom to place the palm of the hand on the hip, so as to relieve the shoulder from the weight of the mantle and keep it away from the feet and from getting involved with the long robe.

The more ample the garments, the more difficult they were to carry gracefully, and it required a complete education—habits learnt from infancy.

Women. The twelfth century brought some innovations into the costume of both sexes and was a period of great extravagance, conspicuous by contrast with the dress of former times.

During the first quarter of the century excessive length of garments was the rage, and, in consequence, gesture and movement became more restrained and subject to the superfluity of material.

At this time also the size of women's waists was much reduced by tightening the gown, which could only be achieved when the gown was made of a substantial material capable of withstanding the strain. Later on, when thinner stuffs became the vogue, it was necessary for women to wear the "corse," or some such strong garment, laced up the back, underneath the bliaut, to retain the bust and constrain the natural shape of the figure.

The introduction of Byzantine modes about 1130 did not change the manner of deportment to any great extent. The body was closely swathed, and much superfluous material clung around the limbs. Plaits of hair hanging to the feet, and long girdles, must have impeded, in a great measure, the movements of the body and limbs, and imparted a certain stiffness to gait and gesture. Dignity, therefore, consisted in great simplicity of attitude, the costume presenting an ensemble of symmetrical perpendicular folds and lines. This was the acme of good taste and characteristic of the complete toilet of a great lady between the years 1130 and 1150, although it remained in fashion until about 1170.

Fig. 6. Ornament, twelfth century

SECTION I.—WILLIAM I. 1066–1087

Nobility—Men

All trace of Scandinavian elements in Art and Costume had disappeared from the Norman race in France by the eleventh century, but they still retained the fierce and turbulent nature, and ardour for war, characteristic of their race. Their costume was like that in use in all other countries in Western Europe, and much influenced by the fashions of Byzantium (*see* Vol. I., p. 255). Many interesting details of this period can be gleaned from the Bayeux Tapestry. Copies are to be found in many museums.[1] For the most part the costumes depicted are military in character, and the English are represented wearing Norman military accoutrements; but this is an ingenuous mistake on the part of the queen and her ladies, who were *not* present on the battlefield, but assumed that the English must have been dressed in the same manner as their own countrymen. Some civilians are included, but only two women.

William I. (born at Falaise, 1027) was exceedingly tall, with a finely proportioned figure. His face was handsome, he had an aquiline nose, quick grey eyes, high forehead, and dark moderately short hair, but his countenance was stern and commanding. When he chose, he could assume a very winning smile, so that few could resist him, but when angry no one dare approach him. By nature he is said to have been cruel, but most of his actions prove him a just judge, a man of great discernment, and even sympathetic. The death of the handsome Earl Waltheof in 1076 has been laid at William's door, but the treachery of Waltheof's wife, Judith, and the greed of his enemies are much more to blame.

In middle age William became bald, and in later life very corpulent.

---

[1] The Victoria and Albert Museum, South Kensington, is one.

Fig. 7. WILLIAM I.

As he rode round the burning city of Mantes, which he had taken, his horse reared and threw him against the pommel of his saddle, inflicting internal injuries. He was removed to Rouen, where he expired on the ides (9th) of September, 1087, and was interred in the Abbey of S. Stephen, Caen. The physicians and others who were present at the death of the Conqueror lost their wits. Alarmed by their anticipation of troubles in the near future, the wealthiest of them mounted their horses and departed in haste to secure their own property. But the inferior attendants, observing that their masters had disappeared, laid hands on the arms, the plate, the robes, the linen, and all the royal furniture, and leaving the corpse almost naked on the floor hastened away.

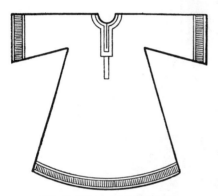

Fig. 8. Shape of the Dalmatic

The state garments of kings at this period can be seen in Fig. 7. It is the type of dress worn by William I. as well as by other kings in Western Europe. The costume consists of at least five garments. Under the mantle referred to below is worn the dalmatic—a vestment of ecclesiastical significance forming part of his regal costume—with wide sleeves. Fig. 8 gives its shape. It is of silk, with an embroidered border of silk and gold decorating the edge, the sleeves, and round the neck. Sometimes a design was powdered, diaper-wise, over the whole garment. A narrow belt encircles the waist, often studded with gold and jewels, the width of the dalmatic being drawn in by it and slightly bulging over it.

The undertunic is of rich material, and about the same length as the dalmatic—to just above the ankles. Under this again would be worn one, two or perhaps three undertunics or shertes.

The sherte worn by the nobility and wealthy upper classes at this period assumed the familiar shape of the shirt of modern times. It was cut straight and descended to the knees, having slits at the sides. Often the slits were at the front and back, and sometimes at the sides as well. The sleeves were close, and reached to the wrists where they were frequently rucked. This garment was made of finely woven linen—"chainsil"—and was invariably white. The Norman nobility set the vogue of ornamenting it by coloured stitching to form a substantial neckband. This stitching was repeated at the wrists.

Worn as an occasional additional luxury, and for warmth, a garment of silk or wool was sometimes used over the sherte, and beneath the undertunic: it was shaped like the sherte, save that the sleeves very often only came to the elbows. When used by the best-dressed people, it was decorated at the edges with needlework. Among the French this garment was known as the JUBE and the blouse worn to-day by the French working-class is its lineal descendant. Over the king's shoulders is draped the semicircular or rectangular cloke, now called in Norman French the "Manteau" or MANTLE. It has an embroidered or gold border, and this garment, like the dalmatic, could have a pattern dispersed over its area. The mantle could be fastened in front, or on the right shoulder, with a clasp or fibula, or tied with cords having metal ornaments at their extremities. *See also* Vol. I., Fig. 121.

Fig. 9. A Norman Noble   Fig. 10. Norman Noble wearing the Cotte

William wears a crown (*see* Fig. 7 and p. 61) on full State occasions, as he did notably at the three great feasts: Easter at Winchester, Pentecost at Westminster, and Christmas at Gloucester. The legs are clothed with hose, or, as they were sometimes called in Norman French, CHAUSSES. They are made of cloth, linen, cotton or silk, and often knitted. The shoes are described under Footgear.

Fig. 9 represents a Norman noble who is dressed in a somewhat similar style. Here the wide-sleeved tunic has a design worked over its surface, in addition to borders at the edge and on the sleeves.

About this time the tunic received various names in the Norman-French language. When short it was called the COTTE; when long, the ROBE; and a little later, when the tunic became a supertunic —the SURCOTE. Fig. 10 shows a Norman noble in everyday dress, wearing the cotte. Its shape is seen in Fig. 11. It should be noticed that the lines on the shoulder and arm are at different angles from

those of preceding diagrams of tunics: this arrangement necessitated either two seams to the sleeve, or joining by a seam to the shoulder, often masked by a band of embroidery. The semicircular mantle in this example is worn fastened in front.

On the legs braies are worn, and over them hose, which appear to be knitted. They are tied below the knees by GARTERS with

Fig. 11. Shape of the Cotte

fringed ends, and the tops of the hose are rolled down over them. This type of leg-covering appears many times in the Bayeux Tapestry.

Nobility—Women

Matilda, born 1031, was the daughter of Baldwin V., Count of Flanders, and a descendant of Ælfred the Great. She was married in 1049 to William, Duke of Normandy, in the Abbey Church of Notre Dame d'Eu. Crowned Queen of England 1068. It has been said of her that she was very fair and graceful, uniting beauty with gentle breeding, and possessing purity of mind and manners. Magnificent and liberal in her gifts, she greatly encouraged the Arts—architecture, painting, embroidery, literature and poetry. Matilda was the first queen of England to sign herself "Regina," although Anglo-Saxon historians, who wrote in Latin, used the word "Regina" in order to avoid introducing so barbarous a word as "Quen" into the Latin text: the king's wife had been known prior to Matilda's time as "The Lady his Companion," or "Quen."

Matilda of Flanders died 1083, and was buried between the choir and the altar of the Abbey Church of the Holy Trinity, Caen.

The Children of William and Matilda

1. Robert Curthose, married Sybilla, whose son William, called "Clito" or Royal Heir, was slain at Alost 1128. Robert died in Cardiff Castle 1134.
2. William Rufus.
3. Henry Beauclerc.
4. Cicelie, a nun of Holy Trinity, Caen.
5. Constance, married Alan Fergan, Earl of Brittany.
6. Alice or Eadwige, contracted to King Harold.
7. Adela, married Stephen, Count of Blois, and was the mother of King Stephen and of Henry, Bishop of Winchester.
8. Agatha, betrothed to Alphonso VI., King of Leon and afterwards of Castile.

It is said that "contemporary" painted portraits of William and Matilda were carefully preserved on the walls of S. Stephen's, Caen, until destroyed by the Revolutionists at the close of the eighteenth century; but the copies which may be seen to-day, published in Montfauçon's *Monumens Monarchie François*, prove them to be works of the thirteenth century. Queen Matilda was dressed in a manner similar to all other great ladies of Western Europe, including the English. Only one new detail of feminine costume was introduced at this time— that was the girdle. In her will, in the register of the Abbey of the Holy Trinity at Caen, kept in the National Library in Paris, we have mention of some items of Matilda's wardrobe:

I give to the Abbey of the Holy Trinity my gown worked at Winchester by Alderet's wife, and the mantle embroidered with gold which is in my chamber, to make a cope. Of my two golden girdles, I give that which is ornamented with emblems for the purpose of suspending the lamp before the great altar. I give my large candelabra, made at S. Lo, my crown, my sceptre, my cups in their cases, another cup made in England, with all my horse trappings, and all my vessels, except those which I may have already disposed of in my lifetime; and lastly I give my lands of Quetchou in Cotentin (Normandy), with two dwellings in England. And I have made all these bequests with the consent of my husband.

It will be seen from this will that the queen greatly valued her gown worked by Alderet's wife, an Anglo-Saxon woman. The royal mantle embroidered with jewels worn by her at her marriage, and probably at her coronation, was kept in the treasury at the Cathedral of Bayeux. It is mentioned in an inventory, dated 1476, of precious effects belonging to that church.

Plate I. (*frontispiece*) represents Queen Matilda, and is founded on this evidence and details derived from other sources. The gown, cut on the plan of the Anglo-Saxon, Vol. I., Dia. 25, is of fine cloth or silk, embroidered in vermilion and gold "by Alderet's wife." It has close sleeves to the wrist, where they finish with a band of similar embroidery; the neck is outlined with the same. The waist is slightly drawn in, and loosely encircling the figure is the girdle, a new article of attire introduced into England at this time. Girdles were made of strands of cord, in gold, silver, or coloured wool, kept together at intervals by metal ornaments, jewelled, or set with enamels and jewels. These ornaments sometimes had emblems upon them. The strands of gold or wool were often connected by knots or twists of wool or gold thread, the loose ends forming tassels. These girdles were generally worn double, with the tasselled ends passing through the looped end at the front. Alternatively, the girdle might be composed of a strip of cloth, possibly stitched with a different colour. 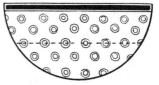 Fig. 12. Diagram of the Mantle More elaborate ones would be made of a twist of silk, plaited with gold. Plate I. shows a gold girdle, strung with gold and enamel ornaments.

The mantle of blue cloth, cut in a semicircle, Fig. 12, has a rich border of crimson embroidered in gold; it is lined with another colour, and fastened across the shoulders by cords connecting circular ornaments.

The undergarments of wealthy women consisted of an undergown, made of rich material, and cut like the over one except that it would not be so full in the skirt part. When the overgown had close sleeves it is very probable the under one was without them. Under this again another gown, called in Norman French the "Camise," was worn, and possibly a second camise under this.

Fig. 13. Norman Noble Lady

The veil in Plate I. is rectangular, made of very soft, floating material,—chainsil, gauze, etc.—embroidered with gold. The crown and sceptre are made of gold, and simple in design.

Fig. 13 shows a noble lady of this reign. Her gown is similar to the one just described.

Norman and English ladies wore a long undergarment to the feet. If worn with a wide-sleeved over-robe, the under one would have tight sleeves rucked at the wrists. The overgarment would be of the same length, and both were cut to fit a little more closely than hitherto round the waist and bust, the skirts widening out towards the hem. The sleeves to the overgarment might be close or wide. Its shape is the same as shown under Anglo-Saxon costume, Vol. I., Dia. 25. The Norman or Old French name for this garment was "robe." This drawing shows the embroidery ornamenting the neck, wrists and upper arm. The last was placed at the edge of, or over, the seam which joined the sleeve to the body part, a seam having become necessary now that the body part fitted closer to the armpit. This lady is wearing a girdle of silk twisted with gold. A mantle would be worn for full dress, attached across the shoulders with cords, while to complete the costume a circular veil would be worn, surmounted by a fillet.

On the head, and round the neck, it was the custom to drape a circular, semicircular, or oblong veil of some soft material, always coloured, and often embroidered. The headcloth or headdress was called COUVRECHEF by the Normans, the origin of our "kerchief." It was also made of fine linen or cambric, draped over the head, and hanging on each side of the face. If the veil was a rectangle, one of the ends, more often than not the right, was thrown over the opposite shoulder, and had almost the same effect as the Anglo-Saxon circular veil. The circular veil with a hole for the face cut in its area (Vol. I., Dia. 26) became obsolete.

The Camise [1] or Chemise (Norman French)

(*Smock*, Anglo-Saxon.) An undergarment falling to the feet or ankles, with close-fitting sleeves, cut on the same lines as the gown. It was generally worn next to the skin. Mention of this garment in its simpler form has been made from time to time, but it became more complicated towards the end of the eleventh century.

The part that covered the shoulders was gathered into a gauging, run on small cords or braids in several rows. This composed the neckband, which usually continued a little way down on to the chest. At the throat it was secured by a button and cord loop. This neckband was frequently decorated with stitching in colours or gold, and often showed above the neck of the gown. The sleeves were finished off in the same way at the wrists, and on the forearm the full material was gauffered so that the sleeve clung close to the arm. A camise of the first half of the twelfth century is shown in Fig. 71: attention is called to the yoke on the shoulder.

The camise was made of various materials: fine wool, linen—particularly chainsil, or silk, when worn by the wealthy and upper classes. The middle and lower classes wore the camise of wool or linen material of inferior make, with less elaborate decoration.

Fig. 14. Border, twelfth-century

Section II.—William II. 1087-1100

Nobility—Men

On the death of the Conqueror, Robert Curthose, his eldest son, succeeded to the Duchy of Normandy (1087-1134). He was incompetent and lazy, and his father had expressed a wish that England, newly conquered and hard to control, should be governed by his second son, William. There was as yet no settled rule of succession to the English crown, and William came immediately to England, seized the treasury at Winchester, and was crowned at Westminster by Lanfranc. He began his reign well; the English, knowing his strength and their need of a

[1] For earlier references *see* Vol. I., p. 81 and p. 274.

king capable of controlling the turbulent Norman barons, rallied round him. When the barons rebelled for the first time, in favour of Robert, whom they knew to be too lazy to keep them in order, William crushed the rebels and banished their leader, his uncle Odo, Bishop of Bayeux. The Court of England's first bachelor king was not graced by the presence of a royal lady to uphold its traditions or refinement.

William, called Rufus from the fact that his face was very red, was stout in figure, strong and big-limbed, with keen restless grey eyes under a broad high brow surmounted by light yellow hair. His voice was loud and he stammered, especially when angry. A faithful son, kind master and a brave knight, utterly fearless, nevertheless William took his share in the Court life of his time, which was passed in the foulest vice. His quarrels with his brother Robert and with the Church, his war with the Scots, and his building operations, engrossed his attention too completely to leave time or inclination to create new fashions.

William II. met his death in the New Forest in 1100 by an arrow discharged by Walter Tirel, Lord of Poix, which is said to have been turned in its flight by glancing from the back of a hart. He was buried in Winchester Cathedral.

Fig. 15. Norman Noble

The nobility and upper classes had become wealthy by confiscation of the estates of the conquered English. Contemporary writers speak of this reign as being a period of great extravagance —not so much as regards new fashion as in the costly materials used for clothing, and also because of the practice of overloading the person with a superabundance of ornament. Nobility, clergy and laity alike were condemned for their love of apparel and extravagance. At this time effeminacy was the prevailing vice "throughout the world." Courtiers as well as wanton youths were sunk in it, and it was then the mode for young men to rival women in delicacy of person, to mince their gait, and walk with loose gesture. The English and French, and particularly the Normans under Duke Robert Curthose, are all censured for these failings.

The tunic was practically the only garment which underwent any change. It was worn longer and fuller than hitherto, extending from the neck to the feet, and hung in many folds. It had wide or close sleeves, and was girded or ungirded at the waist according to the wearer's whim.

Clokes and mantles, of semicircular or rectangular cut, were made of very fine cloth, silk or other rich materials, lined with expensive furs— a new vogue. Legs were clothed, as previously, in braies, but the best-dressed men of the day realised that the closer fitting they were, the more becoming to a well-shaped leg.

Fig. 15 is constructed from an illumination in a MS. of this reign. It shows a noble wearing a long tunic, with wide sleeves embroidered at the edge, worn over an undertunic with close sleeves to the wrist. It should be noticed that the neckband is wider than in earlier examples, and more heavily ornamented. This gentleman had evidently travelled in the East, and had adopted the pallium as worn in Constantinople [1] (*see* Vol. I., Fig. 88). This one measures about twelve feet long by six wide, and is placed on the shoulder so that one-third of its length hangs on the wearer's right. The remaining two-thirds hang to the left. The top border of this portion is caught to the waist-belt on the right side, leaving one-third of it to be carried over the left arm. All round the pallium is an embroidered or woven border, its four corners being plainly shown in the drawing.

The Crusades

It was during the reign of William II. that the first of a series of very important factors in the development of costume occurred—the Crusades.

The exhortations of Peter the Hermit to rescue the Holy Sepulchre from the Infidel, undertaken at the instigation of Pope Urban II. (1088–1099), ignited Western Europe in the autumn of 1096. Thousands of people of all ranks, sewing little crosses of coloured cloth on their left arms in token of their vow, started off in the spring of 1097 on their journey through France, Germany, Bavaria, Austria and Hungary, those who finished the journey reaching Constantinople on 30 August of the same year. "The Welshman left his hunting; the Scot his fellow-ship with vermin; the Dane his drinking bout; the Norwegian his raw fish . . . all was deserted. They hungered and thirsted after Jerusalem alone. Joy attended such as went, while grief oppressed those who remained. But why do I say remained? You might see the husband departing with his wife, indeed with all his family. You would smile to see the whole household laden on a cart about to proceed on their journey. The roads and paths were too narrow for the travellers, so thickly were they thronged with endless multitudes" (William of Malmesbury).

"The rustic," says Guibert de Nogent, "shod his oxen like horses, and placed his whole family on a cart; where it was amusing to hear the

---

[1] William of Malmesbury (1087) writes: "Constantinople was first called Byzantium: which name is still preserved by the Imperial money called Besants." (*See* Vol. I., p. 140.)

children, on the approach to any large town or castle, enquiring if that were Jerusalem " (Fig. 16).

Foulcher of Chartres estimates the number at six hundred thousand pilgrims able to bear arms, besides priests, monks, women and children. "Those who assumed the cross amounted to six millions, but multitudes returned home ere they passed the sea." Pope Urban II. gives the number as three hundred thousand pilgrims.

Fig. 16. Off to Jerusalem, 1097

Numbers of those who attempted the Channel either died of disease or were slain in foreign countries. But those who did undertake the Crusade, and returned, brought back with them new ideas and wider experiences. They had seen many strange peoples, and wonderful cities made beautiful by arts beyond their imagination. Their travels stimulated a desire to compete with the dwellers in continental cities and in the glorious East; and, from the return of the First Crusade in the early years of Henry I.'s reign, we find that a great change penetrated military and social life, architecture, armour and costume. Similar changes, in varying degree, followed each of the subsequent Crusades, covering in all a period of three centuries.

Fig. 17. Detail of Ornament

Section III.—Henry I. 1100–1135

Nobility—Men

Henry was a comparatively young man (thirty) when called to the throne. In view of his renown for refinement and learning (hence his name, Beauclerc), great improvements at Court were anticipated and speedily realised, and these were helped by his marriage with a most cultured woman, Matilda of Scotland, which took place almost immediately after his proclamation. It was fortunate for England that Henry made so wise a choice, and indeed it gave great satisfaction to the people.

In his youth he was despised by the Norman barons, who hated him still more when he outwitted them by his alacrity in seizing the throne on his brother's death. Born (at Selby, Yorkshire, 1070) an English prince, his ways and mode of thought were essentially English, and the English people loved him for it, and supported his claims with enthusiasm. He was knighted by his father at Westminster 1085.

Walter Mapes, chaplain to Henry, distinctly names this reign as the time when the division existing between the two peoples, English and Norman, came to an end, and this he describes as occurring largely through the action of the king himself. Henry I. married secondly Adelicia of Louvaine. He died at S. Denis, and was interred in the Abbey Church of S. Mary, Reading, which he had founded. A contemporary historian prays that "God may give him the peace he loved."

Henry is said to have had a comely face, with a high brow, large eyes, and dark curly hair. He was strongly built, but not tall like his father, whose deep and strong voice, however, he inherited.

On State occasions kings and princes wore a long tunic as described under the last reign. As necessitated by its length, this garment was caught up in front, by passing a portion of it through the girdle at the waist; the undertunic was of rich material, and underneath shertes of very fine linen were worn.

The sleeves of the outer tunic were moderately close to the arm, becoming wider at the wrist, and very long, so that they covered the hand and hung down over it. These tunics were made of woollen material, fine cloth or rich silk—plain or figured, with hand-embroidered borders. It is recorded that King Henry wore on State occasions a tunic or robe of woven gold, studded with gems; and at his coronation "the Legates and Imperial train came gleaming with jewels and gold."

Long semicircular mantles, Fig. 12,[1] were fastened on the right shoulder by a jewelled brooch or clasp, and draped over the left arm.

---

[1] The dotted lines on this diagram indicate seams. When using a material with an up and down pattern, it must be cut and seamed at the centre back also (*see* Fig. 28), and the side pieces reversed. This method applies to all diagrams of mantles.

Fig. 18 is adapted from a drawing in an early twelfth-century psalter, representing a biblical king, who is arrayed in the costume in fashion at the date of the MS.: such as Henry might use. The king is shown wearing a mantle fastened in another way. On the right edge

of the mantle is fixed a ring, often jewelled, through which part of the opposite edge is passed, and either tied in a knot or having the end hanging down. These mantles were so long that to enable the wearer to walk with a certain amount of freedom, a part was carried in whichever hand happened to be free. During the first part of the twelfth century, in both England and France, exaggeration of *length* seems to have been the prevailing peculiarity among wealthy and frivolous men and women. Every article of attire, from the head to the foot, was increased to an absurd and inconvenient length. "They swept the dusty ground with the prodigious trains of their robes and mantles; they covered

Fig. 18. A King, *temp.* Henry I.

their hands with sleeves too long and wide for doing anything useful, and encumbered with these superfluities, they lost the free use of their limbs for active employment."

The materials used for these voluminous mantles were wool and fine silk. Many examples in statuary represent small and abundant folds. These mantles were usually edged with decorated borders, and lined with material of contrasting texture and colour.

Mantles less extravagant in size were frequently worn towards the end of Henry I.'s reign. They were made of thicker materials, and lined with fur—hence they hung in heavier folds, and were worn perforce in a different way. The middle of the straight edge came at the back of the neck, the side edges falling equally on either side of the figure. They were fastened across the chest by cords attached to jewelled ornaments on either

Fig. 19. Cloke-fastening

side, or alternatively, by a cord passing through double metal eyelet-holes inserted at each side of the mantle, Fig. 19. The cord could be drawn tight or loosened at will, according to the wearer's desire to have the mantle enveloping the shoulders and chest, or flowing more open on the shoulders.

Henry I. had one of these mantles presented to him by Robert Bloet, Bishop of Lincoln. It was of exquisitely fine cloth, lined with black sables with white spots, and cost at that time £100, equivalent to £1500 or £2000 of to-day.

It was not customary for boys to wear mantles.

The mantle was a very necessary item of costume for all men of noble birth and position. It belonged historically to the *nobility* and dates from the very earliest times (*see* Vol. I., p. 11). It was a garment of distinction, and the wearing of it was a mark of superiority and nobility, which has continued until our own time. The importance is emphasised by the various customs evolving from its use:

(*a*) To throw the mantle that one was wearing on the ground was an act of defiance. Such a challenge is frequently mentioned in old romances as being given by either men or women.

(*b*) In presenting a petition to any great or noble person, it was customary to bend very low on one knee and touch, or catch hold of the mantle of the notability.

(*c*) Sovereigns presented newly-made knights with mantles. These were often lined with ermine, vair, or sable, and were much prized as heirlooms in the family.

(*d*) On receiving any good news the noble recipient gave the mantle he was wearing, however costly, to the messenger.

Fig. 20. Noble, *temp.* Henry I.

(*e*) The nobility and wealthy landowners were often entertained in their castles after supper by wandering troubadours. If greatly pleased with the entertainment the lord would present his mantle to the poet. But this does not mean that the messenger or the troubadour wore such a rich mantle; he disposed of it as soon as possible to the highest bidder. It was perhaps his only remuneration.

Trailing robes of great length did not long remain in fashion, but they are characteristic of this reign. Towards the end of it, however, Byzantine influence pervaded men's and women's clothes, a result of the return of those participating in the First Crusade, who had sojourned at the Court of the newly-appointed King of Jerusalem, Godfrey de Bouillon.

Fig. 20 shows a noble in a dress of this fashion, and Fig. 21 shows its cut. It fitted quite close on the chest and abdomen, and was tightened round the waist by means of hooks behind, forming transverse folds. The very full skirt part was either cut short at the sides or hooked up at A, which gave an effect of radiating drapery in front and at the back. The back was often cut longer than the front, but did not touch the ground. No belt was worn with this tunic, or undertunic as it often became. A very deep band of embroidery encircled the neck.

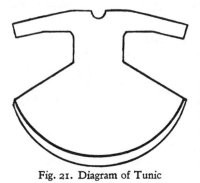

Fig. 21. Diagram of Tunic

The existence of a separate collar, lying flat on the shoulders around the neck, is debatable. Considering that these bands of embroidery must have been very solid, and even stiff, it seems quite impossible that they should have been attached to the tunic, particularly at this period when tunics were made of very fine and soft material. The collar proper did not appear until after the middle of the fourteenth century. A band of narrow embroidery often edged the hem of the tunic, and the sleeves.

About the year 1130 a new garment appeared, called in Norman French the BLIAUT. It was worn by both men and women during the twelfth and thirteenth centuries, and had its origin in the East. Introduced into Western Europe by the nobility returning from the First Crusade, it was a distinctive article of dress, confined to the upper classes between the years 1130–1150. Fig. 22 shows this garment worn by a nobleman. It was cut as a corselet with long fairly wide sleeves, and fitted to the body, forming a curved line below the waist where it was attached to the skirt part. This skirt part was cut in various ways, but Fig. 23 shows its

Fig. 22.
Noble wearing Bliaut

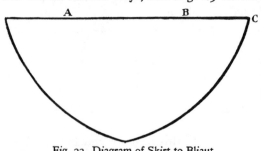

Fig. 23. Diagram of Skirt to Bliaut

most usual shape. There were two parts—the back and the front. They were gathered or pleated from A to B to the corselet at the low waist-line, and fell in graceful folds to a point in front, and to another behind, the sides being open up to the waist-line. It was edged with a border of some soft and heavy embroidery, to assist the hang of the folds, and the same embroidery edged the ends of the sleeves.

This garment was laced, buttoned or hooked at the back, from neck to below the waist-line, so as to tighten it on the chest, around the waist and on the stomach. It was usually cut low at the neck and slit, where it was fastened by a jewelled brooch, to show the neckband of the sherte, or it had a band of embroidery set like a necklace encircling the top edge. A corresponding band of embroidery often rested on the seam around the hips.

Fig. 24 shows an example of an amalgamation of Western and Eastern modes, adopted by noblemen in England and France between the years 1110–1130. It was not a full Court dress, but one that would

Fig. 24. Noble's Dress showing Byzantine influence   Fig. 25. Noble wearing Cotte

be worn at semi-state functions. The under-robe is of Western cut, and of soft material, full in the skirt, with tight sleeves to the wrist, finished with narrow decorative bands at the edge. The over-robe is distinctly Eastern, and is made on similar lines to that of the last figure, *but* instead of two halves of the skirt being joined to the corselet at the front and back as in Fig. 23, they are here worn joined to the sides, with the open edges front and back. In some there was no opening up the back, but the skirt part continued all round except in the front. A band of embroidery is sewn in a line horizontal with the waist. The pallium (*see* Vol. I., p. 191) is worn, thrown over the left shoulder, the hand holding the end (in this drawing). It crosses the back, surrounds the waist, and is kept in place under the right arm and left armpit. A deep collar is worn by this nobleman.

The costume in Fig. 25 is reconstructed from the early twelfth-century painting in tempera[1] on the wall of the crypt under the Chapel of S. Anselm, Canterbury Cathedral. It shows a young nobleman wearing a tunic or cotte, with sleeves cut wide at the armhole but close at the wrists, bound round the waist with a knotted scarf. The front of the tunic is slightly raised. The bands round the neck, wrists and hem are of gold, set with large blue and red stones, with two smaller ones between. The undertunic or sherte is seen below the tunic. Although the figure in the painting represents a biblical character, the dress is of the early twelfth century.

Nobility—Women

Matilda, born about 1079, was the daughter of Malcolm Canmor, King of Scotland, and S. Margaret his wife, sister and heir of Eadgar Ætheling and daughter of Eadward the Exile, son of Eadmund Ironside, King of England—the last of the Saxon princes in succession to the throne. Through this princess the royal family of England is directly descended from Ælfred the Great. The English people hailed her as "Matilda Ætheling." Matilda's first name was Eadgyth. She was destined for the veil, and had lived under the care of her aunt, the Lady Christina, in retirement at Wilton and Romsey. Her piety, charm of manner, unselfishness, and high culture influenced very largely the tone of society during her married life. All the best in the land congregated round the king and queen—scholars, artists, musicians and minstrels always found a welcome, and the Arts were much encouraged—a sure stimulant to the development of Costume. The popularity of the troubadour at a later date owes much to the queen's love of music. She recompensed most liberally all those who practised the arts of Literature and Music, whether English or foreign.

"The Good Queen" died on 1 May, 1118, and was buried in Westminster Abbey. She left four children, "William, born 1102, Richard and Mary, who perished by shipwreck, and likewise Maude, born 1103, who was wife to Henry, the fifth emperor." This Princess Maude is commonly known as Matilda, Empress of Germany; she died 1167.

The queen, being of royal Saxon blood, had, for the most part, ladies of the highest Anglo-Saxon families as attendants. All kinds of domestic accomplishments were practised by them, such as spinning, weaving, embroidery, dressmaking, etc., and it was considered consistent with their dignity to attend to the poultry and dairy. The Countess of Chester, wife of Hugh Lupus, kept a herd of kine and made Cheshire cheeses (Cheese-shire).

[1] This fresco is in the small chapel of S. John or S. Gabriel, in the crypt below S. Anselm's Chapel. Its date is between 1130 and 1150. It is not open to the public, but the author had special permission to study the fresco. Reproductions of it can be seen in Dart's *History of Canterbury*, 1726, or in *Archæologia Cantiana*, vol. xviii.

The noble ladies of Normandy profited by this example, realising that it was a good thing to be useful, and they followed the fashion and adopted similar domestic pursuits. In these and other ways the more conservative and dignified household was self-supporting and self-sufficient, and its ladies therefore lacked the element of serious competition with others which is notoriously a factor in the production of changes in fashion.

Adelicia, the Fair Maid of Brabant, was born about the year 1102. She was the daughter of Godfrey, Duke of Louvaine, and at the time of her marriage with Henry Beauclerc was crowned with him by Ralph, Archbishop of Canterbury, at Westminster Abbey, 30 January, 1121.

This princess was remarkable for her proficiency in feminine accomplishments, and in every way she seems to have been the equal of her predecessor. It was a

Fig. 26. Queen's Costume

triumph of her gentle disposition and lovable nature that she was one of the few who maintained a lifelong friendship with her arrogant step-daughter, the Empress Matilda.

Henry bestowed upon Queen Adelicia the Castle of Arundel, where she lived after Henry's death. Later, in 1130, she married as her second husband Count William d'Albini, whose father, William, was chief butler to the Duchy of Normandy (an office introduced into England at William the Conqueror's coronation), and became the ancestress of the Ducal House of Norfolk. Her young brother, Joseline, was endowed by William d'Albini with the Manor of Petworth. He afterwards married Agnes, the daughter and heiress of the third Baron Percy, and became ancestor of the Ducal House of Northumberland.

Fig. 26 shows the costume of a queen or royal lady of this reign. The gown fits close on the bust and shoulders, and the neck, slit and brooched,

Fig. 27.
Dress of Northern Queen

is low enough to show the neckband of the camise. The skirt part is cut full at the sides and back, and forms many folds around the feet. It is girded at the waist by the girdle now in vogue. The sleeves are small at the armhole, but gradually widen out and hang loose over the forearm, where they are turned back to show the lining, and the rucked sleeve of the under-robe. A mantle is worn over the shoulders, and a rectangular veil, surmounted by a crown, on the head.

A queen of the North—Scotland, Norway or Denmark—is shown in Fig. 27, and the figure is reconstructed from the model of a queen of a set of chessmen now in the British Museum. She is simply though royally robed. The gown has close sleeves and is ungirded, and the mantle is cut like Fig. 28, with the part that surrounds the neck cut away and fastened with a clasp at the throat. A small veil is worn, surmounted by a simple crown.

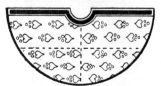

Fig. 28. Shape of Mantle

In contrast with the simplicity of the costume just described, the more frivolous ladies of fashion imitated contemporary masculine extravagance in the length of their garments. Their gowns trailed on the ground in front, and even more so behind, and the wide sleeves grew to such dimensions that it became necessary to knot them, so that they should not drag on the ground, or get entangled with the skirts (Fig. 29). Veils also were very voluminous, and hung so long in front that they were looped or tied in knots.

On top of this trailing mass they placed the mantle, which was often an heirloom and a treasured family possession, of rich material sumptuously embroidered, implying rank and authority in the wearer. When it had been handed down from previous generations, the mantle at this time might well be the one seemly and unexaggerated garment to be worn, yet were a new mantle required, it too would be made to trail on the ground at great length, although at first the semicircular shape was retained.

Fig. 29. Sleeves and Veil in Knots

Whichever type happened to be used, it was fastened as described on p. 30 and shown in Fig. 19; but at this time noble ladies dispensed with the neck folds (shown at A), as being too cumbersome under their veils. A semicircle was therefore cut in the middle of the mantle's straight edge, allowing the material to set better on the shoulders and around the neck. See Figs. 27, 28, and 29.

The more "daring" women of fashion wore their long robes open up the side seams to the hips. The back part was allowed to hang free, but the front was tied in a knot, exposing the legs clothed in long braies of cloth. This style was considered most indecorous, as was also the fashion of tight-lacing, much indulged in by the ladies of this time. Ever since the Norman Conquest there had been a growing desire to reduce the size of the waist. By the year 1130 there appeared an accessory to costume so important that it swayed the vagaries of fashion during many sporadic periods, until the end of the reign of Edward VII.; and although happily it is unlikely to reappear in the present generation, history suggests the unwisdom of prophesying against its recrudescence.

The Corset

Old English *Corse* = a body support or stay, from the French *Corps* = a body.

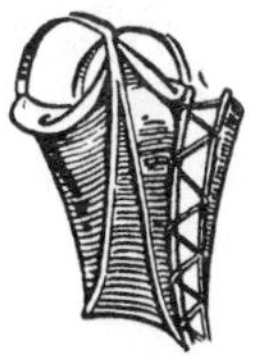

The corse was worn by men at a later date. It was a tight-fitting tunic or "jupe"; a defensive version of it, made of metal or leather, was known as "corselet" or "cuirass."

The corse worn by women at this time consisted of a piece of material or leather (*see* Vol. I., p. 34 for an

Fig. 30.
The Corse

earlier example); and, according to an illuminated manuscript of this period (*Nero*, C. IV., British Museum), depicting the devil tight-laced in corsets, it was stiffened with wood or metal, and laced up the front (Fig. 30).

"Her waist was so fine that your two hands could have girdled her."
From an old French love song of the twelfth century.

A

Sleeves of another curious shape were also worn at this time. They were long, according to the prevailing fashion, even reaching to the ground, cut as shown in Fig. 31; in fact, they were like long tubes open at one end, yet with another opening, A, where the hand would normally come. In cold weather the portion below this opening covered the hands, the sleeves being gathered on the forearm, and the hands passing through the opening at the end B, the folds thus forming a covering for the hands and wrists, which served the

B

Fig. 31.
Shape of Sleeve

same purpose as a muff or gloves. Ordinarily, of course, the hands were passed through the opening at A, half-way down the sleeve, which then hung down to the edge of the gown.

1170–1200
Fig. 32. Border

Section IV.—Stephen, 1135–1154

Nobility—Men

Stephen, the late king's nephew, usurped the throne on his uncle's death, ignoring the fact that he had sworn to obey Matilda, Henry's daughter and his own cousin, acknowledged heiress to the realm. He was supported by many of the barons, and by the citizens of London, who thought order more likely to be maintained by a man than a woman. The ensuing quarrel involved the country in civil war during the greater part of this reign.

King Stephen, born 1104, is described as being very handsome, tall and strong. He inherited from his mother Adela, a daughter of William I., the splendid talents and fine physique of the Norman race, but these attributes did not help him to govern well. England has never been worse ruled. " In his days was naught but war and wickedness and waste." Stephen married before 1114 Matilda of Boulogne; he died at Dover 1154, and lies buried in the Abbey of Faversham, Kent. There was no change in the State garments of his reign of nineteen years. The statue of Henry I. at Rochester, and the effigy on the tomb of his grandson, Henry II., at Fontevrault, show costumes constructed on similar lines: the ordinary everyday attire of the nobility and upper classes was the same as described in the section relating to Henry I.

Fig. 33. Geoffrey of Anjou

The beautiful enamel slab on the tomb of Geoffrey Plantagenet, Count of Anjou, the second husband of the Empress Matilda, and father of King Henry II., gives, however, an excellent idea of the costume of a nobleman of this reign. Fig. 33 is a drawing reconstructed from it. The bliaut is of moderately thin material, probably silk, and is shaped like that worn in Fig. 22, but with sleeves close to the wrist. The skirt part is open neither up the front nor at the sides, but forms an all-round skirt. The decoration is interesting. It consists of bands of embroidery on the skirt and sleeves, with a design placed at intervals between them.

The skirt of the underdress is cut on the circle, and is hitched up at the waist, in places, to produce the box-folds between radiating lines of drapery. The same type of decoration as used for the bliaut occurs on the underdress, but of a different design. The mantle is semi-circular, and is fastened on the right shoulder. The cap is of the old Phrygian type, represented in the original enamel as being embroidered on each side with a lion. (For shoes, *see* Footgear.)

Nobility—Women

Matilda, Queen-Consort of Stephen, was the daughter of Eustace, Count of Boulogne, and his wife Mary, the daughter of Malcolm Canmor of Scotland. Her uncles, Godfrey de Bouillon and Baldwin, were successively kings of Jerusalem. She was a woman possessing a very charming personality, and did much to smooth over the distraught period of her husband's reign.

Matilda died at Castle Hedingham, Essex, in 1151, and was buried in the Abbey Church of Faversham. Her children were:

1. Eustace, Count of Boulogne, married Constance, sister of Louis VII. of France, but d.s.p. 1152. (His widow married secondly Raymond, Count of Toulouse.)
2. William, Count of Montaigne and Boulogne, d.s.p. 1159.
3. Mary, married Matthew, son of Theodore, Count of Flanders.

The characteristic style of women's clothes and hairdressing in Stephen's reign was distinctly different from those in vogue in the time of Henry I. The change occurred actually among the leaders of fashion about the year 1130, but it was not generally adopted until after Stephen's accession. The First Crusade led to the new mode, early in the twelfth century, when many noble ladies accompanied their lords to the confines of the Western world, and remained at Constantinople, Palermo, Venice, etc.—all centres of silk manufacture.

After the consolidation of the Kingdom of Jerusalem, and of Antioch as a Principality, many leaders of the Crusade sent for their wives to join them, and they eventually settled at the Courts of the two Baldwins, or of Fulk of Anjou. It may be assumed safely that these "officers' wives" made the most of their chance of obtaining the gorgeous local products, to be had there at a cost quite reasonable as compared with their price when purchased at home. They bought eagerly silken materials at Constantinople and at Palermo (now fast supplanting the former in the production of fine silks and Oriental materials such as gauze, muslins, crêpe), and stuffs imported from Damascus and Baghdad.

The new mode was a garment adopted by this Western community in the East, and by degrees it found its way through the south of France to the north, and on to England, arriving about 1130. It has the distinction of being the first woman's garment to have a definite shape, and elaborate construction. The gown of the woman of the past was a simple affair compared with this new creation, which was looked upon as a great novelty. At first it was only worn by the highest in the land, but became more general among the upper classes at a later date, and continued in use among them until the end of the twelfth century.

It was composed of very fine material, crimped or gauffered. Its full width, back and front, was joined on the shoulders. Here it was stitched, and stitched again across the bust and back. Round the neck there was usually a band of passement. From this stitching the garment fell in many tiny folds to the feet. The sleeves were treated in the same way; the tiny pleats were fixed into the ARMHOLES (this is the first appearance in history of such a thing as an "armhole"), and stitched a

Fig. 34. The Bliaut　　　　　Fig. 35. Bliaut and Corsage

little way down the upper arm. Thence it fell in many small folds around the arm. The sleeve being cut on the cross, a zig-zag effect was produced at its edge (*see* Fig. 34).

A corsage was worn over this, as seen in Fig. 35. This was a sleeve-less jacket, either open at the neck to show the camise, or close up to the throat. In both cases it was edged by a band of embroidery, and sometimes joined by a small jewelled ornament. This corsage descended well over the hips, where it finished in a downward curve over the stomach. There is a good deal of speculation as to the material used, and also as to the construction of this corsage. It appears to have been composed of two or three thicknesses of moderately thin stuff, pleated around the torso, firmly sewn, and moulded to the figure by means of lacing at the back. There are varying examples of the ways in which these stuffs were sewn together, to form a firm yet supple foundation, besides that described. One very favourite method was to stitch it diagonally with fancy-work either in gold, silver, or colours, which produced a honeycombed effect. Jewels were frequently set at the inter-sections, or in the groundwork between the lines of stitchery, sometimes both, giving the whole a very rich appearance (*see* Plate III.). Other ex-amples of the treatment of this garment suggest that it was made of a knitted or elastic fabric.

Fig. 36.
Bliaut and Hip-belt

Some authorities maintain that a belt of the same or different material was bound tightly around the torso, by means of lacing behind and above the bliaut. This formed a wide hip-belt from below the bust to well over the hips, where it finished in a downward curve (*see* Fig. 36). The materials used for the bliaut were very fine soft silk, silk crêpe, a silk of the nature of very fine crêpe de chine, and a variety of transparent fabrics, as well as gauze. These appear to have been treated in a particular manner—crinkled, crêped, crimped, or even gauffered, and (to use a modern term) accordion-pleated with hot irons, a practice known in the Orient from early times. Almost every colour was then in use, and it was very much the vogue at this time for smart dressmakers to employ shot materials (*see* Vol. I., pp. 216–217).

Fig. 37. Full Toilet of Noble Lady

These fully gauffered, pleated bliauts in which the fashionable ladies of the period (1130–1150) robed themselves, showed the natural form to advantage, the shoulders, bust and hips, etc., being well defined. The clinging suppleness of these fabrics influenced to a considerable extent the gestures and deportment. A slow gliding movement and a dignified bearing, avoiding abrupt and accentu-ated action, became necessary when these filmy materials were worn. Being quickly crumpled, a frequent change of garments was indispensable, to avoid a slovenly appearance.

The toilet of queens, royal and noble ladies, on State and ceremonial occasions (*see* Fig. 37), was still incom-plete until, to the bliaut just described, many accessories were added, and as a necessary finish, of course, the hair would be elaborately dressed according to the prevailing mode (*see* p. 56). First among these accessories was the girdle (*see* Fig. 38), now a very important detail, often of great richness. This belt was placed high in front, just under the bust, and crossed at the back. Thence it followed the seam or lower edge of the corsage, and was brought round to the front. The part of this girdle which encircled the body was generally flat like a belt, and very heavily ornamented with raised gold and jewels. To each end of the belt, which almost met in front, several strands of silk or gold cord were attached. These strands were plaited together, and kept in place at intervals by jewelled rings, finishing off at the ends with rich tassels. They were knotted in front in a particular way, and the two ends fell to the feet.

Fig. 38. The Girdle

At this time the semicircular mantle was attached across the chest in a new way, by a cord fastened on one edge of the mantle, and passing through an eyelet-hole on the opposite side (*see* Fig. 19). These mantles were now made of expensive brocades obtained from Constantinople, damasks from Syria, and samit (a rich thick satin), with elaborate borders worked in gold, and silks of various colours. In addition to these borders, orphreys and passements were lavishly brought into use. Some of the designs used will be found on these pages. The linings of the mantles were very rich, and chiefly of silk in contrasting shades. Furs were not much employed at this time, being too heavy.

Plate III. represents the Empress Matilda as she appeared when visiting Winchester in full State dress in 1141. Some of the details of her costume have been described above. The mantle, of unusual dimensions for the period, is made of "écarlate," embroidered with Saxon knots and bordered with medallions representing saints treated in the manner of Limoges enamels, alternating with the Eagle of Germany. Her escort, A and B, are equipped in very early examples of chain mail, suggested by illuminations in the S. Eadmundsbury Bible (1121–1148) and in the Winchester Bible (about 1150). C is also from the Winchester Bible.

Fig. 39. An Oriental Surcote

Another distinctive garment that boasts of its descendants found its way from the Orient. Originally a Persian coat, it may well have been sent as a present by some crusading lover to his *bel-amie* far away in France or England. It was a loose over-robe, reaching from the neck to the knee, with wide sleeves, Fig. 39. Its shape is seen in Fig. 40. It was made of some light material—silk, or even transparent silk gauze, through which the colour of the underdress gleamed mysteriously; and it was edged all round with a narrow band of heavy gold or bead passement. It hung loose, without a belt, being clasped a little below the waist-line by a brooch or ornament. When Persian coats of this type were introduced into Western Europe, ladies of high rank found them most useful, despite their filmy nature, as an extra wrap on chilly evenings to slip on over their already complete toilet, which included the girdle. Sometimes the girdle was worn outside the wrap, but this was

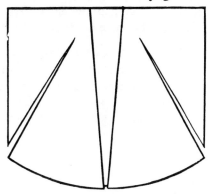

Fig. 40. Diagram of Oriental Surcote

according to the fancy of the individual wearer, and was not the general rule. Needless to say, this dainty garment became very popular, and copies of the original model were made later in thicker and warmer stuffs. Both varieties found an important place in the wardrobe of a lady of fashion during this period (1140–1170).

More will be heard of this garment under its French name of "Peliçon" or "Pelice" (*see* p. 97).

Fig. 41.   Ornament

XII th.

SECTION V.—MIDDLE AND LOWER CLASSES, 1066–1154

The general population of England during this period was made up of many diverse strains. The Anglo-Saxons or English were the original stock, descended from the Celts, Roman-Britons, Jutes, Angles, Saxons, and the Danish settlers in Northumbria and Mercia. To these were now added the Normans, themselves of Danish descent, who had acquired considerable French culture.

The Middle Classes referred to here consisted of:
> Church tenants;
> Military tenants;
> Professional men;
> Merchants;
> Officials;
> Yeomen, owners of free land;
> Socmen, freeholders of land who paid rent instead of service.

The Lower Classes comprised:
> Villeins, freed men holding land at their lord's will;
> Cotters and Bordars, lower villeins holding a cottage and garden or a few acres;
> Serfs, slaves of their owners;
> Peasants.

Temp. William I. 1066–1087

Men. As regards the English of this period, the principal article of dress was, as usual, the tunic or cotte. These tunics were cut either moderately tight-fitting round the body, or loose, with the skirt part cut on the circle or square, and closed or slit up the sides. The sleeves were either wide, showing the close sleeve of the sherte or the bare arm,

Fig. 42. Middle-Class Costume

or else close-fitting. The neck was a little more open than was usual before the Conquest; and sometimes slit downwards in front for about four or six inches, to show the neckband of the sherte. It was usual to finish the neck, sleeves, and the edge of the tunic with a band of conventional embroidery in coloured stitching in wool, or with a band of different-coloured cloth, according to the position and means of the wearer. The tunic was confined at the waist by a belt of leather, cord, or roll of material, and if the tunic was full enough it bulged over the belt. When the tight tunic was worn, it was not uncommon to leave it ungirded, as of yore; the tunic was then pulled in rather tight at the waist.

Under the tunic was worn the sherte or *short* garment (*see* Vol. I., p. 268), now common to all classes of both sexes. When worn by women it was longer and called the camise. The lower classes had shertes and camises made of coarse linen in its natural hue. They fitted loosely, and had close sleeves rucked at the wrists.

Clokes were short, and long, square, circular, or semicircular, and worn as before —fastened with a brooch, or a metal ring on the right shoulder through which a part of the cloke was pushed and tied in a knot. Sometimes they were fastened in front. To these clokes a hood would be attached for use in inclement weather.

Fig. 43. First Knickerbockers

On the legs they wore close-fitting braies of cloth, wool, or linen, with or without crossgartering. Alternatively, loose braies reaching up to the knees were either tied at the ankle and knee, or crossgartered with leather or coloured cloth. Often ropes made of straw were used for this purpose. Gaiters of cloth or wool were in common use among the lower classes.

Fig. 44. A Norman

Fig. 42 is taken from the Bayeux Tapestry, and represents an Englishman or Norman of middle class, wearing a costume of the foregoing description, except that his legs are clothed in hose, having some ornamental stitching round the leg.

The artificers, workmen, shipbuilders, galleymen, stablemen, etc., brought over by William to assist in the disembarkation of his army, wore a useful garment consisting of a tunic with long sleeves and full KNICKERBOCKERS, with a belt round the waist. These knickerbockers, in one piece with the tunic, descended to the knees, and cloth braies were worn on the lower part of the leg (Fig. 43). Often the knickers were separate, and worn with an ordinary sherte, the tails of which were tucked in at the waist. Knickers varied in shape; some were fairly full, suggesting a kilt; others were longer in the leg, but narrow, with a border down the outside of the leg and round the edge (Fig. 44). There were also some very like football shorts; but in all cases the legs were covered with hose, striped round with different colours like football stockings, and in many cases crossgartered. The knickerbockers had their origin in the long loose

Fig. 45. A Peasant

trousers worn by peasants living in England and in the centre of France, and much used by them during the course of the tenth, eleventh and twelfth centuries (Fig. 45).

There are curious examples of these long trousers worn by two figures of Welsh knights, carved upon the architraves of the south door of Kilpeck Church, Herefordshire (Fig. 46).[1] They wear Phrygian caps, close tunics that appear to be wadded, and trousers. Belts are knotted round their waists: one bears a sword, the other a mace. The present building was erected about 1134.

The lower classes usually went bare-headed, occasionally wearing a hood which came to a point at the top. When not in use this hood was thrown back on the shoulders.

Temp. William II. 1087–1100

Men. Fig. 47 represents a citizen or yeoman, called a "vavasour," at the end of the eleventh century. This man is wearing an outer tunic or cotte to the knee, slit up the sides. The sleeves fit close to the arm, and are finished off at the

Fig. 46.
Welsh Knight

Fig. 47. A Yeoman   Fig. 48. An Official of Henry I.'s reign

wrist by a band stitched with a colour. In the original picture this garment is shown brown. The sherte is made of coarse natural-hued

[1] The parts of Herefordshire lying without Offa's Dyke were regarded, until the reign of Henry VIII., as belonging to Wales.

hemp linen. The legs are clothed in braies or chausses, held close to the leg by means of braids or thongs of leather. On the shoulders a rectangular cloke is worn, with a corner pleated into a brooch and fastened on the right.

Temp. Henry I. 1100–1135, *and Stephen,* 1135–1154

Men. Despite the heavy taxation levied upon the people of England by the first two Norman kings, we are told that the middle class—that is, professional men, small officials, wealthy merchants, and those farmers living near the great towns, indulged in much finery and ostentation in their dress.

The tunic was invariably long, reaching to the ankles. Fig. 48 gives a man of the official class, habited in one of these long tunics, fitting close at the shoulders and neck where there is an ornamental band. The sleeves are moderately tight on the upper arm, but widen toward the wrist, where they are turned back to show the sleeves of the sherte or undertunic. (These sleeves were very often close-fitting, with a cuff reaching from the wrist to the elbow. (For cuff *see* Fig. 51.) When worn by rich people, such cuffs are generally shown in illuminated MSS. in gold.) There is a border at the bottom of the tunic, and an opening on the left side, almost to the waist.

Fig. 49.
Physician

Fig. 50.
Student

Above this tunic is worn a bordered cloke, secured on the right shoulder by a brooch, and carried on the arm. The legs are covered with close-fitting braies, and over them chausses of cloth, wool or some easily stretchable material, as the shape of the leg is well defined. The cap is of the soft Phrygian shape, the point flopping on top of the head. The edge is turned up to form a brim.

Fig. 49 represents a physician instructing his pupil. He wears a long tunic, with sleeves cut wide at the armhole and tight at the wrists, over another garment. The upper tunic is bordered and belted with some embroidery in which precious stones seem to play an important part. He wears a cloke, and a headdress with

Fig. 51. Citizen

a peak something like a Phrygian cap. His shoes are described on p. 58.

The student's costume (Fig. 50) displays no great novelty, but his collar and belt should be noticed.

Fig. 51 represents a man of the citizen class, comfortably dressed in a tunic of cloth, shaped about the waist and falling full in the skirt. His sleeves, convenient for business, are tight, with a deep cuff of contrasting colour, or of leather. A pouch or wallet is carried slung over the shoulder. This pouch was called a GYPSIRE, or Gipsere—a corruption of the Norman-French "gibbecière" or "gibecière," meaning a bag used for hawking or for carrying game (French, "giber"). On the legs are worn cloth or woollen hose, probably knitted, fitting tightly and worked with a pattern below the calf. His shoes are of leather, and follow the natural line of the foot.

The hood is a new feature, cut like a funnel, with a hole for the face (see Fig. 52). It is drawn over the head and shoulders, the slit in front on the chest allowing freedom in use, and the point at the top hangs at the back of the head.

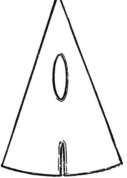

Fig. 52.
Diagram of Hood

At the beginning of the twelfth century, the common people were dressed in simple tunics of rough make, worn over shertes of coarse hemp linen. The sleeves were generally close-fitting, although loose ones were not exceptional. When required, a plain cloke, with hood attached, was fastened by a hook or a metal brooch (Fig. 53). On the legs they wore braies of coarse cloth, or sometimes the legs were bound with leather. The leg bandages seen in Fig. 54 are a reversion to the Anglo-Saxon method of winding.

Fig. 54.   Fig. 53.
Costume of the Lower Classes

Peasants, 1066-1154

Figs. 55 and 56 represent two men of the peasant class, shepherds or swineherds.

The materials used for the garments of these people were wool and hempspun cloth of the coarsest make, so coarse that a romance of the twelfth century speaks of a man as being "wrapped in a cloke which seemed inside out either way on." In a great measure the people had to be content with the skins of some animals not difficult to obtain—possibly those of wolves which had been rash in approaching too near the sheepfold.

Fig. 55 wears a tunic or cotte with close sleeves of coarse stuff, and over it two pieces of skin,[1] with the hair outside: these are joined on

Fig. 55.

Fig. 56.

Costume of Peasants

the shoulders, and belted at the waist with a thong. Over his shoulders is slung his gipsere or satchel of leather. A hooded cape of cloth or fur is worn, exactly the same in shape as the paenula (*see* Vol. I., p. 71), but reaching only to the knees. This garment is sometimes spoken of in Norman French as the CAGOULE. This poor man is obliged to go barelegged, but he has bound his ankles with leather thongs for some protection "against the scratches of the thorns."

The sherte was a luxury in which the labouring class did not indulge. Many illuminations in MSS. represent working men stripped to the waist. Fig. 45 is taken from a contemporary MS., and shows a man at

[1] During the winter months the clergy were permitted to use skin coats, called "pelice." They were worn under the alb, and in consequence the alb became known as the super-pelice, or surplice.

work wearing loose trousers, or bracco untied at the ankles, and nothing else, except that he has bound a piece of stuff round his head to keep his hair away from his face.

Perhaps the shepherd represented in Fig. 56 is more opulent than Fig. 55, as his costume is not so meagre. He wears a respectable tunic of coarse homespun cloth, cut rather on fashionable lines. The sleeves are shorter than usual and display bare arms. The hood is of untanned skin with the hair outside, but the cape part of it is made up of skins of small animals, such as rabbits or badgers. The lower part of the bare legs is protected by ropes of twisted straw, and rough shoes of hide are worn on the feet. When the labouring man was engaged in work on damp or marshy ground, he fastened wooden clogs to his feet over his shoes (Fig. 269). Bare legs were not usual with this class of peasant: many representations show shepherds wearing braies, and some illuminated MSS. show leg-coverings of brilliant colours.

The oliphant (horn) and crook are of this period.

Fig. 57. Border

1066–1154

Women. There were no great distinguishing characteristics in the costume of the English and Norman women of this time. The descrip-

Fig. 58. Middle-Class Costume

tion given in Vol. I., p. 280, serves equally well for this period. They wore the long gown reaching to the feet, cut slightly to the figure, with variously shaped sleeves: some were close-fitting and rucked at the wrist; others were wide, showing the tight undersleeves. For practical purposes the skirt part was often hitched to a cord or girdle round the hips. Ornamental borders of embroidery in colours were much in favour with the better classes.

Many well-to-do women of this period wore a mantle fastened across the shoulders by cords, very similar to those used by the nobility, only not nearly so long. Mantles for common use, clokes, in fact, had attached hoods for covering the head when required.

A long piece of linen was draped round the neck and head; or sometimes the circular veil, now discarded by the fashionable, was worn, with or without a close-fitting cap on top. The hair was parted in the middle, and done in a coil at the nape of the neck.

Fig. 58 is a drawing reconstructed from a figure in the Bayeux Tapestry, representing the Lady Eadwige or Alice, daughter of Duke William,

who was contracted to King Harold but died young. Although a noble lady, her costume is that worn by a woman of the middle class—a gentlewoman. It consists of the gown, cut full in the skirt and with wide open sleeves. In the tapestry the gown is green—a very usual colour for the gowns and other garments of middle-class women. The camise, with tight rucked sleeves to the wrists, is worn underneath the gown. The couvrechef wound round the head and shoulders is a rectangle, and this one is red in colour.

Fig. 59. A Lady of Quality

The lady of quality of the time of Henry I. and Stephen (1100–1154), shown in Fig. 59, is fashionably attired, but not so extravagantly as the noble lady seen in Fig. 29. Her gown is precisely the same in cut as those worn during this and the preceding periods (see Vol. I., Chap. VII.), but the shape of the sleeves is quite original. They fit the arm fairly close until they reach the lower part of the forearm, where they suddenly widen tremendously and extend to some length, curving out at the bottom like the bows of a boat. These sleeves came into fashion at the end of the eleventh century, and continued in use among the upper classes until gradually they became merged, during the latter part of the twelfth century, into the wide sleeve previously described. This boat-shaped sleeve was adopted by Henry, Lord Hastings, about the middle of the twelfth century, as his family coat of arms. The pointed part, indi-

Fig. 60. Woman of the People

cated by the lady, was the side of the gown cut out from under the armhole, as shown in dotted lines. The heraldic sleeve is slightly elongated, to fit the twelfth-century shield.

The hairdressing is a modified version of the prevalent fashion of encasing the two plaits of hair in silk (see Hairdressing, p. 57).

A woman of the people is shown in Fig. 60. Her dark-coloured gown is simply the Norman garment, but, for convenience, reaches only to the ankle. The sleeves with coloured border are wide, showing bare arms, so presumably the sleeves of her underdress or camise have been rolled up to facilitate her work. A small round hat of scarlet, with a narrow upstanding brim of white, covers the head—a survival of the Saxon headgear shown in Vol. I., Fig. 134. Notice the bags, already filled with apples, suspended from a cord round her waist.

Section VI.—Hairdressing, 1066–1154

Temp. William I. 1066–1087

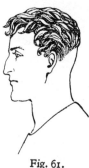

Fig. 61.
Hairdressing

Men. Many of the Norman gentry who accompanied Duke William on his expedition to England had their hair dressed in a very curious manner. The hair was allowed to grow to a moderate length on the top and in front, and was brushed forward. The back of the head was shaved, up to a horizontal line level with the tops of the ears. Many examples are shown in a crude manner in the Bayeux Tapestry. Fig. 61 is a drawing derived from one of them (*see also* Figs. 43 and 44). We are told by Raoul Glaber [1] that the nobility of Aquitaine had been known for many generations before the Conquest for this extraordinary fashion. This style of hairdressing was introduced into Northern France by the Aquitainian nobility in attendance on the Lady Constance, daughter of their earl, when she went to Paris in 998 to marry Robert the Pious. It originated, in a slightly different form, as far back as the fourth century, when it was in use among the early Franks (*see* Vol. I., p. 227).

As a contemporary fashion many Normans wore a natural head of hair, cut moderately short all round, as seen in Fig. 62 and Figs. 9 and 10. With the Normans it was the custom either to shave the face entirely or to shave the beard, except only so much of it as grew upon the upper lip. To wear two locks of hair upon the upper lip (the moustache), without a beard upon the chin, was a fashion of the Normans (Northmen or Norsemen) from the time when they migrated to France in 912. They were worn very large and long, and the Norman-French name for these locks of hair was "guernons" or "gernons." Count Eustace of Boulogne had his upper lip decorated in this manner, and in consequence was surnamed

Fig. 62.
Hairdressing

[1] Historian of the eleventh century, born at the end of the tenth century, died at Cluny 1050.

"Aux-gernons." He is represented in the Bayeux Tapestry, and Fig. 63 is drawn from this source. A great friend of Duke William's, Sir William de Percy, was also noted for his very beautiful gernons, and was nicknamed on this account "Alsgernon," meaning William with the Locks. He was ancestor of the Dukes of Northumberland, and this name "Algernon" has been borne repeatedly by his posterity.

Closely cropped and shaven heads were abandoned by the Normans soon after they established themselves in this country, for a fashion in hairdressing of the opposite extreme (Fig. 64).

When King William returned to Normandy in 1067 he was accompanied by many English nobles and prelates. Among these were Eadgar the Ætheling (d. 1120) (son of Eadward the Ætheling and grandson of Eadmund Ironside), brother of S. Margaret, Queen of Scotland, and heir of the royal line of English kings; Stigand, the ex-Archbishop of Canterbury; Fritheric,

Fig. 63.
Eustace of Boulogne

Fig. 64.
Hairdressing, *temp.* William II.

Abbat of St. Albans, and the Earls Eadwine, Morcar and Waltheof. In the same company were some of the Norman nobles who had crossed the Channel with William only six months previously. They kept the feast of Easter at the Abbey of Holy Trinity, Fécamp, where a great number of bishops, abbats and local Norman and French nobles assembled. They looked with admiration and curiosity upon the long-yellow-haired English, and before long they were converted to this fashion of wearing long hair flowing on the shoulders, a change which soon spread over the whole of France.

Temp. William II. 1087–1100

By the time William II. ascended the throne of England in 1087, the English style of flowing locks and beards (Fig. 64) had become general throughout the whole country. This "effeminate" mode of hairdressing was not limited to England: in Normandy and France it was carried to such excess that in 1095 the Council of Rouen issued a decree forbidding the vogue, but without avail.

Temp. Henry I. 1100–1135

At a council held in London in 1102 by Archbishop Anselm, it was enacted that those who had long hair should be cropped, so as to show part of the ears and the eyes. Although in England measures were taken to limit the wearing of long hair, personages of the highest rank still allowed it to grow to a great length, not only on the head but on the face. Beards fell on the chest in one, two and even three

points, and "moustaches" hung on either side in long lines (*see* Fig. 18). At the beginning of the twelfth century it was the fashion to divide the hair by two partings, springing from the crown on either side of the forehead, the centre hair being brought forward as an irregular fringe. At the back the hair grew long like a woman's, and was curled with hot irons (Fig. 65).

Fig. 65.
Hairdressing, early
twelfth century

As a young man the Scholastic King was very famous for the beauty of his luxuriant black hair. During the year 1104 he was in Normandy, and on a certain occasion attended divine service at Carentan, accompanied by his nobles and retinue, whose flowing locks greatly excited the wrath of the officiating prelate. The bishop preached such an eloquent sermon against the wearing of long hair, and the sinfulness of the fashion, that the king and all his nobles cheerfully assented to these observations, upon which the zealous bishop (Serlo, Bishop of Seez) lost no time in taking a pair of shears out of his scrip, and barbered the whole congregation. On Henry's return to England he published an edict to all his subjects, calling upon them to reduce their ringlets to a more moderate length; but the fashion set by the king himself was of more effect than his edict, and for some time to come the length of the hair became quite moderate.

About 1110 the forehead was worn bare, and to attain this effect it was shaved, or the roots of the hair were plucked out. A writer of the time protests engagingly, "The forepart of their heads is bare, after the manner of thieves, while on the back they nourish long hair like harlots. In former times,[1] penitents, captives and pilgrims usually went unshaved, and wore long beards as an outward mark of their penance, or captivity, or pilgrimage. Now, almost all the world wear crisped hair and beards, carrying on their faces the tokens of their filthy lust, like stinking goats. Their locks are curled with hot irons, and, instead of wearing caps, they bind their heads with fillets. . . .

Fig. 66. Beard worn during
Henry I.'s reign

"They suffer their beards to grow for fear that if they shaved, the short bristles might prick the faces of their mistresses when they were kissing them, and are so hairy that they look like Saracens rather than Christians."

[1] The reign of William I.

Fig. 66 shows the kind of beard fashionable at this time. It is divided into two, with long locks on the upper lip, twisted into points with some sticky preparation. These pointed beards required careful nurture, and at night were enclosed in little bags of silk containing some sort of ointment to keep them in good condition. Nothing that expostulating clergy could say affected the determination of the nobles to retain their "effeminate and goatish appearance." Unhappily, table manners at this time were less dainty than they might have been, and as a consequence, long beards became the abiding-place of much superfluous matter.

The statue of Henry I. at Rochester Cathedral shows him in later middle life, towards the end of his reign. He is wearing long hair, which by that time had returned once more into fashion. His beard, however, is short and clipped.

Temp. Stephen, 1135–1154

During this reign the hair was generally worn long, but not so long as at the time of Henry I.'s accession. It fell upon the shoulders in natural curls. A new style of hairdressing made its appearance in the form of a lock of hair, the origin of which is seen in Fig. 65. It was brought from the crown of the head, and drawn down over the *central* parting, making a point on the forehead (*see* Figs. 25 and 70).

Very long hair was exceptional, and Fig. 67 shows an essentially French style. The side hair was parted and plaited into two tails (during the latter part of the twelfth century these plaits were called "guernons"), which were passed over or under the ears and joined behind the head, above the mass of back hair

Fig. 67. French Hairdressing

which fell behind over the neck and shoulders. This style was not in common use as it required careful dressing, and hair of sufficient length—although, of course, the use of false hair was not unknown even among the men.

King Stephen was famous for his long, luxuriant and crimped beards, so naturally this kind of facial adornment was fashionable. They were worn long, and divided into many crimped locks, with bushy beards on the upper lip (*see* Fig. 67). Figs. 68, 69 and 70 also represent the mode of dressing the hair and beard adopted during the reigns of Henry I. and Stephen. These drawings are taken from an illuminated MS. of this period, and are treated somewhat in the conventional style of the originals.

Fig. 68.   Fig. 69.   Fig. 70.

Hairdressing, *temp.* Henry I. and Stephen

Hairdressing, 1066–1130

Women. The hair of women of the nobility was almost entirely hidden under the voluminous veil. The little that can be seen in contemporary illustrations suggests that it was parted in the middle, and the ends twisted into a coil at the nape of the neck (*see* Vol. I., Fig. 37). Long hair was worn by young women in the privacy of their homes (*see* Vol. I., p. 281).

1130–1154

The hair of ladies of rank at this period was dressed in a particular way—a fashion copied from Byzantium (*see* Vol. I., p. 197, and Figs. 93, 93A). Between 1130 and 1150 they parted it in the middle into two portions, each of which was again divided into three tresses. These three tresses were braided into one long plait, Fig. 34, and the plaits hung on either side of the face in a long line down the front. They were invariably finished off with metal cylinders surrounding the ends of the hair, and terminated with ornaments to keep them weighted.

After a time (1135) the number of tresses was reduced from three to two, and they were not braided, but bound together with a band of gold or coloured ribbon. The method of doing it was to pass the ribbon outside both tresses, then round one, outside both again, then round the other, all the way down, finishing at the bottom in a tapering point (Fig. 71). These plaits were extended to an impossible length, and to attain this effect fashionable ladies had recourse to false hair added to their own, with the result that there was a lively demand for false hair. Unfortunate ones who could not obtain supplies were not to be outdone, so they ingeniously devised concealment of their meagre equipment by using cases of silk, stuffed with tow, in extension of their own locks. These cases they also bound with bands of ribbon, etc., and towards the end of this period (1140) it became the leading fashion to wear plaits of hair so dressed. The dressing of this coiffure took a great deal of time and care, and it was adopted only by noble ladies and women of leisure (*see* Fig. 59).

Fig. 71. Hairdressing and Camise

Over the plaited hair the veil was draped to hang in straight lines with a zig-zag edge, often worked in gold thread all over the surface, and with an edging of gold. On top of this was placed the crown or coronet (Fig. 37 and Plate III.).

Fig. 60—a woman of the people—is exceptional in that the hair is visible. It cannot be said to be "dressed," and hangs untended. At her leisure, such a woman would wear it parted in the middle, and drawn back into a coil at the nape of the neck.

FOOTGEAR, 1066–1154

Temp. William I. 1066–1087

Footgear worn during the reign of William I. was quite normal, following the shape of the foot, as seen in the various drawings of figures under this reign.

High boots — pedules, and later, buskins — formed part of the coronation equipment of emperors and kings of this and earlier times, a practice continued from Roman days, when official boots were the distinguishing mark of magistrates and patricians and, later, of the emperor. They also formed part of ecclesiastical vestments from the sixth century onwards. Such footgear was made of silk and richly embroidered with gold and set with precious stones. They fastened up the front with ornaments, and when of a flexible nature were sometimes tied below the knee with tasselled strings.

Shoes worn with State and full dress were very rich, made of coloured leather, cloth or silk, ornamented with bands of gold. Sometimes the foundation was embroidered, chiefly in squares, lozenges or circles (Fig. 72). In some examples of this time the vamp takes a curved line over the top of the instep without any fastening, the foot being slipped in more easily in consequence (Figs. 10 and 44). In others it rises still higher to above the ankle, the top part being rolled over (Fig. 43). Occasionally this top part had a piece cut out at the sides to make it easier to draw on to the foot (Figs. 9 and 73).

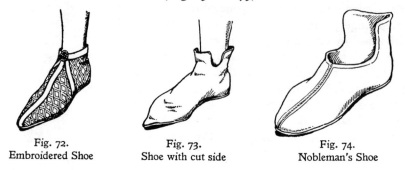

| Fig. 72. | Fig. 73. | Fig. 74. |
| Embroidered Shoe | Shoe with cut side | Nobleman's Shoe |

Temp. William II. 1087–1100

A nobleman's shoe of this reign is shown in Fig. 74. It is cut very high at the back, sloping down towards and open on the instep. To make this kind of shoe fit well it was seamed up the centre, and over the seam a cord was sewn to ensure durability. This style remained in vogue for some time, and is shown in Figs. 78 and 80 under later dates.

Temp. Henry I. 1100–1135, and Stephen, 1135–1154

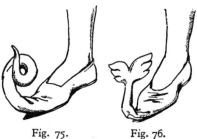

Fig. 75.   Fig. 76.
Scorpion and Fish-tailed Shoes

At the end of the eleventh century long pointed boots and shoes of weird shapes came into fashion, and called forth contemptuous comments from the writers of the times. It happened that the feet of Count Fulk of Anjou were much disfigured in shape by large corns and bunions. To hide these deformities he had shoes made of an unusual length, very sharp at the toes, and elongated so that they might conceal the excrescences. This new fashion became common throughout France, and "wonderfully pleased light-minded persons, and lovers of novelty." A debauched young fellow named Robert, about the Court of William II., introduced the practice of filling the long points of these shoes with tow, and twisting and turning them up like rams' horns. Hence he got his surname of Cornard; and this absurd fashion was speedily adopted by great numbers of the nobility as a proud distinction. In consequence the "coblers" shaped

Fig. 77.
Shoe of Upper Classes

their masterpieces like scorpions' tails, serpents' tails and fish tails, vulgarly called "Pigaces" (Figs. 75 and 76).

A shoe or boot worn by the more staid members of the upper classes is shown in Fig. 77. It is of normal shape, with the sides slit rather like Victorian elastic-sided boots, without the elastic.

Fig. 78 gives a shoe of this and of Stephen's reign, a development of Fig. 74, worn by the nobility. It was made of rich material and jewelled.

Fig. 78.
Shoe of Geoffrey of Anjou

Fashion now demands a more pointed toe. To make the toe part stiff, so that it should not curl under the foot (Fig. 79 shows a pointed toe un-stiffened), separate metal ornaments were sewn up the front: these formed part of the decoration. It should be noticed in many of the shoes (*e.g.* Figs. 78 and 79) that the inner side is higher than the outer. This shoe (Fig. 78) is worn by Geoffrey of Anjou, Fig. 33.

Fig. 80 is a further development of this shoe, fashionable during the reign of Henry II.: it is given here in company with its

Fig. 79. Shoe of Middle Classes

forebears. The only differ-ence is that the toe is less pointed, in fact almost normal, although pointed toes were fashionable at that time. Figs. 79 and 81 show shoes buckled at the ankles, worn by the middle classes during the reigns of Henry I. and Stephen.

Fig. 82 gives the shoe, made of rough leather or felt, worn by the labouring classes.

Fig. 80.
Shoe of Henry II.'s reign

It is buttoned at the side. Figs. 53 and 54 are other shapes. In illuminated MSS. of this time, footgear worn by the peasantry is nearly always shown black.

Legs were protected by pieces of leather or cloth, bound or laced by thongs from the ankle to the knee. This kind of leg-covering was in use from early times, as shown in Vol. I., Fig. 29, which illustrates the primitive form of gaiters or leggings.

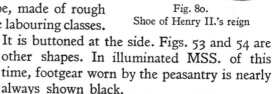

Fig. 81. Middle-Class Shoe

During the Frankish period the name of "Pedules" was given to these articles of leg wear, which continued in use among horsemen,

hunters, etc., until high boots took their place at a later date.
It is stated in a romance of the twelfth century that a horseman "was

shod in leggings and shoes of oxhide, laced with bast to above the knee." In this instance the lacing was done by a cord or string made of the fibres of plants. Such *b o o t s* William Rufus wore on his last hunting expedition in the New Forest. On that morning he was in high spirits, and was "joking with his attendants who were lacing on his boots," when the armourer brought him six special arrows, one of which pierced his heart a few hours later.

Fig. 82.
Shoe of Labouring Classes

Chausses of cloth would be worn underneath these leggings. Sometimes the chausses were of a cloth called "saye," later known as worsted.

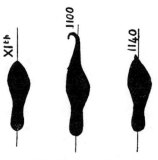

Fig. 83. Sole plans

JEWELLERY, 1066–1154

"Jewellery" may be divided into four sections:

Jewellery of Significance, consisting of crowns, coronets, emblems of Orders, some rings.

Jewellery of Utility: Brooches, buttons, belts, etc., used as fastenings.

Jewellery for Decoration of the Person: Earrings, bracelets, rings, necklaces, pendants.

Jewellery and Goldsmith's Work, applied to the decoration of costumes. (This variety is described in the notes on the costumes concerned.)

Goldsmiths and jewellers of Anglo-Saxon and Norman times were chiefly monks, who were by far the best artists in metalwork. Their art was a labour of love, and their energies were mainly devoted to the decoration of their churches. In addition, however, they undertook orders from the nobility and wealthy, and these were carried out with the same conscientious diligence and good taste. As a consequence of monastic monopoly of the craft, there was a great similarity between ecclesiastical and secular ornaments of goldsmith's work and jewellery produced at this and later periods.

After the Norman Conquest the goldsmith's craft received a considerable impetus and its technique was greatly improved in consequence of the enhanced demand for personal ornaments. Fine jewels were of course an indication of wealth, and for this reason they were accumulated and displayed by the rich upper classes; but by degrees their beauty was appreciated for its own sake.

Jewellery in the form of necklaces, earrings and bracelets was quite unknown to the fashionable men and women of the Norman period.[1] Ornaments of precious metals, set with gems, jewels, and enamels, were limited to brooches, mantle-fastenings, finger-rings, girdles, and, most important of all, crowns and circlets.

Crowns and circlets. Guy of Amiens describes the crown used for the coronation of William I., and Fig. 84 has been drawn from this description. It was made to William's order, by a Byzantine goldsmith, of gold sent from Arabia and gems from Egypt—"a miracle of splendour." Guy's own words best describe the setting:

A carbuncle decks the centre of the front of it; next follows a brilliant jacinth; third in the golden circle gleams a topaz; a glorious sapphire enriches the fourth place; fifth is a sardonyx, which sits over the Royal ears, and next to it comes, sixth in order, a chalcedony. Seventh a jasper—which keeps the foe at bay; eighth is a cornelian, sparkling with ruddy fire; in the ninth cavity is placed a chrysolite; and then, a beryl maketh bright the tenth place. A green emerald fills the eleventh; and thereto brings the chrysoprase its wealth. Supreme on the very top stands a pearl which refills the stones with added light. Placed on the right and on the left of the pearl is an amethyst of double colour. As when the clouds are driven away, the whole sky of heaven, inset with fiery stars, gleams with a ruddy light, so the golden crown, its form picked out with brilliant stones, shines all round about it with bright light.

No authentic drawing of this crown exists, but since we know that it was made by a Byzantine artist, its general character is certain to have been as drawn in Fig. 84. The twelve plates were probably engraved, and hinged together.

The crown shown in Fig. 7 is taken from William I.'s seal. It is a combination of an iron helmet and a golden crown, with four points finishing in three gold balls, or possibly pearls.

Fig. 84.
William I.'s Crown

The crown worn by William's predecessor, Harold, as shown in the Bayeux Tapestry, is reproduced in Fig. 85. It is similar to that worn by Eadward the Confessor in the same work. In

[1] And of the periods covered by Chapters II. and III.

Plate I. the crown worn by Queen Matilda is of plain gold, and its lines follow those of crowns worn by Anglo-Saxon queens.

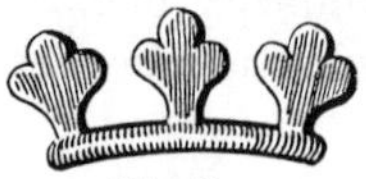

Fig. 85.
Harold's Crown

The little that remains of the crown on the statue of Henry I. suggests that it was of the shape associated with Anglo-Saxon kings, and the crown of Stephen shown upon a coin is very like Fig. 85.

Coronets and circlets worn by the nobility of both sexes were bands of gold, plain or engraved, often with a single stone set in front (Fig. 9).

Fig. 86. An Agrafe

Next to the crown and circlet, the most important article of jewellery worn during the Norman Period was the *brooch* (French, *broche* = an iron pin). It had different names, according to its various uses, and each will be described under this heading. All are descended from the fibulæ of former times (*see* Vol. I., p. 284). Brooches were the most useful adjuncts to dress, and from early times they were decorated in a variety of ways.

The word "agrafe" (Saxon) was applied to a brooch with a long pin, to a circular-topped disc with a pin underneath, and to a circular

Fig. 87.
An Agrafe

or rectangular plaque divided into two notched sections, with a pin set in a slot securing them when put together.

"Fermail" (Norman French) was a name given to a smaller brooch used for fastening the tunic or gown at the throat.

Fig. 86 is a drawing of an agrafe founded on a celebrated brooch in the British Museum, and typical of those used by the English and Norman nobles to fasten their mantles. Such agrafes were ornamented with enamels, often set with jewels of various colours and pearls of all sizes, giving the rich effect of Byzantine jewellery of which they were copies.

During this time the gold and enamelled jewellery made at Limoges was famous all over Western Europe. Fig. 87 shows the frame of a very beautiful agrafe of a distinct type. It is eleventh-century goldsmith's work set with three rubies and three sapphires, all in claw settings, between six groups each of three pearls. In the centre was fixed a cameo of Greek or Roman cutting.

Fig. 88.
An Agrafe

During the reign of Stephen, noble ladies wore large jewelled agrafes at the neck as a finish to the corsage then fashionable. Such agrafes are seen in Fig. 37 and Plate III. They were usually circular plaques of massive gold, ornamented with gold wire and set with jewels (Fig. 88).

The girdle was a fashionable adjunct to dress during this period, and some examples were beautiful specimens of the goldsmith's and jeweller's art.[1] An example of the second half of the eleventh century may be seen in Plate I. where it is described.

During the reign of Stephen, the belt or girdle which encircled the waist and hips was rich and massive, being composed of plaques of gold filigree or repoussé work set with precious stones. One of these girdles is worn by the Empress Matilda (*see* Plate III.); detail is shown in Fig. 38.

Finger-rings. The examples shown here are ecclesiastical, but in style they are not unlike rings worn by the laity. In Fig. 89 the hoop carries a massive square top in gold, set with a deep blue sapphire; it was found in the coffin of Ralph

Fig. 89

Flambard, Bishop of Durham (1099–1128). Another ring a little later in date is shown in Fig. 90. It is of gold, and has a hexagonal top set with a large sapphire; this ring belonged to William de St. Barbara, Bishop of Durham (1144–1153).

Fig. 90

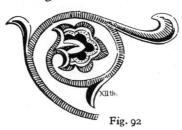

Fig. 91. Buckle

Buckles. An example of buckles in use during the eleventh and twelfth centuries is shown in Fig. 91. Buckles of this type were made of bronze, iron, or often of gold or silver.

XIIth.

Fig. 92

Section VII.—Weaving and Materials
1066–1154

The weaving industry was of good repute during the Anglo-Saxon Period, and by the middle of the eleventh century there were a number of foreign artisans (especially Frankish) and craftsmen, including weavers, living in England. These last were working in conjunction with English weavers, their chief manufacture being a coarse woollen cloth.

Soon after the Conquest a great many weavers emigrated to England from Flanders. The provinces of Flanders and Hainault at an earlier period had acquired renown as the centres of manufacture of woollen fabrics. "The art of weaving seemed to be a peculiar gift bestowed by

[1] The Guild of Girdlers is one of the oldest craft guilds and claims origin in Norman times.

nature upon the Flemings," says Gervase, the monk of Canterbury, at a later date. These Flemings settled round about Carlisle, and in 1111 were transferred by Henry I. to Pembrokeshire, to Tenby and Haverfordwest, and also to Ross, and to the mouth of the Tweed. They introduced many improvements into the craft of cloth-weaving, for which they found excellent material in the fleeces of this country.

It was, however, a domestic industry, its progress slow, and English cloth could not yet compete with that of foreign make. On the other hand, wool produced by English wool-growers was famous throughout Europe. Henry of Huntingdon mentions "fine wool" as the chief export of the English about the end of the eleventh century. "All the nations of the world were at this time kept warm by English wool," says a writer calling himself "Matthew of Westminster."

The craft of the dyer and fuller made but little progress in England after Celtic times until the seventeenth century, although fullers were incorporated under Henry II. Most English woven cloth was shipped to the Netherlands to undergo this process.

A list of names applied during this period to various textiles and materials then in use, with brief descriptions of their natures, is inserted here for guidance. Similar lists will be found in subsequent chapters.

Chainsil (Norman French), *cainsil* or *camisiles*. A fine cloth of flax, similar to cambric, and manufactured on the Continent. The term "chainsil" is used in writings of the time to denote generally "fine linen." Chainsil of a thicker quality was used for making bedsheets and linings of garments. It was generally white, but later it was also made in colours. A more substantial make was used for hangings, and at a later date for covering the walls of rooms. A species of this linen fabric was woven at Rennes in Brittany, and called *Rennes cloth*.

Diaper. A material of silk, linen or cotton, woven in a pattern but of one colour.

Embroideries made in England by the Anglo-Saxon ladies were highly esteemed on the Continent (*see* Vol. I., p. 272), where they were known as "Anglicum opus." The word "opus," though signifying embroidery in general, was also applied to gold embroidery embellished with jewel-work and commonly known as "Orphreys" (French, *ouvré*, meaning wrought, figured or flowered). This latter name was given in particular to the embroidery upon ecclesiastical vestments. When, however, these embroideries formed separate portions and were detachable, they were known as "Apparels" (Vol. I., p. 101).

Fustian (Spanish, *fuste* = a substance) was a material with a linen warp and a cotton woof, woven with a short looped surface which was sheared and formed a close-set pile. Known since cotton was first introduced into the West in the first century B.C. This material was much esteemed as seemly though not costly, and was used for making outer garments of all kinds for the laity, and for vestments for the clergy. Dr. Bock thinks that this manufacture may have suggested to the Italians the idea of weaving silk in the same manner, and so producing velvet (*see* Velvet and Pell, Vol. I., p. 217).

Materials of woven *gold*, imported from Byzantium and the Orient, were used for State and ceremonial costume throughout mediæval times. We are told by Ordericus Vitalis that the French and Norman nobility who assembled to receive William I. on his return from the conquest of England, at Easter 1067, "greatly admired the garments of gold tissue, enriched with bullion, worn by the king and his Anglo-Norman courtiers."

It was usual for the wealthy to purchase fine and rich materials for their clothing, etc., from abroad, although a great deal of all kinds of beautiful fabrics could be bought at the great annual fairs.

The term *homespun* denotes a material woven at home, but at this time and during the Middle Ages it applies more particularly to a plain cloth, something like wool-sacking, woven upon the looms of the lower middle classes and the cottar. The dyeing and fulling of this material were also done at home.

The craft of *knitting* by hand is much more ancient than can be authenticated by direct statements. The existence of the Anglo-Saxon word "cnytan" = to knit, is sufficient evidence that this craft was employed during the period now under consideration.

Passements (*passementerie*). A term frequently applied during the Middle Ages to gold, silver and coloured ornamental braid.

Russet. A coarse homespun cloth of a natural hue, often dyed a brown colour by steeping in a solution of bark. Worn by peasants and poor people. Russet clothes are indicative of country men, who were called "Russettings." "Russettings are clowns, low people, whose clothes were of a russet colour." "Sheep's russet" was spun from undyed wool, and was of a grey colour; it was much used as shepherds' clothing.

Silken materials of all kinds (*see* Vol. I., Chap. V.) were increasingly in favour among the aristocracy and the rich, a preference which has been maintained up to the present day.

Woad. A plant grown in the eastern counties of England and largely employed for dyeing blue cloth, etc., during the Middle Ages.

Woollen cloth was used during this and other periods for making the garments of the nobility and lower classes of society, its texture, quality and colour being the only distinction in use. In these times the term *cloth* was equivalent to the word "stuff," which was used in the Middle Ages to describe all kinds of materials.

Fairs. The markets at which all merchandise and commodities were bartered or sold were held in a small way once a week—on Sundays until the influence of the Church altered it to Saturdays. Besides these, there were the annual markets or fairs conducted on a very large scale.

William Rufus granted permission for an annual fair, for one day only, to be held at Winchester, on St. Giles Hill, mainly, though not entirely, for the sale of wool and woollen goods.

In 1133 Henry I. granted a charter to the Priory of S. Bartholomew, Smithfield, to hold an annual fair at which cloth formed an important commodity. King Stephen confirmed the charter.

(*Continued on p.* 123.)

CRAFT GUILDS AND MERCHANT GUILDS

Guilds were corporations, or associations of men of the same calling established for mutual aid.

The Craft Guilds were unions of artisans and labourers, or *Trade Clubs* among all those of a craft. They also acted as benefit, insurance, and burial societies, and exercised social, educational and even religious functions, besides regulating the hours of work, process of manufacture, wages and prices.

The first Guild of Weavers was founded in London at the beginning of the twelfth century, and by this time English guilds were far in advance of those of any other country in Europe.

The earliest reference to Merchant Guilds is found in documents connected with Burford and Canterbury, dating 1087–1109.

Early in the twelfth century Merchant Guilds or *Unions of Traders* began to appear for the purpose of regulating trade, the exclusion of rivals, and their own protection. They claimed a monopoly of all trade of the town, no one being allowed to trade or deal in any article who was not a member of the guild. The governing bodies of these guilds or corporations consisted of "Aldermen" (compare "Ealdorman," Vol. I., p. 261) or magistrates. The headman or magistrate was called "The Mayor," a name introduced by the Normans in the reign of Henry I. The office superseded that of "Reeve" or "Portreeve," a chief officer of earlier times.

The Hanse of London (distinct from the Teutonic Hanse) originated at this time, and was a society of merchants trading abroad, in association with foreign merchants trading in England. These guilds in course of time made the merchants a powerful governing body, but the craft guilds, in opposition, succeeded in gradually breaking down (for a time) the trade monopoly of the merchants.

(*Continued on p.* 125.)

XIIth

Fig. 93

Section VIII.—Chivalry

The origin of chivalry may be traced, according to Tacitus, a writer of the first century, to the pagan Teutonic tribes of Germania. He says that the investiture of a young warrior with arms was a very important one, and "a sign that the youth had reached manhood; this was his first honour." Indeed, his expressions might have been used with no great differences to describe the actual ceremonies of knighthood.

At the Court of Charlemagne in the eighth century, and later under Henry the Fowler (tenth century), combats at arms were popular—at first simply for diversion, but subsequently with a more serious purpose of training in view. These martial exercises were the origin of the tourney. "Chivalry" may be referred in a general sense to the age of Charlemagne.

About the middle of the eleventh century some French nobles, ashamed of their misdeeds, vowed corporately to consecrate their lives and swords to the service of mankind, and to employ them only in the cause of justice and benevolence. Each member of the group was known as a "Knight," and by the twelfth century the organisation had grown into a recognised and established fraternity.

The term "knight" (see Vol. I., pp. 84 and 105) is derived from the Anglo-Saxon word "cniht" or "cnecht," meaning "one who serves," especially a servant to the king.

It was the custom for all noblemen to be knighted, and knighthood was conferred, with some exceptions, upon all men of the upper classes down to the younger sons of the lower nobility. These latter were frequently devoid of property and without expectations of any, and they took service under some ecclesiastical or secular noble. Some, for pecuniary reward, passed from the entourage of one baron to that of another. In many cases knights acted as a kind of police, and kept law and order in the land.

Before the epoch of the Crusades, chivalry appears to have had no particular reference to religion. At, or after, that epoch chivalry acquired the character as much of a religious as of a military institution.

Under the influence of the First Crusade, the fraternity developed and expanded, and from this origin sprang in time various orders of knighthood, each of which combined the knightly and ecclesiastical elements of a life devoted to God and to arms. The institution of such orders spread rapidly throughout Europe, and they became an important factor in the Second Crusade.

Knighthood was conferred on a man for his moral and physical excellence, after severe trials and proof that the aspirant deserved the honour. First he *must* be a Christian, and obey and defend the Church on all occasions. He must possess all the virtues pertaining to manhood—piety, truthfulness, unselfishness and courage. A champion and devotee of womanhood and of friendship, he undertook by oath to defend the weak and oppressed, to hold his plighted word inviolate, to be faithful to his liege lord, and perform all feudal duties.

Knighthood was a Christianised profession of arms affiliated to feudalism, and may be said to have expired with it. Mediæval romances are largely concerned with the deeds and characters of knights and their ladies, whose exploits and praises were sung by the troubadours, themselves members of the knightly class.

The education of a candidate for knighthood began at an early age. He was placed in the household of some nobleman or knight as a page, and there he learnt the various accomplishments required by

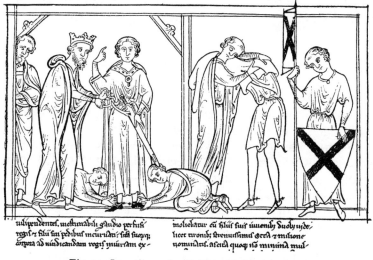

uilipendentes, incstimabili gaudio perfusi
regnf-z filii siu pedibus incuriista: sisi suoyq;
corpora ad uindicandam regif muiistam ex-

moliebatur cu filii suis iuuenibz duoby ujde;
licet tironibz strenuissimis oteia z milione
uomiuistis asciea quoqz iis minima mul-

Fig. 94. Investiture of a Knight; thirteenth century.
Drawing by Matthew Paris.

society at the time—riding, hunting and hawking; the art of playing on the harp or lute, singing and sometimes reading poems and romances for the amusement of the lord and lady on whom he attended. At the age of fourteen he was promoted to the rank of an *Esquire*. He then underwent a full training in all military exercises and pursuits, to which the tourney was an important contribution. Various other duties he had to fulfil—carving at meal-times and handing the dishes round, attendance at the stables to see that the horses were properly cared for, acting as valet to his lord, and bearing his armour ("armiger") or his shield ("scutifer," "escuyer").

Every esquire was *ipso facto* reputed to be a gentleman, *i.e.* a man of gentle or good birth, entitled to armorial bearings, to carry a sword *without* a belt, and to use *silver* spurs.

At the age of twenty-one (some royalties were considerably younger), the esquire was advanced to the dignity of Knighthood. He spent the previous night in the chapel in prayer; in the morning, after a ceremonial bath of purification [1] and several hours' rest, to symbolise his future state of rest in Paradise, he was dressed in a cotte or surcote of white, indicating purity, and a red cloke typifying the blood which he should be ready to shed in defence of Holy Church. He was then shod in black shoes, symbolical of the earth from which he sprang and to which he must return. The ceremony is shown in the accompanying illustration (Fig. 94), a drawing of the early thirteenth century reproduced from Matthew Paris's MS. The king fastens the military belt and sword round the waist of the candidate. Two officers are in the act of securing the *golden* spurs to his shoes. On the right, an esquire holds the shield and banner, and next to him is another candidate having his mailed tunic drawn over his head.

A revised order of investiture of a young knight prescribed from this time is as follows: Procedure is identical with the earlier practice as far as adjustment of the shoes. He is then presented to the assembled company; other esquires and pages array him in his armour and buckle it on. His helmet and golden spurs, which previously had been consecrated and placed on the altar, are now presented to him, and the spurs strapped on. Next he makes his vows, kneeling in front of the altar, and receives from the officiating cleric the consecrated sword and white sword-belt. After this he is "dubbed" a knight. This could be done by the king, by a noble, or a distinguished knight. The postulant knelt before the person conferring knighthood, who, using his own sword, or one handed to him by an attendant, created him a knight, first fastening the military belt, already received, round his waist, then kissing his left cheek, and finally touching his right shoulder (sometimes both) with the blade of the sword, saying: "In honour of the Father, and the Son, and the Holy Ghost, I create thee a knight." This final act is the "Accolade."

Many of the above ceremonies survive, and on occasion are performed in England at the present day.

Some Orders of Knighthood

S. Maurice is the Patron Saint of Chivalry and Knighthood.

Hospitallers. Founded in 1023 a hospital at Jerusalem to provide food and lodging for sick Latin pilgrims. An associated brotherhood was established in London about 1100. Its headquarters were just outside the city walls, near Clerk's Well, in a priory dedicated to S. John and founded by a knight named Jordain Briset. Instituted as a religious order of knights in 1118 and known as *Knights Hospitallers* or

---

[1] The origin of "The Order of the Bath."

Knights of S. John of Jerusalem. After their conquest of Rhodes in 1309, they called themselves *Knights of Rhodes*; but after the island was taken from them by the Turks in 1522, the Emperor Charles V. installed them at Malta (1530), and they were then known as *Knights of Malta.* They sometimes wore a black surcote over their armour; their regular uniform was a black mantle having a white cross of eight points, made of waxed cloth, upon the left shoulder. About 1280 they assumed, when engaged in military duties, a red surcote charged with a Latin cross in white on the breast. For everyday use a black frock and cowl with the cross on the breast was worn (for Banner, *see* Fig. 468).

In 1191, during the siege of Acre, an Order of a somewhat similar kind was founded by some German merchants of Lübeck, who called themselves the *Teutonic Order of Knights.* They wore a white mantle with a black cross.

An English *Order of S. Thomas* was founded by Peter des Roches, under the patronage of a sister of Thomas à Becket, in 1231. This survived until about the end of the fourteenth century. Members wore their own mantles, with a cross divided vertically into red and white halves (heraldic term, "per pale") as a badge.

The Knights Templars. An Order founded to satisfy both the desire for military renown and for the life of a religious—a perfectly possible combination according to the ideas of the period. The Order was founded by nine French knights who in 1118 had followed Godfrey de Bouillon to the Crusades. Lodgings were given to them by Baldwin, King of Jerusalem, in a building near the Temple of Solomon on Mount Moriah at Jerusalem. Their rule was that of Canons Regular. Introduced into England by Hugues de Payens in 1128, their first settlement—the Old Temple, or Oldbourne—was situated where Chancery Lane joins Holborn. In the time of Henry II. they built for themselves a new temple near the Fleet, and founded their Temple Church, which was consecrated in 1185. Although sworn individually to poverty, celibacy and obedience, this noble and aristocratic Order soon grew opulent by donations of land and money, and became eventually perhaps the richest Order in the world.

Roger of Wendover says: "They are said at present to have such immense possessions on both sides of the sea, that there is no province in all Christendom which has not given them a portion of its wealth, and at this day they excel even kings in riches."

It was alleged, however, that prosperity and wealth greatly corrupted them, and under the pretext that their pride, impiety and vices had become so scandalous, Knights Templars throughout England were seized by special command of Edward II. and cast into prison in 1307. Edward took possession of their property, and it formed part of the dowry of his bride, in place of that which he had misappropriated and bestowed upon Piers Gaveston.

Similarly, in France, Philippe IV. suppressed them in 1306. The last grand master was burned alive over a slow fire at the back of the garden wall of the royal palace on the Seine in 1314. Much of the Knights Templars' property fell into the hands of the French king, and some was annexed and incorporated with that of the Knights of S. John of Jerusalem.

There is so much improbability, absurdity and contradiction in the evidence adduced against the Templars at the suppression of the Order, that it is difficult to believe there was any justice in accusing them of impiety and idolatry. Most of the stories against them were told *after* their proscription. They were never denounced by the troubadours, who attacked without fear or pity even popes, clergy and prominent men of all ranks.

Over their armour the Knights Templars sometimes wore a white surcote and always a white mantle, assigned to them by Pope Honorius II. (1124–1130). Pope Eugenius III. (1145–1153) granted them a red cross of eight points to be worn on the left shoulder of the mantle. The sergeants wore black mantles, the esquires brown, each with the red cross. Their banner (Fig. 467) was divided "per fesse" (horizontally) black and white, signifying *terrible to the enemy* and *fair to Christians,* and on their lances they bore a banner of white charged with their red cross.

In the thirteenth century a white coif (*see* p. 176) was worn under a red hat.

The principal distinction between this institution and the Hospitallers was that the Templars added to their monastic and military vows no obligation to tend the sick and relieve the poor. The sole occupation as "Poor Soldiers of Jesus Christ" was to make war with the infidels, and they soon became the head of all Christian chivalry. In every battle and siege they were foremost, the Templars claiming the post of honour on the right, the Hospitallers on the left.

The members of the Orders of Chivalry were under the jurisdiction of no king, and belonged to no country. They were subject only to the emperor (Holy Roman Empire) and to the pope.

The refining effects of chivalry upon the manners and customs of the Middle Ages cannot be overestimated. The youths and young men forming the entourage of a great baron, when free from their various duties, sought recreation in company of the maidens of gentle birth, placed under the charge of the lady of the castle to learn all kinds of domestic and artistic accomplishments. After dinner, about midday or earlier, there was hunting, hawking, archery, ball-play, a primitive golf, and for boys bat-and-ball, quintain; or for the less energetic a walk, each swain probably attaching himself to his particular charmer. Supper was served early, often at sunset, and evenings, when the torches and candles were lit, spent together in various amusements

—music and singing, dancing, romping, and all the games in vogue at the time — chess, dice, hoodman - blind, bowls, kaytes or nine-pins, skittles, etc. For full details of these games reference should be made to *Sports and Pastimes of the People of England*, by Joseph Strutt.

These cheerful pastimes cultivated refinement, elegance and personality, and produced a general improvement of good manners which permeated not only the aristocracy, but also the lower orders. The tone, both moral and physical, of all classes of society underwent an entire change for the better, although the age was no more free than any other from many flagrant instances of viciousness, profligacy, brutality and extreme immorality.

CHAPTER II
1154–1216

CONTENTS

CHAPTER II

1154–1216

CONTEMPORARY EMPERORS AND KINGS

	ENGLAND	FRANCE	GERMANY
1154	Henry II. Eleanor of Aquitaine	Louis VII., 1137–1180	Frederick I. Barbarossa, 1152–1190
1180		Philippe II. Auguste, 1180– 1223 1. Isabella of Hainault 2. Ingelburge of Denmark 3. Agnes de Mérämie	
1189	Richard I. Berengaria of Navarre		
1190			Henry VI. Asper, 1190–1198 Constantia
1198			Philip of Swabia, 1198–1208 Irene, daughter of Isaac II., Emperor of Con- stantinople
1199	John 1. Isabella of Gloucester 2. Isabella of Angoulême		
1208			Otho IV. the Superb, of Brunswick, 1208–1212 1. Beatrix of Swabia 2. Marie of Brabant
1212			Frederick II., 1212–1250 1. Constantia of Arragon 2. Iolande de Brienne 3. Isabella of England

HISTORICAL DATA

1154–1216

1154. Accession of Henry II., first Plantagenet monarch.
Thomas à Becket (1117–1170), Archdeacon of Canterbury; son of Gilbert à Becket, a rich merchant and Portreeve (Mayor) of London; appointed Chancellor.

1155. Frederick I. (Barbarossa) of Germany creates the Kingdom of Bohemia. The *Niebelungenlied* (the national epic of Germany) and other poems composed about this time.
Lambert-li-Cors, author of *Li romans d'Alexandre*, circa 1155, in which "Alexandrines" were first employed.

1158. The University of Bologna founded.

1161. Canonisation of Eadward the Confessor.

1162. Canonisation of Charlemagne.
Thomas à Becket made Archbishop of Canterbury; he immediately "put off the Deacon" and became the champion of the Church.

1163. Gervase, monk of Canterbury; chronicler; died 1210.

1165. William le Breton, continued the writings of Rigord; died 1220.

1167. Geoffrey de Villehardouin, author of *Chronicle of the Fourth Crusade*: "the first real History" (see Vol. I., p. 186). Died 1213.

1170. The struggle between Henry II. and Thomas à Becket continued until their reconciliation, after which Becket returned to England, 1 December, 1170, and on the 22nd of the same month he was murdered in Canterbury Cathedral. A magnificent shrine was erected to his memory by Henry shortly afterwards. This was destroyed by order of Henry VIII., and the bones of S. Thomas were publicly burnt in 1538.

S. Dominic, founder of the mendicant Order of Dominicans, born this year.

1171. Conquest of Ireland (1169–1171) by Henry II.'s general, Richard Strongbow, Earl of Pembroke.

1173. Canonisation of S. Thomas à Becket. Great rebellion headed by Henry II.'s sons, assisted by the Kings of Scotland and France, but subdued by Henry the following year.

Jocelyn de Brakelond, chronicler of S. Eadmund's Abbey; died 1203.

1175. Rebellion in Germany of Henry Welf (Guelf) the Lion, Duke of Saxony, who married Maud, daughter of Henry II. of England. After submission he was granted Brunswick-Luneberg (Hanover); ancestor of the Hanoverian kings of England.

1177. Benedict, Abbat of Peterborough; English historian; wrote lives of Becket, Henry II. and Richard I. Keeper of the Great Seal from 1191 to 1193, in which latter year he died.

1180. Matthew Paris, monk of St. Albans; scholar, poet, divine, traveller, politician, courtier, artist, and the greatest and last of the monastic historians. Died 1259.

The Second Crusade ended with the fall of Jerusalem.

1182. "Il Francesco" (so named from his command of the Provençal tongue) born; son of a rich merchant of Assisi; founder of the Franciscan Order. Canonised as S. Francis. The most beautiful character in the history of Mediæval Christianity. Died 1226.

1188. The Third Crusade undertaken by Frederick Barbarossa.

1189. Wholesale massacre of Jews in England.

1190. Richard I. set out to join the Third Crusade.

1192. On his return he was shipwrecked at Aquileia, and became a wanderer. Eventually he was captured in a cottage in the suburbs of Vienna, and confined in the Castle of Durrenstein on the Danube, by Leopold, Duke of Austria.

1194. King Richard ransomed, and returned to England. He was re-crowned at Winchester to wipe out the stain of his captivity, and left England for the last time 15 July of the same year.

1199. Death of Richard I. Accession of John.

1200. The Fourth Crusade, in which the Marquis Boniface of Montferrat and Baldwin, Count of Flanders, took an active part.

Philippe Auguste excommunicated, and all France placed under an interdict by Pope Innocent III.

The University of Paris founded about this time.

1204. Duchy of Normandy and all other possessions in France lost to England by John "Lackland."

Seventh siege, and sack of Constantinople by the Latins (see Vol. I., p. 138).

1206. Election of Stephen Langton as Archbishop of Canterbury. King John refused him recognition, and quarrelled with the Church.

1208. Pope Innocent III. (1198–1216) placed England under an interdict. William the Clerk, Anglo-Norman poet, flourished; died 1226.

1210. Thibault, Count of Champagne, afterwards King of Navarre. Sometimes called "the Father of French Poetry." Died 1253.

The University of Oxford came into existence early in the thirteenth century.

1214. Roger Bacon, friar, scientist. Studied at Oxford and Paris. Died 1292.

1215. A quarrel between King John and the barons due to the increase in taxation, the number of mercenaries employed, and the plundering of the Church, led to the signing of "Magna Charta," a "Treaty of Peace," at Runnymede, 15 June. John appealed to Pope Innocent III., who warmly took his part, ordered Stephen Langton to Rome, freed John from his oaths, and threatened to excommunicate the barons if they persisted in rebellion.

1216. War arose between the king and his subjects, who were on the point of offering the crown of England to the son of Philippe Auguste, King of France, when John died at Newark Castle in October 1216.

THE ARTS, 1154–1216

ARCHITECTURE

SOON after Henry II. ascended the throne he succeeded, in a great measure, in curbing the power of the lawless barons, by suppressing the strongholds from which they defied their king. He enacted that it was unlawful to erect a castle or fortify a residence without licence.

The castle keep at Newcastle-on-Tyne was begun in 1172 and completed in 1177. It is a typical specimen of combined military and domestic architecture of the period of transition between Norman and Early English.

The style of architecture called "Gothic" came into use in England about the end of Henry II.'s reign, and continued with modifications and variations until the end of the sixteenth century. The name is derived from the fact that this particular style was considered to be founded on barbarian ideas, and the opprobrious word "Goth" was consequently applied to it by the Italians.

The subdivisions of Gothic architecture are:

Early English or Lancet	.	.	.	. began	1150	approx.
Early English fully developed	.	.	.	„	1200	„
Transitional period	.	.	.	„	1250	„
Decorated fully developed	.	.	.	„	1300	„
Transitional period	.	.	.	„	1350	„
Perpendicular fully developed	.	.	.	„	1400	„
Tudor	.	.	.	.	„	1500	„

The Early English is distinguished by the pointed arch, supported on pillars composed of fine clustered shafts, with carved capitals in high relief and moulded bases; long narrow lancet-headed windows inserted in groups, chiefly of three or five; lofty roofs, raised on arch-buttressed walls, and tall spires.

London Bridge. The old timber bridge built by the Romans (*see* Vol. I., p. 17) was replaced in Henry II.'s time by a stone one. It was started in 1176, the architect being a priest named Peter, of S. Peter's, Colechurch. He died in 1205, before its completion, and was succeeded in the office by three citizens of London named Serle Mercer, William Almain and Benedict Botewrite. The bridge took thirty-three years to construct, and consisted of nineteen or twenty arches of various spans, the widest (ninth from the city side) being thirty feet. It had two footpaths on either side of a roadway wide enough for two waggons to pass. About the centre was an apsidal chapel of two stories, rising to a height of sixty feet above water-level, and dedicated to S. Thomas of Canterbury. A drawbridge took the place of the thirteenth arch, defended by a tower, and the bridge had a fortified gate at each end. Dwelling-houses were not built upon the piers until the reign of Edward I., and then only a few. It was not until much later times that the structure became crowded with houses of all kinds. This second London Bridge remained, with many additions and alterations, until pulled down in 1831.

About the middle of the twelfth century a society called the Bridge Building Brotherhood was formed in Southern France, for the purpose of building bridges, maintaining ferries, and establishing hospices near the most frequented fords. The bridge at Avignon was the first con-structed by them, 1176–1188.

SCULPTURE IN FRANCE (continued from p. 11)

For the next stage we must return to Normandy.

The Abbey of Fontevraud, founded 1099, is the burial-place of two kings and two queens of England: Henry II., his wife Eleanor of Aqui-taine, Richard I., and Isabella of Angoulême, wife of King John. The abbey was reduced to a ruin during the Revolution of 1789, but the effigies of these four sovereigns were discovered, hidden away in a cellar, early in the nineteenth century by Mr. C. A. Stothard, the antiquarian. They were in a mutilated condition, but Mr. Stothard restored them and placed them in the safe keeping of the municipality. There they may be seen to-day, with traces of the original colouring still left on the stonework. These monumental effigies supply full details of regal costume of the time, and archæologists, artists and students owe a debt of gratitude to Mr. Stothard.

SCULPTURE IN ENGLAND

A beautiful oaken effigy decorated with colour, at Gloucester Cathedral, is said to represent Robert Curthose, eldest son of William the Conqueror. The armour and other details date the workmanship about the end of the twelfth century (Fig. 445).

The earliest sepulchral effigy of an English king in England is on the monument to King John at Worcester Cathedral, erected shortly after his death in 1216. The nine effigies which originally surmounted altar tombs, and are now on the floor of the Temple Church, furnish very interesting details of military costume, and are well preserved. They do not represent Knights Templars, but "Associates of the Temple"—men who, while not conforming to the rigid rule of the Order during life, yet in death sought the sanctuary of the church in burial within its precincts, a privilege secured by contributions in lands or good coin of the realm. It is not certain either that they were Crusaders.

Standing with one's back to the door and facing the altar, the four on the left date from the end of the twelfth century. The nearest is to the memory of Geoffrey, Baron Magnaville (or Mandeville [1144]), removed from Oldbourne. The other three, executed in Purbeck marble, are unknown. The four on the right are later in date, being of the second quarter of the thirteenth century. Three are to the memory of members of the Mareschal or Marshal family, who were successively Earls of Pembroke. The fourth is unidentified. The single effigy on the extreme right commemorates Baron de Ros (1270).

The four bronze statues in the Middle Temple hall, representing two Knights Templars and two Hospitallers, were cast in 1875.

(*Continued on p.* 136.)

ILLUMINATED MANUSCRIPTS

1154–1216 (*continued from p.* 13)

A marked improvement in the craftsmanship of illuminated MSS., now freed from surviving elements of Anglo-Saxon practice, is apparent from this time. The methods of the older Winchester School disappeared after the Norman Conquest, but were revived, with a blend of English and Norman characteristics, the combination producing work such as that found in a psalter [1] in the British Museum, and in the Winchester Bible,[2] both executed about 1140–1150 under the patronage of the cultured Bishop Henry of Blois (died 1171), brother of King Stephen. Bishop Henry returned from a visit to Rome in 1151, with many examples of all kinds of Byzantine Art,[3] including without doubt many illuminated MSS. which may have exercised some influence on English illuminators of the later twelfth century. The drawing of the figures produced in the second half of the twelfth century is more natural, although they are tall of stature, but the persistence of long thin fingers is very noticeable (*see* Fig. 148). The figures are still drawn in outline, but instead of being left plain they are now filled in with brilliant colour (*see* Plate V.); the draperies have lost their Classic treatment, hanging definitely upon the figure.

Some late twelfth-century work took the form of

Bestiaries. Handbooks on natural history, containing matter and drawings relating to animals and birds; and

Herbals. Similar volumes, but dealing with plants and their medicinal qualities.

The end of the twelfth century closes the transitional period between Anglo-Saxon and Gothic treatment of illuminated manuscripts.

(*Continued on p.* 142.)

---

[1] Cotton MS. *Nero*, C. IV.   [2] In the Winchester Chapter Library.
[3] Compare Benedict Biscop, Vol. I., p. 222.

COSTUME IN GENERAL, 1154–1216

MEN'S AND WOMEN'S DRESS

During the reigns of the first two Plantagenet kings some change took place in the costume of the nobility and upper classes of both sexes. The men discarded their tight-fitting draped bliauts, and long trailing tunics of multitudinous folds, for simpler and more comfortable garments. The younger generation adopted tunics and mantles which allowed a greater freedom of movement—a return to the modes of William the Conqueror's time. This applied also to the women, but in their case the change did not occur until sixteen years later.

The reign of King John is notable for ostentatious display, and in men's dress extravagance ran riot. The women retained the style of costume introduced by Queen Eleanor about 1170.

After the capture of Constantinople by the Crusaders in 1204, and the formation of a Latin Empire (a memorable event in the history of Costume), Western Europe ceased to have any recourse to the East, and adopted in costume an individuality of its own, frankly local in character. This is particularly noticeable in France, after Philippe Auguste returned home in 1191 from his disastrous expedition to the Holy Land; he then devoted himself entirely to the affairs of his kingdom.

Fig. 95. Early Twelfth-Century

SECTION I.—HENRY II. 1154–1189

Nobility—Men

In accordance with the Treaty of Wallingford, Henry FitzEmpress succeeded to the throne of his grandfather Henry I., on the death of Stephen. He was the first of the long line of Plantagenet kings who occupied the throne of England, until Henry Tudor gained the victory at Bosworth in 1485.

Henry was twenty-one years of age at the time of his accession, and had married twelve months previously Eleanor of Aquitaine, the divorced wife of Louis VII., King of France. She was twelve years older than

Henry, a most unscrupulous woman, and the scandal of Europe. The English overlooked this to some extent, by reason of her position as a great heiress and sovereign in her own right of Aquitaine, Poitiers, La Marche, Saintonge, Angoulême, Limoges, Auvergne, Périgord, Guienne and Gascony.

Henry II. (*Henry FitzEmpress. Curt-Manteau*). Born at Le Mans 1133. Created a knight at the age of sixteen, by his great-uncle David I. of Scotland, at Carlisle.

Henry is described as having a ruddy, weatherbeaten countenance, square jaws, a good nose, quick fierce grey eyes, and a round head covered with thick reddish curly hair, kept closely cropped for fear of baldness. In youth he was clean shaven, but in middle life he wore a close beard, as seen in his effigy. He was of middle height, with strong limbs, although his legs were inclined to be bandy. His arms were long and sinewy, and his hands coarse and ill-kept. He possessed a charm of manner which, when he chose to make himself agreeable, was irresistible. When thwarted he was liable to fits of demoniacal passion, and would rend his clothes, and bite and tear with his teeth pieces of straw from the floor.

Henry was first brought to England at the age of eight, and visited this country many times before his accession: nevertheless he seems to have spoken Norman French in preference to English, although he well understood the latter. He was impatient of Court ceremonial. "He never sits down," so one says who knew him well, "he is always on his legs from morning till night." He hardly ever sat, even at his meals, and, as it was not etiquette for anyone to sit

Fig. 96. Henry II.

while the king stood, his courtiers complained most bitterly of being thoroughly tired out.

Henry's latter life was much oppressed by dissensions among his own family. The queen, with whom he lived unhappily, caused him much anxiety. She was chiefly instrumental in fomenting the quarrels between himself and his sons which eventually brought on a fever. Discovering the name of John, his best beloved son, affixed to a list of those in league against him, "his heart was broken, and his death-blow struck." Two days afterwards he died at Chinon, in the arms of his one faithful son (by Rosamund de Clifford), Geoffrey the Chancellor, afterwards Archbishop of York, the only son who behaved to him with gratitude and duty. Henry II. was laid to rest in the Abbey of Fontevraud in Normandy.

Fig. 96 shows the appearance of Henry II. as a young man. The king wears a tunic—the dalmatic—of crimson silk, embroidered or woven with a diaper design of six gold spots "à pois" round a single one, and bordered with a band of gold passement at the neck, on the sleeves, and at the bottom edge. It is lined with white, and girded at the waist. Under this, and showing below the dalmatic, is a close-sleeved tunic of blue, bordered with gold. Under this again is seen a white garment or alb. Over the shoulders, and fastened on the right,

is draped the mantle, in a deep chocolate tint, bordered round the neck and down the front edge with a band of gold about two and a half inches in width. The mantle is lined with white, and the small folds suggest a fairly flexible material, almost certainly a fine rich silk, lined with silk. White gloves of the new shape (with separate fingers) are worn, ornamented with jewels on the back of the hand. On the feet he wears green shoes of a natural shape with pointed toes, embroidered with gold bands, and attached to them are golden spurs secured by red leather straps. The spurs are the insignia of knighthood. Very little of the crown remains in the effigy except the circlet studded with jewels: originally it had motifs of foliage surmounting the circlet. The crown and sceptre shown in the drawing are taken from other sources.

The Emperor Henry V. of Germany exercised an unwitting influence on English costume about this time—but as he did it by dying, perhaps he should not be blamed! On his death, in 1125, his Empress Matilda was recalled to England by her father, Henry I., and, as William of Malmesbury relates,

Fig. 97.
Court Official

"The Empress, as they say, returned with reluctance, as she had large possessions there." The German nobles who formed her escort brought to the notice of the English a German fashion which did not immediately find favour here—but later, when as Duchess of Normandy Matilda held her Court at Rouen, the fashion was adopted there, and ultimately found its way back to this country.

It is illustrated in Fig. 97, which shows an English nobleman in a garment worn on State occasions by an official of the Court. The top part of his tunic is cut as shown in Fig. 11, but the treatment of the lower part, by cutting the edge into long pendent strips, is the first example of the newly-adopted mode called DAGGES.

It became popular among all classes of the English people towards the end of Henry's reign, and it was thought expedient to check the growth of this vogue. In the year 1188 an Act was passed prohibiting the middle and lower classes from indulging in this harmless and not extravagant fancy. Sumptuary laws, however, were frequently disregarded, and instead of restricting the vogue this particular statute tended to foster its growth, for the fashion continued in moderate use until it blossomed forth in the full glory of its eccentricity during the fourteenth century (*see* p. 227).

From the same source came the curious device of having one side, or half, of the garment different in colour from the other. In Fig. 97, not only is the tunic of two colours, or PARTI-COLOURED as it was called, but one side is embroidered. Encircling the waist is a scarf of rich material mounted on a foundation: it is wound loosely round the waist, with one end hanging in front. The sword is attached to a belt which is buckled or hooked to a waist-belt worn under the tunic.

Fig. 98.
Noble, *temp.* Henry II.

The everyday costume of a young noble is seen in Fig. 98. The tunic is cut on the lines of Fig. 11, but the skirt part is shorter and not so wide (Fig. 244). It is ornamented by a broad band of embroidery of

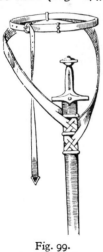

Fig. 99.
Sword Carriage

elaborate design. The same design is repeated on the collar, now assuming the character of a small shoulder cape edged with indentations, an obvious adaptation of the ornament shown at the hem of the tunic in Fig. 97. A belt with a pouch attached (under the cloke) fastens in front by a jewelled clasp. The sword-belt is hooked to it at a point just behind the right hip (Fig. 99). The cloke is similar to the Anglo-Saxon type which fell into disuse among the nobility soon after the Norman Conquest. The fashion for short clokes was revived by the nobles of Anjou, under the names of RHENO, a cloke *without* a hood, and CAPA (cape). When Henry arrived in England at his accession he was wearing one of these short clokes or mantles, hence the nickname of "Curt-Manteau." Short clokes immediately jumped into fashion.

The "Capa" was a short cloke with a cucullus (*see* Vol. I., p. 74) or hood (Anglo-Saxon, *hod* = a head) attached to it. It was a garment (obviously derived from the paenula) in general use among the Normans of the eleventh century, and was adopted in Henry II.'s reign by the English of both sexes, with whom it remained in favour during the latter part of the twelfth, and the thirteenth centuries.

These clokes were made of a very fine material—the "Capa" lined with silk; the "Rheno" with very expensive furs such as sable, ermine or miniver, the latter being worn only by persons of great wealth; indeed, a writer of the time places the Rheno among "Royal Habiliments."

This Fig. 98 illustrates the type of costume worn by the king, as a young man, on ordinary occasions; but the contemporary records mention Henry's preference for simple dress. "He useth boots, without folding caps, and *homely* and short clothes weareth he."

Nobility—Women

Eleanor, born 1118, was the daughter and co-heiress of William X. (1099–1137), Count of Poitiers and fifth Duke of Aquitaine. She married in 1137 Louis VII., King of France.

CHILDREN

1. Mary, married the Earl of Champagne.
2. Alice, married the Earl of Blois.

Eleanor married, secondly, Henry Plantagenet.

CHILDREN OF HENRY II. AND ELEANOR

1. Henry, born 1155, crowned King of England as "Rex Filius," 1170. Married Margaret, daughter of Louis VII. of France. d.s.p. 1183.
2. Richard, succeeded his father.
3. Geoffrey, Earl of Bretagne, 1158. Married Constance, daughter of Conan le Petit, Earl of Richmond and Duke of Brittany. Children: Eleanor, died 1241, and Arthur, born 1186, murdered 1203. Geoffrey was accidentally slain in a tournament in 1186.
4. John, succeeded his brother Richard.
5. Maud, married Henry V. the Lion, Duke of Saxony, ancestor of the House of Guelf. Died 1189.
6. Eleanor, married Alfonso VIII., King of Castile. Died 1214.
7. Joan, married, first, William II., King of Sicily, and secondly, Raymond, Count of Toulouse. Died 1195.

Eleanor's early reputation was of a peculiarly complex and sometimes lurid character. With her the "artistic temperament" ran riot. We are told [1] that "Queen Eleanor as little regarded the married engagements of the persons on whom she bestowed her attention, as she did her own conjugal ties."

Again, [2] "that luxurious lady of the South and heiress of the fair land of Provence—her love of a gay life and sumptuous attire went

---

[1] Miss Strickland. [2] Miss Maud M. Holbach.

hand in hand with culture and refinement such as were unknown in England before she became its Queen."

By way of illustration, the following story deserves record:

While Eleanor was Queen-Consort of France she created a great sensation throughout Christendom. The preachings of S. Bernard (1091–1153; canonised 1174) at Vezelai, in Burgundy, advocating a Second Crusade (1146–1147), attracted huge audiences, including King Louis, the queen, and all the Court. So enthusiastic was the response of all present to the saint's impassioned oratory, that to satisfy the urgent and immediate demand for crosses to sew upon their sleeves or breasts, he was constrained to tear up his own robes [1] to supply material.

The idea of becoming a female Crusader so appealed to Eleanor's emotional temperament that she was completely carried away. Such an attractive, alluring experience would be wonderful! She also, as Duchess of Aquitaine and an independent sovereign, vowed to take the Cross. Eleanor and her fashionable ladies equipped themselves in all the paraphernalia of warriors of the period—in hauberk, heaum and chausses; and it is safe to surmise that they added to this masculine attire some touches of feminine fantasy! Mounted on spirited war horses they practised all kinds of military exercises, and diligently "trained" (in public!) to stimulate their feather-brained zeal and become fully accomplished soldiers of the Cross.

These self-deluded enthusiasts sent their abandoned distaffs to all their less martial friends, to knights, nobles and any "conscientious objectors" who had the good sense to refrain from participation in this disastrous, though possibly well-meant, wild-goose chase. At last Louis and his encumbrances set out, in the spring of 1147, and did the sights of Europe on the way. Hundreds of baggage waggons drawn by oxen, and teams of pack-horses and mules were laden with the battalion's accessories—pavilions of gold-embroidered silk, rich furniture and cushions, cutlery and table plate, to say nothing of innumerable coffers of gorgeous raiment, totally unsuitable for the expedition in hand, followed in the wake of the army. These and the pranks of a regiment of amateur amazons proved a serious impediment when they arrived in the Holy Land, and resulted in the utter failure of Louis's undertaking. It was owing to Eleanor's disregard for the orders of the supreme command that the Saracens completely routed the king's forces, and everything, including Eleanor's magnificent baggage, and the greater part of the army, fell into the hands of the enemy. The queen, her ladies, and poor Louis, who found safety by climbing a tree, escaped only with their lives.

---

[1] He belonged to the Cistercian Order, whose robes consisted of a grey or white frock, and a black scapular with cowl (see Vol. I., p. 173). The crosses therefore would be white, grey or black.

After this disaster the queen fled to Antioch, and, seeking the protection of her young handsome uncle, Raymond of Poitou, Prince of Antioch, she passed her time in pursuing her numerous amours with various princes, including her uncle, and a Saracen emir aged thirteen!

Queen Eleanor returned eventually to Paris, where she first met Count Geoffrey of Anjou, who had come to Court to pay homage to his sovereign lord for the Duchy of Normandy. Chroniclers delighted in scandal, even in those days, and they are responsible for the story that Eleanor lost her head over the handsome count, already, alas, a married man. Two years after, Count Geoffrey having departed this life in the meantime, his son, Henry FitzEmpress, visited Paris to do similar homage, and immediately this royal coquette transferred her former

Fig. 100. Queen Eleanor

infatuation for the father to the son—with a sportive alacrity never difficult to her. The king was annoyed; the prince obligingly retired to Anjou; and the queen made an application for a divorce, on the grounds of consanguinity —they were fourth cousins! Bishop Sugar made some opposition, but the marriage was dissolved. Six months afterwards Eleanor, aged thirty-three, married (1151) Henry Fitz-Empress Plantagenet, aged twenty-one.

As a young woman—she was Queen-Consort of France in her twenties — Eleanor dressed in all the fripperies devised or adopted by the exotic taste of the period. The very latest from the East found a place in the royal wardrobe, and high society followed suit.

The elaborately gauffered bliaut, and its numerous accessories, were still in the height of fashion when Eleanor, then in her thirties, became Queen-Consort of England. Age, however, sobered the Provençal butterfly, and about the 1160's, when she was approaching fifty—an age when all women *should* dress with propriety—she wore a costume which is chastity itself, compared with the elaborate toilettes of noble ladies of the last three decades.

Fig. 100 illustrates the type of costume now fashionable. The gown (Fig. 101) is no longer bound tightly round the figure, but hangs loose over the bust, is confined at the waist by a jewelled belt, and falls to the feet in graceful folds—a return to the mode of the late eleventh century. The gown in the effigy of Queen Eleanor at Fontevraud, from which this drawing is made, is white, covered with gold trellis-work and crescents, either embroidered or woven, and finished at the neck and wrist by bands of gold embroidery. The sleeves are close at the upper arm and tight at the wrist. The camise of chainsil or fine silk shows just above the neckband, and is fastened by a jewelled clasp. Over this is worn a semicircular mantle of blue silk, powdered with gold crescents, and lined with silk of a rose colour. It is attached across the shoulders by gold cords and jewelled plaques.

A rich crown is worn, over a small veil of coloured gauze or fine silk embroidered and edged with gold. Under the veil a piece of fine linen encircles the head, and passes under the chin—the "chin-strap," known at the time as the BARBETTE (*see* p. 119).

Having set this mode of regal attire, Eleanor again misbehaved herself (in 1173), stirring up a mutiny against Henry by his sons. While canvassing for Prince Richard, in Poitou, she was captured, although disguised in male attire, and placed by Henry's orders in close captivity. She remained a perambu-latory State prisoner for the rest of Henry's reign of sixteen years, moving from place to place, but being liberated temporarily only when he required her presence on ceremonial occasions. Eleanor's first imprisonment coincided with the death of Rosamund de Clifford at Godstow Nunnery. Gossips of the time linked the two events together, from which arose the story that the queen despatched her "Fair" rival by poisoned wine or a dagger. The fact is that Rosamund died a natural death, at the age of forty, leaving two sons, William Longespée and Geoffrey.

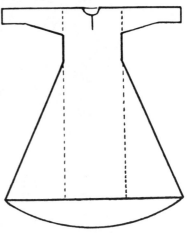

Fig. 101. Diagram of Gown

Fig. 102 shows a noble lady at her cupboard, attired richly, yet in a manner suitable to her duties as chatelaine of a baronial castle. The gown is similar in shape to those worn during the first years of Henry I.'s reign, and the drawing shows the method of lacing it tight round the waist, over the corse. The skirt part is cut in such a manner—with wide gores at the sides—that the folds begin at the level of the hips and fall to the feet in heavy lines in front, as well as behind where they form a train. The sleeves fit close on the upper arms, and are seamed to the shoulders. From the elbow downwards over the forearm, they widen out into long draped folds, finishing at the bottom in a rounded form, *not* in a point, as previously. Girdles might be worn with this type of gown, but there seems to have been no fixed rule. Some illustrations of this period show them, but others do not.

For ordinary wear this gown would be made of Flemish cloth, and in winter a mantle of cloth lined with fur would be added. The fashion-able hairdressing would be worn, while, for out of doors, a cloke with a

Fig. 102. NOBLE LADY AT HOME

hood, worn over the veil, would be used. For full dress such a gown would be made of rich silk, and embroidered or woven as described under Fig. 100. The mantle, too, would be of silk, or even brocade.

SECTION II.—THE HISTORY OF THE GLOVE

The earliest example of the glove is illustrated in Vol. I., p. 46; and the glove worn during the Frankish period is described on p. 233 of the same volume.

During the Anglo-Saxon period the glove trade was the monopoly of German merchants, and in the twelfth century records show that the work of Parisian glovers was of good repute. In the same century London was another centre of the glove trade, and "London gloves" of all kinds were very highly esteemed, as evidenced by entries in many foreign wardrobe accounts of this time. Exportation of these articles, however, was checked by Acts dated 1378 and 1484.

Glovers are mentioned in a list of craft guilds dated 1422; and in 1464 armorial bearings were granted to their association or "Company." The Glovers' Company was not incorporated, however, until 1638.

Eleventh and Twelfth Centuries

Gloves are mentioned in writings of the reigns of William I., William II. and Henry I. They were very rare and costly, and worn only by the upper classes: they were similar to the bag-shaped glove already described (Vol. I., p. 233), and were called "Moufle."

It was not until the twelfth century that a glove with separate fingers was introduced, as a development of the bag-shape. One of the earliest examples of this kind is seen on the effigy of Henry II. at Fontevraud (Fig. 103). It is stated that although this king had coarse ill-kept hands he never wore gloves, except on State occasions, and for hawking.

Gloves at this time fitted well on the hand, but were not so elaborately cut and seamed as the modern variety. The finger part was cut in two pieces, and seamed at the sides (see Fig. 110). At first the line of the seam joining the thumb to the hand was simple (see Fig. 103), but it became more complicated as time progressed (see Figs. 107, 109, and 110).

Fig. 103.
Twelfth-century Glove

In early examples, gloves were sufficiently loose around the wrist to allow the hand to be thrust in with ease. A small cuff covered the wrist part of the sleeve, its edge being decorated with a band of gold. A similar band of gold covered the seam where the cuff joined the glove.[1] On the back of the

---

[1] Gloves stitched with gold thread.
Chanson de Roland, cxciii. 2677.

hand was a circular ornament or piece of embroidery, often set with a jewel (*see* King John, p. 107). Rings were frequently worn on the finger, outside the glove.

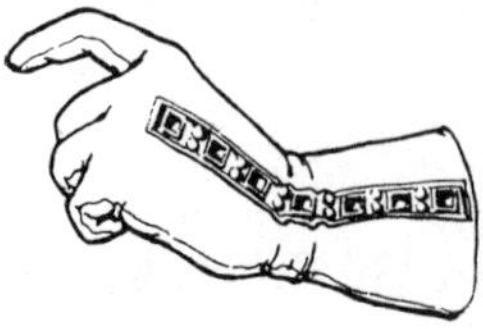

Fig. 104.

Gloves were made of various materials, and many kinds of skins. Those worn by Henry II., Richard I. and King John were white, and in all probability of kid- or calf-skin. Cloth, cotton, a knitted fabric, silk, and (after its introduction late in the thirteenth century), velvet, were the chief materials used. The skins employed were those of the deer, dog, chamois, buck, chicken, sheep, coney, beaver and doe. Gloves made of skin were frequently lined with silk or short-haired fur.

White gloves were very popular, and were considered most elegant for full-dress wear, and from the twelfth century onwards were much worn at weddings.

Fig. 105.
Thirteenth-century
Gloves

At the end of this century, gloves, richly embroidered in gold foliage, set with pearls and other jewels, and retaining the ornamental plaque on the back, were very much in vogue.

Thirteenth Century

At the beginning of the thirteenth century the cuff became deeper, extending over the wrist about four inches, and was sometimes decorated with gold at the edges. The example shown here (Fig. 104) has a band of gold set with jewels along the back, running from the cuff to the knuckles. This shaped glove remained in use throughout the century, but towards its end the cuff lost its circular cut, and became a little more pointed (Fig. 105).

A beautiful pair of gloves worn by Edward I., shown in the painting in the Sedilia at Westminster Abbey, are white, with an embroidered design in black and orange round the cuffs, on the centre of the back, and round the little finger (Fig. 106).

Fig. 106. Glove of Edward I.

Fourteenth Century

The glove shown in Fig. 105 was in common use during this century, except that an ornamental drop, like a button, was attached to the point of the cuff. A fresh variation occurred at this period: the most fashionable gloves were now fastened at the wrists by a button or buttons. In an account dated 1352 there is an item for "48 gold buttons for 2 pairs of dog-gloves covered with kid, with 4 boutons de perles at the bottom." This kind of glove was long, and buttoned up the arm, buttonholes being worked in at one edge, or loops of cord attached, with twelve buttons on each glove (Fig. 107). The cuff was pointed, and finished off with an ornamental drop.

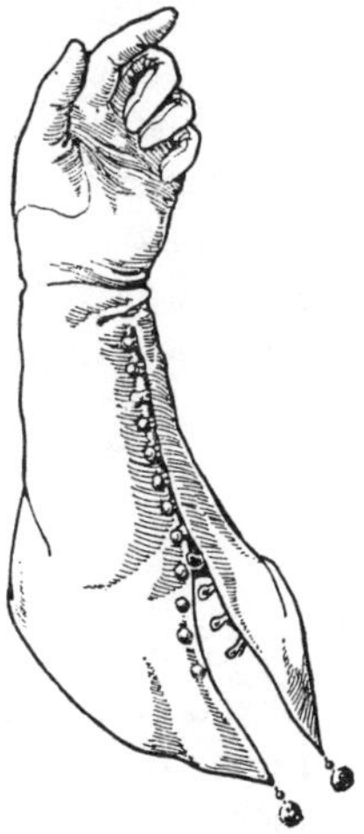

Brown leather riding-gloves with the seams sewn with zig-zag stitches were found in the tomb of Richard II., and are illustrated in Fig. 108. Cuffs became much wider about this time, and developed into what we call the gauntlet, still retaining the pointed edge (Fig. 109).

In the fourteenth century the practice of slashing the glove became the vogue, sometimes in conjunction with the use of embroidery. The "open glove"

Fig. 107.
Fourteenth-century
Glove

(Fig. 109) was a fancy of the Parisian glovers who introduced it. Although from the twelfth century finger-rings were frequently worn

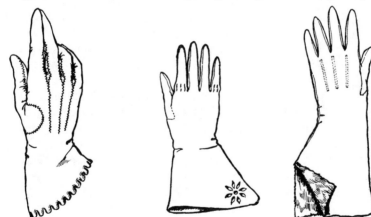

Fig. 108.
Glove of Richard II.

Fig 109.
Fourteenth-century Glove

Fig. 110.
Glove of Henry VI.

outside the glove, it was at this time that slits were cut in the finger of the glove, to exhibit the ring worn on the finger. The cuff also was decorated with these cuts, and at a later date the back of the hand as well.

Fifteenth Century

In the fifteenth century the pendent button when used became very ornate, but it frequently gave place to a tassel. The gloves worn by Henry VI., now in the Public Museum at Liverpool, are simple compared with those already described. They show the finger part cut in four sections, and have a gusset inserted on both sides of the fingers. They are made of brown Spanish leather, lined with deerskin on which the hair had been left in the tanning. The cuff or gauntlet reaches to the elbow, and is open part of the way down the side (Fig. 110). These were strong, useful gloves, used for riding.

Gloves of the Clergy

Gloves as a part of ecclesiastical dress were worn from Anglo-Saxon times. It is said that Charlemagne wore gloves as part of his imperial vestments, and in writings of the tenth century gloves are mentioned as being worn by those performing the liturgy. The clergy, who were tending to become luxurious in their dress, were held in

check at this early date, and the wearing of certain garments, including gloves, was strictly forbidden to any under the rank of bishop. The materials used for ecclesiastical gloves were skin, silk, wool, linen, or a knitted fabric, and they were usually white, as a symbol of purity. Green or purple gloves were worn by bishops on certain occasions, and in the fourteenth century they were worn of the colour of the season.

They were richly ornamented with embroidery in gold and silk, chiefly on the backs, in circles, containing some sacred symbol, a cross or a monogram.

Fig. 111.
Glove of William
of Wykeham

Fig. 111 is a drawing made from the gloves of William of Wykeham (born 1324; Bishop of Winchester 1366; died 1404), now kept at New College, Oxford. These do not differ in shape from the ordinary glove worn by the laity. They are made of crimson purl-knitted silk, and lined with silk of the same colour. The backs are embroidered with a design of a medallion enclosing I.H.S., surrounded by a sun, all in gold. Gold embroidery edges the cuffs, and encircles each finger and thumb.

Hawking Gloves

Gloves of deerskin, with large cuffs, were worn
by the nobility when hawking or hunting, and they
formed an important part of the costume worn by
falconers (Fig. 112). They were strong and thick, as
it was the custom to carry the hawk or falcon on the
wrist. This kind of glove was also much used by the
upper class when riding.

Gloves of inferior yet serviceable quality were
worn by labourers, masons and artisans of all sorts,
and from the twelfth century onwards they were
supplied by the employer.

Fig. 112.
Fourteenth- and
fifteenth-century
Hawking Glove

Mittens ("Moufle")

Mittens (the name is sometimes given to gloves proper), *i.e.* gloves
without fingers, which cover the backs of the hands and wrists, were in
use from very early times, and were worn by all classes as a convenient
method of keeping the hands warm while at work, or by poorer people
in default of the more expensive article. They were made of various
materials, especially leather, and often lined. The quality accorded with
the financial circumstances of the wearer.

Etiquette of the Glove—Customs—Vogues

(From the time of Charlemagne to the end of the fifteenth century)

1. The glove was used as a gage to combat. This custom remained
in use among gentlemen down to the end of the sixteenth century.
2. To strike with the glove was to offer an insult—a defiance to death.
3. To throw the glove at the feet of a person meant a challenge.
4. To give the glove, or the glove and stick, was to entrust with a
mission of confidence, and their possession acted as an authorisation
to represent the giver.
5. From the earliest times it was considered a great insult to address
a high personage, or greet a friend, without first removing the glove.
From the thirteenth century onwards the glove was frequently worn
for that reason on the left hand only; the right glove was then carried
in the left hand, or slung through the waist-belt.
6. To remove the glove or to offer it, signified homage or deference.
This was often presented on bended knee to the object of regard.
7. Part of the toilet of the dead comprised the covering of the hands
with gloves.
8. At a banquet or ceremony the invited guest not infrequently
received gloves from the lord or host.

9. From the eleventh century onwards a present of gloves was a favourite way of recognising indebtedness, or the receipt of a favour.

10. If a lover possessed gloves it was necessary that he should pay special attention to the manner in which they were worn, or *how* they were removed, when paying court to his beloved. There were subtle meanings in the manipulation of the glove, which might have serious consequences.

11. Gloves were not worn by men or women when taking the hands of partners in the dance.

12. At the end of the eleventh century it was regarded as showing a great lack of reverence to enter a church with the hands gloved.

13. The act of picking up the glove of one's lady-love was a sign of deep devotion. Many lovers sought, as sole favour, permission to pick up the lady's glove, and return or retain it.

14. Elegants of the fifteenth century carried both gloves slung in the waist- or pouch-belt.

15. In the same century gloves treated with poison were favourite gifts to one's especial enemy—a practice originating in Italy.

16. "At the Hall door take off your hood and gloves."

Fig. 113. Border

Section III.—Richard I. 1189–1199

Nobility—Men

Fig. 114. Richard I.

Richard, born at Oxford 1157, nicknamed Cœur de Lion. Also King of Cyprus and Jerusalem. Knighted c. 1169. Invested with the Countship of Poitiers and Dukedom of Aquitaine, 1171. Richard was girded with the sword of the Dukedom of Normandy, at Rouen, by Walter, Archbishop of Rouen, 1189.

Richard was at Rouen when in July 1189 his father died. He immediately sent to Winchester, to release his mother from the compulsory retirement which she had been undergoing since 1173, and made her regent of the realm until such time as he himself should arrive in England.

The Third and Fourth Crusades occupied the major part of his reign, and during the king's short visits to this country he was busy raising money for these expeditions. He sold many offices and grants of crown land for very high fees, and even swore that "he would have sold London could he have found a bidder."

Richard spent only eight months of his ten years' reign in England, which accounts for it being an unimportant one in the history of Costume.

Richard was a tall man, six feet two inches in height, shapely rather than massive in build, in fact a well-made man with "a figure like Mars himself." His head was small, his complexion fair, with yellow hair inclined to red flowing about the ears, and he had fierce sparkling blue eyes. He wore a small beard on the upper lip, and a close-trimmed one upon the chin (Fig. 114).

A man of great courage (hence his name, "Cœur de Lion"), he was "a true leader of men, one to whom danger was a luxury, and battle an excitement," and to the end he remained a high-spirited, reckless, over-bearing boy, without sense of responsibility or duty. Poetry and music, rich apparel and show, appealed greatly to his youthful nature.

In 1191, Richard married Berengaria, daughter of Sancho the Wise, King of Navarre. With his usual rashness, Richard exposed himself without armour at the siege of Chalus, and received a mortal wound in the left shoulder from a crossbow bolt. The town fell, but before he died Richard sent for the arbalister, forgave him, and ordered one hundred shillings of English money to be given to him. Hoveden relates that the captain of Richard's mercenaries seized the soldier, without the king's knowledge, and, after Richard's death, first flaying him alive, had him hanged. The body of Richard was buried at the feet of his father in the Abbey Church of Fontevraud.

The effigy of Richard I. at Fontevraud shows him habited in regal garments. He wears a dalmatic of red silk, lined with white, and belted, having a border about one and a half inches in width round the neck, the wide sleeves, and bottom edge. This is worn over an undertunic of green, with close sleeves to the wrist, and slit up the sides. This garment is also bordered with gold. Underneath is a white tunic or alb, bordered with gold. Over the shoulders is a semicircular mantle of sky-blue silk, bordered with a two-inch band of gold embroidery, and fastened in front with a jewelled clasp. His gloves are like those described as worn in Henry II.'s reign, and the red shoes are banded with gold, and have gold spurs attached with black straps. The crown is a circlet set with jewels, and is surmounted by four motifs enclosing a honeycomb design (see Fig. 174, Jewellery).

Some details of the investiture at Richard's coronation are given by two chroniclers.

After administering the oath, "they took off all his cloths from the waist upwards, except his sherte and chausses: after which they shod him in sandals (shoes) embroidered with gold." John Marshal, brother of the Earl of Pembroke, carried the massive spurs of gold. The anointing having been performed, the CAP OF DIGNITY or MAINTEN-ANCE,[1] carried by Godfrey de Lucy, was placed upon his head. He

---

[1] Also entitled "a Chapeau of Estate," an early symbol of high dignity; see Fig. 167.

was then clothed "in his Royal Robes, first a tunic and then a dalmatic
... after this being robed in a mantle ... he himself took the crown from
the altar and gave it to the Archbishop (Baldwin, 1184–1190): on which
the Archbishop delivered it to him, and placed it upon his head, it
being supported by two Earls, in consequence of its extreme weight. . . .
The Royal Sceptre of gold, on top of which was a cross of gold," was
borne by William Marshal, Earl of Pembroke, and William Longespée,
Earl of Salisbury, carried the "rod (*virga*) of gold, having on its top a
dove of gold." These were placed in Richard's right and left hand
respectively. David, Earl of Huntingdon, brother of the King of Scotland, Prince John, Earl of Montaigne and Gloucester, and Robert,
Earl of Leicester, bore the "three golden swords from the King's Treasure,

Fig. 115.   Fig. 116.

The Tunic, *temp.* Richard I.

the scabbards of which were worked all over with gold." A most
distinguished company assembled at Westminster to witness this
coronation, on 3 September, 1189. Queen Eleanor in the full panoply
of royal state, the Princess Alais of France, daughter of Louis VII. by
his third queen, and affianced bride of King Richard (!); the Duke of
Saxony (Henry the Lion), with his son and daughter, the Archbishops
of Canterbury, Rouen, Dublin, and Trèves, "while nearly all the abbats,
priors, earls, and barons of England, Wales and Ireland, were present."

A chronicler of the times who saw King Richard at Cyprus, 1191,
on his wedding day, tells us that he wore a tunic of rose-coloured
samit, and a mantle of silver tissue, striped in straight lines, and nearly
covered with half-moons and shining orbs of solid silver embroidery.
On his head he wore a scarlet cap ("pileum"), embroidered in gold with
figures of animals (probably lions—like his grandfather's, Geoffrey

of Anjou. Fig. 33). He was girded with a sword of fine Damascus steel, with a gold hilt and a scabbard of gold scales (Plate IV.). His Spanish steed was saddled and bridled with gold, set with precious stones, and two golden lions were fixed to the pommel and cantle of the saddle.

A tunic or robe of simple cut, though made of some rich material when worn by a prince or nobleman, is seen in Figs. 115 and 116. The shape is explained in the diagram behind Fig. 115. It was seamed down the sides, the material being folded over the shoulders, and was fastened at the neck by a brooch or clasp, as shown. Alternatively, a short slit or opening was made on one shoulder and fastened with a button (*see* at A). The fullness of this tunic was belted in at the waist, giving some pleasing folds at the side of the figure.

Girdles worn by both men and women were now of considerable length. From one to two inches in width, they were chiefly made of leather in its natural tone, gilded, or coloured, or in silk. Plaques, circular or square, of various designs, in metal, enamelled, or set with jewels, were riveted on to the strap at intervals. The girdle was fastened at the waist by a rich buckle or clasp, with a long end hanging down the front. A pouch or gypiere was often attached to the girdle by looping its cord or strap round the belt, usually on the left side.

Fig. 116 shows the mantle draped over the left shoulder, and the wearer is about to fasten it in front with a clasp.

Nobility—Women

Berengaria, although Queen of England, never came to this country. Had she done so her influence might have been responsible for the introduction of some new fashions. As queen mother, Eleanor held first place among women of the kingdom, a position she retained almost to the end. After the death of her husband in 1199, Queen Berengaria retired to Le Mans, in Normandy, and there superintended the building of the Abbey of Espan, which she founded. This was completed in the year 1230, and at this time she finally abandoned the world, and died some years later, during the reign of Henry III., at an advanced age. Her effigy at Espan, executed about the year 1230, shows the queen wearing the fashionable dress of the first half of the thirteenth century. This is described on p. 156.

Fig. 117.
The Peliçon

The only women's garment to be noticed in this reign is an over-robe called the PELICE or PELIÇON. It was practically a supertunic of silk or cloth, and generally lined with fur—hence its name pelice —*pelice* being the Norman French for fur. It fell in folds to just below the knee; it was not confined at the waist, but a belt, when worn, was fastened round the hips, with a pouch attached.

Fig. 117 shows a pelice worn by a noble lady of this period. It is worn over the ordinary gown, the sleeves of which are seen under the wider ones of the pelice. To this is added a mantle of moderate dimensions, fastened across the shoulders. On the head is the couvrechef or veil, of a fine material, sometimes embroidered and edged with gold, and worn over the WIMPLE.

> Holding up thy train, thine ermine-lined peliçon and camise of fine white linen,
> So that thine ankle may be seen.
>
> *Conte d'Aucassin et Nicolette.*

Fig. 118 illustrates the above lines, written during the second half of the twelfth century. This damsel wears a peliçon of silk, lined throughout with ermine. It is open up the sides, and girded low on the hips. Under the peliçon is worn a gown with tight sleeves, and beneath that the camise, seen at the neck and

Fig. 118. Nicolette

ankle. On the legs are chausses of cloth, and shoes of the fashionable cut. The headdress is a chaplet of fresh roses, and the hair is left flowing.

Section IV.—The History of the Cross

The influence of Christianity on costume, and of the Cross as a Christian symbol on decoration, has been very profound, and for this reason it has been thought that the following record deserves its place in a volume of this character.

The True Cross and Others

In the early part of the year 1187, to the consternation of Christendom, Saladin (or Yusuf) of Egypt took Jerusalem, after an eight days' siege. The Latin king, Guy, or Guido, of Lusignan, was taken prisoner, and the True Cross, or a "convincing imitation of it," fell into the hands of the infidel.

Part of "the Wood of the Cross of Our Lord" had been encased in gold, set with pearls and precious stones, and enshrined in a silver reliquary, by the Empress Helena, mother of Constantine the Great, who is said to have discovered it, among other relics of Our Lord, in 328, buried on or near Golgotha. Its subsequent history is worth recording. On its discovery by S. Helena, the True Cross was divided. The portion described above was enshrined in a chapel especially built for its reception at Jerusalem. The other portion, with the nails, the empress took back to her son. This he is said to have enclosed in an equestrian statue of himself, one nail being fastened to the helmet and another to the horse's bridle. This statue was set upon a porphyry column in the forum at Constantinople. On the other hand, the Church of S. Croce is supposed to have been built by Constantine to receive part of the True Cross. A third nail was given by Pope Gregory the Great to the Catholic Queen Theodolinda, 590, who had it forged into a narrow circlet. This was afterwards enclosed in gold and set with jewels, and is known as the Iron Crown of Lombardy. It was used to crown Charlemagne, then passed into the Austrian Imperial family, and since 1866 has been in the possession of the King of Italy. (It is preserved at Monza.)

As early as the sixth century the "Wood of the True Cross" was carefully wrapped in silk; for Gregory of Tours, the Frankish historian, records that he bought a piece of this silk because he was assured it had been used for that purpose. He cut it up and distributed the pieces in the belief that they would perform miracles. The portion of the True Cross preserved at Jerusalem fell into the hands of Chosroes II., King of Persia and conqueror of Phocas, when he took and sacked the Holy City in 614; but it was returned to the Emperor Heraclius II., who restored it to Jerusalem in 629.

In 647 Jerusalem was captured by the Mahommedans, and the True Cross was removed, but it was eventually returned to its original repository and remained there until Saladin carried it off to Baghdad in 1187. Here it was buried, by order of the caliph, under the threshold of the city gate to be trodden underfoot by the multitude. One author (Bohadin, an Arab, born 1143) asserts that it was shown in Saladin's camp at Acre, and afterwards sent to Damascus. Later it was presented to Isaac II., Emperor of Constantinople (1185–1195).

The next record of the True Cross is of its existence at Damietta, again in the hands of the Saracens. The sultan restored it to John de Brienne, titular King of Jerusalem and Emperor of Constantinople (1228–1237), in 1221. In order to raise money for war upon Byzantium, John's two sons sold it to the Venetians for twenty thousand pounds. However, Baldwin II. (born 1217, died 1274) later got possession of the True Cross and pawned it to a Jew for a still larger sum of money. Baldwin sold it in 1241 to Louis IX. of France, who enshrined it with other relics of Our Lord, including the Crown of Thorns,[1] in the beautiful Church of S. Chapelle, built for that purpose, and completed

[1] See History of the Crown of Thorns, p. 102.

in 1248. There they remained to escape the ravages of the Revolution of 1789. Parts of the True Cross are still preserved in Paris.

Sceptical persons are of the opinion that, if all the fragments of the True Cross were brought together, their bulk would be comparable to that of a battleship. It has been scientifically proved, however, that the known existing pieces amount to only one-third of the original size of the True Cross.

From early times the Cross was the symbol of life, and in many countries it was used, with grim irony, for executional purposes.

The Cross Tau, or "Crux Commissa," was shaped like the letter T, and used for crucifixion of felons, etc. (A similar cross, with a handle or loop at the top, "Crux Ansata-Ankh," is found in Assyrian, Egyptian,

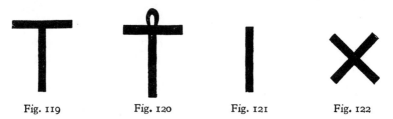

Fig. 119   Fig. 120   Fig. 121   Fig. 122

Persian and Indian monuments and signifies Life. It was used later by Coptic peoples as an emblem of Christianity.) "Crux Simplex" was an upright stake on which the crucified was fastened by the hands crossed above his head. "Crux Decussata" resembles the Roman numeral. Also called "S. Andrew's Cross," and in Heraldry, "Saltaire." "Crux Capitata" or "Crux Immissa," or Latin Cross, has a long upright, and a smaller cross-beam, the three upper members being of equal length. This is the "Cross of Our Lord." The upper member was designed to support the superscription, and this cross was used only for the crucifixion of important criminals. This cross was not used in decoration until the fifth century on account of its painful associations (Figs. 119–123).

Fig. 123

Symbolic Crosses

The Greek Cross had all its arms of equal length, and was used by Crusaders as a badge. A cross of eight points was used in a similar manner. The Patriarchal Cross is formed by an upright shaft crossed by two horizontal bars, of which the upper is the shorter. This type is often seen in illuminated manuscripts used instead of the "Crux Capitata" (Figs. 124–126).

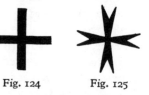

Fig. 124   Fig. 125

The Patriarchal Cross was associated with many holy people. The picture (Plate VIII.B) reproduces a contemporary drawing by Matthew

Paris and shows Louis IX., sick in bed, in 1244. "And as soon as he was in case to speak, he asked that they should give him the Cross, and they did so." The queen mother, Blanche of Castile, a devoted adherent of the Church, is seen touching him with the Patriarchal Cross. The Bishop of Paris is at the foot of the bed and an attendant kneels at the head.

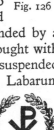

Fig. 126

The cross adopted by Constantine the Great after his conversion to Christianity (312) consisted of the sacred monogram XP, the first two letters of the name Christ. When this was used as a standard, the base of the cross was surrounded by a crown. A vexillum, or banner of purple silk, inwrought with the images of the emperor and his children, was suspended from a cross-bar. This was known as the Labarum (Fig. 127) and used during the period 323–493.

Fig. 127. Labarum

A standard similar to this has been described by Eusebius of Errisa (died 360). "It was a long spear, gilt and provided with a transverse bar like a cross. Above, at the top of this same spear, was fixed a wreath of gold and precious stones. In the centre of the wreath was the sign of the saving Name—that is to say, a monogram setting forth this Holy Name by its first two letters combined, the P in the middle of the X." (Fig. 128.)

Fig. 128. Standard, 4th century

The custom of making the sign of the Cross on the forehead dates from the latter half of the second century. Tertullian (160–230) says: "At every action which we begin, in coming in and going out, when we clothe ourselves, or put on our shoes, when we bathe, when we seat ourselves at table, at lamplighting, on going to bed, we trace on the forehead the Sign of the Cross."

Fig. 129. Agnus Dei

The earliest representation in Art[1] of the Crucifixion is to be found in a panel of an ivory box of the early fifth century, now in the British Museum. The figure of Christ is clothed only in a loin cloth. The earliest crucifixes, which date from the fifth century, show the Lamb on, or holding, the "Crux Capitata"—the "Agnus Dei"; and the earliest crucifix showing Our Lord as the suffering Saviour, clad in the colobium, dates from the end of the same century.

Fig. 130. Crucifix, 13th century

Fig. 131. Altar Cross, 13th century

From the ninth century onwards the loin cloth takes the place of

---

[1] The earliest reference in Literature to a picture of the Crucifixion is in the middle of the sixth century.

the colobium, and up to the twelfth century crucifixes represent Christ alive, with the eyes open. Fig. 129 shows an "Agnus Dei" of the early fifth century. Fig. 130 is a simple crucifix of the thirteenth century. An altar cross of the same period is shown in Fig. 131; it is of very elaborate goldsmith's work, set with jewels.

The Colour and Shape of Crusading Crosses

The thousands congregated in the market-place at Clermont in November 1095 who heard the eloquent exhortation of Pope Urban II. (1088–1099) to undertake the First Crusade were so roused by his vehemence that they shouted with one voice: "God wills it, God wills it!" "It is indeed the will of God," the Pope replied: "His Cross is the symbol of your salvation; wear it, *a red, a bloody Cross,* as an external mark on your breasts and shoulders, as a pledge of your sacred and irrevocable engagement."

In shape, the cross was the "Greek Cross." The fully harnessed knights and warriors of the First Crusade had this cross painted in red upon the side of their helmets (Fig. 132).

Fig. 132

S. Bernard supplied many of the crosses for the Second Crusade (*see* p. 85). As he belonged to the Cistercian Order, which he had just reconstituted (*see* Vol. I., p. 171), his robes were *white.*

When Prince Richard took the Cross in 1187 with Philippe Auguste, King of France, and Philip, Earl of Flanders, "the King of France and his people wore *red* crosses; the King of England with his people *white* crosses; while Philip, Earl of Flanders, with his people wore *green* crosses."

History of the Crown of Thorns

The *Crown of Thorns* is mentioned in the year 409 as being kept in the Basilica on Mount Sion. It shared the vicissitudes of the other relics of Our Lord, but was seen there by chroniclers of later times. In the interval, many thorns had been removed. A great number were presented to earlier Byzantine emperors; one passed from Charlemagne to King Æthelstan as a gift. Several others can be traced without difficulty. The remainder of the original Crown of Thorns was transferred from Jerusalem to Constantinople in 1063. There it remained until the seventh siege and sack of Constantinople in 1204, when it fell into the hands of the Venetians. It was returned to Constantinople and became one of the possessions of the Latin Emperor Baldwin II., who was invested with the title in 1237. The former greatness of the Byzantine Empire had departed, and Baldwin's election was little more than an empty honour, for the much curtailed State was practically bankrupt, and he was forced to spend most of his reign in regal mendicancy. The twenty-five years between his accession and deposition were exhausted in seeking hospitality, always accepted with alacrity, from various European princes. He was forced to add to his funds by the sale of the Holy relics before his deposition by Michael VIII. Palæologus in 1261. (Baldwin's successor was the founder of the Palæologi Dynasty, which lasted until the fall of the Byzantine Empire in 1453 (*see* Vol. I., p. 139).)

The Crown of Thorns and other relics were sold to Louis IX. of France, who deposited them at S. Chapelle. When it was purchased by him, the Crown still had sixty or seventy thorns left upon it, but these were distributed by the saintly king until the remnant consisted only of a circlet of stalks.

The Crown was hidden, as no doubt the other relics were, during the Revolution of 1789, but it was restored to Notre Dame in 1806. In 1896 a new and magnificent reliquary was designed to enshrine the Crown of Thorns.

THE CANDLE

(Latin, *Candela*)

The candle was in use in Egypt, Italy and Greece from very early times. It was a cylinder composed of a fatty substance, wax or tallow, enclosing a wick made of the pith of a rush called "scirpus." The candle or taper was known before the invention of lamps. As a sign of deference and respect to the high officers of Pagan Rome, candles or tapers were carried by the populace on any auspicious occasion. Candles and tapers were carried at baptisms, and of necessity in the darkness of the night at funerals, both Pagan and Christian.

Since they were of pagan origin, candles were *not* used in Christian worship until after the middle of the third century. Candles in candlesticks were then placed on the pavement around the altar to give light. Constantine the Great transformed night into day with "pillars of wax," and Paulinus of Nola (fifth century) mentions the "altar with crowded lights" surrounding it. In the fifth century candles were lit for the reading of the gospels, "even though the sun may shine, as a visible sign of joy and gladness."

During the sixth century it became the custom for devotees to place candles before the shrine of some holy person.

In the seventh century it was usual for acolytes (Greek, *akolouthos* = an attendant—a name first used in the third century to denote an inferior order of attendants of the Church, who ranked immediately below the sub-deacon) to carry lamps or candles in candlesticks during Church ceremonial. These were used in close proximity to the altar, sometimes standing on the pavement beside it, or occasionally upon it. Candles in candlesticks did not become permanent altar furniture until the eleventh century. At this time no less than two were lit for every liturgical service. For Mass there were six, and for Pontifical Mass seven.

Candles used for church purposes were always made of beeswax, bleached for ordinary occasions, but in the natural shade of yellow for Good Friday, Holy Week, and funerals. The beeswax candle symbolised the pure flesh of Our Lord, the wick His Soul, and the flame His Divinity.

Wax candles were expensive, and only used by the wealthy, and then sparingly, for the lighting of rooms. In the ordinary household their place was taken by candles of tallow or by lamps. Torches, either held in the hand or placed in holders or brackets on the wall, were used to light the interiors of castles and halls, from Anglo-Saxon times onwards.

During the fifteenth century, when wax became a less expensive commodity, candles made of this substance were more frequently used.

Candlesticks[1] (Latin, *candelabrum*) were short, intended to be carried in the hand—anything from six to thirty-six inches, and were made of gold, silver, bronze, brass and iron. Others, to stand upon the table or ground, were of various heights. Candelabra of this type were frequently used as stands for lamps, in which case, of course, they were without the usual spike or prick on which normally the candle was pushed down. About 1280 the term "prikett" denoted the candle formed with a corresponding cavity at one end, and *not* the candlestick. It was not until about the end of the fourteenth century that a socket to receive the candle became general.[2]

[1] As early as the middle of the third century, golden candelabra stood in some of the most important churches of Rome.
The Basilica of S. Peter at Rome was erected in the reign of Constantine the Great (323–337) on the spot where tradition affirmed S. Peter had suffered martyrdom. This remained until Pope Nicholas V. (1447–1455) demolished the old church and commenced the new one. It was consecrated 18 November, 1626, having taken 176 years to build.

[2] In 1913 a candlestick was unearthed near Cambridge and is said to be of Roman workmanship. It has a socket!

| Fig. 133. | Fig. 134. | Fig. 135. | Fig. 136. | Fig. 137. |
| Greek, Early | XIIth Century | XIIIth Century | | XIVth Century |

CANDLESTICKS

Nobility—Men

John, born at Oxford, 1166. Prince John was "dubbed" a knight by his father at Windsor in 1185. The ceremony of girding the new duke with the sword of the Dukedom of Normandy was performed at Rouen, by Walter, Archbishop of Rouen, in 1199. "On which occasion the Archbishop placed on the head of the Duke a circlet of gold, having on the top thereof, around the border, rosettes worked in gold."

John was in Normandy at the time of his brother Richard's death, and thereupon seized the Angevin treasury at Chinon, sending two officials over to England to secure his recognition as king. Shortly afterwards John followed, and was first crowned at Westminster in 1199. A second coronation took place at Westminster in 1200, and the third at Canterbury the following year.

The rightful heir to the throne was Arthur, son of Geoffrey, Henry II.'s third son, who at this time was aged thirteen; but his claims were disregarded. His mother, Constance (born 1162, died 1201), placed him in the safe keeping of Philippe Auguste, King of France, by whom he was knighted and invested with his patrimony, the Duchy of Brittany and Countships of Anjou, Maine, Touraine and Poitou.

In 1202, Queen Eleanor, now in her eighty-fourth year, had garrisoned herself in the Castle of Mirabeau (Vienne), in support of John's cause in France; and Philippe, accompanied by Arthur, attacked her there, but John came to her rescue. Arthur became John's prisoner, and was placed under the wardship of Hubert de Burgh, at the Castle of Falaise. John was advised to mutilate his nephew to render him incapable of ruling, and officers were sent to Falaise for that purpose, but Hubert refused to execute the orders. Prince Arthur was then removed to Rouen, to be under his Uncle John's personal "guardianship"; and from that time the boy vanished, and was never heard of again.

The most credible account of Arthur's murder is given by Le Breton, the king's chaplain, who tells how John, returning by water to Rouen, reached the castle steps by night at high tide, and that Arthur was then brought down to the boat from his cell, stabbed, and his body thrown into the Seine, on 3 April, 1203. The victim was aged seventeen.

The suspected murder of Prince Arthur aroused horror and disgust in the minds of the people, who, by this time, were becoming too humane to tolerate such barbarism.

Queen Eleanor suffered some anxiety as to her grandson's danger, and is said to have interceded very strenuously on his behalf. She was spared, however, the knowledge of his fate, and of John's ignominious loss of her inheritance, departing this life at Poitiers on 1 April, 1204. She was buried at Fontevraud. It is reassuring to learn, in the words of a lady historian, that "Eleanor of Aquitaine is among the very few women who had atoned for an ill-spent youth by a wise and benevolent old age. As a Sovereign, she ranks among the greatest of female rulers."

King John's loss of the English possessions in France, in 1204, was not altogether without advantage, according to an historian who writes: "Henceforth the King was mainly, if not solely, King of England, and the welfare of England the main, if not the sole, subject of the English Councils."

With regard to the period of interdiction the chroniclers remain judiciously silent.

Of middle height (5 ft. 6 ins.), King John was a strongly-built, thick-set man. In youth he had a degree of good looks, but the width of the cheek-bones, a family feature of the Norman and early Plantagenet kings, prevented him from being really handsome. In later life he was corpulent and bald, his features hard, and expression soured. His curled hair was of a reddish colour, like that of other members of his family, but, unlike his father and brother, he wore it long and flowing, with a small beard on the upper lip and chin.

At the time of his accession, his appearance is described as follows: "The King of England is about 50 years of age; his hair is quite hoary, his figure is made for strength, compact but not tall."

"Of all kings he was the most vicious, the most profane, the most tyrannical, the most false, the most short-sighted, the most unscrupulous," is the character given to him by an historian. He had all the vices, most of the talents, and none of the virtues of his family. He led a foul and shameless life, was hatefully cruel, torturing his prisoners, even women and children: he was well read, a good soldier, and a cunning statesman.

John married, in 1189, Avisa or Isabelle, daughter and heiress of William, Earl of Gloucester; her grandfather, Robert, Earl of Gloucester, having been a natural son of Henry I. She was never crowned nor acknowledged Queen of England, and within a year of his accession John divorced her on the grounds of consanguinity. Shortly afterwards, King John married Isabella, daughter of the Count of Angoulême. This lady was already betrothed to a young French noble, Hugh de Lusignan, Count de la Marche; but the unscrupulous John carried her off, and their nuptials were celebrated at Bordeaux, 24 August, 1200, by the Archbishop of Bordeaux, who solemnly declared that no impediment to the marriage existed!

King John fell ill at Swineshead Abbey, and a week later, on

19 October, 1216, died at Newark. His soul he bequeathed to God, and his body to St. Wulfstan, in whose minster (Worcester Cathedral) he was buried.

King John was considered by his contemporaries to be the most extravagant prince in the world, both as regards his costume and personal expenses; but where his family was concerned he was parsimonious to a degree. A note, however, by Roger of Wendover, dated 1214, mentions that "King John at Christmas held his Court at Windsor, when he distributed *festive dresses* to a number of his nobles." Stingy John was charitably disposed on occasion!

Fig. 138. King John

He was very fond of new clothes, and these were costly and showy in the extreme. No new ideas were expressed in his attire, and the styles worn by his father and brother were refurbished with abundant decoration. The regal costume seen on his effigy in Worcester Cathedral (the earliest monument of an English king in England) is simple, and exhibits no marked difference from that of Henry II., except that the folds of the slightly shorter tunic are smaller and more numerous—clearly resulting from the use of very soft silk. The tunic is of crimson silk, edged with gold, having a collar, about three inches in width, of gold set with jewels; a band of the same edges the sleeves. A jewelled belt surrounds the waist and falls to the knee. The undertunic and mantle are of cloth of gold, the latter being lined with green. Close-fitting red hose clothe the legs, and golden spurs are fastened by light-blue straps over black shoes. On his hands are white gloves, and a ring is worn on the second finger of the right hand, *outside* the glove. The crown is a band set with precious stones and surmounted by four trefoils (*see* Fig. 175).

Fig. 139. Diagram of the Cloke

When King John's tomb was opened in 1797, the body was found dressed in the robes just described, except that the head was wrapped in a monk's cowl.

King John appeared at a mid-winter feast (Fig. 138) attired in a tunic of white damask, with a gold girdle studded with sapphires, garnets,

Fig. 140.
Noble, *temp.* John

emeralds and diamonds. His mantle was of red samit, embroidered with gold, pearls and sapphires, and the backs of his white gloves were decorated by a large ruby on one and a large sapphire on the other.

The king's mania for rich and extravagant clothing, and for splendid and enormously costly jewels, explains in part the constant raids upon the purses of his people—Church and laity alike being plundered to satisfy his insatiable demands. "The said John never ate flesh, nor did he drink wine or cider or anything with which he might become intoxicated; but for gold and silver he had a considerable thirst."

Following the king's lead, the nobility and upper classes indulged throughout his reign in an ostentatious display of dress and jewellery.

At the end of the twelfth century, another change took place in the shape of mantles worn by French nobles, and adopted also by the English nobility, extra pieces being added to the sides of the original semicircular mantle, as seen in Fig. 139.

The manner of wearing this new-shaped mantle differed from that previously necessary. Instead of the sides hanging in equal lengths, it was now the vogue to draw one side of the edge well over the left shoulder, down over the chest, and tuck a portion of it into the waistbelt, as seen in Fig. 140.

At the same time the prevailing mode was to have these mantles made of very rich stuffs, of Byzantine or Sicilian manufacture, in brocades of bold design, of conventional animals and birds in circles (Fig. 141). Cloth of gold was also very much used, and this was often appliquéd with similar patterns.

Fig. 140 represents a

XIIth & XIIIth Cent.

Fig. 141. Brocade

nobleman—a baron—of the reign of King John or Philippe Auguste, wearing this fashionable mantle for full dress, over the tunic with wide sleeves, cut low in the neck and revealing the sherte. A deep border of embroidery surrounds the bottom edge, and the sleeves just above the elbow. It should be noticed that the tunic is draped on the right side, a portion of it being passed through the waist-belt, thus showing the rich undertunic.

A young nobleman of this reign in ordinary attire is seen in Fig. 142. There is no doubt that he is fashionably dressed, although he is wearing crossgartering, a new mode revived from old styles. The only difference from the earlier fashion is that instead of the legs being bound with leather, as previously, they are now crossed with bands of gold, over tight-fitting hose of a brilliant colour. The long over-robe, embroidered with a conventional design, is slit up the front to display this leg decoration and dagged at the bottom edge. It is girded with a belt carrying a sword. On the shoulders the fashionable hood is worn, fastened at the throat with a jewelled clasp. The head part is thrown back (*see* p. 117, Hood). The headgear is unique. It is a pointed bag-cap, so arranged

Fig. 142.
Noble, *temp.* John

that it forms a turned-up brim, and the point stands up on top of the head. The whole thing has the effect of a turban.

The gloves, of the new cut, are now an indispensable item of fashionable attire.

Nobility—Women

Isabella of Angoulême was scarcely fifteen years of age when she became Queen-Consort of England. Less than half the age of her tyrannical husband, she exercised over him but little influence for good. No small amount of blame was attributed to her for his voluptuous mode of life, and the people even went so far as to suggest that she practised sorcery and witchcraft.

The following is taken from a narrative of the time, and gives a fair idea of the estimation, perhaps prejudiced, in which Isabella was held:

"His Queen hates him, and is hated by him, an incestuous, evil-disposed, adulterous woman, and of these crimes she had been often found guilty, on which the King entrapped her suspected paramours, strangled them with a rope, and had their bodies hung over her bed."

CHILDREN OF JOHN AND ISABELLA

1. Henry, who succeeded his father.
2. Richard (born 1209, died 1272) Earl of Cornwall and King of the Romans; married, first, Isabella, daughter and heiress of the Earl of Pembroke; one son, Henry, born 1235, d.s.p. Secondly, Sanchia, co-heiress of the Count of Provence; two sons, Edmund, Earl of Cornwall, d.s.p., and Richard, d.s.p. 1296. Thirdly, Beatrice, niece of the Elector of Cologne.
3. Johanna, married Alexander II. of Scotland.
4. Isabella, married Frederick II., Emperor of Germany.
5. Eleanor, married, first, the Earl of Pembroke; secondly, Simon de Montfort, Earl of Leicester; their only child, Eleanor, married Llewellyn, Prince of Wales.

Although King John spent vast sums on his own clothes, he exercised rigid economy over the wardrobe of his queen. At the time of her coronation there were orders for "Three clokes for the Queen, of fine linen, one of scarlet cloth, and a grey pelice, costing £12 5s. 4d.; a green robe lined with cendal, 60s.; five ells of cloth, for making two robes for the Queen, one of them to be green and the other brunet. Four white and good gwimples for the use of the Queen, 8 Nov. 1200." There is also an order from King John for four pairs of women's boots, one of them to be embroidered in circles; but apart from these items no other mention is made of the queen's attire. Further details of Isabella and her wardrobe are given in Chapter III., p. 157.

Fashions in women's dress for this reign remained the same as described under date 1170, p. 86.

SECTION VI.—THE MIDDLE AND LOWER CLASSES, 1154–1216

During the course of the last period (1066–1154) the English and Normans had intermarried considerably, and by the middle of the twelfth century it had become impossible to distinguish between the two races.

The people in general were more prosperous, despite the heavy taxes levied on them by Richard I. and King John, and after the accession of Henry III. they became almost affluent.

The Crusades had some sociological effects. Many noble owners sold or leased their castles, manors or lands, to raise funds for participation in these thrilling but expensive undertakings, and thus arose for the first time a new class of owner or tenant. Wealthy merchants or prosperous farmers who had acquired in this way estates and dwellings very different from those to which they had been accustomed, attained a social importance hitherto unknown to them. The era of the "Merchant Princes" was dawning, and this change began to be reflected in Costume. The transition was even more strongly marked in Italy than in England.

Many noble estates were purchased at this time by the clergy, whose financial acumen thus increased materially the wealth they had been accumulating for the past century. This transfer of property from military to ecclesiastical ownership very much improved the status of the lower orders, who were dependent upon their landlords.

Temp. Henry II., Richard I. and John, 1154–1216

Men. A man of good position—a noble-man in ordinary day dress, a knight or rich merchant—is seen in Plate V., a coloured draw-ing copied from the original MS. by Master Hugo, an excellent artist and illuminator, who resided in the Abbey of S. Eadmundsbury (1125–1150). The subjects of his illustrations are representative equally of the middle and end of the twelfth century.

Fig. 143. Yeoman

The cut of the blue tunic or cotte, edged with gold and lined with white, is plainly seen, and although hitched up in front it is most certainly longer behind, in accordance with the prevailing mode (*see* p. 31 under Fig. 20). This also applies to the green undertunic. The scarlet mantle is rectangular, and fastened with a gold brooch. The hose are purple, and the boots blue with gold turned-down tops or folding caps. The arrangement of the hair is very curious, though characteristic.

A man of the *yeoman class* is seen in Fig. 143, which shows the type of dress adopted generally by the well-to-do community.

The tunic, worn by a young man, is short (older men preferred a longer one), and not slit up the sides, although tunics were sometimes treated in this manner. The sleeves are close, and if an overtunic were worn its sleeves would be moderately wide. The sherte, which might be seen at the neck were the hood removed, was buttoned, and in the case of men of some importance would be decorated with needlework. Leather pouches,

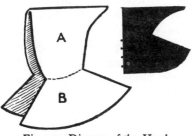

Fig. 144. Diagram of the Hood

hung from leather waist-belts fastened by metal buckles or clasps, were becoming very common, and knives (in sheaths or without) were frequently carried by passing them through the flap of the pouch.

The hood worn by this young man is no longer the funnel-shape

Fig. 145.
Man of the People

Fig. 146. Troubadour, twelfth
century

(see Fig. 51), but of the newer design (see Fig. 144), with its edge, fancifully cut, fastened at the throat with a clasp. In this example the hood is surmounted by a hat; or a cap might be worn, but it was

Fig. 147. Cotte

quite usual to let the hood fall on the shoulders and to wear the hat in the ordinary way. Loose braies were gradually going out of fashion with the middle class, and in their place braies made to fit closer to the leg were adopted. They were made of cloth of all kinds, and sometimes of soft leather, seamed up the sides, with or without the foot part. When not made of an elastic material they were open at the side of the ankle and knee, to allow them to be drawn on to the leg. These openings were laced or tied, and the braies were fastened round the waist by a cord or belt.

Fig. 145 shows a tunic or cotte delineated in the characteristic style of illuminators of the second half of the twelfth century. It also shows very clearly the manner of wearing it, and the folds into which the tunic fell. In the original MS. the tunic is a grey-mauve, with a red border outlined with white. The hose are grey and the boots black.

Although Raoul Glaber tells us the early troubadours were "odd in their ways as in their dress,"
representations of them seen in illuminated MSS.
prove that their attire was simple.

A troubadour (*see* p. 126) of the second half of the
twelfth century is seen in Fig. 146. In no way does the
costume differ from that worn by ordinary people of
the time. The cotte, hitched up as usual, has sleeves
which are shaped in a curious manner. The hood could
be thrown back if necessary, and a cloke might be
added. The colouring of this costume naturally would
be cheerful. The tunic border would be of bands of
various colours. The vielle, played by a bow, is
of a pleasant shape, and comes from a psalter
dated 1170.

Fig. 148.
From an Ill. MS.

Fig. 147 is copied closely from an illuminated MS.
of the end of the twelfth century. The drawing shows
the shape and hang of the cotte worn by many men
of middle class during the second half of the twelfth century. It is by
no means a fashionable garment, such as would be worn by the
nobility, for the skirt part is cut very much on the circle, and the
sleeves are not close-fitting.

Fig. 149. Peasant

Fig. 148 is reproduced from a bestiary of
the late twelfth century, now in the Bodleian
Library, Oxford. It represents a man of the
people. He wears a cotte, and over it a garment
of dark fustian, cut on the lines of the colobium
(see Vol. I., Diagram 13): it has large armholes,
and is confined at the waist by a cord. The legs
are clothed in braies, with foot part attached.

The peasant man or serf in the act of sowing
(Fig. 149) is so simply dressed that details need
no description. The cotte would be made of
very coarse material, the hose either of a knitted
fabric (made by his wife) or rough cloth, and
the boots of leather.

Fig. 150 represents a young gentleman of
the time of King John—a knight in civil dress, a
noble in everyday attire, or an opulent yeoman
—with his wife (?). In general lines the costume
is similar to that of Fig. 143, but the tunic is
ornamented round the neck, wrists and hem with two bands of
different colours, a very usual decoration. The cloke, cut as shown in

Fig. 150.   Fig. 151.
Gentlefolk, *temp.* John

Fig. 28, has an embroidered border. It is made of very good cloth, and lined with a thinner material of contrasting colour. He wears the fashionable hood, and his hose are well-fitting.

Temp. Henry II., Richard I. and John, 1154–1216

Women. Figs. 152 and 153 represent two women of middle class. Their gowns present no variations from the garments of the previous period. The manner in which they cling to the figure is very characteristic of this period. It must not be regarded entirely as a mannerism of the artists who illuminated the MSS. of the time, for it represents fairly closely the mode of wearing these garments.

The sleeves of Fig. 152 hang from just below the elbow, and are edged with a wide border showing the decorated close sleeve of the underdress. There is a similar, but narrower band outlining the neck. The particular way in which the oblong veil is draped over the head, under the chin and tied on the right or left side, is peculiar to this period.

The woman shown in Fig. 153 wears the same type of gown, but made of a material figured *à pois.* The sleeves are cut in the "boat" shape already familiar, and date from the first half of this century. They are edged with some narrow embroidery. The tails of her hair are encased in tubes of material bound with braid.

Figs. 154 and 155 show two gossips of the lower orders, enlivening their toil at the loom with some spicy item of scandal, or embroidery of some astonishing tale heard at the alehouse last night.

In the days when oral tradition constituted the major part of

Fig. 152.   Fig. 153.
Middle-Class Women

"History," conversations of this kind may have been the origin of legends accepted without question by later generations; and it would be interesting to know whether the inventive genius of the lady on the left may not be responsible for solemn statements in our history books to-day.

The clothes of these chatty folk are those with which we have been familiar since Anglo-Saxon times. The gown of Fig. 154 has close sleeves and the "head rail" is an oblong piece of linen with the right-hand side thrown over the left shoulder.

Fig. 55, the lady of more generous proportions, gesticulating with the scissors, wears an ample gown with wide sleeves. She has a cloke of cloth, and a head-covering of linen adjusted in a different manner—the edge is

Fig. 154.

Women weaving

Fig. 155.

bound round the brow and fastened at the back of the head, and the remainder falls at either side, one portion being thrown over the opposite shoulder.

The loom is a simple one, and can be erected quickly (under its permanent shed) whenever the weather is good enough to permit of work out of doors.

The lady friend (Fig. 151) of the young gentleman shown on p. 114 wears a gown somewhat similar to Fig. 100, although her sleeves resemble those of Fig. 153. Over it is worn a mantle with an embroidered border. The oblong veil, the right side of which is drawn round the throat, is surmounted by a felt hat of some bright colour, having an upstanding brim. This hat had quite a vogue about the end of the twelfth century. It must not be confounded with the white coif worn by noble ladies at a later date.

XIIth

Fig. 156

Section VII.—Hairdressing

Temp. Henry II., Richard I. and John, 1154–1216

Men. Long hair falling on to the shoulders was fashionable among the English nobility when Henry II. came to the throne. On his arrival in England the young king was wearing his hair reasonably close to the head, curling naturally, and this was the style adopted by all fashionable men during his reign.

Fig. 157. Hairdressing, *temp.* Henry II.

In middle and later life Henry kept his hair cut closer to the head, but this example was not followed by young men, who continued to wear the hair moderately short, about level with the ears, and waved or curled (Fig. 157).

The fringe on the forehead, first noticed under Fig. 65, and its later development, the lock of hair trained to lie upon the centre parting (*see* Figs. 25 and 70), was still a popular fashion of hairdressing. Fig. 98 shows a young noble wearing this lock.

During the reign of Richard I. the hair was worn a little longer, reaching to about the level of the chin. Beards on the upper lip and chin were not exceptional. Both Henry and Richard wore them. The former did so when he reached middle age, and the latter grew a beard, which he kept closely cropped, on his chin and upper lip, soon after he reached the age of twenty.

In the reign of King John it was again the vogue to wear the hair hanging on the shoulders. Fig. 140 shows it so worn. In his effigy King John is represented as wearing his hair waved and cut off square at mouth-level. On the forehead there is a row of small curls showing beneath the rim of the crown (*see* Fig. 138).

Figs. 115 and 116 give examples of the hairdressing of the nobility, fashionable at the end of the twelfth century. Fig. 145 shows the hairdressing usually worn by men of the middle class. Like the last two figures mentioned, it is parted in the middle, forming waves at the side and back of the head.

The young man shown in Fig. 150 has dressed his hair in the very latest fashion, dating about 1210. This is described under Fig. 251.

Headgear

1154–1216

No great variety of hats and caps is to be found in illuminations of this period. Some appear, and are mentioned under the different drawings. The Phrygian type was in general use during the twelfth

Fig. 158   Fig. 159   Fig. 160

century, and other kinds of hats worn during the second half of the same century are shown here. They were made in felt or cloth (Figs. 158 and 159).

Fig. 160 has the crown elaborately embroidered, and a stiff brim; it rather resembles a dish-cover. This basin-crowned hat (Fig. 161), brown in colour and with a brim, is worn by a house-painter represented in a MS. dating the second half of the twelfth century.

Fig. 161

Towards the latter part of this same century hats and caps usually had a point at the top of the crown. It was a pre-

Fig. 162

vailing custom at this time to remove the headdress by grasping a point on top; therefore points were necessary to headgear, whatever the shape might be. This custom continued during the greater part of the thirteenth century. Fig. 162 shows a hat of this kind. It is shaped like a pointed bag, in silk or cloth, but the way it is put on gives it character. The same applies to the turban-like headdress worn by the young noble in Fig. 142.

The hood. During the reign of Henry II. the hood became an important item in the smart attire of the nobility. Hitherto its use had been confined from the earliest times to the middle and lower classes, who found it a most comfortable and useful head-covering.

The nobility also had worn this plebeian garment as a head-covering in inclement weather, and for use as a disguise. Now, however, they used it not only on the capa, but also for decorative purposes. It was cut as shown in Fig. 163,

Fig. 163. Diagram of Hood

the collar or cape part varying in depth according to fancy (*see* Fig. 143), and sometimes having a gore let in in front or one on each shoulder.

This kind of hood was commonly called an AUMUSE, and was used also as an ecclesiastical vestment (*see* Fig. 166). Fig. 165 shows another version of it.

A hood shaped on slightly different lines was in use among the

Fig. 164.   Fig. 165.   Fig. 166.

The Hood

upper classes at this time. It was cut in two pieces—a bag for the head, A, and a collar or cape for the shoulders, B, seamed together at the neck, as shown in Figs. 144 and 164. These hoods remained in general use until the reign of Edward I.

A cap, composed of a round crown with an upstanding brim of fur, made its appearance among the nobility towards the end of the twelfth century. It was first used as a "Cap of Dignity," or "Chapeau of Estate," and carried at the coronation of Richard I. This particular one had the crown of red silk, with the brim of ermine (Fig. 167). *See also* p. 177.

Fig. 167.
Cap of Dignity

HEADGEAR OF THE MIDDLE CLASSES

1154–1216

Among all classes it was a common practice to carry a hat, as well as wear a hood. These hats were for utility, and had wide brims which could be turned down to shade the face from sun or wind and to protect the back of the head. Invariably a cord was attached on both sides, so arranged that the hat could be pushed back off the head, and would hang behind by the cord passing round the neck (*see* Fig. 143).

Hats shaped somewhat like a mushroom and made of felt, sometimes of fur, and, by the middle of the fourteenth century, of beaver, were worn by travellers, sometimes by peasants (Fig. 243), and always by pilgrims. They had the cord for slinging it on the back when not required for protection.

All Jews were obliged to wear square yellow caps, to distinguish them from Gentiles.

HAIRDRESSING

1170 *Onwards*

Women. The style of hairdressing described on p. 56, under date 1130–1154, remained in use among fashionable women until 1170. About this date a change took place. The hair was

Fig. 168.
The Barbette

parted in the middle as before, and the plaits of hair were reduced to normal length; they were crossed behind, brought round the head, the ends tucked in and kept in place by a band of material or a fillet, as shown in Fig. 168. In the case of short plaits the band or fillet was found very convenient for securing them, but if the plaits were long enough to overlap, or fasten on top of the head, the fillet or band was not necessary. Fig. 102 shows the hair dressed in this manner, forming a kind of circlet of hair around the head, wide and full at the back and almost tapering to nothing on top of the head. This style, with slight variations, remained in fashion during the whole of this period.

HEADDRESSES

Temp. Henry II., Richard I. and John, 1154–1216

The "barbette" or chin-strap. First worn by Eleanor of Aquitaine, this remained in fashion for about a hundred and fifty years. It was a becoming headdress, particularly for elderly women whose profile had lost its early sharpness of line. It consisted of a piece of very fine linen or cambric, folded in such a manner that the part placed under the chin was about an inch or two inches in width, widening out to four or six at the ends. These ends were folded over each other on top of the head (after the hair was dressed as just described under Fig. 168), and secured by a pin. A crease or fold was permissible under the chin. On top of this was placed the veil or couvrechef, surmounted by a coronet, fillet or narrow band of material.

The couvrechef. This was now much reduced in size; it was often cut as a circle, and reached only to the middle of the back. It was frequently of some light colour, in linen, cambric or silk, edged with gold and sometimes richly embroidered. As worn by the nobility it was bound round the head by a gold and jewelled circlet; a coloured silken band or fillet was used by the gentry, and a strip of cloth or braid by the humbler folk.

Temp. Richard I. and onwards

The wimple. The wimple (French, *guimple*; Old English, *gwimple*) was a piece of shaped material, generally fine white linen (sometimes coloured), draped under the chin to fill in the space between the edges of the couvrechef, and pinned to the hair at the side of the head, or fastened to the top of the head, underneath the veil. The wimple is first mentioned at the end of the twelfth century, and was considered a suitable means of veiling female charms! Used by "modest" as well as fashionable women (*see* Fig. 117). It was a convenient covering for the neck and head. For comfort and utility it was often worn with a travelling-hood drawn up over it, especially when riding (*see* Fig. 215).

"Small gwimples for ladies' chyunes," and "gwimples dyed saffron," are mentioned in MSS. of the twelfth century.

FOOTGEAR

Temp. Henry II., Richard I. and John, 1154–1216

Fig. 169

No great change is perceptible in the footgear worn during this period. The shoe (Fig. 80) mentioned in the last chapter, p. 59, was the style worn for full dress. Fig. 169 shows a fashionable shoe worn during these three reigns. It is buttoned at the ankle, cut away on the outside of the instep, and decorated with gold, and sometimes set with jewels, on a foundation of silk, cloth or leather.

The newest shape in boots is seen in Fig. 170, a "boot with folding caps," the type to which Henry II. evidently had some objection (*see* p. 84). These boots were made of silk for full dress, cloth or leather for ordinary wear, and lined with material of a contrasting colour. They were laced for some distance up the front or side, the tops being turned over to show the lining, thus forming "folding caps."

The nobleman in Fig. 97 is wearing boots of soft leather stained some colour. They are buttoned up the front—a rather unusual style.

Fig. 170.
"Folding Caps"

The shoes worn by the noblemen, *temp.* Richard I. (Figs. 115 and 116), are the latest in shape, and came into fashion at the end of

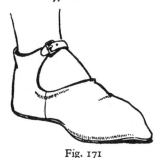

the twelfth century. They follow the form of the foot, having slightly pointed toes, are open on the instep, the strap fastening with a buckle or button (Fig. 171).

Middle classes. The young man seen in Fig. 143 wears ankle boots of leather, with the tops wide enough to turn over to show the lining. The same kind of boot, but a little higher in the leg, also made of leather or felt, is worn by the man shown in Fig. 145.

Fig. 171

Those worn in Fig. 146 are looser, and fall in folds around the ankles.

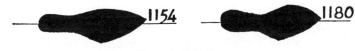

Fig. 172. Sole Plans

JEWELLERY

1154–1216

During this period the art of the English goldsmith made great progress towards perfection—the result of an increasing demand for personal ornaments and for his handiwork for the decoration of costumes. The influence of foreign workmanship grew stronger, particularly that of French craftsmen.

The jewellery of Limoges, noted for its enamels, was eagerly sought by wealthy men and women throughout Europe. A distinct German strain is also noticeable in the work produced here during this time in consequence of the migration of German goldsmiths to this country, in pursuit of the improving market.

The Guild of Goldsmiths dates from the year 1180, and one of the earliest craftsmen whose name has been handed down to us is Anketil, a monk of St. Albans. He was an artist of repute, being highly accomplished in the creation of ornaments of gold and silver, and jewellery. Some of his pieces of plate were presented to his compatriot Nicholas Brakespeare, who was elected Pope as Adrian IV. in 1154. The King of Denmark was another patron of Anketil.

Crowns and circlets. The crown used at Henry II.'s coronation was of German workmanship, for we are told by William of Newburgh that it belonged originally to the Emperor Henry V., and was later acquired by the Empress Matilda, who presented it to the Abbey Church of Bec. It was specially brought over from Normandy for the crowning of her son in 1154. Made "of solid gold and precious stones . . . of such a weight that it is supported by two silver rings when an

Fig. 173.
Crown of Henry II.

Emperor or King is crowned with it. When it is placed in the treasury the whole is divided into two branches, but when it is joined together there is worn on the brow of the wearer a stone of great size and value with a cross of solid gold placed above it." The imperial crown shown in Plate III. may have been "another small crown of gold, which the Emperor (Henry V.) uses in important ceremonies," and was probably lighter in weight. It has an arch, which was first introduced in the reign of the Emperor Henry II. (see Fig. 119, Vol. I.).

Fig. 174.
Crown of Richard I.

The crown worn by Henry II. in Fig. 96 is of plain gold; the drawing is taken from his seal. That shown in Fig. 173 is copied from his effigy, the band being set with oval and lozenge-shaped stones. The crown of Richard I. is well represented on his effigy, and

Fig. 175.
Crown of John

is shown in Fig. 114. Fig. 174 is from another source. Although damaged, the crown on the effigy of King John in Worcester Cathedral is sufficiently intact to enable a copy of it to be made, and this is shown in Fig. 175. In Fig. 100 Eleanor of Aquitaine is shown wearing a crown copied from her effigy; this is the first example of the band surmounted by an escolloped edge of eight points. Four of these points are finished by jewels set in ovals having three pearls on the edges.

Fig. 176. Crown of Clovis.
Twelfth century

Royal crowns used in France were much more elaborate in design and construction than those used in England. Fig. 176 gives one copied from the statue of Clovis, a work of the twelfth century, formerly at Notre Dame de Corbeil, but now at St. Denis. (See also Plate II.A) The lower part is composed of hinged plates, each set with a stone, but the leaf-like motifs surmounting these are rigid.

Circlets, as described in the last chapter, were worn by the nobility during this period.

Brooches. Agrafes similar to that shown in Fig. 88 remained in fashion with the women until about the year 1170, when the style of dress changed; but they were retained by the men to fasten their mantles and clokes, as seen in Figs. 96, 114 and 115; or to fasten the hood, as in Fig. 142. Sometimes two agrafes were used either on mantle or hood, in which case they formed a clasp.

Brooches of smaller size, *fermails,* were used by both men and women to fasten the neck of the bliaut or cyclas (*see* Figs. 115, 116, 193, 214 and 261).

Tasseaux: a term often applied to the circular or square ornaments placed on each side of the mantle in front of the shoulders. Such ornamental bosses were sometimes used by the nobility of both sexes, attached to the shoulders of the mantle on each side, where the retaining cord was fixed (*see* Plate III. and Fig. 100). These were similar in design to the agrafes then in use; like that shown in Fig. 88, but larger.

SECTION VIII.—WEAVING AND MATERIALS
1154–1216
(*Continued from p. 66*)

The weaving industry continued much as described in Chapter I. The most interesting detail concerned with weaving is that, during the reign of Richard I., it was enacted that all woollen cloths—broadcloth —should everywhere be made two ells in width. An ell is a cloth measure equal to one and a quarter yards of to-day. The yard and the ell were originally identical, according to clearly established facts found in old statutes, which suggest that a yard of the Middle Ages was somewhat longer than it is to-day. Henry I. corrected what he termed a false ell, by making the length of his own arm the true standard or ell for the future. This is the yard of to-day.

The money-grubbing John obtained great sums by selling licences to cloth manufacturers and merchants, permitting them to make and sell their cloth as broad or as narrow as they chose, but Magna Charta put a stop to these fraudulent measures.

Almeria, on the coast of Spain, was renowned as a place for the manufacture of "valuable fine silk, called silk of Almeria."

Byssine and *Byssus*. Similar silken material.

Blanchet or *Blanket*. A name given to an inferior woollen cloth worn by the lower classes.

Écarlate. An extra fine quality woollen cloth especially dyed, chiefly scarlet, for which the city of Ghent was famous. It was much used by the nobility for State and full-dress garments.

Gouté à pois. A material woven, stained, or embroidered in spots, either singly or in clusters.

Green was a colour much used during this and the following century for the gowns, clokes and hoods worn by women of the lower orders. *Lincoln green* was first mentioned in the time of Richard I.

Imperial is a name often applied to rich fabrics of silk, in various colours interwoven with gold, and made at the imperial workshops at Constantinople. It was much used for State garments of kings and nobles during the twelfth and thirteenth centuries. Imperial was the earlier name for Baudekyn.

Pers or *Perse*. A cloth of excellent quality of a rich blue colour. Manufactured in Provence, which became famed for its production. Much used by the nobility for their garments.

Raye. Cloth striped horizontally with a different colour and much used during the twelfth and thirteenth centuries.

(*Continued on p.* 187.)

Woad for dyeing was imported in John's reign, the home supply being insufficient.

SOME NAMES OF COLOURS IN USE DURING THE MIDDLE AGES

Aurnola	*Orange*	Mézéreon	*Rose-purple*
Brun	*Brown*	Murrey	*Deep claret*
Brunetta	*Lighter brown*	Paonace or Pavonalilis	*Peacock*
Cendre	*Dark grey*	Pers	*Deep blue*
Cramoisy	*Crimson*	Plombés or Plonquies	*Leaden grey*
Garance	*Madder*	Plunket	*Medium blue*
Graine	*Cochineal red*	Plunket celestyne	*Sky blue*
Gris	*Grey*	Puke or Puce	*Purple of reddish tone*
Grisart	*Light grey*	Sangwyn	*Blood red*
Gris brun	*Drab*	Tanné	*Tan tawny*
Gris cendre	*Ash grey*	Verdulet	*Bright green, bluish in*
Gris pommellé	*Dapple grey*		*tone*
Gros de dos d'asne	*Donkey grey*	Vermeil	*Vermilion*
Herbal	*Brown-green*	Ynde or Inde	*Indigo blue*
Jaune	*Bright yellow*		

FAIRS

(*Continued from p.* 66)

Henry II. granted a charter, confirming that of William Rufus, permitting the fair at Winchester to continue for sixteen days. This fair remained of great importance until the reign of Edward III., when it declined owing to the woollen trade of Norwich and other eastern towns becoming of much greater consequence. Henry II. also confirmed the charter of S. Bartholomew's, which had become a great cloth market, and the place where it was held, the churchyard of S. Bartholomew the Great, is still called Cloth Fair.

But greater by far was the fair held at Stourbridge, near Cambridge. This was originally authorised by King John, and by his instruction the tolls of the fair endowed the Barnwell Hospital for Lepers. At a later date the tolls were paid to the burgesses of Cambridge; the Corporation managed the fair, but the University had the oversight of weights and measures, and the licensing of all booth shows.

Of European renown, this fair opened on 18 September, lasting three weeks, for the sale of all kinds of merchandise. Trading galleys transported from the Flemish, German and French coasts to the River Ouse fine linens and cloths from Bruges, Ghent and Liége; silken fabrics from Antioch; cotton from Tripoli; carpets from Tiberias. Dye, glass and pottery from Tyre, brocades, and later velvets, jewels, etc., passements, were brought from the Orient by Genoese and Venetian merchants; whilst rich furs, raw flax, fustian, buckram, canvas and other materials of foreign make, together with ironwork from Beyrout, oil and soap from Nablus, ginger and musk from China and Thibet, wines from Guienne, Spain, Italy and the Rhine Valley, lemons, oranges, citrons and grapes from Italy, figs, cucumbers, melons, pepper, cloves, aloes, cardamoms, sugar-cane and wines from Palestine, amber, wax, iron, copper, herrings and salt fish, spices, pitch, and ornaments of all kinds, found their places on the booths set up in the various streets allotted to them, according to their different kinds and types, and the countries from which they had come. The English brought their packhorses and mules, laden with home products—wool, hops, corn, barley in sacks, leather, iron, lead and tin, and horses and cattle—to ply a lively trade with the foreigners. This vast fair, and its great concourse of various peoples, continued annually until the end of the nineteenth century, since which time the gathering has dwindled year by year, until in 1925 only three booths were set up, and at the moment of writing there is a proposal before the authorities to abolish it altogether.

John Bunyan took Stourbridge Fair as his model for Vanity Fair in *The Pilgrim's Progress*. For a description of Stourbridge Fair in 1722, *see* Daniel Defoe's *Tour through the Eastern Counties*.

THE GUILDS

(*Continued from p.* 66)

The growing merchants' guilds found that they were powerless without the royal authority, and the first charter obtained was granted to Oxford by Henry II. This king also granted a charter to the weavers, who established craft guilds early in his reign at Winchester, Huntingdon, Nottingham and York.

The first Mayor of London in 1189 was Henry Fitz Alwyn, a man of noble birth and a member of the Drapers' Guild.

For the management of their business, members of the merchant guilds met in their own hall in certain towns. These halls became known as the Guildhall. Feasts and entertainments were also given in these halls, at which the members robed themselves in their "best gowns."

(*Continued on p.* 189.)

Fig. 177

Section IX.—Troubadours and Jongleurs

In the early eleventh century a class of people with a new vocation in life came into prominence: *The Troubadours*—poet-musicians of Provence and Northern France.

Their origin is interesting. Scandinavian "Skalds," reciters or singers of heroic poems or "sagas," found their way to both England and France in the wake of Norse invaders. In England their professional progeny were known as "Gleo-men" or "Gleemen"—itinerant singers and players on various instruments, who flourished from the eighth (and probably earlier) to the tenth century. In Normandy, the skalds' successors were known in Norman French as "Ministraulx," ministers of amusement. After the Norman Conquest of England, the gleemen were supplanted by their Norman "Ministraulx" cousins, whose name became anglicised later into "Minstrels."

Troubadours were in a kind of aristocratic succession to these "Ministraulx."

Troubadours (*Trobador*, or Provençal *Trovador* = one who composes or invents) were poets who wrote their own poems, and they were the first authors who employed their native tongue, Provençal, for their compositions. They went from place to place, visiting the castles or manor-houses of the nobility, enlivening the company after supper with their songs on "the achievements of the Lord and beauty of the Lady." They not only wandered in France, singing their elegant verses, but travelled north into Germany and south into Italy.

"About the year 1000, Southern men began to appear in France and in Burgundy, as odd in their ways as in their dress, and having the appearance of Jongleurs" [1] (Raoul Glaber).

A troubadour often held an official position in the retinue of some great baron, and some of the more accomplished were established more or less permanently as Court poets. As the reputation of this highly-talented and educated class became greater, the aristocracy, especially the knights, joined its ranks. Even kings, princes, and the clergy considered the profession of a singer and poet an honourable one. One of the earliest was a Count of Poitiers; but, on the other hand, some of the distinguished troubadours were the sons of humble parents: Bernart de Ventadorn is a case in point. He was born about 1125, visited England in 1158 and retired to the Abbey of Dalon, dying at an advanced age.

Bertran de Born, born 1140, was of noble birth. "This Bertran was a good knight, a good lover, and a good poet, wise and fair spoken, and well skilled to work either good or evil." On friendly terms with Henry II. of England, it was he who nicknamed the future king "Richard Yea and Nay." In after-life he became a monk, and spent his last years also in the Abbey of Dalon, where he died in 1215. As

[1] *See* p. 113.

a rule, most of the troubadours of distinction, after eventful lives of wandering, ended their days in monasteries.

The troubadour in Germany was known as a "Minnesinger," and one of the earliest lived during the second half of the twelfth century— Dietmar von Aist.

Gottfried von Strassburg. His chief work, *Tristan and Isolda*, was written about 1207–1210. Died 1250.

Walther von der Vogelweide, born 1157–1167 of noble parents. Died about 1228 in the Southern Tyrol. (For arms *see* Plate XVI. A.)

Wolfram von Eschenbach (1190–1220) (Fig. 447) composed *Parzival, Titurel, Lohengrin* and *Willehalm*, and competed in 1207 in the "Waetburg Krieg" [1] at the Court of Hermann, Landgraf of Thuringia.

These two last minnesingers were the most famous German poets of the Middle Ages.

There is no record of any troubadour of English birth, but several came from Southern France to these shores during the twelfth and thirteenth centuries. Mention is made of three troubadours of renown visiting England. They were Bernart de Ventadorn, the "twisted" Marcabru (1150–1195), and Savarie de Mauleon (1180–1233), a powerful baron of Poitou. "A fair knight was he, and courtly and accomplished. No man in the world took such delight in liberality and gallantry and love and jousts and singing and social conversation and poetry and courtly life and in spending."

The legend of Blondel de Nesles discovering the place of Richard's imprisonment is unfortunately pure myth.

By the middle of the thirteenth century the romantic and attractive calling of the troubadour ceased to exist, as a consequence of the decay of feudal society to which it essentially belonged.

Contemporary with the troubadours there flourished *The Jongleurs* (from the Latin *Joculator* = a clown or mountebank), who were a lower order of wandering minstrel. They were in direct descent from the Roman actors and entertainers introduced into Gaul soon after its conquest; but they had made very little progress in their profession since that time, and were regarded in the twelfth century with some contempt. A jongleur of merit and originality might, however, become a troubadour, especially if he possessed any histrionic powers. As a rule he was no poet, but followed and served a troubadour of repute, acting as his accompanist, both vocal and instrumental.

On the disappearance of the troubadours in the thirteenth century, the jongleur survived, but had recourse, of necessity, to other means of livelihood, amusing his audience with antics of all kinds, and feats of prowess. Many who had been on a Crusade had learned tricks of conjuring from the Oriental, and so "Jongleur" in French becomes "Juggler" in English.

[1] Source of Wagner's *Tannhäuser*.

Poetry

The earliest examples of poetry in the Provençal tongue, "langue d'or," date from the middle of the tenth century, but the Provençal school was not established in Northern France until the second half of the twelfth century.

In Provence the principal theme in the songs of the troubadours was adoration and eulogy of one's lady-love. Often the lady was never seen, and frequently imaginary, and, almost without exception, praises were sung to a married woman. Love was a conventional relationship, and marriage was not the primary object in troubadour poetry. After the Albigeois Crusade (1230), the Virgin Mary became the chief theme in their songs of love and praise.

The song-poems of the Provençal troubadours were of two kinds:

First, "Chanzos," songs of love and gallantry, and the subdivision called "Tenson," which was a poetical dialogue. These usually took place after a public joust. The lady of the castle opened her "Court of Love" at which the knights or troubadours contended in poetry and song. A knight would step forward and give a challenge, and another accept it. Two songs were recited or sung, the subject being a special given theme. At the finish the lady would rise, give her judgment and award the prize.

Secondly, "Siventes," songs of chivalry and war.

The songs of the troubadours [1] of the Provençal school of *Northern* France, written in "langue d'oil," were poems of satire, romance and adventure. The romance poems were of three kinds:

Historical, dealing with events in national history;

Traditional, with special reference to the exploits of Charlemagne and his Paladins;

Traditional or *Mystic,* relating the achievements of British heroes, such as King Arthur and his knights.

Adam de la Halle, born 1235, known as the "Hunchback of Arras," was a troubadour of this school, and composed the first pastoral comedy-opera entitled *Li jeu de Robin et de Marion.* He died in 1287.

Music

These wandering minstrels accompanied themselves, or were assisted by one or more jongleurs. They played upon the harp, psalterion or zither (played with a plectrum), vielle, and various kinds of wind instruments.

Part-writing and part-singing being unknown, they usually chanted in unison, and the music in nearly all cases was written in Gregorian notation. Some of their songs are still extant.

The songs of the troubadours are invaluable for their references to costume, accessories, manners and customs.

Illustrations of the dress of troubadours will be found in Figs. 146 and 235.

[1] The name "Trouvère" was given to the troubadours of the North in the eighteenth century.

PLATE VI. SCULPTURE IN ENGLAND. THIRTEENTH CENTURY

A. Margaret of France ⎫
B.   Do.   Do.   ⎬ In Lincoln Cathedral. Photos by S. Smith, Lincoln
C. Edward I.   ⎭

D. ⎫
E. ⎪
F. ⎬ In Wells Cathedral. Photos by T. W. Phillips, Wells
G. ⎭

CHAPTER III

1216–1307

CONTENTS

CHAPTER III

1216–1307

CONTEMPORARY EMPERORS AND KINGS

	ENGLAND	FRANCE	GERMANY
1216	Henry III. Eleanor of Provence	Philippe Auguste, 1180–1223	Frederick II., 1212; deposed 1245
1223		Louis VIII. le Lion, 1223–1226 Blanche of Castile	
1226		Louis IX., 1226–1270 Marguerite of Provence	
1247			William, Count of Holland, 1247–1256
1250			Conrad IV., 1250–1254 Elizabeth of Bavaria
1256			INTERREGNUM
1257			Richard of Cornwall, 1257–1272 1. Isabella, daughter of Earl of Pembroke 2. Sanchia of Provence 3. Beatrice von Falkenstein, daughter of the Elector of Cologne
1270		Philippe III. le Hardi, 1270–1285 1. Isabel of Arragon 2. Marie of Brabant	
1272	Edward I. 1. Eleanor of Castile 2. Margaret of France		
1273			Rudolph of Hapsburg, 1273–1291 Gertrude of Hohenburg
1285		Philippe IV. le Bel, 1285–1314 Jeanne of Champagne, Queen of Navarre	INTERREGNUM
1292			Adolphus, Count of Nassau, 1292–1298
1298			Albert, Duke of Austria, 1298–1308 Elizabeth Meinhard, daughter of Duke of Carinthia

HISTORICAL DATA

1216–1307

1216. Accession of Henry III.
The Fifth Crusade undertaken to assist John de Brienne, titular King of Jerusalem.
1219. Administration of Hubert de Burgh.
1220. Roger of Wendover, flourished 1220,

when he became Prior of Belvoir, Leicestershire; historian and author of *Flowers of History*. Died 1237.
John Hoveden, Latin poet and chaplain to Eleanor of Provence, born about this time; died 1275.

1221. Dominican Preaching Friars, or "Black Friars," settle at Oxford.
John de Fordun, earliest Scottish chronicler, born this year; died 1308.

1224. Sire de Joinville, biographer of Louis IX., born; died 1317.
The Franciscan Friars Minor, or Minorites, or Grey Friars, settle at Oxford and Cambridge.

1225. S. Thomas Aquinas born: the greatest of mediæval theologians. Died 1274; canonised 1323.

1227. Hubert de Burgh created Earl of Kent.

1228. Sixth Crusade undertaken by Frederick II. of Germany.

1230. Robert, monk of Gloucester, born; the first writer who composed verses in English. Died 1285.

1233. Hubert de Burgh, Earl of Kent, dismissed from his justiciarship by the king.

1235. Guillaume de Lorris, celebrated French romancer and author of *Roman de la Rose*. Died 1265.
University of Cambridge founded about this time.

1241. Formation of the Hansa and other Leagues of Free Towns in Germany.

1244. Jerusalem irrevocably lost to Christendom.

1245. Frederick II. of Germany deposed and excommunicated. Empire contested by rival claimants.

1247. Title of Emperor of the Holy Roman Empire given to William of Holland.

1248. Seventh Crusade undertaken by Louis IX. of France.

1250. Louis IX. of France taken prisoner by the Turks, together with a number of his knights and two of his brothers.
Frederick II. of Germany died this year; nominal succession of his son Conrad.
Guillaume de Nangis, chronicler of the kings of France, born about this year; died 1300.

1254. Death of Conrad IV. and end of Hohenstaufen Dynasty. Age of Robber Knights in Germany, 1245–1278.

1255. Rudolph of Hapsburg, an esquire in the army of Ottocar, King of Bohemia, ancestor of imperial family of Austria (*see* 1273).

1256. Double election of Richard of Cornwall, brother of Henry III. of England and Alfonso, King of Castile, to the imperial dignity. The title of Emperor of the Holy Roman Empire went by election, and was not assumed until after coronation by the Pope. Henry II. of Germany (1002–1024) and his successors called themselves before their coronation "Rex Romanorum." This habit continued until Maximilian I. (1486–1519) obtained permission from the Pope to call himself before his coronation in 1493 "Emperor Elect."

1257. Hugh of Balsham, Bishop of Ely, founder of S. Peter's College (Peterhouse), Cambridge.

1258. Great Council, or "Mad" Parliament.

1261. The Barons' War, led by Simon de Montfort; waged in support of the rights of the English people.

1265. Dante born at Florence; died at Ravenna 1321.
"The Full Parliament" summoned by Simon de Montfort, where the "Commons" were present for the first time.

1270. Eighth and last Crusade undertaken by Louis IX. of France and Prince Edward of England.

1271. Capture of Acre, and attempted assassination of Edward.

1272. Death of Richard of Cornwall, King of the Romans and of "Almaine" (1256)
Piers of Langtoft, chronicler, born; died 1307.
Death of Henry III. Accession of Edward I.

1273. Election of Rudolph of Hapsburg as emperor. The first of the non-dynastic emperors of the Holy Roman Empire.

1274. Sir William Wallace, the great patriot of Scotland, born; executed 1305.
Walter de Merton, founder of Merton College, Oxford, appointed Bishop of Rochester.
Robert Bruce born; died 1327, and was buried at Dunfermline.

1280. William of Ockham born: "The Invincible Doctor." Studied at Oxford and Paris. Died 1349.

1282. Edward I. conducted war with the Welsh.

1284. Princes Llewelyn and David captured and executed.

1293. War between England and France.

1296. Edward I. invaded Scotland, and deposed John Balliol (1292–1296).

1297. Walter of Hemingburgh or Guisborough, Canon of the Priory of Gisburn, Yorks, chronicler, flourished; died after 1313.
Canonisation of Louis IX. of France.

1306. Robert Bruce crowned King of Scotland.

1307. Death of Edward I. Accession of Edward II.

PLATE VII. SCULPTURE IN FRANCE AND GERMANY
THIRTEENTH CENTURY

A. Le Roi Mage. In Bourges Cathedral
B. Un Roi.   In Rheims   ,,   } Photos by W. F. Mansell
C. Le Roi David. In Amiens   ,,
D. The Emperor Frederick II.   In Bamberg Cathedral. Photo by Dr F. Stoedtner
E. Comte et Comtesse de Boulogne. In Chartres   ,,   Photo by W. F. Mansell

THE ARTS OF THE GLORIOUS THIRTEENTH CENTURY

1216–1307

ARCHITECTURE

THE thirteenth century was a period of great progress in the arts and culture. Henry III. was "the greatest builder and the greatest patron of the arts who has ever occupied the throne of England. He had an unsatiable passion for architecture, painting and sculpture, and for collecting beautiful materials, goldsmith's work and jewellery." He lavished treasure and spared nothing to make his churches and palaces as sumptuous as the skilled artists of his time could achieve. Many orders and letters of instructions to contractors, etc., for the decorating and beautifying of these buildings are extant.

"All matters, from the size and style of a window to the dimensions of a room, and the paintings on its walls, were executed according to his own directions, often given orally to his officers, and fortunately almost always reduced to writing."

Henry pulled down a portion and enlarged the plan of Westminster Abbey, spending twenty-four years (1245–1269) in building the Chapel of S. Eadward the Confessor. On that saint's day, 1269, Henry, assisted by his sons and brother, bore the coffin containing the remains of the royal saint on his shoulders, and placed it in its new shrine. The "incomparable" Chapter House is another glorious monument to this king. He also built the Traitor's Gate at the Tower of London.

One of the most important works of this time is the western front of Wells Cathedral (1220–1250).

Henry III. introduced coloured glass into the windows of Westminster Abbey, Canterbury, Salisbury and Lincoln Cathedrals.

The Decorated style of architecture which came into use about 1250 retained the same general lines as the Early English. It is so named by reason of its rich decorative development, and its primary stages until the year 1300 are called "Early Decorated" or "Transitional." Pillars were constructed of numbers of grouped shafts, more numerous, and still more slender, than those of the previous style, but the capitals displayed more elaborate carving. The windows were wide, the space divided by mullions, and the head of the arch filled with geometrical tracery, in circles, triangles, etc., of flowing curves.

Edward I. and his queen greatly encouraged workers in all the arts; sculptors, builders, painters, wood-carvers, founders of brass and bronze—all were employed by them, and crafts throve and were brought to a high state of perfection under the royal patronage.

Edward I. erected nine crosses, at places where the body of his beloved wife—his "chère Reine" as he called her—rested during the nights, on its last journey from Lincoln to Westminster. Only three, at Geddington, Northampton and Waltham, remain, and all are now in a mutilated condition. They are excellent specimens of architecture and sculpture, executed by English craftsmen of this time. The cross set up just outside the royal palace at Westminster was always spoken of by him as "my dear Queen's Cross"—Chère Reine Cross, afterwards corrupted into "Charing Cross."

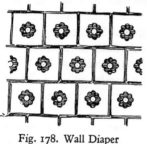

Fig. 178. Wall Diaper

As a house decorator Henry III. deserves great credit. The art of painting made considerable progress under this art-loving monarch, and from his reign onward we have records of orders to supply *oil* and *varnish* for use in wall paintings, which had been carried out hitherto in tempera. The plain flat surfaces of plastered walls, not only as before in churches, but also in domestic apartments, were decorated with elaborate frescoes, and in a new style of ornamentation called "*diaper*," carried out in bright colours and in gold.

Diaper (the derivation of the word is said to be from the Italian *diaspro* = a jasper, a stone which *shifts* its colour), a decoration used for flat surfaces, consisting of a repeated design (Figs. 178 and 179)—usually in alternate squares, diamonds, circles, hexagons, arabesques, or other regular shapes—and contrasting colours (*see* Plates IX., X. and XI., and Fig. 211; also Chapter V., p. 298).

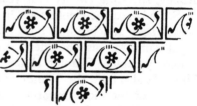

Fig. 179. Wall Diaper

Semée is another word used for a similar decoration particularly applied to textile fabrics (*see* Figs. 12, 28, 139 and 436). It is a pattern spotted over a background or surface, the alternate rows shifted so that each motif comes *between* the motifs in the rows above and below it. It is also a term used in heraldry for the same arrangement (*see* Chapter V., p. 299).

Fig. 180. Painted Drapery

Fresco paintings, when applied to the decoration of domestic interiors, were generally pictures of historical subjects; and the following extracts from records still existing prove not only that historical paintings were then in use, but that they had existed as house decoration at a slightly earlier date:

Henry III. remodelled the old Norman hall at Westminster Palace, which had existed as a royal residence since the time of Eadward the Confessor; and in 1236 an order was given for the walls to be "painted of a good green colour." The painting represented material hung on hooks or nails at intervals, with a gold fringe or border at the bottom edge, and formed a high dado on the plastered stone walls (*see* Fig. 180). A small portion of the original still existing shows it well painted, and the shading of the drapery convincing. This was the style of decoration in use for chambers from the end of the twelfth century.

Instructions were given to Otho, the goldsmith, in the following year, to paint over this old-fashioned wall decoration "a great history," which remained until destroyed by fire in 1262.

The next year a much more elaborate wall painting was begun by Master Walter of Durham, and took fourteen years (1263–1277) to complete. This painting was designed in six bands, increasing in breadth towards the ceiling. The subjects were taken chiefly from Old Testament history, supplemented by allegorical figures. They were painted in brilliant flat colours and gold. The figures are dressed in costumes and armour of the thirteenth century, and form most valuable authorities for the dress of this period. Architecture, and various other details, together with solid colour, form the backgrounds. Another fire considerably damaged these paintings in 1298, and Master Thomas of Westminster, son of Walter of Durham, renovated them, adding new gilding and re-lettering the inscriptions.

The name by which this hall is known is mentioned for the first time in the accounts dated 1307 for payment of this artist; it is called the "Painted Chamber." Sometimes it is also spoken of as "S. Eadward's Chamber," a reference to a very beautiful painting of the coronation of Eadward the Confessor which adorned the north wall.

The later history of this magnificent room is interesting, though melancholy. The brilliancy of its painting became impaired by time, and at the end of the sixteenth century the chamber was "renovated," the walls being papered blue below, and whitewashed above, including the painted ceiling.

During the first half of the seventeenth century tapestries representing the siege of Troy [1] were hung on the lower part of the walls, and the room formed part of the old House of Lords. The tapestries remained in place until the close of the eighteenth century. In 1819 the paintings were revealed, and facsimile drawings of those remaining were made by Mr. C. A. Stothard, and can be seen in *Vetusta Monumenta*, Vol. VI. In 1834 the Painted Chamber was gutted by fire, and now only these reproductions remain for our information.

Other royal residences decorated with wall paintings under Henry III.'s orders were the following:

[1] These were of sixteenth-century workmanship, formerly owned by Charles I., and came from Hampton Court Palace.

In Westminster Palace, besides the apartments already alluded to, "the Queen's Chamber to be beautified and adorned with historical paintings." In the year 1250, an order was given to R. de Sanford, Master of the Knights Templars, to deliver or lend an illuminated book, written in French, on the history of the Crusades, to enable Edward of Westminster, the artist son of Otho the goldsmith, to use the pictures as models for the wall paintings in this room. It was afterwards known as the "Antioch Chamber."

In 1251 instructions were given to the same artist to paint the King's Chamber in the Tower of London, also with representations of the history of Antioch. The Chapel of S. Peter was painted about the same time. Three stained-glass windows had been inserted in the Chapel of S. John the Evangelist some ten years earlier.

At Windsor, the King's Chapel was painted in 1248 with subjects from the Old and New Testaments, and in 1256 the King's and Queen's Chambers were decorated by the artist, William of Westminster, late of Winchester.

"The King's Wainscote Chamber in Winchester Castle to be painted with Saxon Histories, and the same picture with which it had been painted before." As early as 1233, a "painted chamber" at Winchester is mentioned. The Queen's Chapel was painted in the year 1248 by Nigil the artist, and two years later he decorated the King's new Chapel with the story of Joseph. At Woodstock Palace, the chapel (1232) and the hall (1248) were painted, and "the picture now in the Hall to be repaired." At Guildford Castle, the chapel (1235) and the great hall were painted by William of Florence.

In 1255, directions were given for many improvements, including *glazed* windows, to be made, and the castle overhauled, for the reception of the Princess Eleanor of Castile. A wall painting representing the history of Antioch, and especially the incident of King Richard's single combat, was executed in 1250 in the Palace of Clarendon.

"The Queen's Chamber at Nottingham Castle to be painted with the History of Alexander the Great," 1252; and in the same year, the windows in Northampton Castle were filled with stained glass, representing "Dives and Lazarus."

The general advance in culture, as expressed by Henry III.'s orders for wall paintings, tapestries, stained-glass windows, and furniture, with which he beautified his apartments, was furthered by the nobles and wealthy, who followed his example to a very considerable extent, thus promoting the amenities of social life.

SCULPTURE IN ENGLAND
(*Continued from p.* 79)

Among important sculptures of the thirteenth century the statues on the western front of Wells Cathedral rank very high (Plate VI., D, E, F, G). These date not later than 1230–1235. The western front is adorned with

153 life-size statues of saints, kings, queens, knights and nobles, all in the costume of the period. The sculpture is unrivalled by the work of any artist at this date: Nicolas of Pisa is the only contemporary artist whose work is in any way comparable with it.

Many figures in the costume of the period decorated the niches of the crosses erected by Edward I. to the memory of Queen Eleanor.

The latter half of the thirteenth century saw the introduction of effigies in bronze. Those to the memory of Henry III. and Eleanor of Castile, in Westminster Abbey, are considered unsurpassed. They were modelled and cast by William Torel, an Englishman, in 1291.

The monument and effigy erected to the memory of William de Valence (1296) are particularly interesting. (He was the son of Isabella of Angoulême and the Count de la Marche.) The foundation of the effigy is of oak overlaid with copper-gilt—an unusual method. The construction of the chain-mail is well shown. The waist- and sword-belts, a blue ground with gold ornaments, and the armorial shield, are carried out in Limoges enamel. So also is the heraldic cushion, and the plate which covers the top of the oak chest on which the effigy lies. The fillet round the camail is of raised metalwork, originally set with jewels.

The stone effigies on the tombs of Edmund Crouchback (1296) and his wife Avelina (1273), also at Westminster Abbey, are among the many valuable records of costume of the time, especially as they retain much of their decoration in gold and colours. The former is portrayed in military dress, as indeed are the majority of effigies representing men. A painting of the ten knights who accompanied this prince on a crusade originally occupied the north pediment wall beneath the monument. A framed reproduction, made from a drawing dated 1600, is now to be seen adjoining the monument and should be noticed. The picture gives excellent details in colour of the armour and accoutrements worn by knights of this period.

SCULPTURE IN FRANCE

The north porch at Chartres Cathedral, Plate VII. E, built in the middle of the thirteenth century and completed in 1280, contains statues to the number of 700, mostly representing personages from Old Testament history. There are also statues of many queens, representing the Gifts of the Holy Spirit and the Heavenly Beatitudes, all in thirteenth-century costumes.

Between the years 1220 and 1240, Louis IX. renewed all the statues at S. Denis representing his predecessors on the throne of France. In accordance with the custom of artists of the Middle Ages, the statues show these princes all dressed in the fashion of the time when the restoration was done.

The great western triple porch at Rheims Cathedral, Plate VII. B, is also celebrated for its magnificent collection of sculpture, comprising nearly 600 figures representing all classes of the community at the middle of the thirteenth century. The dedication of the cathedral took place in 1215. Louis VIII. was crowned there in 1223, and Louis IX. in 1232, but the building was not completed until 1241. Many French monarchs have been crowned there since that time.

SCULPTURE IN GERMANY

Some admirable statuary of the thirteenth century in Germany is to be found at the cathedrals of Bamberg, Plate VII. D (*see also* Fig. 192), Strassburg, Magdeburg, Nuremberg and Cologne, all of which give interesting details of contemporary costume and armour.

(*Continued on p.* 199.)

MEMORIAL BRASSES

From the latter part of the thirteenth century onwards the student of costume, armour, etc., must survey a wider field; to the many sources of information available before this time is now added the intensely interesting and informative series of memorial brasses in which England is so rich—richer, indeed, than all the other countries of Europe put together.

For about three centuries after their first introduction into England, the material for memorial brasses (the brass or latten plates) was imported, although nearly always cut and engraved by English craftsmen.

Early examples in Western Europe were wrought by engravers of North Germany (where the industry centred in Lübeck, the material being manufactured principally at Cologne) and Flanders. Continental brasses were usually engraved on quadrilateral plates; the inscription, canopy, background, all being depicted on the same plate.

Brasses were the lineal descendants of the incised stone slabs used for memorial purposes in the twelfth century and earlier, and in their mode of construction they reversed the process used in Limoges enamels, for which a copper foundation was cut away to receive coloured enamels, leaving thin dividing lines of copper to "draw" the design. In simple English brasses, the drawing of the figure was achieved by incised lines, and the whole plate cut to the outline of the figure. The plate was then sunk into its prepared stone slab or matrix; accessories to the central figure—borders, canopies, shields, etc.—were similarly treated. In some more elaborate brasses of the late thirteenth and fourteenth centuries, decorations of enamel were introduced, sometimes confined to the shield, but occasionally ornamenting portions of the figure or costume; and in such cases the process was akin to that used in the manufacture of

Limoges enamel, the copper foundation of the enamel being let into the brass flush with its surface.[1]

Personages commemorated by memorial brasses may be divided into four groups:

Ecclesiastical
Military
Court } often with wives and families.
Civilian

All are almost invariably shown full-face (save towards the end of the fifteenth century): usually lying on their backs, and in most cases having the hands together with fingers extended.

The drawing of the faces is generally poor, but the costume and accessories are very well defined, and the folds and drapery excellent. For these reasons brasses are an invaluable source of information on the subject of costume, and their authenticity is beyond question.

The oldest brass extant in England represents a knight in armour —Sir John Daubernon (1277). A few surviving mail-clad knights of the early period are shown with their legs crossed. Contrary to the general belief, however, this does not indicate that they were Crusaders, nor does it necessarily record the fact that they were benefactors to the Church, as some students suggest. Many authorities believe that the cross-legged attitude has no symbolical significance, being simply the expression of a natural and easy posture in repose. Only one brass exists depicting a Crusader—that to the memory of Sir Roger de Trumpington, at Trumpington, near Cambridge (1289), who attended Prince Edward on the last Crusade in 1270.

The earliest brass depicting a woman is that of Margarete de Camoys (c. 1310). A beautiful brass dated c. 1320 is to the memory of Lady Joan de Cobham, and from this are derived the details of costume given on p. 218 and in Fig. 306.

The earliest civilian commemorated on a brass is John de Bladigdone (c. 1325), shown with his wife, but unfortunately only half-length.

(*Continued on p. 200.*)

TAPESTRY

(*Continued from p. 15*)

Even in the writings of the thirteenth century it is difficult to discriminate between embroideries, brocades, damasks, velvets, carpets or coverings of furniture and tapestries properly so called. The following are a few of the names applied to the latter: Tapites, tapytez, tapet, tappis and tapis. "Tapistrie" was always applied to pictorial hangings

---

[1] Enamel decorations of the fourteenth century were not confined to brasses, but applied to monuments and monumental effigies (*see* p. 199).

made at Arras,[1] a town in Flanders which became famous for
their manufacture after the siege and fall of Constantinople in 1204
had driven many tapestry-weavers to settle in that country, bringing
with them specimens of their work. Paris also became a close rival
to Arras.

A method of weaving with a *high warp* was adopted about 1280
in the manufacture of tapestry, and this kind entirely superseded textile
fabrics "painted by the needle" (embroidery) for wall decoration.

Tapestry was first used in England as a covering for the walls of
private apartments in the reign of Henry III. The Infante don Sancho,
half-brother to the Princess Eleanor of Castile and Archbishop-elect
of Toledo, with Don Gracias Madinez, a Castilian grandee, arrived in
England in 1255, in advance of the young princess who was to be the
bride of Prince Edward. They were lodged in the New Temple, and
with them they brought decorations for their apartments. Their attendants unpacked from their travelling-chests rich silks and woollen tapestries
which they hung on the bare stone walls, and carpets of Moorish and
Persian make which they spread upon the stone floors. The hanging of
tapestry on walls was a Moorish luxury and had been adopted by the
Spaniards some time previously. The English were very greatly interested
and fascinated by this mode of decoration which they had not seen
before except in churches. When the princess arrived some time afterwards, she found her apartments at Westminster Palace hung with
costly tapestry "like a church, and carpeted after the Spanish fashion."

Before Queen Eleanor took up her residence at Carnarvon Castle, in
1283, her chamberlain preceded her to
see that the walls of her apartment—the
little room twelve feet square by eight
feet high in which the first Prince of
Wales was to be born, 25 April,
1284—were hung with tapestry, "ut
camerae tapetic et banqueriis ornen-
tur," which had been brought, packed
in travelling-trunks (Fig. 181), by her
grooms of the chamber. This pre-
paratory furnishing became the custom
when the great travelled about the
country.

Fig. 181. Travelling Chest on Stand.
Thirteenth century

From this time tapestry as a garniture for public and private
apartments came into general use in England among the wealthy. In
the dwellings of the lesser aristocracy, the walls of the hall were painted,
whitewashed or wainscoted, with perhaps a piece of tapestry, the pride
of the owner, hung at the back of his seat on the dais, or used for the
decoration of the solar. It is interesting to observe upon the walls of the

[1] The name "Arras" itself came to denote the same thing.

PLATE VIII. TWO DRAWINGS BY MATTHEW PARIS

By kind permission of the Master and Fellows of Corpus Christi College, Cambridge

earliest manor-houses still extant the tenter-hooks for supporting the tapestry which was secured at intervals only at the top edge.

Secular subjects in tapestry were now much used, and the design and draftsmanship considerably improved.

(*Continued on p.* 200.)

PLATE, ETC.

Though one may be tempted to imagine that even the aristocracy of these times were still barbarous in their habits, the following details of personal and household articles should prove that the Court of Queen Eleanor had attained a considerable degree of elegance. In the list of the royal table and household plate, the work of the king's goldsmith named Adam, there is mention of ewers of gold (Fig. 183), enamelled

Fig. 182. Goblet   Fig. 183. Ewer   Fig. 184. Covered Cup

and set with precious stones; chalices and cups (Figs. 182 and 184) of gold and silver; plates, dishes and salts of gold, silver and enamel, and bowls of jasper.

Contrary to common usage, Queen Eleanor evidently did not eat with her fingers, for amongst the items set forth are both knives and forks. Some forks are described as of silver, with ebony and ivory handles, and others of enamel with crystal handles. The knives were encased in silver sheaths.

Chessboards. These were usual and costly presents at this time, and a description of one may prove useful: "A chessboard of Saracenic workmanship, in ivory, ebony and silver, and the chessmen were carved in jasper and crystal." The squares of the chessboard were often in gold and silver, and the chessmen red and gold, occasionally measuring two or two and a half inches in height.

Writing-boards. Writing-boards were about two feet long by fifteen or eighteen inches wide, with rounded corners. In the centre they were covered with green cloth,

Fig. 185. Writing-board

and at the ends there were various holes and receptacles for ink, pens and knives. They were used upon the knees when the writer was seated (Fig. 185).

ILLUMINATED MANUSCRIPTS

(*Continued from p.* 79)

The opening of the thirteenth century saw the birth of a new style —Gothic—in the art of English and French illuminators. Hitherto the French School had not been distinguished for its work; but after the founding of the University of Paris, in 1200, the demand for books produced a great improvement in the craft.

During the thirteenth century it was not always an easy matter to distinguish between English and French work, but by the end of the century the two styles had become distinct, the English culminating in the splendid work of the East Anglian School which became famous in the next century.

The figures have now become almost normal in drawing, the shape of the costume is fairly well defined, and the folds of the drapery are shaded with a darker tone, white being toned down into buff, grey, or sometimes pink shadows. As a rule, the colours are deep and rich, especially blue, which seems to be the favourite.

Backgrounds are of gold, highly burnished, or often panels of colour, generally alternating for adjacent subjects in blue and red. A new treatment of backgrounds had come into use at the end of the last century, namely filling them in Diaper (*see* p. 134); and this pattern gradually became the usual background for illuminations throughout the remaining period of the Middle Ages.

Another thirteenth-century innovation was the *Pendent-tail* to the principal initial letter. Gradually this was highly developed, the curved and scrolled foliated ends extending first down the left-hand margin of the page, and afterwards along the bottom, often returning up the right-hand margin also, and eventually forming a complete border to the page of text. Figures, birds and animals, disporting themselves with all sorts of antics, were entwined in or perched on various details of the decoration. This reached its highest development at the beginning of the fifteenth century.

MSS. dealing with the *Apocalypse* were produced in great numbers during the thirteenth century, and some of the best English work is to be found in them.

Psalters also absorbed a good share of the illuminators' activity, but towards the end of the century a rival was already making its appearance in the "Book of Hours."

Herbals and *Bestiaries* were still popular in the early part of the thirteenth century, and another subject to which thirteenth-century illuminators devoted much attention was the production of *Medicas*: handbooks with numerous illuminations referring to surgery, medicines, and bodily complaints of all kinds.

Some examples of the illuminated work of Matthew Paris, drawn in the second quarter of the thirteenth century, are to be found dispersed throughout Chapter III. In manner these are an interesting survival from an earlier style of outline figure drawing (*see* Plate VIII., Figs. 207 and 247).

The work of English illuminators was also much influenced by French and Flemish artists (who had themselves derived something from English twelfth-century art), and the increasing intercourse between England and Flanders helped in a considerable degree to establish the style of work of the East Anglian School. Very beautiful work was executed by these East Anglian artists towards the end of the thirteenth century, and its high standard was maintained until the middle of the fourteenth century.

Perhaps its most characteristic feature is the use of decorated backgrounds, filled in usually with gold, but sometimes with solid colour, red or blue, and throwing the figures into strong relief—a method practised earlier by Byzantine artists.

(*Continued on page* 201.)

Fig. 186

COSTUME IN GENERAL, 1216–1307

The accession of young Henry III. to the throne, in 1216, marks an interesting stage in the history of Costume. Dress had become more and more elaborate and extravagant during the preceding two centuries, and, as generally happens when a state of over-development and superabundant decoration is reached, there was a widespread reaction.

The costume of the thirteenth century after this event was remarkable for its simplicity, which may be observed amongst the nobility and upper classes of both sexes, more particularly during the period between 1220 and 1270. The cut was simple and better adapted to the needs of the various classes, and the difference between the dress of the noble, citizen and peasant was less marked than before.

Louis IX., born 1215 (1226–1270), canonised as S. Louis 1297, was King of France, and the most virtuous of monarchs at this time. A man of deep religious convictions, he abhorred all worldliness, and set his face against the prevailing extravagance in dress. He set an example, by his simple manners and the plainness of his clothes, which was eagerly followed by his courtiers and subjects, all of whom adored him.

The Court of this wise and good king tended rather to restrain luxury than develop it, and its close relationship with the Court of England (Louis had married, in 1234, Margaret of Provence, Queen Eleanor's sister) without doubt exercised considerable influence on the English fashions.

In both countries sober magnificence, dignity of appearance, and richness of material was the standard to be desired. Long robes, sufficiently ample not to constrain the body or embarrass movement, and capacious mantles, draped in a variety of ways requiring artistic treatment and careful study, were the characteristic features of costume at this time.

Simplicity of apparel remained in favour during the reign of Edward I.; a humble-minded and unostentatious man, his influence on dress was such that the fashions of this reign are noteworthy as being the simplest in history.

Fig. 187

SECTION I.—HENRY III. 1216–1272

Nobility—Men

Fig. 188. Henry III.

Henry was born at Winchester Palace, 1206. In appearance he was not unlike his father, of middle height, and handsome except that his left eyelid drooped somewhat. In early life he was clean-shaven, but after his marriage he grew a close beard on his upper lip and chin. His hair was long, and worn in the fashion of the period (Fig. 188).

He is said to have possessed charming and courteous manners, been graceful in deportment, and of a very kind nature; a great patron of the fine arts, and a lover of poetry.

In character Henry was gentle and mild, but weak and deceitful. He was considered on the whole a pious and good man; brave, but, in the opinion of Hubert de Burgh, not a good soldier; and had faults which made him unfit to wear the crown. Matthew Paris, in his earlier writings, was rather hard on Henry: "Regulus Mendicans," a Beggar Prince, he calls him, and says that he was weak of purpose, but brave in battle, untrustworthy, avaricious,[1] a spendthrift, and devoted to foreign favourites. However, Matthew Paris thought more kindly of him when he came to know his king better, and in later life Paris revised some of his criticisms, deleting many hard words about Henry and modifying others.

Henry was crowned at the age of ten, in the King's Hall at Gloucester, by Peter, Bishop of Winchester, on 28 October, 1216, and was placed under the guardianship of William, Earl of Pembroke, the great marshal.

"In this year (1220), on Whit-Sunday, which was the seventeenth day of May, the said King, in the fifth year of his reign, was again crowned at Canterbury, by Stephen, Archbishop of that place."

At the age of twenty-six it was considered expedient that the king should marry, so with this object in view he scanned the Courts of Europe for a suitable princess. He negotiated with as many as five royal ladies, but without success, until the beautiful Princess Eleanor, daughter of Raymond Berenger, Count of Provence, was brought to his notice by a ruse on the part of her troubadour father and his poet-chamberlain.[2] They sent to Henry's brother, the Earl of Cornwall, an heroic poem written by the young lady. The earl, touched and flattered by this attention, was, alas, already a married man; but he fulfilled the senders' hopes by handing the poem on to his elder brother, with a recommendation that he should follow up its receipt with a proposal. This was done in the year 1235, and in January 1236, Henry III. married Eleanor, with great pomp and much splendour, at Canterbury Cathedral.

Five days later, at Westminster, the nuptial festivities took place, at which Henry wore his crown, and Eleanor was crowned queen. Matthew Paris gives an excellent description of the proceedings:

"The whole city was ornamented with flags and banners, chaplets and hangings, candles and lamps, and with wonderful devices and extraordinary representations, and all the roads were cleansed from mud and dirt, sticks, and everything offensive.

"The citizens, too, went out to meet the King and Queen, dressed out in their ornaments, and vied with each other in trying the speed of their horses. On the same day, when they left the city for Westminster, to perform the duties of Butler to the King (which office belonged to them by right of old, at the Coronation), they proceeded thither dressed in silk garments, with mantles worked in gold, and with costly changes of raiment, mounted on valuable horses, glittering with new bits and saddles. . . . The nobles, too, performed the duties which, by ancient right and custom, pertained to them at the Coronation of Kings. . . . The Earl of Chester carried the sword of S. Eadward, which was called

---

[1] "The King of England hastened his return (from Scotland) into the southern parts of England, and on the road he visited abbeys and priories, commending himself to the prayers of the prelates, and at the same time *enriching himself with their money*"—a disconcerting reversal of their traditional theory of prayer as a marketable commodity! This happened especially at Durham, 1255. (*Vide* Matthew Paris.)

[2] Romeo Cresembini, referred to by Dante as one of the greatest poets of his time.

'Curtein,' before the King, as a sign that he was Earl of the Palace, and had by right the power of restraining the King if he should commit an error. The Earl was attended by the Constable of Chester, and kept the people away with a wand when they pressed forward in a disorderly way. The Grand Marshal of England, the Earl of Pembroke, carried a wand before the King, and cleared the way before him, both in the Church and in the Banquet Hall, and arranged the banquet and the guests at table. The Wardens of the Cinque Ports carried the pall over the King, supported by four spears, but the claim to this duty was not altogether undisputed.

"The Earl of Leicester supplied the King with water in basins, to wash before his meal; the Earl Warrenne performed the duty of King's Cupbearer, supplying the place of the Earl of Arundel, because the latter was a youth and not as yet made a belted Knight. Master Michael Belet was Butler *ex officio*; the Earl of Hereford performed the duties of Marshal of the King's Household, and William Beauchamp held the station of Almoner. The Justiciary of the Forests arranged the drinking-cups on the table at the King's right hand. The Citizens of London passed the wine about in all directions, in costly cups, and those of Winchester superintended the cooking of the feast. . . . The ceremony was splendid, with the gay dresses of the clergy and knights who were present. . . . Why should I describe all those persons who reverently ministered in the Church to God as was their duty? Why describe the abundance of meats and dishes on the table, the quantity of venison, the variety of fish, the joyous sounds of the glee-men, and the gaiety of the servers? Whatever the world could afford to create pleasure and magnificence was there brought together from every quarter."

The marriage of Henry and Eleanor proved a very happy one, but unfortunately this beautiful lady was the most unpopular queen who ever presided over the Court of England.

Henry III. died at S. Eadmundsbury on 16 November, 1272. With his usual simplicity and great reverence for S. Eadward, he had reserved for himself the old discarded coffin of that saint: in it his body was interred, near the shrine of S. Eadward the Confessor at Westminster.

The queen and Knights Templars raised to his memory a magnificent monument of Purbeck marble, Italian marble inlay, porphyry, and mosaic, most of which were brought for that purpose from the Holy Land and the Continent. The monument is surmounted by a bronze effigy of the king.

CHILDREN OF HENRY III. AND ELEANOR

1. Edward, succeeded his father.
2. Edmund, born 1245, Crouchback.
   Married, first, Avelina, daughter and heiress of Earl of Albemarle:
   Secondly, Blanche, Queen-Dowager of Navarre; and left issue.
3. Margaret, married Alexander III. of Scotland.
4. Beatrix, married the Duke of Brittany and Earl of Richmond.

Henry III. was very particular about his own dress, and, unlike his father, he was insistent that his family and the nobles about his Court should be suitably robed in rich and tasteful apparel. He made liberal gifts of cloth, silk, cloth of gold, etc., for their use.

"Nor did the Courtiers and Royal Household appreciate any presents unless they were rich and expensive; such as handsome palfreys, gold and silver cups, necklaces, with choice jewels, imperial girdles, and such-like things."

The effigy on Henry's tomb in Westminster Abbey shows him in State costume, though of a simple character. He is dressed in a long full robe with tight sleeves, and a mantle draped over the left shoulder and fastened on the right with a jewelled ornament. It is devoid of any other decoration whatsoever, so we may conclude the dress was composed of very rich and expensive material.

When his youngest sister married Frederick II., Emperor of Germany, in 1235, Henry supplied her trousseau, and personally supervised with great care every detail. He caused an inventory to be made of the dresses, with a description of the materials used and the style of each one. Even a "robe de nuit" [1] is mentioned! On her wedding-day, the empress "shone forth with such profusion of rings and gold necklaces, and other splendid jewels, with silk and thread garments and other like ornaments which usually attract the gaze and excite the desires of women even to covetousness, that they appeared invaluable.

"With bridal garments of silk, wool and thread she was so well equipped that it was difficult to say which would be most likely to attract the Emperor's affections.

"Her couch was so rich in its coverlets and pillows of various colours, and the various furniture and sheets made of pure fine linen, that by its softness it would invite those lying in it to a delightful slumber.

"All the drinking-cups and dishes were of the purest gold and silver, and, what seemed superfluous to everyone, all the cooking-pots, large and small, were of pure silver."

The costumes made for Henry's bridal coronation, in 1236, were the last word in sumptuousness, and cost an enormous sum. Matthew Paris saw him on this occasion, as he tells us that the king was arrayed in a garment of brilliant tissue of gold—"he sat upon his throne and glittered very gloriously." It is also noted that Henry was the first to wear that very wonderful and costly material called "baudekyn," which was henceforth to become very popular with the nobility.

At Christmas, 1250, "the King (being perhaps saving in his anxiety about his pilgrimage) did not distribute any festive dresses to his knights and his household, *although all his ancestors had made a practice from times of old of giving away royal garments and costly jewels.*" So writes

[1] This garment was not a nightgown but equivalent to the dressing-gown of the present day.

Matthew Paris, disappointed of the show he hoped to see; but later, "in the octaves of the Nativity of the Blessed Virgin (1251), the King came to St. Albans, and going into the church, as was his custom, offered three pieces of silk ('Palls'); and it was reckoned that with those previously offered by him they amounted to thirty. Besides on this

occasion, he offered two very costly necklaces, and ordered them, in memory of him, to be strongly secured to the shrine with nails."

The custom of distributing to their domestics fresh changes of raiment "which we commonly call new clothes" (later, liveries) was practised by the nobility in imitation of their sovereign.

A portrait of a king is painted on one of the panels of the Sedilia erected in 1307, to the right of the Presbytery in Westminster Abbey. Without doubt it is Henry III., as there is a strong resemblance between this and the effigy on Henry's monument. We may suppose it to be the work of Master Thomas, son of Walter, the king's painter.

Henry is represented in full State dress, and Fig. 189 is a reconstruction of this painting. The tunic is modelled on the lines of the garment shown in Fig. 115. The skirt is cut up the front and drawn up into a waist-belt (unseen), giving the edge a wavy effect. It is made of crimson silk and has a pattern (Fig. 190), embroidered in white, orange and gold, round the neck, at the bottom edge and up the sides of the slit.

Fig. 189. Henry III.

The mantle is made of that wonderful new material just invented by the silk-weavers of Italy—velvet—in a shade of olive green. It is edged with a border of the same design and colour as that on the tunic, and lined with miniver. In compliance with the mode, it is very gracefully draped over the right arm, and the left side is brought across and thrown over the right forearm. The king's hair is dressed in the fashionable style, and he wears a circlet surmounted by four leaf-motifs, and four smaller ones. A sceptre is carried. The gloves and shoes are described on pp. 90 and 181. It is altogether a rich though simple costume, exemplifying the good taste displayed in royal dress of the thirteenth century.

Fig. 190. Embroidery, thirteenth century

One of the kings, "Antiochus," painted on the wall of the Painted Chamber, Westminster Palace, is robed in a tunic of gold, with a dark green cyclas over it. A crimson mantle, edged with fur, is fastened by a band of gold across the shoulders, and is lined with white. The white gloves have a band of jewels down the back, like Fig. 104, and the legs are clothed in chausses of red, green and gold fretty-work, with red shoes. The hair and beard are dressed as shown in Fig. 189.

The little that remains of the painting which represents S. Eadward the Confessor being crowned, shows the king wearing a green tunic, and a lilac mantle fastened on the right shoulder. Several interesting gold embroidered borders (Figs. 186, 187, 216 and 230) are seen in places. The hair and crown also bear a striking resemblance to those of Henry III.

The saintly Louis IX. is shown in Fig. 191, seated upon a chair of state. The drawing is taken from one of his seals. Referring to Figs. 101 and 132 of Vol. I., and comparing the design of the two seats there shown, it will be noticed that the style of chairs of state has changed very little during seven centuries. Regal costume also has varied only in a few details. The dalmatic is worn over a tunic shaped in all probability like the one shown in Fig. 115, but the semicircular mantle is fastened on the right shoulder by a brooch in the form of a fleur-de-lys, and a semicircle is cut for the neck and shoulders, as illustrated in Fig. 28. The embroidered border, crown, sceptre and the fleur-de-lys held in the right hand are worthy of notice.

The Sire Jean de Joinville, born 1224, was son of Geoffry de Joinville,

Fig. 191. Louis IX.

Seneschal of Champagne. In early life he was attached to the Court of the King of Navarre, but left him to join Louis IX. on the Seventh Crusade in 1248. He returned to France in 1254, and in 1261 married Alix de Resnel. His *Chronicle of the Crusade of S. Louis* was written at the age of eighty-five. Joinville died in 1317.

The Sire de Joinville was present, in the year 1241, at a State function held at Saumur, in Anjou, and he "can testify that it was the best-ordered Court that I ever saw." He also describes some of the costumes worn by the company. "The King was clothed in a tunic of blue satin, and surcote and mantle of vermeil (vermilion) samit, lined with ermine, and he had a cotton COIF (*see* p. 176) upon his head, which suited him very badly, because he was at that time a young man. . . . My lord the King of Navarre, in tunic and mantle of samit well bedight with a belt and clasp, and a cap of gold. . . . Some thirty of their Knights in tunics of silken cloth . . . and behind these Knights there were a great quantity of

Fig. 192. THE EMPEROR FREDERICK II.

(Drawn from the statue known as "Der Reiter" in Bamberg Cathedral)

sergeants, bearing on their clothing the arms of the Count of Poitiers embroidered in taffeta. . . . And many said they had never, at any feast, seen together so many surcotes and other garments of cloth of gold and of silk."

"After the King returned from overseas (1254) he lived in such devotion that never did he wear fur of beaver or grey squirrel, nor scarlet, nor gilded stirrups and spurs. His clothing was of camlet and blue cloth; the fur on his coverlets and clothing was deer's hide, or the skin from the hare's legs, or lambskin. When strangers of note ate with him, he made them very good company."

Another simple royal costume is shown in Fig. 192, which is adapted from a statue in Bamberg Cathedral. It has been said to represent the Emperor Conrad III., but as the work dates about 1250 it is much more likely to be the Emperor Frederick II.[1] The tunic is of the usual shape, fastened by a brooch at the throat, but the sleeves are cut close to the upper arm. The mantle is attached across the shoulders by a strap, without any decoration. The crown is the only item which is ornamented. The bridle and breast-band of the horse furniture are composed of oblong plates of metal, fixed to leather straps. The spurs, stirrups and saddle are excellent examples of those in use at the period.

THE CYCLAS (Ciclatoun—Syglaton—Gardcorp—Surcote). Matthew Paris relates that at the wedding of Henry III., in 1236, many in the great concourse who witnessed the ceremony were dressed in garments for which he uses the word "cycladibus," worked with gold, over vestments of silk. This garment was usually made of very rich material (especially when it first came into fashion) manufactured in the Cyclades, and the origin of the name Cyclas is attributed to this source.

Other materials frequently used were a fabric of woven gold — baudekyn,

Fig. 193. Cyclas and Diagram

samit, cendal, and siglaton (the origin of another of its names). *See* Vol. I., Chap. V.

Variations and developments of the cyclas appeared from time to time, and will be mentioned in their proper sequence.

----

[1] A very interesting point occurs in regard to this statue. It will be noticed that the statue of "A King" from the cathedral at Rheims (Plate VII. B) bears so marked a resemblance to the figure of "Der Reiter," otherwise the Emperor Frederick II. (Fig. 192), in the cathedral at Bamberg, that there can be but little doubt that they are both portraits of the same individual. *See also* Plate VII. D.

Fig. 193 represents a nobleman of the first quarter of the thirteenth century, wearing the cyclas, a garment of the latest fashion imported from France. It was an over-robe made of a single piece of material and cut as shown in the diagram behind the drawing. It had a hole in the centre (with a slit in front, or on the shoulder) for the head to pass through. The cyclas had its prototype in the cuculla of Imperial Rome, and the monastic scapular, as described in Vol. I., p. 111. At this period it was worn as an extra covering, and for ornament; when girded at the waist it was possible for it to envelop the figure entirely, although the sides were left open, only the sleeves, and sometimes the bottom of the undertunic, being uncovered. This cyclas is worn over the garment described in Fig. 115.

Fig. 194. Noble temp. Henry III.

A nobleman, dating about 1240, is seen in Fig. 194. He is wearing the cyclas just mentioned, which, instead of being left entirely open at the sides, is now joined from below a wide armhole to about knee-level, the remainder being left open. Over this is draped a mantle, and frequently a hood was worn on the shoulders, with the head part hanging down the back.

Fig. 195 shows a further development of the cyclas, worn by Prince John of France, 1247. He wears it over two other garments. The under one of all has tight sleeves to the wrist, which, in the original painted image in front of his tomb, are of gold cloth. The second dress is of purple, fitting the neck and having long hanging sleeves, divided in front to the elbow. The cyclas is mauve, diapered with gold fleurs-de-lys. At this period it was made to fit closer on the chest and in the armhole, slit up the front (a general feature with most long garments, more convenient for the wearer when mounted on horseback), and lined with fur. The sides in this instance are buttoned together (Fig. 196).

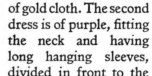

Fig. 196.
Diagram of Second Cyclas

Fig. 195.
Prince John of France

Sleeves were added to the cyclas, and it was then known as the GARDCORP—a surcote or overcoat to be worn for extra warmth. Fig. 197

shows the somewhat complicated sleeves. They were cut with a vertical opening in front, A, for the arm to pass through; if desired, the arm could pass out at the extremity at B. These sleeves are tucked vertically on the shoulders to reduce the width of the material where it was inserted into the armhole; thence they hung in folds to below the elbow, and often to about the knees. The length of the garment varied according to its use, but generally it reached only to just below the knees.

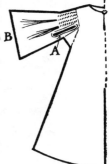

Fig. 197. Diagram of Gardcorp

Fig. 198 is taken from a drawing by Matthew Paris (reproduced in facsimile in Plate VIII. A), and shows King Henry holding, with veiled hands, a crystal vessel containing some drops of the Blood of Christ, which he had received from the Holy Land. Henry carried this relic, under a canopy, in procession to S. Peter's at Westminster, on S. Eadward's Day, 1247. Paris tells us "he carried it above his head publicly, going on foot, and *wearing an humble dress* (and his crown) consisting of a poor surcote without a hood." This was the gardcorp (*see* Fig. 197). Four nobles, habited in the cyclas, carried the canopy. "The Pall was borne on four spears." The name "PALL" used by Paris means a piece of very rich stuff (*see* Vol. I., p. 216).

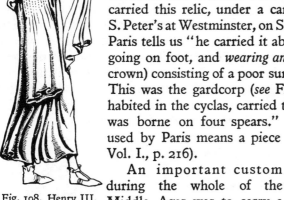

Fig. 198. Henry III.

An important custom during the whole of the Middle Ages was to carry a relic, or offering, in the hands, covered either by a piece of drapery, as in Fig. 198, or by a portion of the mantle.

An unexpected posture adopted by kings and nobles of this period is frequently illustrated in MSS. of the thirteenth century. When seated, one leg is crossed over the other, despite the fact that long robes are worn, in a fashion one would think entirely modern. It was also quite usual for a nobleman to be represented nursing a small lap-dog, and monkeys were frequently kept as pets in the houses of the great.

The seated cross-legged figure, 199, is a young noble at home, wearing a cotte with a gardcorp

Fig. 199. Noble, *temp.* Henry III.

over it. The latter has a hood attached to it, and is fastened down the front with twin ornaments of braid, one terminating in a button and the other in a loop. He is wearing the fashionable coif and hairdressing, with a circlet of jewels round his head. Notice the lap-dog, of the spaniel breed, and the gloves carried in the left hand.

Fig. 200.
The Cointise

Soon after the first appearance of the cyclas its edges were decorated with fringes of silk or gold, and by the year 1254 (in place of fringe) the edges were *cut out* in all kinds of fancy patterns, such as are described in the paragraph relating to heraldic Dividing and Border Lines (*see* p. 299 and Fig. 431), a fashion instigated by the general use of heraldry. To treat the edge of a garment in this fanciful manner was called QUINTISE, from the French, *quinte* = fancy, and *quinteuse* = fanciful, freakish.

The name Quintise, or its equivalent, COIN-TISE, came to be applied to a garment when cut and ornamented in this quaint way; and, as such garments were generally worn on festive occasions and on holy days, holiday clothes were commonly called "cointises." The first mention of this term is made in a description by Matthew Paris of the visit of Henry III. and his queen to France, in 1254; the student-clerks [1] of Paris, especially those of English birth, put on these "holiday clothes (commonly called cointises)" to meet the English royalties.

Fig. 200 shows the first cyclas decorated in a fanciful manner, and for this reason properly called a cointise. The shape is shown in Fig. 115, but it has no slits in the skirt, and is seamed up the sides, leaving large armholes. The novelty is in the bottom edge, which is cut in four points, and in the opening at the neck, fastened on the slant by buttons. This cointise is made of the fashionable "raye" material, in groups of different-coloured horizontal stripes.

Fig. 201 shows the very rich dress of a nobleman about the middle of the thirteenth century. He wears a loose robe to the feet —the peliçon—with pocket slits, and tight sleeves buttoned to the wrists. These peliçons were cut to hang, as shown, with a curious long fold down the centre front

Fig. 201. The Peliçon

of the garment. The pocket slits are a new detail. When the peliçon hung loose from the figure, without a belt, these slits were useful to admit the hand to the pouch attached to the belt underneath. The

[1] University undergrads.

mantle is worn in the ordinary way, being lined with thick fur—vair—
and on the shoulders a narrow cape of the same is worn.

It was a common practice to attach that very useful article, the gypsire, pocket, or purse, to the waist-belt. Purses were made of all kinds
of material (Figs. 202 and 203), including cuir-bouilli—leather boiled in
oil, and stamped or tooled with designs.

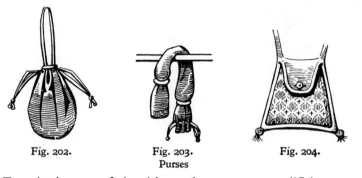

Fig. 202.   Fig. 203.   Fig. 204.
                    Purses

A French chanson of the thirteenth century says: "I have store of
stamped purses, red and green, white and black, that I sell readily at
fairs" (Fig. 204).

Fig. 205 shows a surcote, another development of the cyclas. The
sleeves are cylindrical, and are attached to the armhole on the upper
half only of its circumference. The arm could be
passed through the sleeve (as shown in the left) or
through the armhole. The garment is sufficiently
loose-fitting to be drawn on over the head, and the
skirt is slit in four places. It is lined throughout with
fur, and for this reason might be called a peliçon.
A hood, thrown back on the shoulders, is worn.
The entire costume of this young noble is very
simple, though made of rich material, and typifies
the fashion of the middle of the thirteenth century.
The hair is cut close to the head, and not in the
prevailing mode.

Fig. 206 is from an illuminated MS. dated 1250,
and represents a nobleman in everyday attire. The
tunic of claret colour has moderately close sleeves,
buttoned from elbow to wrist. It is girded at the
waist by a short belt with no end hanging, and is slit
up the front. On top of the ample cloke of scarlet is
a deep collar or narrow cape of vair.

Fig. 205. The Surcote

The hat has a round crown of deep-red velvet, with an upstanding
brim of fur, and it is worn over a linen coif. The boots, with folding
caps, are brown leather, rather pointed in the toe.

The manner in which a tunic or cotte was worn, and the hang of its folds, is shown clearly in Fig. 207, a drawing made by Matthew Paris. Notice particularly the position of the folds drooping over the waist-belt. This drawing also shows the type of cotte worn during the thirteenth century.

Fig. 206. Noble, Everyday Dress

The mantle as worn by men. The new method of arranging the mantle, which came into vogue in the last reign, continued in use during the thirteenth century. Illuminated MSS. and sculptures of this date show many alternative arrangements. The figures in this section also illustrate the various modes. When the mantle was a semicircle of small dimensions, it was worn as a shawl, equally on both shoulders, and gracefully draped over both arms. Another favourite arrangement was to drape the right shoulder and arm with one side of the mantle, bringing it across the back *under* the left arm and holding it in front with the right hand.

Noblemen and noble ladies of this period, through constant use, acquired great skill in throwing the mantle around the figure, and clasping portions of it with one hand, to form very graceful lines and becoming draperies. Numerous statues of thirteenth-century kings, queens and nobles demonstrate the mantle worn with taste, ease and variety, and prove how thoroughly the cultured, well-dressed class understood this knack.

A favourite posture of the hand, adopted by both men and women, is shown in many works of art, illuminated MSS. and statuary of the thirteenth century: the hand is placed upon the breast, with the first finger hooking the strap which attaches the mantle.

Fig. 207

Nobility—Women

The effigies of Berengaria of Navarre at Espan, and of Isabella of Angoulême at Fontevraud, are excellent examples of the costume worn by royal and noble ladies of the first half of this century.

Queen Berengaria (Fig. 208) wears a long gown fastened at the throat

with a beautiful agrafe, with sleeves loose at the armhole and fitting
tight on the forearm, an effect produced either by lacing or buttoning
from the elbow to the wrist. These sleeves are
shaped with one seam down the back, the material
being cut on the cross. A detail to be noticed in
these sleeves is the fold which starts inside the
elbow, and loses itself on the shoulder; this fold
is very pronounced in statuary. The gown is
confined at waist-level by a narrow girdle
(Fig. 209) of leather, having metal ornaments
placed along the whole length; it is fastened with
a buckle or clasp, the long end of the girdle
falling in front to below the knee, and finishing
with a metal ornament. From the girdle hangs
the ALMONER or aulmoniere, a pocket or purse
made of silk or leather, and strung upon a long
cord looped to the girdle. It is so named because
it was used as a receptacle for money intended
for alms. It was the custom at this time, and
earlier, for noblemen and noble ladies to distribute
money or food, particularly bread, to the poor.

Fig. 208.
Berengaria of Navarre

The title "lady" is derived from the Anglo-Saxon *hlæfdige*, meaning
"she who looks after the loaf," or breadgiver. The masculine, *hláf-ord*,
from *hláf* = a loaf, is the origin of "lord."

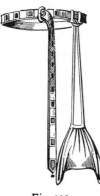

Fig. 209.
Girdle and Almoner.
Thirteenth century

Fig. 208 wears a mantle, but it is thrown right off
the shoulders and attached across the chest by a band
of material. The veil is surmounted by an elaborate
crown.

Isabella of Angoulême was only thirty-four when
left a widow on the death of King John. She was
still a very beautiful woman, regarded by her contemporaries as the "Helen" of the age. She retired to
Angoulême to prepare for the marriage of her daughter,
the Princess Johanna, to the man from whom Isabella
had been stolen fifteen years before—the Count de
la Marche, Lord of Lusignan. Seventeen years of
splendid misery as Queen of England had given her
cause to regret the lover of whom she had been
defrauded in her youth. Circumstances having brought
her once more into the company of the man she had loved, she found
it beyond endurance to allow him to marry any other woman, even
her own child. In 1220, Isabella astonished Europe by marrying him
herself. As an historian [1] remarks: "She completed in her thirty-fifth
year the plight she had broken in her fifteenth."

[1] Agnes Strickland.

In 1242, the Count de la Marche became involved in a plot to assassinate the King of France, and the matter became so serious that it preyed on Isabella's mind and brought on an illness from which she never recovered. She died in 1246.

She had expressed the desire, by way of expiation of her sins, to be buried in obscure simplicity, and was actually interred in the common cemetery at Fontevraud. Several years later, in 1254, her humble grave was shown to her son, Henry III., who was shocked and grieved to find his illustrious mother uncommemorated. He raised for her a stately tomb, with a full-length enamelled effigy, in the choir at Fontevraud, close to those of Henry II. and Eleanor of Aquitaine, her mother-in-law.

Fig. 210.
Noble Lady, *temp.* Henry III.

The effigy of Queen Isabella shows her clad in a gown very much like that of Queen Berengaria, except that the dress of the latter is devoid of any ornamentation, whereas Isabella's is edged with a passement at the wrists, neck, and on the mantle, and the gown is open at the neck, showing the camise. The chin-strap and veil are worn, surmounted by a simpler crown.

Fig. 210 shows the costume of a noble lady wearing a gown exactly like that last described, but the girdle is worn in a slightly different manner.

The girdle. A feature about the waist-girdle which should be noticed, small, yet important, is the variety of ways of wearing it. During the reigns of Henry II., Richard I. and John, the girdle was worn at the waist-line, with the fullness of material of the upper part of the gown bulging over it. During the first half of the thirteenth century, the girdle remained in the same position, but there was no bulge of the gown over it.

After 1250 the girdle sloped downwards, to a point in front, from the top of the hip-bone. There was no bulge of material with the girdle worn in this way, since the gown was held down tight in small pleats by the girdle.

The corse. From a study of the line of women's figures at this time, it is evident that under the gown a corse was worn, which constrained the sides, raised the bosom, and kept the waist small and round. On the Continent this habit was prevalent, and influenced the vogue in Southern England.

At the marriage of Henry and Eleanor's daughter, the Princess Margaret, aged ten, to Alexander III., King of Scotland, aged twelve, the queen and the ladies of her Court appeared in a new fashion, imported from the Continent—the Cyclas. This was the origin of a type of dress worn, with alterations, by noble ladies until the end of the fifteenth century. Its developments during the course of these two centuries will be noted in their proper sequence.

The clothes worn at this "Society" wedding of the year 1251 received almost as much attention from the "Press" as a similar gruesome ceremony does to-day. We are told by Matthew Paris that "because the multitudes of people rushed and pressed together in an unruly manner, in order to be present and behold the grandeur of such a marriage, the ceremony was performed early in the morning, secretly, and before it was expected. There were assembled there so many people of different kinds, such numerous crowds of English, French and Scotch nobles, such hosts of knights dressed in elegant clothing, and glorying in their silk and variegated ornaments, that the worldly and wanton vanity of the scene, if it were to be described in full, would produce wonder and weariness in those who heard it,[1] for a thousand knights and more, clad in vestments of silk, commonly called *cointises*, appeared at the nuptials on the part of the King of England. On the part of the King of Scotland sixty knights and more were dressed in a becoming manner."

The new fashion in which Eleanor and her ladies appeared was, in its first stages, an over-robe without sleeves—the cyclas—shaped like that of the men (*see* Fig. 115). To the cyclas of the women was added a train, especially when worn by noble ladies for full State dress. The queen wore hers "so long in front as well as behind as to trail upon the ground, and was held up with one hand lest her steps should be impeded" (*see* Fig. 211). The "fashion papers" of the day advise, " . . . if the ladies' feet and ankles be not small and delicate, to let their robes fall on the pavement to hide them; but those whose feet are beautiful may hold up the robe in front, under pretence of stepping out briskly." Those tiresome newspaper reporters were anything but complimentary, and compared the fashionable women to "peacocks and pies (pied, or piebald, like a magpie) which delight in feathers of various colours: so do our Court ladies. The pies have long tails that train in the dirt, but the ladies make their tails a thousand times longer than the peacocks' and the pies'."

Fig. 211 shows Queen Eleanor's cyclas, made of some very rich material—a brocade of some brilliant-coloured silk, woven in gold in a pattern of small circles enclosing animals. The pattern is shown in greater detail in the background. The cyclas is lined with silk of a

---

[1] Except, it is hoped, the readers of this book, who doubtless regret that further details are withheld.

Fig. 211. THE BRIDE'S MOTHER

contrasting colour, and edged all round with bullion fringe. Underneath is worn the gown described under Fig. 208 or Fig. 210.

The hairdressing is referred to on p. 178.

Shortly after this time (1251), the cyclas was joined up part of the sides, leaving an opening for the arms, and a short slit from about the knee to the hem. At a still later stage, the cyclas was cut to fit close at the neck, shoulders, armholes and waist, still retaining the seam at the sides, which might or might not reach the hem. The back of the skirt was gored into the waist, to give it the necessary fullness. It was the vogue to bring this back part round to the front and carry it on the arm, close to the side, giving many beautiful folds of drapery (*see* Fig. 212).

Fig. 212.
Gored Cyclas

The mantle of the women. A distinct feature of the costume of noble ladies of the thirteenth century is the long mantle, which came into fashion about the time Henry III. ascended the throne. This new type of mantle, which trailed upon the ground behind, was cut on an oval plan, as shown in Fig. 213. In its construction the width of the material is shown by dotted lines, which indicate the seams. As previously pointed out, when a patterned material with an upright design is used, it is essential to have also a centre seam, and the sides reversed. Alternatively, to reduce the size of the mantle at the *sides* it was sometimes cut on a straight line as shown in the diagram at A B.

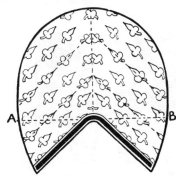

Fig. 213. Diagram of the Mantle

Both men and women of this period attached great importance to the mantle, and the variety of ways in which it was worn show that to drape it gracefully was a study in itself. In this art they bear favourable comparison with the ladies of Classic Greece. It required great skill to adjust an ungainly piece of material, like one of these large fashionable mantles, which tended to hang in ugly voluminous folds, and to dwarf the figure; but illuminated MSS. and statuary show that the wearers were decidedly adept.

The figures in this section illustrate a few ways of carrying the mantle.

When worn by the wealthy these mantles were made of very rich materials, especially that new fabric—velvet. They were lined with silk, a material well adapted for draping; but for warmth, fur lining was used by noble ladies.

The custom that married women *only* should wear the mantle was usually observed, but young girls of the nobility wore it on occasion. This fact is mentioned by many troubadours.

Fig. 214 represents a noble lady in everyday attire. It shows also the type of dress worn by a gentlewoman or rich citizen's wife. The gown or robe is cut like those shown in the previous illustrations, and in the diagram, Fig. 101. The long opening up the front is here turned back to form small revers. This opening could be closed, if required, by fastening it with one or two buttons, or by lacing up the front. The camise, fastened at the throat by a brooch, is seen at the neck. The long girdle, buckled at the waist, has the almoner looped to it by a long cord.

This figure shows another method of wearing the semi-oval mantle, slung loosely over the shoulders and draped over the arms.

The ornament or pendant hanging from the connecting cord is a modish fancy peculiar to this time. The coif and chin-strap complete a very characteristic costume of Henry III.'s reign.

Fig. 214. Noble Lady, Everyday Dress

The camise still remained a very important item of underwear, though it was often unseen. This garment was not always worn next to the skin. Wardrobe accounts throw much light on intimate garments, and from them we learn that ladies of rank and fashion wore "under-garments made of prepared sheepskin."

There are illuminations in MSS. of this period showing ladies mounted on horseback, wearing garments well adapted for the purpose, Fig. 215. Over the gown, with close sleeves and ample skirt, they wore the gardcorp of the men, shown in Fig. 198 and diagram, Fig. 197. A hood, separate or attached, was used with it.

Fig. 215. Riding Dress

As head-covering the chin-strap and coif were suitable for fine weather, but on wet or stormy days, or when in haste, the wimple and small couvrechef were worn under the hood.

The Count de la Marche was implicated in a plot against Louis IX., in the year 1242. At his trial the proceedings were going against him, and word to this effect was brought to his wife, the Queen-Dowager of England, Isabella. In her anxiety for his safety she hurriedly mounted a horse, and, attended by all her retainers, armed to the teeth, galloped to the court of inquiry. On arrival, she found matters so incriminating that she snatched the wimple and veil from her head, in a towering rage, tore them to pieces, and trampled the fragments underfoot.

Ladies of this period rode either side-saddle or astride, much as they do to-day. The horse furniture, and the whip of the period, should be noticed.

XIIIth

Fig. 216. Border

Section II.—Edward I. 1272–1307

Nobility—Men

Edward was born at Westminster, 1239. "Of handsome appearance," he was unusually tall owing to the great length of his legs, hence his name, "Longshanks." He was taller, stronger, bigger than most men, and very deep-chested. Extremely good-looking, but of a stern expression, his only blemish being the falling eyelid which he inherited from his father, his features were masculine, and his forehead broad; his hair was flaxen in youth, dark brown in manhood, and silver-white in old age. For portrait, see Plate VI. c.

Edward was a good and ready speaker, in spite of a slight stammer, and he has been described as brave as a lion, an excellent legislator, thoroughly skilled in the art of war, for which he had too great a predilection, and too fond of arbitrary power. He was knighted by Alphonso, King of Castile, at Burgos, in 1254, and at the same time he was married to the king's half-sister, Eleanor, daughter of Ferdinand III., King of Castile.

In 1270, Prince Edward, who was accompanied by his wife, undertook with Louis IX. of France, Prince Philippe, and the Kings of Navarre and Arragon, the Eighth and *last* Crusade. The King of France,

Fig. 217. King from Byzantine MS.

however, "passed from a temporal kingdom to an eternal one" before he reached the Holy Land, dying from dysentery at Tunis the same year.

The capture of Acre took place in May 1271; and, in the following August, an attempt upon the life of Prince Edward was made with a poisoned dagger by the Emir of Joppa's messenger. The prince, at the time reclining upon a couch in his pavilion, sprang up and wrested the dagger from the assassin's hand, seized the tripod which supported the table, and brained the ruffian on the spot; but not before the dagger had inflicted a wound which would have proved fatal had not a surgical operation been effectual. The tradition that Eleanor sucked the poison from the wound is a fabrication of later chroniclers, for she had to be carried from the tent by her brother-in-law, Edmund Crouchback, in a fit of hysterics.

"It is better, lady, that you should weep than all England should have cause to mourn," Crouchback calmly remarked. Edward's speedy recovery, however, was certainly due to the tender nursing of Eleanor.

Nine years after the death of his first wife, Edward I. married at Canterbury Cathedral the Princess Margaret, daughter of Philippe III. le Hardi.

There is no monument of this king at Westminster, although he was buried there. In 1774, when his tomb was opened, the body was found to be robed with regal magnificence in a dalmatic of red damask, with a mantle of crimson samit fastened on one shoulder by a jewelled gold brooch. Across the breast lay a stole of white and gold baudekyn, decorated with gold quatrefoils and roses of pearls, and on the hands were jewelled gloves. An almost unique point about this costume is the stole, which would appear to be the same article as the Byzantine lorum (see Vol. I., p. 163). There is in existence in England an illuminated MS. of this period, probably of Byzantine workmanship, showing royal personages wearing what is undoubtedly such a lorum.

Fig. 218. Edward I.

Fig. 217 is reconstructed from one of the miniatures. This king is wearing a tunic with the dalmatic over it. Above the latter is placed the lorum. The only possible way it could be put on is explained in Vol. I., p. 163, and shown in Fig. 70. The end, G, instead of being carried over the left forearm, must be attached in some manner at the back. The lorum in the original MS. and in Fig. 217 is heavily embroidered with a pattern in gold, upon a silk foundation of a rich colour. The mantle, slung from the shoulders, is of velvet lined with fur. The crown is not of the usual design worn by English or French kings at this time, but of Byzantine make, which points very clearly to the origin of the MS.

On the great seal of his reign Edward I. is depicted in a dalmatic and supertunic, with the mantle fastened upon the right shoulder.

Despite the splendour of his burial habiliments, Edward I. is shown in a statue at Lincoln Cathedral (Plate VI. c), together with Queen Eleanor, wearing a very simple form of State dress, similar to that illustrated in Fig. 196. It is said that he never wore his crown after his coronation, thinking it a burden, and he went about in the plain garments of a citizen, except on feast days.

Fig. 219. Belt End

Fig. 220.
Noble, *temp.* Edward I.

He declared that it was impossible to add to or diminish real worth by outward apparel.

"What could I do more in royal robes, Father, than in this plain gardcorp?" he once said to a bishop who remonstrated with him on his attire as being unkingly.

The other panel portrait in the Sedilia at Westminster Abbey, erected between 1300 and 1307, represents a king in State dress (Fig. 218): there is every reason for believing it to be Edward I. The tunic of rose-coloured silk, reaching to the feet, has close sleeves, and the opening up the front is edged with a narrow gold trimming like a braid. The tunic is girded with a long black belt, having gold embossed lozenges between small bars of gold (Fig. 219). The mantle, fastened on the right shoulder by a brooch, is semicircular in shape (Fig. 12), of heliotrope velvet lined with vair. It is edged with an embroidered band of simple design, in orange, white and gold. The crown and sceptre are of very delicate goldsmith's work. The gloves are described on p. 90.

Fig. 221.
Livery

Fig. 220 represents a nobleman wearing an ample tunic or robe fastened down the front with buttons, and reaching to the ankles. It has wide sleeves, and an opening is placed at the sides to admit the hand. This robe, of very unpretentious shape, would be made of very rich material, and lined with some equally expensive fabric of a different colour. Underneath the robe a shorter tunic was worn, with tight sleeves which may be noticed on the forearm. The hose, or chausses, are seen at the ankle and were of the best quality. On his head he wears the hood of some brilliant contrasting colour (*see also* p. 177).

Fig. 221 wears a costume similar to Fig. 220. It is parti-coloured in red and white. The drawing represents an important member of the Guild of Saddlers, who took part in the wedding procession of Edward I. and Margaret of France in 1299 (*see also* p. 189).

Fig. 222 shows a young noble wearing a garment similar to Fig. 220. It might be called a robe, surcote, or peliçon, preferably the last, as it is lined throughout with fur. Details for notice are the upstanding band or collar, low on the neck, and its opening buttoned on the chest. Also the slit up the front. The under-tunic shows at the ankles, neck and wrists. He carries gloves in one hand, and a hood in the other.

A surcote (French, " GANACHE ") shown in Fig. 223 is also lined with fur, and is a garment usually worn over a robe or tunic for extra warmth. It has a hood attached to it, and the surcote is cut with wide shoulder-pieces, which form a cape-like sleeve. There is no slit either at the sides or up the front; the garment, being ample, was easily put on over the head. Frequently the seams at the sides were left open —and the garment formed a kind of scapular (Figs. 224 and 225).

With these surcotes capacious mantles made of cloth, silk or velvet, lined with silk or fur, were worn for comfort or full dress. In length they were just off the ground.

Fig. 222
Noble, *temp.* Edward I.

Nobility—Women

Eleanor of Castile died, in 1290, at the house of a gentleman named Weston, at Hardeley, near Grantham, while on her journey to join her husband in Scotland. As soon as the king heard the news of her illness he hastened to Hardeley, but arrived too late. From thence he conveyed her body to London, taking thirteen days to accomplish the journey. At each place where the funeral cortège rested for the night, a cross was afterwards set up by Edward I. The queen was buried in Westminster Abbey, and a monument erected to her memory.

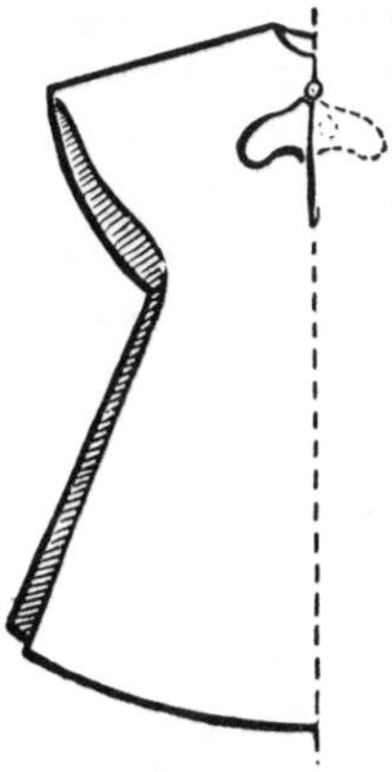

Fig. 223.
Ganache

Fig. 224.
Surcote

Fig. 225.
Diagram of Surcote

CHILDREN OF EDWARD I. AND ELEANOR

1. Edward, first Prince of Wales, born at Carnarvon, 1284.
2. Eleanor, married, first, Alphonso, King of Arragon; secondly, Henri, Count de Bar.
3. Joan, married, first, Gilbert de Clare, Earl of Gloucester and Hereford; secondly, Ralph de Monthermer, Earl of Gloucester and Herts.
4. Margaret, married John, Duke of Brabant.
5. Mary, a nun.
6. Elizabeth, married, first, John, Earl of Holland and Zealand; secondly, Humphrey de Bohun, Earl of Hereford and Essex. The third son of this marriage was William, Earl of Northampton, whose son, Humphrey, was father of Mary de Bohun, who married Henry, afterwards King Henry IV.

Eleanor of Provence, the queen-dowager, resided during her widowhood at her various dower houses at Waltham, Guildford, Ludgershall, etc. Being uncertain whether she would be allowed to retain her rich dower if she took the veil, she postponed that event. However, the *Court Circular* for 1284 announces:

"The generous virago, Eleanor, Queen of England, mother of the King, took the veil and religious habit at Amesbury, on the day of the translation of S. Thomas, Archbishop of Canter-

Fig. 226.
Eleanor of Castile

bury, having obtained leave of the Pope to keep possession of her dower in perpetuity, according to her wish."

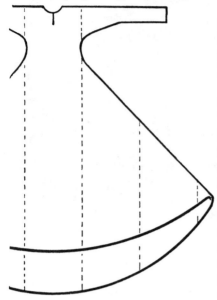

The queen died at Amesbury in 1291, and was buried there, but her heart was interred in the Church of the Friars Minor (The Minories).

The costume of Eleanor of Castile, as shown on her effigy at Westminster, is very simple (Fig. 226). The gown is ungirded and hangs loose; being cut very much on the circle it falls in many folds around the feet (Fig. 227). The sleeves are moderately wide and show those of the under-dress at the wrist. Over the gown is worn a mantle, attached by a strap across the shoulders. The whole costume is without any decoration whatsoever. A crown is worn, and her hair is flowing over the shoulders. This

Fig. 227. Diagram of Gown

style seems exceptional, considering the queen was a woman of about forty-five.

The general style of costume worn by noble ladies of this reign is also very simple, and is shown in Fig. 228. An under-robe, with tight sleeves buttoned from elbow to wrist, is worn. Over this is a gown, with the neck cut moderately low to show a considerable amount of the wimple. The sleeves are wide and finish just below the elbow. The skirt of the gown is very ample and forms a train which is invariably carried over the arm to show a good deal of the underdress.

The decoration of the gown would be a simple though rich border of colour or gold. When a mantle was worn, this too would have some embroidery or passement to edge it, and be lined with silk or fur. The headdress is the same as shown in Fig. 263. In place of the circlet, a coronet would be worn on State occasions.

Fig. 228
Noble Lady, *temp.* Edward I.

Fig. 229 represents a fashionable woman of this reign. Her gown, undecorated, trails upon the ground behind, and is held in one hand, ostensibly to keep it out of the way of her feet, but in reality to show the underdress, which is made of very fine material. The sleeves finish at the elbow with a decided point. A GORGET is worn over the RAMSHORN hairdressing (Fig. 255).

The marriage of Edward I., in 1299, to a French princess, Margaret, daughter of Philippe III. le Hardi, somewhat stimulated French fashions, but no particular style was set by this lady, who, as queen - consort, reigned barely seven years. Her statue at Lincoln Cathedral (Plate VI. A and B) shows her wearing a gown exactly like that of Queen Eleanor (Fig. 226), with a mantle fastened by a strap. Her headdress is described on p. 180 and illustrated in Plate VI. A.

Fig. 229.
Noble Lady, *temp.* Edward I.

CHILDREN OF EDWARD I. AND MARGARET

7. Thomas of Brotherton, born 1301, Earl of Norfolk, First Earl Marshal. Married Alice (daughter of Sir Roger Halys, Knight), whose daughter, Margaret, was created Duchess of Norfolk. The duchess married, first, John Lord Segrave, and, secondly, Sir Walter Manny.

8. Edmund of Woodstock, born 1301, Earl of Kent; married Margaret, daughter of Lord Wake, and had two sons, d.s.p., and a daughter, Joan, the Fair Maid of Kent, who married, first, the Earl of Salisbury, secondly, Lord Holland, and thirdly, Edward the Black Prince.

Fig. 230.   Border

SECTION III.—MIDDLE AND LOWER CLASSES

Temp. Henry III. and Edward I.

Men. Simplicity was the keynote of dress with the middle classes of these two reigns, as well as with the nobility.

A man of professional standing is shown in Fig. 231. He wears the gardcorp with hood attached, over a tunic to ankle length having close sleeves and a narrow stand-up collar. A description of his cap and shoes will be found under their separate headings.

Fig. 231. Physician   Fig. 232. Scholar

A scholar is represented in Fig. 232. His surcote is very simple in cut, fitting loosely rather like a cloke, but it fastens with buttons from neck to waist. Two perpendicular slits allow the arms to pass through

Fig. 233. Merchant   Fig. 234. John Mercer, Architect

if required, but it was quite usual to keep the arms inside. The hood is separate from the surcote, though it might be attached to it. A cotte and hose are worn under the surcote. This garment, made of dark

rough cloth, was much used by professional men. With the addition
of a hat, worn over a coif, and a cloke, the drawing might represent a
medical man.

In Fig. 233 we have a merchant
dressed in the almost universally-worn
gardcorp. This garment, worn at its
longest by the nobility, shrank, by carefully graduated degrees, in accordance
with the social status of the wearer. With
the middle class the material was usually
a cloth or a good stout linen, sometimes
edged with fur. A considerable portion of
the under-garment of dark cloth shows
beneath the gardcorp. The cap is basin-
shaped, with a brim.

Fig. 234 represents a man of some
importance, who wears a cotte shaped
like 207, but it reaches only to the knees,
and is made of heavier stuff, producing
more pronounced folds. The cloke is a
semicircle, fastened across the shoulders

Fig. 235. Troubadour

by a double cord or strap of the same material, knotted at one side.
His hose and shoes are of the usual make, but his headgear, described
hereafter, is somewhat curious.

Fig. 236. Villein

Fig. 235 shows a troubadour (*see* p. 126) of the
thirteenth century. He wears the cotte surmounted
by the cyclas, called in this case a "cointise"
because of its fancy edging. A very distinguished
troubadour would have his clothes made of rich
material, especially some of that very popular
cloth or silk called "raye." The coif and hood, with
a cloke, complete the costume. This troubadour
is accompanying himself on a harp, although the
psalterion or vielle could be used in its place. The
"Harp of Gold" is taken from a "Horæ" dated 1300.

The commonalty dressed much as they had
done before, yet there is a distinction between
the peasants of this era and those of the middle of
the twelfth century. The peasant class was becoming a little more subdivided: the well-to-do
peasants, who were the serfs of the wealthy
farmers, and cottars who acted as henchmen to
the upper classes, were distinct from the lower-
class peasants who worked in the fields, the farm labourers, and these in
their turn were vastly superior to the vagabond and tramp.

The costume of all these varied, of course, according to the means of the wearer; but, generally speaking, the garments consisted of plain

Fig. 237. From a "Medica"

Fig. 238. Farm Labourer

cottes, hoods, hoods and clokes combined, braies or even bracco, strong boots of cloth, leather or felt, and possibly hats.

There is a French influence in the costume of a man of the people —a "villein"—shown in Fig. 236. He is dressed in a cotte with tight

Figs. 239   240   241   242   243
Peasantry

sleeves, open up the front and fastening at the throat. Above this he has a kind of overall of coarse linen, cut with wide armholes, also open up the front; and both are confined at the waist by a leather belt. To this belt would be attached a gypiere containing various articles of necessity, and a knife in a sheath passed through the flap of the pouch. A full cape of coarse cloth or soft felt, with a hood, is worn, and on his head is the usual white coif. He would be thought quite reasonable if he added a hat. His legs are covered with soft leather or felt braies, made to include the foot part.

The man with a pain in his stomach (Fig. 237) might be assumed to be one of the earliest cases of appendicitis. The drawing is taken direct from a "Medica" of the thirteenth century. His garments are a shirt, a loose cotte open up the front and back, and a pair of

Fig. 244. Diagram of Cotte

drawers tied at the knees. These garments were often worn by the lower orders, especially by working men. They are also seen on Fig. 238, a farm labourer who has put on over his shirt a scapular. The legs of both these men are bare, and one has drawn boots of thick felt over his feet, which could be slipped into Clogs (see Fig. 269).

The small boy of the lower orders (Fig. 239) is simply clothed in a cotte and braies of rough material, and shoes of black leather or felt. He

wears a coif, and round his neck is hung a small box containing some charm. The young man holding him (Fig. 240) is a henchman or servitor, and wears a cotte with sleeves, cut wide at the armhole like Fig. 244, and over it a short sur-cote open up the sides to the shoulder. The hood worn over the coif has the shoulder part covered by the surcote, and his braies are in one piece with the foot part.

Fig. 245.   Fig. 246.
Middle-Class Women

Fig. 241 is a peasant, and has a cotte girded by a leather belt, and over it a hood with loose cape. A gypiere is slung over his shoulders. On his legs he has cloth braies which finish at the ankles, leaving the feet bare. These are slipped into black cloth shoes so that the shoes may be easily removed, if necessary, for working. The tool he carries is worthy of notice.

Men of the shepherd type (Fig. 243) often wore the bracco and old-fashioned paenula. To this a hat (*see* Headgear) was added.

Temp. Henry III. and Edward I.

Women. Fig. 245 is a young woman habited in a simple gown which hangs in beautiful folds about her figure. It is cut all in one, on the general plan shown in Fig. 227, and *draped* into the waist-belt. The skirt is long, forming folds over the feet and a train behind.

Another young woman is represented in Fig. 246 wearing a gown exactly like the one just described, but over it is placed a small mantle or cloke, cut as a semicircle. It has a little strap of the same material—

Fig. 247. Two Drawings by Matthew Paris

cloth, serge or russet—and this is buttoned across the chest, and the cloke draped over both arms. The hang of these gowns is well defined in the accompanying contemporary drawings (Fig. 247) of the two daughters of King Lear by Matthew Paris, from which Figs. 245 and 246 are constructed.

The mantle. Although the mantle still belonged theoretically to the nobility, it did not prevent the middle-class wealthy married women from wearing it as well, particularly in France, where a notable extension of this encroachment once led to an unpleasant and embarrassing situation. It is related that on one occasion the Queen of France gave the "kiss of peace," as was the custom, in church, to a woman of evil life, because she was *wearing a mantle*, and was therefore presumably a married woman. The queen complained to the king of the awkward predicament in which she had been placed, and in consequence an Act was passed forbidding women of that persuasion to wear mantles. Like many other sumptuary laws, this enactment was observed only for a time.

A country woman of this period shown in Fig. 248 is garbed in a long loose gown of coarse homespun, with or without a girdle made of leather or a simple cord. The usual habit of holding up the dress displays the undergown of "blanchet." On her head she has twisted and tied an oblong veil or headcloth of coarse linen. It forms a head-covering and wimple combined, an economical idea adopted by women of the humble class. Her boots are of untanned leather, and are buttoned up the front. She carries a distaff and spindle, a domestic article indispensable among the thrifty lower orders.

Fig. 248.
A Country Woman

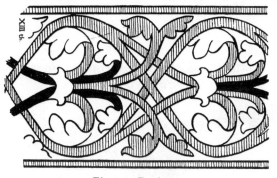

Fig. 249. Border

SECTION IV.—HAIRDRESSING, 1216–1307

Men. At the beginning of the thirteenth century, nobles, gentry, and rich citizens wore their hair cut to a short fringe on the forehead, a return to the style first seen in Fig. 65, and allowed the rest to fall at the sides, showing the lobe only of the ears, to about chin-level at the sides and back, where it was brushed into ringlets. Those at the sides of the face were curled, inwards and then outwards, leaving a background of shadow for the ears (Fig. 250).

Later, about 1225, a distinct fashion was adopted which is the recognised characteristic style of the thirteenth century; first by the nobles, then by the fashionable middle classes, and even by the peasants. The hair was parted *across* the top of the head, just above the brow

(Fig. 251). The treatment of the sides and back was identical with the style just described, but the loose ends left on the forehead—the fringe —were rolled to form one long curl across the top of the forehead.

Fig. 250.

Hairdressing

Fig. 251.

A great number of the nobility and gentry adopted the French fashion of being clean-shaven, although curled beards were worn by many on the upper lip and chin, the ends of the latter being well curled, either inwards or outwards (Fig. 250).

HEADGEAR

A very important and characteristic piece of headgear was worn throughout the thirteenth century. It was the Coif, a cap of cloth, silk, cotton, or linen, fitting close to the head and tied under the chin, enclosing the hair except in front on the forehead and at the nape of the neck (Fig. 252).

In illuminated MSS. all pictures of this headdress show it as being *white*. It was worn by all classes of the community throughout Europe during the thirteenth century, by noblemen, rich citizens, tradesmen, artisans, priests, soldiers and peasants, the only difference being the material of which it was made.

Fig. 252. The Coif

It was a head-covering worn indoors as well as out; probably put on in the morning and worn throughout the day as a fashionable headdress, as it is often seen under a hat or hood. Perhaps it was retained even during the night, to keep the hair in curl, and it is perchance the ancestor of the nightcap, which it very much resembles (*see also* description of Fig. 199).

In 1267, the clergy were forbidden to wear this coif, except when travelling, as it concealed the tonsure, and provided a disguise by which some of them were accused of abusing their calling.

At a later date it was also a distinctive feature of the headdress of doctors of medicine, doctors and officers of the law, and ecclesiastical dignitaries, who wore it during the Mediæval Period, the sixteenth and the seventeenth centuries.

The hood. At the time of Edward I.'s accession the hood underwent a strange development. The head and shoulder parts did not alter in shape, but the point at the top corner began to grow—longer and longer—into a tube called the LIRIPIPE. During this reign it was of moderate length—some three feet or so (*see* Figs. 220 and 222).

A cap, similar in shape to the one described on p. 118, is seen in Fig. 206, representing a noble of about 1250.

Fig. 167 shows a cap taken from a fresco dating a few years later (1262, Painted Chamber). The crown is of crimson velvet, and finishes in a knob on top; in the original painting the upstanding brim is gold, but it was more general to make the brim of ermine. (*Continued on p. 267.*)

A cap with a crown very much like Fig. 167 is worn by the noble in Fig. 194, but the upstanding brim is open in front and curves down on to the forehead. The crowns of these caps were of one colour, and the brims either of another contrasting shade or of fur.

Middle classes, 1216–1307. The man in Fig. 231 is wearing the usual type of cap or hat, with a point at the top. It is made in felt or stiff cloth, and all in one piece. The edge is turned up, forming a brim.

Fig. 234 wears a basin-shaped cap, with bordered edge, and a curious curly point.

A hat or skull-cap made of cloth or felt was much worn during the thirteenth century, especially by children and young men. It was often in very bright colours (*see* Fig. 223).

The hat with roll brim worn over the coif by the man in Fig. 242 is of thick felt, used chiefly by peasants.

HAIRDRESSING

Women. The manner of dressing the hair varied but little, if at all, from that of the latter half of the twelfth century. During the first half of the thirteenth century, the hair was parted in the centre, and divided into two plaits, crossed at the back of the neck and brought round the sides of the head, as before, but now the underlying hair is curled more definitely on the forehead.

A variation of this style, in vogue during the second half of the thirteenth century, was to part the hair *across* the centre of the head,

the back portion being dressed as before described, but the front waved and curled forward on to the forehead (Fig. 253). At the same time another treatment of hairdressing was in fashion. The centre parting was still retained, but the front and side portions of the hair were entwined with coloured *ribbon*, always referred to in these times as a LACE, or gold braid. The rest of the hair was waved, and fastened by an ornament, brooch or slide, low down at the back of the head. As another alternative, the bound tresses from either side were brought round and incorporated with the remainder into one long tail, either loose, or plaited into a pigtail which hung down the back (Fig. 254).

Fig. 253.
Hairdressing, second half thirteenth century

About the end of the thirteenth century, the plaits of hair, which encircled the head, became very large, either by the co-operation of Nature or by artifice. The circlet or fillet being bound tight to the head, the hair on top of it retained its natural shape, but the plaits, whether encased in the CRISPINE or not, formed a large circular pad all round the head (Figs. 258 and 259).

It was not unusual for young married women, as well as girls, to wear their hair flowing over the shoulders and down the back, with the sides waved over the temples and ears (*see* Fig. 118).

Wreaths of fresh flowers were worn upon the head by young girls of all classes from the earliest times. Eleanor of Provence introduced the fashion of wearing chaplets of imitation flowers,

Fig. 254.
Hairdressing, second half thirteenth century

made of gold and silver, and often set with clusters of different-coloured jewels, to represent flowers. These chaplets were very popular with ladies of high rank.

At the end of the thirteenth century a form of hairdressing known as the "Ramshorn" came into fashion. The hair was parted in the middle, and the two portions plaited into tails, which were brought round and twisted over the ears into a scroll like rams' horns (Fig. 255). Particular care was taken to make the suggestion as realistic as possible, the ends of the tails protruding from the centre of the scroll, to represent the tips of the horns (Fig. 245). Greater success in this effort was attained by the use of the headdress described on p. 180.

Fig. 255.
Ramshorn Hairdressing

HEADDRESSES

During the whole of the thirteenth century the "Barbette" was very popular with all classes. About the year 1230 it became, when folded, sufficiently wide to allow a few pleats or folds to radiate from the chin to the sides of the head (Figs. 256, 257).

Fig. 256.

The Coif

Fig. 257.

When the crispine (Fig. 258) was introduced, the barbette was very often worn in conjunction with a fillet. At the end of the century, the barbette was a double piece of linen made up in this shape (diagram in Fig. 260), the sides covering the enormous excrescences formed by the hair encased in the crispine. The coif was frequently worn on top (Fig. 259).

Fig. 258.

Crespinette

Fig. 259.

A new headdress came into fashion about the time of Henry III.'s accession. This was called the Coif. It went through various developments, and lasted until the reign of Edward II. In its first stage it resembled a shallow pill-box, the rim measuring about two to two and a half inches in depth (Fig. 214).

Royal and noble ladies placed their coronets or circlets round this rim, when wearing them on any important occasion (*see* Fig. 210), and sometimes a single band of jewels was so worn. Later an upstanding brim was attached to the pill-box (Fig. 256). At a later date, about 1250, the upstanding brim was gauffered into a series of small pleats or folds (Fig. 257).

At the end of the thirteenth century another version of this coif came into fashion. The upstanding brim was narrower, and a small

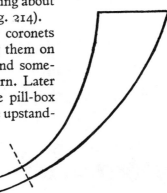

Fig. 260. Diagram of Barbette

pleated frill was inserted behind the brim, which was slightly pulled sideways to attain the modish shape (*see* Fig. 261). Over the coif was placed the veil; the barbette might be worn or omitted.

The statue of Margaret of France, second wife of Edward I., at Lincoln Cathedral, shows the use of a coronet placed round the brim

of a coif of this pattern. Her hair is not confined in a net, but is dressed in curls at the sides of her face (Plate VI. A).

Early in the fourteenth century the coif was enlarged, in circumference only, and became oval in plan. The brim remained from two to two and a half inches in depth. This resulted from the style of hairdressing then fashionable—extreme width, due to the hair being more generously padded at the sides (Fig. 259).

Fig. 261.
Coif, end of 13th century

It is important to remember that in all illustrations of this period these coifs are always *white*.

The headdress called the Ramshorn, in fashion at the end of the thirteenth century, remained in vogue until the end of Edward II.'s reign. It was simply a development of the ramshorn hairdressing described on p. 178. The tails of hair and the top of the head were entirely encased in one long piece of silk; the tails were then twisted into scrolls as before described (Fig. 262).

The ramshorn was a popular and distinct headdress in itself.

In conjunction with it, the couvrechef and wimple were frequently worn (Fig. 263). About 1300, the wimple was very often worn over the ramshorn *without* any other head-covering; it was then called the

Fig. 262.
Ramshorn Headdress

Gorget. A piece of fine soft linen was used, just in the same way as described under the *Wimple*. It was wrapped round the neck, draped up

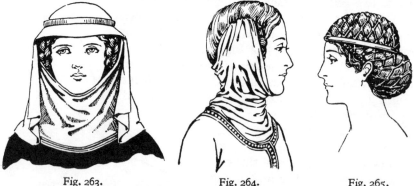

Fig. 263.
Temp. Edward I., Edward II.

Fig. 264.
The Gorget

Fig. 265.
First Crespinette

the sides of the face, and pinned over the ramshorn or pad to the hair at the sides of the head. The edges were fastened by more pins at the nape, leaving a V-shape of hair visible behind the head. As a rule, the bottom edge on the shoulders was tucked in under the neckband of the gown (Fig. 264). By this means the gorget fitted so neatly and closely to the face, head and neck, that it appeared to be "nailed to her chin, or that she had the pins hooked into her flesh."

THE CAUL. Known in the Middle Ages as the "Crispine," or CRESPINETTE; a network cap to confine the hair. The craftsmen who made them were called "crespiniers." *See also* Jewellery, p. 187.

During the second half of the thirteenth century, network caps, more properly called "Cauls," came into fashion for ladies' wear. These headdresses were shaped like bags, made of gold, silver or silk network, and worn over hair dressed as shown in Figs. 168 and 253. At first they fitted fairly close to the head, the edge, band or rim being placed high up on the forehead, to show some hair on the temples and round the nape; they enclosed the head and hair, and were secured by a circlet or fillet (Fig. 265). Jewels were often set at intervals in the band, and also at the intersections of the cross-bars.

About 1300, the plaits of hair became more bulky, and projected on either side of the face. With the caul or crispine, the barbette was worn *under* the fillet of linen (Fig. 258).

The coif, now enlarged in circumference to take the extra width of the coiffure, was frequently worn over the barbette made of a double piece of linen (cut as shown in diagram in Fig. 260), and under this came the caul (*see* Fig. 259).

The crispine or caul developed later into the RETICULATED HEADDRESS of the fourteenth and fifteenth centuries.

FOOTGEAR

12|20   12|60

Fig. 266. Sole Plans

Footgear of this period was not extravagant in shape, following very closely the form of the foot. The materials used were rich, and the shoes often decorated with embroidery.

The style of shoes generally worn is shown in Fig. 171, and a more elaborate pair in Fig. 267. They are of the fashionable shape which came into use about 1240 and remained in vogue until the end of the century. The low-cut opening on the outside of the instep and the

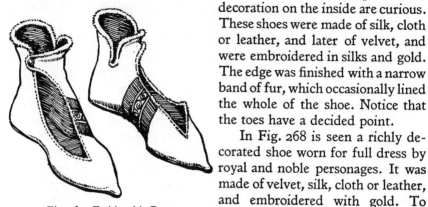

decoration on the inside are curious. These shoes were made of silk, cloth or leather, and later of velvet, and were embroidered in silks and gold. The edge was finished with a narrow band of fur, which occasionally lined the whole of the shoe. Notice that the toes have a decided point.

In Fig. 268 is seen a richly decorated shoe worn for full dress by royal and noble personages. It was made of velvet, silk, cloth or leather, and embroidered with gold. To cover the seam at the side there was

Fig. 267. Fashionable Boots

a vertical band of decoration, and a cord or rib was attached to the front seam to give it extra strength. The shoe fitted close round the ankle, and was secured by a button or buckle fixed to a strap.

In illuminated MSS. of the thirteenth century one frequently sees the feet and legs, to the height of the calf, clothed in boots that closely resemble hose with foot part attached (*see* Figs. 224 and 236). These boots frequently reached to the knee, and sometimes

Fig. 268. State Shoe

above it, and were usually tied round the leg by a string or strap below the knee. They were made of strong cloth or leather, and were usually black.

The general footgear of the middle classes is represented by Figs. 79, 82 and 171. They were made of cloth, felt or rough leather, and were in nearly all cases black. Hose with foot part combined, made of various kinds of leather, were very useful leg-coverings for travellers, horsemen and working men.

Figs. 240 and 242 wear the hose with foot part combined, in a coarse cloth or felt, and the peasant in Fig. 241 is wearing braies of very clumsy make, which fit him ill. When braies

Fig. 269. Clog

were baggy at the knees, or if the wearer wished to raise them from the ankle, he tied a thong round the leg under the knee—a method practised by labourers to-day.

Field labourers left their feet bare when working in wet fields or marshy ground. At other times they wore black cloth or leather shoes, which were easily removed for work. Clogs, Fig. 269, were also used.

The shepherd in Fig. 243 has had recourse to the old method of covering his legs with bracco, and has crossgartered them, including the shoes.

XIII th.

Fig. 270. Ornament

JEWELLERY

During the reign of Henry III. all the Arts made wonderful progress, and in this the craft of the goldsmith and jeweller took a worthy share. The growing importance of the Goldsmiths' Guild was recognised in the reign of Edward I. in an interesting manner, by authority given to them by law to examine all gold and silver articles of plate and jewellery, and to impress all such articles found satisfactory with a "Hall Mark," so called because examination took place at the guild's hall.

The names of three goldsmiths who were successively master gold-smiths to Henry III. and Edward I. have been recorded. They were: Adam, Ade, and Thomas de Frowick.

Crowns in use during the thirteenth century continued to be simple in design, set with a few beautiful jewels. It is stated that Henry III. acquired many crowns during his reign, but for his own crowning at Gloucester he had to be content with a simple fillet of gold, as the crown belonging to his father had been lost in the Wash nine days before. However, he soon replaced it, for it is recorded that he paid £1500 (a large sum in those days) for "a great crown most glorious with gems," to be worn on State occasions. He was lavish with presents of jewellery to his wife, and spent £30,000 at the time of his marriage on various pieces of jewellery for her, including "a Royal crown set with rubies, emeralds, and great pearls; another with Indian pearls, and one great crown of gold ornamented with emeralds, sapphires of the East, rubies, and large Oriental pearls."

The crown worn by Henry III. (Fig. 188) on his bronze effigy in Westminster Abbey had jewels set in it, but these were removed

at a later date. The band is surmounted by eight trefoils separated by points.

Fig. 271 gives an example of a simple crown in use at this time, and similar ones are worn in

Fig. 271

Fig. 189 (Henry III.) and Fig. 218 (Edward I.).

Fig. 272 is a drawing made from one of the frescoes in the Painted Chamber at the Palace of Westminster. It has four large maple leaves separated by four smaller ones, and between each are trefoils. In Matthew Paris's drawing (Plate VIII. A, and Fig. 198) the crown has four trefoils.

Fig. 272

Edward I. possessed a crown of gold set with sapphires, emeralds, rubies and pearls. It was given to him by the King of France.

The crown of Louis IX. (Fig. 191) is one of the first to show the use of the fleur-de-lys. On the statue to Louis VI. le Gros, erected by Louis IX. at S. Denis, is a crown entirely thirteenth-century in character, made of eight plates hinged together, a Byzantine method which went out of use at the end of this century. Four of the plates are surmounted by fleurs-de-lys, the remaining four by maple leaves. A large jewel and four pearls occupy each place. The German crown worn by the Emperor Frederick II. (Fig. 192) has a band deeper than hitherto used, which was probably thickly set with jewels. In design the four floral motifs are a blend of maple leaves

Fig. 273.
Sceptre

and the architectural foliage so frequently used in sculpture.

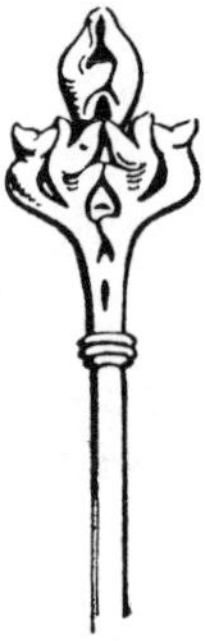

During the thirteenth century *sceptres* were of very beautiful design, as seen in Figs. 189 and 218: the latter is enlarged in Fig. 273.

The crowns and coronets of queens and royal ladies were similar in design to those just described. Eleanor of Provence, queen of Henry III., was renowned throughout Europe for her magnificent jewellery, a great part of which descended to succeeding queens-consort. She introduced the fashion of wearing on her head "guirlands" or "chaplets"— bands of ornament made in gold or silver filigree work, set with clusters of different-coloured jewels to represent flowers. Eleanor had no less than nine of these beautiful chaplets given to her by her husband at the time of her marriage.

Fig. 274.
Chaplet
Band

Later, "eleven more rich guirlands, with emeralds, pearls, sapphires and garnets," were added to the list. These garlands became very popular among ladies of rank and wealth. They frequently wore them round the brim of the coif, in the same manner as the noble lady in Fig. 210 wears her coronet. Fig. 274 shows another kind of chaplet, having leaves of gold and enamel upon a gold band with rubies, sapphires and clusters of seed pearls set at intervals.

Noblemen wore chaplets of gold ornamented by conventional flowers, and Fig. 275 shows one set with roses (*see* John's crowning as Duke of Normandy, p. 105). A larger-scale rose is shown below it. Circlets of gold and

Fig. 275.
Chaplet

jewels were sometimes worn by noblemen over the white coif, as pointed out in Fig. 199.

Fashionable brooches worn by men of the thirteenth century were not always circular in shape. A favourite design was a quatrefoil, often of plain gold (Fig. 276).

Fig. 276.
Brooch

Fig. 277 shows a more elaborate one set with jewels, similar to that worn by the king in Fig. 218. A brooch of this type was shown at the throat of a figure in a fresco which used to adorn the wall of the Painted Chamber, Westminster Palace, and is reproduced in Fig. 278. It is square, and of gold enamelled in different colours.

Fig. 277.
Brooch

Brooches used by ladies to fasten the camise or robe were circular or oval, like those worn in the twelfth century

Fig. 278.
Brooch

(Figs. 87 and 88), but smaller, and called *fermails* (*see* Figs. 210, 214, and 229). Circles of gold set with jewels, having a movable pin attached thereto by a ring, came into fashion after the middle of the thirteenth century (Fig. 279). It is seen worn at the throat in Fig. 254, and a richer one in Fig. 261. These small brooches or fermails were frequently square, sometimes with the corners extended by the heads of animals, as seen in Fig. 280 which is set with four stones. These were used by ladies of fashion to fasten the neck of the camise.

The use of brooches or bosses attached to the shoulders of the mantles as described in the last chapter, p. 123, was retained during this period.

Fig. 279.
Fermail

Another kind of ornament for fastening the mantle, very similar in appearance to an agrafe or clasp, is shown in Fig. 281. It is circular in shape, but divided into two notched sections which are connected by a pin. The two halves were fixed to opposite sides of the mantle. This agrafe is composed of gold, set with enamel on the flat parts, and six jewels and enamel decorate the raised parts. The mantle could be worn fastened by this ornament on the right shoulder or in front.

Fig. 280.
Fermail

A pendant attached to the cord or strap which fastened the mantle became the vogue about the middle of the thirteenth century (*see* Fig. 214).

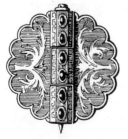

Fig. 281. Clasp

One of these pendants set with jewels is shown in Fig. 282. It is made of gold, with a large stone set in the centre, which probably covered a receptacle for some precious relic.

The buckle shown in Fig. 283 is of gilded bronze set with two garnets. It is of thirteenth-century workmanship and was found in a tomb at Semur.

Pilgrims' signs. In the last century pilgrims or " palmers" (professional pilgrims) who had travelled to the Holy Land fixed an escollop shell in their hats as a sign that they had accomplished their pilgrimage. Other details of a pilgrim's outfit were the staff, wallet, a large hat like Fig. 243, and a cloke. During the thirteenth century this custom of making pilgrimages, not only to the Holy Land but to the shrines of certain saints renowned

Fig. 282. Pendant

Fig. 283. Buckle

for their miraculous power, became more general. Many towns in England, as well as on the Continent, contained the shrines of celebrated saints. Pilgrims visiting these places took great care to procure the badges, brooches, devices or signs peculiar to the patron saint, and, sewing them to their garments or pinning them to their caps, returned in triumph to their native country with these testimonials of holy travel.

These badges or brooches were made of base metal—brass, lead, pewter, etc.—cast in moulds, and had pins attached or holes for sewing them on to garments. The technical name for these brooches was "Signacula," and Fig. 284 shows one associated with the shrine at Canterbury —the head of S. Thomas à Becket. Little shackles of chains came from the shrine of S. Etheldreda, or S. Audrey, at Ely.

Fig. 284. Pilgrim Sign

Fig. 285. Pilgrim Sign

Fig. 285 shows the wheel of S. Catherine, from her shrine on Mount Sinai. The escollop shell was also the sign of the shrine of Compostella in Spain.

These pilgrimages took place throughout the Middle Ages, and pilgrim signs found their way into all countries, to be treasured and revered. Devout persons would kiss these signs on frequent occasions, like Louis XI., of whom it is written that: "He had, besides, his hat quite full of images, mostly of lead or pewter, which he kissed on all occasions when any good or bad news arrived or that his fancy prompted him;

casting himself upon his knees so suddenly at times, in whatever place he might be, that he seemed more like one wounded in his understanding than a rational man." *See* Fig. 566.

A *girdle* of the thirteenth century is shown in detail in Fig. 209 and a description of it given on p. 157. Often the ornaments upon the strap of leather or silk were of gold, and set with jewels, enamels or clusters of pearls. The buckle and chape were also richly decorated in the same manner. Another example of a girdle of this period, which might be worn by either sex, is shown in Fig. 219.

Although *necklaces* are mentioned in writings of the thirteenth century, and jewelled collars were sometimes worn by great ladies on the Continent—a fashion which was not adopted by English or French women for more than a century later—no examples are to be seen upon the necks of figures in illuminated MSS. or sculpture. Such representations of thirteenth-century women as have survived all depict their subjects more or less in full dress, and the couvrechefs and wimples effectively conceal any possible necklaces that may have been worn. It seems likely, therefore, that ornaments of this kind were visible only when comparatively simple costume was worn at home. For full-dress outdoor costume the ornaments most in evidence were agrafes, fermails, and the attachments of mantles.

The *caul* or *crespinette* was an important headdress worn by noble ladies of this period. The network was made of gold or silver, framed in a border of the same metal about half or three-quarters of an inch in width. At the intersections of the network a single stone or a cluster of jewels was set. Sometimes the caul was composed entirely of a network of small pearls, and such a caul often had at each intersection a jewel surrounded by four, five or six pearls.

Fig. 286. Brocade, woven in red and gold

SECTION V.—WEAVING AND MATERIALS
(*Continued from p. 124*)

No startling innovation disturbed the tranquillity of the weaver's craft during the thirteenth century. Quiet progress was made in this transitional period, with but little warning of the amazing development which was to take place in the following century.

Some materials in use were:

Barracus, a striped fabric.

Batiste, a fine thin linen, named after its inventor in the thirteenth century.

Biffe, a material having indefinite or "blotted-out" stripes.

Birrus or *Burel,* a coarse thick woollen cloth used by the lower orders for external clothing.

Broella, a similar material.

Camelot, manufactured in Asia from camel's hair. A fine soft material like cashmere, imported into the West towards the end of the thirteenth century. Another kind was made from the hair of the Armenian goat.

Carised, a coarse fluffy Flemish serge.

Cotton was cultivated in Italy in the twelfth century and exported to other countries. Cotton cloth was made in France in the thirteenth century, and a coarse thick make called Augueton, Hauberjet, or Haberjoun, was used for making jackets, padded with cotton, to be worn under chain-mail armour. It was almost impenetrable and was frequently worn by men-at-arms without any other body armour. This jacket was called a Hoqueton or Hauqueton.

Dimity, a fine cotton cloth or fustian manufactured at Damietta in the thirteenth century.

Estamford or *Estamet,* a heavy woollen cloth of good quality.

Linomple or *Linon,* linen muslin or lawn.

Linsey woolsey, a homespun cloth of linen weft and woollen woof like common serge (of the cheap modern art serge type) imported from Florence at this time.

Lyraigne, a cobwebby light woollen cloth, made in Flanders, and in use during the thirteenth and fourteenth centuries.

Mollequin, a name for cotton muslin.

Raye of the thirteenth and fourteenth centuries had groups of horizontal stripes of different colours. The best qualities were made in Flanders, France or Italy.

Sindon has been variously interpreted to mean satin or very fine linen.

Tiretaine, another name for linsey woolsey.

Velvet, invented about the middle of the thirteenth century (*see* Vol. I., p. 217).

Woollen cloth with a nap upon its surface was the usual material from which the everyday clothes of the nobility and upper classes were made. In the course of wear this nap became tangled and unkempt, and for renovation the garment was sent to be shorn. Many instances are found in wardrobe accounts of the robes of great ladies being sent to be re-shorn.   (*Continued on p.* 280.)

PLATE I.   Matilda Of Flanders (*see* pp. 23–4, 63)

PLATE III. "The Lady Of The English," 1141 (*see* pp. 41–2, 57, 62–3, 122–3)

PLATE IV.   Richard I. (*see* p. 97)

PLATE V. "Elkanah," from the S. Eadmundsbury Bible by Master Hugo, 1121–48 (*see* p. 79)

PLATE IX.   A Noble Lady, TEMP. Edward II. (*see* pp. 215 & 268)

PLATE X.   A Nobleman, TEMP. Edward III. (*see* pp. 226–7, 274, & 278)

PLATE XI.   Queen Philippa, 1350 (*see* pp. 231, 233–4, & 275)

PLATE XIII.   A Nobleman, End of Fourteenth Century (*see* pp. 246 & 385)

PLATE XIV.   A Noble Lady, TEMP. Richard II. (*see* pp. 254, 323, & 369)

PLATE XVI.   A Knight Tilting, Fifteenth Century
(*see* pp. 127, 294, 308–9, 320, 339, 341 & 343)

PLATE XVIII.   Sir Geoffrey Louterell, His Wife and Daughter-in-Law, about 1340

(*see* pp. 229, 263, 269, 308, 321, 323, 329, 337, 340–3)

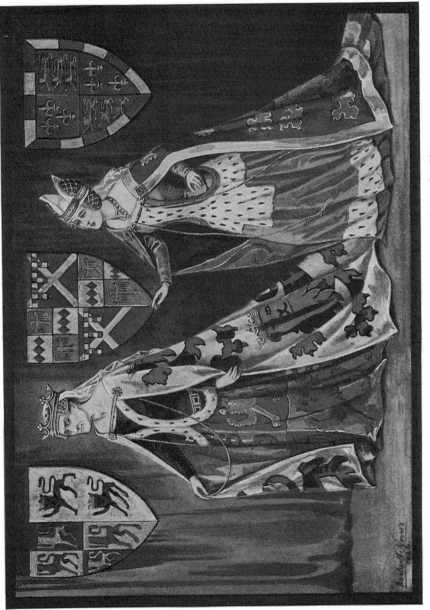

PLATE XIX.   Margaret, Princess of Wales, 1410, and Joice, Lady Tiptoft, 1460
(see pp. 218, 296, 298, 331–3, 338, & 441)

PLATE XX.   Henry, Prince of Wales, 1412–13 (*see* p. 455)

PLATE XXII.   Philippe Le Bon, Duke of Burgundy, and Isabelle of Portugal, 1440–5
(*see* pp. 346, 356, 386, 397, 401, & 441)

PLATE XXIII.   An Interior, Late Fifteenth Century (*see* pp. 356, 408, 417, & 435)

PLATE XXIV.   A Nobleman and Lady, TEMP. Edward IV.
(*see* pp. 346, 397, 401, 408, 415, 417, 435, 447, & 452)

The Guilds

(Continued from p. 125)

By the thirteenth century craft guilds, now becoming dangerous rivals to the merchant guilds, had spread to almost every trade, and purchased the right to make their own bylaws for the betterment of their own particular craft. The training of a craftsman was now regulated: a boy or girl wishing to learn an occupation or trade was bound as an "apprentice" (first mentioned in the year 1270) to a master-craftsman. He or she had to be brought before the mayor and proved to be of good character; and it was the custom that before they completed their term of apprenticeship they must produce a test work or "masterpiece." When the full time had been served the apprentice became a "journey-man" (French, *journée* = a day's work), and could work for so much per day for any master who chose to employ him. Having saved sufficient of his earnings he could set up business for himself by paying a fee to the guild and exhibiting his masterpiece, which proved his right to be enrolled as a master-craftsman.

Liveries. The "best gowns" worn by members of the various guilds were supplied from guild funds, a custom borrowed from the Court and the households of the nobility (*see* pp. 147, 148), and were called LIVERIES, from the French, *livrée* = a delivery.

The first mention of liveries is made in the reign of Edward I., when the Saddlers' Guild rode in procession at that king's second marriage in 1299: "Six hundred of them were in one Livery of red and white, with the cognisance of their mysteries [1] upon their sleeves" (*see* Fig. 221).

After this event all the guilds adopted liveries of different sets of colours, but conflicting accounts suggest that there was no definite rule concerning them: the colours varied according to fashion or the momentary taste of the guild.

In the thirteenth century, a "full suit" of livery consisted of a gown to the ankles, such as was in vogue at the period, usually parti-coloured, and a hood with liripipe, also parti-coloured. (*Continued on p. 284*).

The Guilds and their Entertainments—The Birth of the Drama in England and France.

For two centuries the Church was the home of the drama in England and France, and plays arising out of the Liturgy of the Mass were acted for the instruction and amusement of the people, at first in dumbshow, and later with descriptive verse, by priests, monks, and members of the choir, augmented occasionally by laymen.

The plays, called "Mysteries," were founded on stories taken from Scriptural narrative, and "Miracles," which dealt with incidents from the lives of the saints and martyrs, and were presented in the churches.

[1] *i.e.* guild or craft.

The first miracle play acted in England was produced at Dunstable in 1100.

Mystery and miracle plays became very popular during the thirteenth century and crowded audiences necessitated these plays, or "Pageants" as they were sometimes called, being given in the churchyard. After the middle of the thirteenth century the acting of mystery, miracle, and pageant plays was entrusted to the laity, especially to members of the trade guilds, although the clergy frequently continued to take part in them.

The first of the cycle of Chester Plays (eventually numbering twenty-five) was produced in 1268. It was the custom for a guild to present a play having some reference to its own particular craft; for instance, the Fishmongers' Guild of London presented the story of *The Flood*; the Vintners', *The Marriage of Cana*, etc. By this time the plays were performed in open spaces of the towns, usually the marketplace, upon cars or scaffolds built up into two or three tiers to represent Hell, Earth and Heaven. References still exist which prove the use of properties, special costumes, and simple scenery, all contrived with great care and ingenuity.

About this time the "pageant" proper came into fashion. On the occasion of some great national or civic festival, such as a coronation—the return of a victorious king from the wars—the reception of a new queen-consort, or a foreign potentate—at Corpus Christi—Whitsuntide—May Day—or Midsummer Watch—or at the election of a new mayor or lord mayor—the guilds provided an important part of the entertainment. Wonderful castles and triumphant arches were erected across the streets, and occupied by boys and girls chosen for their beauty, representing mystical and allegorical characters, who performed certain ceremonies as the king or honoured arrival passed by. The guilds also supplied elaborately decorated cars. The Fishmongers furnished one emblematic of their trade to welcome Edward I. when returning from his war in Scotland in 1292.

Mayday games consisted of the acting in somewhat primitive manner of popular stories by artisans, labourers and village folk. The legend of Robin Hood was a favourite theme. The comic element was supplied by jesters, and in addition there was juggling, morris-dancing and horseplay, such as a mock-tourney, hobby-horses, quintain, etc., and general buffoonery.

(*Continued on p.* 284.)

Fig. 287. Border

Section VI.—Widows and their Weeds

Widuwe in Anglo-Saxon means "bereft of a husband."

The word "weed" is derived from the Anglo-Saxon *wæd* = clothing, and is frequently met with in MSS. of the Middle Ages to express clothing of any kind.

At all times a woman bereft of her husband is considered to be at a disadvantage, but this was especially the case in the Middle Ages. If the woman was wealthy she found herself, on the death of her husband, in a very difficult position. Innumerable suitors would press their attentions (after the customary year of her widowhood had expired), many of them with the sole object of augmenting their incomes by marriage with a wealthy widow. More dangerous still was the chance of abduction by some powerful and unruly baron. To guard against these contingencies it was necessary for a widow of wealth to take precautionary measures, and the only way to attain security was to retire to some monastery or nunnery.

Many royal and noble widows built their own abbeys, and retired from the world, often to become abbesses. Widows of less wealth withdrew from the world and sought seclusion from sheer necessity in some monastic establishment.

Repugnance or prejudice against a second marriage may have been a contributing cause, but comfortable shelter from the troubles of the world was often the primary motive.

Hence arose an *Order of Vowesses*. Votaries were obliged to take a vow to lead a single life till death, and became mystically espoused to Christ in a like manner to nuns. It was not necessary for the vowess to adopt the rigid rule of a nun, since a woman's course of life was likely to have become more or less fixed by the time she might be left a widow.

She retained all the freedom and privileges of her married life, with the exception that she was prohibited from marrying a second time.

The Benedictional of a vowess consisted of the postulant taking the vow with her hands placed together between those of the bishop or prelate, before witnesses, after which he gave her his blessing. She then assumed the garments usually worn. They were the *gown*, in shape like those in vogue at the time, to which could be

Fig. 288.
Widow's Barbe and Veil

added the ordinary girdle; a *mantle* with its usual fastenings; and the *couvrechef*. These garments were black. The distinctive garb of the widow was the BARBE, of which the barbette is the diminutive. Until the end of the fourteenth century the barbe was the same as the wimple;

from then onwards it was a piece of white linen fixed to an arrow band encircling the face and covering the shoulders. Its peculiarity was that at the centre, where it covered the chin, it was arranged in small vertical pleats (Fig. 288). The barbe was worn above or below the chin, according to rank.

The following ordinance, although of the fifteenth century, applies to the wimple of thirteenth-century widows and the barbe worn by widows of the fourteenth century:

". . . The Queen, and all ladies down to the degree of a Baroness, are therein licensed to wear the Barbe above the chin. Baronesses, Lords' daughters, and Knights' wives, are ordered to wear the Barbe beneath it, and all chamberers and other persons below the throat goyle" (gullet, or lowest part of the throat). Royal and noble ladies who had become vowesses wore their coronets on special occasions on top of this headdress (see Fig. 571). They may be found thus represented on effigies.

The ring with which the vowess was espoused to Christ was not always a plain gold one; it was sometimes set with jewels, or a "diamante," and worn on the third finger of the right hand.

"The Lady Cecilia, then a widow, in presence of S. Eadmund (Eadmund Rich, canonised 1246), then Archbishop of Canterbury (1234–1240), made a solemn vow of observing perpetual continence and widowhood, and with the ring of betrothal took the russet [1] garment which was worn as a sign of perpetual celibacy."

Vowesses were entitled to be addressed as "Dame."

Nuns. After some vicissitudes, monachism became more firmly re-established in England during the eleventh century. At this time the dress of gentlefolk was simple in shape. For a good example *see* Fig. 58. The gown and veil, with the cloke for superiors, were adopted by nuns, who used them in black, brown, grey and white, according to the Orders to which they belonged (*see* Vol. I., p. 173). To these garments the wimple was added at the end of the third quarter of the twelfth century, and, later, an extra veil of white linen bound tight round the forehead, over the wimple, and under the veil of soft woollen stuff.

---

[1] "Russet" refers to the material, not to its colour.

CHAPTER IV

1307–1399

CONTENTS

CHAPTER IV

1307–1399

CONTEMPORARY EMPERORS AND KINGS

	ENGLAND	FRANCE	GERMANY
1307	Edward II. Isabella of France	Philippe IV. le Bel, 1285–1314	Albert, Duke of Austria, 1298–1308
1308			Henry VII. of Luxemburg, 1308–1313 Constance
1314		Louis X. le Hutin, 1314–1316	Louis the Bavarian, 1314–1347 1. 2. Marguerite, Countess of Holland
1316		Philippe V. le Long, 1316–1322	
1322		Charles IV. le Bel, 1322–1328	
1327	Edward III. Philippa of Hainault		
1328		Philippe VI. de Valois, 1328–1350 1. Jeanne de Bourgoyne 2. Blanche of France	
1347			Charles IV. of Luxemburg, 1347–1378 1. Daughter of Elector-Palatine 2. 3. 4. Elizabeth of Pomerania
1350		Jean II. le Bon, 1350–1364 1. Bonne of Bohemia 2. Jeanne, Duchesse de Bourgoyne	
1364		Charles V. le Sage, 1364–1380 Jeanne de Bourbon	
1377	Richard II. 1. Anne of Bohemia 2. Isabella of France		
1378			Wenceslas, King of Bohemia, 1378 Jeanne
1380		Charles VI. le Bien-Aimé, 1380–1422 Isabeau of Bavaria	
1399	Henry IV. 1. Mary de Bohun 2. Joanna of Navarre		

195

HISTORICAL DATA

1307–1399

1307. The twenty years' reign of Edward II. was one of public disgrace and private calamity, and the most distressing period in the history of England, brought about by the follies of the young king and the violence of his nobles.

While Prince of Wales, Edward had much angered his father, and when called to the throne he greatly annoyed his ministers, and all about him, by his self-will. He recalled his pernicious favourite, Piers Gaveston, son of a Gascon knight, whom Queen Eleanor had befriended and brought to England as a playmate for her son but whom Edward I. had banished. Piers Gaveston was in every way a thoroughly objectionable character, but his share in the changing fashions of the time make him noteworthy from the point of view of this history. His career was cut short by the indignant nobles, who eventually chopped off his head in 1312.

1312. The king's grief and vows of vengeance alienated him from the affections of the nation, with whom in his youth he had been a popular favourite.

1313. Cola di Rienzi born, the great Italian patriot; son of a tavern-keeper and a washerwoman, he became dictator by proclamation of the Roman people in 1347. Murdered by his enemies, 1354.

1314. While the English king wasted his time in frivolous and dissolute pursuits, Robert Bruce took the opportunity to drive the English out of Scotland and seize the Scottish throne. Edward at last roused himself and met Bruce near Stirling with the largest army that had ever marched out of England. By the river of Bannock, on 24 June, 1314, a battle was fought, and won by the Scots, and Bruce firmly established himself as King of Scotland.

In 1314 Hugh le Despenser (the younger) succeeded Piers Gaveston as the king's favourite, and received even more honours and indulgences, until in 1322 Despenser was captured and sent into exile, and later both he and his father were hanged (1326).

1315. Beginnings of Swiss independence.

1320. John Gower, the poet, born; died 1408.

John of Trokelowe, Latin historian, flourished 1307–1323.

1323. Trouble arose between Edward and Charles IV., King of France, over the question of the former doing homage for Guienne, which had been restored to the English crown; and Queen Isabella, Edward's wife and sister to the French king, was sent over to mediate. When in France she met Roger, Lord Mortimer, a man of infamous character, and with him concocted a plan to invade England, overthrow the king's ministry and take over the government. The King of France, not approving of her intimacy with Mortimer, sent her out of the country, and she then applied to the Count of Holland and Hainault, who assisted her with a small fleet. She landed between Orford and Harwich,

1326. Suffolk, 24 September, 1326, with an army including many disaffected nobles, under Lord Mortimer. After King Edward had been pursued for some time, he was caught and taken to Kenilworth, where he was deposed, 30 January,

1327. 1327, and his son Edward proclaimed as Edward III. A Council of Regency appointed by Parliament was put aside by Isabella, and in fact Edward reigned under the regency of his mother and Lord Mortimer, whom she appointed as her Prime Minister. The ex-king was put under the successive charge of the Earl of Lancaster, Lord Berkeley, Sir John Maltravers and Sir Thomas Gurney. His treatment was progressively more and more severe until he was despatched, under most horrible circumstances, in Berkeley Castle, on 21 September, 1327, at the age of forty-three years.

Lord Mortimer, possessing himself of the Despenser estates, was created Earl of March by the queen-mother. Her principal councillor was Adam Arleton, Bishop of Hereford, and between them they ruled the country. Their administration so greatly excited public indignation that the young king was prevailed upon to exercise his

1330. authority, and in October 1330 Edward broke into his mother's apartments at Nottingham Castle, by a secret passage purposely left unguarded, and arrested the Earl of March as a traitor. He was tried, found guilty of the murder of Edward II., of taking upon himself the rule of the realm, and executed on the 20th of the same month. The queen was sent to Castle Rising, in Norfolk, and kept in close confinement.

1332. William Langland born at Cleobury Mortimer, Salop; died 1399. Wrote *Piers the Plowman*; first draft, 1362; second and best, 1377; third and last revision, 1390–8. *Richard the Redeless.*

The most interesting events of the Scotch rising of 1332 were the Battles of Dupplin Moor, Halidon

1333. Hill, 1333; Culbleen, 1335; the wardenship of Walter the Steward, and the courageous defence of her castle against the English by "Black Agnes of Dunbar," the daughter of Randolf, Earl of Moray, rudely referred to by the English soldiers as "The Black Sow."

His uncle Charles IV., King of France, having died childless, Edward turned his attention in earnest to his claim to the French

1337. crown in right of his mother, 1337. This led to the Hundred Years' War, which lasted until the reign of Henry V. Edward III. styled himself King of France and quartered the arms of France with those of England. While Edward was in France, Queen Philippa had been left in command of the English forces against Scotland. The Scotch army was completely

1346. scattered at Neville's Cross, 1346, and their king David II. captured. He was sent to the Tower, and after seeing him safely lodged there, the queen departed next day for Calais, arriving in time to save the six burgesses who had come to Edward to save their town from destruction. The story of her intercession on their behalf is well known.

1337. Sir John Froissart born; died about 1410. Wrote the *Chronicles of England, Scotland, France and Spain.* Priest, canon and treasurer of the Collegiate Church of Chimay. Historian and poet. Private secretary to Queen Philippa, 1360.

1338. Declaration of Reuse, whereby the emperor, or King of the Romans, henceforth derived his title solely from the choice of the electors.

1340. Geoffrey Chaucer, the first great English poet, born. Son of a London vintner. Married in 1366 Philippa, a lady-in-waiting on the queen, shortly afterwards be-

coming valet of the king's chamber. A traveller, soldier, courtier, diplomatist and M.P. Died 1400.

1347. Edward III. was elected Emperor of Germany and King of the Romans on the death of Louis the Bavarian. The only English king who received the offer of this dignity. Edward very wisely declined the honour.

1348. The Black Death, the most terrible plague the world has ever known, swept over Europe and Asia. It reached England in 1348. More than one-half of the population died during this and other visitations in 1361 and 1369.

1356. Renewal of war with France. Victory at Poitiers. King John of France captured.

1360. Treaty of Bretigny. Aquitaine, Ponthieu and Calais ceded to England without feudal obligations to French Crown.

1363. Henry Knighton, or Critthon, flourished 1363. Historical compiler. Died about 1366.

1366. Hubert van Eyck born at Maas Eyck. The first to practise picture-painting in oils, in the modern sense. Died at Ghent, 1426.

1369. Thomas Occleve born; verse-maker, a personal friend of Chaucer, and a clerk in the Exchequer. Died 1450.

1371. Robert, son of Marjory, daughter and heiress of Robert Bruce, and of Walter, the sixth High Steward of Scotland (born 1316), succeeded to the throne of Scotland as Robert II. The first of the Stuart dynasty.

1372. John Lydgate born. Monk of S. Eadmundsbury; "an accomplished scholar with a fair knack of verse-making." Flourished 1430; died 1451.

1374. Struggles against misrule in Church and State filled the last years of Edward's reign. During their course, John Wycliffe (born between 1315 and 1320) came into prominence about 1374.

1377. Death of Edward III.

Accession of Richard II. John of Gaunt chief man in the realm, but disliked and mistrusted by many.

1381. John Ball, a priest of S. Mary's, York, strove hard to get the people to stand up for themselves, the citizens against their feudal lords and the craftsmen against oppressive guilds, and demand reforms, which led to the Peasants' Rising or "Hurlingtime." Wat Tyler of Maidstone made captain of the men of Kent. On the marriage, in 1382, of the king to Anne of Bohemia, a general pardon was granted to all who had joined in the rising.

1382. Rising of the men of Ghent under Philip of Artaveld.

1384. The Lollards, followers of Wycliffe, who died this year. They were called by the friars "hooded men" or Lollards (idlers).

1385. Roger Mortimer, Earl of March and grandson of Lionel, Duke of Clarence, recognised by Richard as his heir to the throne.

1386. Alain Chartier. The Father of French eloquence. Secretary to Charles VI. and VII. Died 1458.
John of Gaunt's Crusade in Spain.

1388. The "Marvellous" or "Merciless" Parliament.

1389. Richard assumes sole rule and many wise laws are made by him.

1390. Jan van Eyck born at Maas Eyck. Brother of Hubert. The Great Master of Flemish painting. Died at Bruges, 1440.

1394. Death of Queen Anne.

1396. Truce with France for twenty-eight years. Richard II. marries Isabella, daughter of Charles VI. of France. The Republic of Genoa is given over to the French.

Thomas Walsingham, historian and monk of S. Albans Abbey. Date of birth unknown. The principal authority for the reigns of Richard II., Henry IV. and Henry V. Died about 1422.

1397. Enguerrand de Monstrelet born about this time of a noble family of Picardy; governor of Cambrai. Wrote *Chronicles* covering period 1400 to the time of his death, about 1453. These were continued by M. d'Escouchy, and terminate at 1461.
Richard crushes the Duke of Gloucester's party and gains supreme power.
Death of John of Gaunt, Duke of Lancaster. Richard denies John's son Henry, Earl of Derby, his estates; thereupon he goes to Brittany.

1398. Richard crosses to Ireland, and Henry returns to reclaim his inheritance, but not to usurp the crown.

1399. Richard betrayed at Flint and made to abdicate, 30 September, 1399.
Accession of the Duke of Lancaster as Henry IV.—the first of the Lancastrian dynasty.

THE ARTS

ARCHITECTURE

THE second subdivision of Gothic architecture starts approximately at the beginning of the fourteenth century, and is known as "Decorated Gothic." Its chief characteristics are the exclusive use of the pointed arch, the pillars and arcade piers of more slender proportions than before, and the more elaborate window tracery. In carving and decoration a very lavish use of leaf, floral and other natural forms is noticeable. The new type of vaulting is known as "Lierne" or binding, and has short ribs inserted at the top of the arch between the longer ones formerly used alone.

The full development of the "Decorated" style was achieved between the years 1300 and 1350. The style of architecture in use during the latter part of the century was called the "Transitional Decorated," the period overlapping the next, known as "Perpendicular Gothic."

SCULPTURE

(Continued from p. 138)

Bronze effigies of the fourteenth century are those on the monuments to the following: Edward the Black Prince (1376), at Canterbury Cathedral, Edward III. (1377), Richard II., and Anne of Bohemia (begun in 1395 and finished in 1397; the work of Nicholas Broker and Godfrey Prest, coppersmiths, of London)—all three in Westminster Abbey. That of Edward III. is surrounded by his children as "weepers"—miniature images of mourners.

Enamelled shields of arms and other details are important factors in the decoration of the monuments to the Black Prince and Edward III., and engraving decorates those of Richard II. and his queen. These deserve careful study, for they are excellent representations of armour, costume and heraldry, and perfect examples of the workmanship of the time. The effigies to Aymer de Valence, Earl of Pembroke (1324), and Prince John of Eltham (1337), both in stone and at Westminster Abbey, and the "weepers" surrounding each tomb, are interesting studies for all manner of details.

(Continued on p. 353.)

MEMORIAL BRASSES

(Continued from p. 139)

The reigns of Edward III. and Richard II. have been called the Golden Age of memorial brasses. Commencing about 1350, it was the best period of brass engraving, some of the finest examples in England being of foreign craftsmanship. All classes were commemorated, chiefly wealthy merchants.

It is interesting to observe that in the late fourteenth and early fifteenth centuries the woolstaplers of the eastern counties and other parts became very prosperous. Business with their Flemish customers took many of them to Flanders, and a number of Flemish brasses were brought back to England by men of this trade, and ultimately erected to their memory. This explains the prevalence of civilian brasses in the eastern counties, and Gloucestershire and Wiltshire.

(Continued on p. 354.)

TAPESTRY

(Continued from p. 141)

The districts in which the tapestry-weaving industry was carried on during the fourteenth century were Flanders and the northern and midland provinces of France, with Brussels, Arras and Paris as chief centres. About this time a tapestry loom was started at Tournai. The oldest piece of Franco-Flemish high-warp tapestry extant is "The Presentation to the Temple," dating from the first years of the fourteenth century and now in the Gobelins Museum, Paris.

From this time onwards, study of the original tapestries, or reproductions and photographs, reveal many interesting details relating to costume, etc. In 1344, Edward III. passed a law regulating the manufacture of tapestry in this country and the inclusion of "Tapissers" in Chaucer's Pilgrims suggests that some tapestry may have been woven in England, although nothing of importance was produced in this country so early.

After the middle of the fourteenth century, the fashion for hanging large rooms with beautiful masterpieces of the art became very general among royal [1] and noble families, especially on the Continent, where great rivalry existed for the ownership of fine sets. Charles V., King of France, was a great collector, as is shown by an inventory of his tapestries compiled in 1379–80. Among them are mentioned one hundred and thirty armorial pieces.[2] Philippe le Hardi (born 1342), fourth

[1] "A great hanging of wool 'dorsorium lanae' wove with the figures of the King and Earls upon it for the King's Hall at London. For the making and sewing of a border of green cloth round the said hanging, for saving the same from being damaged in fixing it up, 6s. 3d. Westminster, 6 Jan. 1318."

[2] "Fifteen pieces of tapestry with divers coats of arms." *See* p. 345.

The above are two entries in a wardrobe account.

son of King John of France, created Duke of Burgundy in 1363—the first of the "Magnificent Dukes"—acquired many rich tapestries from the looms of Arras and Paris, to decorate his several castles.

The most interesting and celebrated series of woven picture-hangings is "The Apocalypse" set made for Louis of Anjou, brother of King Charles V., to hang in his château of Angers. The first pieces were begun in 1376 and were designed by Hennequin or Jean of Bruges, Court painter to Charles V., and copied from an illuminated manuscript of "The Apocalypse" preserved (in 1912) in the Public Library at Cambrai. Each piece of tapestry was fifteen feet high by seventy-two feet wide. These were added to at a later date. *See* p. 355.

Thomas, Earl of Warwick (died 1401), possessed some very valuable pieces of tapestry representing the history of Guy of Warwick: they are mentioned in a charter dated 1397 conferring the earl's property, confiscated on account of the part he had played in the Duke of Gloucester's rising, upon the Earl of Kent. When Henry IV. restored the property to the Earl of Warwick in 1399, he was careful to return this important tapestry to the rightful owner.

The spoils of the Hundred Years' War, which began in 1337, enriched and decorated many an English castle and hall. The ease of transporting them made tapestry and other textiles a very popular form of "loot."

(*Continued on p. 355.*)

Illuminated Manuscripts

(*Continued from p. 143*)

The art of the English illuminators reached its zenith during the first quarter of the fourteenth century. It was characterised by a higher appreciation of the beauty of natural form, and this, coupled with great technical skill, resulted in a harmonious perfection unsurpassed at any period in the history of the illuminator's art.

Drawings lost their hard outline, and were painted in shaded body-colour, on backgrounds of burnished gold or diapered colours. Heraldry played an important part in the decoration of borders, and was often used in the diaper-work of backgrounds. The East Anglian School which came into existence at the end of the thirteenth century, was supreme, centring at Norwich, Ely, Ramsay, S. Eadmundsbury, and also at Peterborough. Its chief features were the use of rich harmonious colours combined with a lavish display of burnished and patterned gold. Ornamental borders became more elaborate, consisting of human figures (often dressed in the costumes of all classes), animals, plants, and particularly figures of a comic and grotesque nature. These last show great originality and imagination, and are invaluable as suggestions for stage demons, gnomes, fairies, goblins, etc.

The Apocalypse still provided the subject for a few English manuscripts, and their decoration maintained its excellence until the middle of the century, when the use of the Apocalypse as a subject for illumination suddenly ceased. At the same time the East Anglian School began to show signs of decay, and after a short interval it died out completely. Of this type of manuscript, the Louterell Psalter, made for Sir Geoffrey Louterell of Irnham, Lincolnshire, about 1340, is a case in point. Although intensely interesting, and most valuable for its authentic detail, the workmanship of this manuscript is considered by some to be below the high standard of technique attained a few years earlier. The extinction of this celebrated school of illumination is accounted for by the Black Death, which ravaged the whole land, particularly the eastern counties where its devastation was very severe.

A new type of illuminated manuscript came into use in the fourteenth century, and by its end had become extremely popular—the "Horæ," or "Book of Hours." It was a little book intended for private devotional use, and divided into various sections. It nearly always contained a calendar, and a long discourse or formula on the Hours or Office of the Virgin. It is from this latter section that the manuscripts take their name. They were very charmingly illustrated, displaying much imaginative work, besides delightful scenes of contemporary life. The most beautiful example dates from the end of this century, or the beginning of the fifteenth, and is known as "Très Riches Heures." It was executed by French artists for the Duc de Berry (1340–1416).

The last quarter of the fourteenth century witnessed a revival of the illuminator's art, although somewhat different in style from earlier work, being perhaps affected by the German influence introduced in the entourage of Anne of Bohemia in 1382. The principal features of this new style are the method of modelling the faces with brushwork, the skilful treatment of architectural ornament, and the natural effect of the landscapes in which the figures are set. This natural treatment, however, did not apply to the sky, in place of which gilded, tapestried, or checkered backgrounds were still retained. This innovation left a permanent influence on English illuminated manuscripts.

The art of the portrait painter may be said to have had its beginnings in the illuminated manuscripts of the early years of the fourteenth century. The first attempt at portraiture is to be found in an illuminated manuscript in the British Museum.[1] It is a very crude drawing of Edward II. Another of this king (Fig. 291) and his queen by a more skilful artist, and much better finished, appears in an illuminated manuscript now in Christchurch College Library, Oxford.[2] There are several other portraits of kings, etc., still extant, the work of illuminators of the fourteenth century; but they are considered by experts to be representative rather than real likenesses. On the other hand, they may rank as authorities for such details as hairdressing, crowns, etc.

[1] Roy. MS. 20, A II. fol. 10.   [2] Reproduced by the Roxburghe Club, 1913.

Towards the end of the fourteenth century, improvement is noticeable, particularly in the portraits of Charles V., the work of French artists, whose manuscripts are now in the Bibliothèque Nationale, Paris. The portrait of John, fifth Lord Lovel of Tichmerch, in a Gospel-lectionary at the British Museum, is recognised as the earliest true likeness. This was executed about the end of the century.

Edward III. bought from Isabella of Lancaster, nun of Aumbresbury, in 1331, a book of Romance for £66 13s. 4d. He kept this book in his own rooms.

Richard II. bought a Bible in French, a "Romance of the Rose," and a "Romance de Perceval" for £28.

(Continued on p. 356.)

PORTRAIT PAINTING

English portrait painting began at the end of the thirteenth or the commencement of the fourteenth century. One of the earliest portraits still extant is that of Henry III. (see p. 148). This and another, perhaps a little later, either of Edward I. (see p. 165) or Edward II., form companion pictures in the Sedilia at Westminster Abbey. Both paintings are attributed to Master Walter and Master Thomas of Westminster, who thus deserve the honour of being the first English portrait painters.

Wall-painted portraits of Edward III., and members of his family, decorated S. Stephen's Chapel, Westminster Palace. These paintings were executed between 1350 and 1363, and are the work of three English artists—Hugh of S. Albans, John Athelard, and Benedict Nightingale. The best reproductions of these paintings may be seen in the House of Commons.

It is generally agreed that the portrait of Richard II. in the Wilton Diptych (see Plate XII. A), and the painting in Westminster Abbey (see Plate XII. B), are the work of an English artist and are the first known examples of English portraiture, apart from wall painting or illuminated manuscript.

(Continued on p. 356.)

Fig. 289

COSTUME IN GENERAL

1307–1399

After the simple fashions worn during the previous century, the fourteenth is notorious for its extravagant and eccentric styles. The modes varied—sometimes close-fitting garments were in favour, revealing the whole shape of the body; at others the figure was enveloped in a "superfluity of clothing" evidenced in trailing gowns and long hanging sleeves. Luxury was unrestrained, especially in France, where the Court of the French kings set the extravagant fashions of the times, and "luxurious habits" were the cause of grave scandal. A French historian remarks that extravagance in dress preceded the misfortunes of a country whose prosperity coincided with wisdom and good taste in clothes. Indulgence in lavish display increased towards the end of the fourteenth century, especially after the death of Charles V. in 1380.

Early in the century England followed the French example, mainly as the result of a French princess becoming queen-consort of the frivolous Edward II. Edward III. is also accused of being extravagant and frivolous, and Richard II. inherited similar characteristics from his great-grandfather. During the second half of the fourteenth century the influence of "fashions from proud Italy" began to assert itself upon French and English costume.

At the end of the first quarter of the century a change in masculine modes took place. Long garments which covered men's legs were discarded in favour of tight-fitting tunics and hose, which revealed the legs, first to above the knee, and, later in the century, the thigh almost to the waist. Staid and sober folk were indeed concerned! These short tight garments remained in vogue until after the accession of Richard II.; at first worn alternatively with long robes, the latter eventually supplanted the former altogether about the end of the century.

Slight but interesting effects resulted from this abrupt change of fashion. The tunic or COTEHARDIE (see p. 221), fitting tightly round the waist and hips (and at a later date padded on the chest), imparted a certain rigidity to the body and produced stiffness of deportment. The cotehardie was so tight, especially at the waist, that the wearer required assistance to get into and out of it. This habitual use of tight hose caused a considerable tension and throwing forward of the leg, which gave a "fine and distinguished air to the gait." Long toes required that the foot should be lifted, and a slight kick employed to throw forward the long toe of the shoe so that it should not fall back under the foot and impede the walk of the wearer. This last difficulty was accentuated with the advent of the HOUPELAND (see p. 247). The fashion for "dagges" reached its climax during the reigns of Edward III. and of Richard II.

The chief novelty in regard to women's costume was its absence from the shoulders. During the first years of the century in France, and about the end of its first quarter in England, women began to wear low-necked dresses, a fashion which lasted for the whole of the century and that which followed. Never, during the whole period covered by this book, was it permissible for women's arms to be bare. Throughout the fourteenth century women wore the "corse," which was bound more and more tightly round the waist and eventually low down on the hips.

Great extravagance is noticeable in costumes throughout the country in the reign of Richard II. It was not limited to the nobility, but extended to their servants and to the wealthy citizens. The king, himself the greatest fop of the age, led the fashions, and adopted all those of continental origin which were in any way eccentric and extravagant.

During the thirteenth century the garments of people of all classes afforded little information as to the wearer's social status, but in the early part of the fourteenth century a revival of class distinction in dress took place, no doubt in some measure due to the changing fortunes which followed the ravages of the Black Death. This distinction differed, however, from that known in the eleventh and twelfth centuries, for the appearance of social position had become largely a matter of acquired wealth and no longer guaranteed high birth. From this time onwards commerce was honoured by dignities and titles, and matrimonial alliances between wealth and well-bred impecuniosity frequently took place. Opulent merchants and citizens tried to assume the extravagant sartorial habits of the nobility, and their example was followed by the lower classes, and even by peasants.

Henry Knighton speaks of the vanity of the common people in their dress, and says it was impossible to distinguish between rich and poor. Satirical poets wrote not only against scandalous luxury in the dress of both sexes, but against the weak and effeminate habits of the nobility, upper classes and rich citizens, the way in which their children were brought up, and the conceit of the lower classes in trying to ape their betters in the luxury of their dress. After the victory at Poitiers, so much priceless booty was taken by the English that the common soldier disdained to accept rich and costly garments of silk, velvet and fur. Froissart describes how all who shared with the Prince of Wales in this great victory "were made very rich in glory and wealth, as well by the ransoms of their prisoners as by the quantities of gold and silver plate, rich jewels, and trunks stuffed full of belts that were weighty from their gold and silver ornaments, and furred mantles. They set no value on armour, tents, or other things; for the French had come there as magnificently and richly dressed as if they had been sure of gaining the victory."

Sumptuary laws passed by Edward III. were not sufficiently forceful to check this passion for finery, which reached its climax under Richard II.

Fig. 290

Section I.—Edward II., 1307–1327

Nobility—Men

So far as the Court was concerned, the simple character of costume worn during the two previous reigns was not continued under Edward II. His reign of twenty years produced a great change in fashions, although this was confined to Court circles, where every description of fantastic style and extravagant idea originated among the king's intimate and foolish companions, each of whom tried to outshine the other. As a consequence of the unsettled state of the country, these developments only came into general use after the accession of Edward III. This section should, therefore, be regarded as a transitional period in costume.

Edward II. was born at Carnarvon, 1284. He is described as resembling his father in the beauty of his person, and his "portrait" in an illuminated manuscript at Christchurch College, Oxford, dated 1326, shows him a good-looking, clean-shaven man with a bright complexion and brown hair (Fig. 291). On the other hand, if the king in the Coronation Manuscript (Fig. 292; *see also* p. 209) is Edward II., as some conclude, he was wearing a small beard on his upper lip and chin when he came to the throne. Although strong, handsome, brave, and well-spoken, he lacked his father's qualities of mind. He was not wicked, but weak, passionate, irresolute, a drinker to excess, headstrong, careless of all but his own pleasures, and given overmuch to the companionship of those beneath him; above all he detested the trouble of public business.

Fig. 291.
Edward II.

He married on 28 January, 1308, at Boulogne, Isabella, daughter of Philippe IV. le Bel and Jane, Queen of Navarre. The coronation of the king and queen by the Bishop of Winchester, in the absence of the Archbishop of Canterbury, took place at Westminster on 23 February,

1308. This was the first instance of the wives of barons being summoned to attend.

THE ORDER OF CROWNING. The Coronation Service, as used from a very early period in England, had its origin in the Christian conceptions of the Middle Ages. It is claimed that the oldest order of this coronation is contained in a manuscript of the tenth, believed to be a copy of one of the eighth century. It is outside the scope of this work to enter into the origin of coronation rituals, which is a matter of strange perplexity.

The "Order of Crowning" is set forth and the coronation robes of a king are described in an illuminated manuscript [1] dating about the commencement of the fourteenth century. The use of many of the forms can be traced back to coronations of much earlier dates, and they continued under the Plantagenet and early Tudor dynasties. The order of the robing and coronation was as follows:

(1) Entrance of king into the church in rich civil costume.

(2) The election and (3) the recognition of the king.

(4) First oblation.

(5) Sermon, and (6) Oath, followed by

(7) *Veni Creator* and *Te invocamus*; (8) the Litany, (9) seven penitential psalms, and (10) four consecratory prayers. During these the king lay "humbly prostrate" at the altar steps.

(11) Consecratory preface for the oil.

(12) The anointing, details of which varied in different countries.

(13) The white coif was then put on, "to protect the Holy Ointment from irreverence." The king was afterwards vested in

(14) The colobium sidonis or alb of fine white linen, reaching to the feet, and having close sleeves to the wrist (*see* A, Fig. 292). Next (15) the tunicle, reaching to below the calf and having close sleeves buttoned to just above the wrist (*see* B). Over this was placed (16) the dalmatic, reaching to just below the knees. The sleeves were wide, descending to half-way down the forearm (*see* C).

(17) Ceremonial shoes or sandals of gold were put on, and (18) golden spurs buckled over them. Then followed

(19) The oblation, and (20) girding on of the sword.

(21) Vesting with armilla or stole, as seen in Fig. 217 (but not shown here), and

(22) The pallium quadrum, or state mantle, of velvet or silk, embroidered round the edge with gold and lined with ermine or vair (*see* D).

(23) Delivery of the ring, symbolical of the marriage between the king and his people, which was placed on the fourth finger of the right hand.

(24) Delivery of the sceptre bearing the cross into the right hand, and (25) the rod surmounted by the dove into the left hand.

[1] In Corpus Christi College, Cambridge, MS. 20.

Fig. 292. KING IN CORONATION ROBES
Early fourteenth century

(26) The crowning by the Archbishop of Canterbury, followed by

(27) The Benediction.

(28) The *Te Deum*.

(29) The inthronisation.

(30) Homage of peers. Then followed:

(31) The coronation of the queen-consort, who was anointed on the hands only.

(32) Introit *Protector noster*.

(33) Second oblation, the king making formal offerings of gold and precious palls.

(34) The Communion.

(35) At the conclusion of these ceremonies the king was conducted back to the palace, where he sat down to a sumptuous banquet.

Fig. 292 is drawn from the miniature and description given in the manuscript. The king, being a bearded man, might be Edward I., but despite this he is more probably Edward II.; he is certainly not Edward III. He wears the colobium sidonis (A); the tunicle (B) of red, bordered with gold and open up the sides, showing a green lining; and the dalmatic (C) of rayed cloth of gold and silver, the gold embroidered with a scroll pattern in orange. Over the shoulders, the square mantle in a pinkish-fawn velvet, having a gold-embroidered border, is fastened by two pleated corners with a large golden agrafe set with rubies. It is lined with vair. When the king was seated it was customary to drape the two bottom corners of the mantle over the knees.

Fig. 293.
Noble in "Quintise"

Other costumes shown in the same manuscript represent the fashions of Edward I.'s and Edward II.'s reigns.

The effigy of Edward II. on his monument at Gloucester Cathedral resembles that of his grandfather, Henry III. The dressing of the hair is exactly the same, and the costume is very similar. The robe fits close on the chest and shoulders, but the skirt part is cut very much on the circle and forms many folds reaching to the ankles. The sleeves fit close on the upper arm, the front part being cut away at elbow-level in the manner shown in Fig. 300. The mantle is attached across the shoulders by a strap or cord, and the whole costume is without ornament.

A nobleman of this period is shown in Fig. 293. He is not one of those who have adopted the most extravagant style, but is wearing a robe similar to those in fashion during the last reign, made of some rich material, with sleeves buttoned tight from wrist to elbow and loose on the upper arm. Over it he wears the "quintise," notched all round the

edge, and lined with a contrasting colour. No girdle is seen, although probably worn under the robe. The absence of a visible girdle was universal with well-dressed people at this period, although it was frequently worn under the robe over the short cotte, to support the gipciere or purse, access to which was through side-slits in the robe. On his shoulders is seen the hood, the bottom edge being ornamented with daggers of the engrailed pattern, and the exceedingly long liripipe is carried in the left hand.

The mantle or cloke. Circular mantles came into use about the beginning of the fourteenth century, and were made of various materials, but chiefly of cloth. They were worn with or without a hood attached to them (*see* Fig. 294). To free the hands the edges were raised and draped over the arm, forming very graceful folds. These mantles were

Fig. 294. Circular Mantle

not open up the front, but were drawn over the head, thus entirely enveloping the figure. Worn by both sexes, these mantles or clokes were very useful for travelling and on horseback, and when lined with fur were very comfortable garments.

A much more ornamental cloke, or mantle, of French origin, was worn during this reign. Similar to the mantle just described, it was cut as a full circle, as shown in Fig. 295, with a hole, A, in the centre for the head, and open all the way up the front. On either side, at a distance from A about equal to the length of the arm, were horizontal or perpendicular slits, B and C, through which the hands might pass if necessary. This mantle usually had three or four ornamental fastenings on the chest, D, and sometimes these continued all the way down the front. This mantle or cloke, worn by both sexes of

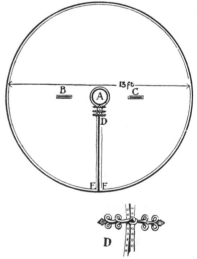

Fig. 295. Diagram of Circular Mantle

the nobility, was composed of rich material, velvet or silk, lined with silk and often fur. It was occasionally decorated with bands of embroidery, sometimes placed at intervals parallel to the circumference, or in a perpendicular or horizontal position on the mantle.

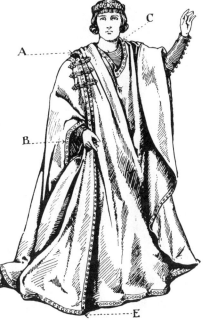

This mantle was first worn in the normal way, *i.e.* enveloping the figure with the head through the opening A, the hands being passed through the openings B and C if required; but one day some fantastic courtier evolved a curious method of wearing it, which he imagined enabled him to carry it more gracefully. The right arm was passed through the right arm-opening B, and *the head through the left arm-opening* C. The normal aperture for the head, A, then fell towards the back, with the ornamental fastenings D over the right shoulder, and the open edges of the mantle, E, D, F, which usually came in front, were now very much on the right side. When the left hand was raised, the

Fig. 296. Later method of wearing Circular Mantle

edge of the mantle was draped over the left shoulder (*see* Fig. 296). The development of this prank will be mentioned later.

The hood. Many curious developments of the hood took place during this reign. First among them was the growth of the liripipe,

Fig. 297. Mummer's Hood

which, when worn by fashionable youth, attained a length of six feet or more. It hung down the back or was carried over the arm. Later, when girdles were worn, the liripipe was draped over the shoulders, with the end passed through the girdle.

Alternatively at this time the liripipe was used to bind the hood on the head, being wound once, twice, or many times round it, and the end tied in a knot at one side, giving the headdress the appearance of a turban. This practice had its use, for it kept the hood secure on the head. It was often worn over the coif (*see* Fig. 293 inset).

About the same time the hood was elongated in an alternative direction—on both sides of the head (Fig. 297). This kind of hood was

Fig. 298.

VARIOUS ARRANGEMENTS OF HOOD AND HAIRDRESSING

considered very quaint, but soon after its introduction its popularity was confined to mummers, jesters and morris-dancers. It then had a small bell attached to each point, and was often made in two colours—parti-coloured or motley. Another curious fashion of wearing the hood was introduced by some Court dandy who, being bored by the conventional way of wearing it, in a frivolous mood conceived the idea of placing the facial opening round the head. In Fig. 298 A the old-fashioned hood (*see* Fig. 52) is shown (diagrammatically) worn in this manner. In Fig. 298 B the later hood (*see* Fig. 144) is shown.

In Fig. 298 c the wearer has arranged the short liripipe to stick out in front, the edge of the facial opening being turned back to form a brim. The shoulder-part has been pleated up and probably fixed with a pin towards the back on the right side, the turned-up brim securing it more closely to the head, and also giving it a certain spring.

Sometimes the position of the hood was changed, the shoulder-part drapery being in front, with the liripipe hanging at the back (Fig. 298 D); or the shoulder-part fell on one side, and the liripipe on the other, as shown in Fig. 298 E. This last method was very generally adopted towards the end of the fourteenth century, and will be referred to again under the hood of that period. The innovation captured the fancy of other courtiers, and these quaint ways of wearing the hood became very general, as may be seen in illuminated manuscripts of this and the following reigns.

Fig. 299. Modern University Hood

A hood shaped like Fig. 163 and Fig. 337 was used from this time onwards as a mark of distinction for university graduates. Originally they were always worn on the head, but later, after the fifteenth century, they were worn on the shoulders and hanging down the back.[1]

Nobility—Women

Margaret of France lost her husband at the age of twenty-six, and, according to her chronicler, John o' London, she greatly lamented his decease. However, her grief did not prevent her appearance in public less than a year after the death of Edward I. (contrary to the prescribed etiquette of the time), to attend the marriage of her stepson, Edward II., and her niece Isabella. She was also present at the christening of Prince Edward, afterwards Edward III. The influence of this charming woman seems to have had some effect, while she lived, upon the behaviour of her niece. Isabella's viciousness did not become notorious until after the death of the queen-dowager, which took place at her residence, Marlborough Castle, in 1317, at the age of thirty-six. She was buried in the

[1] The hood is used to-day for the same purpose, but its shape has deteriorated (Fig. 299).

Church of Grey Friars within Newgate, London, where a monument [1] was erected to her memory. This queen is represented upon the tomb of her great-nephew, John of Eltham, at Westminster Abbey.

Queen Isabella, the wife of Edward II., was a great beauty, and Miss Strickland tells us that no queen since the Saxon Elfrida has left so dark a stain on the annals of female royalty. Although a princess of higher rank (the daughter of a king and of a queen in her own right) than any previous queen-consort, excepting Judith, the wife of King Æthelwulf, she has been handed down to posterity as the "She-wolf of France."

After twenty-eight years of imprisonment, Isabella "went the way of all flesh" in 1358, at the age of sixty-three. Her heart was buried in the Parish Church at Castle Rising, and her body was interred in the Church of Grey Friars. A statuette, or "weeper," of this queen still exists at the side of the monument to John of Eltham, but which of several represents Isabella is not known.

CHILDREN OF EDWARD II. AND ISABELLA

1. Edward, Prince of Wales, born at Windsor, 1312.
2. John of Eltham, Earl of Cornwall, born 1319, died 1336.
3. Joan, married 1328 David II. of Scotland.
4. Eleanor, married Reynald, first Duke of Guelders—ancestors of Mary Stuart, Queen of Scotland.

Some details of the wedding of Edward II. and Isabella, and of the bride's trousseau, are interesting. Eight kings and queens were among the company, and the feasts and tournaments in connection with the marriage lasted a fortnight. The arrangements for the coronation, and the banquet which shortly followed the wedding, were undertaken by Piers Gaveston, but from inexperience in such matters the whole affair was a disastrous fiasco and put the Court in a very bad temper. The bride herself was extremely annoyed that certain valuable presents, jewels, etc., given to the bridegroom by her relatives were immediately bestowed upon the grasping Piers Gaveston.

The magnificent trousseau is described by "Matthew of Westminster," and details are also given in certain wardrobe accounts which afford many interesting particulars of Queen Isabella's costumes. She brought with her from France many dresses made of baudekyn, velvet, all sorts of silk and shot taffeta. Special attention was called to six gowns of green cloth, six beautifully marbled—marbrinus—and six of écarlate, and many costly furs. She had also seventy-two head-dresses, two gold and jewelled crowns, and a quantity of table plate in gold and silver.

At the baptismal ceremony of Prince John of Eltham the queen

---

[1] When, in the reign of Elizabeth, the Church of Grey Friars was made parochial, the Lord Mayor of London, at that time Sir Martin Bowes, sold this monument, together with those of nine other royal personages, and these records were lost.

appeared in a robe (probably a peliçon trimmed with ermine, like Fig. 301) of white velvet, for which five "pieces" were required in the making.

The figures of "weepers" on the tomb of John of Eltham represent kings and queens, relatives of the deceased. It is not certain which is Margaret of France, second queen of Edward I., but all the queens are robed in costumes such as this lady and her niece, Isabella of France, queen of Edward II., would wear. Although the tomb was not erected until 1337, all details of dress are of the first quarter of the fourteenth century. Fig. 300 is a drawing constructed from some of these "weepers." The queen wears a gown cut close on the shoulders and bust, and very circular in the skirt, which has a train (see Fig. 227). The sleeves encircle the arms as far as the elbows, the back portions falling thence in straight pieces with curved ends, displaying the sleeves of the undergown on the forearms. The gown is ungirded, and in accordance with the fashion of the time the skirt is raised and held close to the figure. No mantles are represented on these "weepers," although they would have been worn for full dress by ladies of this rank. The headdress is that described under Fig. 263, surmounted by the royal diadem. A sceptre is carried in the hand.

Fig. 300.
Queen, *temp.* Edward II.

The noble lady seen in Plate IX. is resplendent in the full dress of this reign. The rose-coloured gown has tight sleeves to the wrist, and over it she wears a blue cyclas with openings at each side, treated in a decorative manner and laced with a gold cord, finishing in a tassel at the end. The violet mantle, cross-barred with vermilion, has a gold lining, and borders worked in blue, vermilion and gold. It is attached across the shoulders with gold cords which pass *under* the wimple. The elaborate headdress is described on p. 268, and as usual with this type of wimple it is worn outside the cyclas.

Fig. 301 represents a noble lady garbed in a peliçon. Although of a different shape from that shown in Fig. 117, it is none the less a peliçon, being lined with fur, for by this time the name peliçon was applied to a garment not so much because of its shape as because it was lined with fur. The one shown in this figure is merely a variation of the circular cloke used by the men, and seen in Fig. 294. It is cut,

Fig. 301. The Peliçon

however, in a long oval, since a long train was required. Fig. 302 gives
a diagram of this garment. The chief feature is the very pronounced

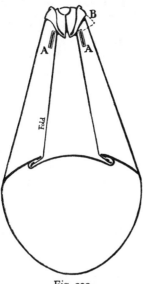

Fig. 302.
Diagram of Peliçon

folds in front on each side of the figure.
These are fixed only at the shoulder seam.
Openings for the hands are situated in
these folds at A. On the shoulders a cape,
or GUEULES, is fixed, also lined with
fur, and it was the mode to turn the
edges of the shoulders upwards to show the
outside material, as shown at B. This gave a
distinctive line to the upper part of the
garment.

Sometimes an ample hood, also lined with
fur, was attached in place of the cape, having
buttons in front to fasten it close up round
the throat. This peliçon was worn by noble
ladies of the period as a State and semi-State
dress, and always had a long train. Being
lined throughout with fur—ermine or sable—
it was very heavy, and somewhat cumbersome; consequently it was usual to have the

train borne by a lady-in-waiting.[1] This garment is worn by Jeanne de Bourgoyne, queen of Philippe VI., and represented in an illuminated manuscript dated 1333. It is also shown in the manuscript at Christchurch College, Oxford, as worn by Queen Isabella.

When the peliçon was of less ample dimensions, *i.e.* cut on a circular plan, the skirt part was raised and held close between the upper arm and side (*see* the brass to Lady de Northwode, Minster, Kent).

The noble lady of the middle of this reign shown in Fig. 303 wears what might pass for a new garment. It is the old cyclas in a fresh guise, with a new cut and different name. At this time the name cyclas fell out of use as applied to a woman's garment, and henceforth was associated solely with the surcote worn by knights over their armour. The woman's version of this garment is known as THE SIDELESS GOWN.

Fig. 303.
First Sideless Gown

The change in shape is almost entirely confined to the armhole, which was cut larger, reducing the width of the

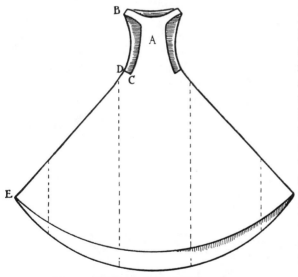

Fig. 304. Diagram of First Sideless Gown

material in front (*see* Fig. 304 at A). The line of the armhole is shown in the drawing at B, C, D. The angle at C was sometimes rounded. The back was wider than the front and fell away from the figure when the wearer moved, thus showing the colour of the lining. In the diagram the shoulder-pieces are marked B, and from D to E the front of the skirt is seamed to the back. It was put on over the head without any fastenings. A more practical

---

[1] No earlier reference to the employment of a train-bearer is recorded in the history of English Court ceremonial. An interesting fact in this connection is that, during the Middle Ages, no trains were carried by attendants in the presence of royalty. On the appearance of the king, or other member of a royal family, trains were lifted by their bearers and placed over the wearer's left arm.

method would be to have hooks and eyes at the back of the left
shoulder. A gown with tight sleeves is worn underneath this gar-

ment. The lady's hair is encased in a gold and
jewelled crespinette, surmounted by the barbette
and coif seen in Fig. 259 and described on
p. 180.

Motifs from the family coat of arms were frequently used as a decoration, powdered over the
whole of the sideless gown. Sometimes the complete armorial bearings were blazoned upon it (*see*
Plate XIX). *See* Heraldry,
Chapter V., p. 332.

The dress worn on ordinary
occasions by a noble lady is
shown in Fig. 305. It consists
of the cyclas in its older form
(*see* Fig. 212) over a gown
shaped like that in the drawing
from the illuminated manuscript Fig. 247. She wears the
fashionable headdress and a

Fig. 305.
Noble Lady *temp.*
Edward II.

wimple which comes well on to the shoulders.

The very simple costume worn by Lady Joan
de Cobham shown on the brass to her memory,
c. 1320, is reconstructed in Fig. 306. It is a gown
of the same shape as seen in Fig. 226, but the neck-
part is cut lower and the sleeves finish just below
the elbow, where they are a little wider and pointed.
There is a border to the neck and sleeves, and the
tight sleeves of the underdress show on the lower
arm. The coiffure is the same as described under
Fig. 393. This costume is utilitarian as well as very
graceful, and is typical of the dress worn by great ladies in the course
of their everyday life.

Fig. 306.
Lady Joan Cobham.

Fig. 307

Section II.—Edward III. 1327–1377

Nobility—Men

Edward III., born at Windsor, 1312. Knighted by the Earl of Lancaster, 1327. Crowned 1 February, 1328.

The drawing (Fig. 308) of Edward III. is reproduced from an illuminated manuscript dated 1331, which shows his hair of a light brown colour. His slight beard upon the chin only is darker in tone, and his complexion is fair. In 1357 another representation of this king is found showing him wearing a flowing beard upon the upper lip as well as the beard on the chin. A description of Edward III. by Walsingham is as follows:

Fig. 308.
Edward III. 1331

He was a shapely man, of stature neither tall nor short, his countenance was kindly, rather like unto an angel than to any mortal, in which there shows the light of a gracious and manly spirit; and if any man were to look him boldly in the eye, or to sleep near him by night, then indeed would he hope to be filled with joy and solace.

Fig. 309.
Edward III. 1372

The portrait corbel head (Fig. 309) of Edward in Ewelme Church, Oxford, shows him late in life, with wavy beard about six inches in length. On his effigy (Fig. 310) at Westminster his hair is much longer, and his beard reaches to his chest. In old age his hair was quite white.

Edward was of a kind disposition and liberal in nature; a good ruler, but not a great monarch like his grandfather, Edward I., though superior in tactical skill to any general he encountered.

Fig. 310.
Edward III. 1377

A consummate knight—his Court was the most brilliant in Europe—he fully justified his position as head of the splendid chivalry that obtained fame in the French wars. His main ambition was military, and he made war flourish by means of trade, of which he was a great supporter. Extravagant, self-indulgent, and eager for power, he prepared for future generations of his house by marrying his sons to wealthy and important heiresses of the noblest families. Unfortunately, these matrimonial alliances resulted in strife, and in a great measure were responsible for the Wars of the Roses of the following century.

In his latter days, Edward gave less and less attention to ruling his kingdom, especially after the death of Queen Philippa in 1369, and left matters largely in the hands of the Earl of Pembroke and John of Gaunt, but their government was not popular. The poor old king was almost entirely left to himself in his last few years, except by his favourite, a woman named Alice Perrers. The death of his eldest son, the Black Prince, in 1376 hastened his end, and his last hours were desolate. His nobles and courtiers were preoccupied with speculations about the future king—would it be John of Gaunt or Richard of Bordeaux, the young son and heir of the Black Prince?

On 2 June, 1377, Edward III. died at the age of sixty-four and in the fiftieth year of his reign. When she saw the king breathing his last, Alice Perrers took the rings from his cold hands and fled, leaving the servants to plunder the Palace of Sheen, known later as the Palace of Richmond.

Description of the effigy of Edward III., which obviously dates at the end of his fifty years' reign and shows him as an old man, is reserved until the end of this section.

Edward, Prince of Wales, called "The Black Prince," was born at Woodstock Palace, 1330. His brilliant career began in 1346, when he was knighted at La Hogue by his father. He married, in 1361, Joan, a great beauty, known as "The Fair Maid of Kent," daughter and heiress of his great-uncle, Thomas of Woodstock, Earl of Kent. This lady had been married previously to William Montacute, Earl of Salisbury, and afterwards to Thomas, Lord Holland, Earl of Kent (in right of his wife), K.G.

CHILDREN OF THE PRINCE AND PRINCESS OF WALES

1. Edward of Angoulême, born 1365, died 1372.
2. Richard of Bordeaux, born 1366, afterwards Richard II.

The prince and princess resided in royal state, chiefly in Gascony, keeping a brilliant Court at Bordeaux and Angoulême. The

Fig. 311. The Cotehardie

princess died at the Royal Castle of Wallingford in 1385. A corbel bust on the vaulting of the Black Prince's Chantry, Canterbury Cathedral, is said to be a portrait of the Fair Maid of Kent.

A typical costume of a nobleman worn during the greater part of this reign is given in Fig. 311. His body garment was known by various

names, sometimes its original "cotte," but more frequently by its later
term, "cotehardie." When worn with military equipment it was known
as the JUPON (*see* p. 321), and this name
was often applied to the civil garment, the
cotehardie. For convenience it is here
referred to as the cotehardie, although a
tight-fitting woman's garment (*see* p. 229)
is called by the same name.

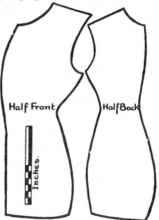

Fig. 312. Diagram of Cotehardie

The cotehardie was a shaped garment
fitting tight on the shoulders and at the
waist and hips. It was constructed in four
parts (*see* Fig. 312), seamed down the back,
sides and front, where it was fastened. The
seams on the hips were sometimes left
undone for about three or four inches from
the bottom and were buttoned with one or
two buttons in the same style as those in
front. The cotehardie shown in Fig. 311 is "parti-coloured" (*see*
p. 317) white and black, and both sides
embroidered ("brayden") or woven in a
gold design. A band of gold on which
buttonholes are worked descends the
front, and the garment is fastened by
jewelled and enamelled buttons all the
way down. The sleeves, which came only
to the elbow, were either inserted in the
armhole, or cut all in one with the side
and back pieces. This particular cotehardie being half white and half black,
the right sleeve is all white and the left
all black. (When the cotehardie was
"quarterly," *i.e.* each front and back piece
alternately of the two colours, the sleeves
would be half and half, the seams being
on the outside and underside, *not* front
and back. This is explained in Fig. 313,
and should be carefully remembered.) At
the edge of the sleeve a piece of material
was attached about three inches in width,
and in length anything up to five feet.
One end was sewn round the arm, the

Fig. 313. Parti-colour Quarterly

remainder falling to the ground in the
form of a long streamer. The name TIPPET was given to these streamers,
and occasionally applied also to the liripipe of the hood. "With his tipet
ybounde about his hed" is a description given later by Chaucer. These

tippets were always white, in cloth, silk or linen, and great care was exercised to keep them without a crease. For this reason they were pressed between planks of wood when not in wear. This applies to women's tippets as well as those of the men.

Underneath the cotehardie a short jacket was worn, with tight sleeves buttoned from elbow to wrist. That worn by the nobleman in Fig. 311 is parti-coloured, the right sleeve being purple and the left blue. To the waist of this short jacket was attached the hose, also parti-coloured, the right leg being blue and the left purple. The hose and foot part are combined, and the toes have long points stuffed with wool. The short jacket referred to above, and seen in Fig. 314, was called a PALTOCK (later POURPOINT, *see* p. 225, which became an important item of apparel). The chief use of the paltock was as a foundation to which undersleeves and hose could be attached. Laces of silk or braid,

A ......

Fig. 314.
Trussing Poynts

with tags or points at the ends, were fixed to the top of the hose or to the shoulder end of sleeves, and these were passed through eyelet-holes inserted at the waist-line or armhole of the paltock. "To truss the POYNTS." [1] "They have a weed (garment) of silk, called a paltock, to which their hosen of two colours, or pied with more, are fastened with white HERLOTS (latchets) without any breeches (drawers)." [2]

The costume in Fig. 311 was not complete until the hood and belt had been added. The former, also parti-coloured blue and purple, had a liripipe quite five feet in length, and a very richly ornamented border round the cape part edged with leaf-like dagges.

A distinctive feature of the costume of this time was a very rich girdle or hip-belt of goldsmith's work and jewels (*see* Fig. 414, and Jewellery, p. 277), worn very low down on the hips (never worn round the waist during this reign), from which sometimes hung a sword or BASELARD on the left side and frequently a dagger on the right, called a MISERICORDE, and so named because it was generally used to inflict the "mercy-stroke" and deprive a wounded antagonist of life.

Fig. 314 shows a young man in the act of trussing his left leg hose by

[1] Sometimes called AIGLETTES.
[2] A book of instructions to a valet, dating about this time, sets forth his duties in dressing his master: "Pull up his hosen and tie them up. Lace his *dublett* hole by hole. Comb his hair with an ivory comb. Set his garment goodly—scarlet or green, satin, cendal, or velvet."

tying his poynts to the eyelet-holes in the paltock; the hose on the right leg is only half on, displaying a bare thigh, and the SLOPS, marked A (*see* p. 245). The holes for inserting the poynts are seen at the waist-line [1] of the paltock, and also up the front where the paltock is laced over the sherte. The sleeves also were sometimes tied on, but it was quite usual to have them fixed to the paltock. Although the method of trussing hose is mentioned under this period, there is no doubt that from early times some such means of supporting leg-coverings was known (*see* Vol. I., p. 269). Positive proof is not forthcoming, however, until the fourteenth century, when evidence is obtained from paintings, illuminated manuscripts, and from the remains of original garments.

Excavations carried out in 1921 at Herjolfsnes, a centre of Danish colonists in South Greenland until the end of the fourteenth century, have brought to light many garments, the shapes of which are identical with the general type of costume worn during the fourteenth century by the middle classes in England, France and Denmark. They are now preserved in the National Museum at Copenhagen, and are very valuable as examples of the cut of the costumes under discussion in this chapter. Four diagrams of these garments are shown in Figs. 315, 324, 325 and 375

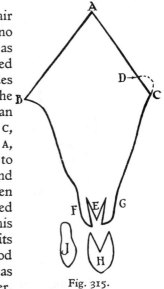

Fig. 315.
Diagram of Hose

Fig. 315 gives the cut of one leg of a pair of hose found at Herjolfsnes, and there is no doubt that this shape, though established as belonging to the fourteenth century, was used for making hose in earlier times. The sides B F and C G were joined up the back of the leg, starting at the heel. As B F was longer than C G, the corner B could not coincide with C, but was drawn up above it and joined to C A, finishing at D. The triangle E was joined to the foot part, H on the instep, the sides F and G to the sides of the foot part, and then joined to the sole J. The point A was attached to the waist-belt at the side of the front. This pattern (Fig. 315) is given because of its interest. It is not one recommended for good fit, but illustrates a useful garment such as was worn by ordinary people. It is, however, an authentic model on which to base the cut of hose of a superior shape as worn by the fashionable upper classes.

Fig. 316 is a diagram of hose, constructed partly from this evidence and from drawings in illuminated manuscripts and partly evolved from practical experience. It is the pattern of hose worn by all well-dressed

[1] Sometimes the hose reached only to just above the hips, where they were trussed to a longer jacket.

men, and gives the front and back of the right leg, with dimensions in inches, to fit an average-sized man. These dimensions do not include turnings. It is necessary to cut the cloth on the cross, so that it stretches where necessary, and to have an opening of eight inches on the inner side of the ankle, so that the hose may be drawn over the foot. This opening can be laced invisibly with a needle and thread after the hose have been pulled up. To cut out the patterns, measurements should be set out from the centre line of each diagram. The lengths from heel to waist (forty-seven inches at back centre) are given in the column between the drawings of the front and back portions. Join the outside seams A B C to D E F, and also the inside seams H I to R Q, leaving an opening of eight inches at the ankle on the inside. The triangle gusset O joins the front and back portions on the inner side of the

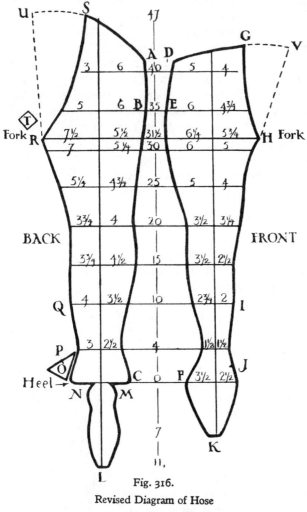

Fig. 316.
Revised Diagram of Hose

ankle, and the sole. At M and N the sole is joined to the heel part, and the remainder of the sole is joined to the instep portion. The parts S A and D G form half the waist-line, leaving an opening back and front as in Fig. 314. The portions included in the dotted lines R U S and H V G should be added if overlaps in front and at the back are required. When long pointed toes were the fashion, the sole at L and the foot part at K were lengthened.

The celebrated psalter of Queen Mary Tudor,[1] dating from the

[1] British Museum, Roy. MS. 2 B. VII.

early years of the fourteenth century, shows in an illumination a young noble being helped by his valet into his hosen of this type.

Should it be desired to join the two legs together to make a pair of hose ("tights" is the modern name), with side-openings from waist to hips, proceed as follows:

Join the outside seams B C to E F: the edges A B and D E form the openings on the hips. Join the inside seams and foot parts as before described, leaving the eight-inch opening at the ankle. Omit the portions included in the dotted lines, and join G H to the corresponding line on the opposite leg, and in like manner join S R. At the fork the gusset T, two inches square, is set at the junction of both legs. The sole and foot part can be cut all in one with the front and back, as this diagram shows, but there is no reason why the method shown in Fig. 315 should not be adopted.

The pourpoint. After the middle of the fourteenth century it was the vogue to stuff out the chest with padding, giving a pigeon-chested effect which was further accentuated by pulling in the waist. The paltock now assumed its later name of "pourpoint" (compare "pourpointed," from the punctures with which it was covered, and "pourpointerie," from the needlework employed in its construction). The shape of the garment— that of a close-fitting, sleeveless jacket to which sleeves could be attached (*see* p. 222)—remained much the same, but the breast part was stuffed between the foundation and an outer piece of material, and quilted with stitching.

The costume of King Edward is noted by Froissart in the year 1346 and his reference is worth quoting: "The King of England being at sea" off Calais, "posted himself in the fore part of his own ship: he was dressed in a black velvet cotehardie, and wore on his head a small hat of beaver, which became him much." It was a simple dress, the cotehardie quite plain, relieved only by a belt of goldsmith's work, and worn with black cloth hose (Fig. 317). Probably a hood of either material was worn on the head, surmounted by a beaver hat like that in Fig. 391; no doubt a cloke of cloth was at hand.

Fig. 317.
Edward III. in 1346

Garters. That usually reticent item of costume, the garter, had been in use to support the hose during the Norman Period (*see* Fig. 10), and a strap or string was frequently used to tie the high boot or BUSKIN securely below the knee. When long robes came into fashion, at the end of the eleventh century, garters disappeared from view, whether worn by men or

Fig. 318. The Mantle

women. With the advent of the cote-hardie garters were worn occasionally by fashionable men, not for utility, but as ornaments, a mode copied from contemporary Italian fashions. Such garters are seen in Plate X. Another method of wearing them, when used by ladies over their short hose (or, as we call them, stockings), was to place the garter below the knee, cross it at the back, and bring it above the knee, tying it with a knot and ends on the outside of the leg.

Fig. 318 shows another nobleman in a similar costume to that shown in Fig. 311. The cotehardie in this illustration has an ornamental edging of dagges. Above it is placed the hip-belt. Over all is worn one of the most fashionable mantles or clokes. It is the circular cloke first worn in the preceding reign, but the slits for the hands are omitted. The cloke could be worn with or without a hood; buttoned on the right shoulder, it envelops the figure, but its opening being on that side leaves the right arm free for immediate action. Frequently the front part was turned back, showing the lining, and draped over the left shoulder and arm. At the bottom of the cloke is a border finished off with decorated dagges.

In 1351 King John of France established the Order of Knighthood of the Star, in imitation of the Garter; and the first chapter was held at the palace of S. Ouen, near Paris. Each knight wore a star on the crest of his helmet or on his hood, another pendent at the neck, and a third embroidered on the left shoulder of his mantle.

Fig. 319 shows a knight of this Order wearing a surcote and a mantle like that described in Fig. 318.

Fig. 319. Knight of the Star

In the following year (1352) the Order of S. Esprit au Droit Désir ou du Nœud was instituted at Naples by Louis of Anjou. The badge was a peculiar knot (Fig. 320) embroidered in purple silk intermixed with gold, worn upon the right arm or breast, and on the mantle. The motto was "Le Dieu Plait." Representations are seen of knights of this Order wearing circular mantles, in the manner described under Fig. 318,

Fig. 320

and this method was adopted by all future orders of knighthood instituted upon the Continent.

A slightly different type of cotehardie had been in use since about 1325, identical with the jupon worn as part of their military equipment by knights (*see* Fig. 449). It was a close-fitting garment to just below the waist, but the lower part was cut on the circle round the hips, and hung in folds to mid-thigh. This cotehardie was worn for ordinary occasions by the nobility, as well as being popular among the middle classes during the first part of this reign (*see* Fig. 361).

Fig. 321.
Edward III. 1375

A noble fop of the period is seen in Plate X. complete in the fashion of the middle of the century. He would be by no means out of date in the reign of Richard II. Although a knight and a gentleman, he well deserves the scornful abuses hurled at his class by the poets, who denounced the evils of this time. They blame "the knights for dressing like minstrels," and "the esquires for wearing great hoods with ridiculously long liripipes, and new-fashioned jupons." His tippets are elaborately decorated with foliated dagges, and the green hood has a border with similar dagges forming four points, one on each shoulder, one in front and one behind.

After the middle of the fourteenth century the wearing of tippets went out of fashion among the upper classes, but they were worn by the middle classes for some time longer, eventually becoming obsolete before the end of the century. The rich jewelled belt in Plate X. hooks round the hips, or is fastened by a clasp. A pendent end ornamented to accord with the belt itself hangs from the right side — not an unusual fashion.

In his effigy at Westminster Abbey, Edward III. is said to be wearing coronation robes. These consist of a long robe hanging straight from the neck, where it is pleated into a neckband. It is slit up the front to a short distance below the waist. The sleeves are close-fitting, and short enough to show at the wrist about three inches of the undersleeve. A semi-circular mantle with a gold border is worn, fastened across the chest by a band of embroidery or jewels. Fig. 321 is a drawing constructed from these details and others—the crown, sceptre, jewelled bosses, cords to the mantle, and shoes have been added from authentic details to show how Edward III. appeared in full state.

Nobility—Women

Philippa, the second daughter of Count William of Hainault, Holland and Zealand, and Lord of Friesland, was born in 1311. She met Edward, Prince of Wales, in 1326, when he accompanied his mother to Flanders. Their marriage took place at York in 1328. The wedding festivities were very magnificent, and had been devised, it is said, by Queen Isabella to divert public attention from the murder of the late king. The principal nobility of Scotland were present, as they had come to arrange a peace treaty with Edward III.

Queen Philippa's eldest son was born on 15 June, 1330, at Woodstock Palace, a favourite residence of the monarchs of England during many generations. The mother and child became very popular with the people, partly on account of her personal charm, and also in view of the great interest she evinced in the welfare of the middle and lower classes. Artists of the time represented the Virgin and Child in the likeness of the young mother and son. This good queen died of that disfiguring malady, dropsy, on 14 August, 1369, and was buried in Westminster Abbey.

"The moost gentyll quene, moost lyberall, and moost courtesse that ever was quene in her dayes, the whiche was the fayre lady Philipp of Heynault, quene of England and Irelande."

CHILDREN OF EDWARD III. AND PHILIPPA

1. Edward, born 1330; married Joan, daughter and heiress of the Earl of Kent. (Their younger child Richard succeeded to the crown.) Died 1376.

2. Lionel, born 1338, Duke of Clarence; married Elizabeth de Burgh, daughter and heiress of the Earl of Ulster. (Their only daughter married Edmund Mortimer, Earl of March, and was ancestress of King Edward IV.) Died 1368.

3. John, born 1340 at Ghent; married, 1st, the Lady Blanche Plantagenet, daughter and co-heiress of the Duke of Lancaster. (Their son, the Earl of Derby, usurped the crown as Henry IV.).

Married, 2nd, Constance, daughter and co-heiress of Peter, King of Castile and Leon. (Their daughter married Henry III., King of Castile and Leon).

Married, 3rd, Katherine, daughter and co-heiress of Sir Payne Roelt, and widow of Sir Otes Swynford. (Their children took the name of Beaufort, and their second son was ancestor of King Henry VII.) Died 1399.

4 Edmund, born 1341, Earl of Cambridge and Duke of York; married Isabel, daughter and co-heiress of Peter, King of Castile and Leon. (Through their only surviving grandson they were ancestors of King Edward IV.)

5. Thomas, born 1355 at Woodstock, Duke of Gloucester; married the daughter and co-heiress of Humphrey de Bohun, Earl of Northampton, Hereford and Essex. Died 1397.

6. Isabel, married Earl of Bedford.

7. Joan, died of plague, 1348.

8. Blanche.

9. Mary, married Duke of Brittany.

10. Margaret, married Earl of Pembroke.

11, 12. Two others died young.

The sideless gown, as described under Fig. 303, continued in fashion until about the middle of the century. The Ladies Louterell (Plate XVIII.) are wearing this garment with their armorial bearings blazoned thereon. Although such heraldic decoration was very much in vogue (*see* Heraldry, Chap. V., p. 332), the sideless gown was frequently worn in plain colours and materials. It was usual to wear it without a mantle, but for full dress it was the custom to fasten the mantle across the shoulders, displaying the whole of the front of the figure. In consequence of the widened openings or armholes of the sideless gown, the under-garment became more important than before, and was known as the "Cotehardie" (Fig. 322). Indeed, its development led to the temporary relinquishment of the sideless gown. One of its features was that it fitted very tight round the waist, being laced at the back or buttoned up the front. The skirt had large gores let into the sides, which made many

Fig. 322. The Cotehardie

folds around the feet, and ended in a train. At each side of the front there were usually perpendicular openings through which the hands could be passed, or which could be used for raising the skirt while walking (*see* Figs. 322 and 327).

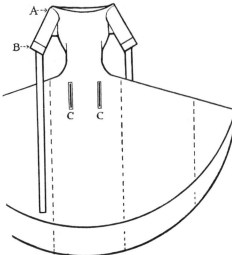

Fig. 323. Diagram of Woman's Cotehardie

Fig. 323 gives a diagram of the shape of the cotehardie hitherto regarded as authentic. This garment fitted the figure as far as the hips and then widened out to form a voluminous skirt and train. On account of the low neck the shoulder-piece at A is very narrow. The "tippet" attached to the elbow sleeve is shown at B, and the pocket slits at C.

A gown shaped almost exactly like the cotehardie, but without a train, was unearthed at Herjolfsnes, and revises our information about the method probably adopted; Fig. 324 gives a diagram of this garment. It is made to fit tight at the waist, with an all-round full skirt, fitting being contrived by side gores cut bottle-necked at the top. An added fullness is given to the skirt by gores which are let into the centres of the front and back pieces. The tightness at the waist depends on how much material is cut away from the centre of the back.

Fig. 325 gives the cut of the long sleeve. It is fairly wide at the arm-

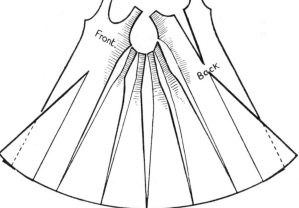

Fig. 324. Danish version of Cut of Cotehardie

Fig. 325. Diagram of Sleeve

hole, but fits close on the forearm, being buttoned from elbow to wrist. The sleeves of the fashionable cotehardie generally finished at the elbow with "tippets" attached to them, as seen in Fig. 323 at B, the sleeve of the underdress showing to the wrist. Frequently the sleeves of the cotehardie reached to the wrists with or without tippets, and were always tight-fitting on the forearm, where they were either buttoned or laced. Here, for the first time (about 1350), the sleeves extended over the hand to the knuckles, forming CUFFS, and were buttoned to the extremity. It was quite usual, however, to wear them unbuttoned from the wrist to the end, with a part of the cuff turned back.

The low-cut neck is another noteworthy feature of this garment. During the reign of Edward III. extremely bare shoulders became the vogue among women of the nobility. This fashion, of course, was but a revival; bare necks and shoulders had been seen last in Europe on women of the barbaric Teutonic tribes of the fifth century. In earlier days, women of the Roman Empire displayed to the full beautifully-moulded necks, shoulders and arms. During the Anglo-Saxon and early English period, it was the custom to veil these charms. Later there was a tendency to disclose them, but the indiscretions of Dame Fashion were checked towards the end of the

Fig. 326. Buttons.
Thirteenth and fourteenth centuries

twelfth century by the introduction of the wimple, and the situation saved, for a time. The wimple was chiefly used during the thirteenth and fourteenth centuries to partly veil the face, and was habitually worn at church by women of good breeding. "Modest women were gwimpled well," says Chaucer; and for this reason it was worn by nuns, and it has continued in use among them, with slight variations, to the present time. It was adopted as the correct veiling for widows (see p. 191).

The neck-line started on its downward course amongst the ladies of Queen Isabella's Court, and soon after Edward III.'s accession the fashion became general. Even Queen Philippa, whose decorum was without question, wore the neck of her cotehardie cut low (see Plate XI.).

Fig. 327. Fashionable Dress, 1330–1350

In order to guard against the risk of untoward exposure, extremely fashionable women utilised ornaments, often of goldsmith's work set with jewels, and fixed at the top of the sleeve on each side below the bend of the shoulder (*see* Brooches, p. 276). Occasionally a third was worn in front (*see* Fig. 327). A simpler version of this contrivance took the form of a band or piece of passement with ornamental hooks at the ends. This is shown in Fig. 322, which represents a fashionable lady of the earlier part of Edward III.'s reign. It should be noticed that the sleeves extend from shoulder to wrist, being buttoned from below the tippets to the wrist. The cotehardie in Fig. 327 exemplifies the description already given. This figure shows a lady of fashion of the

Fig. 328. Noble Lady, *c.* 1350

same period. Her cotehardie is lined throughout with fur, and for this reason the garment could be equally called a peliçon. Rich jewelled brooches clasp the low-cut gown on the shoulders, and a third is fixed on the chest. This leader of fashion has purloined a gentleman's hood, to be used in chilly weather as a graceful shoulder scarf. These hoods with long liripipes were much used by women, either worn on the head, especially for riding, or carried as shown in the drawing.

In Fig. 328 is shown a lady of about 1350. The only detail which marks this date is the cuffs or mitten sleeves, which extend to the knuckles. Her cotehardie is parti-coloured quarterly, *i.e.* divided down the front and back *and* at the sides, including the sleeves. To complete her costume this lady has placed around her hips a very rich belt of goldsmith's work and jewels. The vogue for wearing such belts was copied from the men of the time, and this drawing shows one of the first examples of its kind, very massive in design, and set in such high relief that it projects an inch or two from the figure. Notice the band of jewels on the shoulder, and the mirror. When not held in the hand, the mirror could be placed in the socket at the top of the stand made for that purpose —it is not a candlestick—thus converting it into a standing mirror.

The costume worn by Lady Warwick, wife of Thomas Beauchamp, third Earl of Warwick, and daughter of Roger Mortimer, Earl of March, shown on her effigy, dating 1369, in the Beauchamp Chapel, Warwick, and represented in Fig. 329, is typical of that worn by noble ladies who were not ultra-fashionable. The cotehardie is laced up the front, and the tight sleeves with deep cuffs are buttoned from elbow to finger knuckles. A narrow belt surrounds the hips, and is decorated throughout its length with gold ornaments set each with a single jewel (shown at A), and having a gold pendant-chape or "mordaunt" (B). A mantle hanging on the shoulders is attached by tasselled cords (missing in the original) secured to circular ornaments and knotted across the chest. The headdress is very curious, and is described under Head-dresses, p. 272.

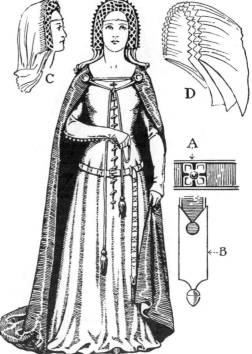

Fig. 329. Katherine, Countess of Warwick, 1360

With slender waists in the height of fashion, it is not surprising to find frequent mention of corsets. It is not known if they differed in shape from that shown in Fig. 30, and it is likely that they were the same. They were made of various materials, and a corset for Queen Philippa is described as being of red velvet, with laces and poynts. "Thirteen pieces of cloth for corsets for our said companion and her damsels," appears in an order of Edward III., which suggests that sometimes bandages were used.

Queen Philippa (about 1350) is represented in Plate XI. The costume is that worn on ceremonial occasions, and consists of the cotehardie of green, brocaded or embroidered in a gold design, with a hip-belt of massive gold-smith's work and jewels. The sideless gown in its latest form is worn over it. The armhole is now very much larger and cut low enough to show the hip-belt, which was always worn *under* the side-less gown—never over it. The shape of this garment is best understood by reference to the back and front diagram of cut in Fig. 330. This shape remained in use until the sideless gown went out of fashion, the only alteration affecting the front marked A in the diagram. That worn by the queen (Plate XI.) is in mauve, and has gold embroidery round the armhole, and over the front of it is a PLASTRON [1] of vair, which narrows to about two fingers in width over the shoulders and round the back of the neck. A band of jewels covers the centre line where it fastens, the

[1] Sometimes called the corset, in writings.

jewelled buttons or band being fixed through holes in the sideless gown to hooks on the cotehardie. The method was found very convenient, as it formed a firm foundation, and secured the sideless gown well in its place in front.

The queen is wearing the mantle of the Order of the Garter fastened by a cord, ending in tassels threaded through holes in a manner peculiar to this Order. The badge of the Garter is about eight inches in diameter, and the "Garter," about three-quarters of an inch wide, is worn round the left arm. Queen Philippa has her hair dressed in the same manner with a coif as seen in Fig. 396 E with the cylinders. A veil hangs at the back from under the crown.

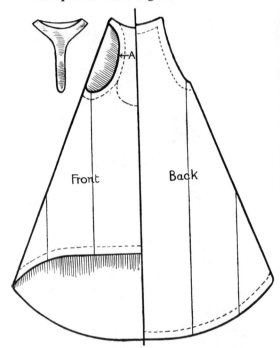

Fig. 330. Diagram of Sideless Gown

The shape of another plastron is shown in Fig. 331. This one also opens up the front, and is fastened by jewelled buttons as described above.

The costume of Queen Philippa shown on her effigy in Westminster Abbey is simple. She wears the cotehardie laced up the front, with a belt round the hips, and over it a mantle. The headdress is very much damaged, but originally it was the same as that seen in Plate XI. Part of the side cylinders still remain.

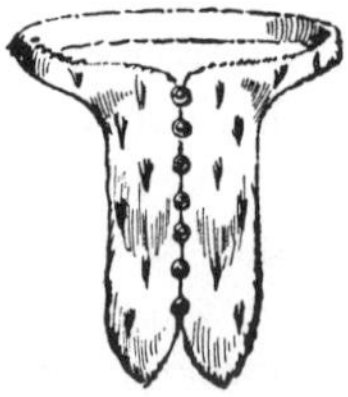

The costume shown in Fig. 332 is taken from a monument of a noble lady dating about 1350. The shape of the large armhole, the fur edging to it, and the reduced width of A (in Fig. 330) should be noticed. The fastening is as last described.

Fig. 331. Plastron

There are a few examples to be found on monuments, etc., of this time showing the side seams of the skirt of the sideless gown left open. When the skirt was edged with fur, the lateral side edges were also bordered with it. A notable instance is that on the statuette of Mary, Duchess of Brittany, which stands as a weeper on the monument of Edward III.

The sporting young lady shown in Fig. 333—taken from an illumination in a Book of Hours dated 1330—has slipped on a peliçon over her cotehardie, the evening being chilly, to shoot rabbits. This peliçon may be of silk or cloth, lined with fur, but differs slightly in shape from those seen in other illustrations. It fits the slim figure rather close, but the skirt part is cut on the semicircle. The sleeves finish at the elbow with wide openings. For pastimes less strenuous this lady would probably fix a flowing veil over her cauled hairdressing, as shown in Fig. 328.

In Fig. 334 is seen a very useful surcote worn as an extra covering over the cotehardie. It is cut as shown in Fig. 336, and worn without a girdle. The sleeves can be buttoned round the sleeves of the cotehardie if required. Fig. 335 shows a lady enveloped in a cloke. It is cut as a semicircle, but the scooped-out top is gathered into a band, fastened low down on the chest by a jewelled clasp. The headdresses in Figs. 334 and 335 are described on p. 272.

Fig. 332. Noble Lady, *temp.* Edward III.

SECTION III.—THE MOST NOBLE ORDER OF THE GARTER

Written in collaboration with G. Ambrose Lee, Esq., C.B., C.V.O.,
Clarenceux King-of-Arms.

The Garter is the premier Order of Knighthood in this country, and membership of the Order may be claimed as the highest honour in the world. It differs from earlier Orders such as the Knights Templars in that its purpose primarily was not service, but to enable the sovereign to confer a high dignity upon distinguished persons whom he wished to honour.

It has been told by the chronicler Agnes Strickland that "the heart of the mighty Edward swerved for awhile from its fidelity to Philippa," and its owner paid marked attention to the beautiful daughter of a Burgundian knight of imperial lineage named William de Grandison. This lady had been married when quite young to Sir William

Fig. 333. Peliçon

Montacute, one of Edward's knights who had been rewarded for his good services by the title of Earl of Salisbury.

Edward III. had first met the countess about 1333 (when he was twenty-one years of age). He had succeeded in relieving Wark Castle, the stronghold of the Earl of Salisbury, from siege by David, King of Scotland, and found her in charge of the garrison, the earl being still a prisoner in France. Lord Berners' (1467–1533) sixteenth-century translation from Froissart is worth quoting: "As sone as the lady knewe of the Kynge's comyng, she set epyn the gates and came out so richly besene (dressed), that every man maruyled of her beauty." The king "was stryken therwith to the hert with a spercle of fyne loue that endured long after."

For a time it was a very serious matter with Edward, "insomuch that he could not put her out of his mind, for love reminded him of her day and night," and it might have had more serious consequences had it not been for the high principles of Katherine the Fair, Countess of Salisbury. But, naturally, people talked—especially the courtiers.

"Out of affection for the said lady, and his desire to see her, he ordered a great feast and tournament to be proclaimed," to be followed by a State ball. To this function the Earl of Salisbury was commanded to bring his lady, and "he willingly complied with the king's request *for he thought no evil,* and his good lady dared not say nay."

What is believed to be the sequel to this love episode is not established with certainty: the loss of the original statutes of the Order of the Garter has left the subject to conjecture, but the tradition is as follows:

Its institution, according to

Fig. 334. Surcote   Fig. 335. Cloke

some writers, is said to have arisen from an accident which occurred at this State ball. While the Lady Katherine was dancing she had the misfortune to drop her garter, much to the amusement of the salacious company and the annoyance of the queen. But the tactful Edward picked it up and restored it to its owner, aptly remarking, "Honi soit qui mal y pense," and adding that he would shortly advance the garter to so high an honour that most of his nobles would be proud to wear it.

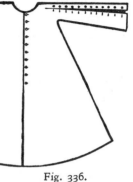

Fig. 336.
Diagram of Surcote

King Edward dedicated the Order to S. George, who suffered martyrdom A.D. 290 under Diocletian, Emperor of Rome. He also built for its service a chapel at Windsor, which was afterwards rebuilt by Edward IV.

At the foundation of the Order in 1348 its insignia were as follows:

1. THE GARTER, which is the principal item. It is formed of a strap of sky-blue velvet, edged with gold; it bears the motto "Honi Soit Qui Mal Y Pense" in gold, and has a buckle and tongue of the same. It is worn by knights on the left leg, and by ladies on the left arm.

2. THE MANTLE[1] of fine blue woollen cloth, cut as shown in Fig. 28, and attached across the chest by a cord originally of blue silk which later was entwined with gold thread, terminating in large tassels. On the left shoulder was embroidered a garter in blue and gold, surrounding "argent a cross gules." The mantle worn by the sovereign was lined with ermine and had a long train, being cut as shown in Fig. 213 without side pieces. The knights had their mantles lined with white damask. In the reign of Henry VI., 1460, the mantle was made of blue velvet.

3. THE SURCOTE, made originally of cloth of the same colour as the mantle, but later four colours were used in yearly rotation—blue, scarlet, sanguine in grain, white. At times of national mourning the surcote was black. Originally, the surcote and hood were ornamented with small garters, made of enamelled metal, or embroidered. Certain specified numbers of these garters were allotted to knights of the Order according to their rank. This continued until about the middle of the fifteenth century, when it was abandoned, as part of the general tendency towards economy necessitated by the Wars of the Roses. The numbers prescribed for use by knights at the time these small garters were discontinued were as follows:

[1] The mantle is the only garment mentioned in the founders' statutes of the Order, but from other sources the original use of hood and surcote can be established.

Henry VI., in 1433, changed the colour of the surcote to scarlet and later in his reign to white. Edward IV. changed it again from white cloth to purple velvet.

4. THE BELT AND SWORD. Around the waist a velvet belt (*see* Fig. 99) of the same colour as the surcote supported the sword.

5. THE HOOD was made of fine cloth, and shaped as shown in

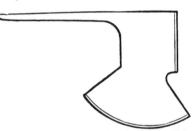

Fig. 337. Diagram of Hood.

Fig. 337. It was the same colour as the surcote, alternating with it, and worn upon the head at all public ceremonies. Originally it was embroidered with small garters, similar to those on the surcote. The wearing of the hood on the head became obsolete (*see* p. 386) in the reign of Edward IV., and it was replaced by the CHAPERON (*see* p. 384), then in fashion. At first the chaperon fitted the head and was worn as shown in Fig. 519, with the liripipe draped over one shoulder.

Fig. 338 shows one of the original knights of the Order in his robes. The surcote is cut on the usual lines, open part of the way up the front. Its sleeve is moderately wide, the close sleeve of the cotehardie showing underneath. The surcote is confined by the sword-belt. The hood is put on next. The mantle is attached *over* the portion of the hood covering the shoulders and chest by a cord threaded in the particular manner shown in the drawing. No contemporary representation of a Knight of the Garter in the time of Edward III. is known to exist. This drawing is, however, constructed from various authentic sources.

The Order consisted of the Sovereign; twenty-five Knights; the Prelate, whose office is attached to the See of Winchester; the Chancellor, whose office was instituted by Edward IV. and conferred originally on the Bishop of Salisbury, subsequently transferred to that of Oxford; the Registrar—the Dean of Windsor; "Windsor Herald,"[1] an

[1] When the Order of the Garter was instituted the founder created a special Officer-of-Arms to be attached thereto, by the name of "Windsor Herald," whose appointment was duly confirmed by Richard II. Henry V., however, perhaps inspired by French ideals,

official supplanted in the reign of Henry V. by Garter-Principal-King-of-Arms (who is also "Principal of the Heralds and Officers of our Illustrious Order of the Garter and King of Arms of England" [1]; and "Black Rod," chief usher of the kingdom, Gentleman Usher of the Black Rod. All these officials have distinctive robes and insignia.

The Prelate was distinguished on official occasions by the wearing of a mantle which was worn over the ecclesiastical cassock and rochet,[2] and may be described as a cope (see Vol. I., pp. 102, 111), without hood, orphreys, or morse. Originally the mantle appears to have been made of woollen cloth, of the same colour as the surcotes of the knights of the Order, and lined with miniver. In the reign of Edward IV. the mantle was of crimson velvet, with a blue orphrey adorned with alternating badges—the rose of England crowned, the "sun-burst," and the crowned fleur-de-lys, in gold and coloured embroidery. On the right shoulder the mantle bore the shield of S. George impaling the royal arms with-

Fig. 338.
Knight of the Garter, *temp.* Edward III.

in the Garter, surmounted by a crown, all in the proper colours. The mitre was worn, but discontinued for some time after the Reformation.

The Chancellor's mantle was the same as that of the Prelate, but the orphrey when introduced was plain, *i.e.* without any embroidered badges thereon, and on the right shoulder of the mantle was worked in gold and colours the cross of S. George, surrounded by the Garter and crowned. The Registrar wore a similar mantle, the original colour of which is unknown, but later it was russet-brown, with a blue orphrey embroidered with alternating "lions passant guardant crowned," and "crowned fleur-de-lys."

created and attached to the Order in question, in the place of Windsor Herald, an official of a higher rank, to be known as "Garter King-of-Arms," and to be the chief of all the Officers-of-Arms attending on the Crown. (The office of Windsor Herald was not abolished but the holder thereof and his successors continued to be attached to the royal establishment.)

[1] Patent appointing John Wrythe to the Office of Garter. 18 Edw. IV.
[2] Ecclesiastical vestments do not come under the survey of this book.

The mantle of Garter King-of-Arms was similar to that of the Registrar, but had twice as many badges embroidered on the orphrey, and the orphrey was of the same colour as the mantle, which was originally russet-brown. The sceptre was of silver gilt, the knob of four rectangular faces, being enamelled with the arms of S. George alternating with the royal arms, surmounted by a royal crown. (For details of the remainder of this costume, see p. 325.)

"Black Rod" wore a similar mantle, and carried an ebony rod mounted with silver, having at the top a crowned lion in the same metal.

In every case the mantle was fastened at the chest by a cord of silk, later twisted with gold, to the ends of which tassels of varying sizes and richness were attached.[1]

At the first chapter of the Order, held at Windsor on S. George's Day, 23 April, 1349, Queen Philippa and the wives of all the new knights accompanied their lords, attired in mantles bearing the badge of the Order. They received as gifts from the king—as did other ladies unconnected with the Order—mantles, surcotes, and hoods, similar to those of the knights, which they wore during the celebration of the Feast of S. George. The Garter was buckled on the left forearm [2] of those ladies who became actual members of the Order.

For about a hundred years after the institution of the Order it was the privilege of a few ladies to be enrolled as Companions. Besides Queen Philippa these were:

Joan, Princess of Wales.
Constance of Castile, wife of John of Gaunt.
Philippa, Queen of Portugal
Katherine, Queen of Castile and Leon} his two daughters.
The Duchess of Guelders, sister of Edward III.
The Countess of Bedford, 1376.
Lady Tankerville.
Anne of Bohemia.
Isabella of Valois.
Joanna of Navarre.
Catherine of Valois.
The Queen of Denmark } sisters of Henry V.
The Duchess of Bavaria }
Margaret of Anjou.
The Duchess of Suffolk, granddaughter of Chaucer, 1432.
Elizabeth, Lady Tryvet, 1433.
Elizabeth Wydeville.

[1] The robes and insignia of the Prelate, Chancellor, Registrar Garter King-of-Arms and "Black Rod" are in use, in slightly varied forms, at the present day.
[2] Sometimes seen represented on the wrist.

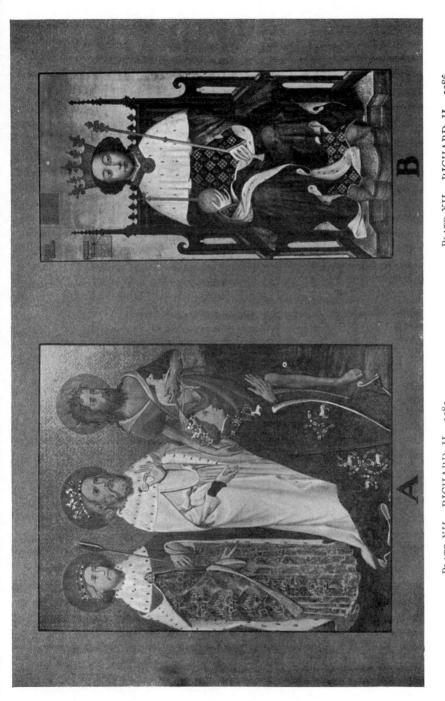

PLATE XII.   RICHARD II., 1382

By kind permission of the Earl of Pembroke and Montgomery

PLATE XII.   RICHARD II., 1386

By kind permission of the Medici Society

Lady Harcourt, 1463.

The Lady Mary Plantagenet ⎫
The Lady Cicely Plantagenet ⎬ daughters of Edward IV.

The Countess of Richmond, mother of Henry VII., 1488.

This privilege fell into abeyance at the end of the fifteenth century, until King Edward VII. created Queen Alexandra a Lady of the Order in 1902, and King George V. created Queen Mary a Lady of the Order in 1911.

Changes in the insignia of the Order took place from time to time, at periods not dealt with in this volume. It has been thought advisable, however, to add these interesting details as an appendix at the end of this section.

_____

Alterations in the colour of the robes and ribbon occurred at different times:

THE GARTER remained sky-blue until George I. altered it to dark blue.

THE MANTLE. Queen Elizabeth ordained that henceforth the mantle should be of purple velvet. It remained this colour until Charles I., in 1637, changed it back to its original shade of blue. During the reign of George II. the shade of blue became darker, to match the garter and ribbon, and has remained a dark blue, called "Garter blue," until the present day. In the reign of Queen Elizabeth the mantle of the knights was lined with white satin, and eventually, about the end of the seventeenth century, with white taffeta.

In the same reign the colour of the Prelate's mantle was changed to murrey, and in 1660 to purple, and the orphrey with its badges disappeared after the second change.

In Queen Mary's reign the mantle worn by the Registrar was made of crimson satin lined with taffety, and the orphrey was omitted. The mantle of "Black Rod" underwent similar changes at the same time.

The mantle of Garter King-of-Arms was changed by Queen Mary to crimson, and by Charles II. to scarlet.

THE SURCOTE in the reign of Queen Elizabeth was of crimson velvet lined with white satin, later taffeta. It has remained so down to our own day.

THE HOOD OR HAT. During the reign of Henry VIII. the chaperon was no longer worn upon the head, but a version of it, at first large enough to fit the head, but later much reduced in size, was laid on the left shoulder. But to avoid obscuring the garter on the mantle, its position was altered to the right shoulder, where it was fixed. The liripipe, or, as it is referred to in documents of the Order, "the Tippet," crosses the breast and is caught on the left side by the sword-belt.

A black velvet hat, of the shape fashionable during the middle of the sixteenth century, was introduced at that time, and worn in place of the chaperon, and to it was added a panache of white ostrich feathers, having in the centre a black heron's plume, all fixed to the hat by a band of diamonds. A modification of this hat is now worn by the knights on all but the most ceremonial occasions.

THE PENDANT GEORGE, Fig. 339. The earliest authentic records associate its adoption with the twenty-second year of the reign of

Henry VII., although tradition suggests its existence somewhat earlier. It is believed by some competent authorities, indeed, that it was probably introduced by Edward IV. after his visit to Louis XI., whom he had seen wearing the pendant insignia of his newly-established Order of S. Michael. It consisted of an enamelled, or plain gold, representation of S. George, mounted on a charger and using a tilting-lance in combat with the dragon.

THE COLLAR OF THE ORDER, Fig. 339, was instituted by Henry VIII. in 1510. It was formed of twelve buckled garters, each encircling the

Fig. 339

Tudor rose, alternating with as many knots of entwined cords. The pendant, or "George," hung from one of these twelve garters. A collar—possibly that of "SS"—was in use a little earlier, perhaps as early as 1506 and possibly with the pendant "George."

THE LESSER GEORGE, Fig. 340, was introduced by Henry VIII. in 1521. It consisted of the pendant, in enamels or plain gold as before, but surrounded by a buckled garter. The "Lesser George" hung from a gold chain, the use of which appears to have ceased early in the reign of Queen Elizabeth. It was then hung round the neck, first on a black ribbon, later sky-blue, but was not used in conjunction with the collar, being a semi-state decoration.

Fig. 340.
Lesser George

THE RIBBON, originally black, about three inches in width, was later, in Elizabeth's reign, sky-blue. Charles II. altered the ribbon to a deep blue, in compliment, it is said, to the beautiful Hortensia Mancini, Duchesse de Mazarin, who came to live in England in 1672; this shade was her favourite blue, and is still known as "Mazarin blue."

The fashion of wearing the ribbon over the left shoulder and under the right arm, instead of round the neck, appears to have been introduced by Charles I. In a portrait by Daniel Mytens, painted in 1631, the king is wearing the ribbon in this manner. It is the only Order of which the ribbon is so worn; in other cases it is worn on the right shoulder. With the introduction of this innovation, its width increased to about five inches. George II. changed the colour of the ribbon to dark blue, the present shade, in consequence, it is said, of the "Old Pretender" having created some knights of the Order by virtue of the right he claimed as "King James III."

THE STAR OF THE ORDER, Fig. 341, was introduced by Charles I. in 1629, and worn by him on the left shoulder of his cloak. (It was perhaps copied from the treatment of the French ensign of the Order of

Fig. 341.
Star of Garter

Fig. 342.
Star of S. Esprit

S. Esprit, Fig. 342, instituted in 1578 by Henry III. of France.) In the centre it had the buckled garter surrounding the cross of S. George surmounting a star of eight points embroidered in silver, or sometimes in diamonds; the irradiation, or "Glory," should, as devised originally, *proceed from the cross* and *not* from the garter, as, however, is often erroneously shown. Charles II. was the first monarch to wear the star upon the left breast of his coat, by this time the outer garment.

THE PRESENT ORDER OF INVESTITURE is as follows:

1. The Garter
2. The Surcote.
3. The Girdle and Sword.
4. The Hood and Mantle.
5. The Collar.
6. The Velvet Hat.
7. The Book of Statutes.

XIVcent.
Fig. 343. Ornament

SECTION IV.—RICHARD II. 1377–1399

Nobility—Men

Richard II. was born at Bordeaux, 1366. Crowned 16 July, 1377.

In his earliest portrait Richard is shown as a good-looking boy of sixteen, with fine features, blue eyes and fair hair (*see* Plate XII. A). As he grew to manhood he was decidedly handsome, his hair becoming light brown. He wore small beards upon his upper lip and a beard of two points upon the chin (*see* his portrait, Plate XII. B).

Richard had great courage, even in youth, as evidenced when he met the mob at Smithfield, and this helped him to withstand the trials and misfortunes of his troublous reign. He was no idle trifler, nor shiftless spendthrift, but a singularly affectionate and gifted man. A great believer in royal rights, but "ill advised when, out of love for art, splendour, and a fair life, he kept up a grand court, and was the patron of poets, painters and architects, though he knew that his people grudged spending money on anything but war." Redelessness (lack of good counsel) ruined Richard; he had his chance, but failed through his limitations, and his subjects would not give him another opportunity.

Richard II. married, first, in 1383, Anne of Bohemia, daughter of the Emperor Charles IV.; and, second, in 1396, Isabella, second daughter of Charles VI. of France and Isabeau of Bavaria.

There are several contemporary portraits of Richard II. still extant. The Wilton diptych (*see* Plate XII. A) represents him as a boy of sixteen, and the date assigned to this painting, in tempera, is 1382. It

Fig. 344

shows him wearing the houpeland (*see* p. 247) of scarlet, lined with miniver and woven or embroidered all over with his badge—a white hart "lodged" (at rest), crowned (round neck) and chained or (*see* Fig. 344) surrounded by wreaths, which he bore in right of his mother, the daughter and heiress of Edmund of Woodstock, Earl of Kent, younger son of Edward I. and Margaret of France. The lavish distribution of this badge among his friends and the loyal gentry was one of the complaints lodged against him by the Duke of Gloucester's party in 1397.

The same badge, upon an enamelled disc, is fastened in front as a brooch, and a collar or necklace is worn (*see* Fig. 420).

The standing figure on the left represents S. Eadmund, who is dressed in the robes of a king of this period. The houpeland is not so long as usual, and is blue, brocaded with a design of birds fronting each other, with their heads turned back and encircled by one coronet. His underdress is of deep blue; only the cuffs show. The mantle, fastened in the centre with a jewelled brooch, is of green velvet lined with ermine, and has an ermine cape. The saint carries an arrow symbolic of his martyrdom. The boots are crimson. The middle figure represents Eadward the Confessor, and is said to be a portrait of Edward III. He wears a robe of a fawn colour, with blue undersleeves showing at the wrist. The mantle is of the same colour as the robe, lined with ermine, and has an ermine cape. The third figure is S. John the Baptist.

The portrait in Westminster Abbey (Plate XII. B) shows Richard at about twenty years of age, wearing a slight beard on the upper lip and chin. Very little of the blue robe is seen, but it evidently hangs straight from the neck as shown in Fig. 321. The close sleeves, with deep cuffs, show at the wrists. The robe bears a repeated woven conventional design in gold, alternating with the letter R surmounted by a coronet. The mantle is of red velvet, lined with ermine, and has an ermine cape. Round the neck and over the cape is a very rich jewelled neck-band and pendant. The crown is a very beautiful specimen of goldsmith's work (see Jewellery, Fig. 404).

The effigy of Richard on his monument in Westminster Abbey shows his appearance at the age of twenty-nine. He wears the small beard as shown in his portrait just mentioned. He is clad in State dress, consisting of a long robe embroidered all over with the royal badge and devices—the white hart, the sun emerging from a cloud, the broom plant (*Planta Genista*, Fig. 345)—interspersed with the initial letters R and A. A hood is worn thrown back off the head, and the shoulder part or cape is seen *under* the mantle.

Fig. 345
Planta Genista

In the time of Richard II. the cotehardie, which had descended halfway down the thigh during Edward III.'s reign, was worn much shorter by men of rank and fashion. It reached to just below the hip-bone, or was sometimes even shorter. Very caustic comments were made upon "the horrible disorderly scantiness of clothing as in the *cuttied* SLOPPES or ANSLETS," [1] meaning that breeches were considerably curtailed or dispensed with altogether.

Fig. 346 represents a young noble wearing a cotehardie of the latest cut—a JAQUETTE, or, as it was sometimes called, COURTEPY (German, *Curtuspije*), a very short overgarment or jacket, which was often parti-coloured or *pied*. Worn over the paltock or pourpoint, it fitted the shoulders and chest, was buttoned down the front, fastened

---

[1] The above quotation from the "Parson's Tale" in Chaucer's *Canterbury Tales* is interesting as being the first reference to "slops." These garments were short breeches, drawers, or codware (see Fig. 314 at A). The name "slops" was applied in Queen Elizabeth's time to the padded trunks worn by fashionable men.

"Anslet," or "hanslein," "hanseline," the diminutive of the German "Hans," equivalent to the French "jaque" or "jaquette" = jacket.

tight round the waist, and descended only a short distance on the hips, revealing a large area of thigh. The upstanding collar is a new feature. It reached to the lobe of the ear, the front part being rounded; and the collar continued the curve of the shoulders. When a headdress of the

hood type was worn, the back of it almost covered the back of the high collar, giving to the latter the misleading effect of a hood cut all in one with the cotehardie or houpeland (*see* Plate XIII.). The sleeves in Fig. 346 are close-fitting, and end in cuffs over the hand. This cotehardie is richly embroidered in a design in gold "enwoven joyously with gems,"[1] for jewels were often introduced into the decoration of such garments as the vogue demanded extravagant, elaborate and quaint ornaments. The phrase, "Apparel broidered of stone," was used in reference to these expensive garments. Another "fashion note" of the period runs, "Decked and bestuck with gems that glance alway, and thereon were the birds of hill and dale cunningly needled, as the popinjay and turtles that sit preening through the summer's day. And true-love knotts that both were deft and fine."[1]

Fig. 346.
The Courtapy

Cotehardies worn by royalty and the nobility cost fabulous sums. One belonging to the Duc de Bourbon was valued at four thousand two hundred gold crowns. A cotehardie worn by Richard II. was estimated at thirty thousand marks. A cotehardie covered with jewels, belonging to John of Gaunt, was looted by the mob during the Peasants' Rising in 1381, and set up as a target. It was afterwards hacked to pieces with agricultural implements borne by the insurgents.

Abbreviation of the upper garments necessitated greater care of the lower. The leg and thigh being so exposed to view, more attention was devoted to the cut of the hosen, so as to define a shapely limb to advantage. The pattern used is shown in Fig. 316, and they could be used either with foot part combined, or finishing at the ankle and worn with shoes. After long practice in the craft, hosiers had now become expert in cut and fit. Fine cloth, silk, and sometimes velvet were the materials used.

The girdle and ESCARCELLE. The position in which the girdle was worn during the second half of the fourteenth century varied at different times. In the reign of Edward III. it was always worn low down on the hips. In the early part of the reign of Richard II. it was worn at a

[1] From *Sir Gawayne and the Green Knight,* a poem dated about 1360.

moderately high waist-level, often in conjunction with a belt round the hips.

An important addition to the waist- or hip-belt at this time was the pouch, purse, or "escarcelle"—often worn at the back—and a knife or misericorde was usually carried with it, the sheath passing through one or both of the loops by which the escarcelle was hung from the girdle. A button or swivel T-piece was fixed to the sheath, and passed through a slot in one of the loops. The escarcelle, usually quadrilateral in shape, when worn by nobles was very richly decorated with

Fig. 347.
Escarcelle

gold and jewels (Fig. 347), but the variety used by officials for carrying despatches, etc., was of stout cloth, leather or cuir-bouilli.

Contemporaneously with the use of this "new curtal weed"—the courtepy—men of fashion also went to the other extreme, wearing gowns and sleeves so long before and behind that unless the face was seen one could not be certain whether the wearer was a man or a woman. This long gown or robe was known as "the houppelande" (Fig. 348). Although a fashion in use in France at the same time, its origin is said to be Spanish, and its name derived from the word "hopa," Spanish for a long gown with sleeves.

Various styles of the houppelande or houpeland are termed the "bastard" (Fig. 350), "long" (Fig. 348), "half-thigh," the variety intended for riding (Fig. 351). The houpeland was cut like a woman's gown (see Fig. 227), but not taken in so much at the waist, and was made in three distinct ways: (1) Without any opening save for a small buttoned slit at the neck to allow the head to pass through; occasionally it is found (2) similar to above, but with the side seams of the skirt opened to knee- or thigh-level; (3) open all the way up the front,

Fig. 348.
The Houpeland

and secured by buttons either all or part of its length. An upstanding collar always surrounded the neck, similar to that described for Fig. 346. The edges of the collar were often indented and had the appearance of a small ruff surrounding the face, in the manner of the Elizabethan ruff.

Hoods were sometimes worn with the houpeland, and, if so, were of a different colour and occasionally lined with fur. The houpeland was worn not only by young men and dandies, but by the most sedate and sober knights and nobles when appearing at Court or any official ceremony. The edges of the houpeland and the wide long sleeves were cut in dagges in designs as eccentric and fantastic as giddy brains could devise. Often each motif or leaf was richly embroidered and set with jewels.

The following modernised quotation from Chaucer's "Parson's Tale" gives a good idea of the practice of decorating garments:

As to the first sin, that is in superfluity of clothing, which makes it so dear, to the harm of the people, not only in the cost of embroidering, but the disguise of indenting or barrying, undying, palying, or bending (heraldic terms; *see* p. 299, Fig. 431 B), and similar waste of cloth in vanity; but there is also costlyer furring in their gowns, so much pouncing of chisels to make holes, so much dagging of cuts; with the superfluity in length of the aforesaid gowns, trayling in the dung and in the mire, on horseback and also on foot, as well of man as of woman, that all the like trayling is verily wasted, consumed threadbare and rotten.

Fig. 349.
Houpeland from *Troilus*

Not content with embroidering their robes with the patterns used by noblemen of a previous generation, they now introduced a method of decorating their long robes with their own family badge or device powdered all over the garment. In like manner they used the initial letter of their names, or their lady-loves', and this often was surmounted by a coronet. The family or personal motto was embroidered on the borders of their robes and sleeves, or on a conventional ribbon set diaper-fashion all over the dress.

A scion of the noble House of de Clare is shown in Fig. 348. He is wearing the houpeland decorated with the family badge—a clarion (an enlarged detail of it is shown in the left-hand corner). It has immense sleeves and is slit up the sides, the edges being decorated with elaborate dagges. The skirt trails on the ground and forms a long train behind. A belt with a short end encircles the waist, and it should be observed that it is now the vogue to wear it in its natural place.

The pourpoint is worn under the houpeland to produce the pigeon-chest effect so much the mode among men of fashion at this time. A pouch with a misericorde stuck through the flap might be added to the belt.

A nobleman standing in the centre of the celebrated illumination of Chaucer's *Troilus*,[1] written during this reign, is wearing a houpeland of gold brocaded in a design of floriated circles about two and a half inches in diameter. Every other circle contains an emerald. The houpeland is lined with miniver. The hat (*see* Fig. 389 c) is of the same brocade, with a band of miniver round the head.

The back view of a nobleman (Fig. 349) is also taken from Chaucer's *Troilus*. The houpeland is of brilliant blue, confined at the waist by a

Fig. 350.
"Bastard" Houpeland

Fig. 351.
Riding Houpeland

wide girdle from which hang numerous small gold and jewelled pendants; these may give place to small round bells. The upstanding collar and the sleeves are edged with a gold embroidery, an inch and a quarter wide, and over the shoulders is a wide cape-like collar of heavy gold embroidery, edged with a row of jewelled pendants or gold bells on chains. The singular fashion of wearing bells in this manner originated in Germany, and was one of the many fanciful details introduced at the time of Anne of Bohemia's marriage in 1383; it was very popular at this period and for some time afterwards. The headdress shown in this figure, although not in the original, is typical of the period. It is bag-shaped with a roll brim, the latter sometimes being made of fur.

[1] In Corpus Christi College, Cambridge.

Fig. 352.
Chaucer's Squire

A shortened or "bastard" houpe-land, with wide sleeves dagged at the edges, is shown in Fig. 350 and was the style adopted by noblemen for ordinary street wear. It could be worn girded or ungirded over a cotehardie, the sleeves of which finish in very long cuffs entirely enveloping the hands and hanging at least six inches below the finger-tips. On his head and shoulders he has a hood worn in the old-fashioned way, sur-mounted by a second hood adapted to the later fashion, its facial opening placed round the head, with the liripipe bound round to form a twisted band, and the cape part arranged to come forward from the back and flop over the front.

Fig. 351 shows a young noble in outdoor dress, wearing the "riding" houpeland open up the front for convenience in sitting his palfrey. In addition to the waist-belt he is wearing another round the hips to carry the escarcelle with the misericorde. A rich jewelled chain and pendant is worn round the neck. The elaborate arrangement of the hood should be noticed. It is put on in the new way, the liripipe binding it to the head, and the ample shoulder part (purposely cut larger than hitherto) made to stand up on the left side of the head like a cockscomb.[1]

Towards the end of the reign a vogue was created for wearing pieces of armour, particularly leg-pieces, with civil dress. It was confined to gentlemen enjoying the privilege of knighthood, who wore thigh-pieces and greaves of steel plate with the houpeland shown in Fig. 351, or the "half-thigh," when riding on certain important occasions.

The young Squire of twenty years, "a lover and a lusty bachelor," from Chaucer's *Canterbury Tales*, is seen in Fig. 352. His cotehardie

Fig. 353.
John of Gaunt, 1385

[1] The name "coxcombe" was given to a fop or dandy at this time.

or courtepy, with wide sleeves, is embellished with embroidery "like a meadow" (which suggests that it is made of a green cloth or silk) "full of white and red flowers." The edge of the courtepy and the high collar are finished with a roll of white fur, and a band of gold embroidery is worked on the edge of the sleeves, the lining of which is of silk in contrasting colour. The slender waist is encircled by a gold belt whence hang small gold bells on chains. The *tout ensemble* of this young man is completed by rich hose, a curious high cap, and another fashionable detail—the necklace. His hair is dressed in the latest fashion "with locks crisp curled, as they'd been laid in press."

John of Gaunt, "time-honoured

Fig. 354. Charles V. of France

Lancaster," in the year 1385, when he was forty-five, is shown in Fig. 353. It is a portrait taken from an illuminated manuscript of that date. He has brown hair and beard, and wears a gold circlet with roundels set with rubies at intervals. The long straight gown is parti-coloured, white and blue, the livery colours of the House of Lancaster. The neck is finished with an ornamental border in scarlet and gold. The sleeves are quite new in shape; the upper part was probably cut all in one with the gown and pleated, just below the elbow, into the close-fitting sleeve which covers the forearm.

Fig. 354 is a portrait of Charles V., King of France, wearing his favourite garment, the "ganache." Reference should be made to Fig. 223 and the description given with it. The ganache worn by Charles is of very fine cloth in one or other of the colours he affected, vermilion or a rich blue; usually its colour was cobalt blue powdered with golden fleurs-de-lys. A hood is attached to the ganache, which opens only on the

Fig. 355.
"Bagpipe" Sleeves and Crackows

chest, and is fastened with two buttons hidden by tabs called PATTES or "paws." [1] The whole garment is lined throughout with ermine. Notice that the king is wearing a linen coif, slightly gathered into a band, and tied under the chin. The crown is described on p. 275. The chair is the new shape which came into use after the middle of the fourteenth century.

A fashionable man of the last decade of the century is seen in Fig. 355. To the short cotehardie are set the latest sleeves, cut in the shape of bagpipes. They fit close at the armhole, develop into a bag at the elbow, and are buttoned tight at the wrists. The whole costume is particoloured, but not in a complicated manner, it being simply half and half, one side black with white embroidery, the other white with black embroidery. He wears the extraordinary long-pointed toes to his hose, called CRACKOWS, fastened by gold chains to his garters (see p. 274).

The full dress of the nobility at the end of the reign is exemplified in Plate XIII. A great many of the nobles represented in an illuminated manuscript [2] dealing with the deposition of Richard II. at Westminster, are wearing this type of costume, including those assembled "with evil intent."

The colourings of the various houpelands in this particular picture are worth noting:

A houpeland, sulphur, lined white, pink underdress.

A houpeland, sky-blue, lined vair, red underdress.

A houpeland, scarlet, lined miniver, sky-blue hood.

A houpeland, deep blue, lined white, scarlet underdress, green cap (like Fig. 349).

A houpeland, gold, lined white.

A houpeland, pale cornflower, lined white, soft green underdress, green cap.

For the most part these noblemen wear the hood folded up like that shown in Fig. 350.

Plate XIII. The houpeland of scarlet is decorated with a double trellis of gold; it is lined with sulphur, and the dagges outlined with gold. The sleeves of the paltock are green, with long dagged cuffs lined with pinkish purple. The hose are green, a black belt with escarcelle encircles the waist, and over the left shoulder a BAUDRIC, "baudry," or baldrick of blue, edged with gold and small gold balls, is worn—a fashion just introduced. The white hood, lined with orange, is put on in the manner described for Fig. 350.

Nobility—Women

The Princess Anne was the eldest daughter of Charles, King of Bohemia and Emperor of Germany, and Elizabeth of Pomerania. She

---

[1] Earliest form of LAPEL.   [2] In the British Museum, Harl. MS. 1319.

was born at Prague in 1367 and married to Richard II. in the Chapel of S. Stephen, Westminster Palace, in 1381–2, after which ceremony there were "mighty feastings."

The queen acted frequently as a mediator between the king, his parliament, and the people. Richard himself writes that "he was reconciled to the citizens (of London) through the mediation of his wife, the queen."

Anne of Bohemia died after a few hours' illness at Shene Palace, Whitsuntide 1394. Her sudden death is supposed to have been caused by the plague then raging throughout Europe. She is buried with her husband in Westminster Abbey. It is said that had the queen been spared, the calamities of later years would have been averted by her gentleness and tact.

The second queen of Richard II. was Isabella of Valois, called "The Little Queen," the nine-year-old daughter of Charles VI.[1] of France and Isabeau of Bavaria. They were married in the Church of S. Nicholas, Calais, in 1396. This child became a widow at the age of thirteen. In 1407 she married the Duke of Orleans, son of Charles V. She died at the Castle of Blois, aged twenty-two, in 1410.

It was mentioned in the section dealing with Henry III. that the fashions in vogue at the English Court in the thirteenth century were only very slightly different from those adopted at the Court of Louis IX. of France. Several succeeding marriages which united the royal houses brought about a closer intercourse between the two nations, and towards the end of the fourteenth century means of communication were much improved. Facilities for travel gradually developed in Western Europe, with the result that differences in manners and customs of the various countries became less marked. In some degree, also, racial distinction in costume was modified by the same cause. When a foreign princess arrived in England, the general style of her costume was more or less familiar to the great ladies of society who came in contact with her. It was only in small details that any novelty appeared—the arrangement of a headdress, a pattern used as decoration on a gown, or a differently-cut shoe, was sufficient to excite the curiosity of those who were interested in the evolution of dress or showed animosity to its vagaries.

Some historians of the mid-Victorian era accuse Anne of Bohemia of introducing the fashion of wearing gigantic headdresses, but it has been proved that they anticipated events, and that the headdresses in question were those in fashion about sixty years later (*see* p. 445).

The chief novelty brought from Bohemia by the queen's attendant courtiers was the "crackow," alluded to hereafter (*see* p. 274). Her

[1] In the ledger of the Royal Treasury of France the following entry occurs under dated 1393: "Given to Jacquemin Gringonneur, painter, for three packs of cards, gilt and coloured, for the amusement of the king, 56 sols (2s.) of Paris." The first packs of cards!

own costumes and those of her ladies were quite in keeping with the modes prescribed by English and French fashions (*see* Plate XIV.). Like

other ladies of exalted position at this time, she generally had her badge—"an ostrich gorged with a coronet and chained or, holding a nail in its beak" (Fig. 356)—a knot (Fig. 357), or one of her husband's badges embroidered on her cotehardie or sideless gown. These may be seen engraved on the bronze effigy to her memory in Westminster Abbey.

Although Richard's second queen, Isabella of Valois, was so young, her

Fig. 356

Fig. 357

trousseau was sufficiently interesting to be noticed by a writer of the time, who mentions a sideless gown of red velvet, embossed with birds in goldsmith's work perched on branches of pearls and emeralds, and bordered with miniver. The mantle was also of red velvet, lined with miniver, having a cape of ermine. Another was of murrey-mézéreon velvet, embroidered all over with pearls. Her plate, wall-

hangings and jewellery were very beautiful, the value of the latter being estimated at five hundred thousand crowns. During her widowhood her jewels were the cause of a lawsuit between France and England.

Plate XIV. represents a noble lady wearing the type of fashionable costume associated with this reign. There is very little difference from the style worn during the preceding reign. The form of the front of the sideless gown is slightly changed; the portion marked A in Fig. 330 is cut away, showing the front of the blue cotehardie, and the skirt-front is suspended from the borders of ermine "purfiled with pelure (fur) the finest in the land" (Piers of Langtoft). The mauve sideless gown hangs from the shoulders at the back *à la sac*, revealing the rose-coloured silk lining, and is embroidered all over with an initial letter—N—surmounted by a coronet. A motto is repeated many times upon the hem. The white coif is still used, but the gold network

Fig. 358.

Noble Lady, *temp.* Richard II.

cylinders of the last reign's headdress are out of date. The plaits of hair brought forward from the back are retained, surmounted by a veil and coronet. This style of costume would be worn by both of Richard II.'s queens, but for full state a mantle might be added.

Although Fig. 358 represents a lady of title, she is dressed simply in a gown cut on the old lines, with wide sleeves lined with a contrasting colour. The high collar is the only fashionable detail, and it is encircled by a necklace with pendant. The sleeves of the under-robe, with deep cuffs, are seen. The headdress is a turban-shaped roll of some rich material, having the centre void for the head to pass through, ornamented with gold (*see* detail) and pearls. The loop of pearls at the side of the face is curious. The short veil, put on first, escapes through the centre of the roll and floats behind.

In the brass to the memory of Elyenore Corp at Stoke Fleming, Devon, 1391, the cotehardie is buttoned from the neck to below the waist, with tight sleeves buttoned all the way down the outside of the arm from shoulder to knuckles. Her headdress is similar to that in Fig. 358 but smaller, and without the pearls there shown.

Section V.—The Middle and Lower Classes
Costume of the Men, 1307–1399
Temp. Edward II., Edward III. and Richard II.

The middle classes copied the fashions of the nobility so far as the cut and general effect were concerned, but the materials used were much inferior. Coarse woollen stuffs, baize, pliable felt, coarse linen and homespun, and a sort of sackcloth, were used.

Fig. 359.   Fig. 360.   Fig. 361.
First Half Fourteenth Century

Fig. 359 shows the type of costume worn generally by the middle classes during the early part of the fourteenth century. It consists of a gown reaching half-way below the knees, open up the front and buttoned down to about the waist. It had wide sleeves and was worn over another gown, which sometimes came below it, having tight sleeves buttoned to the wrist. With this the ordinary hood was worn.

Fig. 360 represents a young man of this class wearing a garment similar to that described under Fig. 223 and Fig. 225. It is a surcote with a hood attached, and has wide openings for the arms, fastening on the chest as described under Fig. 354. This surcote or ganache was a popular garment worn during the fourteenth century by the upper and middle classes. The under-robe buttoned on the chest in the same manner as Fig. 359, and had tight sleeves buttoned to the wrist. The under-robe usually showed below the surcote. This young man wears a hat with a small upstanding brim, the crown sinks slightly, and then rises to a point, which forms the handle for removing it. Leather gloves are carried in the hand.

A young gentleman of the early part of the reign of Edward III. is

shown in Fig. 361, wearing a tunic which fits the shoulders and body to the waist, where it becomes wider, being cut on the circle somewhat in the manner of the Anglo-Saxon tunic. The same shaped garment, when worn by military men, was called the jupon, and is mentioned under Fig. 449. It buttons down the front to the waist, the skirt part being left open and the corners usually turned back to show the lining. A belt with an ornamental fastening confines the waist, and from it hangs the gypsere or escarcelle, with a dagger stuck through the loop or belt. It is important to remember that the middle classes had not yet adopted the fashionable eccentric methods of wearing the hood, as described on p. 213, but the

Fig. 362.   Fig. 363.
Gentleman   Frankeleyn

general way, as shown in the drawing, was to turn the face part back, displaying the lining of a different colour.

The changes introduced by the nobility in the first years of Edward III.'s reign were copied by the middle classes at a little later date, and especially by the younger generation of the well-to-do.

Fig. 362 shows a young man of some position in the fashionable garb of the period. It is the costume that would be worn by the highest nobility for serviceable, every-day use. His cotehardie is not quite so stylish as that shown in Fig. 311, but it is evidently more comfortable. It is buttoned all the way down the front and has tippets of moderate length. It is particoloured, and so are his hose. The tight sleeves of the paltock are of a different colour; they may either match or be parti-coloured. The leather belt from which the gypsere and dagger hang encircles the hips at the fashionable level. Over his hood, which in this case is not parti-coloured, he wears a round hat with upstanding brim. After the middle of the century these caps were of very brilliant colours, especially red.

Fig. 363 represents an important class—the country gentleman whose estates consisted of land free from

any feudal overlord, and known as a "Frankeleyn." They were often men of considerable property, held many official positions, and were noted for their plenteous hospitality. This frankeleyn wears a gown with close

Fig. 364

sleeves, reaching below the calf, buttoned down the front, and confined at the waist by a belt ornamented with metalwork (Fig. 364), from which hangs "his gypsere of white silk" (Fig. 365) and an ANELACE, or long knife, in a sheath. After the middle of the

Fig. 365 century the sleeve of the underdress extended to the knuckles, as shown in this drawing. A circular or semicircular cloke, with a hood attached, fastens on the right shoulder by three ornamental metal buttons, and according to the prevailing custom the front part is thrown back over the left shoulder. The whole costume is free from ostentation or freakish fashion and well suited to a man of substantial condition. The materials of which it was made were expensive and thoroughly serviceable. The brass to the memory of John Corp (died 1391) at Stoke Fleming, Devon, shows the belt (Fig. 366) carrying the anelace worn baudric-wise over the right shoulder and under the left arm. In all other details his costume is the same as shown in Fig. 363.

Fig. 367 is the costume of a citizen or merchant worn during the middle of the fourteenth century. The tunic reaches to below the knees and was sometimes open up the front for convenience in walking. The sleeves are moderately

Fig. 366

wide and show the tight ones of the underdress. The tunic is girded by a leather belt to which is attached a gypsere and a penner, a case containing a pen and an inkhorn. Fig. 370 shows a penner composed of

Fig. 367.   Fig. 368.   Fig. 369.

Second Half Fourteenth Century

cuir-bouilli impressed with a design and attached to an inkhorn made of the same material. They were usually carried slung across the waistbelt. Over the shoulders is worn a short semicircular cloke fastened on the right, and above this again is the hooded cape with a short

Fig. 370.
Penner & Inkhorn

liripipe. The hat with its brim turned down in front is worn on top of this. Boots of leather, pointed in the toe, reach to just below the calf.

Chaucer's Canterbury Pilgrims are representative of the people of the fourteenth century, especially the period from 1384 to 1390, and descriptions of some of the characters and of their clothes are given here.

The "Merchant" (Fig. 368) had a forked beard and was clothed in a motley-coloured (spotted, or it might be parti-coloured or rayed) tunic laced down the front and sides, an unusual manner, the tunic forming an inverted box-pleat in the skirt part; and he "wore a stately Flanders beaver hat, and his boots neatly clasped or laced upon his legs." Hats of this make imported from Flanders were much in favour with people of the well-to-do class.

The "Doctor of Physic" was habited in a gown, and Chaucer states "in sangurin and in pers he clad was al." It was lined with taffeta or cendal. In another part of his works Chaucer speaks of a physician (Fig. 369) who was "clad in a scarlet gown and furred well, as such a one ought to be." In the *Vision of Piers Plowman,* a physician is described as wearing in addition a hood and cloke lined with "calabre," the fur of squirrels in deep brown colour imported from Calabria.

The "Sergeant-at-Law," or counsellor (Fig. 371), wore a gown like Fig. 220, parti-coloured and one side barred or striped with different colours, "a motley cotte," confined by a girdle of silk. The hood was often treated in the same manner, and both were lined or edged with lambskin having the fur dressed outwards, and known as "budge." Sergeants-at-law were originally priests, and as such wore the tonsure (*see* Vol. I., p. 172), but after priests were forbidden to interfere with secular affairs, sergeants continued to shave their heads, and wore the coif (*see* p. 176) of linen, afterwards of silk, for distinction.

Fig. 371.
Sergeant-at-Law

Fig. 372.
Citizen

Fig. 373.
Huntsman

Fig. 372 shows the costume of a young citizen of the reign of Edward III., wearing a cotehardie girded by a leather belt from which might hang a pouch. The tight sleeves of the undertunic show below the square-cut open ones of the cotehardie. On his legs are hose of cloth and boots of leather slightly turned down at the top. His hat, of felt in one colour, is the same shape as that shown in Fig. 362.

The drawing Fig. 373 is taken from an illuminated manuscript of the first quarter of the fourteenth century. It represents a forester who, contrary to what one would expect, is clothed in scarlet, with the exception of the legs, on which he wears grey hose and black shoes. The tunic is of the jupon shape described under Fig. 361, fastened with black buttons down the front, but the sleeves fall from the elbows and are square, lined with white. The undersleeves are scarlet and button to the wrist. The belt is also scarlet and the gypsere black. The liripipe of the scarlet hood hangs about level with the calf. He blows his "oliphant." This was a horn originally made from the tusk of an elephant, and from Saxon times to the end of the twelfth century formed an important item of a noble's equipment. Such horns were highly orna-

mented with carving and bound by two metal bands, often of gold or silver. The oliphant used at this time by huntsmen was usually the horn of some animal.

Chaucer's "Squire's Yeoman" was a forester, or our modern equivalent, a game-keeper. This forester was clothed in the proverbial Kendal green. The baudric from which hung the horn was also green, and he wore upon his breast a "christopher" of polished silver—a clasp or pendant with the image of S. Christopher carrying Our Lord upon his shoulders engraved on it, a very favourite subject at this time. A "mighty bow" was carried, besides a sword, a "handsome dagger," and a small shield or buckler, and beneath his girdle appeared "a bundle of sharp bright arrows plumed with peacocks' feathers." To pro-

Fig. 374.
Chaucer's Shipman

tect the hand and arm when using the bow, a guard was worn in the shape of a glove with a long ornamented leather top, called a "BRACER that was rich and broad."

Another "gay Yeoman" appears "under a forest side, having a bow with bright shining arrows, and clothed in a courtpie of green-coloured cloth and a hat upon his head fastened with black strings."

The "Shipman" (Fig. 374) was captain or commander of a trading vessel. His surcote is of "falding" and comes to below the knee. Its shape is given in Fig. 375 and shows seams at the dotted lines. Buttoning at the throat, it has a low stand-up neckband. In the figure of the Shipman taken from the Ellesmere MS. he has a turned-down collar attached to the neckband. The felt hat has a wide brim turned up in

Fig. 375.
Diagram of Surcote

front; a dagger is carried under the arm by a cord passing over the shoulder.

The "Clerk" is described as wearing "an olde torne court pye. . . . Ful thread bare was his overset courtepy."

Fig. 376 is the type of costume worn by a henchman, or serving-man. It is also the type of costume worn by the well-to-do agricultural class. His body garment is a tunic gathered into the waist by a belt, and having full sleeves finishing in a band at the wrist. The edge of his hood is dagged, and in all probability it is a cast-off of his master's. On his legs he has coarse cloth hose, and strong black leather shoes. His hat is a very usual one, having the brim turned down in front and up behind, or *vice versa.*

The "Miller," Chaucer says, was "a stout chorle and a proud quarrelsome fellow," and when he went abroad he was armed with three weapons of defence—a long PAVADE, or dagger, with a sharp blade, which he wore in his belt; "a jolly POPPER" or bodkin, which he bore in his pouch; and "a Sheffield thwittle," or knife, carried in his hose. He was also armed with a sword and buckler. He wore a white cotte (like Fig. 361), and on holydays a blue hood, "and figured away in red hose made of the same cloth as his wife's gown."

The itinerant tinker (Fig. 377) wears a plain cotte with close sleeves, and hose with foot part combined. He has no hood, but it would be quite

Fig. 376. Henchman

in keeping with his profession to wear one as well as a hat. This drawing is reproduced from the Louterell Psalter.

From another illuminated manuscript come the two peasants on p. 262. Fig. 378 has his ample tunic or cotte in blue, and the close undersleeves are scarlet; the hood with short liripipe is brown, lined scarlet; hose brown, with rough brown shoes, COCKERS, tied about the ankles with white cords. His companion, Fig. 379, is dressed in the same style, except that his cotte is grey and hose blue. A red hat is worn over the blue hood. Gaiters, called HOGGERS, of rough leather are tied about his legs with cord or ropes of straw. This man is playing an instrument

Fig. 377. A Tinker

very much used by peasants, shepherds, etc., and called a "corne-muse," a kind of bagpipe. The costume shown in Fig. 380 is typical of that worn by the peasant or farm labourer. It consists chiefly of a coarse tunic or shirt, reaching to about the knees, pleated in to the neckband, with tight sleeves which button after the usual fashion.

Fig. 378.   Fig. 379.
Peasants

There is evidently a cord or belt round the waist through which the tunic is caught up. On the legs are hose, and the ankles are ornamented with black bands woven into the cloth. There is nothing new about the shoes, but the hat is a novelty. It appears to be of straw, with a wide brim to shade the face from the sun. These hats were made in several shapes, but all had wide brims. He carries his hood over his shoulder by the modified liripipe, quite a common habit at this time.

"Covetousness" in *Piers Plowman* is in the guise of a peasant, and is described as follows:

A hood was on his head, above (it) a lousy hat, and he was in a tawny tabard twelve winters old, all torn to rags and baudy and full of creeping lice. Except a louse were a good leaper she could not have walked on that cloth, it was so threadbare.

An outer garment worn by men and women in the fourteenth century was called a HEUK or "huke." From all accounts it must have been the same shape as the cuculla (*see* Vol. I., p. 111), the scapular and the cyclas. Sometimes it had a hood attached.

TABARD was a name given to this same garment when it reached to the thighs or knees, and was without a hood. It was worn by the lower orders, labourers, peasants, and farm hands during the latter part of the thirteenth century (*see* Fig. 238), and the whole of the fourteenth century, as an extra and convenient covering.

Women

Temp. Edward II., Edward III. and Richard II.

It was not an unusual occurrence in the fourteenth century for the wives of wealthy merchants, frequently the holders of important official positions, to be the daughters of knights or the lesser aristocracy. Many were women

Fig. 380.
Farm Labourer

who had been brought up and lived their lives in castles or manor-houses, and were imbued with the culture and refined taste of the times.

Fig. 381.   Fig. 382.

Gentlewomen

Choice furniture, plate, jewels, portions of tapestry, were parts of their daily environment, and they had at their disposal rich materials for making garments of every description. Such women were often called upon after marriage to act as hostesses to the nobility and sometimes royalty, and did it well — accomplishments perhaps reflected in the honours and dignities conferred upon their husbands.[1] Such a middle-class woman of this period ranked socially as a gentlewoman, and perhaps these earliest alliances with the aristocracy helped in securing for the wealthy merchant class a social position hitherto unknown in their ranks. The de la Poles of Hull are one of the many distinguished families of commercial origin who attained to the highest dignities in the land; their rise in the social scale dates from the year 1339, when William de la Pole lent an enormous sum to Edward III. towards the expenses of his wars with France.

Fig. 383.
Mistress Braunch

A gentlewoman of the first thirty years of the century (Fig. 381) wears a straight gown, wide at the feet, with sleeves that terminate in a point just below the elbows. A wimple and small veil are worn over the fashionable style of hairdressing (see Fig. 393), surmounted by a short hood. As an alternative headdress with this costume, the pointed hood shown in Fig. 398 might be worn.

The young lady in Fig. 382 is dressed in a manner similar to Lady Louterell (Plate XVIII.) and wears a robe and cyclas. Her hair is dressed like Fig. 394, but over it she has placed a scarf folded cornerwise, as described on p. 270.

The brass in S. Margaret's Church, King's Lynn, to the memory

---

[1] Dame Alice, the wife of Sir Richard Whittington, was the daughter of Sir Ivo Fitzwaryn, Kt., and owned large estates in the south-west of England.

of the wife of Adam de Walsokne, 1349 (a corn merchant, judging by the scenes depicted on the brass), shows a similar dress, but with the addition of a mantle. Her headdress is like Fig. 263, but she does not wear the fillet, and the edge of the couvrechef appears to be pinked or indented.

One of the two wives of Robert Braunch, a rich merchant of Lynn, is represented in Fig. 383. It is taken from the very beautiful brass to their memory, dated 1364, in the same church. This lady is wearing a gown like that described under Fig. 300, cut very ample in the skirt, which is held up under the left arm. The sleeves finish at the elbows, whence hang tippets of moderate length lined with vair. On the tight sleeves of the under-robe is some beautiful embroidery in a scroll design, probably carried out in gold. The headdress is the same as Fig. 393, but the couvrechef is longer and falls on the shoulders. It is interesting to note how long this headdress remained in fashion. It must be borne in mind that this lady, of some importance, lived in the eastern counties, far away from Court circles.

Fig. 384.   Fig. 385.   Fig. 386.

Middle-Class Women

A citizen's wife of the middle or latter part of the century, a woman of no social importance, is shown in Fig. 384. Her gown, which fits tight round the waist and reaches to the feet, is cut like the pattern in Fig. 324. It has a stand-up collar, and buttons down the front, and there may be vertical pocket-slits in the skirt. The sleeves, cut like Fig. 325, finish at the elbows with tippets. The headdress is described on p. 273.

Lower Classes

Fig. 386 shows the wife of a small farmer, wearing a gown reaching to the ankles. The young girl (Fig. 385) is habited in the same kind of gown, and both are cut like the pattern shown in Fig. 324. The skirts of these gowns were tucked up, and the sleeves unbuttoned from wrist to elbow and rolled back when working at the wash-tub or other domestic employment. On her head Fig. 386 has a piece of linen shaped like a hood, over which she wears out of doors a broad-brimmed hat of felt or straw.

Under this class, although she would be highly indignant at the suggestion, comes Chaucer's "Wife of Bath," that "bold shameless woman" and gadabout gossip. The style of her dress is the same as described under Fig. 386, but it is composed of expensive materials, which she wove herself; she was an expert at "making fine cloth which surpassed that of Ipres and Ghent." She tells us that "on high days and holy days she was accustomed to a gay scarlet gown." She was "wimpled well," and over her couvrechef she wore a hat as broad as a buckler. Her hose were of fine red cloth and gartered, and when she made her pilgrimage to Canterbury on horseback these attractive legs were comfortably tucked into a BOOT MANTLE—an outer garment (overalls), bound round the hips and ankles, to keep her gown from being splashed and her extremities warm.

Fig. 387.
Peasant

A nicer type is the "Carpenter's Wife," a "handsome well-made young woman. Her body was gentil and small as a weasel, long as a mast and upright as a bolt." A girdle barred and striped with silk, whence hung her gypsere of leather tasselled with silk, was worn around the hips, and "her apron was clean and white and full of pleats." The neckband of her camise and the border of the couvrechef were broidered with black silk, and her hair kept tidy with a fillet of silk. The "fermail" or "ouche," which fastened her gown at the bosom, was of metal "as broad as the boss of a buckler, and her boots were laced high upon her legs."

A peasant or farm hand (Fig. 387) is dressed in a long gown with close sleeves, and over it a heuk tied round the hips by the strings of her apron. Her head is enveloped in a headrail, and over it a hood open at the throat.

1340.

Fig. 388

SECTION VI.—HAIRDRESSING

1307–1399

Men. The style of hairdressing in fashion during Henry III.'s reign, shown in Figs. 250 and 251, was that in vogue during the reign of Edward II. and the early part of that of Edward III. It remained the fashionable mode of hairdressing until about 1340, thus extending over a period of about 130 years. Sometimes the roll was worn on the fore-

Fig. 389. HAIRDRESSING AND HEADGEAR
Fourteenth century

head, and sometimes the fringe. At other times the hair was brushed back off the temples. Fig. 298 F shows the new style adopted about 1340, and it should be noticed that it was still customary to roll the ends of the hair all round the nape of the neck.

Fig. 389 A gives the latest fashion worn during the remainder of Edward III.'s reign. The hair is parted in the middle, waved, or curled by means of curling-irons, and cut off rather square at chin-level.

Noblemen of Richard II.'s Court wore the style of hairdressing just described. A new mode came into vogue in France, copied from the Italian fashion, and was sometimes adopted by the ultra-fashionable young Englishmen; it is shown in Fig. 389 B. The hair, instead of being allowed to hang loose, was rolled round a small pad of stuff, thick behind and diminishing to points in front, where an ornament of gold and jewels, sometimes surmounted by an aigrette, finished it off. With this style the hair was not waved, but worn very smooth and probably oiled.

Fig. 363 shows the usual style worn by country gentlemen of this period. It was parted in the middle, and the sides curled in layers around the head. The more practical members of his class often wore the hair clipped rather close to the head. The lower classes imitated to a moderate degree the fashions set by the nobility.

Beards on the upper lip and chin were very generally worn during this century, as the illustrations in this chapter show. It was entirely a matter of personal choice whether the face was clean-shaven or a beard worn. Beards on the upper lip varied; some were short, others long and wavy. Beards on the chin were nearly always forked, generally in two points but sometimes in three.

Although the effigy of Edward II. shows him wearing a beard, it is known that he was clean-shaven (*see* Fig. 291) up to the time of his deposition. The story is told that he was deprived of proper shaving-water by his gaolers, much to his distress, and that he had to shave in an open field in cold muddy water brought in an old helmet from a stagnant pool.

HEADGEAR

1307–1399

During the first half of the fourteenth century the cap of dignity shown in Fig. 167 underwent a change in shape. The point on top of the crown was omitted from the latest make, and the brim was divided at the back and finished in two points projecting from the cap, thus producing the headgear known as the "Cap of Maintenance" (Fig. 390). It was and still is

Fig. 390

usually carried at the coronation, in front of the sovereign of England, and is always made of crimson velvet with an ermine brim.

The hood, worn in a variety of ways (*see* pp. 211, 213), was still very general, especially among the nobility (*see* illustrations in Sections I. and II.). For ordinary use among all classes there were several kinds of hats and caps, frequently worn in conjunction with the hood (*see* illustrations). Hats made of beaver were much in vogue, and when of Flemish manufacture were considered very smart for ordinary use by the aristocracy (*see* Figs. 317 and 391). A hat formed on the lines of the Greek petasos was popular with the middle classes, being useful and adaptable to all weathers (*see* Figs. 367, 376 and 377).

Fig. 391

Many new shapes in headgear came into fashion during the reign of Richard II. The cap having a roll brim and a bag crown (*see* Figs. 349 and 389 c) had a great vogue. Another kind, having the bag part stiffened, and seen in Fig. 352, was also a favourite. It was the kind of hat much worn by Henry, Earl of Derby, son of John of Gaunt. Both varieties usually had a large cluster of jewels set in front. Fig. 389 D shows a very fashionable hat of Richard II.'s reign, made in beaver of various tones of brown and black; the brim was turned up over one eye and fixed with a jewel surmounted by an upstanding plume.

Fig. 389 E shows a curious circular hat worn by fashionable young men on ordinary occasions; a more usual shape with an upstanding brim is shown in Figs. 362 and 372.

With the lower classes the hood worn in the normal old-fashioned way was most usually adopted; the hat of straw or felt, worn by the peasant in Fig. 380, was in general use among men and women of this class when working in the fields.

HAIRDRESSING AND HEADDRESSES

Temp. Edward II.

Women. During this century the mode of dressing the hair, and the headdress, were almost inseparable. The ramshorn hairdressing was fashionable during the reign of Edward II., but it was generally covered. Fig. 392 shows the extreme fashion of this time. The hair was dressed as described under Fig. 255, or the plaits of hair encased in silk as in Fig. 262. To this is added the wimple placed under the chin and drawn out at the sides over the pads of hair, producing a triangular effect. On the top was frequently placed an oval flat cap of gold network, and above that the veil, the edge forming a straight line across the top of the head. This headdress is also seen in Plate IX:

Fig. 393 is a much simpler headdress. The hair is dressed as described under Fig. 255, and the wimple is worn; but the veil is

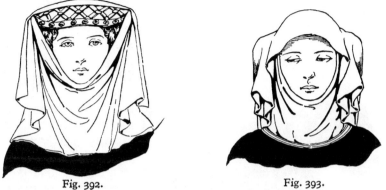

Fig. 392.

Fig. 393.

Early Fourteenth Century

draped on top without a band. It is probably pinned to the hair close to the head to emphasise the line of the pads of hair at the sides (*see also* Fig. 306).

Temp. Edward III.

The ladies Louterell wear the fashionable coiffure of the early years of this reign (*see* Fig. 394 and Plate XVIII.). The hair is parted in the middle and plaited in a very wide braid of sixteen or more strands, ranging round the head from temple to temple. The whole presses somewhat upwards round the skull, under the fillet. The ends of the numerous strands form tiny curls which fall upon the gorget just about level with the lobe of the ear. The gorget is pinned up under the hair-ends all round and tucks inside the neck of the dress. In place of the plain fillet worn by Fig. 394 a jewelled circlet or coronet could be worn; frequently a veil was draped over the whole coiffure and secured by the fillet or coronet. A detail worth remembering is that the gorget or wimple was always worn tucked inside the neck of the dress. The GUIMPE hung *outside* the top of the gown.

Fig. 394.

Temp. Edward III.

Fig. 395 presents a charming coiffure unadorned by any decoration. The hair is parted in the middle and braided into two long plaits. False hair may be added if required. The plaits are each brought forward from the back, low down on the cheeks, and then turned back to form a pad. The remainder of the plait is then taken round the back in the nape to the opposite side, and neatly tucked in with the end of the other plait on top of the head.

This hairdressing was often encased in a gold network bag or crespinette. Another form left the top of the head uncovered, the network only covering the side pads and back (*see* Fig. 333). A thin gauze scarf, some sixty inches long by twenty wide, folded diagonally, was frequently placed on top, secured by the fillet or by two pins. This hung down in two irregular points on each side. In illuminated manuscripts this is often shown blown by the wind, resembling the lambrequins worn by knights on their helmets (*see* Fig. 382).

Fig. 395.
Temp. Edward. III.

Women of the fourteenth century attached great importance to the care of the hair. Their admiration for beautiful hair, especially of a bright gold colour which was the height of fashion, led them to pay especial attention to its cultivation. Paint was used in moderation by ladies of this period to give the effect of freshness, and ointments to preserve the softness of the skin, although we are told that this practice was not very usual among respectable women of the Middle Ages.

About the middle of the century a new mode of hairdressing came into use. In effect it was as though the sides of the face were framed in two stiff perpendicular plaits. Fig. 396 c shows the first version, suitable for hair of moderate length. The hair is parted in the middle and braided into two plaits, puffed up on the temples, and then brought down perpendicularly with the cheeks, the ends being tucked in under the puffing at the sides or in the nape.

For the style shown in Fig. 396 D much longer hair was required—the use of false hair was much patronised—there was no difficulty in adding to it. As before, the hair was parted in the middle and plaited into two, but the plaiting did not start until the loose wavy portion was drawn down the side of the face, covering the ears, to the level of the chin. The plaits were then taken up perpendicularly over the waved portion and *over* the fillet to the top of the head, where the two plaits

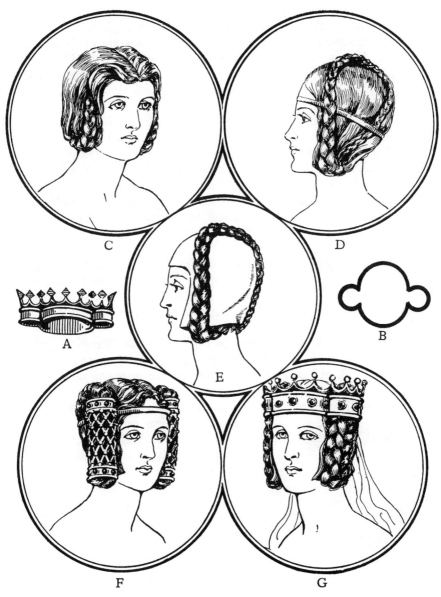

Fig. 396. COIFFURE, *temp.* EDWARD III.

crossed or were interlaced, the ends being brought downward *under* the fillet and neatly tucked into the bottom loops of the side plaits.

Sometimes the under-hair close to the cheek was cut off at mouth-level, and the rest of the hair dressed as just described (*see* Fig. 327). Fig. 396 E shows the same treatment of the hair as described under Fig. 396 D, but before the plaits are arranged on the head a close-fitting linen coif is put on.

Fig. 396 F shows the same treatment as Fig. 396 C, but with the addition of jewelled cylinders. These were fixed to the narrow fillet and the plaits of hair drawn up through them. Queen Philippa (Plate XI.) is wearing these, but on top she has a crown specially designed to include these cylinders. A fine gauze veil of moderate dimensions was usually worn with this headdress, and would be put on either under the fillet or just before the crown. These veils would be decorated with fine gold embroidery and narrow edging, according to the position of the wearer.

Again, Fig. 396 G has the same hairdressing, but it is surmounted by a coronet. Such coronets and crowns not only followed the shape of the head, but were extended by circles at each side of the front, for reception of the plaits. An elevation and plan are shown at A and B, Fig. 396.

A curious headdress is shown in Fig. 329 (Lady Warwick, 1369). It passes round the face, from chin-level on one side, up and over the top of the head, and down to chin-level on the opposite side, and is composed of several rectangular layers of cambric. The outer layer is gauffered, and the inner layers are folded in the manner of accordion

Fig. 397.

Temp. Richard II.

pleating, and sewn to each other at the edges of the folds with French-knots so as to produce a lattice or honeycomb effect. Below the point level with the chin where the lattice finishes, the edges of each layer at right angles to those forming the lattice are left falling free over the shoulders in a series of veils, as shown at C and D in Fig. 329. The whole headdress is kept in place by a narrow fillet, seen across the forehead, to which it is attached at the sides (*see also* Fig. 456). There were several variations in the method of pleating the front part of these headdresses; Fig. 334 shows all the edges pleated into zigzags, and Fig. 335 gives an SS effect. The wife of Thomas, Earl of Warwick, 1406 (Fig. 450), wears a smaller version of this headdress, which only extends across the head between the tops of the ears. Underneath, and just showing in front, is a band of gold which encircles the head.

Temp. Richard II.

The styles of hairdressing described under Edward III. were all in vogue during this reign, but in addition to these a much simpler mode came into use, which is associated solely with this period (Fig. 397). The hair was parted in the middle and done into two plaits, and each plait rolled round into a semi-spherical pad at the side of the face at eye-level, and just showing the lobe of the ear. A fillet round the head helped to secure the pads in their proper places. Sometimes a veil was worn under the fillet or coronet.

Fig. 398.
Hood, Wimple and Barbette

The hood was extremely popular with women of all classes (*see* Figs. 327, 384 and 387). The lower classes preferred the hood without its shoulder cape, and Fig. 398 shows another kind worn by a lady which has almost the appearance of a cap.

FOOTGEAR

1307–1399

One of the most important details to notice in regard to footgear of different periods is the length of the toe, which varied very considerably

Fig. 399. Sole Plans

during the course of the five centuries surveyed in this volume. Reference should be made to the various solid black sole plans, always representing the right foot, which are given in the five sections on Footgear.

During the reign of Edward II. shoes worn by ordinary people were normal in the toe and sole. It was not until about 1340 that the toe began to lengthen; up to this time, therefore, any examples of footgear described in Chapter III. were quite in the mode. The increasing length of the new-fashioned toe may be observed by reference to Figs. 311, 313 and 318.

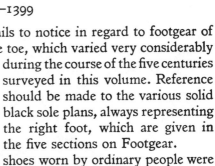

Fig. 400

Shoes are to be found occasionally in illuminated manuscripts of the time worn by the upper classes. Fig. 400 shows one of scarlet cross-barred with gold. A shoe of a little later date, with longer toe, is given in Fig. 401. It is of plain scarlet, and matches the hose. The pair of shoes on the effigy of

Edward III. are normal in shape, and are decorated (*see* Fig. 402) in a very similar manner to the footgear in fashion during the Norman

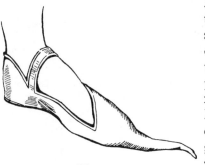

Period. The dandy in Plate X. has toes so long that it required great skill to walk with apparent ease. A certain amount of stuffing—wool, tow, etc.—was used inside the long points of the toes, making them fairly stiff but not rigid. In Plate X. the instep and part of the hose covering the gentleman's toe are gaily decorated, outlining the true shape of the foot.

Fig. 401

Shoes do not appear to have been very much used among the fashionable during the second half of the century save for ceremonial occasions (*see* Plate XII. B and Fig. 400). It was more usual to have the foot part all in one with the hose in order to continue parti-colour, then so popular, without a break. For this reason also, parti-coloured footgear, when one leg was of two colours, was not decorated.

Fig. 402. State Shoe

In the reign of Richard II. pointed toes reached their greatest length. Long toes were not introduced, as some affirm, by the courtiers attending Anne of Bohemia; but these gentlemen are responsible for the device of fastening their excessively long

toes to their garters by gold or silver chains. Sometimes the toes were of such length that they had to be attached to the waist-belt.[1]

A French shoe of this period is given in Fig. 403. Compared with those just described it is almost normal, besides being cut very open, with the vamp and

Fig. 403. French Shoe

back rising into points. A cord passing through the loop at the back ties round the ankle and over the front of the shoe, keeping it secure. Sometimes the toe was long enough to be curved round and attached to the point over the instep.

Footgear of the middle and lower classes can be best studied by reference to the drawings and descriptions given under the various figures.

[1] Crackows.

JEWELLERY

1307–1399

In the fourteenth century the first English sumptuary law, regulating the wearing of jewellery, was passed in the year 1363. It provides that "no person under the rank of a knight, or of less property than £200 in lands or tenements, should wear rings, buckles, ouches, girdles, or any other part of their apparel decorated with gold, silver or gems." This suggests that the wearing of jewellery had become much more general, not only with the nobility but with the middle classes.

Figures in gold, silver or enamel, or any combinations of these materials, were introduced at this time into the decoration of jewellery. Metal figures were often modelled in high relief upon enamelled backgrounds with precious stones set around them or used as part of the design. Ornaments were sometimes made entirely of enamel, these being imported from Limoges, which still retained its world-fame for this style of jewellery. Goldsmiths of France, Northern Italy and Northern Spain were the best craftsmen and jewellers of this period, and their work was in great demand and commanded large prices.

Crowns, coronets and circlets. For the design of royal crowns in use at the beginning of the fourteenth century, reference should be made to Figs. 291 and 292. The crown worn by Edward III. in Fig. 308 is similar to these, but that shown in Fig. 309, of a later date, is more elaborate and has a greater number of leaf motifs surmounting the band. These are better displayed in Fig. 321.

The crown shown in Fig. 301 is taken from an illuminated manuscript depicting Jeanne de Bourgoyne, and is of the type worn also by Isabella of France. The crown worn by Queen Philippa, Plate XI., is very elaborate. The band is surmounted by eight leaf motifs, separated by small trefoils, and is set with many jewels, chiefly rubies and emeralds. This crown is copied from a reproduction of a fresco formerly in S. Stephen's Chapel, Westminster. The sides of the crown in Plate XI. have additional rings to fit the tops of the hair cylinders; a plan may be seen in Fig. 396 at B.

The crown worn by Charles V., Fig. 354, is of beautiful design, having six fleurs-de-lys raised on points above the band, and between each two large pearls set one above the other on upright gold wires.

Fig. 404.
Crown of Richard II.

The portrait of Richard II. (Plate XII. B) shows the king wearing an elaborate crown (Fig. 404), and this is the first example of the more highly decorated style worn by later English kings. The crowns worn by the two kings in the Wilton Diptych (Plate XII. A) are very similar to this, but not quite so high; and that worn by Richard in the same diptych is slightly simpler than the others.

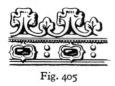

Fig. 405

Coronets were worn by noblemen, often fixed round their helmets; and the earliest example of one worn in this manner is to be found on the effigy of Prince John of Eltham, 1334. The one given in Fig. 405 is from the effigy of the Black Prince. Such a coronet was of goldsmith's work set with jewels.

The coronet worn by the nobleman in Fig. 318 is of plain gold, rising in four points, the edges being rolled. Fig. 311 shows a circlet —a narrow band not quite half an inch in width—set with a single fine jewel. Chaplets such as are described in Chapter III. were still worn by the nobility. They were sometimes composed of one or two strands of pearls encircling the head, with a single jewel or cluster of stones worn on the forehead. Froissart tells that Edward III. "toke the chapelet that was upon his heed beyng bothe fayre goodly and ryche," and gave it to Sir Eustace de Ribeaumont "as the best doar in armes." It was of two strands of perfectly matched pearls.

The circlet returned to fashion among ladies of the upper classes about 1360; but not as a revival of the simple gold circlet with perhaps a single stone worn in earlier days. Those in use during the second half of the fourteenth century were much more massive than their fore-runners; in fact, they were miniature versions of the hip-belt described on p. 277, composed of plaques hinged together to fit the head. Fig. 328 shows one of these new circlets of goldsmith's work in filigree set with jewels—possibly a cameo or intaglio. These gems returned to popularity towards the end of this century and during the whole of that which followed. Not only was there a revival of the neglected art of cutting cameos and intaglios (see Vol. I., p. 64), but there was also a craze for acquiring antiques of all kinds [1]—from the collections of impecunious royalties and nobles. No small number came from the vast but fast-diminishing imperial treasury at Constantinople.

Fig. 406.
Clasp

Brooches. During this period brooches were used for the same purposes as described in Chapter III. One of a pair of clasps for fastening a belt, or a cloke or hood at the throat, is shown in Fig. 406. It could be made of gold, silver or brass, and perforated in a design.

Fig. 407.
Buckle

There is a hole in one portion and a hook is attached to the end of the corresponding ornament. The two halves could be sewn or riveted to the garment. Fig. 407 gives a typical buckle of the fourteenth century, made in any of the three metals above mentioned. A clasp, a pair of which was used to secure

---

[1] The age of the art-collector had begun.

the low-necked cotehardie tight round the bust, is shown in Fig. 408. It is of gold, enamel, precious stones and pearls. These clasps or brooches had small teeth set underneath them, which gripped the material and kept it tight round the bust, counteracting the tendency of these low-cut neck-openings to slip. Often a third was fixed in front of the bust (*see* Fig. 327), and for this reason breast brooches were sometimes called "*Pectorals.*"

Fig. 408

Two fermails of the fourteenth century are shown in Figs. 409 and 410; the originals cover an area of just over one square inch and are of silver gilt, but these types were also made of gold or silver. They are engraved, one with initials and the other with an inscription. Frequently they had a scriptural quotation, some word or sentence, engraved on them as a protectional charm against evil.

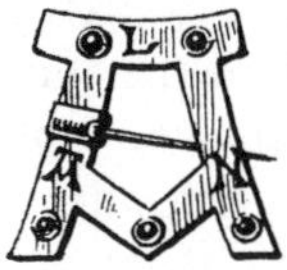

Fig. 409

Small, useful, yet ornamental brooches of the type shown in Fig. 280 were much used at this time. Fig. 411 is very similar, but more elaborately jewelled and set with emeralds. Heart-shaped fermails were also very popular, and Fig. 412 shows one entwined with a band or ribbon on which might be engraved an inscription. A develop-

Fig. 410

ment of this heart-shape came into fashion about the middle of the century, having the point terminating in two small hands, often holding a precious stone. Fig. 413 shows this idea developed still further, and has a human head projecting from the ring opposite the hands.

Hip-belts. A new article of jewellery came into fashion with the cotehardie in the early part of Edward III.'s reign. This was the belt that was worn low down on the hip. These hip-belts were composed entirely of goldsmith's work, and in design were a series of square, circular or lozenge-shaped plaques united by joints to give the belt a certain flexibility. The plaques were ornamented with engraving,

Fig. 412

Fig. 413

repoussé or filigree, often in conjunction with enamel, and set with many rich jewels. The belt was fastened in front by a pin passing through slots behind the central medallion and kept in its place by hooks inserted in the cotehardie. Fig. 414 shows one of these belts which is ornamented with circular and lozenge-shaped plaques in gold set with rubies, emeralds, diamonds and pearls. Between the plaques are groups of three large pearls. A belt less rich would have gold links attaching the plaques to each other. These plaques were often in such high relief that they projected an inch or two beyond the hips. From the belt the misericorde was hung on the right side, and, when the occasion required, the sword on the left.

Fig. 414. Hip-belt

Towards the end of the reign it was the vogue to have a long end to the belt hanging on the left side; this is seen in Plate X.

Noble ladies also wore very ornate hip-belts over the cotehardie, as seen in Fig. 328. They were made like the belts worn by the men, or else composed of separate plaques sewn to a band of silk or velvet. Two plaques forming part of a lady's hip-belt are shown in Fig. 415. They date from the end of the four-teenth century, and the same type was worn during the fifteenth century. When the sideless gown was worn over the cotehardie it became the vogue to retain the hip-belt *underneath* it, visible only through the side openings.

Belts worn at the waist by wealthy and unfashionable men were beautifully decorated with silver, sometimes gold or other metal, riveted or sewn on to leather straps usually having an edging or rim of pliable metal. One such belt is shown in Fig. 416. Fig. 364 gives the detail of part of the belt worn by the gentle-man in Fig. 363, taken direct from the memorial brass. From a similar

Fig. 415. Detail of Hip-belt

Fig. 416
Gentleman's Belt

source comes Fig. 366, the belt worn by John Corp. Both have ornamental mordaunts. The buckle in Fig. 364 is wider at the end than where it is fixed to the belt, to allow the raised ornaments of the belt to pass through with ease.

During the second half of the fourteenth century, ladies sometimes wore a perpendicular band of jewels down the centre of the plastron or upon that portion between the bands of fur which outlined the wide openings of the sideless gown (*see* Fig. 332). The different sections of the band were linked together, and secured to the plastron or cotehardie by small hooks. Fig. 417 gives a detail of this ornament, which was much used for full dress by noble ladies in the fifteenth century. These bands sometimes encircled the neck-opening as well as decorating the plastron.

Fig. 417.
Plastron Band

Two or three *finger-rings* were worn by wealthy men and women. By this time they were not so massive in design as the last shown (*see*

Figs. 89 and 90). A hoop of gold was set with gems and precious stones much in the manner of modern ring designs. A description of the rings worn by a fine lady of the fourteenth century given by Piers of Langtoft is as follows:

> On all her fine fingers daintily adorned were fretted with gold wire. Thereon red rubies and diamantz of greatest worth and two-fold kind of sapphire, Orientals[1] and beryls to destroy venom.

Fig. 418 shows a betrothal-ring having a design of clasped hands and a motto or posy inscribed on the band. This type of ring very often had the hoop made in two, sometimes three sections, which turned on a pivot and could be easily detached and shared by two people as a pledge of troth. These rings were generally called "Gemmel-rings." Signet-rings

Fig. 418.   Fig. 419.

Rings

were usually worn on the thumb, and for that reason were somewhat heavy in design, as shown in Fig. 419.

Chains of gold or silver began to make their appearance around the necks of noblemen during the reign of Richard II., the high collar then in fashion being well adapted to show them to advantage.

Detail of the *necklace* worn by Richard II. in the Wilton Diptych (Plate XII. A) is given in Fig. 420. It is composed of a band, about one inch in width, edged with gold and set with pearls. Square jewelled ornaments are fixed about three inches apart all round the band, and it is clasped in front with a larger square ornament in gold, having a large jewel surrounded by pearls set in high relief. The ends of the band hang a short distance below this clasp.

Pendants, reliquaries or crosses were sometimes hung from neck chains and used by both sexes. Fashionable young men of the time carried their jewelled daggers on neck chains: a "dainty conceit" peculiar to the reign of Richard II. Badges were frequently hung round the neck in a similar manner.

Fig. 420.

Necklace, Richard II.

Badges. For many years it had been the custom for the retainers of great lords to wear their master's badge. This led to a practice among the nobility of the latter half of the fourteenth century of having their own individual badge made of gold, enamel and jewels, and wearing it as a personal ornament. Similar ornaments were frequently presented to their friends, and to

[1] Any rich stone from the East.

lukewarm adherents with whom it might be desirable to curry special favour. This method of propitiation was a favourite one with Richard II., whose various badges were wrought in gold and enamels and framed or studded with jewels of various kinds, chiefly rubies and pearls or diamonds, red and white being the livery colours of the Plantagenets.

A list of a few family badges is given on p. 310.

Although English women did not wear visible necklaces until the end of the century, they made up for their absence in other ways. *Garters* worn by noble ladies of Edward III.'s reign were very rich, made of silk or velvet, heavily embroidered in gold or silver, and decorated with enamels and jewels, often finishing in tassels of silk strung with precious stones. Men also wore elaborate garters, set with jewels and furnished with beautiful buckles and mordaunts.

Section VII.—Weaving and Materials

1307–1399

(Continued from p. 188)

The development of the weaving industry in England advanced very greatly during the fourteenth century, largely due to the attention devoted by Edward III. to the welfare of his subjects. In the year 1331 Edward invited, among many others, a Fleming named John Kemp to bring "his servants and apprentices in his mystery" to settle at Norwich. This man brought with him many dyers and fullers, and afterwards removed to Westmoreland, founding there a manufactory for the famous "Kendal green," which appears to have been a rather coarse cloth of a good green colour.

Other Flemish weavers settled in the eastern counties about this time. Remembering the trade which had brought prosperity to her own country, Queen Philippa established a large colony of weavers at Norwich in the year 1336, from which a considerable development of the industry sprang. Before this time the neighbouring village of Worsted had been a centre of weaving, but it was from this date that it became famous for the manufacture of cloth made from long-stapled wool, called by the name of the village, "worsted." Plain worsted, known earlier as "saye," was the material usually worn by the population in general.

Before long, weaving was definitely established in certain places, each associated with some particular type of manufacture: baizes were manufactured at Sudbury; cloths in Worcestershire, Gloucestershire, Hampshire, Sussex and Berkshire; coarse cloths in the West Riding of Yorkshire; friezes in Wales; fustians at Norwich; kerseys in Devon; and serges at Colchester and Taunton.

Trade between England and Flanders (the great manufacturing

country of Europe at the time) greatly increased in the latter part of the fourteenth century, especially as sheep-farming developed in England after the Black Death; nine-tenths of the raw material was supplied to the looms of Bruges and Ghent. Revenues from this source became so important (the king alone receiving £60,000 annually from the wool tax) that it was judicious to keep amicable and diplomatic relations between the two countries. When Edward III., and later Henry V., contemplated attacks on France, they took good care to gain the friendship of the counts of Flanders: firstly, so that their country might be used as a base for operations against France, and secondly, because a large proportion of the expenses of the Hundred Years' War was raised in England by the wool tax, which depended upon the trade and goodwill of Flanders.

Export of English wool extended to Italy, and we find it on record that a company of Florentine merchants entered into a contract with Cistercian monks, who were large wool-growers owning vast sheep ranges on the Yorkshire moorlands, to purchase their whole year's growth of wool.

The development of weaving in England altered these conditions, and gradually the export of wool declined. Manufactured cloth became the basis of national wealth in place of raw wool. At intervals the export of wool was forbidden altogether, so that more might be left for the looms at home.

Stoppage of supplies of raw wool brought the looms of Flanders to stagnation, and half the population were thrown out of work, which, as Bacon tells us, "pinched the merchants of both nations very sore."

Materials, 1307–1399

Alexander. A striped silk of Oriental manufacture, which took its name from Alexandria, though not exclusively made there. *Bord, bourde, burda* are earlier names for the same kind of material.

Aurum in serico. Gold and silk tissue.

Chainsil. Now woven and dyed in colours—red, vermilion, green, yellow, orange.

Cameline. A material very like cashmere, made in Flanders.

Canzi. A material obtained from China and probably of silk.

Carda. As oft fluffy cotton cloth, like short swansdown, used for lining. The best quality was made in Flanders, France, and Italy.

Carry-marry. A coarse serge cloth used by peasants.

Cashmere. Woven from the hair of the Tibet or Armenian goat. During this century the factories for weaving it, in Cyprus, were worked by French craftsmen, and in Armenia by Venetians. Some cashmere was made at Rheims.

Caurimawry. Same as carry-marry.

Cogware or *Cogmen.* A coarse material like frieze, a homespun.

Cordetum. A coarse cloth.

Cottum. A woolly material woven from the hair of cats and dogs.

Écarlate. A name used during this century for a richer quality silk than given in Vol. I., p. 217.

Echiqueles. Checked; a fourteenth-century name for cloth woven in squares.

Falding. A coarse cloth like serge or frieze.

Flanella or *Flannen.* A woollen material, the origin of flannel.

Gold, Cloth of. Much used in this century as at other times for making State and ceremonial garments.

Kersey. A coarse make of saye, said to have been first made at Kersey in Suffolk.

Kerseymere. A finer make of kersey.

Lake, Cloth of. A cloth of Liége or Luye, a fine linen, but not so fine as lawn.

Marbrinus. A material of silk woven to look like the veins of marble. It was rich in substance, and sometimes adorned with figures.

Mattabas or *Marramas.* A cloth of gold.

Oldham. A cloth of coarse make.

Osterni. A silk cloth dyed purple.

Raffata. Taffeta.

Tars, Cloth of. A costly material, but its nature is uncertain. *Tarsicus, tartarinus, tartaryn* are other names for it.

Tartaire. A silk stuff made originally in Tartary, but later imitated in the West.

Fur

"Fur" was originally a verb meaning "to line." The phrase "furred with ermine," = lined with ermine, is frequently found in mediæval writings.

Latin, *Pellis* = a skin. Old French, *Pelles* = skins or furs. Old English, *Pelure.*

Furs or skins had been in use among the peoples of Western Europe ever since the Stone Age, but precious furs were not used in the West for the lining or decoration of garments until the beginning of the twelfth century, and then only occasionally. The first appearance of sable, in the time of Henry I., is recorded on p. 31, and ermine was used a little later.

Sable, ermine and miniver were used sparingly during the succeeding 150 years. About the middle of the thirteenth century the use of rich furs was much more fashionable, and by the first half of the fourteenth century their use had greatly increased, as proved by the enumeration of many kinds in a charter of Edward III., 1328. The following furs are mentioned in the writings of the Middle Ages.

The four most valuable furs were:

SABLE (*Saphilmas pelles*), ZIBELINES, ZORNBOLINES. The fur of an animal of the weasel kind.

ERMINE (*Hereminæ pelles*). A northern animal of the weasel family, reserved by Edward III. for the use of the royal family and nobles possessing £1000 per annum. In the reign of Henry IV. its use was extended to the nobility generally. The winter skin of this animal is white, the tip of its tail only remaining black.

Often the paws of the black Astrakhan lamb were used instead of ermine tails. "The sayde surcote overt furred with iij tymbr di' and v. ermyn bakks and viij ermyn wombes, the said furre powdered with ccccxxv powderings maade of *bogy shanks* and the sayde furre lyneth perfourmed with xxxij tymbr' of wombes of menyver pure." This quotation from a wardrobe account of the fifteenth century is enlightening. "Tymbr" (timber) is a measure equivalent to forty skins. "Bogy" is another name for budge (lambskin), and "bogy shanks" means lambs' legs.

MINIVER, MINEVER, MINEVEER, MENU VAIR. The fur of the white ermine, without the tails or spots. It was highly esteemed during the Middle Ages, and was much worn by the nobility, their high social position being indicated by its use.

VAIR. A composite fur, consisting of the white of the ermine and the bluish-grey of the squirrel, called "Gris." It is said to have derived its name from "Verre," since the best quality was almost iridescent and shone like glass. Its appearance is represented in heraldry by heater-shaped shields of alternate white and grey or blue (*see* Fig. 427, Nos. 4 and 6). This fur ranked with sable and ermine, and was much valued in the Middle Ages. Another kind of vair was the skin of a species of squirrel, grey on the back and white on the throat and belly. This fur was imported from Hungary in the twelfth century, and in great quantities during the following century.

Other furs mentioned as being in use in the fourteenth century are:

Gris or *Bise*, *Byses*, *Bysettes*. The fur of the gray or martyn, or of the back of the squirrel in winter.

Martyn, *Marten*, *Marters*, or *Martrons*.

Rabbit. Importance was attached to this fur, which is mentioned as being worn by "nobles and gentlemen."

Stradling, *Bison*, *Foynes*, *Fur of bethes* (used for liveries), skins of *beaver* and "*bogyleggs*," are named in records.

Budge or *Bogy*. Lambskin with the fur dressed outwards; much used for legal robes and livery gowns. Budge Row in the City of London is "so called of the Budge furre, and of skinners dwelling there."

(*Continued on p. 462.*)

THE GUILDS

(Continued from p. 189)

In the fourteenth century guild organisations extended over the whole country, and brought the craftsmen together in organised bodies. Early in the century it was an enforced rule that no one should be admitted to the Freedom of the City of London unless he were a member of one of the trades.

During the reign of Edward III. an entire reconstruction of trading fraternities took place. They were now assuming a distinctive dress or livery [1] and came to be called "Livery Companies." The name "Guild" was changed to "Crafts and Mysteries" (the word "mystery" was used in the reign of Edward I. to denote trade or calling; *see* p. 189), and the old title "Alderman" changed to "Master and Wardens." The name "Alderman" was restricted to the heads of the City wards.

In the year 1376 there were forty-eight City companies in London, and the right of election of all City dignitaries, officers and Members of Parliament was in the hands of these livery companies. At this time the richer companies separated from the poorer; the former gained control of the Common Council, and the existing custom of choosing the mayor exclusively from among them dates from this time. The importance of the Mayor of London was recognised in 1354 when Edward III. granted to Adam Francis, of the Mercers' Company, the prefix of "Lord." It was his second year of office.

(Continued on p. 464.)

Entertainments of the Livery Companies and Guilds

(Continued from p. 190)

Mystery and miracle plays were still very popular and were the most important dramatic entertainments of the fourteenth century. The following is a description of a mystery or pageant play given every year from 1378 on the Feast of the Purification of the Blessed Mary by the Guild of S. Mary at Beverley:

For the principal character, that of the Virgin Mary, "a fair youth, the fairest they can find, is picked out, and is clad as a Queen. . . . One of the Gild shall be clad in comely fashion as the Queen, like to the glorious Virgin Mary, having what may seem a son in her arms; and two

---

[1] *Livery colours of the various' companies.*—Distinct colours for the liveries of various companies were fairly general during the first part of the fourteenth century; but in many instances these colours were frequently changed. An attempt has been made to compile a complete list of the livery colours of the guilds and City companies, but it has been found that conflicting accounts, and the lack of records of fixed rules, make it impossible to do so.

If it be necessary to suggest these livery colours for any production, they may be deduced with reasonable accuracy from the tinctures of the armorial bearings of the company concerned.

others shall be clad like to Joseph and Simeon; and two shall go as
Angels, carrying a candlebearer, on which shall be twenty-four thick
wax lights. With these and other great lights borne before them, and
with much music and gladness, the pageant Virgin and her son, and
Joseph and Simeon, shall go in procession to the church. And all the
Sisteren of the Gild shall follow the Virgin; and afterwards all the
Bretheren; and each of them shall carry a wax light weighing half a
pound. And they shall go two and two, slowly pacing the church; and
when they have got there, the pageant Virgin shall offer her son to
Simeon at the high altar; and all the Sisteren and Bretheren shall offer
their wax lights, together with a penny each. All this having been
solemnly done, they shall go home again with gladness."

Street pageants developed into elaborate processions. On the birth
of a son and heir to Edward II. in 1312 the Fishmongers
celebrated the joyful event with a noble pageant. "They
caused a boat (on wheels) to be fitted out in the guise
of a great ship, with all manner of tackle that belongs to
a ship, and it sailed through Chepe as far as Westminster, where the Fishmongers came, well mounted and
costumed very richly, and presented the ship to the
Queen." The mayor and aldermen were richly robed "in
like suits," and they were accompanied by the Guilds of the Drapers,
Mercers and Vintners.

Fig. 421.
Trestle-end

Feasts and banquets, so universally associated with corporations,
have been popular forms of entertainment from early times; and some

Fig. 422.
A Golden Dish

of those given by the aldermen and guilds
of the City of London were magnificent
and costly beyond description. Mayors
of other towns also gave elaborate banquets. Robert Braunch, Mayor of Lynn,
Norfolk, 1349 and 1359 (died 1364), was
celebrated for the "Peacock Feast" with
which he regaled Edward III. This event
is depicted on his brass in the Church of
S. Margaret, King's Lynn.

Some tantalising details of a banquet
of this time are given in the following lines:

There came in at the *first course*, before the king's self,
Boars' heads on broad dishes of burnished silver,
Flesh of fat harts with noble furmenty,
And peacocks and plovers on platters of gold,
Herons and swans in chargers of silver,
And tarts of Turkey full pleasant to taste.
Next hams of wild-boar with brawn beglazed,
Barnacle-geese and bitterns in embossed dishes,
Venison in pasties, so comely to view,

Jellies that glittered and gladdened the eye.
Then cranes and curlews craftily roasted,
Conies in clear sauce coloured so bright,
Pheasants in their feathers on the flashing silver,
With gay galantines and dainties galore.
There were claret and Crete wine in clear silver fountains,
Wine of Alsace and Antioch and Hippocras enough,
Vernaccia from Venice, a wine of great virtue,
Rhenish wine and Rochelle, and wine from Mount Rose,
All in flagons of fine gold, and on the fair cupboard
Stood store of gilt goblets glorious of hue,
Sixty of one set with jewels on their sides.

. . . . . .

Spices (dessert) were dispensed with unsparing hand,
And Malmsey and Muscatel, those marvellous drinks,
Went readily round in fair russet cups.

Fig. 423
Goblet and Cover

In 1357 Sir Henry Picard, Lord Mayor of London and Master (1363) of the Vintners' Company, entertained in lavish manner Edward III. and the Kings of France, Scotland, Denmark and Cyprus, at a banquet. A mural painting of this festivity is to be seen in the Royal Exchange, and, although by a modern artist, gives a most accurate idea of the proceedings.

About the middle of the fourteenth century the river became the chosen scene of some of the most effective pageantry. The various guilds and livery companies decked out barges of different shapes and sizes, manned by watermen, each wearing the colours and badges of the company he served, which formed a procession up the Thames, usually making for the king's palace at Westminster.

(*Continued on p. 465.*)

CHAPTER V

HERALDRY

(Written in collaboration with G. Ambrose Lee, Esq., C.B., C.V.O.,
Clarenceux King-of-Arms)

Section I.—Introduction

Heraldry may be defined as the science of recording genealogies, and interpreting charges and devices on shields, banners, etc. In days past it was chiefly used in connection with military equipment, and, from this circumstance, early heraldry has also been called *Armory.* Its most important function was that of distinction. It was a symbolic and pictorial language represented in figures, devices and colours. Every heraldic composition has its own definite and complete significance conveyed through its direct connection with some particular individual, family, dignity, or office.

Heraldry became hereditary, like other real property, in accordance with certain precedents and laws of inheritance. It admits of augmentation and expansion.

Origin and development. In all ages of the world, and amongst all races of men, some form of symbolic expression has been in use and favour. Warriors of distinction have adorned their shields with devices, sometimes significant of their own condition or exploits, country or family, and the use of these devices has been retained in many cases by their descendants. In like manner it has been a universal custom to display devices and figures on military standards. The systematised form evolved by the science of Heraldry about the middle of the twelfth century was a superstructure built up on these earlier forms of family insignia, which had acquired an hereditary quality.

The heraldry of Europe evidently derived its origin from the East, and was intimately associated with religion and superstition. The eagle belongs to the ensign of Vishnu, the bull to that of Siva, the falcon to that of Rama, the goose was an incarnation of Buddha, etc. Migrating tribes carried with them their respective emblems.

In the same manner the Assyrians and Egyptians used various devices as decoration or cognisance. Greek warriors are shown on vase paintings carrying shields ornamented with various animals and objects, used as distinguishing emblems—a fact alluded to by Homer.

287

The Romans copied the Greeks and went still further, adopting the eagle as a national standard (*see* Vol. I., Fig. 35). Their military leaders sometimes wore distinguishing symbols on their armour or shields. Seals and signet-rings, engraved with a personal device, were also used by the Romans, and the emblems so employed have certain features in common with the system which developed much later into the definite science of heraldry.

The Israelites had certain devices, and even hereditary symbols, displayed on their standards.

"And the children of Israel shall pitch their tents, every man by his own camp, and every man by his own standard" (Num. i. 52). "Every man of the children of Israel shall pitch by his own standard, with the ensign of their father's house" (Num. ii. 2).

It was the custom among Teutonic tribes, the ancestors of the Anglo-Saxons, to bear standards, ensigns and shields, all decorated with a distinctive device, and this is true also of the Normans.[1]

Various countries in ancient times had their recognised standards, which were borne at the head of the army in battle, or flown as banners from the masts of the ships.

National emblems. The *Egyptians* adopted the eagle and the vulture as a national standard.

The *Greeks*, the owl.

The *Dacians*, the dragon.

The tribe of *Benjamin* adopted the wolf, which is also the *Norman* standard.

The tribe of *Dan*, a serpent and an eagle.

The tribe of *Ephraim* adopted the unicorn.

The tribe of *Judah*, the lion, as if sleeping.

The *Mexicans*, the swan.

The *Teutonic* tribes adopted the horse, as borne by the House of *Hanover*.

The *Scandinavians*, the raven.

The history of modern heraldry begins about the middle of the twelfth century, with the use of hereditary devices for practical purposes of distinction. This was necessitated by three factors:

(*a*) The system of Feudal Overlordship (*see* Section II.).

(*b*) The growing popularity of the tournament (*see* Section III.).

(*c*) The first Crusades (*see* p. 318).

---

[1] "The two princes, William and Geoffrey, give a mutual challenge; each gives the other notice of the garb and shield that he will wear, that he may not be mistaken."

Section II.—Feudalism

Feudalism was the system by which a certain man, called a *Vassal*, held land from the owner, the king, or from an overlord, or *Suzerain*, on condition that the vassal rendered military service to his overlord when required.

The owner of some vast estate, himself a vassal to the king, found it to his advantage to parcel out land among vassals, who, in return, agreed to accompany him to war, attend his Court, and guard his castle, and, if necessary, assist him when he was put to any great expense. Land granted on these terms was said to be "infeudated," and called a "Fief."

Originally the "fief" was granted for a certain number of years or for the life of the grantee, and reverted at his death to the owner. As early as the tenth century, there was a strong feeling that what the father enjoyed should pass to his children, and shortly afterwards the usual tenure was amended so that the possession of land became hereditary in the family of the vassal, and passed down to the eldest son from one generation to another. So long as the vassal remained faithful to his lord and performed the stipulated services, and his descendants did the same, neither the lord nor his heirs could rightfully regain possession of the land.

The holder of a fief might himself become an overlord by granting a portion of his fief to another upon the same terms as those on which he held from his lord. By these means the superior overlord drew around him a number of people of various grades, and this not only enhanced his prestige, but proved very useful in keeping up his estate in time of peace. In time of war, they formed a small standing army, and were essentially *his* men and *not* the king's. If the overlord warred against the king, his vassals could support him without being guilty of treason.

The vassal acknowledged his dependence on his feudal lord by the act of rendering "homage" (Latin, *homo* = man). He knelt before him, and, placing his hands between those of the lord, he swore to be his "man" (*see* Selous' *Hereward the Wake*, Pl. 19). Thereupon the lord gave his vassal the kiss of peace, and raised him. The vassal then took the oath of fidelity upon the Bible or some holy relic, solemnly binding himself to fulfil all his duties towards his lord. Refusal by a vassal to do homage for his fief (when it changed hands) was equivalent to a declaration of revolt or independence by the new heir. The overlord or suzerain was the immediate vassal of the Crown, since the king was recognised as the proprietor of the whole land.

When William I. conquered England, he claimed the whole country with himself as chief or superior landlord. The Anglo-Saxon nobles and gentry who supported him continued to hold their estates under him. The lands of the Saxon nobles and gentry who *took arms against William* were confiscated and given to the Norman nobles and military attendants who had helped him to conquer the country.

The overlord was of the class known as "Barons," equivalent to the "Peers" of later times. The greater barons were the king's chief tenants, and in most cases enjoyed the offices of "Comes" and "Dux." The lesser barons held from the greater by tenure of military service.

The Origin of Early Titles

"Comes" or "Count" was a title of Imperial Rome, and referred to a State official. An Imperial Roman officer was stationed in Britain during the fourth century A.D., and was styled "*Comes Littoris Saxonici*"— Warden or Guardian of the Saxon Coast, *i.e.* the east coast of Britain, which at that time was exposed to the ravages of Saxon pirates.

In Saxon times Comes was a title of honour and implied a "Companion of the King's Household." The Anglo-Saxon name was "Thegn," afterwards "Gezith," meaning "The King's Guard" (*see* Vol. I., p. 259).

Eorl or *Æthel* (*Yarl*, Scandinavian), later *Earl*, was a Saxon title for the head man of the shire, and each shire had its Ealdorman (older or elder man, a civil magistrate, from which our word alderman is derived). Before the use of the title Earl, the older Saxon name of Æthel was general, and had an undermeaning equivalent to the Roman *nobilis* or primary class of noble blood, and from it the title "Ætheling," the king's kin, was derived. After the time of Canute (1014) the term Earl began to be used instead of Eorl or Æthel. The Norman successors to the deposed Anglo-Saxon earls were known for a time as "counts," since they preferred to follow the practice of the country whence they came. Until 1138 earls appear to have been officials, each in charge of a county, but those created by Stephen seem to have been often merely titulary. Up to the year 1337 the title of earl ranked as the highest after royalty, but it is now the third degree of rank and dignity in the British peerage. The title *Count* has now disappeared from the British peerage, or, more correctly speaking, it is merged in the title of earl. The wife of an earl, however, retains the title of Countess.

Viscount (Latin, *Vice* = instead of, and *Comes*) was originally the title of a sheriff of a county, or the *Earl's Vice-agent*. It was first bestowed upon John, Baron Beaumont, by Henry VI. in 1440 as an hereditary dignity. It now ranks fourth in the order of the peerage.

Dux, later Duke, a military title of the Roman Empire, was created by Constantine the Great and used as the equivalent of the civil title of *Comes* on the separation of the military and civil command in A.D. 330. The general in command in Britain was styled *Dux Britannium*. The title of duke was not used in England until Edward III. created the Black

Prince "Duke of Cornwall" in 1337. It was then merely a title of honour; in the British peerage it now ranks first after the Royal Family and the Archbishops of Canterbury and York.

Marken, Markisii, later *Marquess,* was a Teutonic word meaning the limit or border of a land or district, and afterwards the territory that adjoined that limit. The officers in charge of these districts (called Marken or Marquisates) were styled *Markisii* and in German *Markgrafen.* This office was assigned to the families of Percy and Douglas as Wardens of the English and Scottish Borders or *Marches.* As a title of honour it was first introduced by Richard II., who created his favourite Robert de Vere, Marquess of Dublin. It now ranks second in the order of the British peerage.

Baron. To-day the title of baron has declined from its original importance and is the fifth or lowest order in the peerage.

All peers and peeresses other than dukes and their consorts are usually referred to as Lord and Lady So-and-so. The wife of a baronet or knight, properly called *Dame,* is also addressed *by courtesy* as Lady.

The sons of dukes and marquesses are called by their Christian names and their surnames, with the prefix of "Lord," and the daughters of dukes, marquesses and earls in like manner, with the prefix of "Lady." But the *eldest son* of a peer holding more than one title is known by his father's secondary title. Younger sons of earls, and all the sons and daughters of viscounts and barons, are styled "The Honourable — —."

It should be borne in mind carefully that in England there is no "nobility" except the actual holding of a peerage; all the sons of peers of every rank being, in the eyes of the law, nothing but commoners with no privileges whatsoever, except a barren title and a certain precedence.

Differencing

The overlords of the middle twelfth century, who had inherited these early titles, were the first to adopt *Coats of Arms* when heraldry originated. As time went on, it became necessary that the more important vassals living on an estate should be distinguished also by a device or badge. These vassals were men of every grade of gentle birth, and were the next to appropriate coats of arms for themselves.

At this juncture feudal dependence had a great effect upon heraldry and provided the means of meeting these increasing demands, introducing a treatment of armorial bearings based on and denoting

Feudal Alliance

The method generally adopted was for the vassals to take for their coats of arms some charge or detail from their overlord's shield of arms, and to arrange, concoct or develop armorial bearings at once different from and complementary to those of their overlords. This is called in heraldic language *D i f f e r e n c i n g*. As an example, it should be noted that

Randolph, Earl of Chester (*temp*. Stephen and Henry II.), bore three golden garbs or wheat-sheaves upon a blue field (Fig. 424). The garb is still to be observed on the shields of a great number of the nobility and gentry of the County Palatine of Chester.

The *Counties Palatine* are those frontier counties where the count or earl exercised inde-pendent jurisdiction. This privilege was granted to Hugh the Fat, Earl of Chester, by William the Conqueror. Durham and Lancaster were also

Fig. 424. Chester

Counties Palatine. The Palatine jurisdiction of Chester was abolished in 1830, and that of Durham in 1836. Lancaster alone (forfeited to the Crown in Edward IV.'s reign) still retains its Court. Palatinates of Pembroke and Hexham were dissolved in the reigns of Henry VIII. and Elizabeth respectively.

Section III.—The Tournament and its Relation to Heraldry

In the time of Charlemagne (800) it was the custom for nobles attached to his Court to amuse themselves with entertainments taking the form of combats at arms. Later on, Henry the Fowler, Emperor of Germany (917–936), adopted this pastime seriously. He inaugurated meetings of all his subjects whose estates qualified them for knighthood (*see* Chivalry), to practise military exercises in order to improve the efficiency of his cavalry; by this means he hoped to overcome the turbulent Hungarians who threatened invasion of his dominions. These gatherings proved very popular, and from them originated the Tourna-ment, a conflict between many mounted knights divided into two parties. The name is derived from the French, *tourner* = to turn round. Great agility was necessary on the part of both horses and men in swerving round to ward off thrusts, as well as considerable military skill.

In the eleventh century, jousts were invented by a certain French knight, Geoffrey de Prenilly (died 1066). These were friendly trials of strength and skill between two mounted or unmounted knights, advancing on each other, lance in rest or sword in hand (*see* Plate XV.).

Tournaments or jousts do not appear to have been practised to any great extent in England until early in the twelfth century. William of Malmesbury, the historian, mentions one as having taken place in the

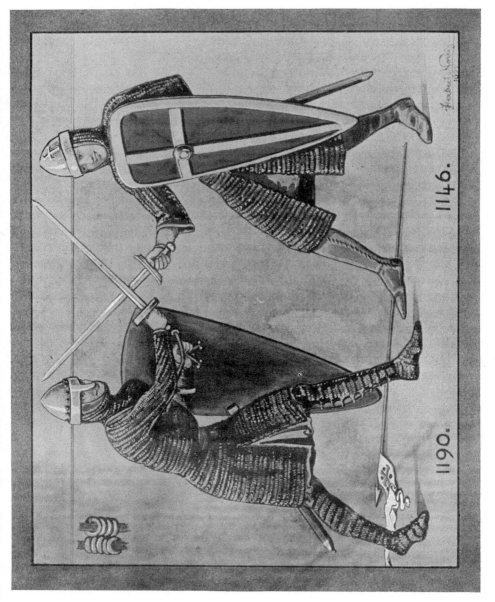

1146.

1190.

PLATE XV.   A FRIENDLY JOUST

year 1142 (Stephen), but such entertainments did not receive the royal authority until it was granted by Richard I. From this time onwards, both tournaments and jousts became more general, and many rules and regulations were introduced.

A *Herald* in mediæval times was an officer who bore messages from one king or noble to another. He also laid out the Lists (the enclosed space reserved for the combat) in preparation for jousts or tournaments, and superintended matters relating to ceremonial and the bearing of coats of arms. A trumpet was blown and the herald announced a new knight when he appeared at a tournament. The German for "to blow a horn" is *blasen,* and the term "blazon" in heraldic language means to describe, interpret, or represent any armorial figure, charge, device or composition in an heraldic manner.

A *charge* is any heraldic device or figure.

An *emblem* is a concrete or pictorial expression of a symbolic idea.

If a new knight appearing at a tournament wished his identity to be kept secret, he kept the visor of his helmet closed. It was then the duty of the herald to interpret to the spectators the significance of the charges or devices upon the knight's shield, without divulging his name. This explanation, given in Norman French, came to be known as *Heraldry,* and its technical language is used to-day when describing coats of arms. While awaiting his turn a knight always hung up his helmet, with his shield below it, in the *Lists,* and the familiar decorative treatment of armorial bearings is copied from this custom (Fig. 425, also Figs. 439, 443 and Plate XVII.).

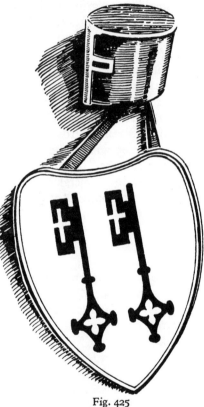

Fig. 425

During the early Christian centuries, it was the habit among Teutonic warriors to mark their shields with a distinctive brilliant colour. Knights of the eleventh century also coloured their shields, often adopting for the early tournament the colours favoured by the lady of whom the bearer proclaimed himself the champion, and occasionally a portrait of the lady herself. These colours are known in heraldic language as *Tinctures* (*see* p. 296).

A shield is blazoned or described in the following order. First, the shield or field, its character and tinctures, beginning, if divided, with the dexter side. Secondly, the charge, its position (sometimes), number, nature, and tincture (where necessary this is described quarter by quarter).

Plate XV. represents a friendly joust with swords. The combatant knights wear chain-mail hauberks, with attached hoods, of the twelfth century. The small diagram in the top left-hand corner of the illustration shows the method of stringing steel rings on strips of leather attached at intervals to the leather foundation, the rings on alternate strips being reversed in direction. The knight dated 1146 has been to the Crusade—see the cross on his helmet. Notice the construction of the shields, the grip on the inner side, 1190, and the metal bands in cross form and border, strengthening the face of the wooden shield, with primitive heraldic charges and tinctures: "azure a cross within a bordure argent."

Plate XVI. shows a knight of the fifteenth century fully equipped for a tournament. His armorial bearings are "quarterly argent and gules, in the second and third quarter a frette or, over all a fesse azure." Crest, an eagle. This illustration shows the surcote, or jupon, housing of the period, and rein-guards, all charged with the knight's arms—the crest on the helmet, and on the horse's head, crest-wreath and mantling. The shield shows the "bouche" or aperture through which the lance passes. The vamplate or metal guard protects the handle of the lance. Notice the latest development of the chamfron (see p. 341).

Section IV.—The Shield

The most important part of the whole paraphernalia of a knight or gentleman of the Middle Ages next to his sword was the *shield*. It was the first of all military accoutrements to bear family charges. Armorial bearings on the shield were common during the reign of Richard I. As Earl of Poitou he bore in his father's lifetime "or two lions combatant vert." In later times, when armour ceased to be worn, right up to the present day, the shield has continued to be regarded as the most appropriate vehicle for the same display.

The shield, with its armorial devices, constitutes a "Shield of Arms," and always displays its charges upon its face. It was held by the knight before his person, its face presented towards any who confronted him. The right and left sides of the knight were thus covered by the right and left sides of the shield, and consequently were severally *opposite* to the left and right hands of the observer. (In heraldic language the right side of the *shield* is known as the *Dexter* side, and the left as the *Sinister*.) For the most part these shields were made of wooden planks, linden or elm, framed to the required shape and strengthened by an extra piece, fixed perpendicularly or horizontally — sometimes both. They were often set in a frame or border. Shields used in warfare varied in shape at different periods.

Fig. 426, No. 1, shows the shape and construction of a characteristic shield of the thirteenth century.

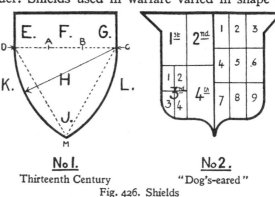

No. I.
Thirteenth Century

No. 2.
"Dog's-eared"

Fig. 426. Shields

Describe an equilateral triangle, D C M, and with a centre, D, draw the segment of a circle, C M. Repeat with centre C, and draw segment D M. Divide the top, D C, into three equal parts. Raise the top of the shield one of these thirds.

The parts, or points, of the shield are distinguished thus:

> E. The Dexter Chief, the most important position.
> F. The Middle Chief.
> G. The Sinister Chief.
> H. The Centre or Fesse Point. Also important.
> J. The Base.
> K. The Dexter, or right side.
> L. The Sinister, or left side.

Fig. 426, No. 2, gives the shape of a shield sometimes used in modern heraldry, being more convenient for displaying the numerous quarterings which have accumulated as time progressed. It is divided "per pale." The dexter side is quarterly of four, and the third quarter is again quarterly. The sinister side is quarterly of nine. This shape of shield is not considered to be in good heraldic style — and is referred to contemptuously as a "dog's-eared shield."

Returning to the construction of the shield, it is natural that the constructional lines were the first to be brought into use as an armorial charge. For example, by painting the surface one colour and the border or bar across it another, a conspicuous distinctive mark was obtained. This method created what is heraldically termed

The Ordinaries (Fig. 427.)

N.B. These drawings contain other details mentioned later.

> 1. The Chief, and three PILES.
> 2. The Fesse.
> 3. The Bar or Bars.
> 4. The Pale.

5. The Cross.
6. The Bend.
7. The Saltire.
8. The Chevron.

As the number of knights and important people who adopted these charges increased, it became necessary to augment the ordinaries; consequently, there were introduced

The Subordinaries (Fig. 428)

1. The Canton: and three Besants.
2. The Quarter (Quarterly).
   First and fourth, the Bordure.
   Second, Flanges.
   Third, the Tressure.
3. Rustre (with circular opening) and Mascles.
4. The Orle.
5. The Escutcheon.
6. Lozenges (three) and Billets (five).
7. Gyron.
8. The Frette.

These subordinaries proving insufficient,

Miscellaneous Charges

such as human figures, animals, birds, fish, natural objects and imaginary beings were added.

The term *quartering* means dividing the shield in the centre "per pale" or perpendicularly; dividing it again "per fesse" or horizontally, across the middle.

If one of the quarters is again quartered, it is termed *quarterly quartering* (see Fig. 426, No. 2, 3rd quarter, and centre shield, Plate XIX.).

If there are an uneven number of quarterings in a family coat of arms, the paternal coat or quarter—usually the dexter top one—is duplicated at the end to make up the even number.

Tinctures (Figs. 427 and 428). In English heraldry the tinctures comprise two metals, five colours, and seven furs. They are as follows:

Metals

	Heraldic Term		Represented in black and white, Fig. 428, by
Gold	Or	No. 7	Spots
Silver	Argent	No. 8	Plain

Fig. 427. ORDINARIES AND FURS

Fig. 428. SUBORDINARIES AND TINCTURES

Colours

	Heraldic Term		Represented in black and white, Fig. 428, by
Blue	Azure	No. 1	Horizontal lines
Red	Gules	No. 1	Perpendicular lines
Black	Sable	No. 7	Solid black or criss-crossed lines
Green	Vert	No. 5	Lines bending to left, *i.e.* from dexter at top to sinister at bottom
Purple	Purpure	No. 5 but reversed. Lines bending to right

These metals and colours are represented in black-and-white drawings as shown in the shields in Fig. 428; but this convention was not in use during the Middle Ages, nor in Tudor times. *It was introduced by an Italian heraldic artist about the year 1630.* It is used, nevertheless, in some of the illustrations in this chapter, to enable the student to decipher the coats of arms.

It is the rule that a colour is superimposed on a metal and *vice versa;* never a colour upon a colour, nor a metal on a metal. This rule has its exceptions in the case of varied fields upon which may be charged a bearing of either metal or a colour. Also the armorial bearings of the Latin kings of Jerusalem bore "argent five crosses or": the object of this exception was to provide a unique shield unlike that of any other sovereign.

The *furs* are shown in Fig. 427 and are as follows:

Ermine	Black spots on white	No. 1
Ermines	White on black	No. 2
Erminois	Black (another form of "spot") on gold	No. 3
Vair		No. 4
Countervair	as shown in	No. 6
Potent		No. 8

"Counter" means reversed. "Counterchanging" is to divide the shield in such a manner that it is in part of a metal and in part of a colour,

Fig. 429. Chaucer

and then arranging the charges in such a manner that they shall be reciprocally of the same colour and metal. The armorial bearings of Geoffrey Chaucer, Fig. 429, give a simple example of counterchanging: "argent and gules a bend counterchanged." A more elaborate example is shown in Fig. 430: "per saltire a griffin coward, sable and argent, all counterchanged." Another shield showing counterchanging is that of Owain Glendower, Plate XIX.

Diaper is a term denoting a style of decorating the surface of the shield (*see* Chapter III., p. 134). It is merely a fancy treatment of plain

Fig. 430. Counterchanging

surfaces, and does not alter the symbolism of the shield of arms, nor of the charges. It may be of a geometrical, floral or arabesque character.

Semée is a term applied to a small charge, strewn or scattered over a field (Fig. 436—the ancient shield of France). The word *powdered* may also be used in the same sense.

Dividing and border lines. There were many different kinds of lines, apart from the straight and curved, used to divide the tinctures, etc., upon the face of the shield.

Fig. 431 gives eleven varieties with their heraldic names. Similar dividing or border lines were also used to decorate the edges of the cyclas or "quintise," a fashion which started towards the end of Edward I.'s reign, and was afterwards carried to excess (*see* p. 154).

Charges. Space will permit only a few of the multitude of charges to be dealt with: the *Cross*, the *Lion*, and the *Eagle*.

The Cross

The simplest, and the one most frequently used, is that known as the Greek Cross, or Cross of Saint George (*see* Fig. 427, No. 5).

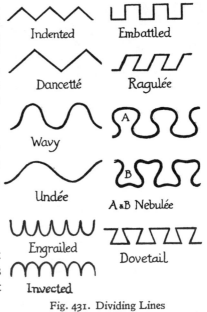

Indented

Embattled

Dancetté

Ragulée

Wavy

A

Undée

B

A & B Nebulée

Engrailed

Dovetail

Invected

Fig. 431. Dividing Lines

Various crosses (*see* Fig. 432):

1. The Cross Fleurie.
2. The Cross Moline. Also stands for the eighth son in cadency. ("Azure a cross moline or," is borne by the family of the de Molines, or later the Molineux, who in 1771 were created Earls of Sefton.)
3. The Cross Pommée.
4. The Cross Botonée.
5. The Cross Crosslet.

6. The Cross Patée.

7. The Cross Portent.

8. The Cross Crosslet Fitchée. "Fitchée" applies to the pointed arm or end, and is frequently used with other crosses, *e.g.* Cross Botonée Fitchée. (*See also* Crosses, Chapter II., p. 100.)

Fig. 432. Various Crosses

The Lion

The *lion* symbolises in heraldry courage and command. Ever since heraldry made its first pretensions to being a science, the lion has been held in the highest estimation, and was adopted as a charge on the shields of many of the European sovereigns, princes, nobles and men of gentle birth. The lion figures in the royal arms of England, Scotland, Wales, Norway, Sweden, Denmark, Spain, Hungary, Austria, Holland, Belgium, Bavaria, Bohemia, Luxemburg, Hesse-Darmstadt, Nassau, Schleswig, Venice, Swabia, Thuringia, Guelph of Saxony and Bavaria, etc. It is to be found also in the old English families of de Bohuns, Carew, Fitzalan, Howard, de Lacy, Percy, Mowbray, Segrave, le Strange, Talbot, Herbert, etc.

Being so much used, it was necessary to show it in different attitudes and in different tinctures:

Rampant. Erect, one paw on the ground, the other three elevated, its head in profile and its tail standing up. Originally the term "a lion" denoted a lion rampant, as this was its most characteristic attitude.

Rampant guardant. As above, but looking out from the shield.

Rampant reguardant. As above, but looking backward.

Passant. Walking. Right fore-paw elevated, looking forward, with tail displayed over the back.

Passant guardant. As the previous, but looking out from the shield, which attitude was originally termed "a leopard" ("gules three leopards or": England).

Passant reguardant. As above, but looking backward.

Statant. Standing on all fore-paws, looking forward, and tail drooping behind.

Statant guardant and *reguardant.* Variations as before.

Sejant. Sitting; *i.e.* with the hind-quarters only on the ground.

Couchant. At rest; stretched on the ground.

Dormant. As couchant, but with the head laid between the fore-paws.

When several lions appear on a charge and are therefore drawn on a smaller scale, they are called *lioncels* (Fig. 33).

A lion's head is a frequent charge, either *erased* (cut or jagged) or *couped* (cut off straight). Such heads may be in profile or full-face.

The *paw* or *jamb* is often used, and may be also erased or couped.

A *demi-lion* is the upper part of the body cut off at the ribs, showing the tuft of the tail only at its back.

Lions are termed *armed* when the claws and teeth are of a different tincture. The term *langued* is applied to the tongue in like manner.

The term *proper* means in its natural form and colour.

These descriptions of different attitudes, etc., are applicable also to most other animals.

Fig. 433. England

The lions of England. "Gules three lions" (or leopards), passant guardant, "in pale or" (Fig. 433). The lions of England authentically date from the middle of the twelfth century and were first borne by King Henry II. The kings of England before this date are said to have borne lions as armorial bearings, but it is possibly mere legend, as they were invented for them by the heralds of the thirteenth century at a time when heraldry was so generally popular. All sorts of heroes of the past, including Saxon kings, saints, biblical personages, and even Adam and Eve, had coats of arms assigned to them.

Whether it be legend or fact that William I. bore the two lions of the Norman duchy is uncertain, but the question arises, had the Normans of the eleventh century a conviction that they were descended from part of the lost tribes of Israel, and with this idea in mind did they adopt the lion of Judah as their standard? Be that as it may, when Henry II. ascended the throne of England, he is supposed to have added a third lion, the lion of Aquitaine, in right of his wife Eleanor.

The royal arms, "gules three leopards or," were first blazoned upon the shield of Richard I.

The Royal Arms of England, 1154–1485

Henry II., Richard I., John, Henry III., Edward I., Edward II., and Edward III. (until the thirteenth year of his reign) bore "gules three lions passant guardant, in pale or" (Fig. 433). In 1340 Edward III. made claim to the crown of France (through his mother, on the death of all her brothers) in opposition to Philippe VI. de Valois, and in consequence he quartered France Ancient (Fig. 436) with the three lions of England, giving precedence to the arms of France by placing them in the first and fourth quarters. The three fleurs-de-lys of France (Fig. 437) superseded France Ancient in or about 1405 (see p. 306) and remained in the first and fourth quarters of the royal arms of England until 1801.

Richard II. retained the arms of his grandfather and sometimes impaled, at other times quartered, the arms attributed to Eadward the Confessor, "azure a cross fleurie, between five martlets or," with those of France and England. Henry IV., Henry V., Henry VI., Edward IV., Edward V., and Richard III. all used France Modern (Fig. 437), quartered with England (Fig. 433).

In the course of the several centuries during which heraldry was universal, the heraldic lion and eagle went through a series of changes as regards their shape and decorative treatment. Each century had more or less its own style in lions and eagles (see Figs. 434 and 435). In its earliest form in heraldry (middle twelfth and early thirteenth centuries) the lion was much more like a leopard. Later, the lion achieved a more decorative and decided mane, and its legs began to acquire hair on the back part. The eagle also grew a more generous supply of feathers on its wings and tail. This development was more pronounced during the fifteenth and sixteenth centuries, when both became very much more ornate.

It was during the fourteenth and fifteenth centuries that the work of heraldic artists reached its highest standard.

The most important point to be borne in mind by an heraldic designer or artist is that the style of the heraldry introduced should harmonise with the *period* of the incident represented. Until the Gothic revival in the Victorian era, it was possible to recognise the date of any heraldic achievement by the style in which it was represented, each preceding period having had a distinctive style of its own. It also should be remembered that a different style also characterised the heraldic draughtsmanship of the various countries of Europe, which in like manner can be recognised by connoisseurs.

A competent heraldic artist designs his lions, eagles, or in fact any charge, to fit the space or area of that part of the shield which it is to occupy. If that space be square, then his lion or eagle must be square

FIG. 434. THE EVOLUTION OF THE LION

Cent.
1. 12th. Enamelled slab to Geoffrey of Anjou, Le Mans Cathedral. Rampant.
2. 13th. Tomb of William Longespée, Salisbury Cathedral. 1226. Rampant.
3. 13th. Tile in Chapter House, Westminster. Passant.
4. 13th. From MS., National Library, Paris. 1300. Rampant.
5. 13th. From MS. by Matthew Paris. 1250. Passant.
6. 13th. Banner from the *Chroniques de Saint Denys*. 1250. Rampant.
7. 14th. From the seal of Thomas of Lancaster. 1322. Passant.
8. 15th. From a French MS. dated 1400–1420. Rampant.
9. 16th. From a roll of arms dated 1542. Rampant.

(see Fig. 434, No. 9, and Fig. 435, No. 1); if banner or shield shape, the charge must be adapted accordingly (see Fig. 434, Nos. 6 and 8, and Fig. 435, No. 4).

Nothing detracts so seriously from the value of heraldic detail introduced into pictorial works or stage productions as the slipshod and ill-informed treatment so often seen. Indifferent drawing, total neglect of the necessity to adapt the shape and size of the charge to that of the "field" (see p. 313), inaccurate detail, and painfully inartistic treatment are the chief faults only too frequently found. A floreated sixteenth-century lion in a thirteenth-century setting is no more inappropriate than a "portrait" of Charles I. painted by a cubist. Perfect examples of ideal treatment are to be seen for the trouble of visiting Westminster Abbey; Edward III.'s tomb, for instance, the tiles in the Chapter House, and innumerable other specimens well repay study. Armorial bearings of various periods in Flanders and Germany, and even modern reproductions—the arms of the Counts of Flanders in the Hôtel de Ville, Ghent (modern work), for instance—are excellent models to follow.

The Eagle

The *eagle*, although one of the earliest heraldic charges, does not appear in English heraldry as frequently as the lion. It symbolises royal power, courage and magnanimity. It is associated almost entirely with the Holy Roman Empire, and is thus borne by many ruling houses and princes in Germany, and figures in the royal arms of Germany, Russia, Austria, Prussia, Saxony, Lorraine, Leiningen, etc. It also figures in the arms of old English families such as the Monthermers, Montgomeries, d'Ernfords, De la Meres, Grandisons, Gavestons, etc.

The form is almost always "displayed," that is with its wings expanded, legs apart, and tail between the legs (with the head erect and in profile it is called the *royal eagle*). The *double-headed* or *imperial eagle* has two heads, arranged symmetrically in profile, looking outwards, and later examples are sometimes crowned or encircled by a nimbus.

Legs or *jambs* were used as charges and treated either erased or couped.

Wings, either double or single, called a *vol*, frequently occur.

Heads, erased or couped, were also used.

These descriptions of attitudes, etc., apply to all birds.

Persian. The eagle appeared in Persia in the fifth century B.C., when it was used as a military standard. Xenophon (443–357 B.C.) mentions that they carried on a spear in front of their army when on the march, a golden eagle with outspread wings.

Egyptian. The eagle was adopted by the Egyptians at a very early date, and was in use later under their Macedonian king, Ptolemy Soter, early in the third century B.C.

Roman Republic. It became the emblem of the Roman Republic about the second century B.C., and was permanently adopted as the Roman military standard during the second consulship of Marius, 104 B.C. The eagle with outspread wings, grasping the lightnings of Jupiter, was fixed to a long staff and carried in the van of the cohorts when on the march. In camp, the standard stood in the prætorium, fixed in the earth.

PLATE XVII. A MODERN FULL ACHIEVEMENT OF ARMS

A. A Tabard   B. A Banner

Imperial Rome. Under the Empire it was the insignia of Imperial Rome.

Byzantium. When the seat of empire was removed from Rome to Byzantium, or Constantinople, in 328, the imperial eagle went with it, and became the standard of the Byzantine Empire. To exemplify the

FIG. 435. THE EVOLUTION OF THE EAGLE, FLEUR-DE-LYS AND MAUNCH

Cent.
1. 13th. From *Chroniques de Saint Denys.* 1250.
2. 13th. The Emperor Otho IV., from Matthew Paris MS.
3. 14th. From the MS. of Baldwin of Luxemburg.
4. 14th. The Emperor Henry VI., from Minnesinger MS.
5. 16th. The Emperor Maximilian, 1521, after Albert Dürer.

FLEUR-DE-LYS
6. 13th. Tomb of Fulk de Cantelupe, Abergavenny Church.
7. 13th. Tomb of Eva de Cantelupe, Baroness Bergavenny, Abergavenny Church. 1257.
8. 15th. Brass in Bray Church, Berks.
9. 15th. From Beaufort tomb, Southwark Cathedral.

MAUNCH
10. 14th. Brass to Sir Hugh Hastings, Elsing, Norfolk. 1347.
11. 16th. Tomb of Talbot, Earl of Shrewsbury, Sheffield Cathedral. 1528.

Eastern and Western Empires, the double-headed eagle looking to the left and right came into use at this time.

Russia. The Russian imperial eagle did not make its appearance until the fifteenth century A.D. The Czar of Muscovy, Ivan III. (1462–1505), had married the niece of the last emperor of Byzantium, who was butchered by the Turks. After the fall and sack of Constantinople in

1453, Ivan considered himself heir to the Byzantine, or Greek, Empire, in right of his wife, and took the imperial Byzantine eagle as his royal arms.

Holy Roman Empire. After Charlemagne had been crowned Emperor of the Holy Roman Empire by Pope Leo III. at Rome on Christmas Day, 800, he adopted the eagle (single-headed) in support of his claim as successor to the Roman Cæsars. Having seen the double-headed eagle on the imperial standard when on a visit to Constantinople in 1147, Conrad II. adopted it as the arms of his empire. The earliest representation still extant appears in a drawing made by Matthew Paris of the arms of the Emperor Otho IV., some time before 1259 (*see* Fig. 435, No. 2). It next appears on an imperial coin struck in 1325 by the Emperor Louis the Bavarian.

Germany and Austria. The emperors of Germany and Austria inherited their imperial double-headed eagle from the emperors of the Holy Roman Empire.

France. The Emperor Napoleon revived its use for his army in 1804 as a fitting symbol of Imperial France. It retired under the rule of the Bourbons, but was revived once more by Napoleon III. in 1852.

America. Its use by the United States of America was intended to express the ideas of freedom and courage.

Some other Charges

The fleur-de-lys. A lily or iris, taken by Louis VII. of France (1137–1180) as his royal ensign. In 1190 Philippe Auguste adopted

Fig. 436. France Ancient

Fig. 437. France Modern

"azure semée (*see* p. 299) of fleurs-de-lys or" (*see* Fig. 436), which remained the royal coat of arms of France until Charles V. reduced their number to three, in 1365 (Fig. 437).

The dolphin (*see* Fig. 438, No. 13). First borne by Charles de Valois, son of Philippe VI. of France, in 1349. From this date the eldest son of the King of France bore the title of "Dauphin." It originated in a misfortune which befell the last Count of Vienne in Dauphiné, who accidentally caused the death of his only son by letting him fall out of a window. In his inconsolable grief, he sold his estates to the King of France on condition that the eldest son of the king should always bear the title of Dauphin; and then retired from the world into a monastery.

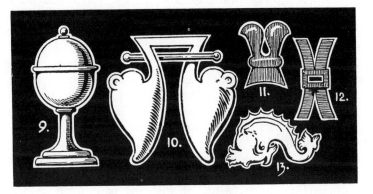

Fig. 438. Some Charges

The covered cup (Fig. 438, No. 9). Borne by the family of Butler, hereditary cupbearers to the kings of England.

The water bouget (Fig. 438, No. 10). A charge representing the vessels used in the East at the time of the Crusades for carrying water. Borne by the family of Bourchier.

A chess-rook (Fig. 438, No. 11). Borne by the family of Roke-wood and others.

The fer-de-moline or *mill-rind* (Fig. 438, No. 12). The iron affixed to the centre of a millstone, a modification of the "cross molines."

Manche or *maunche* (Fig. 435, 10). A sleeve from a lady's gown, fashionable in the reign of Henry I. (*See also* Fig. 59).

Section V.—The Crest

The *crest* (Latin, *crista* = a tuft) was an ornament placed on the highest point of the helmet, and was a sign of distinction and exalted position. The use of the crest was restricted in early days to a few persons of eminence. In later heraldry it is represented above a shield of arms.

In very early times the crest consisted chiefly of feathers. The Ionians are said to have been the first to wear tufts and feathers in their helmets, but the Greeks or Achæans of a previous age, the Homeric period, wore crests of coarse hair dyed scarlet. Homer relates that Agamemnon wore a "studded helm with a fourfold crest and plume of horsehair . . . with its new scarlet dye . . . and terribly the crest nodded from above" (Iliad, ix. 15).

Alexander the Great wore on his helmet a ram's head, the emblem of Jupiter Ammon, in support of his claim to descent from that deity. Julius Cæsar wore a star to indicate his relationship to Venus. In the Roman army a plume or crest was the distinguishing mark of a centurion.

The heads of wolves, bears, oxen with huge horns, and the spread wings of eagles were used by the chieftains of the Teutonic tribes, and later the Anglo-Saxons decorated their helmets of leather with combs of metal and the horns of various animals (see Vol. I., Figs. 86, 109, and 110, also pp. 239 and 242). The custom of wearing ornaments of distinction and honour on the helmet was discontinued during the Norman period, but revived in the middle of the thirteenth century, some hundred years after heraldry had first come into use, at a time when it had become thoroughly established and the right to armorial bearings recognised as hereditary.

An ornament in the nature of a crest was added to the helmet by the Earl of Boulogne at the Battle of Bovines in 1214. It consisted of two curved upstanding horns, made of stiffened parchment stuffed with wool.[1] This was regarded as a ludicrous innovation; but later on, particularly in the reign of Edward I., such artificial horns became very fashionable.

Horns standing up from the helmet were frequently used in foreign heraldry (especially German) in conjunction with a crest, or alone (Plate XVI. B, "per fesse sable and or. Crest, two buffaloes' horns conjoined to combs, the whole also per fesse as in the arms," for Tannhäuser).

Dating from the middle of the thirteenth century, crests were almost without exception in the shape of a fan or quadrangle fitted into the apex of the helmet. On this fan-shaped or quadrangular crest was a repetition of the armorial bearings of the shield (Plate XVIII.). By the middle of the fourteenth century figures and devices used as adjuncts to the shield of arms were employed in place of the fan.

These later crests were sometimes identical or modified forms of some detail of the shield, but occasionally quite distinct features. The significance of the charge on the shield (the *family* cognisance) was considered complete *without* addition of the crest, which was associated exclusively with the person who bore it. It was not until the end of the fourteenth century that the right to bear a crest was identified with the right to bear arms; and even then, although crests were recognised as hereditary, it was quite usual for any member of an armorial family to adopt one of his own if he thought it a more

---

[1] Crests were generally made of this material during the Middle Ages. A useful modern substitute is papier-mâché.

distinctive mark of his individuality. This was often the case in a family of several sons.

Women, except *sovereign* princesses, were, and are, not entitled to crests.

One, two, or three long waving ostrich feathers, rising from the apex of the helmet, came into use only at the end of the fifteenth century. During the sixteenth century they were very fashionable.

The crest wreath came into use about the third quarter of the fourteenth century, and consisted of a roll formed of two pieces of material of the principal colour and metal of the arms twisted together, worn round the top of the helmet level with the base of the crest (Plate XVI.). When a crest is represented without any other detail of armorial insignia, the wreath represented as a twisted bar is usually placed horizontally below it. This alternative shape came into use at the end of the fifteenth century.

Mantling or *lambrequin*. This was a pennon-shaped scarf of material, usually silk, lined with another colour, and placed on the helmet underneath the crest and crest wreath. It dates from the early fourteenth century. It hung in two long ends terminating in tassels. It was usually represented with jagged edges, a fashion which originated from the scarf being cut and jagged by the sword or lance in battle or tournament. In conventionalised form, it was used also in armorial achievements as a design round the shield. In colour it was of the principal tincture and metal of the shield (Plates XVI. and XVII.).

The helmet. During the course of the Middle Ages the helmet underwent many changes in shape, a fact which must be borne in mind in designing an armorial achievement, as the helmet should be of the same period. It is placed as an accessory above the shield of arms, and bears the crest, crest wreath and mantling. Before 1600, helmets were generally set in profile facing towards the spectator's left, but in more modern heraldry the practice is as follows:

The sovereign. Helmet of gold, with six bars in the visor, set full-face.

Princes and nobles. Helmet of silver, garnished with gold, five bars, set in profile.

Baronets and knights. Helmet of steel, garnished with gold, visor raised, no bar, set full-face.

Esquires and gentlemen. Helmet of steel, visor closed, set profile.

The badge. A single charge with a decided heraldic significance, in use long before the establishment of any definite usage in heraldic matters. When the code of heraldry had come into being, the badge took the form of a figure or device, distinct from the crest. It often consisted, though not necessarily, of some detail adopted from the family shield, and was borne without any shield or other accessory, except perhaps a motto (Figs. 462, 463 and 471). Badges were of two kinds; the one, personal, peculiarly significant of the owner; the other, borne by all persons connected with the owner or dependent upon him.[1] The first category was often applied, during the fourteenth and fifteenth centuries, to the decorations of costume (*see* Fig. 348), household furniture and plate, horse equipment and military gear, banners, etc.

The badge can be used by the women as well as the men of the family to which it appertains. It has been, from this circumstance, called "The Woman's Crest."

Some Badges

Arundel: An acorn.
Beauchamp: Bear and ragged staff.
Beauforts: A portcullis.
de Bohun: White swan.
de Clare: Black bull. Clarion.
Clinton: Gold mullet.
Courtney: A bell.
Dacre: Silver escollop attached by cord to ragged staff.
Douglas: A red heart.
Edward II.: Castle.
Edward III.: A fleur-de-lys.
Edward IV.: A white rose *en soleil*. White lion.
Edward the Black Prince: An ostrich feather.
Henry IV.: White swan crowned.
Henry V.: A chained antelope.
Henry VI.: A panther.
Holland: A fetlock.
Howard: Silver lion.
Hungerford: A sickle.
John of Gaunt: Two falcons holding fetterlocks in their beaks.
Lancaster: Red rose.
Neville: A dun cow.
Pelham: A buckle.
Percy: Silver crescent. A double manacle.
Peverel: A golden garb.
Richard III.: A white boar.
Stanley: Griffin's leg erased gold.
Tudor: White and red rose.
York: White rose. Shackle and padlock.

Supporters. Figures of various kinds, so placed in connection with the shield of arms as to appear to be protecting or supporting it.

In the early days of heraldry (thirteenth century) angelic figures were sometimes introduced, apparently as "guardian angels" to shields

[1] Early in the thirteenth century badges were worn upon the garments of the military and domestic retainers of great lords.

of arms, and these typified the great respect with which the family coat
of arms was regarded. During the reign of Edward III., figures of men,
beasts, birds, fishes, or imaginary animals were introduced on seals
only, but these did not become general in the armorial insignia of persons
of very high rank until the middle of the fifteenth century. They were
only granted by express command of the sovereign.

Fig. 439. From the Seal of Earl Edmund de Mortimer, 1400

Fig. 439 is a reconstruction from the seal of Earl Edmund de
Mortimer (1400) showing the shield: "barry of six or and azure, an
inescutcheon argent; on a chief or, gyroned of the second, two pallets
of the same"; quartering: "or a cross gules" for de Burgh of Ulster.
The crest: "a panache of many feathers rising from a coronet all proper."
The helmet is mantled, and the whole supported by "two lions or."

Commoners are allowed the privilege of using supporters only if
they are Knights Grand Cross of one of the great orders of knighthood,
or otherwise by special permission and licence of the sovereign.

Armorial banners were often placed in the hands or paws of supporters.

Supporters, of course, had some reference to the bearer of the coat of arms, as, for example, in the case of the House of Tudor: the earlier royal arms of England were supported by two lions. On the accession of Henry VII. the sinister lion was replaced by the Welsh dragon; and, in like manner, on the accession of James I., the dragon was superseded by one supporter of the Scottish royal arms, the unicorn.

Mottoes (Italian, *motto* = a word). In an heraldic sense, a motto is a word or phrase accompanying a badge or coat of arms, and usually inserted on a scroll. Derived from the "war-cries" of early times, a motto may be emblematical, or it may have some allusion to the character of the person bearing it, or to his name or armorial insignia.

Richard I. was the first monarch to adopt the hereditary motto of our kings: "Dieu et mon Droit," the field-word or war-cry used by him at the siege of Gisors, 1198.

> *Fare, fac.* "Speak, act." Fairfax.
> *Cave.* "Beware." Cave.
> *Set on.* Seton.
> *Festina Lente.* "On slow—push forward." Onslow.
> *Perse Valens.* "Strong in himself." Percival.
> *Do no yll.* Doyle.
> *Ich Dien.* "I serve." [1]

Mottoes may express a moral or religious sentiment, or they may record some historic fact, as "Grip Fast," borne by the Earl of Rothes, which alludes to the rescue from drowning of Queen Margaret by Bartholomew Leslie.

A motto need not be hereditary, and thus a different one may be assumed by each member of an armigerous family without any formality.

SECTION VI.—SOME RULES OF HEREDITARY ARMORIAL BEARINGS

Heritage

Heraldry recognised as a science, circa 1210. At the beginning of the thirteenth century the development of systematic charges led to the recognition of heraldry as a social necessity. The great number of armorial bearings that had been invented and assigned to various people during the latter part of the preceding century made it essential that

---

[1] A more probable interpretation of the meaning of "Ich Dien" is that it resembles in pronunciation the Welsh "eich dyn" meaning "your man," part of the phrase "Here's your man," used by Edward I. in presenting his infant son, the first English Prince of Wales, to the Welsh. It was first adopted as his motto, so far as we know, by Edward the Black Prince, and retained by all subsequent Princes of Wales. This is a more likely meaning than that commonly accepted, which offers a doubtful translation from the old German, "I serve."

a record of the names and bearings should be made, and this was prepared on long rolls of parchment. These were called *Rolls of Arms*, and to-day they give us most valuable information on this subject. The oldest roll extant dates about 1250, and is now kept at the College of Arms.

Popularity of armorial bearings. Each heraldic charge upon a shield had (in the beginning) its own definite significance with reference to the *bearer*. By it he was known, and his feats of daring upon the battlefield, or distinction in tournament and joust, were associated with his coat of arms, of which, therefore, he was justly proud. He displayed the armorial bearings in a decorative sense during periods of peace and in old age. The son and heir was proud of his father's *Achievements*; in right of birth he took the paternal shield and strove to prove himself worthy of it, emulating his father's knightly deeds, possibly adding to the family fame, and so acquiring an *Augmentation* to his paternal coat. Thus the hereditary nature of armorial bearings was soon established.

The field. It should be noted here that the groundwork, or entire surface of the shield, is spoken of in heraldic language as *The Field*, because upon it were placed the honourable emblems won on the field of battle.

Marshalling

Armorial bearings having become hereditary, the eldest son bore the family shield of his father. To distinguish the shield of the son from

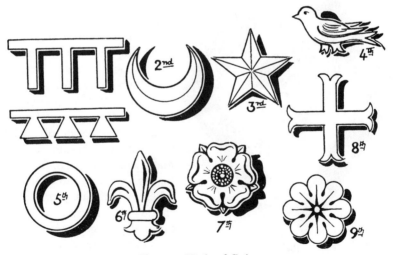

Fig. 440. Marks of Cadency

that of the father, a *Difference* was placed upon it in the form of a *Label* (*see* Fig. 440, No. 1).[1] This was borne by the eldest son until the

---

[1] If the label has more than the usual three points, the number should be specified in the blazon. The Dovetail label is of later date, and was not much used.

death of the father; the shield of arms then reverted to its original design, that is, *the label was removed.*

This process continued from father to eldest son during the course of generations.

The *younger sons* also placed various definite charges upon the family shield for "difference," a process referred to as *Marking Cadency.*

The "differences" illustrated in Fig. 440 are as follows:

2nd son	.	. .	Crescent
3rd son	.	. .	Mullet
4th son	.	. .	Martlet
5th son	.	. .	Anulet
6th son	.	. .	Fleur-de-lys
7th son	.	. .	Rose
8th son	.	. .	Cross Molines
9th son	.	. .	Octofoil

These marks of cadency were placed upon the point of honour on the shield (centre top), or in some other conspicuous position. One of these marks might be charged upon another; for instance, the

Fig. 441. Lozenge

fourth son of the second son of the head of the house would bear a martlet upon a crescent, and so forth. The use of the label, or in fact any mark of cadency, was by no means universal. Such marks were used by the most punctilious, but the complications occurring in a few successive generations defeated the object for which the system was devised.

Cadency charges occasionally permanent. In course of time these marks of cadency, used in conjunction with some main charge, often, but by no means always, became themselves inherent hereditary factors in the shields of descendants of the original younger sons.

Daughters do not carry "differences."

Arms of daughters. When there were daughters in the family of an "armiger," as the possessor of armorial bearings was called, *as well as sons,* the unmarried daughters were entitled to use the family coat of arms during their lifetime. They

were blazoned on what was called a *Lozenge* or *Diamond* (Fig. 441):
"argent two corbies proper, within a bordure sable charged with fourteen
plates," for Corbet. This rule dates from the
fifteenth century, but some time previous to
this—thirteenth century—lozenges were used
for displaying on seals the armorial bearings
of men and women.

When an armiger married a woman who
possessed brothers, the family arms borne by
him and his wife went through the process of
"dimidiating," or "halving," the two coats of
arms, which were then joined together. The
shield of arms shown in Fig. 442 illustrates
this method, and is interesting, as it was borne

Fig. 442. Dimidiation

by Edward I. and Margaret of France, and also by Edward II. and Isabella
of France. From the
middle of the thir-
teenth century on-
ward this method was
gradually changed to
Impalement, that
is, the shield was
divided "per pale,"
down the middle,
and the husband's
family arms were
blazoned on the
dexter side, and the
wife's family arms on
the sinister side
(Fig. 443): the arms
of Sir Richard Whit-
tington: "gules a
fesse componée or
and azure; an anulet
of the second," im-
paling those of his
wife: "quarterly per
fesse indented,
ermine and azure,"
for Fitzwaryn. He
took the busy bee as

Fig. 443. Impalement

his crest. By the third quarter of the fourteenth century impalement had
entirely superseded dimidiation.

Heraldic heiresses. When there were no sons in the family, the married daughters were entitled not only to inherit the arms of their father, but to transmit them to their descendants. An only daughter and child was called a "sole heir"; if more than one, they were "co-heirs."

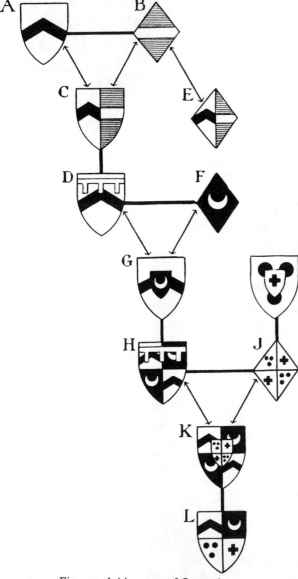

Fig. 444. Achievement of Quarterings

Heiress: escutcheon of pretence. If the armiger married an heir, or co-heir, then the wife's family arms were blazoned on a small shield, called an *Escutcheon of Pretence,* and placed in the centre of the husband's own family shield (Plate XVII.). Strictly, the escutcheon of pretence ought not to supersede impalement until a child is born—in fact not until the husband has good "pretensions" of having his wife's arms quartered hereafter with his own by his sons and their descendants.

Arms of an heiress transmitted to her children. The children of these parents inherited the maternal family arms [1] "quartered" with the paternal. This method is adopted each time a descendant marries an heir (Fig. 444). Should an heir possess any number of quarterings, obtained by her ancestors' marriages with heirs, these are all transmitted. The wife of the fourth Viscount Townsend brought in 250 quarterings, including the royal one of Plantagenet.

[1] But *not* the crest (which the woman did not possess and therefore could not transmit).

A simple example of the achievement of quarterings is given below and illustrated in Fig. 444:

Sir Primus Aye, who bears "argent a chevron sable" (A), marries the daughter of Sir James Bee, bearing "azure a fesse argent" (B). After marriage their coat of arms appears as (C). They have a son, Secundus, and when he assumes the paternal arms he adds the label (D). In course of time his father dies and the label is removed. His widowed mother assumes the armorial bearings on a lozenge (E). At a later date Sir Secundus Aye marries the daughter and co-heir of William Dee, who bears "sable a crescent argent" (F) and his shield bears his wife's arms in pretence (G). A son, Tertius, is born to them, and when his mother dies he assumes his paternal coat, quartered with the maternal, on his labelled shield (H). Afterwards he marries the daughter and heir of Sir Basil Epsilon, who bears quarterly "argent three pellets," and, because her mother was an heir, "argent a cross sable" for Effe (J). His father conveniently dies about the same time, and, having removed the label, Sir Tertius Aye takes his wife's escutcheon of pretence and places it on his own shield (K). Before their son Quartus receives knighthood, the father goes the way of all flesh. No label is required when Sir Quartus Aye assumes his family coat of arms of four quarterings for Aye, Dee, Epsilon and Effe (L).

NOTE.—Although these sections are written mainly in the past tense, the rules relating to Heritage and Achievements of Arms remain the same to-day.

Plate XVII. shows a modern "Full Achievement" of arms showing the family coats quartered and the escutcheon of pretence, the crest of a family representing two families and bearing, by virtue of a licence from the Crown, the crest as well as the arms of the family of an ancestress. The helmet and lambrequins are used as decorative mantling.

SECTION VII.—HERALDRY AS APPLIED TO COSTUME, FLAGS, HORSE FURNITURE AND WALL-HANGINGS

Parti-colour or Pied

Reference has been made (p. 166) to the attendance at Edward I.'s marriage procession (1299) of the Saddlers' Guild, in "livery" of red and white. Over a hundred years earlier (*see* p. 83) the first example of Parti-colour appeared in England, but it did not become popular until this time. Garments were "parted per pale," that is, divided vertically into halves of contrasting colours.

At first, *i.e.* in Edward I.'s reign, this method was adopted by the great as a livery (*see* pp. 166 and 189) for their retainers; the colours used were the principal tinctures from the family coat of arms. Later, in the time of the volatile Edward II., the king's foolish and dissolute companions were greatly intrigued by this fashion, and in their levity adopted it for themselves, taking from their own unrespected armorial bearings the tinctures for their festive garments, and presently introducing "counterchanging," *e.g.* the red half of a garment had a white sleeve or leg, and the white half a red one. The younger ladies fair fell victims to the same craze, which added to the colourful picturesqueness of joust and tournament. Later still, in Edward III.'s reign, and for a century afterwards, the vogue originated by gay and irresponsible youth spread to more serious-minded folk, and parti-colour was accepted as orthodox wear for young and old, courtier and citizen.

On the other hand, it is possible that in some—perhaps many—cases the effect in question arose fortuitously, *i.e.* when, owing to a lack of some of the original material, some other of a contrasting colour was used, *e.g.* to patch or replace part of a valuable garment, the bizarre effect thus obtained being approved and copied deliberately.

Costume of the Men

The Surcote

Armorial bearings, as distinct from badges and mottoes, were worn by gentlemen only on their military surcotes, shields, helmets and horse-trappings.

The armour in use during the First Crusade was of the type worn by the Normans when they invaded England in 1066, and was made mostly of leather with iron bosses; but after the return of the Crusaders, in the early part of the twelfth century, armour, and arms offensive and defensive, underwent a great change, which marks the commencement of the period of chain-mail armour.

Nobles and knights participating in the Second and Third Crusades (1146–7, 1188) covered their bodies and arms with tunics (*hauberks*) and their legs with *chausses*, both of chain mail. So equipped, they found that the powerful sun of the Syrian plains, shining upon the polished iron,[1] caused a heat beyond the wearer's endurance; therefore a covering became necessary, and this not only to protect the iron from the burning rays of the sun, but also to prevent it rusting. The surcote, made of white linen or silk, was introduced, and worn over the armour to overcome this difficulty. It was sometimes called the cyclas.

The cylindrical helmets which were worn at this time concealed

---

[1] Their armour shines beneath the sun's clear ray,
Hauberks and helms throw off a dazzling flame
And blazoned shields, flowered in bright array,
Also their spears, with golden ensigns gay.
Song of Roland, Laisses 137, lines 1808–11.

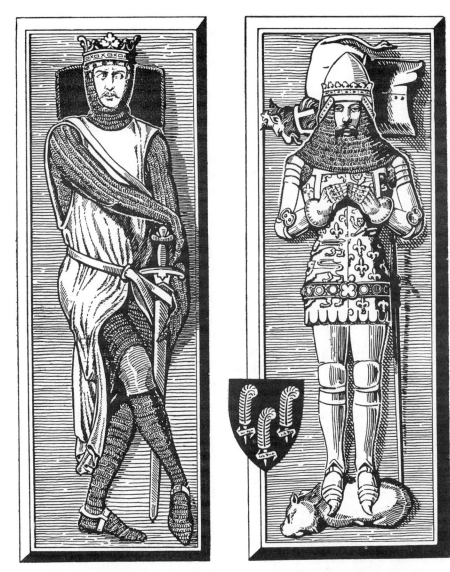

Fig. 445. Robert Curthose, Gloucester
Cathedral. 1150–1200

Fig. 446. Edward the Black Prince,
Canterbury Cathedral. 1379

the face, and the use of uniform white surcotes made it very difficult to identify the wearer. To obviate this, the idea of placing some dis-

tinguishing mark or "charge" upon the already tinctured shield (see p. 293) was evolved.

The Italians appear to have been the first to adopt the surcote, in the twelfth century. Later it was used by the French, but it was not worn by the English until the reign of Henry II. Surcotes did not become general until the time of John.

Military surcotes were cut on almost the same lines as the cyclas shown in Fig. 193, but wider. Being made of soft material, they hung in many small folds around the hips, and were girded at the waist by the sword-belt. In length the surcote reached half-way down the leg (Fig. 445); the shorter variation, called the cyclas, generally came to knee-level and was sometimes shorter in front than at the back.

The seal of Alexander II. of Scotland (1214), and the effigies of Robert Curthose at Gloucester, Fig. 445 (executed in the second half of the twelfth century), and William Longespée (1224) at Salisbury, and of knights in the Temple Church,

Fig. 447.
Wolfram von Eschenbach

show examples of the surcote in its earlier form. These early surcotes were always white, but during the first part of the thirteenth century coloured surcotes were worn to distinguish certain groups of knights. Louis IX. was attended by forty knights clothed in "surcotes simply of green." The surcote is also shown in the drawing (Fig. 447) of the troubadour-knight, Wolfram von Eschenbach (1210), who bears upon his shield and banner "gules two axes endorsed argent." The two axes used also as a crest should be noticed. The arms borne by another trouba-dour, Walther von der Vogelweide

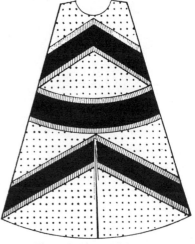

Fig. 448. Armorial Surcote

(Plate XVI. A), are: "gules a birdcage or, and within it a bird vert: crest, a birdcage and bird as in arms."

At this time also, charges, identical with those on the shield, were first placed upon the surcote (first examples: de l'Isle, Rampton, Cambs, effigy; Sir Robert de Setvans, Charlham, Kent, 1306) and occupied its whole surface, which became the "field." Since for this purpose it became necessary for them to be more substantially made, surcotes were often mounted on another material as a foundation, and lined with a contrasting colour. In this process they were reduced in width, and cut precisely as shown in Fig. 193 and in Fig. 448. This surcote is "or a fesse between two chevrons sable barrulée gules," for de l'Isle. "Barrulet" is a diminutive bar or fesse (and "cotise" a diminutive bend).

Early in the reign of Henry III. an order was given for a cyclas to be made for the king "of the best *purple* samit embroidered with three leopards in front and three behind"—the royal arms of England, which are charged upon a red field. The use of the word "purple" to denote the variety of shades mentioned in Vol. I., p. 106, at so late a date is interesting.

Plate XVIII. is taken from the Louterell Psalter, which (from internal evidence) "bears date prior to the year 1340." It represents Sir Geoffrey Louterell being armed for a tournament by his wife and daughter-in-law, and gives all details of the equipment for such an occasion of a knight and ladies during the second quarter of the fourteenth century.

Sir Geoffrey wears the surcote and ailettes, charged with his armorial bearings, "azure a bend between six martlets argent," over armour of the period. The tilting helmet of gold being handed to him by his wife has the fan-shaped crest, displaying the Louterell arms between two uprights— a curious, yet not uncommon decoration. Each item in the illustration is described under its separate heading.

Fig. 449.
Lord St. Amand

After the first quarter of the fourteenth century, the surcote became closer fitting on the shoulders, chest (where it was often padded) and at the waist, but it retained the full though shorter skirts. This was the first form of a variety of the surcote called the *Jupon*, shown in Fig. 449: "or fretté sable, on a chief of the second three besants," for Almeric, Lord St. Amand (1347). The besant is a golden roundle and had its origin in the gold coins in use in Byzantium (*see* Vol. I., p. 214, and p. 27, this volume). With the exception of the helmet, Fig. 449 is taken from the Hastings brass at Elsing, Norfolk.

Gambeson, Haugueton, or Haburgeown and its variation, the Jupon, Gipon, Gypown,[1] or Gypell,[1] later called the Pourpoint

A tight-fitting jacket or vest, worn under armour. It was often padded and quilted (and was then said to be "gamboised"; hence one of its names, "Gambeson") between two layers of thick cotton material called "augueton," from which comes another name—"Haugueton." This jacket or gambeson was worn by warriors of the eleventh and twelfth centuries, usually under their armour, but appears to have been worn sometimes without armour, being sufficiently tough to resist ordinary sword- or lance-thrusts. The jacket or haugueton was used by men-at-arms as defensive armour during the thirteenth century. In the fourteenth, it was not only worn by foot soldiers, but became, in conjunction with the surcote or cyclas, the ordinary garment of knights.

At this time the haugueton followed the shape of the fashionable cotehardie, fitting close over the body, without **body armour,** and was known as the "Jupon." The jupon was drawn tight to the figure by lacing at the back or sides, the bottom edge often being ornamented with dagges. The surface was covered with rich material, and armorial bearings embroidered upon it. Fig. 446 shows the jupon worn by Edward the Black Prince in his effigy at Canterbury, quartering France Ancient and England. A similar jupon still hangs over the prince's tomb, and is made of blue and crimson velvet, quilted in longitudinal stripes,

Fig. 450.
Fourth Earl of Warwick and his Countess

on a foundation of padding and canvas. The fleur-de-lys and lions are in gold embroidery.

Fig. 450 represents Thomas Beauchamp, fourth Earl of Warwick (1406), and his wife Margaret, daughter of Lord Ferrers of Groby. It is reconstructed from the brass in S. Mary's Church, Warwick. The

[1] Chaucer.

earl bears upon his jupon, "gules a fesse between six cross-crosslets botonée or," for Beauchamp. This is repeated on the mantle of the countess, and on her gown she bears her father's arms, "gules seven mascles or."

During the early part of the fifteenth century the haugueton or jupon went out of use in England as a military garment. Knights then appeared in full plate armour. At this time a similar tight-fitting jacket, padded on the chest and shoulders, came into fashion among civilians, under the name of "Pourpoint."

The Houpeland

The end of Edward III.'s reign saw the introduction of a fashion of decorating noblemen's long robes—houpelands—and the dresses of the ladies with their family badge or device, powdered all over the garment (see Fig. 348). In like manner, the initial letter of the wearer's name, or that of his or her beloved, might be used, often surmounted by a coronet (see Plate XIV.). The family or personal motto was frequently embroidered as a decoration on the borders of robes and sleeves; and sometimes, worked on a conventional ribbon, it was set diaperwise over the whole dress.

Ailettes

Ailettes came into use about the end of the thirteenth century. Their function was to protect the front of the shoulder and armpit, and they consisted usually of pieces of thick leather or wood, and later of plates of iron, generally quadrangular, but sometimes circular, pentagonal or lozenge-shaped. They were attached to the chain mail by two laces, which passed through holes in the ailettes, and tied together. Before going into combat the knight sometimes secured the upper edges of the ailettes to the helmet by transverse straps, making a gable roof of his head and shoulders and thereby protecting himself from attack. Ailettes were blazoned with armorial bearings which occupied their whole surface, as seen in Plate XVIII.

The Tabard

The tabard was first adopted as an item of military dress at the commencement of the reign of Henry VI. It was worn over their armour by royalties, nobles and knights, and blazoned with the arms of the wearer. The earliest representation of a military tabard is seen in the brass of John Wantele (1424). That of William Fyndern (1444) shows a tabard of the usual shape, similar to that illustrated in Fig. 451. Henry VI. is represented upon one of his seals wearing this garment blazoned with the royal arms.

During this reign, and until the beginning of the sixteenth century, the tabard was frequently worn by nobles on the battlefield, when attending a tournament, or at some military State function. Fig. 451 represents the tabard worn by Richard Beauchamp, fifth Earl of Warwick (1381–1439), and is taken from the Cottonian MS.[1] in the British Museum. The blazoning is "quarterly, gules a fesse between six crosslets or," for Beauchamp, and "chequée or and azure, a chevron ermine," for Newburgh. These armorial bearings were repeated on the back, and on the two cape-like sleeves. Richard III. is represented in the "Warwick Roll" illuminated by John Rous) wearing a similar tabard, blazoned with the royal arms.

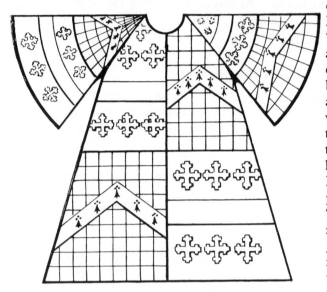

Fig. 451. Diagram of Tabard

At about the close of the fifteenth century the tabard as an item of military equipment went out of use. It survived as the official costume of heralds, worn over ordinary or secular ceremonial dress. The herald's tabard was blazoned with the arms of the sovereign, indicating that the wearer was in a sense a representative of the Crown.

Officers-of-Arms, under the generic name of Heralds, had formed part of the establishment of the sovereign, as well as of some of the great nobles, from very early times. Those in the royal household were incorporated first by Richard III., and consisted of three ranks: (a) Kings-of-Arms (three); (b) Heralds (six); and (c) Poursuivants (four).

There were (and are) three Kings-of-Arms, originally heralds:

The Garter, or Principal, created by Henry V.

The Clarenceux, anciently styled "Surroy," his province lying south of the River Trent. Formerly a herald, created King-of-Arms by Edward IV.

[1] This MS. is the work of (?) John Rous, between the years 1485–1490, all details in it being of this period, irrespective of the dates of the incidents portrayed. As an example, it is interesting to note that in folio 19b Henry V. is depicted wearing a crown of a pattern which was not used until at least sixty years after his death, and a tabard of a cut unknown before 1440. Henry V. died in 1422!

The Norroy, anciently styled "North-Roy," his province lying north of the Trent.

The jurisdiction of the provincial Kings-of-Arms corresponds roughly to the provinces of Canterbury and York.

The six Heralds are:

Windsor, instituted by		Edward III.
Chester,	,,	Edward III.
York,	,,	Edward III.
Lancaster,	,,	Edward III.
Richmond,	,,	Edward IV.
Somerset	,,	Henry VIII.

The four Poursuivants are:

Rouge-Croix, so styled from the Red Cross of S. George.

Bluemantle, so styled by Edward III. in allusion to the French coat of arms, or to the blue mantle of the Order of the Garter.

Rouge-Dragon, instituted by Henry VII. to commemorate his descent from the Welsh Prince Cadwallader, whose badge it was.

Portcullis, so styled by Henry VII. from one of his badges.

Costume of Heralds. The surcote worn by every rank of herald is called a "Tabard," or "Houce [1] des Armes." For its shape, *see* Fig. 451. The tabard of the kings-of-arms, technically known as a "Tunique," is made of velvet and cloth of gold, embroidered and appliquéd with the royal arms of the period on the front, back and sleeve-capes.

The kings-of-arms wear crowns, formed of a circlet of gold, bearing the words, *Miserere mei Deus secundum magnam misericordiam tuam.* The circlet is surmounted by sixteen oak leaves alternately about three and two inches in height. [2]

The collar of "SS" in gold is worn round the neck, and, from the reign of Elizabeth onward, with pendent royal badges both back and front, and with a portcullis on each shoulder.

The Arms of the office of Garter King-of-Arms are: "argent a cross gules, on a chief azure a crown, surrounded by a garter between a lion passant and a fleur-de-lys or." Those of the office of Clarenceux King-of-Arms are: "argent a cross gules, on a chief of the last a lion passant guardant crowned or"; and those of the office of Norroy King-of-Arms: "argent a cross gules, on a chief per pale gules and azure a lion passant guardant crowned between a fleur-de-lys and a key wards upwards or." On his official seal each king-of-arms impales his personal coat with his official.

The tabard of the heralds, technically known as a "Placque," is made of satin and cloth of gold. Collars of "SS" in silver, with royal

---

[1] Same as "Heuk" (*see* p. 262).   [2] This form, still existing, was settled in 1660.

badge attached both back and front, but without the portcullises on the shoulders, are worn. The badges were added in Elizabeth's time.

The tabards of poursuivants were originally worn athwart, *i.e.* with the sleeves back and front, and the chief parts of the garment over the arms. They were made of silk throughout. When a poursuivant was created a herald his tabard was readjusted—the chief parts of the garment hanging back and front, and the sleeve part on the shoulders. This practice was in use until the Commonwealth.

All officers-of-arms in the English royal service wore beneath their tabards, at full State and on ceremonial occasions, indoors, and when on horseback, surcotes of scarlet cloth; in the case of Garter King-of-Arms richly embroidered with a decorative pattern of the period, and furred. When the tabard was worn at a funeral, a "mourning cloke" with a hood and liripipe of black was worn with it.

Late in the eighteenth century a uniform in the prevailing fashion, and of dark blue, was devised for the use of all officers-of-arms, to be worn under the tabard. About 1860 the uniform was changed to scarlet, with gold embroidery indicative of the various ranks of the wearers, and designed in keeping with that worn by all other officers of State.

From the time of Edward III., Messengers-of-Arms, "certain servants, or inferior officials, employed by the Officers-of-Arms," were known as "Courrours des Armes," who passed or repassed on foot on official business. They wore cottes parted "per pale" back and front, "azure and gules," with the king's badge on their backs. After seven years' service in this capacity they were set on horseback, given spurs, and called "Horsemen-at-Arms," and the badge, hitherto shown on the back, was moved to the left shoulder. The exact date and circumstances of the extinction of these and many other minor officials are not known, but they did not come into prominence again after the reorganisation of the royal households in the interests of retrenchment by Henry VII. at the end of the fifteenth century.

An important point to be remembered is that no herald ever blew a trumpet, nor did any trumpeter ever wear an *armorial* tabard or coat of arms.[1] When making a proclamation, a herald or officer-of-arms was preceded or accompanied by a trumpeter to call attention to the proclamation about to be made, and here the association of heralds and trumpeters ends.

About the fourteenth century, surcotes, jupons, tabards, ladies' dresses, and sometimes horse-housings, were treated in elaborate stitchery. The whole surface—the field and the charges—was worked in a decorative manner, on the same principle as diaper or semée (*see*

---

[1] It is possible that these misrepresentations, which originated only in the nineteenth century, are the inventions of some theatrical producer or popular weaver of "historical" romance.

p. 134, Chapter III.). Some of the earliest tabards in existence [1] show, for example, the "field or" of *yellow* silk, embroidered with a line or diaper design in gold thread with tiny gold spangles introduced. A similar method was sometimes adopted for tinctures on elaborate heraldic garments. For example, "azure" might have a groundwork of blue linen embroidered in decorative squares, lozenges, etc., with a stitching of blue silk in perhaps a deeper shade. And it was not unknown to have a jewel—a sapphire of the same colour—set in the centre; a ruby might be used similarly on a ground "gules." This treatment was known as "Purfling."

Plate XVII. A is a photograph of the tabard worn by heralds attached to the Court of Isabella Clara Eugenia, "The Great Infanta," daughter of Philip II. of Spain, wife of the Archduke Albert of Austria, and Governess of the Low Countries from 1588. It is of elaborate sixteenth-century workmanship in velvet, silk and gold appliqué. The quarterings are interesting, and the method of repeating on a smaller scale the full coat on each sleeve-cape should be noticed.

The Mantle or Cloak of Arms

The mantle or cloak of arms was an uncommon garment worn by kings and nobles on State occasions during the latter part of the fourteenth and the whole of the fifteenth century. In shape it was three-quarters of a circle, and armorial bearings were twice displayed upon it, in front and at the back. Fig. 452 shows one of these mantles of arms laid out flat. It is blazoned quarterly "azure a cinqfoil ermine" for Astley, and "gules two bars or" for Harcourt. It was worn in the manner shown in Fig. 318, with the opening on the right side and fastened on the right shoulder.

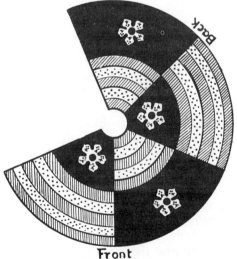

Fig. 452. Diagram of Coat of Arms

A PRACTICAL HINT may be given here for the guidance of those wishing to introduce armorial bearings economically into banners, surcotes, or other garments, or wall-hangings, for stage, film and pageant purposes. To its simplicity is added the virtue of authenticity.

[1] The earliest tabards—English—extant date from the first part of the sixteenth century, but these were treated in the earlier manner.

Remnants of an armorial surcote dating about 1240 still exist. It is of very fine linen, golden yellow in colour, and on it a lion in blue linen ("or a lion rampant azure" for Rivers) is appliquéd, the edges being sewn down securely with a solid chain-stitch in dull orange. Various parts of the animal are stitched and darned with deeper blue threads, to suggest the anatomy.

This method is still the simplest way of working armorial bearings on dresses, etc., and is more satisfactory than other methods where cost is a consideration. The fabric retains its suppleness better than if painted, the colourings are more intense than stencilling, and it is not such laborious work as embroidery, although the last, of course, is best, and, as a matter of historic fact, was employed in elaborate stitchery of coloured silks, gold and silver threads, for the decoration of the richest armorial dresses, etc., in the Middle Ages, and also for banners.

In the decoration of banners, also, the artist of to-day may combine economy with accuracy by the use of paint. It was indeed usual for all but the most important banners to have their armorial bearings blazoned in this manner. It is well to remember that the charge (except the lettering) is reversed on the side displayed when the staff is to the right of the banner (see p. 336 and Fig. 466), and this is aided if the paint from the other side shows through.

COSTUME OF THE WOMEN

The Cyclas

The women of France were the first to adopt the fashion of displaying armorial bearings upon their garments. The earliest illustration extant is to be found in a French MS. dating about 1285,[1] and shows a lady, the wife of Sir Joifrois d'Aspremont and daughter of Sir Nicolas de Kievraing, in the dress she probably wore at the Tournai de Chauvency which took place in that year.

A tournament was a very popular function, and always attracted a fine assembly of ladies—wives, relatives and friends of the contesting knights—who were present in great numbers at so important a social event. It was natural that they should wish to see their lords triumphant, or perhaps discomfited; and interest did not necessarily confine itself to the immediate family circle. Many ladies declared their sympathies by displaying the armorial bearings of the combatants, or they might contribute to the general decorative effect by wearing those of their own family. The husband of this lady, Sir Joifrois himself, was taking part in this particular tournament.

The drawing (Fig. 453) shows the Lady Aspremont, and is reconstructed from a miniature in this illuminated MS. She wears the

[1] The "Aspremont Horæ" in the National Gallery of Victoria at Melbourne.

cyclas, charged with the arms of her father, "or a chief bendy of six argent and gules" (*see also* Shield), over a gown having tight buttoned sleeves to the wrist. Her hair is encased in a crespinette, fashionable at this time, and she wears a barbette. She was accompanied by her daughter and her sister-in-law, both of whom wore a costume similar to that described, but blazoned with the arms of Aspremont, "gules a cross argent."

Whether these ladies originated the fashion signifies little, but it is certain that at the end of the thirteenth century armorial bearings were frequently used as decoration for festive dresses. The earliest record of this fashion in England is a brass to Margarete de Camoys, about 1310, which shows her wearing a long flowing gown, with sleeves terminating a little below the elbows, showing the tight buttoned sleeves of the under-gown. Her gown is charged with a "semée of escutcheons," being her father's (*not* her husband's) arms. Her headdress is the couvrechef draped over the ramshorn hairdressing.

Plate XVIII. shows two ladies, the wife and daughter-in-law of Sir Geoffrey Louterell, both of whom are wearing the cyclas. That of Dame Louterell impales Louterell with "or a lion rampant vert," for Sutton, her

Fig. 453.
The Lady Aspremont, 1285

father. The "display" of the lion should be studied, as it is an excellent example of the manner in which heraldic beasts were adapted to suit the field. The front of the cyclas being narrow on the chest and divided down the middle "per pale," it is necessary that the back of the animal's head should be cut off by the left arm-opening. This is not a usual practice, but as the lion is the only charge it is consequently of large dimensions, and covers half of the garment. The tail extends in graceful curves up the left side of the back. The "bend argent" of the Louterell arms starts on the lady's right shoulder-blade, passes the right arm-opening, and slants across the skirt to the pale line, terminating just below the knee. The three martlets follow in a line more or less parallel with the bend.

The lady holding the Louterell shield was the daughter of Sir Geoffrey Scrope, and wife of one of Sir Geoffrey Louterell's sons. Her cyclas impales Louterell and Scrope, "azure a bend or, a label [1] argent,"

---

[1] This label has the usual *three* points; presumably her "slim outline" was insufficient to display the five points which would have been correct in this case (*see* second shield in left-hand top corner).

although her father's shield shows a label of five points. The line of the Scrope "bend or" is clearly seen in the illustration. Both ladies wear the cotehardie then in fashion. The younger lady carries her hood of black and gold, faced with ermine, over her arm.

The Mantle

The mantle was used late in the thirteenth century as a means of displaying armorial bearings. It represented the shield; and the blazoning was always arranged to be viewed from the back—the pale line, where present, dividing the mantle in the centre of the back. From the front, therefore, the blazoning, so far as it can be seen, is reversed. The earliest known illustration is to be found in another miniature from the Aspremont Horæ, already referred to, where the Lady Aspremont wears her father's arms upon her mantle, and her daughter the Aspremont coat of arms on hers, *i.e.* both wear the paternal arms.

Fig. 454 gives a diagram of a semicircular armorial mantle which was in use during the period from about 1280 until the middle of the

Fig. 454. Diagram of Tiptoft Mantle

sixteenth century. The mantle remained in use among women as the sole garment on which armorial bearings were displayed, for at least fifty years after such ornamentation on the cotehardie and the sideless gown was discontinued. The mantle in this figure is typical of those worn during the whole of this period. It is taken from the brass at Enfield to the memory of Lady Tiptoft, which dates about 1470. She was the daughter and heiress of Sir Edward Charlton, Lord Powis, and Eleanor, daughter of Thomas Holland, Earl of Kent, and widow of Roger Mortimer, fourth Earl of March. Lady Tiptoft's mantle bears her father's armorial bearings, and their arrangement illustrates one of those exceptional cases sometimes encountered in heraldry. Owing to the exalted rank of her mother, the maternal arms—Holland—are marshalled upon the dexter side: "gules three lions of England or, within a bordure argent," for Holland, and "or a lion rampant gules," for Charlton, on the sinister side (*see* centre shield, Plate **XIX**. The "bordure," it will be observed, only surrounds two sides of the coat, *i.e.* it was never placed adjacent to the pale line. The design of the charges to fit the quarter-circles calls for attention. Charges normally horizontal, when arranged on a semicircular mantle always took a line parallel to its circumference, as exemplified in the three lions of the Holland family and the hind legs of the Charlton "lion rampant." The elongated bodies and lower limbs lost their distorted effect when the mantle was fastened on the shoulders of the wearer and hung in folds to the feet (*see* Plate **XIX**.). This manner of treating the charge became a little more difficult when only one coat of arms was blazoned on the mantle; a number of quarterings needed less distortion of charges to cover the field.

It must be borne in mind that the lines dividing such quarterings are always adapted to accord with the shape of the garment. Those normally per-pendicular are straight, but radiate from a common centre at the neck of the mantle; those normally hori-zontal are arcs, all parallel to the circumference.

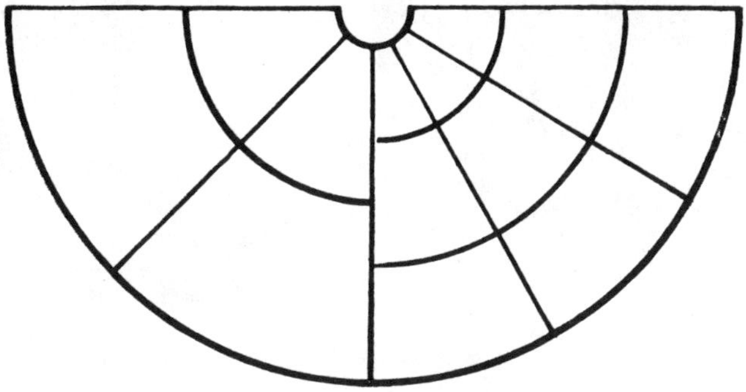

Fig. 455. Diagram of Mantle

Fig. 455 gives a diagram of a semicircular mantle divided "per pale," the dexter being quarterly of four, the sinister quarterly of nine.

The Cotehardie

By the middle of the fourteenth century, when the cyclas had ceased to be the height of fashion among women, armorial bearings were frequently blazoned on the cotehardie. Sometimes the arms of the lady's father only, and sometimes those of her husband alone, were used, and often the impaled coat.

The same difficulty occurred here as with the cyclas in adapting the upper part of the coat of arms to the body part of the garment. The lower part of the charge, whatever it might be, widened out to cover as much as possible of the skirt. When a single coat of arms was used, the charge occupied the front and sides of the cotehardie. An impaled coat had the "per pale" line in the centre of the front, the fields joining at the back (*see* Fig. 456). A mantle might be worn with this treatment of an impaled coat. The blazoning is "gules on a chevron or, three lions sable," for Cobham, impaling "or three torteaux, a label azure," for Courtney.

Fig. 456.   Fig. 457.
The Heraldic Cotehardie, fourteenth century

Fig. 457 shows an alternative treatment of an impaled coat, which was always worn without a mantle. In this instance the impaled coat is blazoned on the front and repeated on the back, the fields joining at the sides.

The Sideless Gown

The heraldic sideless gown, cut as shown in diagram, Fig. 330, was seldom worn without the mantle. From about the third quarter of the fourteenth century until the reign of Henry VII. these two garments constituted official or State dress for ladies of high rank. Such dresses are to be seen, however, on brasses and monumental effigies to the memory of great ladies down to nearly the middle of the sixteenth century. Armorial bearings were blazoned on the front and sides of the skirt (see Plate XIX.), covering an area shaped like the paludamentum (see Vol. I., Diagram 17, p. 110).

Plate XIX. represents Margaret, Princess of Wales, about 1410. She was the wife of Owain Glendower, Prince of Wales, and daughter of

Sir David Hanmer of Flintshire. Her husband's impaled shield is on the left: "quarterly or and gules four lions passant guardant, counterchanged," for Glendower, and "argent two lions passant guardant azure, crowned or," for Hanmer. The Glendower arms are blazoned on the sideless gown of the princess, and her father's upon her mantle.

Plate XIX. is reconstructed from the brass to the memory of Joice, Lady Tiptoft. The mantle has been described already on p. 330.

The centre shield is that borne by Richard Nevill, son of Ralph, Earl of Westmoreland, and of the Lady Joan Beaufort (1424). He married Alice, daughter of Thomas, Earl of Salisbury, and in right of his wife became Earl of Salisbury, Lord Montagu and Lord Monthermer. Accordingly, the earl quartered ("quarterly quartering") his own arms, "gules a saltire argent" and the label of the Beauforts "componée argent and azure," for Nevill, with "argent three fusils conjoined in fesse gules" for Montagu, and "or an eagle displayed vert," for Monthermer. It will be noticed that the wife's greatly superior rank (through which he derived his earldom) is recognised in the placing of her arms in the dexter position—a method sometimes adopted in such cases. The third shield is that borne by the family of Beaufort, descendants of John of Gaunt, fourth son of Edward III. and Katherine, widow of Sir Otes Swynford. The royal arms are differenced with "a bordure componée argent and azure."

Study of the many examples of heraldic dresses to be seen in illuminated MSS., sculpture, and on brasses, reveals no definite rule as to which coat of arms—the father's or that of the husband—should be displayed upon the cyclas, cotehardie, sideless gown, or mantle. One or other or both might be used, apparently at the whim of the wearer.

FLAGS

From the Anglo-Saxon, *fleogan* = to fly, so called from their manner of flying or fluttering in the wind.

From pre-Christian times there are records of the use of flags—sometimes decorated with emblems. In their earliest form they were always attached to the spear-shaft, close to the head, and later developments are all derived from this beginning.

The modern term "flag" covers a number of forms, *e.g.*:

> Oriflamme
> Pennon
> Banner
> Guidon
> Standard
> Gonfalon

The Oriflamme

From the Latin, *aurea flamma* = a flame of gold; a name given to a certain flag in use during the eighth century. It was square or horizontally oblong, one end being decorated with the addition of pointed tongues. Usually made of red silk, it had the effect of a golden flame when fluttering in the sunshine.

Fig. 458

Perhaps the earliest existing representation of a flag in Europe is in the ninth-century mosaic on the façade of S. John Lateran, Rome. The figures of both Constantine the Great (in ninth-century costume) and Charlemagne hold flags in their hands. These are shaped like the oriflamme, and are of red silk, powdered with circles and other minute motifs which *might* represent golden flames. The staff of one flag is surmounted by a Greek cross, that of the other by a fleur-de-lys (Fig. 458).

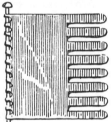

Fig. 459.
Oriflamme,
thirteenth century

It is said that William Duke of Normandy "allowed his oriflamme, made of *simple* red tissue of silk, to float in the air" at Senlac. The name "oriflamme," given to the banner which was carried before the French kings and preserved in days of peace in the Treasury of the Abbey of S. Denis, seems to have been originally the designation of any royal standard.

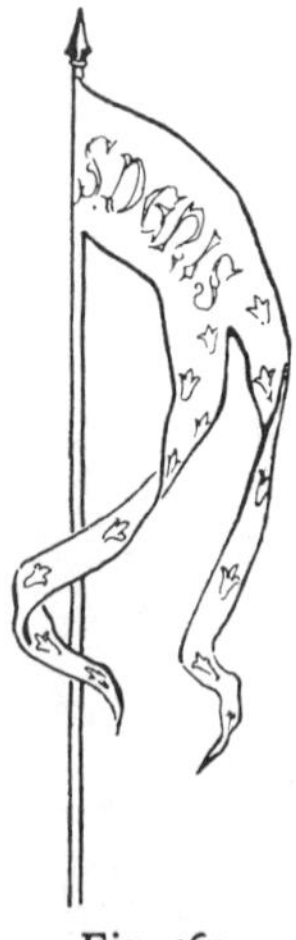

The oriflamme or sacred banner of the Abbat of S. Denis was of red silk, extended by three tongues or flames, having a silk tassel between each. The office of oriflamme-bearer was an important and honourable one. Before receiving the oriflamme from the hand of the abbat, the bearer partook of the Sacrament and made a vow to guard his trust faithfully.

In 1119 the oriflamme of S. Denis was carried as the French national standard at the Battle of Brenneville. The oriflamme of France, made of red silk, is shown in Fig. 459, copied from a drawing by Matthew Paris which dates about 1240. It has undergone a change in shape, in accordance with the fashion of the time.

Fig. 460

At the Battle of Cassel (1328), under Philippe VI. de Valois (1328–50), "Messire Miles de Noyers was mounted on a great destrier covered with a 'haubergerie,' and carried in his hand a lance to which was attached the oriflamme of vermilion samit in the shape of a gonfannon with three tails, and surrounded by bands of green silk."

Fig. 460 shows the oriflamme of France and S. Denis as it appeared in the fifteenth century. It has assumed the shape of a pennon with swallow-tail. It is of red silk embroidered with gold flames and the motto, "Montjoie [1] Saint Denis." This oriflamme is said to have been lost at Agincourt, 1415.

The Pennon

From the Latin, *penna* = a wing, or a feather; a small flag either single-pointed or swallow-tailed. In the eleventh century the pennon was square, one end being decorated with the addition of pointed tongues, Fig. 461; it was used by the Normans as a distinguishing mark of knights. Many of these are represented on the Bayeux Tapestry. This one shows a Greek cross in a border embroidered on the pennon. The pennon remained for about a hundred years the ensign of the knight, and towards the end of the twelfth century it was charged with some motif from the

Fig. 461.
Norman Pennon

Fig. 462.

Fig. 463.

Pennons with Badge

armorial bearings of the owner—a badge (*see* badges on pennons in Fig. 462 and 463). This was placed in such a position—at right angles to the lance—that it could be deciphered when the lance was "at charge." The pennon was frequently surrounded by a narrow gold or coloured fringe.

During the reign of Henry III., the pennon acquired the distinctive swallow-tail, Fig. 462; (badge, a Cornish chough proper, for Scrope), or the single-pointed shape shown in Fig. 463 (badge, a sickle, for Hungerford). Another version of the single-pointed pennon was introduced in the thirteenth century. In shape this was a scalene triangle, Fig. 464, obtained by cutting diagonally the vertically oblong banner (*see* p. 337).

Fig. 464

[1] "Montjoie," the war-cry of France. "Renounèd word of Pride" (*Chanson de Roland*).

The Pennoncelle

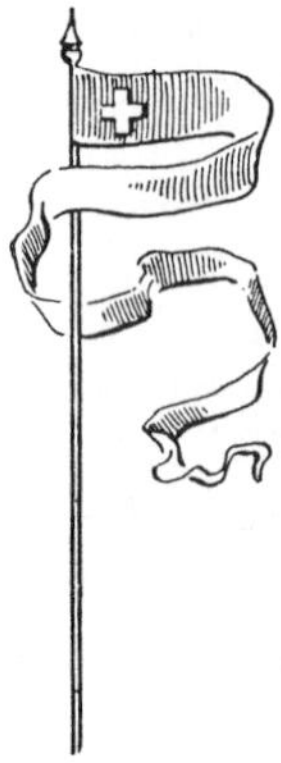

A long narrow pennon or streamer, usually single-pointed. Frequently flown from the masts of ships (Fig. 465).

The Banner

Low Latin, *bandum* = a standard; French, *bannière*. A perpendicularly oblong flag. It was the ensign of the king, barons, overlords, and "knights banneret," carried before the owner as a sign of his feudal rights.

The banner bore the complete coat of arms of the owner, and represented his shield.

Fig. 465

The charges were so arranged that the dexter side was always next to the staff, no matter which way the banner flew. *This rule holds good with armorial flags and banners of all kinds.* See Fig. 466, "barry of argent and sable per bend counterchanged: on a chief sable a lion rampant argent"; and Fig. 467, "argent a chief sable"—the banner of the Knights Templars.

Banners were sometimes tongued; for example, see the banner of the Hospitallers (Fig. 468), "gules a cross argent." This latter style of banner resembles its ancestor, the oriflamme (Fig. 459). Banners were generally

Fig. 466

made up on a stiff or rigid foundation to prevent flapping; this had the advantage of displaying the coat of arms more effectively. They were frequently decorated with a gold or coloured fringe all round the edge, save at the staff.

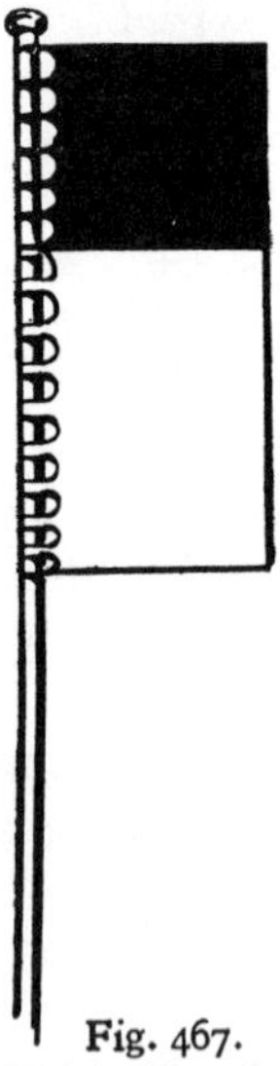

It was usual to carry the banner fixed to a spear, and sometimes to a staff. Banners were also attached to long trumpets, and were blazoned with the arms of the lord who employed the trumpeters, and thus corresponded generally with the arms on the tabards of the heralds when the two worked in conjunction.

Some time in the seventeenth century the arms on these trumpet banners were replaced by "Full Achievements" (*see* p. 317 and Plate XVII.), with crest, helmet, mantling, supporters and motto, set out with decorative accessories and elaborately embroidered. It is interesting to note that banners used on trumpets might have their charges either parallel or at right angles to the trumpet.

Fig. 467.
Knight Templars'
Banner

Towards the end of the thirteenth century a superior rank of knight was created, it is said by Edward I. At the same time this new rank was adopted in France. When a knight distinguished himself by any deed of valour he was ordered to present his pennon on the field of battle to the king, or to the commander-in-chief, who cut off its ends—the tongues—thereby converting the pennon into a square banner, and returned it to the owner, who was thus created a "Knight Banneret." On this banner he had the privilege of blazoning his armorial bearings. Henceforth the knights of inferior rank were known as "Knights Bachelor," a name derived from "bas Chevalier."

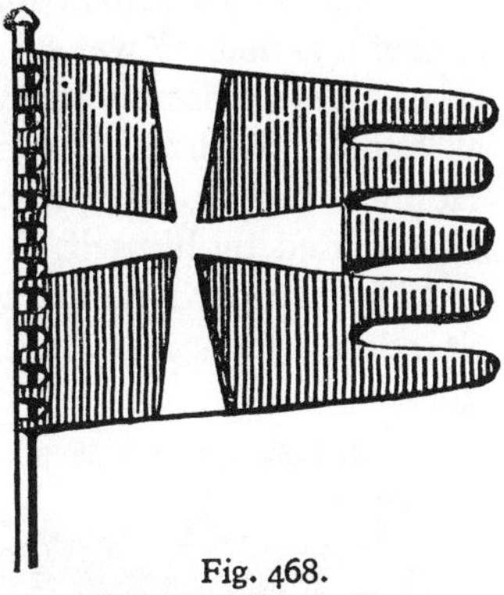

Fig. 468.
Banner of Hospitallers

An alternative practice brought the triangular pennon into use at the end of the thirteenth century. The oblong banner was *cut diagonally*, converting the retained portion into a scalene triangular pennon.

In the first years of the fourteenth century the oblong banner gave place to a square one (Fig. 469, "gules three crescents argent," for Oliphant). The knights bachelors' pennon therefrom took the shape of a right-angled triangle, *i.e.* half the square.

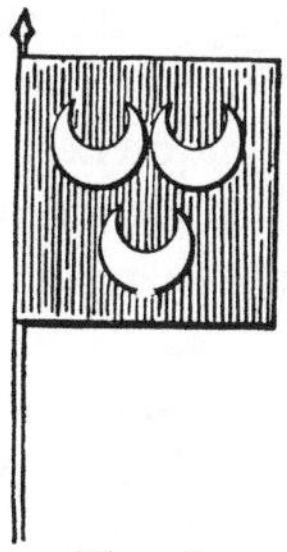

Fig. 469.

Although the general rule seems to have been that the pennon was charged with the badge *only*, and the banner with the armorial bearings, several illustrations of the first half of the fourteenth century are to be found (Plate XVIII. is one of them, and this is of the old-fashioned shape) showing the pennon blazoned with the coat of arms.

The explanation of many variations to be noticed in the use of flags and other heraldic details appears to lie in the fact that the rules and practices governing their use were nearly always transmitted orally from one generation to another. When the traditional practice died out, very few records, if any, remained for the information of the curious of later days.

The Guidon (*Guydon*)

An enlarged edition of the pennon. Still used by cavalry regiments in the British Army.

The Standard (Norman French, *Estendard*)

The original meaning is an ensign—that which stands, such as the Roman "Signa" (*see* Vol. I., p. 80). Later it signified a staff with a flag. It was a name given in the Early Middle Ages to the most imposing kind of flag.

Harold, King of England, possessed one "made of gold tissue having the image of an armed man upon it." Another contemporary description of it is that it "was sumptuously embroidered with gold and precious stones, and represented the form of a man fighting." After his victory at Senlac, William I. sent this standard to Pope Alexander II. His Holiness had already presented the Duke of Normandy with a standard consecrated by himself.

The standard raised at Northallerton in 1138 (the "Battle of the Standard") was a staff surmounted by a crucifix above a silver casket

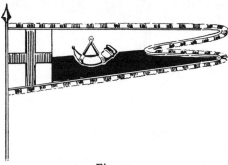

Fig. 470.
Standard, fourteenth and fifteenth century

(or pyx) containing the Host, fixed in a four-wheeled car. From the staff below the pyx were flown the sacred banners of S. Cuthbert of Durham, S. Peter of York, S. John of Beverley and S. Wilfrid of Ripon.

The standard in use during the reign of Edward III. was an heraldic flag of pennon shape, usually terminating in two rounded ends, and sometimes swallow-tailed. It varied in size according to the rank of the owner. A typical standard of the fourteenth and fifteenth centuries is illustrated in Fig. 470. Such a standard would be decorated and charged as follows:

Next to the staff comes the red cross of S. George on a silver field,[1] and the rest of the surface is usually divided, "per fesse," or "per bend" or "bendy," into the two principal tinctures of the owner's coat of arms, or livery colours, with the badge, and sometimes also the motto, blazoned in the centre. The whole standard is surrounded by a fringe of gold, of colour, or what is called *componée*—a single row of small alternating squares of two tinctures of the shield. (*See also* Beaufort shield, Plate XIX.)

The standard shown has the red cross of S. George and the livery colours, argent and sable, charged with the badge of an oliphant proper. The fringe is componée of argent and sable.

The standard was usually carried rolled up. Not only was it too sacred to display without reason, but also its great length made it awkward to carry. It was hung from a window or high tower in the owner's castle.

[1] All standards had the S. George's Coat, and at later dates the Union device, next the Staff, to identify the owner as an Englishman or Briton. In 1606 the Cross of S. Andrew was added to that of S. George; and in 1801 that of S. Patrick was incorporated with the earlier union, to form what is now known as the Union Jack.

The photograph, Plate XVII. B, shows the banner of the city of Ghent, 1482, which varies from those previously described in an interesting way. It shows the lion familiar in Flemish armorial bearings.

The Gonfannon or Gonfalon (Italian, *Gonfalone*, the bearer of this flag was called a "gonfalonier").

The gonfannon was a long flag, pointed, or swallow-tailed, or of several tongues, displayed from a transverse bar slung to a pole or spear. It was used for various purposes, chiefly decoration. It could be either charged with a badge or coat of arms, or ornamented with a fancy design. The gonfannon in Fig. 471 has four tongues, and is charged with a badge—a castle. *See also* Plate XVI. showing one charged with a coat of arms. The gonfannon was much used for ecclesiastical ceremonies and processions.

Fig. 471

Sails of Ships

Coloured sails had been in use by the Romans from pre-Christian times. A vermilion sail was used on the ship of the chief military consul, and a purple one on that of the chief civil consul.

During the period of the empire, the emperor used a purple sail, which was often decorated with imperial devices. Black sails were used by the Romans during a period of national mourning.

Purple and red sails were used for important ships for many subsequent centuries.

The Scandinavians used sails made up of alternate widths of two colours, and this style was adopted by their descendants, the Normans, for their ships' sails (*see* Bayeux Tapestry).

Bohadin the Arab mentions that at the siege of Jaffa, 1192, King Richard's ship "was distinguished by its red sail."

In the reign of Henry III., a warship's sail was frequently blazoned with the arms of the knight in command—the "Ammiral"—a rank of naval officer [1] which came into existence about this time. The whole sail was used as the field, and the charges displayed upon it in the same manner as the armorial bearings on a shield. Sometimes the knight's badge instead of his arms was powdered over the surface of the sail. This was especially the custom during the latter part of the fourteenth and in the fifteenth century.

The standard of the knight was flown from the mast, and pennoncelles from other points. The royal banner was not flown from ships unless the king was on board.

[1] William de Leybourne was the first "Ammiral of the Seas" in 1286.

Military Horse Furniture

War horses or chargers were called "destriers." Sir Samuel Meyrick says this name was used because they were led by the right hand of the page, but it appears more likely to have been derived from the Old French, *destruire* = to destroy, since such horses were trained to take part in battle, and to use their heavily shod forefeet as remarkably formidable weapons.

At the beginning of the thirteenth century, knights' chargers wore (sometimes over armour) silk or cloth coverings, called "housings"

Fig. 472. Housing

(French, *housse*). Housings consisted of two pieces, both strongly lined, one of which, having apertures for the eyes, went over the head and neck where it was fixed to the saddle. It was divided in front, and fell over each foreleg, reaching almost to the fetlock. The other part covered the back, haunches, tail and hindlegs. At first (1220), the back part was not so long as the front, Fig. 472. Later (about 1260), the front was shortened and made level with the back part. Early in the fourteenth century both parts were further reduced, and reached only to a short distance below chest-level, Plate XVIII. This housing was of any colour, and many of them were without any decoration. At the time Louis IX. was taken prisoner by the Saracens in 1250, it was reported by Joinville "that he was mounted on a little courser, covered with a housing of silk." However, at a much earlier date it was not unknown for the coat of arms of a knight to be blazoned upon this item of horse furniture, for the seal of Seiher de Quincey, first Earl of Winchester, 1216, shows his armorial bearings, "or a fesse gules, a label of seven points azure," displayed upon the housing of his charger. Fig. 472 shows a housing charged with "azure three buckles argent."

At the end of the fourteenth century and beginning of the fifteenth, the sumptuous decoration of harness and horse furniture knew no bounds. Housings were of the richest silk and brocade, and cloth of gold and silver. Bits, stirrups and all metal fittings were made of gold, often set with pearls and jewels of all kinds, and beautiful enamels.

Housings were frequently powdered all over with the badge of the owner—king, noble or knight. At the beginning of the fifteenth century, this fashion became as general as the earlier one of blazoning the housings with coats of arms.

Plate XVIII. shows perhaps one of the first examples of a piece of horse furniture called the "chamfron," which took the place of the portion of the housing covering the horse's head. It is here shown blazoned with armorial bearings, and made of stiff material such as leather. It fitted the front and cheeks of the horse's head, and had openings for the eyes. This one has coverings for the ears. The chamfron was afterwards developed, and became an important item of plate armour for horses: a small one is shown in Plate XVI.

Trappers of Chain Mail

By the second half of the thirteenth century horses were sometimes armoured in coverings made of chain mail, called "trappers." In shape these trappers were shortened versions of the housings, and were worn over a "gambeson" made of quilted linen, cloth or leather with wool or cotton stuffing between the two thicknesses, Fig. 473. These chain-mail trappers were not very generally used, partly on account of their great cost, and partly because of their weight. The gambeson alone usually proved sufficiently effective as a protection. Housings, either of plain colour or blazoned, were frequently placed over the trappers, or the gambeson, as a protection from the sun and rain.

Fig. 473. Trapper

In the fifteenth century a horse was said to be "barded" when it was protected with plate armour.

The Saddle

Horsemen of Greek and Roman times were so highly skilled that it was possible to keep a "good seat" without a saddle. A saddle with a "tree"—that is, a rigid foundation or seat—was unknown until the fourth century A.D. It was used by the Anglo-Saxons, but it was not of any definite shape until the Normans introduced their pattern.

The saddle of the Normans consisted of the "seat" and side-flaps, the latter being wider at the bottom edge than at the top where it joined

the seat. The pommel or burr (French, *arçon* = saddle-bow or front piece) and cantle—the front and back upstanding portions—curved outwards and were about four to six inches in height (*see* Fig. 474).

During the twelfth century, the saddle for civil use consisted of a framed seat or tree, a thick square pad, often decorated, and an ornamental

Fig. 474

saddle-cloth (placed under the saddle), first used in the reign of Henry I. The pommel and cantle returned into use in military saddles about the first quarter of the twelfth century in a much enlarged form, both at the front and at the back, the cantle changing into a chair-back support, as seen in Plate XVIII. and Figs. 472 and 473. It was necessary that these should be very strong so that the rider had a firm seat to withstand the shock of the lance-thrust. This was especially the case during the fourteenth century, when combat with the lance attained considerable importance.

The fixing of a saddle by a strap round the chest and crossed girth-straps is shown in Fig. 473. The former was usually placed under the trapper.

About the middle of the thirteenth century, the pommel and cantle were used to display armorial bearings (*see* Plate XVIII.).

The Crest

From the end of the thirteenth century onwards, the crest surmounting the knight's helmet was repeated on the horse's head. The horse was always supposed to be looking towards the dexter, and the charges on all items of furniture were blazoned accordingly. This treatment should be noticed in Plate XVIII., where the ladies are facing the dexter and the knight and horse are looking towards the right of the picture.

Bits and Bridles

The ordinary bit in use from the Roman Period to the fourteenth century was a bar of iron with large rings at its extremities, to which the reins were attached, Fig. 475.

Fig. 475

From the eleventh to the end of the twelfth century a branch was attached to the bit, having an ornamental disc where it joined the mouth bar, and an open square at its extremity to take the rein, Fig. 476. In the thirteenth century the branch took a slightly curved line, Fig. 477. About the end of the thirteenth century an interesting quadrilateral bit came into use, *see* Plate XVIII., and remained for the greater part of the fourteenth century.

During the latter part of this century and the fifteenth, bits with straight or curved branches, Fig. 478, were both used, with or without the addition of ornamentation of various kinds, Fig. 479. The bridle also became more ornate and sumptuous.

Fig. 476.   Fig. 477.   Fig. 478.   Fig. 479.

Bits, Bridles and Reins

Reins

For some considerable time reins had consisted of a strap of leather, often coloured. This is known as the curb rein, and was used alone until the fourteenth century. During the thirteenth century reins were decorated in various ways—with metal studs, square, round, or lozenge-shaped.

The snaffle, *see* Figs. 478 at A, and 479 at B, was introduced about the end of the fourteenth century, and used in conjunction with the curb. It was frequently decorated when used for either civil or military harness. At a little later period the snaffle had a band of material, about four to six inches in depth, attached to the rein for a distance of about fifteen to eighteen inches from the bit, *see* Fig. 479 at B. This was richly ornamented, and when used for war-horses, or at the tournament (*see* Plate XVI.), was blazoned in quadrangles with the owner's armorial bearings. In the fifteenth century military reins were sometimes protected by metal rein-guards.

The civil snaffle rein had ornaments of an elaborate nature, such as tassels, metal discs, or bells, etc.

Spurs

Spurs were used by the Greeks in the fifth century B.C. and by the Romans in the fourth century B.C. These were small spikes, fixed to an

iron half-hoop or shank having apertures at the ends through which a
strap passed to buckle them to the foot (*see* Fig. 480). This is the
origin of what is known as the "prick spur." During the eleventh and
twelfth centuries, the prick was at the end of a short and straight

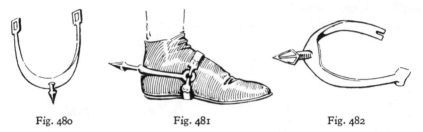

Fig. 480   Fig. 481   Fig. 482

neck (Figs. 481 and 482). In the thirteenth century the neck took a
line downwards, and the shank a decided curve upwards (Fig. 483).
Towards the end of the century the neck became longer.

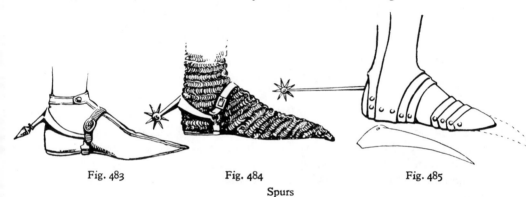

Fig. 483   Fig. 484   Fig. 485

Spurs

A small wheel with spikes set at the end of the neck, called the
"rowel spur," was introduced about the middle of the thirteenth
century (Fig. 484).

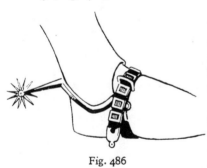

Fig. 486

In the fourteenth century, when
war-horses were fully barded, the
spur was at the end of a very long
neck. This was attached to the shank
and strapped to the foot, or riveted
to the heel of the soleret (Fig. 485).

Fig. 486 is a drawing of a spur
from the bronze effigy of Edward the
Black Prince on his tomb in Canterbury Cathedral. The straps, which
would be of leather, are set with
quadrangular ornaments of blue enamel surrounded by gold borders.
The buckles and chapes are also in gold.

Stirrups

Stirrups did not come into use until the sixth century, and were not generally used until the eleventh century. From early times up to this period horsemen were so skilled that it was beneath their dignity to require such aid. During the Carlovingian Epoch, when expert horsemanship was severely tested in combats of arms (*see* p. 292), stirrups of hoop or ring shape, Figs. 487 and 488, were used, hung from straps. The triangular stirrup, Fig. 489, was known at this time, and came into general use among the Normans. This shape continued up to the end of the fourteenth century.

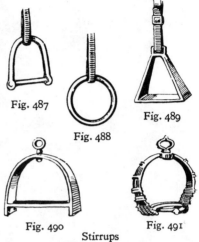

Fig. 487

Fig. 488

Fig. 489

Fig. 490

Fig. 491

Stirrups

A simple stirrup of bow shape, with two bars for resting the foot, is of the fifteenth century, Fig. 490, and an elaborate one of the same period is shown in Fig. 491.

Wall-hangings

The decoration of walls with armorial bearings was introduced into England from the Continent, where it had been in use for some short time, by Isabella of France, when she came in 1308 as the bride of Edward II. The new queen brought with her some wall-hangings designed in lozenges, certain of which were blazoned with the arms of England, France and Navarre. Fig. 492 shows a reconstruction of this heraldic tapestry, and its blazon is: "gules three lions passant or," for England; "azure semée of fleurs-de-lys or," for France; "gules an escarbuncle or," for Navarre. In alternate lozenges badges were added: the Star issuing from a crescent, of Richard I.; the Rose, of Edward I.; the Castle, of Edward II.

After this date it gradually became the fashion for the nobility to garnish their apartments with this kind of wall decoration, especially that part of the wall space behind the high seat set upon the dais at the end of the great hall. Alternatively, the hangings might be diapered with the owner's badge, and his achievement of arms placed in the centre, immediately above the seat or throne.

Every noble had the right, in his own house, or anywhere not in the presence of the king, to a "Chair of Estate," raised on a dais, and set under a canopy with his arms blazoned behind it on a hanging called a "dorsal," or "Cloth of Estate," close up against *the wall*, the chair being set immediately in front (*see* Plate XXII. and Fig. 517). The obvious reason for this was to guard against attack from behind. Enthronement at a coronation was the only exception to this practice. If the king honoured him with a visit, the nobleman's arms were removed, the royal arms substituted, and the seat occupied by the king.

Fig. 492. Wall-hanging

Designs for armorial wall-hangings, particularly of the fifteenth century, were of different types. Sometimes the breadth of the tapestry was divided into perpendicular panels about four or five feet in width. On these were displayed two alternating coats of arms, each coat occupying the whole area of its panel (*see* Plate XXI. A). Another very general treatment of armorial tapestry was to divide it into squares or oblongs. In an illuminated MS.[1] dating about 1445 the dorsal behind the throne of Henry VI. is designed in oblongs about twelve by ten inches, with the arms of France and England in alternating spaces.

In Plate XXIV. is seen a wall-hanging composed of lozenges of red and white. The white are charged with the red rose of the House of Lancaster, and the red lozenges with the white rose of the House of York. The badges of noble houses were often used in this manner on wall-hangings.

> The boast of heraldry, the pomp of power,
> And all that beauty, all that wealth e'er gave.

[1] Roy. MS. 15, E. VI.

CHAPTER VI

1399–1485

CONTENTS

CHAPTER VI

1399–1485

CONTEMPORARY SOVEREIGNS

	ENGLAND	FRANCE	BURGUNDY	GERMANY
1399	Henry IV.	Charles VI., 1380–1422	Philippe le Hardi Marguerite, Countess of Flanders	Wenceslas of Bohemia, 1378–1400
1400				Rupert, Count Palatine of Rhine, 1400–1410
1404			Jean sans Peur, 1404–1419 Margaret of Bavaria	
1410				Jossus, Marquess of Moravia, 1410
1410				Sigismund, King of Hungary, 1410–1438 1. Marie of Hungary 2. Barbe of Cellei
1413	Henry V. Catherine of France			
1419			Philippe le Bon, 1419–1467 1. 1409, Michele of France, daughter of Charles VI. 2. 1424, Bonne of Artois, Comtesse de Nevers 3. 1429, Isabelle of Portugal	
1422	Henry VI. Margaret of Anjou	Charles VII., 1422–61 Marie of Anjou		
1438				Albert II. the Great, 1438–1439 1. Elizabeth, daughter of the Emperor Charles IV. 2. Beatrix of Nuremberg
1439				INTERREGNUM
1440				Frederick III. the Pacific, 1440–1493 Eleanor of Portugal
1461	Edward IV. Elizabeth Wydeville	Louis IX., 1461–1483 1. Margaret of Scotland 2. Charlotte of Savoy		

ENGLAND	FRANCE	BURGUNDY	GERMANY
1467		Charles le Téméraire, 1467–1477	
		1. 1439, Catherine of France	
		2. 1454, Isabella of Bourbon	
		3. 1467, Margaret of York	
		Killed at Nancy, 1477	
1477		Marie, only child and heiress, b. 1457	
		1477, Maximilian I.	
1483 Edward V.			
1483 Richard III.			
Anne of Warwick			

HISTORICAL DATA

1399–1485

1400. Henry IV.'s reign started amidst opposition and conspiracies. On Twelfth Night the Earls of Kent, Huntingdon and Salisbury, and Lord Despenser concocted a plot to reinstate Richard; or, if he were really dead, to place on the throne the rightful heir, Edmund Mortimer, Earl of March (born 1393, the great-grandson of Lionel, Duke of Clarence). This plot was unsuccessful; and on 14 February, Richard II. was murdered in Pontefract Castle. To convince the public of his death, his corpse was exhibited in the Chepe. Many thought the body to be that of some other person, and rumours that Richard was still alive, and under the protection of the King of Scotland, were current for some time.

Manuel II. Palæologus, Emperor of Constantinople (1391–1425), visited Charles VI. at Paris, and later Henry IV. in England, to "sollicit succours" against Bajazet, the Turkish sultan. He was met at Blackheath by the king and nobility in great state; and entertained splendidly during Christmas at Eltham Palace, where twelve aldermen and their sons amused the Court with a mystery. On his departure he received from Henry only 3000 marks.

1402. Welsh war begun by Owain Glendower, Prince of Wales (born 1364; knighted by Richard II., 1387; fifth in descent from the last Prince of Wales; crowned prince in 1402; died 1415).

1403. Troubles with Irish and Scots. Victory won over the latter by the Percys, Lords Warden of the East and Welsh Marches. They plotted with Douglas and Owain Glendower for the restoration of Richard II. or the next rightful heir, the Earl of March. Death of Percy (Hotspur) and Douglas at the Battle of Shrewsbury, 23 July, 1403.

1406. Henry acknowledged the power of the Commons. The executions of Scrope, Archbishop of York, and of Thomas Mowbray, earl-marshal, freed Henry from his English enemies.

1407. Thomas Elmham, historian, Benedictine monk of S. Augustine's, Canterbury. Birth unknown. First mentioned in 1407 when he was "arrested for excessive zeal in the discharge of his duties." Died 1440. Beginning of Civil War in France. Regency of the Prince of Wales and the Beauforts—John, Earl of Somerset; Henry, Bishop of Winchester; and Thomas, Duke of Exeter.

1413. Death of Henry IV. and accession of Henry V. Edmund Mortimer, Earl of March, a claimant to the throne, liberated by Henry V.

1414. Body of Richard II. transferred to Westminster Abbey. Henry determined to crush the Lollards (of whom Sir John Oldcastle was chief). He tightened up the laws against heresy; and on discovering a plot against his life, he executed summarily all the conspirators who were captured. Oldcastle remained in hiding until 1417, when he was seized and burnt. Council of Constance, to discuss reform of the Church.

1415. Scrope's conspiracy to place the Earl of March on the throne. Its instigators, Lord Scrope, Sir Thomas Grey and the Earl of Cambridge, were all executed.

Invasion of France; siege and fall of Harfleur, despite heroic defence by the French. Henry marched on Calais.

Battle of Agincourt, 25 October. A sweeping victory for the English.

Henry returned to England and was received with enthusiasm.

1416. Visit of Sigismund, Emperor and King of Hungary, to London, "out of a pious design to make peace between England and France."

To secure Harfleur, Henry sent his brother John, Duke of Bedford, to France.

1417. Henry returned to France, and completed the conquest of Normandy; Caen was taken by storm; all Normandy, except Rouen, followed; Henry enforced order and justice, and Rouen fell on 19 January, 1419.

1420. Treaty of Troyes, which disinherited the dauphin, bestowed the crown of France on Henry at the death of Charles VI. and stipulated for the marriage of Henry and Catherine of France.

1421. Henry returned to France.

1422. Death of Henry V. at the age of thirty-five from a "long-suffered illness." Accession of Henry VI.

Death of Charles VI. Henry VI. acknowledged King of France. During the king's minority the Duke of Bedford Regent of France; the Duke of Gloucester Regent of England.

1424. Edmund Mortimer, Earl of March, d.s.p. in Ireland, where he was imprisoned, thus leaving his nephew Richard, Duke of York, next in succession to the crown.

James Stewart (born 1394), son of Robert III. of Scotland, captured by the English at sea (1404); confined, first in the Tower; Nottingham Castle (1407); Evesham (1409); sent back to the Tower by Henry V. (1413); afterwards removed to Windsor. Married Lady Joanna Beaufort, daughter of John, third Earl of Somerset, and returned to Scotland, 1424. Assassinated at Perth by the Earl of Athole, 1437.

1428. War in France. Bedford had conquered all France north of the Loire, except Orleans; to this he laid siege.

1429. Jeanne d'Arc (born 1412) led army to relief of Orleans, which she accomplished 29 April. (She received a wound—the only time she shed blood for France till her martyrdom.)

Immediately Orleans was safe for France, Jeanne conducted the vacillating dauphin to Rheims, and saw him crowned as Charles VII., 17 July.

1430. Jeanne d'Arc continued the war till she was taken by the Burgundians at Compiègne, 23 May, and sold to the English, who handed her to the civil authorities. She was burnt

1431. as a witch at Rouen, 31 May, 1431. "She stands alone on the page of history." Canonised 1921.

Coronation of Henry VI. in Paris, 17 December.

The Medici became powerful in Florence.

1435. Death of the regent, Bedford.

Hans Memling born. One of the greatest painters of the old Flemish School. Fought at Granson and Morat under Charles le Téméraire. An inmate of St. John's Hospital, Bruges, where he died in 1495.

1442. John Beaufort, first Duke of Somerset (created 1443), appointed to French command.

1444. Truce of Tours.

1447. Death of the Duke of Gloucester, and of the Duke of Somerset, the last real statesman who supported Henry VI.

Calais the sole French province remaining to England.

1448. Lorenzo di Medici born: known as "The Magnificent"; a man of great culture and renowned for his munificence. Died 1492.

1449. Great discontent prevalent throughout England, owing to the huge subsidies demanded for carrying on the unsuccessful wars in France. Chief among resulting troubles was the rebellion headed by Jack Cade, who led the Kentish peasants to London with a "complaint," but the insurrection proved abortive and Cade was killed in the retreat.

1450. The Duke of Suffolk impeached for high treason and banished for five years, but murdered (30 April) at sea on his way to the Continent by Henry Holland, Duke of Exeter, admiral, and heir-presumptive to the House of Lancaster. Buried at Wingfield, Suffolk.

Wars of the Roses. Richard, Duke of York, boasted double descent from

1453. Edward III. In 1453, a son was born to the king. Henry VI. fell ill, and York was appointed protector, and thus was given to him the power he wanted to further his own claim to the throne. On Henry's recovery, Edmund, second Duke of Somerset, unpopular since the loss of Guienne and Gascony, was restored to favour; and York took up arms, supported by the Earls of Salisbury and Warwick the "Kingmaker."

Girolamo Savonarola born, a Dominican preacher and politician. Strangled and burnt at the instigation of the di Medici in 1493.

Capture of Constantinople by the Turks (see Vol. I., p. 138).

First Battle of S. Albans, 23 May. Somerset slain.

Henry VI. insane: York's second protectorate.

1456. King recovers: York resigns post. Battle of Bloreheath, Yorkist victory.

1459. Battle of Northampton, Yorkist victory. Henry VI. taken prisoner; Queen Margaret fled to Scotland.

1460. Duke of York urged his claim to the throne through descent from Lionel, Duke of Clarence. Parliament voted for House of Lancaster, and though London and the merchant towns were for York, the barons refused to dethrone Henry VI., but promised York the crown on Henry's death.

Battle of Wakefield, 31 December; Lancastrian victory. Duke of York slain. Warwick espouses the cause of the duke's son, Edward, Earl of March. Execution of Salisbury.

John Skelton born; English poet. Died 1529.

William Dunbar born; Scots poet. Died 1520.

1461. Battle of Mortimers Cross, 2 February. The Earl of March victorious.

Second Battle of S. Albans, 17 February; Lancastrian victory. The licence of Queen Margaret's unruly army prevented her from following up her victory; and the Earl of March came first to London. He rallied the citizens while Warwick barred the Lancastrian march. A council of Yorkist lords in Parliament deposed the absent King Henry and offered the crown to the earl, 2 March, but the final issue lay with the sword.

Battle of Towton, 29 March; a terrible struggle ended in a Yorkist victory. Edward, Earl of March, crowned king as Edward IV., 29 June. Henry and Margaret fled to Scotland; a rising in the north crushed by Warwick.

1464. Battle of Hexham, 15 May; complete Yorkist victory. The deposed King Henry fled to Lancashire, and Margaret and her son Edward to Kirkcudbright and, later, to Flanders.

Edward IV. married Elizabeth Wydeville, and advanced her kinsfolk to honours and estates, in gifts and marriages, so angering and estranging Warwick and his other earlier supporters.

1465. The deposed King Henry captured and lodged in the Tower.

1469. Warwick, disgusted with Edward IV.'s behaviour and his personal extravagance, and furious at his own failure to negotiate a marriage for Edward with the sister of Louis XI., rallied the discontented Yorkists round Edward's brother, Clarence, whom he married to his own daughter, Isabel, and fomented risings against Edward. In the first outbreak in Yorkshire, the insurgents defeated Edward's forces at Edgecote and afterwards took and executed the Earls of Pembroke, Devon and Rivers (Queen Elizabeth's father). Edward advanced on Warwick and Clarence; was kept by Warwick under some restraint for a considerable time at Warwick Castle and other places, until he escaped to London. England was again his own, and Warwick and Clarence fled in alarm to France. Warwick began to treat with the Lancastrians and returned to England. He liberated Henry VI. once more, imbecile as he was, and Edward IV. fled to Burgundy, leaving his queen, Elizabeth Wydeville, at the Tower, whence she escaped to the Sanctuary, Westminster, where their son Edward was born. Edward IV. returned, was joined by Clarence, who had deserted Warwick, and marched on London. Henry VI. was sent once more to the Tower.

Sir Thomas Malory, birth unknown, compiler of *The Most Ancient and Famous History of the Renowned Prince Arthur.*

1471. Battle of Barnet, 14 April. Edward gained a decisive victory over the Lancastrians. The Earl of Warwick and many other distinguished men were killed.

Battle of Tewkesbury, 4 May. Edward IV. captured Henry's queen, Margaret, and sent her to the Tower. Her son Edward, Prince of Wales, was either slain in battle or murdered after the fight was over.

Death of Henry VI. in the Tower.

1474. Edward IV. prepared for war with France, in alliance with Charles le Téméraire, Duke of Burgundy.

Gawin Douglas born; Scots poet. Bishop of Dunkeld, 1516. Died of plague, 1522.

1475. Invasion of France. Edward bought off by Louis XI. Queen Margaret ransomed, and returned to France.

1478. Edward accused his brother Clarence of treason; he was condemned and died secretly in the Tower.

1480. Quarrel between Edward and James III. of Scotland.

Sir Thomas More born, only son of Sir John More, a judge of King's Bench. Beheaded 1535.

William Tyndale, translator of the Bible, born between 1480–90. Arraigned before the Imperial Commission of the Emperor Charles V., imprisoned at Vilvorde, and strangled by the public executioner, 1536.

1483. Further trouble with Louis XI.; preparations for war interrupted by the death of Edward IV., 9 April.

Accession of Edward V.; placed under the regency of his uncle, Richard, Duke of Gloucester, who removed the young king from the custody of his mother's family. Later, by threats, Edward's brother, the Duke of York, was also secured, and both were lodged in the Tower. Gloucester disputed Edward's legitimacy, and after much intrigue he was accepted by Parliament (25 June) as the lawful heir to the throne. He was crowned as King Richard III. on 6 July, 1483.

Richard III.'s enemies were chiefly to be found among the nobility. The Duke of Buckingham, Constable of England, was the first to revolt. He was descended from Edward III. through the Duke of Gloucester (Thomas of Woodstock) and considered claiming the crown for himself, but afterwards supported Henry Tudor, Earl of Richmond, in his claim to the throne. Buckingham was betrayed to Richard, and beheaded at Salisbury.

Murder of Edward V. and the Duke of York in the Tower.

1485. Battle of Bosworth, 22 August.

THE ARTS

ARCHITECTURE

THE Perpendicular style of Gothic architecture belongs exclusively to the fifteenth century, and is so called from the persistent use of perpendicular lines, dominating the mullions of the windows, which often continue upward into the arch itself, and the use of panelling on vertical lines. The arches are less pointed, and open timbered roofs are of high pitch and frequently ornamented with elaborate carving. Flying buttresses are a distinct feature of this period of architecture. The vaulting is extremely ornate, and known as "Fan Vaulting," a style in which English architecture is unsurpassed.

SCULPTURE

(Continued from p. 199)

The only existing example of the work of fifteenth-century coppersmiths is the effigy to the memory of Richard Beauchamp, Earl of Warwick, in S. Mary's Collegiate Church, Warwick. The building of the Beauchamp Chapel was begun in 1443 and completed in 1464. The monument, with its effigy and fourteen images, "embossed, of Lords and Ladyes in divers vestures, called Weepers, to stand in housings made about the Tombe," was finished at the same time. These figures were the work of William Austin, founder, Thomas Stevyns, coppersmith, and Bartholomew Lambrespring, a Dutchman and goldsmith of London. The last was responsible for the enamelled escutcheons of arms which decorate various parts of the monument. The effigy of the earl, in full plate armour, is the outstanding authority for a nobleman's war equipment of this period, and both drawings and photographs are reproduced in many works on the subject.

Numerous monumental effigies in stone, scattered over the British Isles, provide most valuable material for the study of costume—military, court and civil—to be found. It is possible to examine at leisure the most minute details—the design of an ornament on a lady's headdress, or the method of lacing the camail to the helmet—from all points of view. The subject is endless and cannot be carried further in the present volume. There are, however, numerous works dealing with mediæval statuary and monumental effigies, and it is hoped that these few notes may encourage students to pursue their investigations into this fascinating subject.

Many details of costumes given in this volume are derived from the statues alluded to in these sections; reproductions of the originals may be studied in books relating to the subject.

Memorial Brasses

(Continued from p. 200)

A marked deterioration is noticeable at the beginning of the fifteenth century in the work of memorial-brass engravers, and this increased as time went on. It was due to a change in the personnel of the departed —great numbers of brasses were erected at this period to the memory of civilians, whose social ambitions were gratified by the adoption of this type of monument, but whose commercial parsimony prevented them from loosening their purse-strings sufficiently to ensure good work.

At the same time, some brasses of this period still retained the highly-finished and careful treatment displayed by work of the craftsmen of the last century. Some of the finest and most elaborate brasses were in memory of wealthy woolmen. During this century many professional men—judges, doctors, sergeants-at-law, notaries, etc.—were commemorated by engraved brasses, and these are very useful for the study of academic and legal costume.

During the reign of Richard III. an interesting departure from the established rule occurred. Hitherto, all brasses represented the deceased full-face. This continued, so far as the men were concerned; but brasses to the memory of fashionable women showed the face "three-quarters," in order to display the elaborate headdress (see p. 448) then in vogue, since it was impossible to depict it full-face.

Tapestry

(Continued from p. 201)

By the commencement of the fifteenth century, the art of weaving picture-hangings had reached its highest standard of perfection. Arras still remained pre-eminent in the industry; Brussels, Bruges and Tournai were also famous for their workshops.

To continue the history of "The Apocalypse" series of tapestries (mentioned on p. 201), new panels were added in 1417 under the direction of Yolande of Arragon. René I., Duke of Anjou, titular King of Naples and Duke of Lorraine, caused the work to be continued between the years 1431–1453. The last piece was made in 1490 by order of the Princess Anne, daughter of Louis XI. of France. It was presented in 1498 by René II. to the Cathedral of Angers. Of the ninety scenes, seventy are still in existence.

Philippe le Bon, centre of the cultured Court of Burgundy, was a very lavish purchaser of tapestry, and his collection was considered unique at the time. Many of his specimens were brought from Brussels, whose products by this time rivalled, and eventually supplanted, those of Arras.

A series of tapestries, very useful for the study of costume of the first part of the fifteenth century, is that known as "The Burgundian Sacraments." [1] These were woven at Bruges, about 1440, by order of Philippe of Burgundy for his son Charles, Count de Charrolois (Charles le Téméraire).

Tapestries representing hunting scenes were very popular in the fifteenth century. The four panels of "Hunting Tapestry" belonging to the Duke of Devonshire, originally at Hardwicke Hall, measure forty feet wide by twelve high. Some authorities consider that they were woven at Arras or Tournai about the middle of the century; others suggest that they were made in England as they depict much local colour. Whichever may be correct, they show a great variety of costumes worn during the reign of Henry VI.

On the death of Charles le Téméraire [2] at Nancy in 1477, Louis XI. of France took possession of the Duchy of Burgundy, and from that time onwards Arras ceased to create the wonderful picture-hangings for which it was once so famous.

The tapestry made to celebrate the admission of Henry VI. and Margaret of Anjou to the Trinity fraternity still hangs in its original position on the wall of S. Mary's Hall, Coventry. This was designed in Flemish style, but was possibly woven in England towards the end

---

[1] Now in the Metropolitan Museum, New York.

[2] The tapestry representing "The Condemnation of Banquet and Supper," stated by M. Viollet-le-Duc to have been found in the tent of Charles le Téméraire in 1477, and to-day on view in the Musée Historique Lorrain, Nancy, is now pronounced to be of early sixteenth-century workmanship.

of the fifteenth century. It shows Henry VI., his queen and court, but the costumes and accessories are definitely those of the reign of Henry VII. This is another instance of the many pitfalls open to the amateur costume designer who relies on the period portrayed rather than the date of the workmanship.

During the second half of the fifteenth century, in addition to the figure subjects mentioned above, designs used for tapestries included armorial bearings (*see* p. 346) as well as conventional floral patterns, formal trees and geometrical designs, usually woven upon plain colour grounds. Typical examples are shown in Plates XXII., XXIII., and Fig. 571.

ILLUMINATED MANUSCRIPTS
(Continued from p. 203)

During the fifteenth century the art of the English illuminators declined, despite the fact that some good work by English artists belongs to this period.

The wars with France, which took place in the first half of the century, created a taste among the wealthy English for manuscripts by French artists, whose work during this time attained the high excellence hitherto monopolised by English illuminators.

Towards the end of the century the taste of manuscript-collectors shifted from France to Flanders—that country of highly-skilled painters who renounced imaginative symbolism for the minute representation of natural beauty—and the great demand for work by Flemish artists left English art to decay and perish for lack of encouragement. All the same, such illuminated manuscripts of English workmanship as were produced at this time are useful as authorities on English costume.

PORTRAIT PAINTING
(Continued from p. 203)

Unfortunately no English portrait painters belong to the fifteenth century. There are a fair number of portraits of some of the kings and queens, and of noble personages of this time, still existing in various collections. Many of them are well known, but, almost without exception, they are either the work of foreign artists or were painted early in the sixteenth century. It is disappointing to learn that this applies to the familiar portraits of Henry IV., Henry V., Henry VI., Edward IV., Richard III., Margaret of Anjou and Elizabeth Wydeville. It is suggested that these were all painted for his collection to the order of Henry VII. (died 1509) by an artist, possibly English, who was much influenced by Flemish or French technique.

Edward IV. was a great patron of the arts, and encouraged portrait painting, mainly by Flemish artists. The art had been widely practised on the Continent for some time, especially in Italy and Flanders.

PRINTING

William Caxton, born 1412, was a mercer of London. In 1464 he was sent by Edward IV. as "ambassador and special deputy" to frame a commercial treaty with Philippe, Duke of Burgundy. He spent some considerable time in Flanders, and had opportunities of learning the craft of printing. Later he resided in the household of Margaret of York, wife of Charles le Téméraire, Duke Philippe's successor. The duchess brought Caxton to the notice of Lord Rivers, Elizabeth Wydeville's brother, and on Caxton's return to England, Rivers greatly helped in furthering his work. A printing-press was set up in the Almonry at Westminster, and here Caxton spent the remainder of his life, printing in old black-letter type books to the number of sixty-four in twenty years. He died in 1491.

Fig. 493

COSTUME IN GENERAL

1399–1485

In the fifteenth century the state and ceremonial of the great nobles and feudal lords attained its zenith of brilliant splendour.

No particular new style in costume, either for men or women, is noticeable during the first quarter of the fifteenth century. The fashions of Richard II.'s reign were worn with slight variation throughout the reigns of Henry IV. and Henry V.

During the French wars of the first four decades of the fifteenth century, when in fact a large portion of France became an English possession, the nobles of France wore the most sumptuous garments and splendid jewellery. This luxurious habit continued throughout the stirring times when Jeanne d'Arc had the dauphin crowned at Rheims as Charles VII., and during the reign of that monarch. It continued, indeed, until Louis XI. became king in 1461, for, although he in earlier days had been a devotee of fashion, a more economical spirit actuated him after his accession, and extravagance was checked in his time—to bloom afresh under Charles VIII., 1483–1498.

Men. The new style which came into use in England when Henry VI. reached manhood had its origin in the reign of Henry V., and is exemplified in Fig. 515. For about ten years, from 1440 onwards, the tunics of the fashionable nobility reached to just above the knee (Fig. 533), and were of rational cut and style; but during the next decade they became excessively short (Fig. 535), a revival of the garment called in the fourteenth century the "Courtepy."

An incursion of Italian modes into France about the middle of the century had its effect upon the clothes of the English upper classes. About the same time it became the vogue among the English nobility to imitate the manners, customs, and costume in favour at the Court of Burgundy, which, although essentially French, incorporated elements of Flemish and German taste. Among the factors derived through the Burgundian Court, although originating in Germany, was the use of stuffing for padding of sleeves, shoulders and chest, which grotesquely distorted the masculine form, making the most elegant figure look ridiculous (*see* Figs. 535 and 562).

Short tunics were in fashion from the middle of the fifteenth century until well on in the next. At the end of Henry VI.'s reign, long straight robes, houpelands and peliçons reappeared, and these, thickly padded on the shoulders and narrow in the skirt, were adopted by the fashionable upper classes, and worn over the short tunics mentioned above. The very tall hat usually worn with these narrow robes gave immense height to the wearer, and, in conjunction with the padded shoulders, produced a curious effect. The "line" desired by all fashionable men is indicated in Figs. 494, 537 and 562.

The vogue for wearing armour on the legs, mentioned on p. 250, Chapter IV., continued during the whole of the fifteenth century.

Fig. 494

Women. The costume of women during the whole of this period was almost uniform in character. The cotehardie, sideless gown and mantle were the garments in general use among the nobility during the first quarter of the century. During the second decade, ladies adopted the houpeland of the men and wore it, sometimes in conjunction with the mantle, as an alternative to the sideless gown—a mode borrowed from Italy—and this gradually superseded the earlier combination. An undergarment, the cotehardie, continued to be worn with them, and variations in its sleeves are referred to in individual examples. By the end of Henry V.'s reign, the cotehardie, sideless gown and mantle were reserved for full state dress for important ceremonies, and their use, especially that of the sideless gown, was denied to any save ladies of the Court. It is interesting to note that a little later, the first two of these garments were referred to in records of Henry VI.'s time by different names—the cotehardie being called the KYRTLE, and the sideless gown mentioned as the "Surcote."

At the beginning of the second half of the century, sleeves of the houpeland or robe underwent a change, the long open and the poky varieties giving place to a close-fitting sleeve with deep cuff falling over the knuckles.

During the whole period, except from about 1415 to 1425, bare necks were the correct mode. The introduction of the houpeland (Figs. 507, 541 and 543) modified the neck-opening. The turned-down collar of the houpeland revealed the throat in a V; but by degrees the opening became wider (Figs. 545 and 547), and presently the collar was worn round the shoulders—a return to the fashion of the middle of the previous century. By 1450 necks and shoulders were extremely bare, especially at Court functions, when the cotehardie and sideless gown, or the fashionable amended version of the houpeland, now called the "robe" or "gown" (Fig. 549), were worn. When ladies of the Court presented themselves "immodestly attired" before Henry VI., he turned away and rebuked them: "Fie, fie, forsooth ye be much to blame."

The ideal pursued by fashionable women from the middle of the fifteenth century onwards was to have a high forehead, narrow chest, low sloping shoulders, long neck, high small waist and prominent stomach.

Although the style of dress may be considered somewhat monotonous, ladies of the fifteenth century gave full rein to fancy in regard to their headdresses. Never before or since did these display such fantastic shapes, equalled only perhaps by the outrageous erections worn at the Court of Marie Antoinette. It is important to remember that, although the dress worn during this century may not indicate to the student its precise date, this may be adduced within a limit of ten years from the headdress. For this reason attention is directed to the chronological series of fifteenth-century headdresses given in Section VIII. of this chapter.

Little change in costume took place during the short reigns of Edward V. and Richard III., and therefore these brief periods are included in Section VI.

Early XVᵗʰ.

Fig. 495

SECTION I.—HENRY IV. 1399–1413

Nobility—Men

Henry IV. was born at Bolingbroke in 1367; crowned 1399; created K.G. 1377; attended the jousts at S. Inglevert 1390, and pronounced by the French "the best of the English knights."

Fig. 496 is taken from a portrait of Henry when Earl of Derby. A man "of a mean stature," but "well proportioned and compact. Strong, handsome, proud of his good looks," Froissart calls him "Beau Chevalier." His hair was of a deep russet-brown colour.

All through life he was brave and active, an orthodox, devout and good-living man, though somewhat hot-tempered. A great lover of literature, he doubled Chaucer's pension, patronised Gower, and invited Christine de Pisan to England because he took such delight in her poetry. He married first in 1380 the Lady Mary de Bohun, daughter and heiress of Humphrey, Earl of Hereford, who died in 1394. He married secondly in 1403 Joanna, daughter of Charles II., King of Navarre, and widow of John de Montfort, Duke of Brittany. Henry was taken ill while at his devotions at the shrine of Eadward the Confessor, and died in the Jerusalem Chamber, Westminster Abbey, on 20 March, 1413. He is buried in Canterbury Cathedral.

Fig. 496. Henry IV.

CHILDREN OF HENRY IV. AND MARY DE BOHUN

1. Henry of Monmouth.
2. Thomas, Duke of Clarence; married Margaret, daughter of Thomas, Earl of Kent, d.s.p. 1421.
3. John, Duke of Bedford, born about 1389. The celebrated Regent of France during Henry VI.'s minority, 1422–1435. Married first, 1423, Anne, daughter of Jean sans Peur, Duke of Burgundy (she died 1432), and second, Jacqueline of Luxemburg, daughter of Peter, Count de St. Pol. This lady married as her second husband Sir Richard Wydeville, Kt., and was the mother of Elizabeth Wydeville, later wife of Edward IV.

 The duke died in 1435. Like all the family of John of Gaunt, he was a great lover of the arts and literature. He purchased the library of Charles V. of France and sent it to London.
4. Humphrey, Duke of Gloucester. Regent of England during the minority of Henry VI., and sole guardian after Bedford's death. Married first, 1425, Jaqueline of Luxemburg, daughter and heiress of William, Duke of Bavaria, and second, Eleanor, daughter of Lord Cobham. He presented to the old Oxford University Library so large a number of valuable manuscripts that a special library was built for their accommodation, the original of what is now known as the Bodleian Library. The duke fell into disgrace through the intrigues of the Bishop of Rochester, the Earl of Suffolk and Queen Margaret. He was accused of high treason in 1446, imprisoned, and was found dead in his bed, 1447.
5. Blanche, married, 1402, Louis, Duke of Bavaria.
6. Philippa, married, 1405, Eric, King of Denmark, K.G.

Although perhaps the costumes of this reign were not so fantastic as those of the last, they were equally extravagant so far as richness of material and decoration were concerned, for the sumptuary laws were revived in 1403. The king was fond of outward display of power, and maintained and instituted various rites and ceremonies.

It goes without saying that costume played an important part in these; naturally, the courtiers followed the king's example, and the general population were influenced by the manners of their betters.

The houpeland remained much in favour during this reign. Fig. 497 shows Henry IV. in the costume he usually wore, consisting of the houpeland of some rich material, with long open sleeves lined with another colour; the sleeves of the underdress, extending to the knuckles, show underneath. The skirt part is opened up the sides, displaying the hose, and down the centre there is a band of gold embroidery set with jewels; this band encircles the neck, and the high collar of the paltock shows above it. It should be noticed that dagges are conspicuous by their absence, and the whole costume is very dignified and without exaggeration.

Fig. 497. Henry IV.

After Henry became king, he usually wore the hood in the manner now orthodox for ordinary dress. The old-fashioned way of wearing the hood was used only with ceremonial robes. The face part of the hood is worn round the head, with a jewel set in front, and the cape part screens one side of the face (*see also* Fig. 298 E). The liripipe falls on the other side, often caught by the girdle of gold set with jewels. The escarcelle hung from the waist-belt or from an additional hip-belt which might be worn with this costume.

Fig. 498 is a drawing taken from an illuminated manuscript, and shows a young noble of the reign of Henry IV. wearing the new modified houpeland of scarlet, with bagpipe sleeves (less extravagant than Fig. 355) finished at the wrists with bands of white fur. The waist-belt carries the fashionable bells suspended on chains, as well as a dagger hung by cords. The embroidery in blue and gold round the shoulders, back and chest is quite new in style. He wears a blue collar of SS,

Fig. 498. Noble, Henry IV.

and a beautiful chaplet, detail of which will be found under Jewellery (Figs. 639, 640).

Since the last years of the fourteenth century, France had had political and domestic relations with Italy, in consequence of Genoa having become the property of the King of France. Many of the fantastic Franco-Italian styles made their appearance in England during the reign of Richard II. and remained in use among the ultra-fashionable until the end of the war with France.

Louis, Duc d'Orléans, assassinated 1407, is represented in Fig. 499, wearing a "bastard" houpeland with wide sleeves. The decoration round the shoulders is much more elaborate than that shown in Fig. 498, and motifs ending in rectangular bells or ornaments hang from the main ornament.

Fig. 499. Louis, Duc d'Orléans Decoration of the long wide sleeves with an heraldic animal or bird, embroidered in gold or colours, was a curious fashion of the early years of the fifteenth century. Parti-coloured hose, and the hat referred to on p. 268 as being a favourite of the Earl of Derby, are still the height of fashion.

Fig. 500 represents a French noble of the first twenty years of the century. To understand the shape of the garment, a surcote or houpeland, reference should be made to Fig. 528, which is made in the same shape but does not appear so complicated. The surcote is but a circular cape cut up laterally as shown in Fig. 531, the front panel only being secured by the waist-belt, and the back portion forming a cape over the back and sides. The surcote in Fig. 531 has a fur border round all the edges. In Fig. 500 all the edges are dagged, and the front panel is slit part way up the centre. The high collar so fashionable in Richard II.'s reign is now lower; and the belt, carrying the escarcelle (often worn at the back), has returned to the hips and is frequently worn so

Fig. 500. French Noble

low that it gives the body abnormal height—an effect very much the mode. Over the surcote this noble has placed a baudric of gold, from which small bells are hung, in a peculiar yet obvious way, over the right shoulder and left forearm and cape. Under this surcote the paltock or pourpoint would be worn, little being seen except at the sides and sleeves.

Inset is the latest style of hat, copied from the Italian, composed of a skull-cap surrounded at the edge by rosettes of different colours, looking like chrysanthemums or gold flowers. In the original manuscript from which this is taken the rosettes are of alternate white, emerald green and black.

Fig. 501 illustrates another type of French houpeland worn by a

Fig. 501. The French Houpeland

nobleman of the same period. It has sleeves the shape of which is clearly shown in the drawing. They are dagged, not in the customary leaf design, but the edges are cut vertically at intervals. The sleeves are put into the armholes by pleats or gathers, they are lined throughout with fur, and a design in gold is embroidered on the upper parts. The fullness of the houpeland is confined by the belt worn very low down on the hips, and forms regular folds in the skirt, which reaches just below the knee. Under the houpeland this nobleman wears a garment having a high collar of black, with lines of gold on it, but the full white undersleeves gathered into a black band at each wrist are a novelty. Hose of two different colours are worn, and a hood is slung over the shoulder. It was the mode to arrange the hood on the head in one of the ways shown in Figs. 398 and 608 A. The hair (see Fig. 607 A) is dressed in a new style much in vogue during the first half of the century.

Fig. 502.
Noble, Henry IV. and V.

Fig. 502 depicts a courtier attired for

hawking. He is dressed in a houpeland of blue and gold brocade, lined with fur. The decoration on the shoulders, and the wide sleeve open a short distance at the seam above the wrist, should be noticed. The belt is worn round the waist, convenient for riding, and a neckband or collar finished with a gold ornament is worn in a manner similar to the collar of SS.. The large hat is made of straw and has two upright feathers, one white, the other scarlet, fixed by a jewelled ornament. The hawking-gloves are of white leather, the points of the cuffs finishing with scarlet silk tassels.

Parti-colour was still in favour, and Fig. 503 shows a noble wearing a houpeland of moderate length, with wide long sleeves. It is parti-coloured, diagonally, from the left shoulder to the right foot. This

Fig. 503.   Fig. 504.
Nobility, Henry IV. and V.

costume might be carried out in purple and blue, with the lining of the sleeves counterchanged or of a different colour. A hip-belt hangs on the slant, carrying the escarcelle; a collar or necklace of twisted gold-smith's work, and a baudric hung with bells, are worn. Many noblemen wore chains and twists of gold, with ornaments and bells, hanging over their shoulders or from the waist. The hair in Fig. 503 is worn in the normal fashion, waved, and cut level with the mouth.

Henry, Prince of Wales, a young man of exuberant spirits, added to his other follies an inordinate passion for dress, as is borne out by the following episode. It must be remembered that, taking into consideration the extraordinary fashions that had been in vogue for over half a century, he was not so eccentric in his dress as we moderns might think.

At the age of ten he was sent to Queen's College, Oxford, under the care of his step-uncle, the Chancellor, Henry Beaufort. Queen's Hall was founded in 1340 by Robert Eglesfield, chaplain to Queen Philippa, whose armorial bearings are "argent three eagles or eaglets displayed gules, armed or." AIGLETTE is a French term for a small eagle, and "aiglet" or "aiguillette" is also a name given to the metal tag or point of a lace, and to a needle. "Aiglette et fils" was a canting motto of the founder; and it was the custom for the bursar to present aiglettes or needles to students of Queen's College each New Year's Eve, with the exhortation, "Take this and be thrifty." [1]

Henry IV., sinking fast under the worries and anxieties of a usurped throne, had taken to his bed, and, as the custom was whenever the king was ill, the royal crown on a cushion was placed beside him, for his successor to take on his death. A relapse into unconsciousness was mistaken by the attendants for death, and they covered the king's head with a cloth. When the Prince of Wales was told that his father had expired, he placed the crown on his own head and took it away. Henry, reviving, asked what had become of it, and, being informed that his son had taken it, had him brought into his presence.

"My fair son," said the king, "what right have you to it? For you well know I had none."

"My lord," replied the prince, "as you have held it by right of your sword, it is my intent to hold and defend it the same during my life."

It is said that this episode took place on New Year's Day, 1413, and that when the Prince of Wales presented himself before his father he was dressed "in a gowne of blewe satin full of aiglet holes, at every hole the needle hanging by a silken thread by which it was worked." This was a subtle, if flippant, method of expressing to his father his intention to lead a new life, and that he would henceforth mend his ways by the needle of thriftiness, as his decorations showed.

In Plate XX. is seen the Prince of Wales attired in the fashionable dress of the time—the houpeland of blue satin lined with white. The wide sleeves are dagged at the edge, and at the neck is a band of gold passement. A belt of gold set with rubies and edged with pearls encircles the waist. The garment is worn over a paltock of green, and scarlet shoes show at the hem. The prince is represented in a miniature illustrating a set of poems by Occleve wearing a dress exactly like this, and in the same colours. Added here to these details is the decoration of aiglet-holes, outlined or overcast with silver thread, having needles hung at the ends.

The background is composed of the armorial bearings of the Prince of Wales and three examples of his badge: "an ostrich feather, pen and all argent."

The arms borne by Robert Eglesfield are shown in the top right-hand corner.

[1] This custom is still followed to-day.

The Order of the Bath

The significance of bathing was early recognised in devising the ritual for the investiture of a knight. As early as the time of Henry I., a bath "according to custom" appears to have preceded the other ceremonies of the initiation of a knight-elect (*see* p. 69, Chivalry), if this took place otherwise than on a field of battle, when, of course, the proceedings necessarily were curtailed. At the coronation of Richard II. a number of new knights were created, and they were solemnly bathed before the actual ceremonies of investiture occurred. The same observance took place at the coronation of Henry IV., when forty-six knights were formally invested in the Tower of London, rode with the king to Westminster, and sat with him at a special table at the coronation banquet in Westminster Hall. The king presented them with magnificent ceremonial robes, and from these circumstances the foundation of "The Order of the Bath" generally is attributed to him, "Knights of the Bath" being traditionally first thus designated by name in the annals of his reign. However this may be, from this time forth (with the exception of the coronation of Edward VI.) until the reign of Charles II., investiture of Knights of the Bath invariably formed part of the coronation ceremonies of every English sovereign.

During the latter half of the seventeenth century the Order fell into abeyance, but it was revived, as now constituted, by George I. in 1725, although this recrudescence bears but the faintest resemblance to the famous Order whose designation it assumed.

Robes of the Order

Apart from clothing, girdle, sword, spurs, etc., there does not appear to have been any insignia of the original Order of the Bath; and changes in the colour of the robes tend to suggest that no significance was attached thereto, and that magnificence was all that was aimed at. Gowns or surcotes, hoods and mantles are mentioned, and it is therefore possible that the robes of this Order were similar to those of the Order of the Garter—surcote, hood, mantle, sword and swordbelt, spurs.

At the time of Henry IV. the surcote, hood and mantle of the Knights of the Bath were of green silk lined with miniver or white samit. At the coronation of Henry VI. they were clad in scarlet; at that of Edward IV. thirty-two new Knights of the Bath rode before the king in the procession from the Tower, wearing blue silk surcotes, hoods and mantles, lined with white, and laces (ribbons) of white silk upon their shoulders.

The appearance of Knights of the Bath in Henry IV.'s time is shown in Fig. 518.

Changes subsequent to the period covered by this volume are noted below as a matter of interest:

At the coronation of Henry VIII. and Katherine of Arragon, twenty-four Knights of the Bath were created, and nineteen more when Anne Boleyn was crowned, and these rode in her procession through the city, clad in violet gowns and hoods "purfiled" with miniver. In the time of Queen Mary, blue mantles appear to have been used again, with shoulder laces of white silk. In the seventeenth century crimson robes lined with white satin became the custom, and these were continued in the new or revived Order as constituted in the reign of George I., when also the existing arms, ensign, or badge, and collar of the Order were devised and inaugurated: "azure three imperial crowns or," being the arms ascribed to King Arthur, the fabled founder of the Order of "Knights of the Round Table."

Nobility—Women

Joanna of Navarre was the second daughter of Charles, King of Navarre, and Jane of France, daughter of King John of France. Born about 1366, she married John de Montfort, "the Valiant," Duke of Brittany, in 1386, and was left a widow in 1399.

Their children were: John, born 1388, died 1442; Arthur, created Earl of Richmond by Henry IV. and referred to in the archives of France as the Valiant Count de Richemonte, died 1412; Jules; and Richard, Count d'Estampe, died 1438.

Joanna, who had been appointed regent for her son, Duke John, with his entire charge, assumed the reins of government in his name. She took him to Rennes, where he was knighted by Oliver Clisson, Count de Penthowaes, a powerful and wealthy noble, whose influence as Constable of France was far-reaching. Thereafter he was invested with the ducal habit, circlet and sword at S. Peter's, Rennes, on 22 March, 1401.

Joanna had known Henry of Lancaster during her married life, in fact he was a friend of her tyrannical husband, and Henry had greatly admired the way she managed him. After the duke's death, the betrothal of Henry (now King Henry IV. of England) and Joanna was announced. It was in consequence of the approaching marriage that for political reasons Philippe le Hardi, Duke of Burgundy, compelled Joanna to resign the regency of Brittany and the custody of her sons. After her resignation of these powers the young Duke of Brittany joined the enemies of Henry IV. and remained an opponent of his son, Henry V.

Joanna's marriage took place on 7 February, 1403, at the Church of S. Swithin, Winchester,[1] "in great pomp."

She was a great patroness of the arts and poetry and was instrumental

[1] The Cathedral Church of S. Peter, S. Paul and S. Swithin.

in the granting of the manors of Wotton and Stantesfield to Thomas, son of Geoffrey Chaucer, whose only daughter, Alice, married as her third husband, William de la Pole, the celebrated Duke of Suffolk, and is buried at Ewelme.

Queen Joanna was not the proverbial stepmother. A pleasant association between this queen and another historic personage (in some ways perhaps better known) is recorded in official documents of the time. The Issue Rolls preserve for us the fact that Richard Whittington supplied the wedding trousseau of the Princess Blanche, Henry IV.'s eldest daughter, for her marriage in 1402 to Louis, Duke of Bavaria; and again in 1405 (presumably having "given satisfaction" on the earlier occasion) he did the same for the Princess Philippa when she married Eric, King of Denmark. At the time of the first marriage, of course, Joanna was not yet Queen of England, and it is interesting to conjecture whether Whittington found it more or less difficult to satisfy the new stepmother when Princess Philippa was wed, than to please the motherless Blanche three years before. Queen Joanna did her utmost to promote an understanding between her husband and her madcap stepson, the Prince of Wales, as well as to patch up the differences between her own son, the Duke John, and her husband. In the former attempt she was so successful that later, when Henry V. went to the wars in France, he deputed to her a share in the government. This was characteristic of his treatment of her in the early years of her widowhood, which took place in 1413. It was quite an exceptional mark of favour to a queen-dowager, who was not also queen-mother, to grant her permission to reside in any of the king's royal castles.

When Joanna first came to England, numbers of foreigners, Frenchmen, Bretons, Lombards, Italians and Navarrese, followed in her train, and received appointments in the royal household. These appointments gave rise to general complaint, and many of them had to be rescinded. Upon her widowhood she began again to appoint foreigners to her household, having received so many marks of the new king's favours that she hoped to live in peace. This was ill-judged, and had unfortunate consequences, for it was one of the reasons, in conjunction with the friendship of her sons with the King of France, for an accusation of witchcraft and conspiracy to the king's harm being brought against her in 1420. On these charges she was condemned without a chance of justifying herself. She was deprived not only of her rich dower, but of all her money, furniture and personal property, even to her wearing apparel, and committed as a close prisoner to her jointure palace of Leeds Castle, Kent (and afterwards at Pevensey), while a proclamation of her alleged offences was made throughout England. The queen-dowager was released by Henry's orders a few weeks before his death, and the following extract from the king's instructions is interesting: ". . . and ordain her that she have, of such cloth and of such colour

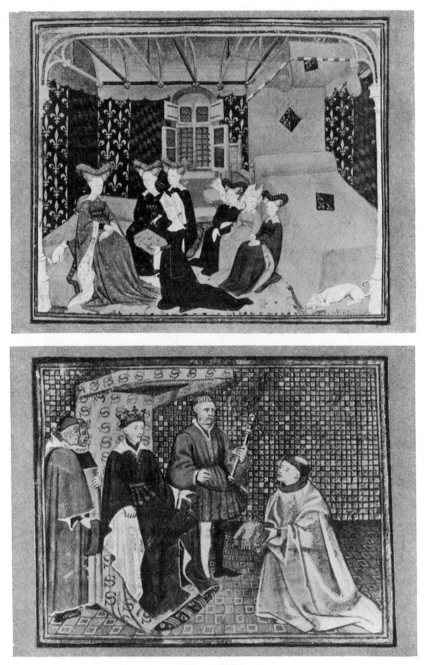

PLATE XXI.

FIG. A. ISABEAU OF BAVARIA AND CHRISTINE DE PISAN

FIG. B. HENRY V. AND JOHN GOLOPES

By kind permission of the Master and Fellows of Corpus Christi College, Cambridge

as she will devise herself, v. or vi. gowns such as she useth to wear"
(Parliamentary Rolls).

The remainder of her life was passed "in all princely prosperity,"
and she died at her favourite residence, Havering Bower, in 1437.

Fig. 505 represents the second wife of Henry IV., Queen Joanna of
Navarre, and is a drawing adapted from her monument in Canterbury
Cathedral. The sideless gown worn
over the cotehardie is very similar
to that in Plate XIV., the only
difference being that the bands of
ermine round the huge armholes
do not meet at the waist in front,
but allow the material of the skirt
to continue to the neck, where it is
finished by a straight band of
embroidery — passement set with
jewels, similar to that on the edge
of the skirt. Gold-jewelled ornaments like buttons are arranged
down the front. Over this is the
mantle, with a narrow border,
fastened just above the armpits by
two square jewelled ornaments.
These are connected by a cord, and
from each side the loose ends,
looped over the connecting cord,
hang down, finishing with tassels.
A band of jewels, broad or narrow,
often took the place of this con-

Fig. 505. Joanna of Navarre

necting cord; detail of such a band is given in Fig. 656, Jewellery.
This arrangement is frequently seen on monuments, etc., of this
period. Notice that the queen is wearing the collar of SS. A network
caul, which projects on either side of the face from beneath the crown,
is worn, but it does not extend below the lobes of the ears and is
covered at the back by a veil surmounted by an elaborate crown.

The costume of a noble lady of this reign is shown in Fig. 504. She
is simply though richly dressed in a cotehardie, and over it is a mantle
fastened by square mantle tasseaux. The headdress is the only new
feature about the costume. Over this cotehardie the sideless gown
would be worn on any important occasion.

A noble lady attired for ordinary occasions is shown in Fig. 506.
She wears the cotehardie, but over it has a gown fitting high and
close to the neck. Here it is gathered into the neckband, and the
gown is cut to fall in folds from the neck to the feet, buttoned all
the way down. It is drawn in at the waist by a long girdle, the

end of which falls some distance down the front. The headdress has the side cauls of network, which in this instance extend over the whole head, and are partly covered by a veil.

About the beginning of the fifteenth century noble ladies of France adopted the houpeland, and in every way, with the exception that they omitted the high collar, it was exactly like the houpeland worn by the men. The fashion was copied by English noble ladies before the end of the reign of Henry IV. Fig. 507 shows one with wide sleeves and girded rather high at the waist. A new feature is the square turned-back collar, sometimes worn turned up, and always of the same material or fur as that used to line the garment. Bagpipe sleeves were sometimes worn with the houpeland. The houpeland was worn over the cotehardie, and often for full state a mantle, attached under the collar, was also worn. The headdress shows another variety of that described under Fig. 613 E.

Plate XXI. A is reproduced from the title-page of a book of poems written by Christine de Pisan (*see* p. 427) and presented by her to Isabeau of Bavaria, Queen of France, who is seated on the

Fig. 506. Noble Lady, Henry IV. and V.

left of the picture which shows the presentation. The queen wears a houpeland of sanguin in grain, woven with a gold design and lined with ermine. A black-and-gold belt encircles the waist, the long end hanging behind. The ladies in attendance from left to right wear houpelands of black, blue, purple, blue, vermilion and green, and five of the headdresses are the early type of the HEARTSHAPE HEAD-DRESS (*see* p. 439). (The well-known portrait of Isabeau of Bavaria which shows her wearing a very high headdress, an exaggerated version of this type, is not contemporary, being a work executed between the years 1440 and 1450.) Madame de Pisan is in a blue gown, with a folded linen headdress like those worn by two of the noble ladies.

The interior is worthy of notice.

Fig. 507. Noble Lady, Henry IV. and V.

The stone walls are hung with armorial bearings, the fleur-de-lys of France, and "paly bendy argent and azure" for Bavaria. The bed, canopy, dorsal and couch are in vermilion, with the arms of France and Bavaria "per pale" blazoned on lozenges. A bed of this period usually had curtains at the head, as well as two at the feet, which latter were kept rolled up in the daytime as seen in the illustration. The rafters are alternately vermilion and green. Observe the window, with the frames open at the bottom, and the shutters only open at the top; the chair, cushions, carpet, and, last but not least, the hounds of the period.

It is useful to note here some details of other rooms occupied by the aristocracy of a slightly later period. Cardinal Beaufort, who died at Winchester in 1447, bequeathed the hangings of his State chamber at his house in Waltham Forest to Queen Margaret. They were of cloth of gold of Damascus, and probably considered at the time an original scheme for room decoration. In the reign of Edward IV. it is told that the royal apartments at Windsor and Westminster were hung on State occasions with cloth-of-gold arras, and that the floors were covered with rich Oriental rugs, and carpets of velvet. The chief article of furniture in the principal living-room of the great was the "dressoir" arranged in tiers, the greatest number for a king or queen being five, and these were garnished with magnificent gold plate, including the "drageoir" or comfit-dish full of sweetmeats for the entertainment of visitors, covered with a fine napkin, all laid out on linen cloths embroidered with gold. Edward IV. occupied at Windsor a bed "upholded" in cloth of gold, with the royal arms embroidered on the dorsal. The counterpane was also of gold cloth, lined with ermine, and the sheets and pillow-cases of the finest Rennes cloth. The bedding was stuffed with feathers.

Fig. 508. Border

SECTION II.—HENRY V. 1413–1422

Nobility—Men

Henry V. was born at Monmouth in 1388; knighted by Richard II. in 1399; Knight of the Bath, 1399; crowned, April 1413.

In appearance he had a comely oval face, long straight nose, dark brown eyes, and smooth hair, with a fresh ruddy complexion. Fig. 509 is drawn from his portrait which, although pronounced an early sixteenth-century painting, carries out the contemporary description. In figure he was tall and slender, well-proportioned and stoutly knit. He was active and took a keen pleasure in all manly sports. As a general he

surpassed all his contemporaries, and was considerate for the welfare
of his soldiers, sharing all their hardships and encouraging them by his

conspicuous valour. Temperate and frugal in private
life, he was generous and courteous, though brusque,
straightforward and brief in speech. In dealing with
others he made it a point of honour to be affable
to all men. "He was in his youth a diligent follower
of idle practices, much given to instruments of
music, and fired with the torches of Venus herself,"
so Elmham says. Reading and music were his chief
recreations, particularly the harp. He was also a
composer, and took great delight in church music,
which he played on the organ.

Fig. 509. Henry V.

Henry V. married in June 1420, Catherine, daughter of Charles VI.
of France and Isabeau of Bavaria. The king died of dysentery at Bois
Vincennes on 31 August, 1422, and was buried in Westminster Abbey.

Henry forsook the riotous behaviour for which he was notorious
in youth when he ascended the throne, and he gave up the company
of the plebeian associates, familiarity with whom had been the outcome
of his poverty. Henceforth he devoted himself to the kingdom and its
enlargement. The war with France forced him to raise money; this he
did by pawning the royal gold plate and jewellery, personal sacrifices
which he made in order that his soldiers should receive pay, rather than
applying for pecuniary assistance to his Parliament. Military preoccupa-
tion required so much attention from king and people that there was
no time to think of new clothes; and therefore very few interesting
details of costume are associated with this reign of nine years.
One of the most important functions of which we have any record was
the reception of Henry V. by the citizens of London after the Battle of
Agincourt, when "the Mayr of London was redy bown, with alle the
Craftes of that Cite, alle clothyd in red through out the Town" (Lydgate). Henry, mounted upon his palfrey (probably the "small grey horse"
which he rode on the battlefield), was robed on this occasion in a riding
houpeland (see Fig. 351) of purple velvet, and may have worn golden
greaves upon his legs, according to the mode still in fashion mentioned
in the description of that figure. A new crown set with jewels was upon
his head.

When Henry took Rouen in 1419 and made his State entry into the
city, "he was followed by a page mounted on a beautiful horse, bearing
a lance, at the end of which, near the point, was fastened a fox's brush
by way of a streamer, which afforded great matter of remark among
the wiseheads."

Peace between England and France was restored in 1420 and "Fair
Catherine and most fair" became the queen of Henry V. At his marriage
Henry is said to have worn a complete suit of gold armour. In Fig. 511

HENRY V. AND COURT

he is shown wearing a houpeland of velvet, with wide sleeves which are lined with fur and almost touch the ground, the edges being dagged. It is confined at the waist by a belt from which hang gold bells. His undergarment consists of a paltock with tight sleeves, though the high collar is the only part seen. He wears a necklace and crown, and the hair is dressed after the peculiar fashion of the time, which recalls that of the Norman Period. This is shown to better advantage in Fig. 512. This nobleman, the Duke of Bedford (a portrait taken from an illuminated MS.), wears a houpeland of velvet, with full sleeves like Fig. 498, gathered into cuffs of fur at the wrists; a loose belt with a falling end encircles the waist. The collar is described under Fig. 515. In the *Bedford Book of Hours*, dated 1423, the duke, then Regent of France, is shown wearing a houpeland with wide long open sleeves. His dress and that of the duchess are of brocade of the same pattern and colour (*see* p. 394). The duke's houpeland is lined and has a square turned-down collar of grey squirrel, "gris," like that shown in Fig. 511. It is worn over a black velvet tunic or pourpoint, confined by a crimson velvet belt low down at the waist. This type of costume was worn by noblemen, not in the prime of life, for at least the first twenty years of Henry VI.'s reign.

The tunic and sleeves worn by Fig. 513—Richard, Earl of Cambridge, father of Richard, Duke of York, the Protector—are of the same colour and material, and the high collar of the paltock shows at the neck. The ornamentation on the shoulders is formed of leaf-shaped pieces of metal depending from crescents hung by chains from a band on the shoulders. The twisted gold necklace or collar is studded with pearls and precious stones, and the waist-belt is of gold lattice-work, from which an embroidered purse and dagger were sometimes hung. In this portrait of the earl, taken from an illuminated MS., he is wearing his hair flowing and cut level with the chin, confined by a very fine jewelled circlet. He evidently did not approve of the new fashion of hairdressing which was now all the rage. The hose are of different colours and so are the ankle-boots.

A young French nobleman is represented in an illuminated MS., dating about 1410–1415, wearing metal shoulder ornaments similar to those just described. He is dressed in a dagged houpeland and hood, both precisely as shown in Fig. 351.

The costumes shown in Figs. 498, 499, 500, 501, 502 and 503 of the preceding reign were also worn in this, but the latest style is shown in Fig. 515, the costume of a gentleman and the fashion usually worn by the upper middle classes during the reign of Henry V. The houpeland has almost disappeared and is replaced by a gown fitting the shoulders, its slight fullness being caught in at the waist by a belt and hanging to the ankles in few folds. At the sides vertical openings give freedom to the legs. The sleeves are a familiar detail, and the neck-opening, cut in a V in front, has a shaped collar of fur which narrows to points at the bottom of the V and shows the upstanding collar of the pourpoint inside. The gown was usually made of cloth, but when worn by the nobility might be of silk or velvet, and in each case trimmed with fur. This gentleman carries a curiously-shaped hat in his hand.

Plate XXI. B is a photograph of an illumination in a MS. now in Corpus Christi College, Cambridge, and shows Henry V. seated on a throne under a blue canopy fringed with gold and powdered with gold SS. The king wears a crimson houpeland lined with miniver, with a falling square collar of the same fur; his belt, from which hang gold bells on chains, has been described under Fig. 511. His tunic is green and hose black, and he wears the Garter round his left leg. The picture shows the presentation to the king of a French translation of Cardinal Bonaventura's *Life of Christ* by John de Galopes. The translator wears a doctor's robe of light purple. Two ecclesiastics stand at the king's left hand. One is thought to be Louis, Cardinal of Luxemburg, Chancellor of France, afterwards Archbishop of Rouen, and perpetual administrator of the Diocese of

Fig. 515. Gentleman, Henry V.

Ely. He died in 1443, and is buried in Ely Cathedral. The courtier on the king's left might be the Duke of Exeter, uncle of the king. He wears a green tunic, parti-coloured hose white and red, and holds a mace of office. The wall-hangings are of blue-and-gold arras, the carpet green, white, black and gold, and Henry's feet rest on a red-and-gold cushion.

When the King and Queen of England were in Paris they held their Court at the Louvre, and "it is impossible to detail its magnificence or that of the princes who attended them. The French nobility came from all parts to do them honour, with the utmost humility." The King and Queen of France resided at the Hôtel de S. Pol, "but their state was very different, for the King of France was poorly and meanly served compared with the pomp with which he used to keep open court in former times, and attended only by some old servants and persons of low degree, which must have been very disgusting."

Details of the funeral procession of Henry V. are given by the historian Monstrelet as follows:

The body of King Henry was carried in great pomp, attended by the English princes, his household, and a multitude of other people, to the church of Notre Dame in Paris, where a solemn service was performed; after which it was conveyed to Rouen in the same state, where it remained for a considerable time.

The royal coffin was placed within a car drawn by four large horses, having on its top a representation of the deceased monarch, of boiled leather, elegantly painted, with a rich crown of gold on the head: in his right hand a sceptre, in his left hand a golden ball, with his face looking to the heavens. Over the bed on which this representation lay was a coverlid of vermilion silk interwoven with beaten gold. When it passed through any towns, a canopy of silk (like to what is carried over the Host on Corpus Christi Day) was borne over it. In this state, and attended by his princes and the knights of his household, did the funeral proceed from Rouen straight to Abbeville; the procession proceeded to Hesdin, and thence to Montrieul, Boulogne, and Calais. During the whole way there were persons on either side of the car, dressed in white, carrying lighted torches: behind it were his household clothed in black, and after them his relatives in tears, and dressed in mourning. At about a league distance followed the queen, with a numerous attendance. From Calais they embarked for Dover, and, passing through Canterbury and Rochester, arrived at London on Martinmas Day.

When the funeral approached London, fifteen bishops dressed *in pontificalibus*, several mitred abbots and churchmen, with a multitude of persons of all ranks, came out to meet it. The churchmen chanted the service for the dead as it passed over London Bridge, through Lombard Street to St. Paul's Cathedral. Near the car were the relations of the late king uttering loud lamentations. On the collar of the first horse that drew the car were emblazoned the ancient arms of England: on that of the second, the arms of France and England quartered, the same as he bore during his lifetime; on that of the third, the arms of France simply. On that of the fourth horse were painted the arms of the noble King Arthur, whom no one could conquer: there were three crowns or, on a shield azure. When the funeral service had been royally performed in the cathedral, the body was carried to be interred at Westminster Abbey with the kings his ancestors. At this funeral, and in regard to everything concerning it, greater pomp and expense were made than had been done for two hundred years at the interment of any king of England; and even now, as much honour and reverence is daily paid to his tomb, as if it were certain he was a saint in paradise.

Nobility—Women

Catherine of Valois, born on 27 October, 1401, at the Hôtel de S. Pol, was the youngest of Charles VI.'s daughters. In early youth her mind was set on being queen of England, an idea suggested by the wooing of her eldest sister Isabella (widow of Richard II.) by her hero Henry V., whom Isabella rejected for the Duke of Orleans. As early as 1413 Henry IV. sent Edward, Duke of York, on a private mission to demand the Princess Catherine in marriage for his son. The following year Henry V. demanded her hand, together with an enormous dowry, which, being refused, he determined to win by the sword. The marriage was celebrated at S. Peter's, Troyes, in June 1420, and the following year the king and queen made a great progress throughout England. Their only child, Henry, was born on 6 December, 1421, and in less than a year Queen Catherine was left a widow. At some date unknown she married as her second husband, Owen Tudor,[1] son of Meredith ap

---

[1] The cradle of this race of kings who ruled England for 118 years can be seen to-day but half a dozen miles across the bare hills of Anglesey. It is the farmhouse of Permynyd, where still stand the ancient gateway and the walls of the hall, with its great chimney-piece decorated with their family coat of arms: "gules a chevron between three helmets argent," for Tudor (*see* Fig. 516).

Tudor and the Lady Margaret, daughter and co-heiress of Thomas ap Llewelyn, Lord of South Wales. This marriage was kept secret for some time, but was tacitly acknowledged in 1428. The young man who so captivated Catherine belonged to a family celebrated for the comely and handsome appearance of its menfolk. He had fought as a common soldier in a Welsh band, and had received preferment as squire of the body to Henry V., which office he retained under the infant king, Henry VI. Later he was appointed head of the guard at Windsor, and also clerk of the wardrobe. In this latter capacity it was his duty to guard the queen's jewels and to superintend the purchasing of materials, etc., for her costumes. Although friendly disposed towards his stepfather, Henry VI. never officially recognised his marriage, and the early death of Queen Catherine at Bermondsey in 1437 (she was buried with royal state in Westminster Abbey) was a great misfortune for the Tudor family of three sons and a daughter.

Fig. 516. Arms of Tudor

CHILDREN OF CATHERINE AND OWEN TUDOR

Edmund of Hadham, created Earl of Richmond by Henry VI. in 1453; married Margaret, daughter and co-heiress of John, first Duke of Somerset, great-granddaughter of John of Gaunt. He died in 1455, aged 20, leaving an infant son, afterwards Henry VII.

Jasper Tudor, created Earl of Pembroke; d.s.p. 1493.

Another son lived and died a monk at Westminster.

Tacina Tudor, married Reginald, Lord Grey de Wilton.

After the death of their mother these children remained until 1440 under the protection of Katherine de la Pole, sister of the Duke of Suffolk, and Abbess of Barking. The father was placed in Newgate, but escaped, and later appeared suddenly before the Privy Council then sitting at Kennington Palace. He defended himself with such spirit and manliness that the king pardoned his "offences," and Owen returned to Wales. His next appearance was at the Battle of Wakefield, where he and his son Jasper fought under the Lancastrian banner. At Mortimer's Cross they were defeated; Jasper retreated, but Owen stood firm and was taken prisoner with some others of his kinsmen and comrades, the Lloyds and Howels. They were taken to Hereford, and, in the market-place of that city, were all executed, 1461.

Armorial bearings were still used on costume, especially on Court dress. The fleur-de-lys is seen on the queen's mantle in Fig. 510, and the lady in attendance has her husband's coat of arms and her own embroidered on the sideless gown.

Queen Catherine wears a gold network caul (*see* Fig. 613 A) over the ears, surmounted by a veil; the crown, quite simple in comparison with that worn by Queen Joanna in Fig. 505, is separate, and put on over the veil; otherwise the two costumes are identical in most details. The headdress of Fig. 514 is of the end of the reign; it appeared in France in 1420, and remained in fashion only ten years. The principal part consists of some rich material, cross-barred with gold and studded with jewels, with a deep border on the upper edge. It resembles the opening valves of a shell, the cavity at the top being filled by the billowing folds of the voluminous veil, which hangs half-way down the back. Little or no hair is visible, and a stiffened muslin under-veil hangs round the back of the head, and curves up to the ornament over the forehead; sometimes this part was not worn, but a huge wing of gauze, like a butterfly, was folded instead round the back of the head, leaving the face unshaded (*see* Fig. 616 B).

XV d.

Fig. 517. Border

Section III.—Peers' Parliamentary Robes of the Fifteenth Century

(Written in collaboration with G. Ambrose Lee, Esq., C.B., C.V.O., Clarenceux King-of-Arms)

"Peers" is derived from the Latin, *pares* = equals, and the word was always so used in Norman and early Plantagenet days. The earliest record of its use in the sense of denoting members of the baronage is contained in records of proceedings against the Despensers in 1321, and since that date a restricted use of the word, denoting membership of the Upper House of the "Parliament Chamber," in which all are politically equal, has remained its commonly accepted sense.

The exact origin and the earlier stages of development of the British Parliament have long been, and continue to be, subjects of much acrimonious controversy. Some writers claim for it an almost immemorial antiquity, but for the purpose of this work it is unnecessary to go into the merits of the question, and we therefore may confine ourselves to the general statement that the Parliament assembled at the "Full Parliament" of 1265 was as representative of the various classes of the kingdom, practically speaking, as the Houses of Lords and Commons in the beginning of the eighteenth century. So far back as the thirteenth century it would appear unlikely that any special ceremonial costume was used to distinguish the members of this assembly, with the possible exception of those officials who supervised and directed its proceedings. No details of such costumes, however, have been preserved. Indeed, thirteenth-century illuminated MSS. show that barons attended Parliament in armour, with their armorial bearings displayed on their surcotes.

In the following century—the fourteenth—a regular system of official costumes, of definite cut and colouring, and marked in a special manner to indicate different ranks, appears to have been evolved in the neighbouring kingdom of France, and in due course to have been adapted for use in this country, and formed the nucleus of the English system which in essentials has survived to the present day. When exactly such adaptations began has not been ascertained, but the reign of Richard II. may be taken as the earliest, and that of Henry IV. as the latest, probable date of the establishment of special ceremonial costumes for the peers of this country. The earliest form of such robes would appear to have been a plain circular cloke or mantle, having in the centre an opening for the head, and the sides caught up by the arms on either side, exactly similar to the manner in which the paenula was worn. Early French robes of this description were marked at the shoulder or shoulders with bars of contrasting colour and material, to indicate differences in the rank of the wearers; and in some cases, where an addition to the plain mantle in the form of a hood was made, these bars were shown on the hood instead of on the mantle itself. The addition of a hood to be drawn up on the head when required, either separate from or attached to the mantle, early became necessary, and thus with some minor adjustments we arrive at the two varieties of peers' robes still in actual use in England. The three estates of the realm are known as Lords Spiritual, Lords Temporal (originally military, as having the Lieutenancy of England and Wales committed to their charge), and Commons. The Parliament robes of the temporal peers, according to the earliest account which has survived, were as follows:

Fig. 518.
Early form of Peers' Robes

The first example of costume bearing anything in the nature of a distinguishing indication of noble rank is found in an illuminated MS.

dating 1396–1407. Fig. 518 represents this forerunner of what came later to be known as "Peers' robes." Froissart says that "at the corona-tion of Henry IV. the lords put on houpelands of scarlet with long mantles over them." The houpeland was the fashionable garment at that time, and the name was frequently applied to the surcote shown in Fig. 338 and described under the Order of the Garter. The mantle was of the shape then in vogue, such as is seen in Fig. 318, but without the elaborate decoration. These two garments are shown in Fig. 518—a drawing reconstructed from that of a nobleman in the illuminated MS. just mentioned. He wears a scarlet surcote, with open sleeves edged with white fur, and over it a circular mantle of scarlet fastened on the right shoulder. A scarlet hood lined and edged with white fur is thrown back off the head, with the liripipe (from this time frequently referred to as the tippet) hanging down the back.

Fig. 519. A Marquess

Figures on the Chantry of Henry V. at Westminster Abbey supply the earliest representations of robes bearing GUARDS or bars to denote the specific grade of peerage to which the wearers belong. Fig. 519 shows a peer—a marquess —of the fifteenth century, in his Robes of Estate. The surcote of scarlet cloth is open up the front, and girded with a sash of blue silk knotted in front. The sleeves are moderately wide at the wrists (about twenty inches in circumference) and the garment is lined with white fur—miniver—which shows at the edges. The hood, cut like Fig. 337, also of scarlet cloth and

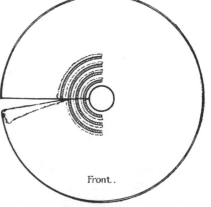

Front.

Fig. 520. Diagram of Peer's Mantle

lined with white fur, is worn on top of the surcote, and the mantle over it, with the liripipe or tippet of the hood falling down the back outside. The shape of the scarlet cloth mantle with its three and a half guards for a marquess is given in Fig. 520. The headgear is described on p. 385.

The mantle of scarlet cloth is a complete circle with a hole in the centre for the head, and is slit from the neck to the hem. It is similar to the cloke illustrated in Fig. 295, except that there are no openings for the hands and that "bars" have been added. This mantle was worn in the fashionable manner of the fourteenth century, fastened upon the right shoulder, leaving the right arm free. The left side was draped over the left arm.

About the first quarter of the fifteenth century, marks distinguishing the rank of the wearer were introduced in the form of guards or bars placed upon the top half (back and front) of the right side of the mantle. These guards were of gold lace (braid) about one and a half inches in width, each set above a narrow band of miniver.

> A Duke had four guards.
> A Marquess had three and a half.
> An Earl had three.
> A Viscount had two and a half (title created 1440).
> A Baron had two.

In the setting out of the mantle of a marquess and a viscount the half-guard starts at the middle of the back and ends at the opening for the arm; consequently, seen from behind, a marquess might pass for a duke, likewise a viscount for an earl, affording yet another example of the fact that many may present a more distinguished appearance from behind than in front!

During the fifteenth century the parliamentary mantles of dukes, marquesses and earls were of purple (violet) velvet, lined with ermine, worn over silk surcotes of the same colour, confined by girdles or sashes of blue silk tied in front, slightly to the left.

Dukes carried a "verge" or rod of gold, about six feet long.

Peers' robes of the reign of Henry VI. were completed with the addition of the fashionable chaperon, made of scarlet cloth or crimson velvet, and it is to be noted that all peers wore this headgear when sitting in the "Parliament Chamber." In the reign of Edward IV. the chaperon gave place to the new style of headgear then in vogue (see p. 436).

A coronet worn at investitures or coronations was originally a plain gold circlet set in a cap of scarlet velvet lined and turned up with miniver, and had no distinctive design. Later, in an illuminated MS. of the reign of Henry VI., a group of peers is shown, and they wear two kinds of coronets. Some are as shown in Fig. 645, others wear similar coronets without the balls. Towards the end of the fifteenth century some peers wore coronets composed of circular discs, and others had the discs surmounted by points as seen in Fig. 646. It was not until early in the sixteenth century that peers' coronets were regulated in design. The modern series of peers' coronets, ranging according to rank from a duke's eight strawberry leaves to a baron's six pearls, was not introduced until later in the century, and, indeed, was not finally settled until the middle of the sixteenth century.

Dukes, marquesses and earls had, formerly, at their installation or creation, a sword put over their shoulders or girt about them which viscounts and barons had not. Dukes and marquesses are styled "Princes," and all other peers "Lords."

The parliamentary mantles worn by the Archbishops of Canterbury and York were complete circles of scarlet cloth, lined with miniver and having a hole in the centre for the head, and a vertical slit about twenty-four inches in length midway between the neck and hem in front. (This type of mantle, in scarlet cloth, was also worn by Doctors of Divinity of the University of Cambridge until the eighteenth century.)

A few details regarding the quantity of materials used for making the robes of peers and peeresses for the coronation of Richard III., taken from a royal wardrobe account dated 28 June, 1483, are given below. It should be remembered that all peers and members of the royal household received these materials at the expense of the royal wardrober, who, on this occasion, was Piers Courteys. This custom, of course, was in use from early times; *see* p. 147 of this volume.

"To the mooste Reverend Fader in God, Lorde Thomas (Bourchier) Archiebysshop of Canterbury and Cardynall of England, for to have for his liveree of clothyng agenst the saide mooste noble coronation of our sayde Souveraine Lord the Kyng xviii yerds of scarlet, and xviii yerds of grene damask."

The length allowed to peers varied according to their rank. A duke had twelve yards of crimson velvet for the mantle, besides eight yards of cloth of gold and eight of black velvet.

A duchess or a countess was allowed six and a quarter yards of blue velvet purfiled (lined) with six yards of crimson cloth of gold "for a long gown," and six yards of crimson velvet purfiled with six yards of white cloth of gold. Besides these materials the official allowance for a duchess or countess included "a tymbr di' of ermyn bakks, a tymbr di' of ermyn wombes, and xxxiiij tymbr di' wombes of menyver pure."

Fig. 521. Border, early fifteenth century

Section IV.—Henry VI. 1422–1461

Nobility—Men

Henry VI. was born at Windsor in 1421; crowned at Westminster in 1429 by Archbishop Chicheley; crowned at Notre Dame, Paris, in 1432 by Cardinal Beaufort.

In appearance Henry was "tall of stature and slender of body, whereunto all his members were proportionately correspondent, of comely visage, wherein did glisten his bountifulness of disposition."

The king was fitter for a cloister than the throne.

This monarch was the first to bear the title "Moste Cristen King" and to be styled "Magestee Royall," each king before him being called "Soveraygne Lorde Highness."

Fig. 522. Henry VI.

Fig. 522 is a portrait derived from an illuminated MS. in which he is shown with a pale complexion and light brown hair which he always wore flowing and cut level with the mouth.

Henry VI. married in 1445 at Titchfield Abbey, Margaret, daughter of René, or Regnier, Duke of Anjou and titular King of Sicily, Naples and Jerusalem.

He has the distinction of being the youngest English king on record, ascending the throne in 1422 at eight months old. When he opened his

first Parliament, at the ripe age of twelve months, he was seated upon his mother's knee, enthroned among the Lords. In 1425 the infant king made a progress through the city, held securely on a great white horse. On arriving at Westminster, his mother awaited him seated on the throne in the Great White Hall, and received him on her lap to open his second Parliament. There is no contemporary drawing[1] of this king showing the robes he wore at his coronation in 1429, but there is a MS. illumination of him, aged about eight years, in a psalter made for his use, and in this Henry is represented enveloped

Fig. 523. Henry VI.

in a "cloke of arms" (see p. 327) emblazoned with the arms of France and England, quarterly, on the front and back. In another illuminated

[1] There is one by John Rous; see footnote, p. 324.

MS. he is shown at the age of twelve years, wearing a long robe (*see* Fig. 523). It is similar to the garment shown in Fig. 524 except that it

is ungirded, and although Henry is shown kneeling, the robe of rich brocade, lined with miniver, appears to be very long, as much of it lies upon the ground. He wears a crown similar to that shown in the portrait of his father (Figs. 509 and 641). Another illumination in the same MS. shows Henry at the same age, wearing a houpeland of cloth of gold, with sleeves gathered at the wrists into white fur cuffs; and over it a mantle of white velvet, lined with ermine, and having a cape and hood of the same fur. The crown is the same in all these portraits.

Fig. 524 is taken from a fifteenth-century illuminated MS. by John Lydgate, representing S. Eadmund (ninth century) dressed in the manner appropriate to a king of the artist's time (1420–1440). The king wears a gown or houpeland of a familiar shape with sleeves such as were in fashion during Henry IV.'s reign (*see* Fig. 498). The brocade of which the gown is made has a diagonal stripe: black with a white feather design on it, and vermilion with a white flower pattern. It is edged with white fur. The cape bears

Fig. 524.
A King, *temp.* Henry VI.

a similar feather design, and is lined and bordered with ermine; the hood is turned back to show the lining. A pouch, of a new shape, hangs from the belt which encircles the waist, and a crown of simple design is worn.

Fig. 525 represents a nobleman of the same period, wearing a houpeland almost exactly like the one just described. It is not quite so long and the brocade is of white and red stripes with a black design. The cape is omitted, and the new-fashioned headgear is worn.

The Chaperon

The hood, and the variety of ways in which it was worn, has been described on p. 213, and illustrations of costumes worn in the reigns of Edward II., Edward III., Richard II., Henry IV. and Henry V.

Fig. 525. Noble, Henry VI.

show many of the fantastic arrangements adopted by the fashionable and by ordinary men. Although this style of headgear had been in use for nearly a hundred years, it was not easy to manipulate, especially that part which formed the cap, as it was frequently removed from the head and carried over the shoulder. At last someone's patience gave out, and it was converted into a fixed article of headgear. The shoulder part and liripipe of the hood were cut off, and the material of the head part used to make a circular padded roll, like a miniature motor tyre, the inside fitting the head, leaving the crown uncovered (*see* at A, Fig. 526—a diagram of this headgear looked at from below). To the inside of this roll was fixed the portion of the cape which normally encircled the neck. The cape itself was frequently exaggerated in shape and size (*see* at B). The liripipe was attached to the roll, generally at the side (*see* C); an ornament, D, fixed to the front of the roll, and the headgear was complete. In wear, the cape portion was folded and thrown to one side, covering the crownless roll as shown in Figs. 525, 528 and 533. This development of the hood took place about the year 1420, and was called "the Chaperon." It was a French idea originated

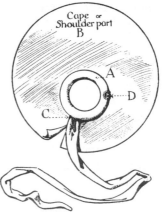

Fig. 526. Diagram of Chaperon

by the citizens of Paris, and was copied about the same time by the Italians, but one does not find an example worn in England during the reign of Henry V. It is represented, worn by the Duke of Bedford, made Regent of France in 1422, in his *Book of Hours*, a French work dated 1423. Fig. 528, which represents an English nobleman, is taken from an English illuminated MS. of about 1430, and is perhaps the earliest record of the chaperon worn in this country. Another example worn in the same manner is shown in Fig. 525 of about the same date. Fig. 529 shows the way it was carried over one shoulder by the liripipe, which was often draped across the chest, its end hanging over the opposite shoulder. In Fig. 533 (dating 1440) the cape part sticks up a little more than earlier, and, as was quite usual, the edge is dagged. It was frequently lined (as of old; *see* Plate XIII.) with a contrasting colour. A rich gold ornament or brooch, such as is seen in Fig. 651, was worn attached to the front of the roll.

After 1450 the liripipe gradually lost its original tubular shape, becoming simply a long scarf, which was sometimes cut in dagges as shown in Fig. 535. The liripipe to the chaperon worn in Fig. 537 is a piece of the same material, about eight or nine feet long, cut at the free end as an obtuse-angled triangle, the acute end being fixed at the side, *inside* the roll. The smartest way of wearing this piece of material was to drape it gracefully across the chest and on to the shoulder, where it was often fixed by a jewelled brooch, the remaining long end floating behind (Fig. 537). Another way was to pass it under the chin (in the manner of the barbette of the early fourteenth century), on to the opposite side of the roll, and over the top of the head, whence it hung down at the side. This arrangement was sometimes worn by Philippe, Duke of Burgundy. In Plate XXII. he has the liripipe passed close round his neck and over the left shoulder.

It was the mode to arrange the cape part, B, as an upstanding fan (see Fig. 537). When the chaperon was made of soft silk, this effect was achieved by the insertion of stiffening, usually parchment, or wires.

The chaperon was much in vogue in England during the whole of the reign of Henry VI. and on the Continent at the same time. It was also used as official headgear, but by the year 1483 it had ceased to be worn as a fashionable item of civil dress, remaining in use only as part of the robes of the Orders of the Garter (see p. 238) and of the Golden Fleece.

Many of the figures on Henry V.'s Chantry are wearing the chaperon, accounted for by the fact that this work was begun in 1422 and finished about 1431, a time when this headgear was coming into fashion in England.

Italian XV

Fig. 527. Border

During the minority of Henry VI. (1422–1440), the style of costume worn, first seen in Fig. 515, was less fantastic than that in use among the fashionable for the first twenty years of the fifteenth century. But later a strong Italian influence on fashions was apparent among the French nobility, as a consequence of intercourse dictated by the Duke of Orleans' [1] hope of succeeding to the Duchy of Milan on the death of his uncle, Filippo Maria Visconti (1447). This hope did not mature, but these relations, nevertheless, had their effect upon French and English costume.

Fig. 528 shows an English noble wearing a surcote similar to, though less exaggerated than, that described under Fig. 500. It is also identical with that worn by the Italian nobility of this date, and is to be found represented in many paintings by Italian artists of this epoch (Fig. 531 gives a diagram of the cut of this garment, which in shape is a circular

---

[1] This was Charles (1391–1466), son of Louis, Duke of Orleans, before mentioned. He was captured after Agincourt, and imprisoned at Groombridge, Kent, obtaining his release in 1439. He married as his third wife Mary of Cleves, and their son became later King Louis XII. After his disappointment in 1447, Charles retired to his Castle of Blois, and devoted himself to the writing of poetry, in which he excelled.

cloke and front panel combined). The noble is wearing the latest style in headgear, called the chaperon.

Another young English noble is shown in Fig. 530 wearing a garment

Fig. 528.

Fig. 529.

Fig. 530.

Three Nobles, Henry VI.

shaped like Fig. 532, with the bottom edge of the pleated skirt decorated by dagges of a new design. Each one overlaps the other, which helps to accentuate the flared effect of the skirt. The sleeves, however, are the latest fashion and resemble deep and wide hanging bags with vertical openings for the arms. Much abuse was hurled at these new sleeves, which were written of as "the devil's receptacles," because they conveniently held anything that was stowed away in them; whatever was stolen could be secreted in their ample recesses, and for this reason they were called POKY SLEEVES. Fig. 529 gives a back view of the same garment showing how the

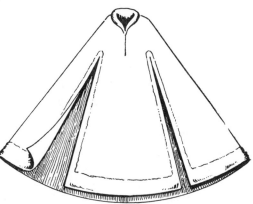

Fig. 531. Diagram of Cloke-Tunic

ends were sometimes finished off, either with a hole bound with fur or material through which the hand could be passed, or else with a large button, such as is sometimes seen at the end of a bolster. The skirt of this garment is longer than that in Fig. 530 and extends to below the knees.

Tunics in fashion in Western Europe and Italy at this period were

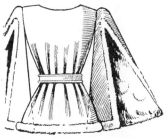

frequently cut as shown in Fig. 532. They fitted the shoulders and widened out towards the hem, where they finished about knee-level; the fullness, confined by the girdle, formed a regular-pleated short skirt. The sleeves were cut funnel-shape, having a vertical slit up the front, and were fixed into the armholes with few if any gathers or pleats.

Fig. 532. Diagram of Tunic

A fashionable young man of about 1440 is shown in Fig. 533. The tunic is shorter than that in Fig. 529, and drawn in to the natural waist-line; the skirt, slit up the sides, sometimes to the hip, at others to the waist, still takes a moderate flare. The neck-opening and collar are similar to those seen in Fig. 515.

The sleeves are not exaggerated. They are full and pleated into the armholes and at the wrist. A padded band of fur usually outlined the skirt, neck and wrists. This young man is wearing the fully-developed chaperon evolved from the older "draped hood" (*see* Fig. 351) and its prototype, the hood proper (*see* Fig. 298 B).

The drawing, Fig. 534, represents Henry VI. as he appeared on various State occasions between the years 1445 and 1453. He wears a long robe, the houpeland, of purple velvet with wide open sleeves, lined with ermine. The robe is confined at the waist by a gold belt set with rubies and diamonds and having a long pendent end. A semicircular or semi-oval mantle of the same materials is worn, together with an ermine cape and hood, fastened by a jewelled ornament. Over the cape is worn a handsome collar and pendant cross of jewels. The headgear, peculiar to this king, is the French BONET (*see* p. 435) of purple velvet with an ermine brim, "void"

Fig. 533.
Fashionable Man, Henry VI.

at the front, revealing the crown set inside it. On full State occasions Henry wore the crown shown in Fig. 642.

In the illuminated MS. presented by the Earl of Shrewsbury to

Margaret of Anjou, Henry VI. is represented in State robes similar to those just described, but in different colours. He wears a blue mantle over a heliotrope houpeland, and a crown without a cap.

Although always well dressed in a seemly manner, considering his position Henry VI. was very economical in the matter of his costume. His impoverished circumstances compelled him to pawn most of his jewels and household plate to provide the essentials for his marriage and the coronation of his queen in 1445.

This same year, when Henry VI. gave an audience at Westminster Palace, he was attired in a long robe or houpeland of vermilion cloth of gold. As each ambassador presented his credentials, on one knee, the king put his hand to his chaperon and slightly raised it, saying in a soft

Fig. 534. Henry VI.

tone, "S. John, thanks! Great thanks to S. John." On the following day at an audience in his privy chamber the king was dressed in a long robe of black velvet. Both this robe and the houpeland of vermilion cloth of gold were shaped like those worn by Henry VI. in Fig. 534, and were probably lined with ermine, miniver or sable.

But such magnificence was not to last. Henry was in such reduced circumstances in the year 1459 that when he bestowed the only gift in his power—his best robe—on the Prior of S. Albans Abbey as a recompense for hospitality received during his Easter sojourn, his treasurer, well knowing the poverty of the royal wardrobe was such that Henry had no other garment for State occasions, privily redeemed it for fifty marks.

In his most dire distress one may picture the saintly king attired like the humble man shown in Fig. 594, mounted on a broken-down

Fig. 535. Shorter Tunic

horse, with his feet tied to the stirrups, and an abusive placard fixed to his shoulders. So was he conducted to the Tower in 1465.

Fig. 539 gives an excellent example of Court dress worn during the greater part of the fifteenth century. It represents Talbot, Earl of Shrewsbury, offering his book, *Fais d'Alisandre*, to Queen Margaret, about 1445. His costume is similar to that shown in Fig. 533, but the earl's tunic is made of brocade—a blue ground woven with a gold design. Over this is worn a houpeland of sanguin in grain, lined with

Fig. 536. English Noble   Fig. 537. French Noble   Fig. 538. Henry VI.
THE LONG ROBE

sable and powdered with a hundred garters in blue and gold. These are not worn as part of the insignia of the Order of the Garter—it was the custom for knights to appear at Court sometimes wearing garments decorated with the badge. The scarlet chaperon, carried over the left shoulder, is unadorned except for a jewel and pendant pearl in front. It was not unusual for the chaperon also to be powdered with garters.

In Fig. 535 one sees the newest style in vogue about 1450. The tunic or cotte had become so short in the skirt that it was frequently alluded to, first, as the petticotte, and later as the pourpoint, which it much resembled. The original paltock, worn underneath, to which the collar and undersleeves were attached, was now called the "Dubblet."

The chief feature of this pourpoint is its brevity; the shoulders of the sleeves are showing the first signs of padding.

At the same time, in France the long robe was revived, but quite different in nature from the houpeland. It was introduced into England about 1460. Fig. 536 gives the first version. This robe was made to fit the chest, back, and under the arms, the material being fixed into three padded folds or tucks, diminishing in size from the shoulder to the waist, then gradually widening to the bottom of the robe. The superfluous material inside the seams of these folds was cut away to make the garment fit better. The same arrangement of folds was repeated at the back. Fastenings of the robe—hooks and eyes—were disguised under the first fold on the left-hand side, and at first it opened from the shoulder to the waist. No belt was worn with this close-fitting robe, as it was considered that the presence of a belt might discredit the perfect tailoring it required. A cord to carry the dagger or pouch was sometimes slung loosely round the waist. The sleeves were large at the armhole, and padded, descending well on to the hand and fairly close-fitting. The mode demanded wide shoulders, slender waists and hips, and the skirt part as narrow as possible. It did not take the fashionable Frenchman long to exaggerate this mode, and Fig. 537 shows the extraordinary effect of increasing the width of the shoulders by padding the sleeves; and to prevent this padding from being displaced it was quilted at right angles to the shoulders. These robes, of less eccentric form, were adopted by fashionable young Englishmen. Henry VI. is represented in an illuminated MS. dating about 1455–1460 wearing this long robe in a modified style, and in addition a belt with long end round the waist and a pouch slung from it by a cord (Fig. 538).

Nobility—Women

Margaret of Anjou was born at Pont-à-Mousson in 1429, the daughter of René and of Isabella of Lorraine, "a woman of commanding talents, great personal endowments and conjugal tenderness."

Margaret's beauty was famous, and Henry VI. sent an embassy, headed by the Marquess of Suffolk, with an offer of marriage, which was accepted. The princess was conducted to England after some inevitable delay, since it was necessary for the king to convene a special Parliament in order to obtain funds for the expenses of his marriage.

When the new queen landed at Southampton her wardrobe was so scanty that the marquess sent post haste to London for a "tiremaker," "who came into the presence of the Lady Queen for divers affairs touching the said Lady Queen," or, in other words, to supply her deficiencies with the latest English fashions. This entry in a wardrobe account is the first record of the name of an English dressmaker, Margaret Chamberlayne.

The marriage ceremony was performed at Titchfield Abbey on 22 April, 1445, and Margaret was crowned at Westminster "with a degree of royal splendour little suited to the exhausted treasury of her enamoured consort." Two years later she found practically the whole executive power left in her hands, because Henry was much more interested in his studies and his new foundation, Eton College, than in the government of his kingdom; the opportunity thus arose for the partisans of the House of York to attribute the nation's losses in France and Normandy to Margaret's alleged misgovernment.

The birth of her son, Edward, in 1453, gave Margaret an ideal to fight for which her studious husband had not provided, and her conduct during the Wars of the Roses earned for her the praise of Charles, the poet-Duke of Orleans, who said, "No woman surpassed her in beauty, and few men have equalled her in courage." There is no doubt that she was the most important personage on the Lancastrian side during the wars. Throughout all the dangers and trials of civil war, in which the lack of discipline in the Lancastrian army probably lost her the final victory, Margaret never failed in hope and courage, as is shown by the well-known story of her flight from the disastrous field of Hexham. After a more than adventurous journey she arrived at Ecluse (or Sluis) with her son, and seven ladies in attendance, clothed only as befitted peasants, in clokes and hoods, and gowns decidedly the worse for wear, the shape of which can be seen in Fig. 385. The unfortunate queen had no means to procure a new wardrobe until the Duke of Burgundy sent her relief and offered her hospitality. In spite of her sufferings Margaret did not fail in loyalty to her husband. Once, when the Duchess of Burgundy was commiserating with her upon his failings, she replied, "When, on the day of my espousals, I took the rose of England, was I not aware that I must wear it entire, with all its thorns?" With her son, the Red Rose Prince of Wales, and his wife, Anne Nevill (born 1454), daughter of the King-maker, whom he had married at Angers in the preceding year, the queen returned to England accompanied by a fresh army, and arrived at Weymouth the day before the fatal Battle of Barnet, 1471, joining forces with the Lancastrian adherents. With this composite army Margaret met the White Rose at Tewkesbury. Although both Margaret and her son rode from rank to rank of her army encouraging the men, she suffered a decisive defeat. When Margaret saw how the battle went, "she was with difficulty prevented from rushing into the mêlée," but swooning she was carried to a religious house close to the gates of Tewkesbury Park.

Edward, her son, it is said, was taken prisoner by Sir Richard Crofts, who, to win the promised reward of £100 a year for life, brought him to King Edward. When questioned, the prince was rash enough to reply that he had fought to win back his father's crown and his own inheritance, a sufficient pretext for his immediate murder.

Fig. 539.   Fig. 540.

MARGARET OF ANJOU AND TALBOT, EARL OF SHREWSBURY

Margaret was brought to Coventry, where she learnt of the murder of her son. In a transport of passion she cursed the king and all his posterity, with the result that he would have put her to death but for the fact that no Plantagenet had ever shed the blood of a woman.[1] He took her in his triumphal procession to the Tower, together with the Princess of Wales, and that same night Henry VI. was murdered under the same roof.

Fig. 541. Anne, Duchess of Bedford

By arrangement with Louis XI., Margaret was ransomed in 1475, and she returned to France, where she lived in the deepest seclusion, keeping alive the interests of the Lancastrian party for her kinsman, the young Earl of Richmond.

She died at the Château Damprière on 25 August, 1482.

Fig. 541 is a drawing of Anne, Duchess of Bedford, 1423, reconstructed from an illustration in the *Bedford Book of Hours*.[2] It is described in this section because it was the type of costume worn by noble ladies from about 1420 to 1460. The duchess is wearing a houpeland with very long sleeves of cloth of gold brocaded in a design (of which a detail is shown in Fig. 542) in vermilion, shown black, with green leaves, shown hatched, and blue stars with diamond centres. Rubies are used to suggest berries. The houpeland is lined with ermine and has a square turned-down ermine collar; it is girded rather high at the waist by a black-and-gold belt. A

Fig. 542. Detail of Brocade

detail of the headdress will be seen in Fig. 614 B. The richness of the costume, and especially the headdress, is, of course, exceptional, but it

---

[1] A Tudor did!

[2] This book was presented to her nephew, Henry VI., in 1430. She died in 1432.

must be borne in mind that the social position of this lady was of the highest. She was the daughter of Jean sans Peur, Duke of Burgundy, and wife of the renowned Regent of France, and so practically "the first lady in the land," for under the conditions prevailing in France at that time it is doubtful if Queen Isabeau could be said to have retained that status.

A lady-in-waiting depicted in the same *Book of Hours* (Fig. 543) wears a similar houpeland, with wide sleeves dagged in points, of scarlet lined with white fur, with a collar of white fur having another smaller collar of fine linen over it. The undersleeves are black velvet, and so is the waist-belt, which is worked with gold. These belts were excessively long and buckled behind, the long end hanging down the back on to the ground. The headdress is similar in shape to that of the duchess, but carried out in black velvet, gold and rubies. The poky or bagpipe sleeve was sometimes used in a lady's houpeland of this description.

Some authorities maintain that the illuminated MS. presented by Talbot,

Fig. 543. Noble Lady, Henry VI.

Earl of Shrewsbury, to Margaret of Anjou was made in 1445; if so, the queen was then aged sixteen. In the illumination from which Fig. 540 is taken she certainly looks older, despite the fact that her fair yellow hair is flowing over her shoulders—a custom with fifteenth-century queens when wearing a crown. In the original drawing her cote-hardie is of cloth of gold, and the sideless gown, purfiled with ermine, is of blue cloth of gold. A detail to be noticed is that the skirt part of the sideless gown is gathered into the ermine bands. Over the queen's shoulders, fastened in an unusual manner, is a heliotrope mantle edged with a gold band headed by a leaf design, and lined with ermine. The crown is clearly of thirteenth-century design (*see* Fig. 271), but rises to eight points instead of four, the customary four decorated points alternating with plain points. The crown worn on several occasions by this queen is shown in Fig. 644. The sceptre is very similar to that illustrated in Fig. 273. Margaret's badge of a daisy flower in white enamel with red centre is given in Fig. 544.

Fig. 544

Fig. 545 represents the latest fashion in France and England between the years 1445–1455. The gown is a modified houpeland, using less material than heretofore, and consequently there are fewer folds in the skirt, which followed the form of the body and finished in a train.

It cannot be determined with any certainty at what date the body and skirt of the gown were made in separate parts. The houpeland

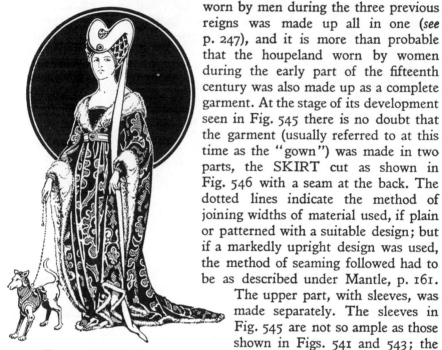

Fig. 545. Noble Lady, 1445–55

worn by men during the three previous reigns was made up all in one (*see* p. 247), and it is more than probable that the houpeland worn by women during the early part of the fifteenth century was also made up as a complete garment. At the stage of its development seen in Fig. 545 there is no doubt that the garment (usually referred to at this time as the "gown") was made in two parts, the SKIRT cut as shown in Fig. 546 with a seam at the back. The dotted lines indicate the method of joining widths of material used, if plain or patterned with a suitable design; but if a markedly upright design was used, the method of seaming followed had to be as described under Mantle, p. 161.

The upper part, with sleeves, was made separately. The sleeves in Fig. 545 are not so ample as those shown in Figs. 541 and 543; the collar has developed into revers, low down on the shoulders, leaving the neck much exposed. At the back, the collar descends in a curved or V line almost to the waist-belt. The portion of the underdress covering the chest is cut circular at the top, and is visible where the points of the collar meet the waist-belt in front. The belt is still worn very long, buckling at the back, the end falling to the ground. The material of this dress may be a silk brocade, or a velvet pattern upon a silk or gold ground, or velvet upon velvet, all of a large design; and the revers, narrow border and sleeve linings are of fur. A variety of headdresses might be worn with this attire, *e.g.* Figs. 614 D, 616 C, 616 D and 619 (2) and (3).

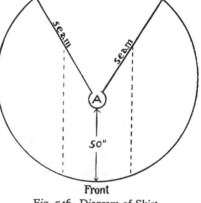

Fig. 546. Diagram of Skirt

A simpler dress worn by a noble lady is seen in Fig. 547. Although of the houpeland variety it is less ample, and illustrates the transitional period. The sleeves are the only feature worth mentioning; they show the gradual diminution in size, and may be contrasted with the preceding figure, and with the later stages illustrated in Plates XXII. and XXIV.

Dresses without belts, fitting close at the waist, were worn by young girls of the upper classes (Fig. 548). They were not cut so low as those worn by their seniors, and were sometimes open up the sides, showing the skirt of the undergarment. In this drawing there is some gold or silk embroidery around the edge of the opening, which is closed for a short interval at thigh-level.

About this time, 1440–1450, fashions in Western Europe were dictated by the Court of Burgundy. Whatever its duchess wore was noted with jealous interest by all ladies with any pretensions to being well dressed. Plate XXII. is an illustration derived from various sources. The head is taken from a contemporary portrait (*circa* 1440) of Isabelle of Portugal in the Musée des Beaux-Arts, Ghent. Madame wears a

Fig. 547. Noble Lady, Henry VI.

dress of gold, silver and black brocade bordered with miniver, cut on lines which did not become fashionable in France until later, nor in England until about 1460. The loose-fitting sleeves show the stage of transition between the long hanging ones of the houpeland (*see* Fig. 541) and the close sleeves seen in Plate XXIV. The headdress is a narrow version of the heart-shape (*see* Figs. 614 B and C), having the roll and short hanging end (an imitation of the liripipe) in black and gold brocade. A band of pearls, edged with pearl drops, ornaments the sides and back of the head in an unusual manner. Another illuminated MS. portrait of this duchess, dated 1454, shows the headdress with double square veils, as illustrated in Figs. 549 and 619 (3).

Fig. 548.
Young Lady, Henry VI.

"1457. For this day Madame the Duchess" (of Burgundy, Isabelle of Portugal) "had put on a quite ROUND DRESS, for at that time she did not wear the silken train (*queue de drap de soye*), nor do I remember whether anyone wore a train." This entry in the diary of the Viscomtesse de Furnes records the advent of a dress without a train; an illustration is shown in Fig. 573. It was in fashion in France and England at a later date.

Fig. 549.

FULL TOILETTE, NOBLE LADY, 1450–60

The full toilette of a lady of fashion between the years 1450–1460 in England or France is illustrated in Fig. 549. Her neck, shoulders and back are bare. The gown might be made in silk, velvet or brocade: the colour indicated in the original illuminated MS. is pale green. It consists of a body part with sleeves, and a skirt. Fig. 550 gives a diagram of the cut of one-half of the upper part of this dress—one of A PAIR OF BODIES.[1] A B is the centre front and G is the centre back. H passes over the shoulder. C D and F E are seamed to form the armhole. The front waist-line B C is either gored as shown by the dotted lines, or slightly gathered into the waist-band. J K L, when joined to A H G, forms the rever. The skirt is cut as shown in Fig. 546, but having a very long train and lying on the ground in front as well as behind, its shape is an oval instead of a circle. The only decoration is the ermine revers, cuffs and deep border at the hem, and a very rich waist-belt of goldsmith's work, made of jointed plaques set with jewels, in the manner of the hip-belts described on p. 278, but not quite so massive.

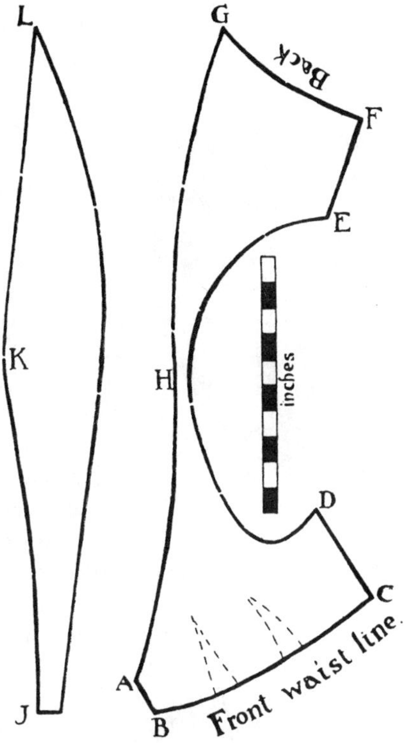

Fig. 550. Diagram, One of a Pair of Bodies

Great dignity is given to this lady by the wonderful headdress, described under Fig. 639 (3), and made of translucent gold and coloured tissue, which gleams through the transparent veils of white "linomple" or lawn, bordered with a decorative edging.

[1] Later "Bodice."

SECTION V

THE DUKES OF BURGUNDY [1]

During the fifteenth century a very important influence affected the countries of Western Europe—the cultured Court of the Dukes of Burgundy.

The dukedom of Burgundy was created in 1032 and bestowed upon

Robert, the fourth son of Robert the Pious, King of France. This ducal house became extinct on the death of Duke Philippe (I.) in 1361, whereupon King John of France annexed the duchy to the Crown, and in 1363 gave it to his youngest son, Philippe (II.) le Hardi, born 1342, Duke of Touraine. At that time the duchy comprised Burgundy, Boulogne, and Artois, and by the marriage of Philippe le Hardi in 1366 to Margaret, Comtesse de Flandre, Flanders, Rethal in Champagne, Nivers in Nivernais, and Franche-Comté were added to

Fig. 551. Arms of Burgundy   these possessions. By far the most powerful duke in history was the grandson of Philippe le Hardi—Philippe (III.) le Bon, born 1396, who succeeded his father, Jean sans Peur, a firm ally of England, who had been assassinated in the streets of Paris in 1419. To avenge this outrage, and in concert with Queen Isabeau, Duke Philippe (III.) offered the crown of France to Henry V. of England. This "Grand Duke of the West" acquired in divers ways Namur in 1429, Hainault, Holland, Zeeland, Brabant and Limburg in 1435, and some French territory and the Duchy of Luxemburg in 1445. To celebrate his third marriage, with the Infanta Isabelle of Portugal, he instituted the Order of the Golden Fleece (*see* p. 402). His Court was the most brilliant in Europe—the model on which others were based. Its etiquette, Court ceremonies and precedence set the standard for Europe. A description of Court and social life, and of costume worn in this brilliant circle, is given in a little book written by a lady of the Court—Madame la Viscomtesse de Furnes. An excerpt from it reads as follows:

The said Madame de Namur,[2] so I have often heard, had a big book in which were written all the ceremonies of France, and the Duchess Isabelle always acted on her advice in such matters. For the ceremonial of Portugal and that of France are not uniform.

---

[1] The armorial bearings of the Dukes of Burgundy, Fig. 551, are as follows:
Quarterly. 1st and 4th, France ancient within a bordure componée gules and argent (for Burgundy).
2nd, Bendy of six azure and or within a bordure gules (for Burgundy ancient), impaling sable a lion rampant or (for Brabant).
3rd, Bendy of six azure and or within a bordure gules (for Burgundy ancient), impaling argent a lion rampant gules (for Limburg).
In pretence, or, a lion rampant sable (for Flanders).

[2] A niece of Jeanne de Bourbon, Queen of France.

The great duke was always magnificently attired, and the fashions of Burgundy were eagerly adopted by all well-dressed men and women of Europe. Plate XXII. shows him seated on a chair of state, beneath a vermilion canopy, with a dorsal of vermilion and gold brocade. The pattern should be noted, as its design is characteristic of the period. His duchess, the Infanta Isabelle of Portugal, is standing beside him. The duke, who is in the Burgundian fashion of the period 1440–1445, wears a tunic of blue and gold brocade, of a bold floral design, edged with sable. This tunic shows an arrangement of pleats not adopted in England until about twenty years later, and then only applied to the long robe in fashion about 1460 (*see* Fig. 536); a short tunic pleated in like manner appeared for the first time in the reign of Edward IV. (*see* Plate XXIV.). The chaperon is of blue velvet having a jewel on the brim, and the collar of the Golden Fleece is worn (*see* Fig. 552).

When Louis XI. made his public entry into Paris in 1461, the Duke of Burgundy rode behind the king, "so splendidly dressed, himself and his horse, that the whole of his equipment was valued at ten thousand crowns. Nine pages attended him, magnificently appointed, each having a light but superb helmet, and the frontlet of the duke's horse was covered with the richest jewels. On his left hand was his nephew, the Duke of Bourbon, handsomely dressed and mounted; and on his right his son, the Count de Charrolois (afterwards Charles le Téméraire), most superbly dressed. . . . The Duke of Burgundy was lodged at his Hôtel d'Artois, which was hung with the richest tapestries the Parisians had seen: and his table was the most splendid any prince ever kept, so that all the world went to see it, and marvelled at its magnificence. Even when he rode through the streets or went to pay his devotions at church, crowds followed to see him, because every day he wore some new dress or jewel of price—and he was always accompanied by seven or eight dukes or counts, and twenty or thirty of his archers on foot, having in their hands hunting-spears or battle-axes. In short, whether the duke remained in his hotel or came abroad, everyone pressed to see him, on account of his noble appearance and great riches."

This magnificent duke, the wealthiest prince of his age, died in 1467, and was buried in the Church of S. Donnast, Bruges. The funeral procession "was preceded by sixteen hundred men, in black clokes emblazoned with the arms of the duke, each with a lighted taper in his hand."

The Count de Charrolois (born 1433) succeeded his father as Duke of Burgundy, but spent most of his ten years' reign, and his father's huge fortune, in extravagant and unnecessary wars. He married in 1467,[1]

---

[1] *See* Letter CCLVIII. of "J. Paston the younger" to his brother under date, Bruges, Friday, 8th of July, 1468; 8. E. IV., in which the writer describes the costumes worn at the wedding festivities as: "richly beseen, and himself also, as cloth of gold, and silk, and silver, and goldsmith's work, might make them; for of such gear, and gold, and pearl, and stones, they of the Duke's Court, neither gentlemen, nor gentlewomen, they want none."

as his third wife, Margaret of York, sister of Edward IV., but was a lukewarm supporter of the King of England. This Duke of Burgundy —Charles le Téméraire—met a violent death at the Battle of Nancy on 5 January, 1477, fought against the Swiss under the command of the Duke of Lorraine. His nude body was discovered in the snow on the battlefield, and conveyed to Nancy, where it was "placed on a table and dressed in a vesture of cloth from the neck to the feet, with a pall of black velvet over the body, in a dark chamber hung with black velvet. Under his head was a pillow of black velvet; and at the four corners of the table were large lighted tapers, with the crucifix and holy water at his feet. While he lay in state, the Duke of Lorraine came to see him, dressed in mourning and wearing a large golden beard that descended to his girdle, in imitation of the ancient Preux, and in honour of the victory he had gained over him. Having taken one of his hands from under the pall, he said, 'May God receive your soul! You have done us many and grievous injuries and vexations.' After which he took some holy water and sprinkled it over the corpse" (Monstrelet).

Louis XI. of France immediately took possession of the duchy and annexed it to his own domains, and the young heiress of Charles le Téméraire, Marie of Burgundy (born 1457), was wedded shortly afterwards to the Archduke Maximilian, afterwards Emperor (1493) of Austria, thus conveying the greater part of the "Cercle de Bourgogne" to her husband. The young archduchess died in 1482 from injuries received in the hunting-field, leaving a son Philippe (born 1478), father of the Emperor Charles V. (born 1500), and a daughter Marguerite (born 1480), Regent of the Netherlands.

THE ORDER OF THE GOLDEN FLEECE, LE TOISON D'OR

The Order was instituted on 10 January, 1429, at Bruges, and dedicated to the Virgin and S. Andrew,[1] the patron saint of Burgundy. It was restricted to the sovereign, who was hereditary Grand Master, and twenty-four knights, who had stalls in the choir of Notre Dame, Bruges. It is set forth in the statutes of the Order "that whoever is the object of the choice of the Sovereign, possesses, in virtue of his so being, every requisite which may entitle him to his admission therein." The office of Hereditary Grand Master was transmitted to the Hapsburgs in 1477 by Marie of Burgundy's marriage with the Archduke Maximilian. In 1555, on the abdication of the Emperor Charles V., the Netherlands were annexed to Spain, and the Order of the Golden Fleece passed to the Spanish Crown. The Treaty of Utrecht, 1713, left the Netherlands sovereignty with Spain, but the treasury and records of the Order remained at Ste. Gudule in Brussels, which had become an

---

[1] A silver S. Andrew's cross formed the badge of Philippe le Bon.

Austrian possession. In 1725 the Order was divided into two branches, Spanish and Austrian, the latter retaining the original records and insignia. These were transferred in 1793 to Vienna during the French Revolution. Although some agitation occurred in 1920 to have them returned to Belgium, the author is informed by an official at Ghent (December 1926) that no action has been taken, and so far as is known these historic insignia and records are still in Vienna.

The original motto of the Order, "Aultre n'aray, Dame Isabeau tant que vivray," was afterwards changed to "Je l'ay emprins." The insignia and robes were as follows:

Fig. 552. Golden Fleece

The collar, formed of flintstones or fire-steels alternating with flames, all in gold, the latter sometimes set with rubies. To this was attached

The pendant, a fleece in gold, representing the staple industry of the country (*see* Fig. 552).

Fig. 553. Charles le Téméraire

The robes consisted of surcote, chaperon, and circular mantle cut like Fig. 295 but made of écarlate, a cloth of superior quality, dyed scarlet, and manufactured at Ghent.

In 1445 Oliver de la Marche, steward to the duke, records that the mantle was of black velvet, and, later, that Charles le Téméraire changed the surcote, chaperon and mantle to crimson velvet. The drawing Fig. 553 represents Duke Charles in his robes as Grand Master. The long surcote of crimson velvet is lined with white silk, and confined at the waist by a gold cord; the sleeves are long and do not fit close to the arm. The mantle, also of crimson velvet lined with white silk, has a border all round embroidered in a gold design; it fastens on the right shoulder, in the manner fashionable in the fourteenth century and described under Figs. 318 and 319. It was customary to drape the left side of the mantle high up on the left shoulder. The collar and pendant of the Order are worn above the mantle. The chaperon of crimson velvet afterwards gave place to the fashionable "bonet" of black velvet.

A description of a banquet given in 1445 by Philippe le Bon in the Great Hall of the Château des Comtes de Flandre at Ghent on the seventh reunion of the Knights of the Golden Fleece is given by Oliver de la Marche as follows [1]:

There a very large table was laid, covered and backed with black velvet, embroidered with the arms of the Duke of Burgundy, and on the left side was a lower table prepared for the four officers of the Order of the Golden Fleece. The dinner ready, the knights came in from the meeting. The Duke of Burgundy sat in the middle of the table, on his right the Duke of Orleans, and on his left the Seigneur de Saintes; and the other knights sat in their due order. The two dukes were each served separately, as were also the knights, each his separate dish, and there was an abundance of wine and meat. At the lower table sat the Chancellor, the Treasurer, the Registrar and the King-at-Arms, and these were served separately like the knights. The serving of the dinner lasted a long time. There was the sound of fiddles and trumpets, and the heralds received gifts and shouted for largesse. The tables cleared, spices were brought in, and the princes and the knights retired to their rooms. At three o'clock they returned, clad in their robes and long black clokes, the collar of their Order round their necks; they mounted on horseback and went in their accustomed order to the church, to hear Vespers and to pray for their sins and for the dead and dying.

The duke's steward also gives an account of an audience granted to the ambassadors of the Duke of Milan:

The audience took place on Wednesday afternoon, the 13th June, 1449. The hall of the château of the counts was richly decorated; tapestries of great value covered the walls. The duke was seated at the end of the hall, resplendent with all the richness of majesty. On his left was the Duke of Cleves,[2] on his right the Chancellor, and the people of the court were ranged on the two sides of the hall, according to their rank and quality.

The ten ambassadors approached; the two principal were wearing coats of cloth of gold which hung to the ground, while the others wore coats of silk, of velvet, or other rich material; thirty-six servants followed them.

FlemishXV

Fig. 554

SECTION VI.—EDWARD IV., EDWARD V., AND RICHARD III. 1461–1485

Nobility—Men

Edward IV. was the eldest son of Richard Plantagenet, Duke of York, grandson of Richard, Earl of Cambridge, and great-grandson of Edmund, Duke of York, the son of Edward III.

He was born at Rouen in 1442. He was chosen King of England by

[1] From M. Alphonse van Werveke's *Château des Comtes de Flandre*.
[2] Nephew of Duke Philippe.

the lords of his party, and the Commons, and crowned at Westminster on 4 March, 1461.

"Fort beau prince, plus que nul que j'aye jamais veu en ce temp la" (Philippe de Conigues).

In his youth Edward IV. was exceedingly good-looking and reckoned the handsomest man in Europe. He had a tall elegant figure, which showed off to great advantage the costume fashionable at the time. His thoughts, we are told, were wholly employed upon dressing, hunting, and the ladies. Towards the end of his reign he was inclined to corpulence. Fig. 555 is derived in part from illuminated MSS., and shows him at about the age of thirty.

Fig. 555. Edward IV.

Skilled in all manner of manly feats, a kind husband and father, he, like Henry V., made a point of being always courteous to all classes. He was extremely popular with the people, mainly by reason of his good looks, bravery and charming disposition, but he was thoroughly selfish and too fond of pleasure. He married Elizabeth Wydeville in 1464.

Fig. 556. Edward V.

Edward IV. died at Westminster Palace in 1483. It is said that his death resulted from disappointment caused by the Treaty of Arras, which forced Maximilian to promise his young daughter Marguerite to the dauphin, and provided for the cession to France of some territory in the Netherlands; but it is more likely that he died as a consequence of his dissolute life. This king is buried at Windsor, but there is no monumental effigy of him.

His son Edward succeeded him as Edward V., but his reign lasted less than three months (*see* p. 410). Fig. 556 is a portrait of this king taken from an illuminated MS.

Richard III., Duke of Gloucester, the brother of Edward IV., was born at Fotheringay Castle in 1450. He was made Protector to his nephew, Edward V., after whose death he was chosen king. In the meantime he had paid his addresses to Anne Nevill, his cousin, widow of the Red Rose Prince of Wales, son of Henry VI. and Margaret of Anjou, whom he married in 1472. Sir Thomas More

Fig. 557. Richard III.

describes Richard as "little of stature, ill fetered of limmes, croke backed, his left shoulder much higher than his right, hard favoured of visage, and such as is in states called warlye, in other men otherwise." "A noble soldier, mean in form and of feeble strength. He was short in stature and had a shape short above and left twisted below," says John Rous. These masculine descriptions do not tally with that of a lady—the Countess of Desmond—who danced with Richard as a young man, and declared in her letters that he was the handsomest man present on that occasion, with the exception of his brother the king (Fig. 557). Restless by nature he was continually sheathing and unsheathing his dagger while in conversation. His fingers were never still; when not fidgeting with his dagger he would draw off and push on his finger-rings.

Richard is said by those who knew him to have been a powerful man, active and agile. Like most of the Plantagenets he was very fond of music, and encouraged the arts and learning. He had great schemes for the welfare of his people, and a policy superior to that of his brother Edward, "and laid down the lines upon which the Tudors ruled England for six score years, to the people's liking and their own good-fortune —yet he has left his own name to become a by-word and a reproach" (York Powell). It seems certain, however, that Richard's memory has been unjustly vilified by time-serving supporters of the Tudor usurpation.

After the death of his queen, Anne, Richard determined to marry his niece, Elizabeth; but before he could do so he was killed at Bosworth.

Costume of the Nobility—Men

Temp. Edward IV. 1461–1483

Like other sovereigns before him, Edward IV. introduced a collar of honour, which he bestowed upon his faithful followers and adherents. It was composed of alternate suns and white enamel roses of the House

of York, either set, like the collar of SS, upon a ribbon, or linked together with chains. Some examples show six oak leaves set between the suns and roses. The white lion badge of the House of March was attached to the collar when bestowed by Edward IV. (Fig. 558), but later, when Richard III. awarded it, his own badge of a white boar was used as the pendant (Fig. 559).

Fig. 558.
Collar of Suns and Roses, with Edward IV.'s Badge

Edward was very interested in ceremonial forms and practices of all kinds, ancient and modern, a taste probably inspired by the customs observed at the renowned Court of Philippe le Bon. Many changes in minor details of heraldic formulæ, garter and peers' robes, etc., took place in this reign, all due to the monarch's enthusiasm for archæological research and formal display.

From miniatures in illuminated MSS. representing this king he appears to have worn robes of State identical with those shown in Fig. 534.

From this reign onward, the royal crown was always used in conjunction with the cap of maintenance (*see* Fig. 643). In its original form, however, this cap, as shown in Fig. 390, was frequently worn by Edward IV. with his parliamentary robes.

Fig. 559.
Richard III.'s Badge

A description of the costume worn by gentlemen in the year 1467 is given by Monstrelet as follows:

At the same time, the men wore shorter dresses than usual, so that the form of their buttocks, and of their other parts, was visible, after the fashion in which people were wont to dress monkeys, which was a very indecent and impudent thing. The sleeves of their outward dress and jackets were slashed to show their wide white shirts. Their hair was so long that it covered their eyes and face; and on their heads they had cloth bonets of a quarter of an ell in height. Knights and esquires, indifferently, wore the most sumptuous golden chains. Even the varlets had jackets of silk, satin or velvet; and almost all, especially at the courts of princes, wore peaks at their shoes of a quarter of an ell in length. They had also under their jackets

large stuffings at their shoulders, to make them appear broad, which is a very vanity, and, perchance, displeasing to God; and he who was short-dressed to-day, on the morrow had his robe training on the ground. These fashions were so universal that there was not any little gentleman but would ape the nobles and the rich, whether they dressed in long or short robes, never considering the great expense, nor how unbecoming it was to their situation.

The dress of a nobleman of the early part of this reign is represented in Fig. 560, which is taken from a portrait of the king's brother, the Duke of Clarence. It is shown worn without a girdle, although narrow girdles, sometimes simply a cord, were usually worn. The sides of such robes were frequently slit vertically from the hem to about waist-level, and a vertical or horizontal slit often appeared on the sleeve at elbow-level, either back or front. The collar of the undertunic shows at the neck, and a beaver hat of red, blue, green or black is worn. The

Fig. 560. Duke of Clarence

materials used for these robes were plain silk, velvet or cloth, but a little later large-patterned brocades in designs of the period became the height of the mode.

Long robes reaching to the ankles, referred to at this period as "gowns," were in general use among the English nobility from about

1468 onwards. Fig. 561 shows one of brocade, or velvet upon velvet, in two colours, and in a design distinctly Eastern in treatment. The gown is lined or faced with fur, the fronts turned back to form deep revers on the chest. These robes were belted, and a pouch with dagger carried at the side. The tubular sleeves were moderately padded on the shoulders, and had vertical or horizontal openings at elbow-level, which enabled the arm to be passed through. Alternatively, the hand could emerge at the end, the long sleeve being pushed well up the arm.

Fig. 561.
English Noble, Edward IV.

A robe like Fig. 561 was frequently worn, during the latter part of the fifteenth century, by a knight over his complete suit of armour. This type of robe or gown, with long sleeves, continued in general use among the upper classes, with slight modifications, until the middle of the sixteenth century. After that time its use was restricted to official costume of dignitaries. From the beginning of the seventeenth century onwards it was the model on which legal, academic and municipal gowns were founded.

A fashionable Frenchman of the middle of the reign of Edward IV. is shown in Plate XXIII. wearing a long gown of black velvet without any trimming. The pleats or tucks descend from the shoulders to the waist in a tapering line, thence becoming larger as they approach the hem. This gown opens up the back to the waist, displaying the undergarment of red silk, pleated in the centre back. The black velvet sleeves are narrow and open and hang straight from the slightly padded shoulders, revealing the full length of the close-cut red sleeve of the undergarment. The long hanging oversleeves were often loosely tied behind. A cord through which a dagger is passed binds the waist, and a gold chain encircles the neck.

The most up-to-date fashionable garb, an example of the general style of costume worn by young nobles of this reign, is shown in Plate XXIV. The tunic or dubblet is padded, or "double-clothed," with stuffing between, on the chest and shoulders, in order to accentuate the slender waist — a great feature among smart men of the times. This is also enhanced by the arrangement of tucks which descend from the shoulders, converging towards the centre of the waist, but they continue in parallel lines to the front edge of the short basque. The dubblet or pourpoint is of purple velvet, edged with gris, which also outlines the neck and openings of the sleeves. The undergarment is of crimson silk, seen through the openings and at the high neck-band. Hose of purple are almost covered by the very long soft leather boots, which ruck round the leg and are turned down to show the grey silk lining.

It is stated that Edward IV. wore a dubblet of this kind, made of white velvet embroidered with black, and another one of orange velvet decorated with black and white; no doubt this type of garment well became his elegant figure.

Although so fond of dress, Edward attempted to check extravagance in apparel by enacting sumptuary laws. One dated 1464 forbade anyone below the rank of baron wearing cloth of gold, purple silk or sable. Gentlemen and esquires were restricted from the use of velvet upon velvet, unless they were Knights of the Garter. Also they might not wear velvet, damask or brocade unless they possessed a yearly income of £100,[1] or were attached to the king's household.

A fashionable man wearing a Flemish or French gown is represented in Fig. 562. The garment is a development of that shown in Fig. 537. This gown is of silk, having a border of a contrasting colour, nine or twelve inches in depth, at the bottom edge. It has a cord girdle and is open up the front to the waist, and the wide sleeves, padded on the shoulders, are slit and laced loosely at the back to show the full undersleeve of the pourpoint, the high collar of which is also seen. It will be noticed that height is the mode of the day, and to accentuate this, slimness of body is aimed at, except as regards the shoulders. One of the fashionable high hats, described later, is worn. The triple chain necklace, of gold, is typical of this period.

Fig. 562. Flemish Noble

A loose coat called a JOURNADE or "Jornade" was worn, without a belt, by English, Flemish and French men of all classes during the second half of the fifteenth century, made of every kind of material, rich or coarse, according to the wearer's status. It was a very short garment, frequently worn for riding, and sometimes put on over full or demi-armour. Fig. 563 shows a journade worn over civil dress. It is cut circular, and the pleats, in this figure, arranged on the shoulders back and front to form an inverted box-pleat under the arm. A similar

[1] £1 equals about £15 to-day.

Fig. 563. Journade

box-pleat is repeated in the centre of the back. The sleeves to this journade are of the usual shape, long, wide, and very much padded on the shoulders.

It was considered by the dandy extremely smart to carry the hat on the end of the cane, and even to place it on the head by this means.

Fig. 564 depicts a fashionable young man at the end of this reign and throughout that of Richard III. He is wearing a journade cut circular and buttoned at the neck, with long slit sleeves less grotesquely padded than the last. It is made of silk and lined, or edged only, with ermine. In cut this garment is the forerunner of the coat which came into fashion in the reign of Henry VIII. The hat, of felt, velvet or beaver, is a style much worn at this period.

The costumes of the poor little prince who was for a brief two and a half months King Edward V. were in the fashions just described. Of robes for his intended coronation we have an account in the book of the wardrobe. It does not appear extravagant or ostentatious.

A short tunic made of 2¾ yards of crimson cloth of gold, lined with black velvet. A long robe of the same lined with green damask. Another short tunic, of 2¼ yards of purple velvet, lined with green damask; and a purple velvet "bonet." His coronation mantle was to have been of purple velvet.

For this projected ceremony, as in Henry III.'s time, all the officers of State and nobility received benefactions of cloths of gold, silver, scarlet, and silks of various colours, specified as liveries, etc. "The Duke of Bukks who stands first, 8 yards of blue cloth of gold: 8 yards of black velvet, and 12 yards of crimson velvet" (*see* Peers' Robes, p. 382).

Fig. 564. Later Journade

All these were provided by Uncle Richard for the coronation that never took place—so they were probably used for his own, 5 July, 1483.

Fig. 567 shows Edward V. in ordinary attire.

In France the model for masculine attire was the king, Louis XI. Born in 1423, he married, in 1436, Margaret, daughter of James I. of Scotland, who died in 1444 of a broken heart due to her husband's unkindness. He married secondly, in 1457, Charlotte of Savoy. Their family consisted of:

> Charles, born 1469, who succeeded as Charles VIII.
> Anne, married Pierre de Bourbon.
> Jeanne (deformed), married Duke of Orleans, born 1462, afterwards Louis XII.

As the dauphin, Louis was always well dressed, so Madame la Viscomtesse de Furnes tells us.

During the funeral obsequies of King Charles VII., Louis, of course, wore mourning robes of black, but these were set aside after the ceremony, and, according to Monstrelet, "the dauphin, now king, immediately dressed himself in purple velvet, which is the custom in France."

Louis started his reign as a well-dressed man. A few days after his accession the new king made his public entry into Paris, mounted on a white steed caparisoned in blue velvet decorated with gold and golden fleurs-de-lys, and "dressed in a white silk robe, without sleeves, his head covered with a chaperon and liripipe." Louis XI. did not approve of luxurious habits, and it was not long before he became particularly careless about his appearance, wearing the most threadbare, coarse and dilapidated old clothes (Fig. 566), a sure symptom of acute eccentricity. Mean-looking and physically weak in middle age, his life was characterised by subtlety, selfishness, superstition (see p. 186) and vindictiveness, and his matchless capacity for intrigue earned for him the title "the universal spider."

As he grew old he trembled at the thought of assassination and shut himself up in his Castle of Plessis, protected only by his faithful Scots guards, a regiment of three hundred archers who had been instituted in 1419 by Charles VI. Louis created the Virgin "Honorary Colonel" of the Scots guards, as well as "Comtesse de Boulogne," a conciliatory favour dictated by his fear of death.

He had deceived all Europe; he now tried hard to deceive himself, to cheat the Almighty and bribe the devil in his effort to ward off death. To aid in his rejuvenation he arrayed himself in magnificent attire, hoping thus to conceal his failing health. "Before his decease he was sorely afflicted with different disorders, for the cure of which his physicians prescribed many extraordinary remedies." He gave up the ghost on 30 August, 1483.

THE ORDER OF S. MICHAEL

This Order was instituted in the year 1469 by Louis XI. of France. The king was Grand Master of the Order, and at its institution created thirty-six knights. It was intended as an honour for the recognition of all kinds of merit.

The insignia consisted of:

The grand collar, composed of twelve escollop shells, connected and linked together with cords of gold tied with two loops and four ends (Fig. 565).

The pendant. The figure of S. Michael trampling upon the dragon, all in enamels.

The robes consisted of:

The mantle, circular, open up the right side, made of white damask, bordered all round with embroidery

Fig. 565. Collar and Pendant of S. Michael

in gold and colours representing the collar of the Order, and lined with ermine. The left side was draped over the shoulder. The mantle was worn over ordinary dress.

The chaperon, of crimson velvet, was not worn, but carried on the back behind the right shoulder, the broad flat liripipe descending in front to hip-level.

Temp. Richard III. 1483–1485

Richard III. took a delight in rich clothes worn by those around him, but his own dress was relatively simple. Details of the coronation robes of Richard and his queen, extracted from a wardrobe account dated 1483, include the following:

For the king to wear on his ride from the Tower to Westminster, a dubblet of blue cloth of gold wrought "with netts and pyne apples," [1] and lined with green cloth of gold: a mantle of purple velvet furred with ermine. For the coronation ceremony, sherts of "reyns" cloth and crimson "sarsynet": crimson satin hosen lined with white sarsynet, and shoon of crimson cloth of gold; a closed surcote, mantle and hood of red satin lined with "menyvere pure," and purfiled with "venys gold." A purple velvet mantle, lined with miniver: a hood and a long gown lined with purple satin, and wrought with garters and roses.

Figs. 566 and 568 represent respectively Louis XI. and Richard III.

[1] A favourite motif in patterns for brocades of the late fifteenth and early sixteenth century. *See* Fig. 571.

as they appeared when not in full State. The costumes are very similar in shape, but in material they are widely different. That of Louis, in the language of the time, is "lewd," *i.e.* extremely shabby. The king wears the collar of S. Michael, and his favourite skull-cap, over which rests a moth-eaten high-crowned beaver hat adorned with images of the saints for whom he entertained the highest veneration. The costume of Richard Plantagenet is rich. The tunic of gold brocade fits comfortably, its skirt reaching to just above the knees, and has close sleeves.

Fig. 566. Louis XI.   Fig. 567. Edward V.   Fig. 568. Richard III.

Its square-cut neck, the latest innovation, reveals the fine white cambric shert, with neckband embroidered in fine black silk stitching. Over the tunic is worn a surcote or coat of purple velvet lined with sable. It is a shortened version of the gown shown in Fig. 561, cut on the circle to knee-level, thus establishing a certain kinship with the journade recently described. The sleeves are open at the ends, slit vertically in front, and both openings edged with sable. The moderately padded shoulders are convenient for hiding Richard's deformity, and over the turned-back sable revers is worn a rich jewelled collar, or the "Suns and Roses." The fashionable "bonet" of purple velvet with a jewelled brooch is worn.

XVth

Fig. 569. Diaper Pattern

Nobility—Women

Cicely, youngest daughter of Ralph Nevill, Earl of Westmoreland, and of Joan Beaufort, daughter of John of Gaunt, married Richard, Duke of York, the Protector, and was the mother of Edward IV., Richard III., and the Duke of Clarence. Her youngest daughter, Margaret, married Charles le Téméraire, Duke of Burgundy.

The Duchess of York was a woman of remarkable beauty and indomitable pride. Near her home, Raby Castle, she was called "the Rose of Raby," but in the neighbourhood of her later residence, Fotheringay Castle, she was known as "Proud Cis." There she lived in state like a queen, being the second lady in the land before her husband's death; the Castle of Fotheringay had a throne room, in which she gave State receptions.

Edward IV.'s queen, Elizabeth, had an interesting history prior to her marriage. She was the daughter of Sir Richard Wydeville (Baron Rivers, 1448, and Earl Rivers, 1466) and his wife Jacqueline of Luxemburg, widow of the Regent John, Duke of Bedford. Elizabeth married first, in 1452, Sir John Grey, afterwards Lord Ferrers of Groby, and became one of the four ladies of the bedchamber to Margaret of Anjou. By this marriage she had two sons, Thomas, Marquess of Dorset, and Richard, both of whom were born at Bradgate. Lord Ferrers was killed under the Lancastrian banner while leading a cavalry charge which gained the day at the second Battle of S. Albans, 1460. Elizabeth's character and courage were shown when she visited Warwick's camp in that year, ostensibly to ask a personal favour, but in reality to spy out the land on behalf of her own Lancastrian associates. In 1464, Edward, a young man of twenty-two, fell violently in love with her, and married her secretly, since no king of England had previously married one not of royal blood. However, when the marriage was announced it was thought expedient to make much of her mother's kinship to the Holy Roman Emperor. Among the children of this marriage were Edward, Prince of Wales, afterwards Edward V., and Richard, Duke of York, both murdered in the Tower by their uncle Richard III., and Elizabeth, thus left heiress to the crown. Queen Elizabeth died in 1492 and was buried at Windsor.

Anne Nevill, the widowed Princess of Wales, resented the Duke of Gloucester's attentions, and to avoid them disappeared and remained in hiding until the cunning duke discovered her in a house in London disguised as a cook-maid. He immediately put her into sanctuary, under threat of attainder for being a Lancastrian rebel. In these circumstances she was obliged to accept his assistance, and reluctantly married him in 1472. After a miserable married existence of two years, the birth of a son, Edward, Prince of Wales, reconciled her to her fate. In some strange manner this boy met "an unhappy death" at the age of ten in 1484, but this was not by the hand of his father, who idolised him. This loss, combined with the knowledge that her husband desired to get rid of her, brought on a decline, from which Anne slowly died. Her lingering death is sufficient proof that her husband was not guilty of poisoning her, although he is accused of that crime by many writers. She died at Westminster in March 1485.

In a very interesting and little-known illuminated MS. of Edward IV.'s reign is a portrait of Elizabeth Wydeville in coronation robes; Fig. 570 is drawn from that portrait.
Queen Elizabeth wears the conventional cotehardie and sideless gown, both of vermilion cloth—écarlate. The ermine which surrounds the armholes continues as a plastron in front, finishing in a horizontal line at hip-level. A deep border of the same fur surrounds the hem of the skirt. She is enveloped in a mantle of deep blue velvet, having a border of gold, which lies upon the ground in heavy folds and is lined with ermine. It fastens across the chest with tasseaux, cords and tassels. An orb and sceptre are carried, and a crown surmounts hair flowing on the shoulders.

Fig. 570. Elizabeth Wydeville in Coronation Robes

Queen Elizabeth in everyday attire would be dressed as shown in Plate XXIV., but the gown would probably be in her favourite black velvet purfiled with sable, ermine, or miniver. In her portraits [1] at Windsor, Queens' College, Cambridge, and the Ashmolean Museum, she is depicted wearing the headdress shown in Fig. 619 (6), but without the veil, in place of which is worn a long veil similar to that shown in Fig. 577. In one portrait the queen wears sable, but in the Windsor and Ashmolean pictures the revers (like those shown in Fig. 573) and cuffs of her gown are of black and gold brocade. As a widow it is more than probable that she wore the headdress, Fig. 619 (4), with the addition of the widow's barbe seen in Fig. 288.

The lady seated in the chair of state, Fig. 571, is that "Grande Dame" of the fifteenth century, Cicely, Duchess of York, mother of Edward IV. and Richard III. She was left a widow in 1460 and died in 1495. In this drawing the duchess is shown as an elderly lady; her widowhood prevented the use of garments fashionable at that time, yet her temperament and dignity required something not unfitting to her age

---

[1] See p. 356. The correctness of details in the costume of Elizabeth Wydeville suggests strongly that these portraits are contemporary (Flemish) art.

Fig. 571.

DUCHESS OF YORK, AND PRINCESS MARGARET OF CLARENCE

and rank. The gown is similar in shape to that in Fig. 545, but with close sleeves and a high neck, made of black velvet or silk, having cuffs and border at the skirt hem of ermine or sable. The mantle of velvet is lined with ermine. A widow's barbe is worn *over* the chin, with a white veil under a second of fine black cashmere. On State occasions a coronet similar to that shown in Fig. 649 would surmount the veils.

The little child is her granddaughter, the Princess Margaret, born 1469, styled "the last of the Plantagenets," who afterwards became the Countess of Salisbury and married Sir Richard Pole. She was attainted on suspicion of conspiracy, and beheaded by order of Henry VIII. at the age of seventy-two, in 1541. This little princess wears a gown fashioned on the lines of that shown in Fig. 548, but with hanging open sleeves. A gold fillet with a jewel confines her flowing hair. Notice the candelabra, cloth of estate, and chair of state.

A royal lady or lady of the Court of King Edward IV. is shown in Plate XXIV. attired in a gown of orange velvet. There is no new feature about the upper part, which is cut very low in the neck as usual, except that the close-fitting sleeves extend over the hands, forming circular cuffs (*see* Fig. 572). The skirt is similar to that described in Fig. 549, having a long sweeping train. This, or the front of the voluminous skirt, was usually held in one hand. The revers, cut low on the shoulders,

Fig. 572. Circular Cuff

sometimes two or three inches below them, are of sable, and the edging of the sleeves and the deep border round the skirt hem are of the same fur. Any kind of fur could be used: miniver was fashionable, especially on a gown of black velvet. Velvet was used in the same manner as fur. A rich waist-belt of silver, set with turquoise, encircles the waist only, and at this period does not fall to the ground behind. The underdress shows on the chest, and fine white folded gauze inside the revers gives a very soft line to the décolletage. The headdress, Fig. 619 (4), is described on p. 447.

The lady in Plate XXIII. is dressed in a plain mauve gown of the same shape as that just described, having the revers and cuffs only of white fur. A small veil, open up the front and turned back, is worn under the headdress, which is described under Fig. 619 (4).

The following passage from Monstrelet, dated 1467, gives some details of costumes worn by women at this time:

In this year also, the ladies and damoiselles laid aside their long trains to their gowns, and in lieu of them had deep borders of furs of miniver, marten, and others, or of velvet, and various articles of a great breadth. They also wore hoods (hennins) on their heads of a circular form, half an ell, or three-quarters, high, gradually tapering to the top. Some had them not so high, with kerchiefs wreathed round them, the corners hanging down to the ground. They wore silken girdles of a greater breadth than formerly, with the richest shoes, with golden necklaces much more trimly decked in divers fashions than they were accustomed to wear them.

Fig. 573.
The Round Dress

In the 1460's ladies adopted a "quite round dress." It was not used for full Court costume, but was much in evidence at this period as indicated by illuminations found in MSS., etc., of this decade. It was introduced at the Court of Burgundy in 1457; the damoiselle with flowing hair in company with the Flemish lion depicted on the banner shown in Plate XVII. B is wearing this kind of dress, made in a rich brocade of the period, deeply bordered with ermine. Fig. 573 illustrates the same type of dress in black and gold brocade. The skirt is cut on the circle, although not full, and pleated or gathered at the waist to form a fold on either side, and one or two down the centre of the back. The body and sleeves are of the same shape as before described, but the revers do not meet in front in a point, but are rounded off without meeting the waist-belt. When the skirt was made of a large-patterned material, as in this illustration, the body and sleeves were frequently of a plain fabric matching in colour the groundwork of the skirt. The chest is filled in by a separate shaped piece of velvet taking the place of that portion of the underdress which covers the chest in Fig. 545. This was called the PLASTRON, although entirely different from the article so described at an earlier date (see p. 233). Over the shoulders, and tucked under this piece of velvet, is a fold of linomple or gauze. Examples of the headdresses worn with this costume are given in Fig. 619 (3), (4), (5) and (6).

Fig. 575 is a drawing made from an illumination in a MS., the "Roll of Fraternity of Our Lady," in the possession of the Skinners' Company, and shows Margaret of Anjou as a widow in 1475,

Fig. 574.
Noble Lady

Fig. 575.
Margaret of Anjou, 1475

or, as some suggest, in the sisterhood habit. The costume consists of a gown hanging straight from the neck and falling in many folds at the feet. It is of grey cloth, with a narrow gold edging to the sleeves. Over this is worn a very voluminous mantle of black velvet lined with ermine, and having a narrow gold border. An ordinary wimple, not the widow's barbe, is surmounted by a curious hood of black velvet, lined with black silk and edged with narrow gold.

The lady in attendance, Fig. 574, is fashionably garbed in black velvet, with leopard-skin revers and cuffs. The plastron and belt are of gold. The headdress has its veil mounted upon a gold-embroidered fez cap (*see* Fig. 619 (6)), with a frontlet of black velvet, seamed at its bottom edge to the front half of the lower edge of the cap.

John Rous gives in the "Warwick Roll" a portrait of Anne of Warwick, queen of Richard III. She is shown wearing a dress identical with that given in Fig. 570. She wears the head-

Fig. 576. Noble Lady, Richard III.

dress seen in Fig. 619 (6) surmounted by a crown. Details of the costumes worn at her coronation are recorded as follows in a contemporary wardrobe account: "xx yds. of purple cloth of gold wrought with garters. For a mantle, with train, surcote and kyrtle, xi yds. of crimson velvet furred with miniver pure, the mantle and surcote garnished with Venys gold, with tassels of silk and gold." The same garments were repeated in purple velvet for another set of robes. These materials were made into costumes similar in shape to those worn by Elizabeth Wydeville for her coronation, and shown in Fig. 570.

Fig. 576 shows a noble lady in the type of dress that came into fashion about the year 1480. It was a revival of the cotehardie, although that name had become obsolete, and the garment was now called the "kyrtle." It fitted close to the figure round the bust, waist and hips, and fell in many folds around the

Fig. 577. Alice Harleston

feet. Its shape may be understood by reference to the original diagrams given in Figs. 323 and 324. The chief feature of this new version, however, is the opening for the neck; it is cut very low in front and on the shoulders, as shown in the drawing, and moderately low behind, edged either with fur, velvet or brocade. A piece of velvet of contrasting colour shaped on the curve—the plastron mentioned in describing Fig. 573—shows on the chest. This eventually developed into the stomacher of later times. The hip-belt is of the latest pattern; the part surrounding the body is flat, made of silk or leather, and was sometimes decorated with metal; at the junction of the belt-ends and hanging portion are metal ornaments, and the long end is composed of sectional ornaments in metal. A pouch might be attached to the end, and sometimes other articles of utility kept it company—it was not uncommon for a book to be suspended at the end. This lady is wearing the fashionable headdress of the time, described under Figs. 619 (5) and (6).

Armorial bearings were blazoned on this type of dress, in the way described under the cotehardie (p. 331). On a brass to the memory of Alice Harleston, 1480, in Long Melford Church, Suffolk, this lady is depicted wearing the fashionable headdress, and upon her kyrtle she bears the arms, "argent a saltier between four crosses gules," for Harleston, and on her mantle, "sable a bend ermine cotised indented or," for Clopton (see Fig. 577).

1450

Fig. 578. Border

SECTION VII.—MIDDLE AND LOWER CLASSES, 1399–1485

The fifteenth century is marked by several distinct features which had their bearing on the social life of the country and a consequent influence on costume, particularly that of the middle and lower classes.

A growing importance was acquired by the manufacturing and merchant class—the latter very largely concerned with buying and selling cloth, for which England had a world-wide reputation.

In France, under the Valois, the citizen class had attained an importance previously unknown to them. The king favoured many of them and ennobled some, and by the beginning of the fifteenth century the leaven of practical good sense which their advancement had imported into the ranks of the nobility began to make its influence felt, to the great advantage of all concerned, for the older type of nobles were conspicuously deficient in these staid and useful characteristics.

The beginning of the century saw the growth of a distinct "labour class" in England, living on wages and not on the land. The emancipation of the villeins which followed the Plague and the Peasants' Rising of the previous century brought about a time of considerable prosperity for the English labourer. It is interesting that the term "villein" is not found in the Statute Book after the reign of Richard II., and the name speedily lost its earlier significance. The yeoman class, for centuries the backbone of the nation, came to the fore in the fifteenth century.

Great nobles and feudal lords were at the height of their splendour during this century. They kept enormous retinues of officers and servants, divided into distinct grades, entitled to regular allowances of food and clothing. It was indeed an ideal period for the domestic servant.

Men

The old gentleman shown in Fig. 579 does not differ much from some of those illustrated under Middle Classes of the fourteenth century. His gown is long, with close sleeves, and buttons part of the way up the

Fig. 579.   Fig. 580.   Fig. 581.
Temp. Henry IV. and V.

front. A hood, with the usual hat and gloves, and a cloke if necessary, were worn.

Fig. 580 represents a well-to-do young citizen of the reign of Henry IV. or Henry V. He wears a tunic buttoned on the chest and reaching to just below the knees, having dagges at the bottom edge and round the armholes, over another garment with bagpipe sleeves of a contrasting colour. It was the mode among these young people to have the tunic of a dark and the sleeves of a light colour, or *vice versa*. He has a belt ornamented with metalwork to which a pouch might be attached. If required, a hood would be worn, and a hat of any of the shapes given in the last chapter. The one in the illustration is a new shape, having a beehive crown with a brim cross-cut at the sides so that the front or back could be turned up or down. The hose are of cloth, and boots with moderately long toes fit the ankles and are turned down at the top.

Fig. 582.
Gentleman, fifteenth century

Fig. 583. Fig. 584.
Merchants, fifteenth century

Fig. 581 represents a man of a lower grade of society than the last, wearing a tunic of practically the same shape, cut in points at the bottom only and made all in one neutral colour. The liripipe of his hood is tied round his head.

Fig. 582 shows the costume of an opulent man of the middle classes, a gentleman of some position. It was a style that came into favour during the first quarter of the fifteenth century and was in general use among superior folk during the whole century. Many brasses to the memory of important commercial men depict this gown, first seen in Fig. 515. It was made of very good cloth, in quiet colouring, edged and often lined with fur, and confined at the waist by a belt ornamented with metalwork. For use out of doors a chaperon would be worn, or any of the hats given under Headgear.

Two merchants suitably dressed for travelling are given in Figs. 583

and 584. They have probably arrived from the Baltic or Flanders to dispose of their merchandise at Stourbridge Fair, and to buy English horses, tin, wool, leather and what not for their distant markets. The man in Fig. 584 is wearing a warm outer tunic, often lined with fur, which he would remove when he had arrived at the inn. His pouch is of strong leather and so are his boots. The hose are substantial and the hood lined with fur is comfortable in a biting wind. The one in Fig. 583 is similarly dressed, but wears a travelling-cloke with a fur-lined hood over it, and a beaver hat.

Fig. 585 is a yeoman or huntsman, dressed in a poke-sleeved tunic of Kendal green. Underneath this is an ordinary tunic with stand-up collar and close sleeves, buttoned only at the wrists, showing inside the sleeves of the shert.

Fig. 585

The hat is of grey beaver, the hose are green cloth, and the boots black leather. A horn and hunting-spear are carried.

A young French or English citizen of the first half of the century

(Fig. 586) wears a tunic of cloth with full sleeves pleated into the armhole and turned back at the wrists to form cuffs. The neck is surrounded by a band of fur of the usual shape (probably grey, as this colour was a favourite), and three buttons fasten the tunic on the chest. An ordinary belt encircles the waist, and to it a pouch might be attached. Although he is wearing a fez-shaped cap of scarlet, he carries his hood over his shoulder. The chaperon did not take the place of the hood among the middle classes until the second quarter of the century. The hose with foot part combined are dark in colour and made of cloth or soft leather.

When Henry VI. went to Paris for his coronation in 1431 he "was met at La Chapelle, half-way between Paris and S. Denis, by Sir Simon Morier, Provost of Paris, with a numerous company of the burghers, dressed in crimson satin

Fig. 586.
Citizen, first half fifteenth century

Fig. 587.
A Man of Substance

dubblets with blue hoods, to do him honour and respect; there were also very many of the inhabitants dressed in scarlet."

Fig. 587 represents a very important personage of the middle and second half of the fifteenth century, wearing a superfine cloth gown lined with fur. He has a gold chain round his neck which probably indicates that he is a mayor, or even the lord mayor, since chains of office were in use at this time for such dignitaries. From the chain is suspended a circular pendant bearing the arms of his guild or town in enamels and gold.[1] On official occasions a mayor would add to this costume a hood and a mantle, both of scarlet cloth lined with white fur, usually rabbit or budge. Spectacles, "gasingis," are believed to have been known in China in remote times. Roger Bacon, who died in 1294, refers to them, and they were in fairly general use in England in the fifteenth century (Fig. 588).[2]

John Lydgate, in *London Lycpeny*, mentions "spectacles to reede," and they are seen in pictures of the second half of the fifteenth century. At this time they had no bars at the sides.

Fig. 588. Gasingis

Fig. 589 represents an English or French citizen, a well-dressed man of good standing. The style of costume is that in vogue between the years 1445 and 1460. His body garment is shaped as shown in Fig. 531, and would be lined with fur if the wearer could afford it. It is worn over an undertunic of cloth in a subdued, contrasting colour. As an alternative a garment similar to that shown in Fig. 532 could be worn over the same undertunic. The universal hood is worn even at this date, in fact it was as popular with the middle and lower classes as the chaperon was with the aristocracy. The hat of cloth, beaver, or occasionally of velvet, is of a new shape, decorated with an ornament, which might be a livery badge (an enseigne) or that of his party, fixed in front. It should be

Fig. 589.
Citizen, middle fifteenth century

[1] The portrait of Sir Richard Whittington, engraved by Elstrack, is late sixteenth-century work, and the details of the elaborate mayoral collar shown in it give features introduced at a date considerably after Whittington's time.

[2] The Spectaclemakers' Guild received its charter from King Charles I. in 1629.

noticed that this man is wearing a second, different, badge fastened on the cape part of his hood—quite a usual practice.

The only detail of the costume shown in Fig. 590 which differs from that worn by the same class of man—a fairly well-to-do tradesman—during the past hundred years, is the sleeves. Following the example of the upper classes, this person, who belongs to the middle and second half of the fifteenth century, has had his sleeves made with a vertical slit on the upper side, or, to be more precise, the seam has been left undone. The tunic is edged with inferior fur, and the hat, of beaver of a cheap make, is carried in the hand.

Fig. 590. Citizen

The citizen in Fig. 591, of the period 1475–1485, is simply and adequately garbed in the style of the time. The tunic is buttoned down the front and has an upstanding collar of moderate height. It fits close to the figure, as do the sleeves and skirt part. A waist-belt holds the pouch on one side, and a knife in a sheath on the other. The cap is on the lines of those in vogue at this time, and his high boots of soft leather fall around his legs in rucks over well-fitting hose of cloth.

Fig. 591. Citizen, 1475–85

The successful angler in Fig. 592 is a man of lower standing than the last. His buttoned tunic, with looser sleeves turned back in cuffs, has a fuller skirt; the general effect is similar to Fig. 591, but more clumsily made. His hose are coarse, and he wears heavy leather shoes. His felt hat has a wide shady brim. The day appears to be Thursday!

The farm-hand with the scythe is typical of the appearance of this class of the community during the course of the fifteenth century. He is to be found depicted in many illuminated MSS. of this period. The

Fig. 592. Man of the People, latter half fifteenth century

particular one from which Fig. 593 is taken dates about 1420–1440. He wears a brown linen or cloth tunic or cotte, with loose sleeves rather short in the arm. Blue chausses, rolled at the knees over garters, leave the knee and thigh bare, and coarse heavy black boots are tied with cords round the ankles. From the waist-belt hangs a wooden receptacle to carry necessaries, and in it can be seen the steel for sharpening his scythe. The hat of black straw has a wide brim. In addition to these garments, no doubt this man has at home an ordinary hood and a short cloke.

The farm-hand, Fig. 594, wears a similar tunic in light brown, but the sleeves are longer and turn back at the wrists. The leather pouch

Fig. 593.   Fig. 594.   Fig. 595.
Peasants, fifteenth century

hung from the belt has a strap buckled round it to keep the contents secure. The hood is a faded red, and the braies of dull blue are tucked into black boots. The implement carried in the hands was used for scooping grain.

Fig. 595 represents a country-man on his way to work in the fields. His tunic is of the same shape as shown in the last drawing, but the close sleeves at the wrist suggest that he wears an undergarment as well as a shert. In the cold early morning he wears his hood, but his straw hat is slung over his back ready to protect his head from the midday sun. On his legs he has chausses shaped after the pattern given in Fig. 315. These are attached to the band which binds his sloppes about his waist. They are also bound round the knee, and frequently when engaged in strenuous labour they were undone at the waist, the top part then hanging from the knee. When made of substantial material the foot part was combined with the chausses, but when this wore out the chausses were tied under the foot inside a rough leather shoe. In very damp fields the working-man slipped his feet into wooden clogs. An example of these may be seen in Fig. 269. A meal is carried in the crescent-shaped bag tied round the waist, and water or ale in the pewter bottle slung across the shoulder.

Women

Temp. Henry IV. and Henry V.

Early fifteenth-century examples of the costume of well-to-do middle-class women are to be found in the numerous representations of Christine de Pisan (born 1363, died 1431). She was the daughter of Charles V.'s astronomer, and married M. de Pisan in 1376, but was left a widow in 1386. At the end of the fourteenth century she attracted attention by her poems. She is seen kneeling in the reproduction, Plate XXI. A. Fig. 596 is a drawing constructed from various representations of this lady. She is usually shown wearing the same kind of dress, which may be accepted as the general style worn by gentlewomen during the first thirty years of the fifteenth century. The cotehardie is of deep blue, having sleeves close-fitting on the upper arm to just above elbow-level, whence they form long bands from nine to twelve inches in width, frequently lined with fur, sometimes with silk, reaching to the hip, and often to the feet. These bands, of course, have their origin in the tippets of the last century. The sleeves of the under-gown show at the wrists. The headdress most favoured by Madame de Pisan is that shown in Fig. 616 A, but, since she was a widow, the wimple was worn with it.

Fig. 596. Middle-class Woman, first half fifteenth century

The chair is taken from an illumination in one of her books, and is made of wood, simply polished. Some other chairs represented in her works are painted. The "quysshon" of velvet, cloth, or soft leather, "garnissht" with tassels at the corners, is worthy of notice.

A nurse bathing a baby is shown in Fig. 597. Her gown is the usual close-fitting garment with close sleeves, and she wears an apron, such as is described on p. 265. A couvrechef, now referred to as KERCHIEF, is draped round her head, surmounted by a white cap, the crown pleated into a band.

The costume of a matron of the citizen class is illustrated in Fig. 598.

It was a style in general use during the greater part of the fifteenth century, and was made of various materials of the coarser kind. The gown is cut all in one, with sleeves wide enough to roll up if necessary, and the skirt reaches to the ankles. This · good woman's best gown might have one or two bands of bright colour round the edges of the sleeves and skirt. A cord or belt would fasten at the waist, and in this example for house or rough work an apron

Fig. 597.   Fig. 598.
A Domestic Episode, fifteenth century

is tied round the waist. The quaint hood is cut as shown in Fig. 617, and often worn over a wimple and kerchief.

Temp. Henry VI.

A young gentlewoman of the middle of the century (Fig. 599) wears the fashionable houpeland, having bagpipe sleeves (other sleeves, such as those shown in Figs. 543 or 547, could be worn as alternatives to these), and the gown is made of good cloth—her best gown might even be of silk and lined with fur—having a fur or cloth collar and perhaps a second one of linen. The dressing of the hair is uncommon, and an ornamental roll of stuff is worn on the head. Any of the simple headdresses shown in Figs. 613 c, 613 f, 614 a, 615 and 616 a could be worn with this dress. The little boy is dressed exactly like the men of the same period, in tunic and hose, and his hair is cropped in the prevailing style.

The gentlewoman in Fig. 600 [1] is the wife of a country gentleman of the middle of the century. Her dress, such as was worn by people of

[1] Mistress Jenny, of Knodishall, Suffolk, died 1440.

her class until about 1460, is very similar to that shown in Fig. 547, and is of cloth, with revers and wide cuffs of fur. The underdress is close at the neck and its sleeves fit tight at the wrists. The headdress is reticulated, and similar in shape to Fig. 614 c, but without any roll; a semicircular veil is arranged in a manner somewhat resembling that in Fig. 615.

The wife of a citizen or small farmer is shown in Fig. 601. She wears a gown fitting close at the waist and in the sleeves; these unbutton so that they can be rolled up, and the skirt, being cut on the circle, is easily raised when walking or attending to domestic duties. About this time

Fig. 599.
Gentlewoman, first half fifteenth century

Fig. 600.
Gentlewoman, middle fifteenth century

the top part of the underdress or cotte was detached from the skirt part, and for a while discarded, and the latter—the petticotte, or PETTICOAT (sometimes referred to as the kyrtle), was worn alone as an undergarment. For economy's sake it was a rectangular piece of rough stuff, seamed at the back and gathered into a waist-band. The girdle, of leather, cloth or cord, was only worn over the gown when the wearer was in her "best." Consequently that indispensable article, the purse or pouch, was attached to the end of a strap or cord and fixed to the waist-band of the petticoat. Her head is tied up in a kerchief, but even this woman takes care to arrange it on fashionable lines, because "it's so becoming."

The wife of a citizen or retainer attached to a great house at the middle or latter part of the fifteenth century wears a gown (Fig. 602) modelled on the lines of those worn by the upper classes, and made of cloth with revers and cuffs of a different colour, or perhaps of fur. Over the bare neck is a square piece of linen, a kerchief, folded cornerwise, the ends tucked in under the revers. The hair would be parted in the middle and done in a knot on the crown of the head, with a hood (*see* Fig. 618) with flat liripipe worn over it.

A lower-class woman of the country or town is shown in Fig. 603 carrying her baby in swaddling bands. Her gown might be all in one

Fig. 601.   Fig. 602.   Fig. 603.
Women of the People, fifteenth century

piece, or the top with long loose sleeves might be of one colour, and the skirt of another, with a border round the hem. An apron and a pouch are hung from the waist-line. A garment with short sleeves, resembling a modern jumper, in cloth or possibly knitted material, is worn over the upper part, and reveals the long loose sleeves of the undergarment made of coloured stuff, or perhaps those of the white camise. A piece of linen, slightly stiffened, is worn over the head; and it should be noticed that this woman has contrived its arrangement in such a manner as to suggest the line of headdresses worn by fashionable women of the time.

Temp. Edward IV., Edward V. and Richard III.

The costumes of the lower orders given in this section were worn throughout the fifteenth century, but the better-class women of the reigns of Edward IV. and Richard III. followed more or less the vogue adopted by the aristocracy.

Sir John Crosby, a grocer and wool merchant of the City of London, was alderman and sheriff in 1470. His wife, Dame Agnes, is seen in Fig. 604 talking to Mistress Smyth. Dame Crosby wears a dress like that in Fig. 576, but the neck-opening is not so revealing and is cut rather on square lines. A rich necklace is worn. The girdle is slung loosely in the fashionable way round the waist, the end hanging on one side, with a purse attached at its extremity. The headdress is the cap shown in Fig. 619 (6), but, in place of the veil there seen, a wide band of black velvet edged with gold embroidery is fixed to the cap over the forehead (*see* Fig. 574), and a similar band or folded piece passes over the head and falls at the back. A mantle lined with fur is worn, giving this lady a distinguished appearance, as was seemly in the wife of a city magnate.

Mistress Smyth (*c.* 1480) of S. Eadmundsbury (Fig. 605) wears a headdress like Fig. 576, but her gown is shaped high in the neck and

Fig. 604.   Fig. 605.

Gentlewomen, second half fifteenth century

is open for some distance down the front, where it is edged with fur. A girdle at normal waist-level keeps the garment closed, and close to the figure. The sleeves are wide and edged with fur. The underdress is visible at the chest, and its tight sleeves show at the wrists. The husband of this lady must have held some important position, as she wears a mantle, no doubt of good Flemish cloth, lined with fur.

Italian 1450

Fig. 606. Border

SECTION VIII.—HAIRDRESSING: MEN—HEADGEAR—HEADDRESSES—FOOTGEAR—JEWELLERY

Hairdressing—Men, 1399–1485

At the commencement of the century men dressed their hair and beards as described in Chapter IV., under Richard II. Towards the close of Henry IV.'s reign, however, a change in the fashion of hairdressing took place which lasted until the end of the reign of Henry VI. It first appeared in France, and Figs. 500 and 501 are the earliest examples of this curious mode. Fig. 607 A shows it on a larger scale. The nape was shaved up to about the level of the ears, and the hair was brushed to radiate from the crown, and trained to curl under at the ends. It was unusual to have it waved, although some drawings in illuminated MSS. show it so treated, and the most fashionable wore the hair straight.

Fig. 607

The effigy of Henry IV. shows what has sometimes been mistaken for a roll of material, but there is no doubt that it is a rather archaic treatment of hair dressed as shown in Fig. 389 B. The scapegrace Prince of Wales encouraged the new style by having his own hair cropped in this manner, and the whole world followed the example of the hero of Agincourt.

Young Henry VI. is shown in early portraits wearing his hair dressed in the prevailing style, but when he grew to manhood he objected to it, and before he reached the age of twenty-four let his hair grow, and wore it curled at the sides and back in the more conservative fashion shown in Figs. 522, 534 and 607 B. This, of course, was the older style which had been in use throughout many reigns: the most truly representative hairdressing in the Middle Ages.

For a few years after the new style of cropped hair was introduced, beards were worn, but before Henry V. came to the throne beards went entirely out of fashion among the nobility and upper classes for the remainder of the fifteenth century. This style of hairdressing, with clean-shaven faces, was also adopted by certain of the middle class, and no self-respecting man, except those of the lower and peasant class, wore long hair until the reign of Edward IV., nor beards until Henry VIII. brought them again into fashion.

Some time about 1460, the Flemish mode of hairdressing was adopted by the English nobility. The hair was long, touching the shoulders at the back, and brushed forward from the crown on to the forehead, where it formed a fringe "so long that it covered the eyes and face," so Monstrelet says, but this statement is slightly exaggerated. Fig. 607 c shows this hairdressing at its greatest length. In many examples, especially in England, the hair was not worn so long, and frequently to just below the ears (Fig. 607 B). Variations in the length of this hairdressing were adopted by the French and Italians of this same period.

Headgear, 1399–1485

Foremost amongst headgear of the fifteenth century is the chaperon, described under a separate heading on p. 384. It entirely superseded the earlier fantastic arrangement of the hood on the head, in favour among fashionable people up to the end of the second decade.

In the reign of Edward IV. the chaperon went out of fashion, but its useful liripipe was retained, and attached to hats of various shapes.

Fig. 608. Headgear, first half fifteenth century

Illustrations of sundry hats and caps in use during the fifteenth century are given in Figs. 608, 609, 610 and 612. The first series (Fig. 608) belongs roughly to the first half of the century, and the remainder mainly to the second half.

Fig. 608 A shows a very original and unusual way of arranging the hood in vogue at the end of the fourteenth and beginning of the fifteenth century. The short liripipe is bound round the head, under the shoulder part on the wearer's right and over it on the left, where the end is fixed with a brooch. The original drawing shows this headgear scarlet. Although men of fashion were adept in arranging the hood in a series of fantastic ways, it seems certain that this one must have been fixed on a foundation of the skull-cap nature: a basis which perhaps suggested the form of construction used for the later chaperon.

Fig. 608 B is a very smart hat, in fashion between 1395 and 1410. The crown is surrounded by an upstanding fold of material fixed in front with a jewel; and the brim, turned up at the back, comes to a point in front.

A black felt hat, Fig. 608 C, is shaped on similar lines to that shown in Fig. 499, but with a narrow brim, and has a white and a scarlet feather fixed in front by a jewel. This hat was in fashion from about 1400 until 1420. Of the same period is the floral headgear described under Fig. 500.

Fig. 609. Headgear, second half fifteenth century

Fig. 608 D shows a useful hat of black, green, fawn or brown beaver, having a gold chain round the crown and a jewelled ornament set in front. This style of hat was very generally worn throughout the fifteenth century.

A cap worn by royal and noble persons with State dress, such as the nobleman in Fig. 518, is shown in Fig. 608 E. It has a scarlet cloth or velvet crown, with an ermine brim, either upstanding all round, turned up in front, or turned up behind. It was called the ABACOT, and was a Cap of Estate or Dignity (see Fig. 167, and the Cap of Maintenance, Fig. 390). It was worn with the early type of peers' robes at the beginning of the century and will be encountered later in discussing crowns.

Hats of beaver like that shown in Fig. 389 D continued to be worn during the first twenty years of the fifteenth century. The hat of straw worn by the noble in Fig. 502 was an uncommon one, and used only by certain of the nobility out of doors.

The tall hat seen in Fig. 609 A made its appearance in France about 1435–1440, and was soon adopted by Englishmen, chiefly those of the middle classes. It was made of felt, soft, yet sufficiently stiff to stand up straight. If the wearer chose, he could fold up this hat and tuck it under his arm or in his pouch, replacing it by the hood, which was frequently carried also, slung over the shoulder.

The hat like a baby's indiarubber mouthpiece, Fig. 609 B, is the latest from France, about 1450, and the original was a creation of rose-pink felt.

Fig. 609 C shows a nobleman's hat, in fashion during the second half of the fifteenth century, made of rough beaver and decorated with a gold chain round the brim, a jewel set in front, and a second jewel holding a quill on the right side.

Fig. 609 D is made of softer shaggy beaver, so that the high crown flops backwards or towards the front. It is of the familiar shape, turned up at the back and standing out in front. This hat is adorned with a gold chain and small bells. The height of its brim at the back is the climax of a general increase (*see* Figs. 608 B and D, and Fig. 609 C).

Fig. 609 E is a different shape from the others, being lower in the crown and made of felt or cloth, with the brim turned up and of moderate proportions. It was in fashion towards the end of Edward IV.'s reign.

Beaver hats such as that worn by King Edward III. (Fig. 317, and also shown in Fig. 391) returned to fashion during the reign of Edward IV. The only difference in the shape was that the crown was higher, and it was decorated by an ostrich plume, frequently two, standing up from the back of the brim where they were fixed by a jewel (*see* Plate XXIII.). It was also the vogue at this time to ornament the stem of the feather with pearls or diamonds.

The last of the liripipe for civil wear is seen in the long band attached to hats of all shapes and sizes—"the liripipes or tippets which pass round the neck and hang down before reaching to the feet all jagged." Many figures illustrating the fashions of Henry VI.'s reign show the liripipe used in this way. In the reign of Edward IV., when the chaperon went out of fashion, the liripipe in the form of band or drapery was attached to such hats as are shown in Figs. 563, 564, and 609 E. An example is shown in Fig. 610, attached to a hat that would complete the toilette of the young noble depicted in Plate XXIV.

Fig. 610.
Late
form of
Liripipe

A cap of a new style came into fashion about the end of Henry VI.'s reign. It was of Italian origin, adopted by the French, and copied by the English nobility. The French name was "Bonet." It had a crown cut as a slight oval large enough for the circumference to be pleated into a headband. To this a brim, cut on the curve about 2½ or 3 inches in width, was attached. This cap with the brim turned *down* is shown in Fig. 611, and in Figs. 561 and 612 it is seen worn in the proper way. Shortly after its introduction the brim was cut vertically, and the

edges overlapped and were fixed by a jewelled brooch. These bonets were usually made of black velvet, having a fur brim when worn by the nobility; but after the middle of the reign of Edward IV. the brim was invariably of velvet to match the crown. The lower classes had the bonet made of cloth or felt.

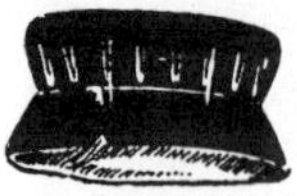

Fig. 611.
Diagram of
Bonet

The chaperon previously worn with peers' robes gave place to this bonet during the reign of Edward IV.

In a letter written before 1460, the Earl of March, afterwards Edward IV., asks his father, the Duke of York, that they, the earl and his brother, may have "some fyne bonetts sente on to us by the next sure messengers, for necessite so requireth." He was always a dressy man! By 1469 the young bloods of the middle classes took to these caps, for young Paston writes, "I prey you send me an hat and a bonet by the same man, and let him bring the hat upon his head for (fear of) mis-fashioning of it; I have need of both, for I may not ride nor go out of the doors with none that I have, they be so lewd; a murrey bonet, and a black or a tawney hat." "Hats of wolle" cost viii_d._ to xii_d._ each, and bonets ii_s._ vi_d._ to iii_s._ each in the year 1480.

Fig. 612. Bonet

The bonet shown in Fig. 612 continued to be generally worn by all classes throughout Europe, with but slight variations, until late in Queen Elizabeth's reign. The name survives in Scotland to-day, though the bonnet has lost its brim.

Records of the fifteenth century contain some interesting rules for certain ceremonies, customs and etiquette connected with headgear.

When presenting anything, a gift or letter, to any person of high degree, the giver knelt on one knee and held his hat in his hand. If both hands were occupied, the hat was placed on the ground beside the giver. These two rules also applied to any man when offering a gift at a shrine, or to a holy person. If the giver was attended by others, they also knelt bareheaded.

Kneel on both knees to God, and on one to Man.

When approaching a Noble, take off your cap or hood and fall on your right knee twice or thrice. Keep your cap in your hand till you are told to put it on.

When two men met in greeting, each pushed off his chaperon so that it fell behind the shoulder; they then clasped hands, or gripped each other's forearm in an embrace.

Henry VI. touched his chaperon when receiving ambassadors.

When hats were worn in place of the chaperon, they were lifted and held in the left hand, and the right hands of those greeting were clasped, *but never shaken.*

At the hall door take off thy hood and gloves.

Observe in Curtseie to take
A rule of decent kind,
Bend not thy body too far forth,
Nor backe thy leg behind.

Curtesy came from Heaven when Gabriel greeted Our Lady. All virtues are included in it.

Headdresses

The Reticulated Headdress (Latin, *Reticulum* = a net)

This form of headdress may be said to have made its first appearance in the age of Classic Greece. Ladies of Rome also wore nets of gold thread, called "Reticula," to cover their hair, a fashion copied from the Greeks.

The headdress which came into fashion during the second half of the thirteenth century was of this nature, although it was known as the crespinette. It went out of use during the early years of the reign of Edward III., surviving thereafter for only a short time as the side cylinders. The third appearance of this headdress occurred at the end of Richard II.'s reign, following on the introduction of the style of hairdressing shown in Fig. 397. In the time of Henry IV. the side pads of hair were encased in net bags—cauls—often composed of gold thread with pearls or jewels set at the intersections. These are seen worn by Queen Joanna in Fig. 505, and at this time they left the ears exposed. A little later the cauls increased in size and left only the lobe of the ear visible, as shown in Fig. 504.

In both these examples, and in all cases where side cauls were worn, they were attached to a fillet or band round the head. Fig. 506 shows the network which covers the side pads extending also over the top and back of the head. In this case the network is shaped in one piece. A roll of stuff entwined with pearls and set with jewels was worn by noble ladies on top of this type of caul, as shown in Fig. 507. Another version is given in Fig. 613 E.

An elaborate headdress worn during the reigns of Henry IV. and Henry V. is shown in Fig. 613 A. The shape of the side caul has changed to that shown in Fig. 613 B (a truncated cone, flattened on the upper surface), and it was made of gold wire set into narrow metal frames in three connected pieces. In this the hair was confined. In Fig. 613 A, the fillet or band A B is wide and richly chased (sometimes the visible part of the back portion B was omitted) and the side cauls leave the ears exposed, a detail peculiar to the reign of Henry IV. In this model the top of the head is covered with network having square plates set with jewels at the intersections. A coronet is worn over this headdress, its bottom rim being shown at C. Before the coronet was placed in position

Fig. 613. RETICULATED HEADDRESSES

it was usual to drape a veil over the back part of the head, and this the coronet kept secure.

A reticulated headdress of the same reign, without the side pieces, is seen in Fig. 613 C. The head is covered by a cap of large mesh, having square ornaments at the intersections. A rigid frontal piece, decorated with metal studs or jewels, is placed high on the forehead, and below it appears a narrow wirework or gold thread band, which fits close on the brow.

Fig. 613 D shows the well-known reticulated headdress taken from the monument of the Countess of Arundel, in fashion during the reigns of Henry IV. and Henry V. The wirework frames project more at the sides than in the examples just described, and cover the ears. Above them and at right angles to the head a piece of wire curves upwards to carry the rectangular veil, with pinked edging, which hangs at the back like a casement curtain. Surmounting this is a coronet. Ladies of less exalted degree used a circular roll of material ornamented with jewels, pearls, and plaques of enamel, in place of the coronet. Fig. 613 E gives another version of this same headdress, but without the wires and the veil (see also Fig. 507). The top of the head is covered by a shaped piece of linen or coloured silk, surmounted by a roll decorated with plaques of enamel and twists of cord, or with jewels as shown in Fig. 507. Fig. 613 F has the cauls covered by a circular veil caught at the sides to the band on each temple, and so arranged as to give very graceful folds on each side.

All these headdresses were worn in the following reign, that of Henry V., together with another illustrated in Fig. 614 A. In this the outer edges of the cauls extend upwards into vertical points. Over these is draped a circular veil. A square veil, hemmed or pinked, could be used in the same manner; the only resulting difference would be in the hang of the folds on either side. In arranging the veil, of either shape, care was taken to preserve the outline of the top of the head, as seen between the two points. A wimple was generally worn by matrons with this headdress, and arranged in position before the cauls were put on. The wimple was worn similarly by elderly women with the other types of headdresses previously described. This headdress (Fig. 614 A) remained in use among the middle classes during the greater part of the reign of Henry VI., but the others just described went completely out of fashion amongst the "smart young things."

During the reign of Henry VI. a reticulated headdress of a different shape was worn. It was in favour in France from about 1410 onwards, and an illumination in a MS. of this date (see p. 370) shows Isabeau of Bavaria, Queen of France, wearing it (see Plate XXI. A). Her appearance is generally similar to that of the lady shown in Fig. 541. This latter figure is reproduced from the Bedford Book of Hours, 1423, wherein one sees the front view of the headdress given in Fig. 614 B. The network takes

Fig. 614. RETICULATED HEADDRESSES

the shape shown in Fig. 614 C, encircling the sides of the face, exposing the lobes of the ears, and continuing round the nape of the neck. The side pieces take a curved line upwards, forming stunted horns on either side. This is usually referred to as the "Heart-shaped headdress." An oval roll of rich material is placed on top of this framework, as seen in Figs. 541 and 614 B, resting on the forehead, surmounting the horns, and descending in a large curve at the back of the head. The network and roll in this particular case (Fig. 614 B) are richly decorated with jewels. The band which edges the network is set with oblong rubies and groups of three pearls, and the network itself is composed of two rows of pearls having circular rubies alternating with emeralds at the intersections. The spaces between show the foundation of gold tissue, and occupying the centres are lozenge-shaped rubies alternating with emeralds, each with pearls at their points. On the forehead, under the roll and emerging from the caul, is a narrow band of brilliant colour, in contrast to the roll; this is set with pearls. The roll of some rich-coloured silk is entwined with a double row of pearls, one row white pearls, the other black; and between are clusters consisting of a ruby with six pearls, alternating with a sapphire and six pearls.

Fig. 615. Headdress, Henry IV. and V.

The headdress worn by the young noble lady in Plate XIX. is heart-shaped, but in that example the side cauls are separate, being fixed to a band round the head. Between the cauls a small semi-circular veil is arranged, folded somewhat in the manner shown in Fig. 615. An ornamental band of gold, 2½ or 3 inches in width, encircles the complete headdress, including, in this case, the veil behind, although sometimes the veil was worn hanging over the band at the back.

About 1440 the liripipe of the men was added to the ladies' heart-shaped reticulated headdress. This fashion, adopted from Burgundy, may have originated in Spain or Portugal, as it is worn by the Duchess of Burgundy (see Plate XXII.). In this example it is of no great length and made of the same black and gold brocade as the roll. Fig. 545 shows a longer liripipe of plain colour, starting from the back part of the roll. In Fig. 547 the liripipe is attached at the back on the right, and a piece of material, in imitation of the cape part of the men's hood, hangs on the left, almost converting the headdress into the masculine chaperon.

Dennington Church, Suffolk, contains a monument to the memory of William, Lord Bardolf, K.G., a hero of Agincourt, treasurer of the household of Henry V. and chamberlain and privy councillor to Henry VI. He died in 1447. The headdress worn by his wife is given in Fig. 614 D, and is another elaborate example of the reticulated style. Its sides and back are covered with a wide trellis-work of gold and red enamel, the intersections set with jewels, and the intermediate square spaces filled in with four pearls set in gold. Before the cauls were placed on the head one side of the veil was fixed tight round the forehead, and, when the headdress was put on, the back part of the veil fell outside it at the back. Over all was set the coronet, shaped to surround the semi-circular side pieces. A view of the top of the head is shown in Fig. 614 E. This lady wears a cotehardie, a sideless gown edged with fur, and a mantle bordered with gold passement.

The heart-shaped headdress, reticulated or in various materials, continued to be used by the middle classes during the greater part of the fifteenth century, even after fashionable women had discarded it about 1465–1470.

Other Headdresses of the Fifteenth Century

Several other headdresses of this period cannot be classified under the two main categories, the Reticulated and the Hennin. The following are some examples.

Fig. 615 is a headdress in fashion during the reigns of Henry IV. and Henry V. It entirely enclosed the hair and consisted of an oval-shaped cap of some material—cloth of gold, silk or cloth—mounted on a stiffened foundation and edged with a narrow band of passement or other trimming. Its chief feature is the semicircular stiffened veil, about forty-eight by twenty-four inches, the straight edge so arranged, turned back, and pinched here and there, as to give the lines clearly indicated in the drawing. It was fixed to the cap by two pins under the turned-back edges.

The headdress shown in Fig. 616 A was in general use among women of the nobility and middle classes. It is familiar by reason of the various portraits of the poetess Christine de Pisan, who is always depicted wearing this style. First the hair (unseen) is dressed to the form outlined in Fig. 614 C. This is done naturally or by artifice. Around this erection of hair is placed a rectangular piece of stiffened linen about thirty by sixteen inches, the long edge passed round the nape of the neck, over the ears, with the two corners A and B sticking up in front. The centre of the corresponding long edge is bent round to meet the top of the fore-head, and the two edges on each side are pinned together on the temples; by this method two points are formed standing up one on each side of the head, C and D. At these points it is necessary to pin the two edges together. A second piece of stiffened linen, about thirty by thirty-two inches, has a fold about four inches deep on its thirty-two-inch edge,

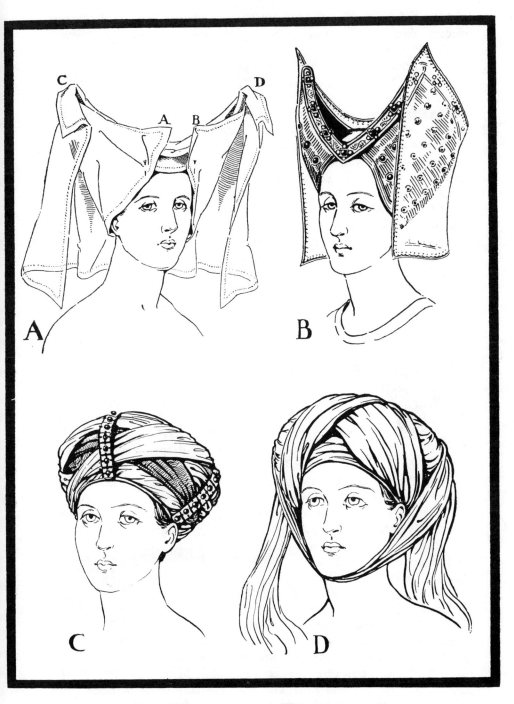

Fig. 616. HEADDRESSES, FIFTEENTH CENTURY

and is fixed by pins to the two upstanding points c and d of the first piece, sinking in a curve on to the top of the head, as clearly indicated in the drawing.

The description of the headdress worn by the noble lady in attendance on Queen Catherine, given on p. 378 (Fig. 514), applies also to the headdress shown in Fig. 616 B, in fashion during the reign of Henry V. and the first years of Henry VI. The opening "valves of a shell" are made of gold tissue studded with jewels, and mounted on a light framework, having a border of patterned gold passement set with jewels and pearls. Instead of the billowing veil shown in the first figure, this has some very transparent gauze stretched upon an ornamental wire frame, which is bent round the headdress and attached to its top edge.

A lamentable event at this time gave an opportunity to those whose function in life is the creation of "new modes" (though history usually shows a precedent for each innovation). The fall and sack of Constantinople by the Turks in 1453 inspired the ladies of Western Europe to adopt a version of a Byzantine headdress. This was the coiffure resembling an Oriental turban, described in Vol. I., p. 169.

It was composed of all kinds of rich materials made up on a foundation. Fig. 616 c shows a turban headdress of this kind. The folds of gold or silver tissue are fixed in place by bands of jewels. They might

Fig. 617. Diagram of Hood

cover the head completely or be hollow in the centre, the turban surrounding the head roll-fashion. Frequently the wearer's long plait of braided hair passed through the roll and fell down the back over the rim. Fig. 616 D shows another kind of folded turban, with a veil draped under the chin and caught at the top, whence the long ends fall and float in the breeze. Rolls of fur often composed this turban headdress; they were usually hollow in the centre, and had a cluster of jewels placed in front, from which arose, sometimes, an upstanding plume. Great originality was displayed in the designs of these turban headdresses, which remained in fashion in England, and on the Continent, until the end of the century. Many of them, worn by great ladies of Italy, are seen in portraits of this time.

Fig. 618. Diagram of Hood

Hoods of various shapes continued to be worn by women of the middle and lower classes throughout the fifteenth century. Two examples are illustrated in Figs. 598 and 602, their respective shapes being shown in Figs. 617 and 618. They were usually made of black cloth lined with a colour visible where the front edges were turned back. Well-to-do women sometimes had these hoods made of black velvet.

The Development of the Hennin

1430–1485

The HENNIN, sometimes referred to as the CORNET, was a high steeple cap, like a candle extinguisher. It first appeared in France about 1428 (Fig. 619 (1)), and was made of a stiffened fabric covered with a rich material, and worn tilted back on the head, its upper surface at an angle of about forty-five degrees to the vertical. The hair was entirely concealed, being drawn back and covered by the hennin. Over the hennin was placed a circular veil, draped in such a manner that its edge came just above the eyes, the greater part falling behind the head.

It was this early type of hennin which inspired Friar Thomas Conecte of the Carmelite Order, in 1428, to pungent invective against "the noble ladies, and all others who dressed their heads in so ridiculous a manner, and who expended such large sums on the luxuries of apparel." Not content with abuse, he incited rude street boys to pursue with jeers fashionable women and to pull down these monstrous headdresses, wherefore the poor things had to seek shelter while their servants dealt faithfully with the offenders. For a time, to avoid further disturbances, hennins were laid aside. (This same zealous friar devised a plan of dividing the men and women who came to hear his sermons by a cord, "for he said he had observed some sly doings between them while he was preaching." He was burned for heresy in Rome, 1432.) "But this reform lasted not long, for like as snails, when any one passes by them, draw in their horns, and when all danger seems over put them forth again—so these ladies, shortly after the preacher had quitted their country, forgetful of his doctrine and abuse, began to resume their former colossal headdresses, and wore them even higher than before."

About 1440, a much higher version of the hennin was worn by noble ladies of France. The higher the rank of the wearer, the higher the hennin; some were as much as forty-five inches from base to point. The circular veil also increased in size, and was usually caught up with a jewel at a point in the centre of the forehead (Fig. 619 (2)).

Temp. Henry VI,

The latest fashion at the French Court, about 1450, was to cover the hennin with two rectangular veils of gauze or fine linen, edged and embroidered, and stiffened into angular folds as shown in Figs. 549 and 619 (3). These very transparent veils, when worn over hennins of rich gold or silver brocade, had a wonderful effect. The headdresses allowed no hair to be seen, except a small ring or loop in the centre of the forehead, designed to show the colour of the hair. Ladies of fashion of this period were convinced that their ideal of a spotless alabaster-like

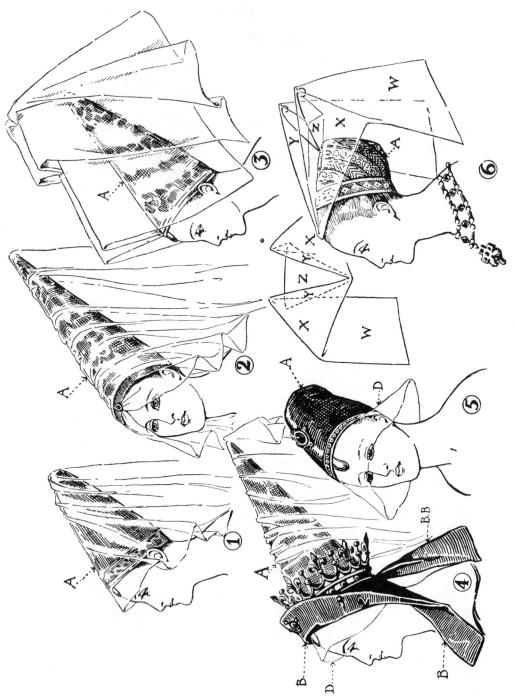

Fig. 610. DEVELOPMENT OF THE HENNIN

complexion was best realised by concealing the hair, and having their faces slightly veiled.

At this date, 1450, the hennin with double veil was adopted for full dress by English noble ladies.

The first veil, Fig. 620, measuring about fifty-six by twenty-four inches, was attached at B to the hennin's edge at the centre of the forehead, and it was necessary to have an invisible wire frame, Fig. 621, fixed

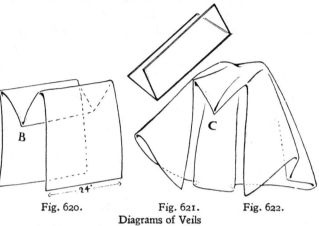

Fig. 620. Fig. 621. Fig. 622.
Diagrams of Veils

along the top of the hennin at A, Fig. 619 (3). The second veil, Fig. 622, was semicircular, about fifty-six inches in diameter. It was folded as shown, and its centre point C was attached to the hennin, through the first veil, about half-way along its upper surface. The circular portion of the veil hung in folds at the back of the headdress.

Temp. Edward IV.

About 1460 the hennin was made of brilliantly coloured silk, or of gold or silver tissue. The current fashion was to put it on in the following manner:

1. All the hair was drawn back off the face and twisted into a chignon on the crown of the head.

2. Over this was placed a piece of very fine and delicate white lawn (Fig. 619 (4)), shaped so as to form a shade or frame for the face (D). It was firmly fixed to the hair by pins.

3. On top of this was set a long strip of double velvet, B, always black, about five inches wide by thirty inches long. It was placed round the head as shown, and the inner edge was attached to the hennin, save at the back quarter, to which another piece of black velvet, B B, was attached and hung from the centre of the hennin down the wearer's back. The front part of the velvet band B was turned back at the top to form a point and so fixed with a jewel. A jewelled pin was often used to fasten one or both of the side pieces of the black velvet band to the hennin. Finally,

4. A voluminous rectangular veil (about five feet by ten or twelve feet) was thrown over the top of the hennin, a few inches being allowed to hang beyond the point. See also Plate XXIV.

Royal and noble ladies wore their coronets around the base of the hennin, just behind the black velvet band.

The hennin was very rarely worn with the wimple, except in the case of old ladies and widows (*see* Widows and their Weeds, p. 191).

A simpler kind of hennin is seen in Fig. 619 (5). Its use became very general in England about 1470, when fashionable women decided to dispense with the cumbrous headdresses lately in vogue. The tall hennin had been abandoned in France at an earlier date. In shape this new type of hennin was either cylindrical or a truncated cone; it was made of silk or velvet on a soft foundation, and had a band of embroidery at the bottom edge and a jewelled ornament in front towards the top. A circular transparent veil (D) was often worn on the head under this hennin.

About 1470 more hair was allowed to be seen, and the fashion of the pretentious hennin approached its end.

A headdress introduced about 1470 and known as the BUTTERFLY was in general use for the remainder of the reign of Edward IV. and during that of Richard III. It is seen in Fig. 619 (6).

It is a reduced version of the last, Fig. 619 (5), in shape very like a flower-pot. It was made usually in silk heavily embroidered in gold, and worn very much at the back of the head, the hair being drawn back under it. This cap was sometimes worn alone, but usually a veil of

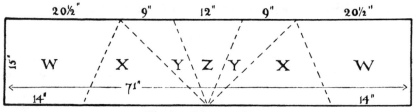

Fig. 623. Diagram of Veil

stiffened gauze was used with it, oblong in shape and measuring about seventy by fifteen inches. A series of zigzag foldings gave it the form seen in the diagram Fig. 623 and drawing, and to support it two gold wires were attached to the top of the cap as shown, and the veil evidently pinned to the hair in front. Noble ladies wore their coronets above the flat centre portion of the veil (z), and illuminated MSS. show Queen Anne, wife of Richard III., wearing this cap and veil, surmounted by the royal crown matrimonial.

Fig. 623 explains the folding of this veil, and its lettering, w x y z, is the same as in Fig. 619 (6) and its diagram. More hair than formerly was seen, as a consequence of the cap being worn so far back on the head. The hair was brushed right off the forehead, and its ends confined inside the cap. High foreheads were in favour, and to attain this end ladies of fashion to whom Nature had been unkind remedied the defect by plucking out their forelocks by the roots.

FOOTGEAR, 1399–1485

Writing in 1739, William Maitland, F.R.S., gives some entertaining details about the Cordwainers:

This Fraternity was incorporated in Letters Patent of the Eleventh of Henry the Fourth, anno 1410, by the Name of Cordwainers and Coblers, the latter whereof at that Time was no despicable Epithet as at present; for the genuine Meaning thereof then, was that it not only signified a Shoemaker, but likewise a Seller or Dealer in Shoes; for it does not appear that the Word Shoemaker was then in Use.

Sometime after, the Fashion of Shoes was so preposterous, that it occasion'd the making of an Act of Parliament (4 Edward IV.) to restrain the same, wherein it was enacted, "That no Cordwainer or Cobler within the City of London, or Three Miles of the same, shall make any Shoes, Galoshes, or Huseans (Boots or Buskins) with any Pyke or Poleyn, passing the Length of Two Inches, to be adjudg'd by the Wardens or Governors of the Mystery in London, nor shall they presume to sell, or put upon the Legs or Feet of any Person, any Shoes, Boots or Buskins on Sundays, or Feasts of the Nativity and Ascension of Our Lord or Corpus Christi, on the Penalty of Twenty Shillings for each Offence.

Fig. 624. Sole Plans

Fig. 625

Before the close of the fourteenth century the grotesquely long toes of men's shoes began to diminish, and by 1410 they were approaching normal shape. The length of the toes again gradually increased, as seen in Fig. 624 above, attaining their maximum length about 1460, to decline once more during the following twenty years.

Fig. 625 gives an example of a shoe in use during the first quarter of the fifteenth century. It was made of various kinds of material, generally leather, having a strong leather sole for ordinary wear when used by all classes. For the nobility and upper classes this shape of shoe was made of velvet or silk, upon a substantial foundation, and often embroidered. A band of ornamentation surrounded the ankle, and

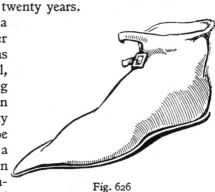

Fig. 626

descended the opening where the shoe was laced at the side, either right or left.

Fig. 626 gives a shoe or boot in use from about 1415 to 1430. The foot part was that worn for a considerable period, the length of the toe varying at different dates as Fig. 624 shows. These ankle boots could be laced at either side or fastened by straps and buckles, as seen in the drawing. The materials of which they were made differed according to the rank and means of the wearer. In many cases, as illustrated in various figures in this chapter, no shoes were worn, but the hose were made all in one with the foot part, and the length of the toe varied according to the fashion of the time.

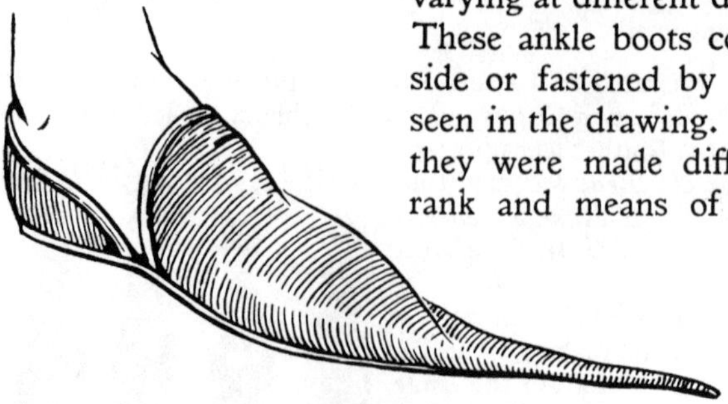

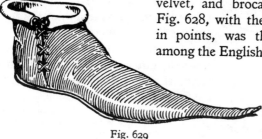

Fig. 627

There was more variety in the styles of shoes worn from 1450 to 1470, as Figs. 627, 628, and 629 illustrate, and illuminations in numerous MSS. indicate that they were made of all kinds of materials, including leather, silk, velvet, and brocade. The shoe shown in Fig. 628, with the front and back finishing in points, was the shape in general use among the English nobility and upper classes during the second half of the fifteenth century; the toe varied in length at different times.

Fig. 628

A shoe of the reign of Edward IV. is given in Fig. 629. It laces down the side, and the top is slightly turned down to show the lining of silk or fur. It was quite usual to omit this turned-down part, and, if the shoe was made of the same material as the hose, being laced tightly round the ankle, it would have the effect of hose with foot part cut all in one.

Fig. 629

Fig. 630 is a low-cut indoor shoe

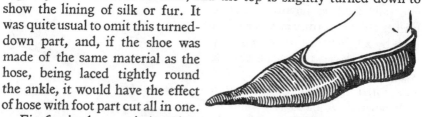

Fig. 630

of the second half of the century, usually made of velvet, silk or leather, but occasionally seen represented white in conjunction with dark-coloured hose.

A shoe of modern appearance, used by the middle and lower classes towards the end of the fifteenth century, is given in Fig. 631. It follows the natural shape of the foot, has a slightly pointed toe, is buckled across the instep, and has a low heel. Such shoes were made of leather or cloth, and some examples are in light colours.

Fig. 632 is a drawing of a GALOCHE or clog, which came into use towards the end of Henry VI.'s reign. It is made of wood, its top covered with leather, and

Fig. 632. Galoche

has an attached ornamental strap through which the foot was passed. The long point of the clog helped to support the toe of the shoe and kept the shoe from the mud and damp. Another kind of clog, called a POULAINE or "Poleyn," was in fashion at the Court of Burgundy, and is said to have been introduced from Poland. It was generally made of thick leather and was fairly flexible. One is shown in plan in Fig. 633, and another, Fig. 634, fastened to a foot (see also Fig. 564). The top of the sole was very often richly decorated in inlays of different woods, ivory, gold and silver, and the point of the toe was curved round and fastened by an ornament to the sole. These poulaines were worn by fashionable men and women in the streets, and slipped off when entering the house. With the disappearance of long toes about 1480, these poulaines went out of fashion.

One of a pair of very smart boots is shown in Fig. 635. Made of fairly substantial leather, it laces up the leg and fits the calf closely, being turned down below the knee and forming a point behind. The foot is slipped into a simple galoche of wood, with a leather loop.

Boots covering the lower part of the leg had been worn for some time, and mention of buskins is first made on p. 57. These only reached to below the knee, or in exceptional cases just above it. They were in general use during the whole course of the fifteenth century among horsemen and others desirous of being comfortably shod.

About the middle of the century the high boot was

Fig. 633.
Poulaine

introduced. The young noble in Plate **XXIV.** is wearing a pair of high boots made in soft leather, so long that they would reach the thigh. They are turned down to show the rich lining, and being soft they ruck around the leg—a much-desired effect. These fashionable long boots

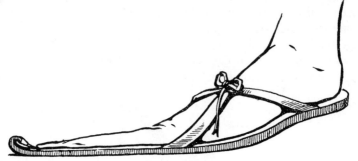

Fig. 634. Poulaine

were not only used for riding; they were also worn indoors, and were made in dark- or light-coloured soft leather, and were laced up the side, inside or out, for a distance of ten to twelve inches from the ankle, to make them fit, although not too closely. The length of the toe varied, of

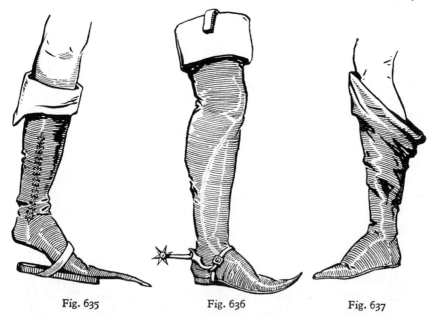

Fig. 635   Fig. 636   Fig. 637

course, according to the period. Fig. 636 shows one of these boots of the latest style—one very welcome to a busy man of society or commerce who spent much time in the saddle. Spurs were buckled on as shown in the drawing. The dotted line should be noticed; occasionally the high boot was made to open along this line, and fastened all the way by hooks and eyes. The toes of these boots turn upwards, a feature not unusual in footgear of the second half of the fifteenth century.

Fig. 637 shows a boot worn by all classes as an alternative fashion, in use at the same time as the high boot. Made of soft leather, the top was allowed to fall in many creases around the ankle.

Another freak of fashion in which dandies indulged was to wear a long boot on one leg and a low shoe on the other.

JEWELLERY, 1399–1485

A much more lavish display of jewellery is noticeable during the fifteenth century, although examples of this time do not differ much from the style used in the fourteenth century. The Middle Ages were not cursed with a craze for re-setting beautiful jewels in "modern" settings; antique examples were thoroughly appreciated. It seems incredible that the disturbances which took place in England and France —the French Wars and the Wars of the Roses—in no way diminished the extravagance of the nobles in the wearing and acquisition of jewellery. The French perhaps more than the English were noted for this "vice." The House of Valois were all devoted lovers of works of art, and the Dukes of Berry, Burgundy and Orleans, rivals in display, had an insatiable passion for jewels of great price. The lesser nobles followed their example, greatly to the stimulation of the art of the jeweller. Sumptuary laws enacted by Louis XI., and his dislike of extravagance, affected the art for a time. As a consequence, its development passed to the states of Burgundy and Flanders, where it rapidly achieved a surprising degree of intricacy, richness and elegance. At his death in 1467 Philippe le Bon possessed a vast quantity of jewellery and precious stones of inestimable value; all these passed to his son, Charles le Téméraire, and when he died they were dispersed throughout Europe, chiefly through the agency of the three brothers Fugger, descendants of the original Johann Fugger, a wealthy weaver of Graben near Augsburg, who had become great bankers and moneylenders, receiving the titles of Counts of the Holy Roman Empire. In England, Henry V. and Edward IV. were the greatest patrons of the jeweller's art, although some of the wealthiest nobles were very close rivals.

Crowns and Coronets

The very ornate crown worn by Henry IV. is shown in Fig. 638, copied from his effigy in Canterbury Cathedral. It consists of eight strawberry leaves and as many fleurs-de-lys alternating with sixteen groups of pearls. The band is deeper than in earlier examples, and is engraved and set with jewels. This may have been the "Harry" crown that was dissected and pledged piecemeal by Henry V. to raise money for his French expedition. This crown is said to have contained fifty-six pink rubies, called balays, forty sapphires, eight diamonds and seven large pearls. It was redeemed by Parliament in 1430–1.

Two coronets or chaplets are illustrated here. Fig. 639 shows one of twisted blue silk and gold, alternating with gold cinqfoil ornaments. Fig. 640 shows a band of blue set with gold discs, with rubies in the centre of each. Both these chaplets are of the type in use by noblemen during the first quarter of the fifteenth century. Another

Fig. 638. Crown, Henry IV.

is seen in Fig. 513, composed of quatrefoil motifs alternating with quaint shaped uprights, each set with a jewel. By the middle of the century head ornaments for men went out of fashion.

The Byzantine Empress Irene was the first monarch to add an arch to her crown (see Vol. I., p. 203); and Henry II. of Germany was the first Western emperor to adopt this innovation (see Vol. I., p. 265). Henry V. was the first English king to wear a "closed" crown, that is, one having two arches—probably made to replace the one (Fig. 638) belonging to his father, which he had previously pawned. The crown shown in Fig. 641 is reproduced from a portrait of Henry V., but whether the painting is contemporary or not is uncertain.

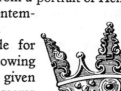

Fig. 639

Fig. 640

A crown without an arch was made for Henry V., to fit round his helmet. The following enumeration of jewels, with their cost, given in the Parliamentary Rolls dated 1423, seems prodigious, remembering the value of money in the fifteenth century, when £1 equalled £15 of 1914. The "workmanship" alone seems very reasonable—but the craftsman appears to have adjusted matters by charging £20 too much in the total!

Fig. 641. Crown, Henry V.

	£	s.	d.
4 balays (pink rubies)	133	6	8
4 sapphires at £10 each	40	0	0
80 large pearls at 60s.	240	0	0
128 pearls at 10s. each	64	0	0
4 balays at £13 6s. 8d. each . . .	53	6	8
16 sapphires at £4 each . . .	64	0	0
6 oz. of gold at £10 per oz. . . .	60	0	0
Workmanship	4	11	8
TOTAL	£679	5	0

A ruby, originally brought from Spain in 1366 by the Black Prince, was set in this crown.[1]

The coronet of Henry as Prince of Wales is shown in Plate XX.

The crown used by Henry VI., and shown in Fig. 642, has several arches set with pearls, surmounted by a mound and a cross. In place of the strawberry leaves seen in Fig. 638, are four crosses patée, and the deep band is set with oval and lozenge-shaped jewels and pearls. Towards the end of this reign the cap of maintenance or abacot was amalgamated with the crown, and formed a cap of crimson velvet inside the arches, its ermine brim showing beneath the band. Edward IV. is represented with a crown of six arches; six large fleurs-de-lys and six smaller ones

Fig. 642. Crown, Henry VI.

rise from the band, and the ermine brim is deeper than usual.

Fig. 643 shows the crown worn by Richard III., which is similar to that of Henry VI., but has only four arches. The crown seen in the badge, Fig. 682, has six arches, and these are crocketed.

The crown worn by Queen Joanna is like her husband's, and those worn by Catherine de Valois, Margaret of Anjou, and Elizabeth Wydeville may be seen in drawings representing them.

Fig. 643. Crown, Richard III.

A very beautiful crown worn by Margaret of Anjou is shown in Fig. 644. The band is edged top and bottom by a row of pearls, and on the band are four enamelled coats of arms, the one with France and England impaling Lorraine being in the centre, alternating with white enamelled roses having rubies set in the centres, and between each of these is an initial letter in raised gold. Above this band rise six points surmounted

Fig. 645. Peer's Coronet

Fig. 646. Peer's Coronet

Fig. 644. Crown, Margaret of Anjou

by cinqfoils bearing five sapphires surrounded by diamonds on each. Between these are six shorter uprights bearing trefoils, with large sapphires in the centres. At the bases of the high uprights are white enamelled roses, alternating with groups of five pearls. At the bases of the shorter uprights are single large pearls. This crown was made by Clement Deck of Vézelai, goldsmith to King René of Anjou, by whom he was ennobled,

[1] Now set in front of the crown made for Queen Victoria's coronation.

i.e. granted armorial bearings, in 1496, "or an annille azure between four thistles proper."

Fig. 647. Countess of Clarence

For peers' coronets, *see* Figs. 645 and 646 and p. 381.

Although coronets designed to indicate the precise rank of the wearer were not in use until the sixteenth century, noble ladies wore coronets of an elaborate form. Coronets seen in Figs. 613 A and 613 D are of the time of Henry IV. and Henry V. That in Fig. 614 D is of about 1440.

The fine coronet of the Countess of Clarence, Lady Margaret Holland, daughter of Thomas, Earl of Kent, and widow of John Beaufort, Marquess of Dorset and first Earl of Somerset, is to be seen on the beautiful altar tomb, 1440, to her memory and her two husbands in Canterbury Cathedral. Fig. 647 shows it worn above an elaborate reticulated headdress, and Fig. 648 gives a detail. The mantle tasseaux—a quatrefoil rose in gold, set with a ruby or emerald mounted on enamel, the lozenge framed in gold—should be noticed.

Fig. 648. Detail of 647

Fig. 649 gives a detail of the coronet represented in the effigy on a very beautiful monument in Ewelme Church to the

Fig. 649.
Coronet, Duchess of Suffolk

memory of Alice (born 1404), only child of Thomas Chaucer, son of the poet. She married, first, Thomas Montacute, Earl of Salisbury, who was killed at the siege of Orleans, 1428, and later became the wife of William de la Pole, first Duke of Suffolk. The duchess was made a Lady of the Garter in 1432. She died in 1475.

Brooches and Enseignes

During the fifteenth century the brooch became a very favourite decoration for the headdress. Henry IV. usually wore a very rich brooch fixed to the front of his hood. It is on record that he possessed an "ouche" representing in white and coloured enamel a young girl holding a popinjay in her hand, on a background of white flowers, and surrounded by diamonds, rubies, sapphires and pearls.

Fig. 650 shows a very elaborate ornament worn during the first half of the century, usually in a rather tall hat, such as is seen in Fig. 499.

Fig. 651 is the type of brooch used in the last reign, and in this, for ornamenting the front of the bag- or bolster-shaped cap seen in Figs. 349 and 389 c.

From the first part of the reign of Henry VI. onward, no gentleman was fully dressed without a

Fig. 650. Brooch

very rich brooch decorating his chaperon or bonet. These often had a small pendent jewel, as in Fig. 652, but it was more usual to have a rare pearl hung on one or two chain links, hanging from the ornament

Fig. 651.   Fig. 652.   Fig. 653.   Fig. 654.

Hat Brooches

(Fig. 653), which fell just over the edge of the cap on to the forehead above the left eye. Fig. 654 shows one of these bonet ornaments with three peardrop pearls suspended from it.

Tasseaux or Mantle Bosses

A larger version of Fig. 651 might be used also as one of a pair, fixed to the mantle where the cord or band of embroidery fastened it on the shoulders.

Fig. 655 gives one of a pair of circular mantle bosses in gold, three or four inches in diameter, ornamented with leaves and flowers in enamel, and set with different-coloured jewels. A section is given to show how the cords which fasten the mantle pass through each boss. Often a band of embroidery

Fig. 655. Mantle Tasseau

or cord gave place to a piece of goldsmith's work, made up of two or three hinged plaques. Fig. 656, showing one end-ornament and part of the hinged plate, explains this arrangement. One end was fixed to one side of the mantle, and the other to the opposite side. At the side of the

Fig. 656. Mantle Fastening

central ornament is a pin, A, which passes through slots. The whole ornament is of gold, having four white enamelled roses set with large rubies. The central ornament is of a beautiful shape, enclosing rubies, emeralds and pearls.

Fig. 657 shows another mantle boss, lozenge-shaped, also in gold, enamel and jewels; and Fig. 658 a simpler one having concave edges of gold surrounding an enamelled centre in a deep rich colour, surmounted by a leaf pattern in gold set with a coloured jewel. Fig. 659 is in gold, with a gold floral design set in enamel. Fig. 660 shows a very beautiful brooch worn by William of Wykeham, Bishop of Winchester. It is formed of the letter

Fig. 657. Tasseau

M in gold, the symbol of the Virgin, patroness of the diocese, surmounted by a crown, and is set with cabochon rubies and emeralds, and Oriental pearls, in compartments outlined with granular work. The vase in the centre is cut from a large ruby, from which spring three lilies of white enamel with cabochon emeralds set as leaves. Standing in the open arches are the figures of the Virgin and S. Gabriel, of gold in full relief, the wings of the angel being set with translucent green enamel.

Fig. 659. Tasseau

Fig. 658. Tasseau

The protection of sundry saints was further ensured by wearing their images, either fixed to some portion of the dress, or forming part of the decoration of a brooch or pendant.

Enseignes of the fifteenth century were brooches having either pins fixed to them or holes for fastening or sewing on to caps. They bore heraldic ornaments in enamel and gold, and were similar to badges, previously described. These were much used during the political disturbances in England and France, and were worn chiefly to denote the wearer's party.

Hip-belts worn over the cotehardie during this century were similar in design to those shown in the last chapter, but narrower and in less high relief. The bands of jewels which extended down the plastrons of fur were the same as described under Fig. 417. Other examples are shown on the various figures illustrating costumes of the fifteenth century.

Fig. 660.
Brooch, William of Wykeham

Finger Rings

Many rings were worn upon the fingers by men and women (especially the latter) of the second half of the fifteenth century, a fashion probably set by Queen Margaret, who was very fond of loading her hands with jewels. Illuminations, etc., of this century often show five or seven rings on each hand, and some, two or three on each finger, generally leaving one of the eight fingers without any. Frequently rings were worn on the middle joint as well as the third, and some men wore rings on the thumb. In design finger rings at this time were very similar to those worn to-day, set either with single or groups of jewels in the centre, or covering the half-hoop. Amongst other jewels of great value belonging to the Dukes of Burgundy were three marvellous diamonds each set in a finger ring. One was given by Charles le Téméraire to Pope Sextus IV., another in the shape of a heart held by two hands was given by him to his treacherous neighbour, Louis XI., and the third he always wore himself, and this was possibly the only clue to the recognition of his corpse on the battlefield of Nancy. Three other diamonds belonging to this duke were picked up on the battlefield. One eventually found a place in the Pope's tiara, and is valued at £12,000. A second, the "Sancy Diamond," was set in the crown of France, but sold at the Revolution. A third was bought by Henry VIII. for £5000. His daughter, Queen Mary, handed it over to Philip II., since when it has remained in the possession of the House of Hapsburg.

Fig. 661

A ring of uncertain date is shown in Fig. 661. It is of gold set with an irregular oval Oriental ruby, and five triangular diamonds in their native crystallised state, at equal distances round the circumference. Around the upper and lower edges is a Latin inscription, in black Gothic lettering: "Who wears me shall perform exploits—and with great joy shall return."

Jewelled rosaries were much used, hung from the girdle, or sometimes attached to the finger ring or round the wrist (*see* Fig. 576).

Pendants of various kinds, or small reliquaries, were attached to the rosary in the same manner as the crucifix.

Fig. 662 shows a *reliquary* dating about 1400. It measured about two by three inches, the front being of filigree gold foliage, mounted upon enamel of some rich colour, and framed to contain a relic. These reliquaries were hung on gold chains round the neck. Another reliquary of a later date is shown in Fig. 663.

Fig. 662.　　　Fig. 663.

Reliquaries

A *pendant cross tau* of Spanish workmanship, seen in Fig. 664, is worn by the noble depicted in Fig. 533. It is of silver set with jewels in each arm, having a filigree tassel hanging from the lower one. This same noble has a purse, Fig. 665, hung from his waistbelt, ornamented with silver set with precious stones.

Fig. 664

Neck chains were very generally worn by men and women during the fifteenth century. Primarily these consisted of links of gold or silver, but towards the end of the fourteenth century sections were inserted at intervals, made in enamel or set with jewels, and necklaces so made were called "Carcanets," a name also applied to the ordinary neck chain.

The fashion of wearing necklaces was revived, both by men and women, towards the end of the fourteenth century, and

Fig. 665. Purse

their use became an important part of full dress about the first quarter of the fifteenth, especially for women. The necklace of the men was generally referred to in the fourteenth and fifteenth centuries as a collar.

The Collar of SS, said to have been instituted by Henry IV., actually made its appearance toward the end of the fourteenth century, before Henry came to the throne. It is said to refer to the initial letter of Henry's motto, "Souvenez," "Remember me." The first example is found on the

Fig. 666. Collar of SS

effigy of Sir John Swinford, who died in 1371. The SS collar shown in Fig. 666 is taken from the effigy of John Gower, in Southwark Cathedral (1408). The SS fixed to an edged band resemble snakes, and the swan badge of the de Bohun family hangs from the trefoil link. The custom of suspending a badge from this collar came into use at the end of the fourteenth, and remained in vogue during the fifteenth century. The colour of the band is sometimes shown red, blue, or black, and often the S's were linked together without a band. Fig. 667 shows a collar so linked, dating 1446. Fig. 668 shows another of the fifteenth century, with the S's linked on a band.

Fig. 667

Fig. 668

The necklace shown in Fig. 669 is drawn from the portrait of Isabelle, Duchess of Burgundy. It is composed of rectangular plaques linked together, each set with a circular jewel. Along the top and bottom edges are single rows of small gold globules; motifs hang from the lower edge, and an ornament of three circular jewels set in gold is hung from a group of four circular-set jewels.

Fig. 669

Fig. 670 is a drawing made from a necklace of the first half of the fifteenth century. This also is composed of rectangular plaques linked together, each set with a jewel. Pendant pearls and enamel motifs hang alternately from each link.

Fig. 670

A very delicate necklace of strung pearls, having jewel pendants surrounded by pearls, is illustrated in Fig. 671 and dates about 1470.

Fig. 671

The necklace worn by Elizabeth Wydeville in her portrait in the Ashmolean Museum, Oxford, is a band designed in gold leaves worked in bullion, and outlined with black velvet or enamel. A quatrefoil ornament composed of the same materials has a ruby in the centre, with a pearl between each foil; a detail is given in Fig. 672. Hung round the neck by a black silk ribbon or "lace" is a beautiful reliquary of gold and enamel, set with five jewels and three pendant pearls (see Fig. 663).

Fig. 672

Fig. 673

More than one necklace was worn at this time, and the portrait said to represent Jane Shore, the wife of a Lombard Street jeweller and mistress of Edward IV., shows her wearing a double string of pearls round her throat, and below it a necklace of pierced circular medallions linked together, having a pendant similar in design but set with pearls.

The necklace shown in Fig. 673 is copied from the portrait at Holyrood Palace of Margaret of Denmark, Queen of Scotland (married

Fig. 674

1469). Enamelled lozenge-shaped ornaments are set at intervals between two rows of alternate pearls and enamel tubular beads. The gold pendant is set with jewels, and from it hangs a large pear-shaped pearl threaded on gold wire.

A necklace taken from a painting by Hans Memling is given in Fig. 674. Motifs designed as roses, in alternate red and white enamel, are each set with a central ruby or pearl in claw settings, surrounded by five pearls. These are linked together by twisted gold wire, headed by a row of cut jet beads or black pearls, with topaz pendants hung from the bottom edge.

German 1480

Fig. 675. Border

SECTION IX.—WEAVING AND MATERIALS, 1399–1485

(Continued from p. 283)

The Wars of the Roses had an interesting effect on the social and commercial development of England. Carried on almost exclusively by the barons and their retainers, these wars resulted in the destruction of the old feudal aristocracy by suicidal conflict, and led to a growth in the influence of the merchants and manufacturers. Despite the disturbance caused by these almost entirely political quarrels, the weaving industry steadily progressed, although checked from time to time by restrictions imposed on export and import as a consequence of continental differences, until at last the "Great Treaty" between the English and Flemish rulers in 1496 allowed trade to proceed unchecked once more.

Belainge. A common woollen stuff much in use during the fifteenth century.

Caddis. A kind of flock, used for stuffing. Caddis was also spun into yarn and used for quilting, stitching, etc. Another name for this latter kind was "Crull."

Camacas, cammaca. See Vol. I., p. 216. A costly material used during the fifteenth century.

Camelots were made during the fifteenth century of silk, either plain or with patterns.

Canvas. A hempen cloth used for outer clothing by the poor, and for lining garments by the rich.

Carda. The best quality of this fluffy cotton cloth in white was used as lining for the official dress of sergeants-at-law, and usually given for lining liveries.

Furs in use during the fifteenth century are noted on p. 282.

Gold, cloth of. The terms "Vermilion Cloth of Gold," "White Cloth of Gold," etc., are often found in writings of the fifteenth century. It was a material having a ground of gold with a very narrow rib of coloured silk, woven so closely that it had the effect of a colour shot with gold. Blue, crimson, green and purple cloth of gold were other varieties in use.

Gold thread, not unlike the fine Japanese make of the present day, was sold for decoration and embroidery, wound on rolls or "pipes" of some composition: "I prey you to buy for me two pipes of gold" (Agnes Paston, 1440).

Lawn. A very fine make of linen, first mentioned by this name in an inventory of effects of Henry V., dated 1423. John Lydgate refers to it in *London Lycpeny.*

Mahoitres, mahotoitres. A German name for wadding used as stuffing.

Mustyrdderyllers, musterdevelers. A cloth mentioned in records of the fifteenth century. The name undoubtedly refers to a make of woollen cloth (not to the colour) manufactured originally at the town of Muster-de-Villiers, near Harfleur, France. It is conjectured that the name may be also derived from "Mestier de velours," meaning half velvet—probably a kind of velveteen.

Velvet came into more general use at the beginning of the fifteenth century: previous to this time it is seldom mentioned, on account of its great rarity. The manufacture, chiefly in Italy, Spain and Flanders, greatly improved about this time and different kinds were invented. Velvet upon velvet was of two piles, that of the pattern being raised above the pile of the groundwork. The richest and most costly was of three-pile, and was stiffish in texture. To give this effect to velvet of an inferior quality, it was sometimes stiffened with a solution of gum.

"Venys gold." Passement or guipure, decorated braid, plaited, knotted or looped and woven in bright and dull gold to form a pattern which had a very rich effect. Made in Venice (hence its name), Milan

and Genoa. Very much used for ornamenting mantles and other garments worn during the Middle Ages.

Worsted. The quality of worsted was much improved in the fifteenth century, and some of the best had a surface of a silky nature: "fine worsted which is almost like silk."

Italian 1480

Fig. 676. Border

THE GUILDS AND LIVERY COMPANIES

(*Continued from p. 284*)

A register of craft guilds, compiled during the reign of Henry V., shows their number as one hundred and eleven. All were imbued with the aggressive spirit of the times, and strife between the merchants and the craft guilds was frequent and bitter, largely as a consequence of the former's endeavour to suppress the guilds. At other times the merchants sought a surer means of controlling the crafts by affiliating them with their own guilds. By the middle of the century the merchant guilds had gained supremacy, in many cases becoming identified with the governing bodies of the towns to which they belonged, and so continued to regulate trade.

During the second half of the century amalgamation of some of the smaller craft guilds under one head took place: thus the Glovers, Pursers, Tawyers, Pouchmakers and Whitawayers combined with the Leathersellers, under that name; and so forth. By 1528 the craft guilds were mainly represented by *The Twelve Great City Companies*, although a number of others still existed,[1] and some had died out altogether.

In order of precedence the twelve companies are as follows:

	First mentioned	*Charter*	*Incorporated*	*Grant of Arms*
1. The Mercers . . .	1172	1190	1393	1568
2. The Grocers . . .	1160	1345	1345	1531
3. The Drapers . . .	967		1439	1439
[2] 4. The Saltfishmongers .	1433 } Edward I.		1536	1575
The Stockfishmongers .	1509 }			

[1] In 1739 there were seventy-nine other companies in London, some of which had come into existence since 1528. At the present day there are sixty-seven.

[2] United in 1536: now known as the Fishmongers.

	First mentioned	Charter	Incorporated	Grant of Arms
5. The Goldsmiths	1180		1396	1396
6. The Skinners	1319		1327	1327
7. The Merchant Taylors	1300	1327	1466	1480
8. The Haberdashers			1447	1447
9. The Salters	1355		1558	1530
10. The Ironmongers	1351		1462	1455
11. The Vintners	1154	1365	1436	1427
12. The Clothworkers			1482	1530

These twelve great City Companies, and the guilds, used armorial bearings, many of them for a long time before they were officially granted. For the armorial bearings, *see* Fox Davies, *The Book of Public Arms.*

Entertainments of the City Companies and Guilds

(Continued from p. 286)

Important plays of the mystery and miracle type [1] were produced throughout the fifteenth century, chief among them being the Wakefield or Townley Plays, thirty-one in number; fifty-one others of the York Cycle, dating from 1415; and forty-two Coventry Plays, of which the first was written about 1468.

To this type of play, *Moralities* were added early in the fifteenth century. Morality plays were sermons in disguise, dealing seriously with abstractions and allegory, the characters representing certain qualities, such as "Good Deeds," "Avarice," etc. The first morality play dated about 1400.

Pageants.[2] When Henry V. returned from his French campaign in 1415, a great pageant was devised by the people of London for his reception. The Lord Mayor and aldermen in "red gowns with hoods of red and white," and the City companies and guilds in their variously-coloured liveries, rode out to meet him.

Again, in 1432, "scarlet gowns and sangwyn hoods were worn by the Aldermen, and white gowns with scarlet hoods and the cognisance —divers—embroidered on their sleeves, by the commonalty, when they met Henry VI. on his return."

In the Lord Mayor's Water Pageant of 1436, Robert Otteley, a

---

[1] These continued to be represented on the traditional lines of earlier periods. In like manner they were continued after this time, but with the rise of English drama in the Elizabethan era, mystery and miracle plays went out of fashion.

[2] The days of Elizabeth and James I. witnessed very wonderful pageants, and the reign of the latter is considered the Golden Age of the Lord Mayor's Show. Towards the end of the seventeenth and beginning of the eighteenth century these pageants lost a great deal of their original glamour, and festival processions gradually disappeared. The only one that has survived until the present day is the Lord Mayor's Show of 9 November.

member of the Grocers' Guild, was the first to use the Lord Mayor's State barge.

Sir Richard Whittington (born 1370), of the Mercers' Company, Alderman of London, 1392; Member of Parliament, 1416; and four times Lord Mayor, added to his renown by giving a banquet [1] of the

Figs. 677, 678, 679.   Fig. 680.
Table with Jugs and Salt   Stool, Ewer and Basin

most elaborate nature to Henry V. and Catherine of Valois in 1419. Even the fire in the centre of the hall was fed with spiced woods, and, responding to the queen's comment upon such luxury, he made the fuel more costly, it is said, by taking a bundle of the king's own bonds to the value of £60,000 and committing them to the flames. He died in 1425.

The Interlude was added to the list of dramatic performances during the reign of Henry VI. This had a decidedly comic element, and was given solely for amusement.

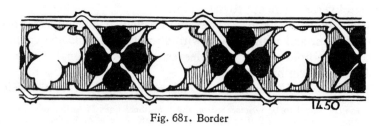

Fig. 681. Border

[1] Before the Great War, various City companies maintained this tradition and gave splendid banquets and receptions to favoured and appreciative gatherings, but to-day even these rejoicings have been curtailed.

At Bosworth Field, 22 August, 1485, Richard III. fought desperately, and when his friend, the Duke of Norfolk, was slain, he cut his way alone to the spot where the Duke of Richmond's standard of S. George was set up. Killing the standard-bearer, Brandon, he hoped to encounter Harry of Richmond personally, but "was borne down by numbers." His body was plundered of its armour and ornaments, and the crown that was about his helmet was picked up and hidden in a hawthorn bush. It was afterwards found by Sir Reginald Bray and carried to Lord Stanley who, taking Richmond to a little hillock close by, placed it on the head of his stepson, saluting him as King Henry VII.

Cleave to the crown  though it hang on a bush.

Fig. 682. Badge of Henry VII.

The dead king's stripped and mutilated body was flung head downwards over the back of a horse and taken back to Leicester, where it was buried in the Abbey of the Grey Friars.

The latter part of the fifteenth century marked the close of the mediæval feudal system, and a new régime, which dispensed with the little kingships of the great nobles, began. Europe in its modern form was being born, and concurrently the modern political machinery came into being. In England, the Wars of the Roses had resulted in the rule of the barons being entirely swept away, while the king, Henry VII., having now entire control of the existing artillery, strengthened the position he had won in battle by understandings, or alliances, with Scotland, France and Spain. France had become consolidated by the union of north and south, following on the conclusion of the Hundred Years' War, the practically complete expulsion of the English, and the abolition of the great feudatories of the kingdom. In Spain, the union of the Kingdom of Arragon (and Sicily) with that of Castile and Leon concentrated in one great power the whole of the

Iberian peninsula. In 1453 the Turks captured Constantinople, driving Greek scholarship to take refuge in Italy, and thus bringing about the great upheaval to be known subsequently as the "Renaissance" or Revival of Learning, which also was stimulated beyond measure by the invention of printing. The impetus thus given to art, literature, and science carries us beyond the scope of the present work, and leaves us anticipating the epoch-making discovery of the Americas and the Indies, and the setting of the stage for new acts and new actors in the world's drama.

END OF VOL. II

GENERAL INDEX

Note:—For names of individuals and places, see separate Index, p. 480.

INDEX OF NAMES

Names in the *Historical Data* are not indexed here.

A CATALOG OF SELECTED
DOVER BOOKS
IN ALL FIELDS OF INTEREST

A CATALOG OF SELECTED DOVER
BOOKS IN ALL FIELDS OF INTEREST

CONCERNING THE SPIRITUAL IN ART, Wassily Kandinsky. Pioneering work by father of abstract art. Thoughts on color theory, nature of art. Analysis of earlier masters. 12 illustrations. 80pp. of text. 5⅜ x 8½.   23411-8 Pa. $4.95

ANIMALS: 1,419 Copyright-Free Illustrations of Mammals, Birds, Fish, Insects, etc., Jim Harter (ed.). Clear wood engravings present, in extremely lifelike poses, over 1,000 species of animals. One of the most extensive pictorial sourcebooks of its kind. Captions. Index. 284pp. 9 x 12.   23766-4 Pa. $14.95

CELTIC ART: The Methods of Construction, George Bain. Simple geometric techniques for making Celtic interlacements, spirals, Kells-type initials, animals, humans, etc. Over 500 illustrations. 160pp. 9 x 12. (USO)   22923-8 Pa. $9.95

AN ATLAS OF ANATOMY FOR ARTISTS, Fritz Schider. Most thorough reference work on art anatomy in the world. Hundreds of illustrations, including selections from works by Vesalius, Leonardo, Goya, Ingres, Michelangelo, others. 593 illustrations. 192pp. 7⅛ x 10¼.   20241-0 Pa. $9.95

CELTIC HAND STROKE-BY-STROKE (Irish Half-Uncial from "The Book of Kells"): An Arthur Baker Calligraphy Manual, Arthur Baker. Complete guide to creating each letter of the alphabet in distinctive Celtic manner. Covers hand position, strokes, pens, inks, paper, more. Illustrated. 48pp. 8¼ x 11.   24336-2 Pa. $3.95

EASY ORIGAMI, John Montroll. Charming collection of 32 projects (hat, cup, pelican, piano, swan, many more) specially designed for the novice origami hobbyist. Clearly illustrated easy-to-follow instructions insure that even beginning papercrafters will achieve successful results. 48pp. 8¼ x 11.   27298-2 Pa. $3.50

THE COMPLETE BOOK OF BIRDHOUSE CONSTRUCTION FOR WOOD-WORKERS, Scott D. Campbell. Detailed instructions, illustrations, tables. Also data on bird habitat and instinct patterns. Bibliography. 3 tables. 63 illustrations in 15 figures. 48pp. 5¼ x 8½.   24407-5 Pa. $2.50

BLOOMINGDALE'S ILLUSTRATED 1886 CATALOG: Fashions, Dry Goods and Housewares, Bloomingdale Brothers. Famed merchants' extremely rare catalog depicting about 1,700 products: clothing, housewares, firearms, dry goods, jewelry, more. Invaluable for dating, identifying vintage items. Also, copyright-free graphics for artists, designers. Co-published with Henry Ford Museum & Greenfield Village. 160pp. 8¼ x 11.   25780-0 Pa. $10.95

HISTORIC COSTUME IN PICTURES, Braun & Schneider. Over 1,450 costumed figures in clearly detailed engravings–from dawn of civilization to end of 19th century. Captions. Many folk costumes. 256pp. 8⅜ x 11¾.   23150-X Pa. $12.95

STICKLEY CRAFTSMAN FURNITURE CATALOGS, Gustav Stickley and L. & J. G. Stickley. Beautiful, functional furniture in two authentic catalogs from 1910. 594 illustrations, including 277 photos, show settles, rockers, armchairs, reclining chairs, bookcases, desks, tables. 183pp. 6½ x 9¼.   23838-5 Pa. $11.95

AMERICAN LOCOMOTIVES IN HISTORIC PHOTOGRAPHS: 1858 to 1949, Ron Ziel (ed.). A rare collection of 126 meticulously detailed official photographs, called "builder portraits," of American locomotives that majestically chronicle the rise of steam locomotive power in America. Introduction. Detailed captions. xi + 129pp. 9 x 12.   27393-8 Pa. $13.95

AMERICA'S LIGHTHOUSES: An Illustrated History, Francis Ross Holland, Jr. Delightfully written, profusely illustrated fact-filled survey of over 200 American lighthouses since 1716. History, anecdotes, technological advances, more. 240pp. 8 x 10¾.
25576-X Pa. $12.95

TOWARDS A NEW ARCHITECTURE, Le Corbusier. Pioneering manifesto by founder of "International School." Technical and aesthetic theories, views of industry, economics, relation of form to function, "mass-production split" and much more. Profusely illustrated. 320pp. 6⅛ x 9¼. (USO)   25023-7 Pa. $9.95

HOW THE OTHER HALF LIVES, Jacob Riis. Famous journalistic record, exposing poverty and degradation of New York slums around 1900, by major social reformer. 100 striking and influential photographs. 233pp. 10 x 7⅞.
22012-5 Pa. $11.95

FRUIT KEY AND TWIG KEY TO TREES AND SHRUBS, William M. Harlow. One of the handiest and most widely used identification aids. Fruit key covers 120 deciduous and evergreen species; twig key 160 deciduous species. Easily used. Over 300 photographs. 126pp. 5⅜ x 8½.   20511-8 Pa. $3.95

COMMON BIRD SONGS, Dr. Donald J. Borror. Songs of 60 most common U.S. birds: robins, sparrows, cardinals, bluejays, finches, more–arranged in order of increasing complexity. Up to 9 variations of songs of each species.
Cassette and manual 99911-4 $8.95

ORCHIDS AS HOUSE PLANTS, Rebecca Tyson Northen. Grow cattleyas and many other kinds of orchids–in a window, in a case, or under artificial light. 63 illustrations. 148pp. 5⅜ x 8½.   23261-1 Pa. $5.95

MONSTER MAZES, Dave Phillips. Masterful mazes at four levels of difficulty. Avoid deadly perils and evil creatures to find magical treasures. Solutions for all 32 exciting illustrated puzzles. 48pp. 8¼ x 11.   26005-4 Pa. $2.95

MOZART'S DON GIOVANNI (DOVER OPERA LIBRETTO SERIES), Wolfgang Amadeus Mozart. Introduced and translated by Ellen H. Bleiler. Standard Italian libretto, with complete English translation. Convenient and thoroughly portable–an ideal companion for reading along with a recording or the performance itself. Introduction. List of characters. Plot summary. 121pp. 5¼ x 8½.
24944-1 $3.95

TECHNICAL MANUAL AND DICTIONARY OF CLASSICAL BALLET, Gail Grant. Defines, explains, comments on steps, movements, poses and concepts. 15-page pictorial section. Basic book for student, viewer. 127pp. 5⅜ x 8½.
21843-0 Pa. $4.95

BRASS INSTRUMENTS: Their History and Development, Anthony Baines. Authoritative, updated survey of the evolution of trumpets, trombones, bugles, cornets, French horns, tubas and other brass wind instruments. Over 140 illustrations and 48 music examples. Corrected and updated by author. New preface. Bibliography. 320pp. 5⅜ x 8½. 27574-4 Pa. $9.95

HOLLYWOOD GLAMOR PORTRAITS, John Kobal (ed.). 145 photos from 1926-49. Harlow, Gable, Bogart, Bacall; 94 stars in all. Full background on photographers, technical aspects. 160pp. 8⅜ x 11¼. 23352-9 Pa. $12.95

MAX AND MORITZ, Wilhelm Busch. Great humor classic in both German and English. Also 10 other works: "Cat and Mouse," "Plisch and Plumm," etc. 216pp. 5⅜ x 8½. 20181-3 Pa. $6.95

THE RAVEN AND OTHER FAVORITE POEMS, Edgar Allan Poe. Over 40 of the author's most memorable poems: "The Bells," "Ulalume," "Israfel," "To Helen," "The Conqueror Worm," "Eldorado," "Annabel Lee," many more. Alphabetic lists of titles and first lines. 64pp. 5³⁄₁₆ x 8¼. 26685-0 Pa. $1.00

PERSONAL MEMOIRS OF U. S. GRANT, Ulysses Simpson Grant. Intelligent, deeply moving firsthand account of Civil War campaigns, considered by many the finest military memoirs ever written. Includes letters, historic photographs, maps and more. 528pp. 6⅛ x 9¼. 28587-1 Pa. $12.95

AMULETS AND SUPERSTITIONS, E. A. Wallis Budge. Comprehensive discourse on origin, powers of amulets in many ancient cultures: Arab, Persian Babylonian, Assyrian, Egyptian, Gnostic, Hebrew, Phoenician, Syriac, etc. Covers cross, swastika, crucifix, seals, rings, stones, etc. 584pp. 5⅜ x 8½. 23573-4 Pa. $15.95

RUSSIAN STORIES/PYCCKNE PACCKA3bl: A Dual-Language Book, edited by Gleb Struve. Twelve tales by such masters as Chekhov, Tolstoy, Dostoevsky, Pushkin, others. Excellent word-for-word English translations on facing pages, plus teaching and study aids, Russian/English vocabulary, biographical/critical introductions, more. 416pp. 5⅜ x 8½. 26244-8 Pa. $9.95

PHILADELPHIA THEN AND NOW: 60 Sites Photographed in the Past and Present, Kenneth Finkel and Susan Oyama. Rare photographs of City Hall, Logan Square, Independence Hall, Betsy Ross House, other landmarks juxtaposed with contemporary views. Captures changing face of historic city. Introduction. Captions. 128pp. 8¼ x 11. 25790-8 Pa. $9.95

AIA ARCHITECTURAL GUIDE TO NASSAU AND SUFFOLK COUNTIES, LONG ISLAND, The American Institute of Architects, Long Island Chapter, and the Society for the Preservation of Long Island Antiquities. Comprehensive, well-researched and generously illustrated volume brings to life over three centuries of Long Island's great architectural heritage. More than 240 photographs with authoritative, extensively detailed captions. 176pp. 8¼ x 11. 26946-9 Pa. $14.95

NORTH AMERICAN INDIAN LIFE: Customs and Traditions of 23 Tribes, Elsie Clews Parsons (ed.). 27 fictionalized essays by noted anthropologists examine religion, customs, government, additional facets of life among the Winnebago, Crow, Zuni, Eskimo, other tribes. 480pp. 6⅛ x 9¼. 27377-6 Pa. $10.95

FRANK LLOYD WRIGHT'S HOLLYHOCK HOUSE, Donald Hoffmann. Lavishly illustrated, carefully documented study of one of Wright's most controversial residential designs. Over 120 photographs, floor plans, elevations, etc. Detailed perceptive text by noted Wright scholar. Index. 128pp. 9¼ x 10¾. 27133-1 Pa. $11.95

THE MALE AND FEMALE FIGURE IN MOTION: 60 Classic Photographic Sequences, Eadweard Muybridge. 60 true-action photographs of men and women walking, running, climbing, bending, turning, etc., reproduced from rare 19th-century masterpiece. vi + 121pp. 9 x 12. 24745-7 Pa. $10.95

1001 QUESTIONS ANSWERED ABOUT THE SEASHORE, N. J. Berrill and Jacquelyn Berrill. Queries answered about dolphins, sea snails, sponges, starfish, fishes, shore birds, many others. Covers appearance, breeding, growth, feeding, much more. 305pp. 5¼ x 8¼. 23366-9 Pa. $9.95

GUIDE TO OWL WATCHING IN NORTH AMERICA, Donald S. Heintzelman. Superb guide offers complete data and descriptions of 19 species: barn owl, screech owl, snowy owl, many more. Expert coverage of owl-watching equipment, conservation, migrations and invasions, etc. Guide to observing sites. 84 illustrations. xiii + 193pp. 5⅜ x 8½. 27344-X Pa. $8.95

MEDICINAL AND OTHER USES OF NORTH AMERICAN PLANTS: A Historical Survey with Special Reference to the Eastern Indian Tribes, Charlotte Erichsen-Brown. Chronological historical citations document 500 years of usage of plants, trees, shrubs native to eastern Canada, northeastern U.S. Also complete identifying information. 343 illustrations. 544pp. 6½ x 9¼. 25951-X Pa. $12.95

STORYBOOK MAZES, Dave Phillips. 23 stories and mazes on two-page spreads: Wizard of Oz, Treasure Island, Robin Hood, etc. Solutions. 64pp. 8¼ x 11. 23628-5 Pa. $2.95

NEGRO FOLK MUSIC, U.S.A., Harold Courlander. Noted folklorist's scholarly yet readable analysis of rich and varied musical tradition. Includes authentic versions of over 40 folk songs. Valuable bibliography and discography. xi + 324pp. 5⅜ x 8½. 27350-4 Pa. $9.95

MOVIE-STAR PORTRAITS OF THE FORTIES, John Kobal (ed.). 163 glamor, studio photos of 106 stars of the 1940s: Rita Hayworth, Ava Gardner, Marlon Brando, Clark Gable, many more. 176pp. 8⅜ x 11¼. 23546-7 Pa. $14.95

BENCHLEY LOST AND FOUND, Robert Benchley. Finest humor from early 30s, about pet peeves, child psychologists, post office and others. Mostly unavailable elsewhere. 73 illustrations by Peter Arno and others. 183pp. 5⅜ x 8½. 22410-4 Pa. $6.95

YEKL and THE IMPORTED BRIDEGROOM AND OTHER STORIES OF YIDDISH NEW YORK, Abraham Cahan. Film Hester Street based on Yekl (1896). Novel, other stories among first about Jewish immigrants on N.Y.'s East Side. 240pp. 5⅜ x 8½. 22427-9 Pa. $6.95

SELECTED POEMS, Walt Whitman. Generous sampling from *Leaves of Grass.* Twenty-four poems include "I Hear America Singing," "Song of the Open Road," "I Sing the Body Electric," "When Lilacs Last in the Dooryard Bloom'd," "O Captain! My Captain!"—all reprinted from an authoritative edition. Lists of titles and first lines. 128pp. 5⁵⁄₁₆ x 8¼. 26878-0 Pa. $1.00

THE BEST TALES OF HOFFMANN, E. T. A. Hoffmann. 10 of Hoffmann's most important stories: "Nutcracker and the King of Mice," "The Golden Flowerpot," etc. 458pp. 5⅜ x 8½. 21793-0 Pa. $9.95

FROM FETISH TO GOD IN ANCIENT EGYPT, E. A. Wallis Budge. Rich detailed survey of Egyptian conception of "God" and gods, magic, cult of animals, Osiris, more. Also, superb English translations of hymns and legends. 240 illustrations. 545pp. 5⅜ x 8½. 25803-3 Pa. $13.95

FRENCH STORIES/CONTES FRANÇAIS: A Dual-Language Book, Wallace Fowlie. Ten stories by French masters, Voltaire to Camus: "Micromegas" by Voltaire; "The Atheist's Mass" by Balzac; "Minuet" by de Maupassant; "The Guest" by Camus, six more. Excellent English translations on facing pages. Also French-English vocabulary list, exercises, more. 352pp. 5⅜ x 8½. 26443-2 Pa. $9.95

CHICAGO AT THE TURN OF THE CENTURY IN PHOTOGRAPHS: 122 Historic Views from the Collections of the Chicago Historical Society, Larry A. Viskochil. Rare large-format prints offer detailed views of City Hall, State Street, the Loop, Hull House, Union Station, many other landmarks, circa 1904-1913. Introduction. Captions. Maps. 144pp. 9⅜ x 12¼. 24656-6 Pa. $12.95

OLD BROOKLYN IN EARLY PHOTOGRAPHS, 1865-1929, William Lee Younger. Luna Park, Gravesend race track, construction of Grand Army Plaza, moving of Hotel Brighton, etc. 157 previously unpublished photographs. 165pp. 8⅞ x 11¾. 23587-4 Pa. $13.95

THE MYTHS OF THE NORTH AMERICAN INDIANS, Lewis Spence. Rich anthology of the myths and legends of the Algonquins, Iroquois, Pawnees and Sioux, prefaced by an extensive historical and ethnological commentary. 36 illustrations. 480pp. 5⅜ x 8½. 25967-6 Pa. $10.95

AN ENCYCLOPEDIA OF BATTLES: Accounts of Over 1,560 Battles from 1479 B.C. to the Present, David Eggenberger. Essential details of every major battle in recorded history from the first battle of Megiddo in 1479 B.C. to Grenada in 1984. List of Battle Maps. New Appendix covering the years 1967-1984. Index. 99 illustrations. 544pp. 6½ x 9¼. 24913-1 Pa. $16.95

SAILING ALONE AROUND THE WORLD, Captain Joshua Slocum. First man to sail around the world, alone, in small boat. One of great feats of seamanship told in delightful manner. 67 illustrations. 294pp. 5⅜ x 8½. 20326-3 Pa. $6.95

ANARCHISM AND OTHER ESSAYS, Emma Goldman. Powerful, penetrating, prophetic essays on direct action, role of minorities, prison reform, puritan hypocrisy, violence, etc. 271pp. 5⅜ x 8½. 22484-8 Pa. $7.95

MYTHS OF THE HINDUS AND BUDDHISTS, Ananda K. Coomaraswamy and Sister Nivedita. Great stories of the epics; deeds of Krishna, Shiva, taken from puranas, Vedas, folk tales; etc. 32 illustrations. 400pp. 5⅜ x 8½. 21759-0 Pa. $12.95

BEYOND PSYCHOLOGY, Otto Rank. Fear of death, desire of immortality, nature of sexuality, social organization, creativity, according to Rankian system. 291pp. 5⅜ x 8½. 20485-5 Pa. $8.95

A THEOLOGICO-POLITICAL TREATISE, Benedict Spinoza. Also contains unfinished Political Treatise. Great classic on religious liberty, theory of government on common consent. R. Elwes translation. Total of 421pp. 5⅜ x 8½. 20249-6 Pa. $9.95

MY BONDAGE AND MY FREEDOM, Frederick Douglass. Born a slave, Douglass became outspoken force in antislavery movement. The best of Douglass' autobiographies. Graphic description of slave life. 464pp. 5⅜ x 8½. 22457-0 Pa. $8.95

FOLLOWING THE EQUATOR: A Journey Around the World, Mark Twain. Fascinating humorous account of 1897 voyage to Hawaii, Australia, India, New Zealand, etc. Ironic, bemused reports on peoples, customs, climate, flora and fauna, politics, much more. 197 illustrations. 720pp. 5⅜ x 8½. 26113-1 Pa. $15.95

THE PEOPLE CALLED SHAKERS, Edward D. Andrews. Definitive study of Shakers: origins, beliefs, practices, dances, social organization, furniture and crafts, etc. 33 illustrations. 351pp. 5⅜ x 8½. 21081-2 Pa. $8.95

THE MYTHS OF GREECE AND ROME, H. A. Guerber. A classic of mythology, generously illustrated, long prized for its simple, graphic, accurate retelling of the principal myths of Greece and Rome, and for its commentary on their origins and significance. With 64 illustrations by Michelangelo, Raphael, Titian, Rubens, Canova, Bernini and others. 480pp. 5⅜ x 8½. 27584-1 Pa. $9.95

PSYCHOLOGY OF MUSIC, Carl E. Seashore. Classic work discusses music as a medium from psychological viewpoint. Clear treatment of physical acoustics, auditory apparatus, sound perception, development of musical skills, nature of musical feeling, host of other topics. 88 figures. 408pp. 5⅜ x 8½. 21851-1 Pa. $11.95

THE PHILOSOPHY OF HISTORY, Georg W. Hegel. Great classic of Western thought develops concept that history is not chance but rational process, the evolution of freedom. 457pp. 5⅜ x 8½. 20112-0 Pa. $9.95

THE BOOK OF TEA, Kakuzo Okakura. Minor classic of the Orient: entertaining, charming explanation, interpretation of traditional Japanese culture in terms of tea ceremony. 94pp. 5⅜ x 8½. 20070-1 Pa. $3.95

LIFE IN ANCIENT EGYPT, Adolf Erman. Fullest, most thorough, detailed older account with much not in more recent books, domestic life, religion, magic, medicine, commerce, much more. Many illustrations reproduce tomb paintings, carvings, hieroglyphs, etc. 597pp. 5⅜ x 8½. 22632-8 Pa. $12.95

SUNDIALS, Their Theory and Construction, Albert Waugh. Far and away the best, most thorough coverage of ideas, mathematics concerned, types, construction, adjusting anywhere. Simple, nontechnical treatment allows even children to build several of these dials. Over 100 illustrations. 230pp. 5⅜ x 8½. 22947-5 Pa. $8.95

DYNAMICS OF FLUIDS IN POROUS MEDIA, Jacob Bear. For advanced students of ground water hydrology, soil mechanics and physics, drainage and irrigation engineering, and more. 335 illustrations. Exercises, with answers. 784pp. 6⅛ x 9¼.
65675-6 Pa. $19.95

SONGS OF EXPERIENCE: Facsimile Reproduction with 26 Plates in Full Color, William Blake. 26 full-color plates from a rare 1826 edition. Includes "TheTyger," "London," "Holy Thursday," and other poems. Printed text of poems. 48pp. 5¼ x 7.
24636-1 Pa. $4.95

OLD-TIME VIGNETTES IN FULL COLOR, Carol Belanger Grafton (ed.). Over 390 charming, often sentimental illustrations, selected from archives of Victorian graphics—pretty women posing, children playing, food, flowers, kittens and puppies, smiling cherubs, birds and butterflies, much more. All copyright-free. 48pp. 9¼ x 12¼.
27269-9 Pa. $7.95

PIANO TUNING, J. Cree Fischer. Clearest, best book for beginner, amateur. Simple repairs, raising dropped notes, tuning by easy method of flattened fifths. No previous skills needed. 4 illustrations. 201pp. 5⅜ x 8½.   23267-0 Pa. $6.95

A SOURCE BOOK IN THEATRICAL HISTORY, A. M. Nagler. Contemporary observers on acting, directing, make-up, costuming, stage props, machinery, scene design, from Ancient Greece to Chekhov. 611pp. 5⅜ x 8½.   20515-0 Pa. $12.95

THE COMPLETE NONSENSE OF EDWARD LEAR, Edward Lear. All nonsense limericks, zany alphabets, Owl and Pussycat, songs, nonsense botany, etc., illustrated by Lear. Total of 320pp. 5⅜ x 8½. (USO)   20167-8 Pa. $7.95

VICTORIAN PARLOUR POETRY: An Annotated Anthology, Michael R. Turner. 117 gems by Longfellow, Tennyson, Browning, many lesser-known poets. "The Village Blacksmith," "Curfew Must Not Ring Tonight," "Only a Baby Small," dozens more, often difficult to find elsewhere. Index of poets, titles, first lines. xxiii + 325pp. 5⅜ x 8¼.   27044-0 Pa. $8.95

DUBLINERS, James Joyce. Fifteen stories offer vivid, tightly focused observations of the lives of Dublin's poorer classes. At least one, "The Dead," is considered a masterpiece. Reprinted complete and unabridged from standard edition. 160pp. 5³⁄₁₆ x 8¼.   26870-5 Pa. $1.00

THE HAUNTED MONASTERY and THE CHINESE MAZE MURDERS, Robert van Gulik. Two full novels by van Gulik, set in 7th-century China, continue adventures of Judge Dee and his companions. An evil Taoist monastery, seemingly supernatural events; overgrown topiary maze hides strange crimes. 27 illustrations. 328pp. 5⅜ x 8½.   23502-5 Pa. $8.95

THE BOOK OF THE SACRED MAGIC OF ABRAMELIN THE MAGE, translated by S. MacGregor Mathers. Medieval manuscript of ceremonial magic. Basic document in Aleister Crowley, Golden Dawn groups. 268pp. 5⅜ x 8½.   23211-5 Pa. $9.95

NEW RUSSIAN-ENGLISH AND ENGLISH-RUSSIAN DICTIONARY, M. A. O'Brien. This is a remarkably handy Russian dictionary, containing a surprising amount of information, including over 70,000 entries. 366pp. 4½ x 6⅛.   20208-9 Pa. $10.95

HISTORIC HOMES OF THE AMERICAN PRESIDENTS, Second, Revised Edition, Irvin Haas. A traveler's guide to American Presidential homes, most open to the public, depicting and describing homes occupied by every American President from George Washington to George Bush. With visiting hours, admission charges, travel routes. 175 photographs. Index. 160pp. 8¼ x 11.   26751-2 Pa. $11.95

NEW YORK IN THE FORTIES, Andreas Feininger. 162 brilliant photographs by the well-known photographer, formerly with *Life* magazine. Commuters, shoppers, Times Square at night, much else from city at its peak. Captions by John von Hartz. 181pp. 9¼ x 10¾.   23585-8 Pa. $13.95

INDIAN SIGN LANGUAGE, William Tomkins. Over 525 signs developed by Sioux and other tribes. Written instructions and diagrams. Also 290 pictographs. 111pp. 6⅛ x 9¼.   22029-X Pa. $3.95

ANATOMY: A Complete Guide for Artists, Joseph Sheppard. A master of figure drawing shows artists how to render human anatomy convincingly. Over 460 illustrations. 224pp. 8⅜ x 11¼. 27279-6 Pa. $11.95

MEDIEVAL CALLIGRAPHY: Its History and Technique, Marc Drogin. Spirited history, comprehensive instruction manual covers 13 styles (ca. 4th century thru 15th). Excellent photographs; directions for duplicating medieval techniques with modern tools. 224pp. 8⅜ x 11¼. 26142-5 Pa. $12.95

DRIED FLOWERS: How to Prepare Them, Sarah Whitlock and Martha Rankin. Complete instructions on how to use silica gel, meal and borax, perlite aggregate, sand and borax, glycerine and water to create attractive permanent flower arrangements. 12 illustrations. 32pp. 5⅜ x 8½. 21802-3 Pa. $1.00

EASY-TO-MAKE BIRD FEEDERS FOR WOODWORKERS, Scott D. Campbell. Detailed, simple-to-use guide for designing, constructing, caring for and using feeders. Text, illustrations for 12 classic and contemporary designs. 96pp. 5⅜ x 8½. 25847-5 Pa. $3.95

SCOTTISH WONDER TALES FROM MYTH AND LEGEND, Donald A. Mackenzie. 16 lively tales tell of giants rumbling down mountainsides, of a magic wand that turns stone pillars into warriors, of gods and goddesses, evil hags, powerful forces and more. 240pp. 5⅜ x 8½. 29677-6 Pa. $6.95

THE HISTORY OF UNDERCLOTHES, C. Willett Cunnington and Phyllis Cunnington. Fascinating, well-documented survey covering six centuries of English undergarments, enhanced with over 100 illustrations: 12th-century laced-up bodice, footed long drawers (1795), 19th-century bustles, 19th-century corsets for men, Victorian "bust improvers," much more. 272pp. 5⅝ x 8¼. 27124-2 Pa. $9.95

ARTS AND CRAFTS FURNITURE: The Complete Brooks Catalog of 1912, Brooks Manufacturing Co. Photos and detailed descriptions of more than 150 now very collectible furniture designs from the Arts and Crafts movement depict davenports, settees, buffets, desks, tables, chairs, bedsteads, dressers and more, all built of solid, quarter-sawed oak. Invaluable for students and enthusiasts of antiques, Americana and the decorative arts. 80pp. 6½ x 9¼. 27471-3 Pa. $8.95

HOW WE INVENTED THE AIRPLANE: An Illustrated History, Orville Wright. Fascinating firsthand account covers early experiments, construction of planes and motors, first flights, much more. Introduction and commentary by Fred C. Kelly. 76 photographs. 96pp. 8¼ x 11. 25662-6 Pa. $8.95

THE ARTS OF THE SAILOR: Knotting, Splicing and Ropework, Hervey Garrett Smith. Indispensable shipboard reference covers tools, basic knots and useful hitches; handsewing and canvas work, more. Over 100 illustrations. Delightful reading for sea lovers. 256pp. 5⅜ x 8½. 26440-8 Pa. $8.95

FRANK LLOYD WRIGHT'S FALLINGWATER: The House and Its History, Second, Revised Edition, Donald Hoffmann. A total revision–both in text and illustrations–of the standard document on Fallingwater, the boldest, most personal architectural statement of Wright's mature years, updated with valuable new material from the recently opened Frank Lloyd Wright Archives. "Fascinating"–*The New York Times.* 116 illustrations. 128pp. 9¼ x 10¾. 27430-6 Pa. $12.95

PHOTOGRAPHIC SKETCHBOOK OF THE CIVIL WAR, Alexander Gardner. 100 photos taken on field during the Civil War. Famous shots of Manassas Harper's Ferry, Lincoln, Richmond, slave pens, etc. 244pp. 10⅝ x 8¼.   22731-6 Pa. $10.95

FIVE ACRES AND INDEPENDENCE, Maurice G. Kains. Great back-to-the-land classic explains basics of self-sufficient farming. The one book to get. 95 illustrations. 397pp. 5⅜ x 8½.   20974-1 Pa. $7.95

SONGS OF EASTERN BIRDS, Dr. Donald J. Borror. Songs and calls of 60 species most common to eastern U.S.: warblers, woodpeckers, flycatchers, thrushes, larks, many more in high-quality recording.   Cassette and manual 99912-2 $9.95

A MODERN HERBAL, Margaret Grieve. Much the fullest, most exact, most useful compilation of herbal material. Gigantic alphabetical encyclopedia, from aconite to zedoary, gives botanical information, medical properties, folklore, economic uses, much else. Indispensable to serious reader. 161 illustrations. 888pp. 6½ x 9¼. 2-vol. set. (USO)   Vol. I: 22798-7 Pa. $9.95
                                                                                 Vol. II: 22799-5 Pa. $9.95

HIDDEN TREASURE MAZE BOOK, Dave Phillips. Solve 34 challenging mazes accompanied by heroic tales of adventure. Evil dragons, people-eating plants, blood-thirsty giants, many more dangerous adversaries lurk at every twist and turn. 34 mazes, stories, solutions. 48pp. 8¼ x 11.   24566-7 Pa. $2.95

LETTERS OF W. A. MOZART, Wolfgang A. Mozart. Remarkable letters show bawdy wit, humor, imagination, musical insights, contemporary musical world; includes some letters from Leopold Mozart. 276pp. 5⅜ x 8½.   22859-2 Pa. $7.95

BASIC PRINCIPLES OF CLASSICAL BALLET, Agrippina Vaganova. Great Russian theoretician, teacher explains methods for teaching classical ballet. 118 illus-trations. 175pp. 5⅜ x 8½.   22036-2 Pa. $5.95

THE JUMPING FROG, Mark Twain. Revenge edition. The original story of The Celebrated Jumping Frog of Calaveras County, a hapless French translation, and Twain's hilarious "retranslation" from the French. 12 illustrations. 66pp. 5⅜ x 8½.
                                                                                      22686-7 Pa. $3.95

BEST REMEMBERED POEMS, Martin Gardner (ed.). The 126 poems in this superb collection of 19th- and 20th-century British and American verse range from Shelley's "To a Skylark" to the impassioned "Renascence" of Edna St. Vincent Millay and to Edward Lear's whimsical "The Owl and the Pussycat." 224pp. 5⅜ x 8½.
                                                                                      27165-X Pa. $5.95

COMPLETE SONNETS, William Shakespeare. Over 150 exquisite poems deal with love, friendship, the tyranny of time, beauty's evanescence, death and other themes in language of remarkable power, precision and beauty. Glossary of archaic terms. 80pp. 5³⁄₁₆ x 8¼.   26686-9 Pa. $1.00

BODIES IN A BOOKSHOP, R. T. Campbell. Challenging mystery of blackmail and murder with ingenious plot and superbly drawn characters. In the best tradition of British suspense fiction. 192pp. 5⅜ x 8½.   24720-1 Pa. $6.95

THE WIT AND HUMOR OF OSCAR WILDE, Alvin Redman (ed.). More than 1,000 ripostes, paradoxes, wisecracks: Work is the curse of the drinking classes; I can resist everything except temptation; etc. 258pp. 5⅜ x 8½. 20602-5 Pa. $6.95

SHAKESPEARE LEXICON AND QUOTATION DICTIONARY, Alexander Schmidt. Full definitions, locations, shades of meaning in every word in plays and poems. More than 50,000 exact quotations. 1,485pp. 6½ x 9¼. 2-vol. set.
Vol. 1: 22726-X Pa. $17.95
Vol. 2: 22727-8 Pa. $17.95

SELECTED POEMS, Emily Dickinson. Over 100 best-known, best-loved poems by one of America's foremost poets, reprinted from authoritative early editions. No comparable edition at this price. Index of first lines. 64pp. 5 3/16 x 8¼.
26466-1 Pa. $1.00

CELEBRATED CASES OF JUDGE DEE (DEE GOONG AN), translated by Robert van Gulik. Authentic 18th-century Chinese detective novel; Dee and associates solve three interlocked cases. Led to van Gulik's own stories with same characters. Extensive introduction. 9 illustrations. 237pp. 5⅜ x 8½. 23337-5 Pa. $7.95

THE MALLEUS MALEFICARUM OF KRAMER AND SPRENGER, translated by Montague Summers. Full text of most important witchhunter's "bible," used by both Catholics and Protestants. 278pp. 6⅝ x 10. 22802-9 Pa. $12.95

SPANISH STORIES/CUENTOS ESPAÑOLES: A Dual-Language Book, Angel Flores (ed.). Unique format offers 13 great stories in Spanish by Cervantes, Borges, others. Faithful English translations on facing pages. 352pp. 5⅜ x 8½.
25399-6 Pa. $8.95

THE CHICAGO WORLD'S FAIR OF 1893: A Photographic Record, Stanley Appelbaum (ed.). 128 rare photos show 200 buildings, Beaux-Arts architecture, Midway, original Ferris Wheel, Edison's kinetoscope, more. Architectural emphasis; full text. 116pp. 8¼ x 11. 23990-X Pa. $9.95

OLD QUEENS, N.Y., IN EARLY PHOTOGRAPHS, Vincent F. Seyfried and William Asadorian. Over 160 rare photographs of Maspeth, Jamaica, Jackson Heights, and other areas. Vintage views of DeWitt Clinton mansion, 1939 World's Fair and more. Captions. 192pp. 8⅞ x 11. 26358-4 Pa. $12.95

CAPTURED BY THE INDIANS: 15 Firsthand Accounts, 1750-1870, Frederick Drimmer. Astounding true historical accounts of grisly torture, bloody conflicts, relentless pursuits, miraculous escapes and more, by people who lived to tell the tale. 384pp. 5⅜ x 8½. 24901-8 Pa. $8.95

THE WORLD'S GREAT SPEECHES, Lewis Copeland and Lawrence W. Lamm (eds.). Vast collection of 278 speeches of Greeks to 1970. Powerful and effective models; unique look at history. 842pp. 5⅜ x 8½. 20468-5 Pa. $14.95

THE BOOK OF THE SWORD, Sir Richard F. Burton. Great Victorian scholar/adventurer's eloquent, erudite history of the "queen of weapons"–from prehistory to early Roman Empire. Evolution and development of early swords, variations (sabre, broadsword, cutlass, scimitar, etc.), much more. 336pp. 6⅛ x 9¼.
25434-8 Pa. $9.95

AUTOBIOGRAPHY: The Story of My Experiments with Truth, Mohandas K. Gandhi. Boyhood, legal studies, purification, the growth of the Satyagraha (nonviolent protest) movement. Critical, inspiring work of the man responsible for the freedom of India. 480pp. 5⅜ x 8½. (USO) 24593-4 Pa. $8.95

CELTIC MYTHS AND LEGENDS, T. W. Rolleston. Masterful retelling of Irish and Welsh stories and tales. Cuchulain, King Arthur, Deirdre, the Grail, many more. First paperback edition. 58 full-page illustrations. 512pp. 5⅜ x 8½. 26507-2 Pa. $9.95

THE PRINCIPLES OF PSYCHOLOGY, William James. Famous long course complete, unabridged. Stream of thought, time perception, memory, experimental methods; great work decades ahead of its time. 94 figures. 1,391pp. 5⅜ x 8½. 2-vol. set.
Vol. I: 20381-6 Pa. $13.95
Vol. II: 20382-4 Pa. $14.95

THE WORLD AS WILL AND REPRESENTATION, Arthur Schopenhauer. Definitive English translation of Schopenhauer's life work, correcting more than 1,000 errors, omissions in earlier translations. Translated by E. F. J. Payne. Total of 1,269pp. 5⅜ x 8½. 2-vol. set. Vol. 1: 21761-2 Pa. $12.95
Vol. 2: 21762-0 Pa. $12.95

MAGIC AND MYSTERY IN TIBET, Madame Alexandra David-Neel. Experiences among lamas, magicians, sages, sorcerers, Bonpa wizards. A true psychic discovery. 32 illustrations. 321pp. 5⅜ x 8½. (USO) 22682-4 Pa. $9.95

THE EGYPTIAN BOOK OF THE DEAD, E. A. Wallis Budge. Complete reproduction of Ani's papyrus, finest ever found. Full hieroglyphic text, interlinear transliteration, word-for-word translation, smooth translation. 533pp. 6½ x 9¼.
21866-X Pa. $11.95

MATHEMATICS FOR THE NONMATHEMATICIAN, Morris Kline. Detailed, college-level treatment of mathematics in cultural and historical context, with numerous exercises. Recommended Reading Lists. Tables. Numerous figures. 641pp. 5⅜ x 8½.
24823-2 Pa. $11.95

THEORY OF WING SECTIONS: Including a Summary of Airfoil Data, Ira H. Abbott and A. E. von Doenhoff. Concise compilation of subsonic aerodynamic characteristics of NACA wing sections, plus description of theory. 350pp. of tables. 693pp. 5⅜ x 8½. 60586-8 Pa. $14.95

THE RIME OF THE ANCIENT MARINER, Gustave Doré, S. T. Coleridge. Doré's finest work; 34 plates capture moods, subtleties of poem. Flawless full-size reproductions printed on facing pages with authoritative text of poem. "Beautiful. Simply beautiful."–*Publisher's Weekly.* 77pp. 9¼ x 12. 22305-1 Pa. $7.95

NORTH AMERICAN INDIAN DESIGNS FOR ARTISTS AND CRAFTSPEOPLE, Eva Wilson. Over 360 authentic copyright-free designs adapted from Navajo blankets, Hopi pottery, Sioux buffalo hides, more. Geometrics, symbolic figures, plant and animal motifs, etc. 128pp. 8⅜ x 11. (EUK) 25341-4 Pa. $8.95

SCULPTURE: Principles and Practice, Louis Slobodkin. Step-by-step approach to clay, plaster, metals, stone; classical and modern. 253 drawings, photos. 255pp. 8⅛ x 11.
22960-2 Pa. $11.95

THE INFLUENCE OF SEA POWER UPON HISTORY, 1660–1783, A. T. Mahan. Influential classic of naval history and tactics still used as text in war colleges. First paperback edition. 4 maps. 24 battle plans. 640pp. 5⅜ x 8½. 25509-3 Pa. $14.95

THE STORY OF THE TITANIC AS TOLD BY ITS SURVIVORS, Jack Winocour (ed.). What it was really like. Panic, despair, shocking inefficiency, and a little heroism. More thrilling than any fictional account. 26 illustrations. 320pp. 5⅜ x 8½. 20610-6 Pa. $8.95

FAIRY AND FOLK TALES OF THE IRISH PEASANTRY, William Butler Yeats (ed.). Treasury of 64 tales from the twilight world of Celtic myth and legend: "The Soul Cages," "The Kildare Pooka," "King O'Toole and his Goose," many more. Introduction and Notes by W. B. Yeats. 352pp. 5⅜ x 8½. 26941-8 Pa. $8.95

BUDDHIST MAHAYANA TEXTS, E. B. Cowell and Others (eds.). Superb, accurate translations of basic documents in Mahayana Buddhism, highly important in history of religions. The Buddha-karita of Asvaghosha, Larger Sukhavativyuha, more. 448pp. 5⅜ x 8½. 25552-2 Pa. $12.95

ONE TWO THREE . . . INFINITY: Facts and Speculations of Science, George Gamow. Great physicist's fascinating, readable overview of contemporary science: number theory, relativity, fourth dimension, entropy, genes, atomic structure, much more. 128 illustrations. Index. 352pp. 5⅜ x 8½. 25664-2 Pa. $8.95

ENGINEERING IN HISTORY, Richard Shelton Kirby, et al. Broad, nontechnical survey of history's major technological advances: birth of Greek science, industrial revolution, electricity and applied science, 20th-century automation, much more. 181 illustrations. ". . . excellent . . ."–*Isis.* Bibliography. vii + 530pp. 5⅜ x 8¼. 26412-2 Pa. $14.95

DALÍ ON MODERN ART: The Cuckolds of Antiquated Modern Art, Salvador Dalí. Influential painter skewers modern art and its practitioners. Outrageous evaluations of Picasso, Cézanne, Turner, more. 15 renderings of paintings discussed. 44 calligraphic decorations by Dalí. 96pp. 5⅜ x 8½. (USO) 29220-7 Pa. $4.95

ANTIQUE PLAYING CARDS: A Pictorial History, Henry René D'Allemagne. Over 900 elaborate, decorative images from rare playing cards (14th–20th centuries): Bacchus, death, dancing dogs, hunting scenes, royal coats of arms, players cheating, much more. 96pp. 9¼ x 12¼. 29265-7 Pa. $12.95

MAKING FURNITURE MASTERPIECES: 30 Projects with Measured Drawings, Franklin H. Gottshall. Step-by-step instructions, illustrations for constructing handsome, useful pieces, among them a Sheraton desk, Chippendale chair, Spanish desk, Queen Anne table and a William and Mary dressing mirror. 224pp. 8⅛ x 11¼. 29338-6 Pa. $13.95

THE FOSSIL BOOK: A Record of Prehistoric Life, Patricia V. Rich et al. Profusely illustrated definitive guide covers everything from single-celled organisms and dinosaurs to birds and mammals and the interplay between climate and man. Over 1,500 illustrations. 760pp. 7½ x 10⅛. 29371-8 Pa. $29.95

Prices subject to change without notice.

Available at your book dealer or write for free catalog to Dept. GI, Dover Publications, Inc., 31 East 2nd St., Mineola, N.Y. 11501. Dover publishes more than 500 books each year on science, elementary and advanced mathematics, biology, music, art, literary history, social sciences and other areas.